"Women in the Military w... authoritative account on the subject for decades to come"

★ ★ ★

A commendable and monumental work. . . .This book is fascinating to read with so many intriguing details and facts that surely would have been lost without her diligent research. *Women in the Military* will stand as the authoritative account on the subject for decades to come.

Marine Corps Gazette

Examines contemporary controversy over the presence of women in the military forces, notably women's role in Grenada, Panama, and the Gulf War.

ARMY Magazine

General Holm has updated the original version [of *Women in the Military*] to reflect the progress made, and new problems encountered since the book's original publication in 1982. Particularly significant is her discussion of the role of military women in Grenada, Panama, and the Persian Gulf War.

U.S. Naval Institute *Proceedings*

Exemplifies advocacy scholarship at its best. . . .This updated work makes a major intellectual contribution to a major national debate. Recommended for all collections.

Library Journal

[The author] shines both as scholar and as journalist, and her account of how women have earned the right to be treated as "members of the first team rather than as a protected subclass" is eloquent, inspiring, and richly informative.

Publishers Weekly

Throughout, the book is distinguished by clear writing, thorough research, common sense, the voice of experience, and strong commitment both to equality for women and to strength in the American armed forces.

American Library Association *Booklist*

Major General Jeanne Holm has written the definitive history of the vast contributions made by American women to this nation's defense. From the American Revolution through Desert Storm, she has unfolded the rich fabric of women's battle to gain admittance into what until recent times has been the special world of men: the armed forces.

Brig. Gen. Evelyn P. Foote, USA (Ret.)

Jeanne Holm's the one person with the right experience to have written this book. It's the "Bible" on women in the military. Putting emotion aside, she lays out the facts on every issue. Her grasp of the issues is unparalleled.

Brig. Gen. Wilma L. Vaught, USAF (Ret.)
President, Women in the Military Service for
America Memorial Foundation

A uniquely comprehensive chronicle of depth, insight, and balance . . . [which provides] an authoritative, factual, and well-researched historical perspective.

RAdm. Fran McKee, USN (Ret.)

General Holm brings a refreshing analytical objectivity to a debate that for too long has been in an emotional crossfire. As one whose career spanned the evolution of the contemporary role of women in the nation's armed forces and who was one of the principal architects of the expansion, she is uniquely qualified to separate rhetoric from reality. This book will be invaluable to legislators grappling with the thorny issue of women in combat.

Martin Binkin, Senior Fellow of
The Brookings Institution

WOMEN
IN THE
MILITARY
An Unfinished Revolution
Revised Edition

Maj. Gen. Jeanne Holm, USAF (Ret.)

PRESIDIO

Copyright © 1982 by Jeanne Holm
Revised Edition © 1992
Quality paperback printed 1993

Published by Presidio Press
505 B San Marin Dr., Suite 300, Novato, CA 94945

Library of Congress Cataloging-in-Publication Data

Holm, Jeanne, 1921—
    Women in the military : an unfinished revolution / by Jeanne Holm.
— Rev. ed.
      p. cm.
    Includes bibliographical references and index.
    ISBN 0-89141-513-0
    1. United States—Armed Forces—Women. I. Title.
    UB418.W65H64 1992
    355'. 0082—dc20   92-17981
                                        CIP

The photo of Maj. Marie Rossi on the dedication page is reprinted courtesy of her family. All other photos courtesy U.S. Department of Defense.

Printed in the United States of America

To Maj. Marie T. Rossi
(January 3, 1959—March 1, 1991)

And All Who Serve

Contents

Acknowledgments

While responsibility for the contents of this book rests with its author, I am nonetheless mindful of the considerable debt owed to many others who have contributed in countless ways to this project during both the initial 1982 publication and this revised edition. Many were acting in their official capacities, but most contributed out of a belief that it was a story that needed to be told and they wanted to help.

First, I must thank the many present and former officials of the Defense Department and the military services—Army, Navy, Air Force, Marine Corps, and Coast Guard—who made it possible to obtain contemporary and historical materials without which it would not have been possible to reconstruct the events described in this work. In this respect, I am especially grateful for the cooperation of the Office of the Assistant Secretary of Defense (Force Management and Personnel) under four administrations. Particularly helpful were the directors and staffs of the Defense Advisory Committee on Women in the Services when it came to identifying the key issues and background materials essential to researching what is a highly complex area of military personnel management cutting across the five services.

I am deeply indebted to military and civilian colleagues who have furnished information, shared their recollections of events, and provided personal insights. Among those who contributed to the original publication were: Capt. Louise K. Wilde, USN (Ret.) and Col. Jeanette I. Sustad, USMC (Ret.), both of whom have since passed away; Col. Julia Hamblet, USMC (Ret.); RAdm. Fran McKee, USN (Ret.); Maj. Gen. Mary E. Clarke, USA (Ret.); Brig. Gen. Sally Wells, USAF (Ret.); Brig. Gen. Margaret Brewer, USMC (Ret.); Col. Bettie Morden, USA (Ret.); Capt. Patricia Gormley, USN (Ret.); Col. Diane Ordez, USAF (Ret.); Col. Roberta Patrick, USMC (Ret.); Capt. Maria Higgins, USN (Ret.); Lt. Col. Welda Smith, USAF (Ret.); and Capt. Mary Bachand McWilliams, USCG (Ret.).

For assistance in up-dating this book I owe a great deal to individuals, both within and outside the armed forces, who provided background information, documentation, and informed insights into contemporary events and issues, many of which continue to be controversial and contentious. Among those who helped are: Col. Mary C. Pruitt, USAF; Brig. Gen. Evelyn "Pat" Foote, USA (Ret.); Capt. Patricia Gormley, USN (Ret.); Brig. Gen. Wilma Vaught, USAF (Ret.); Comdr. Rosemary Mariner, USN; and especially Carolyn Becraft, who has researched and spoken out on the problems facing women in the U.S. armed services. And I am grateful to the many other former and active military members whose recollections added perspective and human interest to the narrative.

Various persons, including several cited above, have kindly read and critiqued individual chapters of the manuscript while it was in progress, particularly Mary C. Pruitt, Carolyn Becraft, Bettie Morden, Welda Smith, Norma M. Loeser, Nonna Cheatham, and Patricia and Matthew Gormley. A special thanks to my editor, Adele Horwitz of Presidio Press, who initially persuaded me to put pen to paper on this project and came out of retirement to edit the up-dated version. She is a joy to work with.

Finally, beyond the direct assistance provided, I would not have undertaken the task of up-dating this work had it not been for the warm words of encouragement from military women of all ranks—active and retired—who expressed their belief in the importance of recording the decisions and events that have touched their lives and professional careers. It is they who are the unsung heroines of this book.

But with all of the help I have had along the way, I alone bear full responsibility for the final work, for the accuracy of my facts, for the authenticity of my reconstruction of events and dialogue, and for the soundness of my interpretations.

Abbreviations

AAA	antiaircraft artillery
AAC	Army Air Corps
ACLU	American Civil Liberties Union
AEF	American Expeditionary Forces (Europe)
AFROTC	Air Force Reserve Officers' Training Corps
AFSC	Air Force Specialty Code
AGF	Army Ground Forces
ASF	Army Service Forces
AVF	all-volunteer force
AWACS	Airborne Warning and Control System aircraft
AWOL	absent without leave
CBI	China-Burma-India theater of operations
CCC	Civilian Conservation Corps
CNO	Chief of Naval Operations
DACOWITS	Defense Advisory Committee on Women in the Services
DOD	Department of Defense
DOPMA	Defense Officer Personnel Management Act
ERA	Equal Rights Amendment
ETO	European Theater of Operations
GAO	General Accounting Office (federal)
GCA	ground-control approach landing system
G.I.	government issue, also refers to enlisted men
ICBM	intercontinental ballistic missile
JAG	Judge Advocate General
LORAN	long-range aid to navigation
LST	landing craft-tank
MACTHAI	Military Assistance Command in Thailand
MACV	Military Assistance Command in Vietnam
MCWR	Marine Corps Women's Reserve
MEDCAP	Medical Civil Action Program
MOS	military occupational specialty
MSTS	Military Sea Transportation Service
NATO	North Atlantic Treaty Organization
NCO	noncommissioned officer
OCS	Officer Candidate School
OMB	Office of Management and Budget (federal)

OTS	Officer Training School
PACAF	Pacific Air Force
P.L.	Public Law
POW	Prisoner of War
R&R	rest and rehabilitation
ROTC	Reserve Officers' Training Corps
RVN	Republic of Vietnam
SAC	Strategic Air Command
SEA	Southeast Asia theater of operations
SNAFU	situation normal—all fouled up
SOS	Services of Supply
SPAR	Coast Guard Women's Reserve (from the Coast Guard motto "Semper Paratus—Always Ready")
SWPA	Southwest Pacific Area
UPI	United Press International
UPT	undergraduate pilot training
USAF	United States Air Force
USARV	United States Army Headquarters, Vietnam
USCGC	United States Coast Guard Cutter
USNS	United States Naval Survey ship
USO	United Service Organization
V.A.	Veteran Administration
V.C.	Viet Cong
VVA	Vietnam Veterans of America
WAAC	Women's Army Auxiliary Corps
WAC	Women's Army Corps
WAF	Women in the Air Force
WASP	Women's Airforce Service Pilots
WAVES	Women Accepted for Voluntary Emergency Service. Acronym connoting women serving in the line and staff corps of the Navy.
WEEM	Women Enlisted Expansion Model
WMSC	Women's Medical Specialist Corps
WR	Women's Reserve of the Marine Corps
WREN	Women's Royal Naval Service (U.K.)

Introduction

Defense Secretary Les Aspin announced at a press conference on 28 April 1993 that he was ordering the military services to open assignments in combat aviation to women as a first step toward allowing them into virtually every combat position short of those in front-line ground combat units. He added that he would also ask Congress to repeal the law banning women from serving on Navy warships at sea.

"The steps we are taking today are historic," Aspin said. "The results . . . will be that [for the first time] the services will be able to call upon a much larger pool of talent to perform the vital tasks that our military must perform."

Aspin's announcement amounted to a sea change in the rules governing women's long history of participation in America's national defense establishment. The stage had been set two years earlier when Congress repealed a 1948 law excluding women from assignment to military aircraft engaged in combat missions. But the new law had not yet been implemented.

Actually, the concept of allowing military women to perform in combat roles had been visible on the horizon for several years, but it was given strong impetus by the experiences of the Persian Gulf War.

Operations Desert Shield/Storm were recognized as a defining moment for women in the U.S. armed forces. Of all the new realities brought home to Americans by the nightly news from Saudi Arabia, none had been more startling than the image of a U.S. woman soldier in full battle gear, M16 rifle slung over her shoulder, on duty in the Gulf. It was the first realization for most people that wives, sisters, daughters, and mothers could actually be sent off to a combat theater to serve side-by-side with men in the tough, gritty, risky jobs of war. That some became casualties and prisoners of war was perhaps the biggest surprise of all.

Of the 540,000 Americans who served in Operation Desert Storm, nearly 41,000 were women—more than 7 percent of the U.S. forces in the theater. It was the largest wartime deployment of American military women in history. They did just about everything on land, at sea, and in the air except engage in the actual fighting, and even there the line was often a fuzzy one. They piloted and crewed jet planes and helicopters over the battle area, refueled fighters in mid-air, serviced high-tech equipment on the ground,. and loaded laser-guided bombs on F-117 Stealths for raids on targets in Baghdad. They directed Patriot missiles, drove trucks, ran enemy prisoner of war facilities, refueled M1 tanks on the side of the road, and guarded bases. They served on naval replenishment and repair ships, fleet oilers, and hospital ships offshore. And in the process many old myths that had hindered their progress in the military were demolished and replaced with surprising new realities.

"Women have made a major contribution to this [war] effort," said Secretary of Defense Dick Cheney when the Persian Gulf War was over. "We could not have won without them." Commanders in the field echoed similar praise of the women's performances under fire. Gen. H. Norman Schwarzkopf, the Coalition Forces commander, said they were "magnificent."

More than any other event could have, the Persian Gulf War spotlighted the extent to which the United States has come to rely on women in national defense, and it refueled a long-simmering debate over just what should be the outer limits, if any, of their roles in the armed forces.

Women's participation in the military is not, as many believe, of recent origin; it goes back to our nation's beginnings. However, the extent of women's involvement and the degree to which they have been "militarized" and integrated into the services are significant departures from the past.

Since the United States abandoned conscription in the early 1970s, the numbers of women on active duty in the Army, Navy, Air Force, and Marine Corps rose from a token 40,000, or roughly 1 percent, in 1971 to 223,000, or 11 percent, in 1991. There were another 151,000 in the selected reserves, or 13 percent of that force, many of whom were called to active duty during Operation Desert Shield/Storm. The Coast Guard, under the Department of Transportation, had 2,700 on active duty and another 1,200 in its reserve. Altogether, there were nearly 378,000 women in uniform, the largest in the history of the U.S. armed forces.

Previously confined to mostly traditional jobs and to a few selected shore bases, women by the 1990s were serving in nearly all noncombat jobs in each of the services. They were stationed at nearly every U.S. military installation in the world, were flying a vast variety of aircraft, and were serving aboard noncombat Navy and Coast Guard vessels at sea. In fact, women were so integrated into the armed forces that the U.S. could not have gone to war without them; their involvement in combat was inevitable and unavoidable.

These changes did not come easily or without considerable controversy at each step. As the decade of the eighties ended there was growing debate within and outside the military about the wisdom of placing so much reliance on women for defense. Although the Persian Gulf War laid many of the issues to rest, it raised new questions about what should be the outer limits of their involvement in the military, particularly in actual combat.

The United States faces crucial choices for the balance of this century as defense requirements change to meet the new realities of the post–Cold War period within an environment of diminished dollars and manpower resources and systems of ever-increasing technological sophistication. In that context, fundamental policy decisions concerning women's participation in the armed forces will have to be made.

We start with the basic questions to be resolved: the degree to which women can and should be involved; whether they should share, as a matter of citizenship, the same rights and obligations as men for their nation's defense; and, if not, what the legitimate parameters for their participation should be.

To deal intelligently with all these issues requires an understanding on the part of policymakers and the general public of how we got to where we are today and, more importantly, w*hy?* These are the questions this book explores. It is not intended to be a history—that is a job best left to professional military historians. It is not intended as a detailed chronicle of everything that happened—that would take volumes. It is an attempt to identify and shed light on the key events and issues, to explain the crucial decisions, and to relate how the people most involved felt about the policies and decisions that affected their lives and their careers.

Since obviously none of this could have occurred in a vacuum, an attempt has also been made to place each phase in its historical context and to show how what was happening to military women was influenced by the contemporary military situation and the social climate of the time.

It is a marvelous tale of persistence, courage, and foresight in the face of repeated frustrations and the built-in institutional resistance of the tradition-bound military subculture. It is set against the background of peace and war, of social evolution, and of advancement in the technology of warfare. The scope of the subject is so broad as almost to defy condensation into a single volume. Many of the issues have had to be ignored and others dealt with only superficially.

This book nonetheless provides a framework for future research in the hope that others will pick up the threads in various areas or specific issues and explore them in greater depth before the material is forever lost in the dusty files of the defense establishment.

In selecting material for this book, the author has had to rely, to a large extent, on unpublished works, unclassified government materials, and personal files not readily available to the general public. An effort has been made to acquire original source materials, wherever possible, and to interview people with firsthand knowledge of events. But research of this kind is a dynamic process, and it is inevitable that these references will become outdated before this publication is in print. Indeed, as we go to press some of the issues discussed in these pages have already been overtaken by events.

It is also realized that the events described are seen through the eyes of one who spent some thirty-three years in the armed forces, as many of the events in this book were unfolding, and who was often directly involved in the issues and the controversies, and therefore makes no claim to being a totally unbiased observer. She has nonetheless made an attempt to present all sides of the issues and, wherever possible, to let the facts and events speak for themselves.

Also, if this book does not deal as fully as it might with the women officers in the health professions (nurses and the medical sciences), it is because the major issues beginning in World War I concerned enlisted women and officers in the line—until the 1970s known as WACs, WAVES, WAF, and Women Marines.

And finally, a conscious decision was made to confine this story to the active duty forces, to the exclusion of the thousands of women who serve in the Reserves and the Guard. Their story is worthy of a volume in itself.

PART I

REVOLUTION
THROUGH
WORLD WAR II

CHAPTER 1

IN MOLLY'S WAKE:
THE EARLY DAYS

THE STORY OF America's military women begins with the birth of our nation.

It was a hot and sultry June day at Monmouth Courthouse in the year 1778. General George Washington was there with his troops, the British forces were there, and so was "Molly Pitcher." To the weary, parched soldiers on the battlefield the woman with her water pitcher must have seemed like an angel as she moved among them binding wounds, dispensing water, and giving encouragement. Many of the soldiers recognized her as Mary, wife of John Hays, an artilleryman of the 7th Pennsylvania Regiment.

In the thick of battle, John Hays' gun position ceased firing. Mary found the crew lying mutilated and John seriously wounded. Although not trained in the arts of war, she probably had seen enough action to know what had to be done. She put down her water pitcher, grabbed the ramming staff, swabbed out the hot gun barrel with water to extinguish sparks and remove unexploded powder, rammed home a charge and fired. Replacements soon arrived, but she stayed at her station as rammer until relieved by an artilleryman.

Joseph P. Martin, who claimed to have been an eye witness to this (or a similar) episode, elaborated:

> While in the act of reaching for a cartridge and having one of her feet as far before the other as she could step, a cannon shot from the enemy passed

directly between her legs without doing any other damage than carrying away all of the lower part of her petticoat. Looking at it with apparent unconcern, she observed that it was lucky it did not pass any higher, for in that case it might have carried away something else, and continued her occupation.[1]

Historians agree about the battle's outcome, and about the behavior of the generals on both sides—one, an American, disgraced himself early in the day by leading a retreat in the face of the enemy—but are less certain about the true identity of Molly Pitcher. Most often cited is Mary Ludwig Hays McCauley, the heroine of Monmouth, but there were others known to have accomplished similar feats during the war. Some claim that the "real" Molly Pitcher was Margaret Corbin who, a full two years earlier, distinguished herself in the battle of Fort Washington by taking over the gun position of her husband (also named John). Before the fort fell to the enemy, Margaret was wounded and disabled for life.

Although the identity of the real Molly remains indefinite, she cannot simply be written off as a romantic legend. She represents the women who served with the Continental Army during our war for independence. And she was not an anomaly.

During the 18th and 19th centuries, women were routinely present with the armies in battle. Indeed, with the constant notorious manpower shortages, sustaining Washington's army in field or in garrison would have been next to impossible without the women. Moreover, it was common and accepted practice for poor but respectable wives, mothers, and even daughters, to go along with their men when they went off with the army; often they had no other practical alternative. The army authorized a certain number of women—usually three to six per company—to draw rations for themselves and their children in return for their services, which generally included cooking, sewing, and laundry.

Women were also hired employees. The medical service, for example, was allowed one matron and ten nurses per hundred wounded. Although paid a regular wage, like the other women with the army, these were civilians with no military status as such. The women's civilian status did not shield them from the grit, grime, and hardships, nor did their lack of military training protect them from the horrors of war and the personal risks they faced in the daily performance of their assigned tasks.

However, the colonial mind would never have thought to

militarize these women even when the army was in the most desperate straits. Such a conceptual breakthrough would have to wait until the 20th century.

Despite Army regulations that provided only for male enlistments, women got around the rules by masquerading as men—or more probably as boys, since there were many fresh-faced boys as young as twelve in uniform. Many of these women acquitted themselves very well as soldiers. Some passed undetected; others were unmasked. The best known of these was Deborah Samson who, in 1780, joined the 4th Massachusetts Regiment as Robert Shirtliffe and served three years as a common soldier, fighting in a number of battles and being wounded at Tappan Bay, Tarrytown, and Yorktown. While an orderly to a general officer, "Shirtliffe" was hospitalized with fever. The surgeon soon discovered that "Robert" was really Deborah Samson, and she was quietly discharged.

We do not know how many women, or how many men, served with the American forces during the course of the Revolution. Available data are sparse and unreliable. We do know that when the war was over, the Continental Army was disbanded, leaving a force the size of a Corporal's guard—some eighty men. This set the pattern that the United States would follow until 1948: that of rapid mobilization for war and equally rapid demobilization at war's end. Not until that pattern changed would women be granted full and permanent military status in the U.S. armed forces.

THE NINETEENTH CENTURY

In the early years of nationhood women's interest in the military in times of crisis was always evident—as was the military's need for their services. While most women contented themselves with civilian status, others determined to follow the only other course available to them and masqueraded as men. Thus, in the War of 1812, Lucy Brewer, later acknowledged by the Marine Corps as the "first girl marine," served for three years as a marine on the USS *Constitution* as George Baker. In 1846, during the Mexican attack on Fort Brown, Sarah Borginis achieved the rank of brevet colonel under Gen. Zachary Taylor.

During the Civil War women on both sides became active on an unprecedented scale. Many of the restrictions and social conventions with respect to women's activities were set aside or simply ignored to meet the unusual demands of this all-pervasive war. In addition to undertaking the usual functions of cooking, sewing, and foraging for supplies, many women, both black and white, served as saboteurs, scouts, and couriers. They blew up bridges, cut telegraph wires, burned arsenals and warehouses, and helped prisoners and slaves escape.

We do not know precisely how many women disguised as men actually joined the armies on both sides. Some estimates put the figure at four hundred. The most famous was Sarah Edwards, who served as a nurse, spy, courier, and soldier in the Union Army. Frances Hook enlisted in the 90th Illinois Infantry, was wounded, and was captured at Chattanooga. Anna Carrol was a self-styled military strategist who is supposed to have suggested the plan followed by Grant in his Tennessee campaign, which was one of the turning points of the war.

Female spies were common. Mrs. Rose O'Neal Greenhow, a Washington society hostess, was arrested and imprisoned for supplying the Confederate Army with information that contributed to its victory at the First Battle of Bull Run. Pauline Cushman, a New Orleans actress who publicly toasted Jefferson Davis from a Louisville stage while active as a Union spy, was ultimately discovered and sentenced to execution, only to be saved in the nick of time by the arrival of Union troops.

One of the most colorful and enterprising characters of the period was Loreta Velasques. Beautiful, well educated, and affluent, she had been born in Cuba, where her father was a diplomat. When her husband, who was an army officer, left for the war, Loreta, over his objections, bought a Confederate uniform, glued on a moustache and chin beard, recruited a troop of soldiers, and set herself up as their commander under the name of Lt. Harry T. Buford. Before she was discovered, she had fought in a number of battles, including the First Battle of Bull Run, and had served a brief stint as a self-styled spy. After being wounded and unmasked, Loreta enlisted as an infantryman but soon decided she would prefer being an officer on horseback and secured herself a commission in the cavalry. She led patrols into enemy territory and on many occasions demonstrated competence and courage, but after being badly wounded was again unmasked. Unable to get promoted, she finally decided to call it quits. After being widowed twice, Loreta was last seen heading west for gold.

By far the most significant and lasting contributions made by women during the Civil War were in the fields of health care and medicine. Individually and collectively, women stepped forward to provide vitally needed medical supplies and to improve standards of sanitation and patient care.

Clara Barton emerged as one of the giants of the Civil War. She was an individual of prodigious energy, resourcefulness, and organizational ability. On her own initiative, and often at her own expense, she became an important supplier to the Union Army. She personally collected supplies and medical equipment and supervised their delivery and distribution directly to the troops in the field. In addition, she ministered to the wounded and dying on the field of battle even after narrowly escaping death in the Battle of Antietam. After the war, Barton was responsible for establishing the first National Cemetery, at Arlington, Virginia, where she personally marked some twelve thousand graves. She also organized the American Red Cross and served as its first president for over twenty years.

Dr. Mary Walker, a maverick and an early feminist, gave up her medical practice to go with the Union Army as a nurse since female doctors had not yet become acceptable but female nurses had. She was taken prisoner but was later exchanged. In 1864, she was commissioned as a lieutenant in the Medical Corps, thus becoming the first woman doctor in the Army. She served as an assistant surgeon and was awarded the Congressional Medal of Honor. Her medal, along with those of a number of male recipients, was withdrawn in 1917 when the Army raised its criteria for the award, but was finally restored by a special act of Congress in 1976.

At the beginning of the war, women in the North organized to support the Union Army and formed, to coordinate their efforts, the Women's Central Association of Relief. Under pressure from this association, the Union Army established the first official agency to devise and enforce sanitation regulations in the Army. The Sanitary Commission became the official channel through which Northern women could organize patient care, collect and distribute hospital supplies and equipment, and enforce standards of sanitation. The women also obtained permission to convert transport ships into the first primitive hospital ships to care for the wounded. The women volunteers serving on those ships worked under the most difficult of circumstances—without staff, provisions, or even mattresses for the wounded who jammed the ships.

Supplies and equipment were so scarce that the women often had to scrounge their own; and on many occasions, they worked around the clock with no relief in sight.

Throughout the war, the shortage of nurses presented severe problems for both the North and the South. At her own suggestion, Dorothea Dix was appointed by the U.S. Secretary of War in 1861 as Superintendent of Women Nurses with the primary job of organizing and recruiting a corps of nurses to serve with the Union Army. Dix was already well known for her work in the reform of insane asylums. The standards for nurses that she originally established reflect the social practices of the times rather than the rigors of wartime nursing. To serve as a nurse, a woman had to be over thirty, very plain looking, and wear plain brown or black dresses. No previous nursing experience was required. Later, Dix revised requirements. The only criterion was "a willingness to work." Largely through Dix's prodigious efforts, some six thousand nurses were recruited and trained for service with the Army of the North.

The record of Civil War nurses provides one of the finest examples of dedication, organizational ability, and simple courage to be found in American military history. Largely through their efforts, Army patient care took a quantum leap forward. But even though the Army may have appreciated the women's contribution, military leaders were not ready to accept the obvious fact that nurses were a necessary and integral part of any effective medical service. True to tradition, when the war ended in 1865, the Army reverted to the practice of using enlisted men for patient care in its hospitals, and the female nurses went home.

At the outset of the Spanish-American War, the Army faced an epidemic of typhoid fever in its camps and attempted vainly to recruit six thousand or more men to handle patient care. Its only alternative was then to recruit women. So, at the request of the Surgeon General, Congress authorized the Army to appoint women as nurses—but under civilian contract, not military status.

Within the space of two months, some twelve hundred women volunteers were recruited under the direction of Dr. Anita Newcomb McGee. More than fifteen hundred eventually were to serve between 1898 and 1901 in the United States, overseas, and aboard the hospital ship *Relief*.

The pioneering done by women in patient care and preventive medicine during the Civil and Spanish-American wars was to have a lasting impact on the military medical services. And whether military doctors liked it or not, and most did not, nurses had carved out a niche for themselves—a permanent niche, as it turned out. Enlisted hospital corpsmen had their place, but clearly they were no substitute for trained nurses. Moreover, much of the confusion in patient care during the wars could be attributed to the lack of a single uniformed nursing corps, with official status, under direct military control. Even so, opposition to granting military status in any form to nurses remained strong simply and only because they were women. Most medical officers were opposed to the idea, as was Surgeon General George M. Sternberg—at least initially.

General Sternberg was reluctant to have women with the troops in the field. He also expressed some concern about the probable expense of luxuries for the women: bureaus, rocking chairs, and other special items not previously requisitioned for men. However, the indisputable contribution of the contract nurses in 1898–99 was enough to convince the general that having the nurses as a more permanent part of his medical services was the way to go. So, at his request, Dr. McGee (then Acting Assistant Surgeon in charge of the newly established Nurse Corps Division) drafted the legislation necessary to give nurses quasi-military status.

In 1901, Congress established the Nurse Corps as an auxiliary of the Army. In this ambiguous quasi-military status, nurses still had no military rank, equal pay, or other benefits normal to military service such as retirement or veterans' benefits. Seven years later, on 12 May 1908, the Navy followed the Army's example. Although full military status would have to wait until 1944, the nurses were officially recognized as a necessary and permanent part of the Army and Navy. So by the time World War I approached, the nursing services were organized and ready to go.

WORLD WAR I

In 1916, Secretary of the Navy Josephus Daniels asked his legal advisor, "Is there any law that says a yeoman must be a man?" The answer was no. "Then enroll women in the Naval Reserve as yeomen," he said, "and we will have the best clerical assistance the country can provide." It was a decision born of pragmatism.

Daniels was convinced that, as the United States headed for inevitable involvement in World War I, the Navy simply would not be able to meet its requirements for clerical personnel. He believed that as the men were drained off for duty with the fleet, shortages in the shore establishments and headquarters would grow critical, and the Civil Service system would not be able to keep up with the demand. He was right.

On 19 March 1917, the Navy Department authorized the enrollment of women in the Naval Reserve in the ratings of yeoman, electrician (radio), or such other ratings as might be considered essential. Thus, when the United States entered the war on 6 April, the Navy was in a position to enlist women. The Marine Corps came to the same conclusion a year later as its stateside bases were drained to man combat units. The War Department, however, despite the urgings of Army commanders, could never quite bring itself to make so radical a decision. Women other than nurses did not serve in the Army during World War I. Nurses were one thing, but enlisted women quite another.

By the end of the war, 34,000 women had served in the Army and Navy Nurse Corps, the Navy, the Marines, and the Coast Guard. World War I not only confirmed the ability of women to serve as nurses but brought women into other traditionally male preserves when the services found that they could not obtain the necessary numbers of men.

Any questions about the wisdom of the Army and Navy in establishing nursing corps were swept away by the numbers of women recruited as nurses and the high quality of their service during World War I. By war's end, the Army Nurse Corps had expanded from 400 to 20,000 and the Navy Nurse Corps from 460 to 1,400.

The first 400 Army nurses sailed for Europe in May 1917 to serve with the British Expeditionary Forces in France. By Armistice Day, more than 10,000 had served overseas in Belgium, England, Italy, and Serbia, as well as in Siberia and various U.S. territories—in field hospitals and in mobile, evacuation, base, and convalescent hospitals. They were also assigned to troop trains and transport ships.

Many Army nurses were decorated, including three who received the Distinguished Service Cross, a combat medal second only to the Medal of Honor, and twenty-three who received the Distinguished Service Medal, the highest noncombat award. Many received foreign medals: twenty-eight were awarded the French Croix de Guerre. Some were wounded; thirty-eight remained overseas, buried in U.S. cemeteries, most of them casualties of the flu rather than of enemy action.

The Navy Nurse Corps was much smaller, and possibilities for duty overseas were limited by the number of Navy overseas facilities. However, many nurses were stationed in hospitals in the British Isles and in field hospitals in France.

Certainly the acceptance of nurses, even with their dubious status, was the first breakthrough for women insofar as a military profession was concerned. It had not, however, led military planners to the next logical step. The armed forces remained relatively untouched by and unconcerned with the major evolution in women's roles that was occurring during the last part of the nineteenth and the early part of the twentieth century. They accepted, as society in general did, the premise that the military was a male institution whose social and occupational context was permeated by the cult of masculinity. So it was in 1900. So it was in 1917. And so it is to a great extent in 1982. Acceptance of women as full and equal role participants in this masculine milieu is seen by many as the ultimate test of society's willingness to compromise with long-established traditions.

By the end of the nineteenth century, with industrialization, urbanization, and, more importantly, mass education, a new, more self-sufficient American woman had emerged. By the time the First World War hit Europe, American business and industry were hiring and training female clerks, typists, factory workers, telephone operators, and technicians. In fact, by the time the United States was drawn into the war, some fields had been taken over almost exclusively by women.

One of the most profound changes was the "feminization" of office work at the turn of the century. Before the invention of the typewriter and telephone, the office had been a male domain. But when Philo Remington introduced the typewriter in 1873, he hired women to demonstrate it. Businesses that bought the machines hired women to operate them. By 1902, the Bell telephone system employed 37,000 women switchboard operators as compared to 2,500 men.

Preparations for the war gave impetus to women's migration into the skilled and semiskilled industrial labor force on an unprecedented scale. As demands for manpower increased in both the public and private sectors, women went to work in shipyards, steel mills, and aircraft plants, performing a wide variety of higher-paying "men's jobs." Acute shortages began to appear in the skills generally classified as "women's jobs," particularly in the clerical skills. It was this shortage that precipitated the enlistment of the first groups of women into the U.S. armed forces.

As Navy Secretary Daniels had foreseen, as the war neared— and particularly after hostilities began—the Civil Service could not meet the mounting demands of both the government and the military for skilled clerical personnel. To fill the void, the Navy, the Marines, and the Coast Guard—in varying degrees—turned to enlisting women, primarily to perform clerical duties at headquarters. The number of women enlisted in each service was determined both by its size and nature and the timing of its decision. For example, the relatively small Coast Guard, chiefly responsible for patrolling coastal waters, enlisted only a few women for its headquarters.

The Navy Department, due to Daniels' foresight, authorized the enlistment of women—"yeomen (F)"—in March 1917 before U.S. entry into the war. Popularly known as "yeomanettes," Navy enlisted women not only performed clerical duties but also moved into diverse fields as draftsmen, translators, camouflage designers, and recruiters. Some of the 12,500 yeomanettes saw duty with hospital units in France and with intelligence units in Puerto Rico and overseas.

The Navy had a special problem in assigning its yeomen (F). At that time all yeomen were supposed to be assigned to ships, but Navy regulations forbade women at sea. To solve this dichotomy, the Navy assigned the yeomanettes to tugs resting on the bottom of the Potomac River.

The Marine Corps did not begin to recruit women until August 1918, two months before hostilities ended. The three hundred women who enrolled as marine (F) were dubbed "marinettes." The Marine Corps' action was taken in desperation and only after overseas casualties caused acute shortages of combat personnel, and after the completion of a survey that indicated that while combat-ready marines were holding down clerical jobs in headquarters, about 40 percent of the clerical work could be done equally well by women. (In the survey, experienced male clerks estimated that it would take a ratio of about three women to replace two men: the reverse turned out to be the case.)

Despite the action of the Navy and the Marines, the War

Department held firm, determining that the Army could not legally enlist women for any purpose. Although resigned to female nurses, the War Department balked at enlisted women even though many commanders and chiefs of branches clearly recognized the need.

One reason for the War Department's entrenchment was its deep hangups about women employees in general and military women in particular. Before the war, Army and National Guard posts were specifically forbidden to employ civilian women in any capacity except as nurses. Only after commanders who were faced with severe personnel shortages pleaded with the War Department were they authorized to employ civilian women in essential work for which men employees could not be obtained. The War Department had concluded that "with careful supervision, women employees may be permitted in camps without moral injury either to themselves or to the soldiers," provided the women were "of mature age and high moral character."

Given this official paranoia about having civilian women on Army posts, military women would have been viewed as pariahs. Although the British had already successfully established a women's military auxiliary, and despite many pleas from military planners, chiefs of branches, and field commanders, the War Department remained adamantly opposed. Even entreaties from Gen. John J. Pershing, Commander of the American Expeditionary Forces in Europe (AEF), fell on deaf ears.

In October 1917, Pershing cabled the War Department for 100 female uniformed telephone operators. He received contract civilians. Gen. James G. Harbord, Commander of the Services of Supply in Europe, requested 5,000 military women as clerical workers to release combat-capable enlisted men for duty at the front. He was sent 5,000 limited-duty, unskilled enlisted men instead. To help ease the desperate shortage of skilled personnel, the United Kingdom loaned Pershing members of its Women's Auxiliary Army Corps, the largest of several such British auxiliaries; and American female civilian contract employees were dispatched to a number of Army agencies in Europe.

At the same time, Pershing had to contend with some 5,000 American women volunteers recruited by welfare organizations for service in Europe over whom he had absolutely no control. The overlapping functions and lack of coordinated supervision of these diverse, independent groups running loose in Europe added to the general confusion of the theater. In sharp contrast were the organized and disciplined British WAAC and the U.S. Army's own Nurse Corps. Pershing yearned to make some kind of order out of the chaos.

Meanwhile, back in Washington most of the chiefs of Army branches were pressuring for a corps of women to ease their skill shortages. But the War Department remained unconvinced of the desirability or feasibility of making this radical departure in the conduct of our military affairs. A proposal by a committee of Congress to establish such a corps was rejected by the Secretary of War, Newton D. Baker, who considered it unwise, undesirable, and exceedingly ill-advised. When the Surgeon General, who had grown accustomed to having female nurses, decided he would like to commission female doctors to ease the shortage of qualified medical officers, he was advised that only persons "physically, mentally and morally qualified" could be appointed and that women obviously were not physically qualified.

The fact that the Navy and Marine Corps had taken the initiative by enlisting women rankled many Army agency heads and commanders. Although all the services were working within essentially the same legal constraints, the critical element of difference between the decisions of the Navy and those of the Army on enlisting women was the attitudes of the two service Secretaries. The Navy Secretary saw the need for military women, and, if he had reservations, he overcame them; the Secretary of War was unalterably opposed to the idea and would not concede the need despite overwhelming evidence to the contrary.

Had the war continued much longer, the manpower crunch, coupled with pressures from his commanders and from such powerful groups as the Young Women's Christian Association, the Women's League for Self-Defense, and the American Council on Education, might have forced the Secretary of War to capitulate. But the war ended in November 1918, and the subject was shelved with an official sigh of relief:

> In view of the present military situation it is believed no longer desirable that arrangements be made to form military organizations composed of women. . . . A continuation of the war would have required the United States . . . to make a much more extended use of women . . . to replace men sent overseas or men shifted to heavy work which men alone can do.[2]

Though the issue was officially shelved, the controversy was not. The war-to-end-all-wars had ushered in a new era for women and it would never be quite the same again.

NOTES

1. As with most such accounts of that period, the statement is of uncertain origin. Henry Steele Commager and Richard B. Morris attribute it to Martin in *Spirit of 'Seventy-Six* (New York: Harper and Row, 1958), p. 714.
2. Mattie B. Treadwell, *U.S. Army in World War II: Special Studies—The Women's Army Corps* (Washington, D.C.: Department of the Army, 1954), p. 10.

CHAPTER 2

BETWEEN THE WARS: DEMOBILIZATION 1919-25

On 11 NOVEMBER 1918 the Armistice was signed and World War I ended. Immediately, demobilization of the enlisted women in the Navy, the Marines, and the Coast Guard began. Of the military women, only the nurses survived the postwar demobilization, reduced to their peacetime strength.

"But why?" we might ask. The AEF experience clearly showed a need for American women with any U.S. military deployment overseas in time of war—to operate telephone switchboards, type letters, and perform other administrative duties. The American G.I. simply lacked the necessary skills, and there were too few local "nationals" who possessed both a knowledge of English and the needed security clearances. Civilian contract labor had also proven undesirable because it did not allow for sufficient military control.

Despite their obvious value to the military, the women were demobilized—not surprisingly, for their service had always been viewed as temporary; in the early 1920s the concept of women serving permanently with the military was an outlandish one. Likewise, military women were, as were military men, tired of war and anxious to resume their peacetime activities. However, if they had wanted to stay, they would not have been welcome.

One of the barriers facing women then, as now, was the prevalence in the military of the masculine mystique, the idea that the military is a man's world and warfare is a man's business, not a fit or proper place for a woman. The influx of 34,000 military women into the armed services during World War I had had no perceptible effect on this cult of masculinity.

Military nurses were accepted, but they were viewed differently from enlisted women. Nursing was accepted as women's work, and nurses were considered a necessary evil. In 1920, in recognition of their wartime services, the nurses were granted the status of officers with "relative rank" from second lieutenant through major. They were allowed to wear insignia of rank but were not given full rights and privileges, such as base pay equal to that of male officers of comparable grades. Their lack of full military status would keep them safely isolated from the military mainstream, somewhat like members of a ladies' auxiliary.

Yeomen (F) and Marines (F) were a different matter. They enjoyed full military status and had replaced male personnel in military jobs, hence could have been perceived as a threat to the male status quo. In 1925, the wording in the Naval Reserve Act of 1916 authorizing the Navy to enlist "citizens," which had permitted women to be eligible for the Navy and Marine Corps, was changed to limit eligibility to "male citizens." This ensured that the Navy Department could not enlist women again without Congress's express approval.

The 1920s became a period of reaction against war as Americans retreated into isolation. At the same time the military was demobilizing, the powerful women's organizations that had emerged during the suffrage movement started to become active in the pacifist, antimilitary establishment movements. The Army believed that women were very susceptible to the mounting public sentiment to dissolve the "ruthless military machine." The one thing the Army did not need was a group of suffragettes suggesting that the Army disband. To head off any such problems the War Department launched a public relations effort, and Secretary of War Newton D. Baker established the position of Director of Women's Programs, United States Army, appointing Anita Phipps director.

Her task was to maintain liaison between the War Department and women's organizations such as the American War Mothers, Daughters of the American Revolution, the League of Women Voters, and the National Federation of Business and Professional Women. She was to get the message to these women that the U.S.

Army was not a ruthless machine that constituted a threat to the peace but a progressive, socially minded institution interested in women's contributions. It would be a part of the overall drive to stem the drift of public opinion toward pacifism and abolition of the military by propagandizing for a strong defense.

However, instead of being placated, the women acquired a means through Phipps of demanding that the Army give greater recognition to women. What they wanted was to have women appointed as civilian aides to the Secretary of War.

Because her duties in the staff were never clearly defined, Phipps took it upon herself to plan for a women's service corps, presumably with herself as its first director.

In developing her plan, Phipps assiduously queried commanders, branch chiefs, and staff agencies and determined that 170,000 military women could be used in the event of war. No attempt was made to determine whether such numbers could realistically be recruited.

Almost half would perform clerical duties and a few would carry out technical tasks. The rest would be laborers, seamstresses, cooks, messengers, charwomen, and the like, since military women were perceived by many not only as the solution to overseas skill shortages a la AEF but also as an answer to the critical lack of menial labor at bases in the United States.

Because the Women's Service Corps, as Phipps called it, would be part of the Army, and its members would receive full military status, its proposed establishment was viewed with suspicion and hostility. To many old hands in the General Staff, the suggestion, coming from Phipps, smacked of empire-building and would result in a powerful machine difficult to control and endowed with the possibilities of hampering and embarrassing the War Department.

In 1926, the plan was submitted to the War Department and rejected. Phipps, who had managed to alienate most of the staff, found herself without the support of her superiors, isolated and in ill health. In 1931, the new Chief of Staff, General Douglas MacArthur, had her position abolished as of "no military value."

Phipps's plan was the first of three developed in the between-the-war period. Maj. Everett S. Hughes, chief Army planner for a women's corps in the General Staff personnel office presented the second in 1928; Gen. George C. Marshall, when he became Chief of Staff, ordered a third in September 1939. The first two approaches were similar in that they envisioned a women's corps that would be *in* the Army rather than attached to it as an auxiliary. With the third plan, by contrast, under no circumstances would the women be given full military status. They would be set up in quasi-military female organizations but would not be members of the Army.

Whereas Phipps's plan had been directed toward proving personnel needs, Hughes's was geared to the psychological and managerial aspects of incorporating vast numbers of females into the male milieu of the Army. His study for the General Staff, "Participation of Women in War," proposed that the Army accept the inevitability of large numbers of women taking part in the next war—the more nearly total the war, the greater the part.

Hughes focused on ways to make that participation more effective. He considered advance training essential for both women and men so that women setting up the corps in wartime could comprehend Army thinking and men making decisions about women could understand the problems of militarizing women. Hughes said that if the women who were to head the new corps were ignorant of Army ways, "this ignorance, coupled with man's intolerance, may be fatal."

Hughes's plan, like its predecessor, soon disappeared into the files of the War Department. In the words of Army historian Mattie Treadwell, "Major Hughes' prophetic efforts were embalmed with endorsements, laid out for observation for a period, and then buried so deep in the files that they were recovered only after the WAAC was six months old and War Department planners had already made most of the mistakes he predicted."

Some years later in England, Hughes, then a major general, asked Oveta Culp Hobby, Director of the Women's Army Corps, who was on an official visit to his headquarters, about what had happened to his "masterpiece." She had to admit she had no knowledge of its existence.

It was not until September 1939, shortly after Gen. George C. Marshall became Chief of Staff, that the matter surfaced once again. Marshall clearly saw the inevitability of severe manpower shortages in the armed forces if and when America was drawn into the war, which at that point seemed only a matter of time. The personnel staff was asked to do a study on the use of military women. The result was a plan for a corps patterned after the all-male Civilian Conservation Corps (CCC). As the Army staff visualized it, the women's corps would include "hostesses, librarians, canteen clerks, cooks and waitresses, chauffeurs, messengers and strolling minstrels." As mentioned before, the chief difference between this plan and its two predecessors was that under no circumstances would the women be given full military status. As with the Nurses Corps and the CCC, the women's corps would serve *with* not *in* the Army. Fortunately for all concerned, this plan too got buried in the files.

Nothing came of any of them until May 1941, when the Marshall plan was dragged out of War Department files as proof to Congress that the Army was indeed studying the problem. But it would take a major national emergency to cause policymakers in all the services and in Congress to cast aside preconceived notions in favor of pragmatism. World War II produced just such an emergency.

CHAPTER 3

THE FIRST
BREAKTHROUGH:
WORLD WAR II

In 1956, AFTER extensive study of women in the work force, manpower expert Dr. Eli Ginzberg observed that "the increasing participation of women in the labor force does not take place on an even, slow-moving pace, but rather through a series of breakthroughs."[1] The Second World War was one such breakthrough.

In September 1940, the first peacetime selective service became law, and pressures continued to build from women's groups to become part of the mobilization effort. Women's patriotic organizations sprang up around the country, training women in military drill, discipline, and other skills that would be needed by the armed forces. Among the groups were the Women's League of Defense in Chicago, the Women's Ambulance and Defense Corps in Los Angeles, the Oregon Women's Ambulance Corps in the Northwest, and the Green Guards in Washington, D.C. When in May 1941 a bill to establish the Women's Army Auxiliary Corps (WAAC) was introduced, they followed its progress in Congress and lobbied for its passage.

H.R. 4906, the bill that established the WAAC, was introduced by Congresswoman Edith Nourse Rogers in May 1941. Rogers first became interested in the matter in World War I, when women had served overseas without the protection of military status. After the war, she became involved in legislation to obtain financial relief for women who had lost their health as a result of war service but who, because they had no military status, were not entitled to veterans' gratuities or care. She was therefore convinced that "women would not again serve with the Army without the protection the men got."[2]

When in early 1941 Rogers informed General Marshall that she intended to introduce such legislation, Marshall gave the General Staff the job of coming up with something. Seeing the handwriting on the wall, the staff called Rogers with the promise that they had been studying the same proposal and would be willing to have her introduce an Army bill that the War Department could support. "The purpose of this study," wrote the Assistant Chief of Staff for Personnel, "is to permit the organization of a women's force along the lines which meet with War Department approval, so that when it is forced upon us, as it undoubtedly will be, we shall be able to run it our way." The Army's plan called for a women's auxiliary which, while it provided for military control over the members, would tend to avert the pressure to admit women to actual membership in the Army. Rogers, they knew, wanted to have the women *in*—not *with*—the Army. The War Department's unwillingness to go the whole way and provide women with full status, combined with opposition from members of Congress to the idea, convinced Rogers that compromise on this point was the only way to get any legislation at all.

The bill, prepared by the General Staff, provided for only a small auxiliary corps "for the purpose of making available to the national defense the knowledge, skill, and special training of the women of the nation." It was not intended to release large numbers of men for combat. Rather, it called for a small, elite corps of educated, technically qualified women in order to "quickly attain the highest reputation for both character and professional excellence." The plan's provisions for using many of these women in unskilled work—as, for example, charwomen and laundresses—seemed not to have struck anyone as inconsistent or illogical.

Moreover, this notion that women should be of high moral character and technical competence while no such standards were used for men set the tone for the double standards that were to characterize the women's programs for the next forty years.

The Rogers' bill languished for months in the War Department despite the Chief of Staff's obvious enthusiasm for it. Marshall believed that manpower shortages, especially in certain skills, would become a major bottleneck to the war effort, and he recognized that some of these skills were possessed almost exclusively by women in the civilian sector. He pointed out that it would be uneconomical and a waste of valuable time to train men in such skills as typing and operating telephones when those jobs had been taken over by women. He also pointed out that women wanted in. While he could see no immediate need to take in women, he felt he needed the authority to do so as an important part of his overall mobilization planning for the Army. "It is important that as quickly as possible we have a declared national policy in this matter," Marshall told the Congress. "Women certainly must be employed in the overall effort of this nation. . . . We consider it essential that their status, their relationship to the military authority, should be clearly established."

In late November 1941, as the war grew more imminent, Marshall, aggravated over the foot-dragging in his own staff, shook his finger at one staff officer and demanded, "I want a women's corps right away and I don't want any excuses."

With the attack on Pearl Harbor, War Department resistance disappeared in the general scramble to mobilize resources for what suddenly appeared to be war on a global scale. As Marshall had predicted a year earlier, the armed forces in 1942 were headed for a manpower crisis of unprecedented proportions. Although the draft had been put into effect in September 1940, the Army ground forces alone were already short 160,000 men by the summer of 1942 and were faced with either slowing the activation of new units or sending them to the field under strength. Either action could jeopardize plans for the African invasion already in the making. The shortages were further aggravated by a shift in the ratio of combat personnel to support and overhead personnel. Men who could have filled positions in combat units were being siphoned out of the training pipeline to fill military jobs in noncombat units—jobs that many people believed could be performed by women. Similar trends were developing in all the services.

But even with the obvious strains on manpower post–Pearl Harbor and despite Marshall's enthusiasm for it, the WAAC legislation had a rough go of it in Congress. There, opposition to women remained strong, and emotions ran high. According to Brig. Gen. John Hilldring, who was charged with shepherding it on Capitol Hill, "In my time I have got some one hundred bills through the Congress, but this was more difficult than the rest of them combined."[3]

The bill passed the Senate with relative ease. The comments were of a humorous vein: "Are you going to start a matrimonial agency?" or "You are going to have a few generals, aren't you?" and "No, the women generals will remain at home."

The House was where the real opposition developed. Fears were expressed about men and women going into battle together and about how the men would be more concerned with the women's welfare than fighting. One member said:

> I think it is a reflection upon the courageous manhood of the country to pass a law inviting women to join the armed forces in order to win a battle. Take the women into the armed service, who then will do the cooking, the washing, the mending, the humble homey tasks to which every woman has devoted herself. Think of the humiliation! What has become of the manhood of America?

The bill passed and in May 1942 the WAAC was under way. From the very beginning, the auxiliary status did not work. The women were neither in nor out, neither fish nor fowl. The WAAC was not part of the Army, but it was run by the Army. Its members did Army jobs in lieu of soldiers but were administered under a separate, parallel set of regulations. This legal status was dubious, and there was no legally binding contract that could prevent a woman from leaving anytime she chose to. (Fortunately for the Army, most women did not realize this.) If they went overseas, WAACs did not have the same legal protection as the men, nor were they entitled to the same benefits if injured.

Under the WAAC, military women were not entitled to the same pay as their male counterparts, to entitlements for dependents, or to military rank. While this was not of much concern to the women when the Corps was first established because their primary motive was to serve in any way they could, once the other women's components were established with full military status, the WAACs came to resent the inequities.

Also, the relative advantages of the other services became readily apparent to prospective recruits. Their effect on WAAC recruiting as the other services began to move into the market was soon obvious. By the spring of 1943, many WAAC basic training facilities were sitting idle, and shipments to stateside bases had come to a near standstill.

In June 1943, after much debate and numerous attempts to impose crippling amendments, a bill was passed to establish a Women's Army Corps (WAC) with full military status. It was signed by the President on 1 July and Oveta Culp Hobby was sworn in as the director four days later. For the next ninety days, members of the WAAC were offered the option of either joining the new WAC or going home. This period soon came to be known as "The Conversion." During it, most of the inequities and organizational problems were resolved, and recruiting got a much needed boost.

During all the congressional furor over the WAAC bill, the Navy stayed on the sidelines. As with the Army staff, there was something less than enthusiasm for the whole idea within the higher levels of the Navy, with the exception of the Bureau of Aeronautics. The Naval Reserve Act, which was in effect at the onset of World War II, had, for example, repeated the phrase of the 1925 Naval Reserve Act that limited eligibility to male citizens. In December 1941, the Army sought Navy support of a joint bill to provide for auxiliaries in both services. Not only would the Navy not go along with it, but it tried to persuade the War Department not to sponsor the WAAC bill. One of the Navy personnel chiefs told his Army counterpart, "You are going to take a beating in Congress and we'll wait and see what happens."

Although it did not support the WAAC bill, the Navy had embarked on a separate course toward using women for its own reasons. In mid-1941, the Navy had come to the alarming discovery that it too would have a manpower problem if the United States were drawn into the war. Manning the fleet and forward bases would require releasing men from bases in the United States, thereby creating serious shortages in the shore establishments. The Bureau of Aeronautics proposed that military women be used and recommended that legislation be proposed to permit this. The Bureau of Personnel was not interested until Pearl Harbor, and an inquiry from Congresswoman Rogers in December 1941 got their attention.

In the months following Pearl Harbor, the U.S. naval forces in the Pacific were taking the brunt of the action in an effort to stem the Japanese expansion toward Australia. In May and June 1942, they fought and won the battles of Coral Sea and Midway Island. In August, they would begin the long, grueling struggle for

Guadalcanal and the Solomon Islands. Although victorious, the Navy and Marine Corps would pay a heavy price in men and equipment and, like the Army, were facing manpower shortages of growing magnitude. By the spring of 1942, the Navy had concluded reluctantly that it would have to resort to the utilization of military women to release men for duty with the fleet and also to man forward bases. One observer noted that certain of the older admirals would have preferred "dogs or ducks or monkeys" to women if it had been possible to use them. But despite the Navy's natural, built-in conservatism, its women would be members of the Naval Reserve rather than an auxiliary group.

In January 1942, seeing the handwriting on the bulkhead, the Bureau of Personnel recommended to the Secretary of the Navy that Congress be requested to authorize creation of a women's organization. The Secretary agreed but made it quite clear that he wanted the Navy women *in* the Reserve, not in an auxiliary such as the Army was proposing.

With some behind-the-scenes help from members of the Bureau of Aeronautics who were tired of the Navy staff's foot-dragging, Congressman Melvin Maas introduced the required enabling legislation in March 1942 (H.R. 6807); an identical bill was introduced in the Senate by Sen. Raymond Willis. The Maas bill sailed smoothly through the House, but unexpected opposition developed in the powerful Senate Naval Affairs Committee. Certain conservative committee members were firmly convinced that the armed forces were no place for women and that military service would somehow destroy their futures as "good mothers." This despite the fact that thousands of women were working in defense plants all over the country.

Also, pressures were brought to bear on the Navy to go for an auxiliary patterned after the WAAC and similar to the Navy's own Nurse Corps, whose members had not yet been granted full military status. Right up to the last, an attempt was made to end-run the Secretary of the Navy on this point by getting the President to favor an auxiliary. Joy Bright Hancock, later to become a director of the WAVES, described what happened:

> And right here, the fine "Italian hand" of a woman handled the delicate matter. On May 30, 1942, Dean Harriet Elliott of the University of North Carolina wrote Mrs. Roosevelt to explain the need for legislation as requested by the Navy [giving women full military status] and to ask the First Lady's help in getting presidential approval.[4]

It was only through the intercession of Mrs. Roosevelt with the President that the Navy Secretary got the nod for a Women's Naval Reserve.

The WAAC bill was signed on 15 May 1942 as Public Law 554—77th Congress. Two and a half months later, on 30 July, the Navy bill, P.L. 689, was signed, authorizing the establishment of the Navy Women's Reserve. These women would be identified as WAVES, a contrived acronym for Women Accepted for Volunteer Emergency Service. Mildred McAfee, the first director of Navy women, did not want them to have an acronym: they would simply be women in the Navy. But after the legislation was passed, a headline appeared in a Washington paper: "Gobletts Come to Town." McAfee then reluctantly agreed to calling her women WAVES—which many men soon interpreted to mean "Women Are Very Essential Sometimes." The Marine Corps Women's Reserve was authorized by the same law as the Navy Reserve but there would be no acronym, at least not officially. According to the commandant, they would be marines. Four months later, the Coast Guard Women's Reserve was established using the acronym SPAR, derived from the Coast Guard motto, "Semper Paratus— Always Ready."

NOTES

1. Speech before the Defense Advisory Committee on Women in the Services, spring meeting, April 1956.
2. U.S. Congress, *Congressional Record*, Vol. 87, No. 100, 28 May 1941, p. 4693.
3. Treadwell, p. 24.
4. Joy Bright Hancock [Capt., USN (Ret.)], *Lady in the Navy* (Annapolis: Naval Institute Press, 1972), p. 56.

CHAPTER 4

GETTING IT TOGETHER

THE MORALE OF the women who gathered at the old fort at Des Moines that steaming Iowa summer in 1942 was extraordinarily high, particularly considering the circumstances that had brought them together and the uncertainty of their futures. Never before had any of them experienced anything like it. Most of them had come by train. Many from the West Coast had been riding in hot, un-airconditioned coaches for two days, wearing the same clothes.

The commander of the new WAAC training center, which had recently been an Army cavalry post, stables and all, had told the swarming dignitaries and reporters that "it will be no glamour girls' playhouse" and that there would be few concessions to "feminine vanity and civilian frippery." To the women who were unloaded from G.I. trucks and herded into the processing center, that was an understatement, to say the least.

The first group of 400 white and 40 black women had been selected from among 30,000 applicants. The competition was keen. Although they came from every state in the Union and a variety of circumstances, they had a number of things in common besides a desire to serve: they were all volunteers; 99 percent had been successfully employed in civilian life; 90 percent had college training—most had degrees, some had several degrees; most were between twenty-five and forty years of age, although 16 percent were younger and 10 percent older. One in five was married, usually to a serviceman, and some were mothers of grown children. Because none of them had ever done anything like this before, they had little, if any, idea of what to expect or of what would be expected of them. The only things about which they were certain were that their country was at war and that they were needed.

Like most of the thousands who would follow, they had given up good jobs as sales managers, lawyers, college faculty members, office executives, reporters, editors, teachers, social workers, and executive secretaries. They had had only two weeks' notice to get their personal affairs in order, close out their jobs, take the oath, and get to Fort Des Moines by 20 July 1942, the opening day for the first class of female officers in the history of the U.S. armed forces.

Certainly, none of the thousands of women who would converge on Fort Des Moines that summer to attend Officer Candidate Training and enlisted basic training had the remotest idea that they were embarking upon a road that would eventually lead to the permanent integration of women into the U.S. armed forces. As they sat there perspiring in their civilian clothes, still in a state of shock, the newly appointed Director, WAAC, spoke to them of having a "debt to democracy and a date with destiny." It was heady stuff—one of those rare, emotion-packed moments that none of them would ever forget. Although each had been reminded often enough that she was "making history" and that she was a "pioneer," it never occurred to any in the group, least of all to the director, that some among them were on the threshold of professional military careers. Each had joined to contribute to the war effort. They were committed "for the duration plus six months." When it was all over, the women, like most of the men, expected to go back to pick up their lives where they had left off. Some of the men thought they might "go career" but, except for the nurses, that option was not yet open to women.

As might have been expected, establishing the first women's components in the armed forces did not go smoothly. Women were unfamiliar with military ways, having grown up to believe the bearing of arms was a masculine profession. Military men, having been conditioned to the same view, were simply unprepared to fully accept women—manpower shortage or not. Even General Marshall, the earliest and most ardent military male supporter, had initially viewed the WAAC only as an experiment. Yet, one by one, the services began absorbing women into the ranks.

On the morning of 16 May 1942, the day after the WAAC bill

was signed, Mrs. Oveta Culp Hobby was sworn in as the Corps' first director. At the age of thirty-seven, Hobby was a newspaper and radio executive, publisher, lawyer, writer, and civic leader. She was the wife of the former governor of Texas and mother of two. A year earlier, she had been "virtually drafted" by the War Department to set up a women's interest section in the Bureau of Public Relations to deal with the concerns of mothers and wives of draftees. General Marshall was so impressed that he persuaded her to help get the stalled WAAC legislation through Congress. Once success seemed assured, Marshall asked her to serve as its first director. What had started out as a brief separation from her job and family turned into an extended stay and then an ordeal.

Hobby stepped into a difficult, almost an impossible, situation. In the weeks leading up to the WAAC bill's final passage, the man charged with WAAC preliminary planning had been a lieutenant colonel with twenty years in the cavalry and without any qualifications whatsoever to plan a women's program. Assisted only by a female civilian, the colonel had to rely on the various agencies of the War Department to do the necessary preliminary planning for the WAACs. For example, the Quartermaster General was tasked with the design and procurement plans for uniforms and equipment, and the Adjutant General was asked to develop recruiting plans. Most of these agencies were also without the necessary expertise and experience to deal successfully with women's needs and, in general, could not have cared less. Moreover, the Army was going through an explosive expansion that had imposed staggering burdens on all of the agencies of the War Department.

Plans called for recruiting 12,000 women the first year and for peaking at 25,000 within two years. However, the recruiting offices were deluged with applicants from the moment they opened their doors. Also, requisitions for some 80,000 WAACs began pouring in from commanders in the field and other agencies. So, in June, before the first officers and enlisted women had completed their initial training, plans were under way to expand the program to 25,000 the first year and to an ultimate strength of 63,000 to be reached within two years. Accordingly, recruiting and training schedules were revised, and new facilities were planned to accommodate the accelerated buildup. Within three months, the 63,000 figure was discarded in favor of a still further expansion. The new figure soon bandied about the General Staff was a whopping

1.5 million. These recruitment goals were to prove unrealistic and to create tremendous burdens on the fledgling WAAC program.

Less than a month after the WAVE legislation was passed, the officer training school was ready for business with a class prepared to enter. In just over two months, three schools for specialty training for enlisted women were ready to go.

Apparently recognizing the absence of in-house capability, the Navy made the wise decision to turn to the academic community for advice and assistance in organizing the women's programs, as they had done in the past in setting up new male recruiting and training programs. Virginia Gildersleeve, dean of Barnard College, agreed to organize and chair an advisory council of prominent women college presidents, deans, and civic leaders from various parts of the country.

Because of the prestige of its members, the Advisory Council was able to call upon national experts in any field in making recommendations on the women's programs during the crucial early phase. Council recommendations on the WAVES went directly to the Chief of the Bureau of Personnel without having to overcome normal bureaucratic hurdles. Not only did this group furnish sound advice, based on years of experience with women's programs, which gave realism to the initial phases of Navy planning, but they also opened the campuses of some of the nation's most prestigious women's academic institutions, giving the WAVES an image of "class."

The Midship School, for indoctrination of officers, was set up at Smith College in Northampton, Massachusetts, and later augmented by nearby Mount Holyoke College. Recruit (boot) training for enlisted women was set up at Hunter College in New York City.

On the advice of the Advisory Council, Mildred McAfee was selected to head the WAVES program. President of Wellesley College, McAfee was an outstanding educator with impressive credentials and a knack of getting along with people—qualities she would need in abundance in the months ahead. She was appointed a lieutenant commander in the Naval Reserve, the highest rank authorized under the law. To help plan and organize the recruiting, training, and administration aspects of the WAVES program, a number of highly qualified, experienced women were selected and commissioned as lieutenants, lieutenants junior grade, and ensigns.

Another important and, as it turned out, crucial decision made by the Navy was to establish realistic, achievable recruiting goals and to stick with them. Initially, the Bureau of Personnel had estimated a total strength of 10,000 women, filled primarily by those with clerical skills. After the Bureau of Aeronautics alone indicated a need for 20,000, the personnel chief upped the figure to 75,000 enlisted women and 12,000 officers.

The Coast Guard and Marine Corps closely followed the Navy example and even proselytized some of the WAVE personnel as nuclei for their own women's programs. The Coast Guard, normally a part of the Treasury Department, was transferred to the Navy Department during the war to man invasion barges and troop and supply ships. By August 1942, coast guardsmen had seen plenty of action in the South Pacific, North Atlantic, and the Aleutians and were taking heavy casualties. In November, when the legislation authorizing the women's reserve in the Coast Guard was passed, the SPARs were organized. Like the WAVES, their purpose was to release men from the shore establishments for duty at sea and overseas, and their structure and training reflected that similarity. Shortly after the law was signed, twelve WAVE officers resigned from the Navy to accept commissions in the Coast Guard. Among them was Dorothy C. Stratton, who was appointed as director of the SPARs with the rank of lieutenant commander. Later, thirty-four enlisted WAVES also transferred over.

From the start, the Coast Guard found itself in competition with the other services, particularly the Navy since the average prospective recruit could not distinguish a SPAR from a WAVE because they wore the same uniforms and were recruited for the same kind of jobs. Pending establishment of their own facilities, the SPARs even trained with the WAVES. Then, the Coast Guard requisitioned the plush Biltmore resort hotel in Palm Beach, Florida for SPAR recruit training. Eventually, training for enlisted women moved to the regular Coast Guard training station at Manhattan Beach, and officer training was moved to the Coast Guard Academy. Thus, the Coast Guard became the first service to train women officers at its academy.

A smaller service with correspondingly fewer and smaller shore establishments, SPARs recruiting goals were more modest than the WAVES'. A first tentative survey of Coast Guard districts to determine how many women they could employ produced conservative numbers. After the commandant notified his district commanders that they were expected to use women to release men wherever they could, a second survey produced an 80 percent increase in the demand. Goals of 1,000 officers and 10,000 enlisted persons were set.

The Marine Corps was the most reluctant to accept women as a means of freeing men for combat, although a women's reserve was authorized on 30 July 1942. The battle of Guadalcanal in August, however, made it clear that more combat marines would be needed for the grinding battles that loomed in the Pacific. Ironically, the Marine Corps had a precedent in the marine (F) of World War I, when women first wore the forest green uniform with its famous globe-and-anchor insignia. But the commandant, Lt. Gen. Thomas Holcomb, knew in 1942 that admission of women marines this time would be on a much larger scale. Like many others, he was concerned that it would create "untold problems." In November, Holcomb, bowing to the inevitable and to persistent pressures from his own staff, recommended to the Secretary of the Navy that "as many women as possible should be used in noncombat billets thus releasing a greater number of the limited manpower available for essential combat duty."[1] The Secretary agreed, and plans were made to establish the Marine Corps Women's Reserve (MCWR) beginning in February 1943.

Strength goals, which were first set at 500 officers and 6,000 enlisted women, were soon raised to 1,000 and 18,000, respectively, because of requests from commanders for women and the favorable recruiting climate.

Following the Coast Guard example, the Marine Corps persuaded nineteen WAVE officers to transfer over as the nucleus of its Women's Reserve. Mrs. Ruth Cheney Streeter was appointed as director in the grade of major. At forty-seven, Streeter was an active, energetic woman who held both private and commercial pilot licenses. She had four grown children; three of her sons were in the service, two in the Navy and one in the Army.

As the Coast Guard had, the Marines trained the first female marine officers and enlisted women at the WAVE schools until their own training programs were set up at Camp Lejeune Marine Base, North Carolina.

With the establishment of the fourth and last of the women's "line" components, the U.S. military services embarked upon a new uncharted course for which they were not fully prepared.

THE LINE DIRECTORS

A decade earlier, Major Hughes had expounded the necessity of prior training for women and men so that the women would understand military thinking and the men would comprehend the problems of militarizing women. His warning had not been heeded. Now the first directors, grappling with problems in the unfamiliar, often hostile territory of the military staff and command system, often found themselves at odds with the organizations and their deeply rooted traditions.

The burden that lay on the women line directors was no small one. It was made all the heavier by their lack of military experience and the ambiguity of their positions within the organization which McAfee, the WAVE director, accurately described as "the dangling link in the chain of command."[2] Unlike the heads of the Nurse Corps, responsible for providing nursing services, the line directors had no functional responsibilities. Their jobs were initially ill defined, and the scope of their responsibilities and authorities was fuzzy. They were regarded by the service staffs with a mixture of bemused tolerance and suspicion. As neophytes to the military, they had to find their own paths in vast, unfamiliar bureaucracies overlaid with entrenched masculine traditions. Furthermore, the military bureaucracies, overwhelmed by the problems of building an enormous wartime force from scratch, were instinctively resistant to any innovations that might compound their problems or further threaten the status quo. So, understandably, the first twelve to eighteen months were a period of mutual adjustment, of trial and error.

There was no aspect of the women's programs that did not fall naturally within the responsibility and authority of some existing staff agency. So, whatever issues the directors pursued, they were treading on someone else's turf. Theoretically, whatever aspect of the male personnel program was handled by an agency would likewise be assumed for women. For example, the Quartermaster General was responsible for uniform, design, and procurement for Army men, so that office would do the same for WAAC uniforms. The Judge Advocate General would likewise handle disciplinary policies, and the Chief of Personnel would establish personnel policies for women as well as men. However, because of pressures of other, more pressing business and a tendency not to take women's programs seriously, what needed to be done did not always get done. On the other hand, some agencies, eager to charge ahead, often miscalculated and erred badly for lack of understanding of women's needs.

Without clear-cut authority, the directors' ability to influence decisions and coordinate actions depended on perceptions of their relationship to the power structure. In this respect they shared a number of severe handicaps. Because they were totally without military experience, their credibility was always in doubt. Because they held low rank in a hierarchy of top brass, they lacked military clout. Because they were women, it was difficult to be taken seriously.

The best things the line directors had going for them were: their backgrounds and personal qualities—experience with women, basic intelligence, and ability to get along with people; the fact that the men were basically unsure of themselves where women were concerned; and the general assumption in the service staffs that the directors had powerful connections—and they did. In fact, despite the high level of competence of these exceptional women, had they not had complete support from the top—from the President, the First Lady, the service Secretaries, and service Chiefs—it might have been a different story. Because of the uniqueness of their positions and the general perception of their power, the directors were able to exert considerable influence on the policies and procedures for women in the services. And when they acted jointly on issues unique to women, their influence was usually irresistible. For example, policies having to do with discipline, marriage, and pregnancy were worked out cooperatively.

Of the four directors, Hobby's situation was the most difficult and complex, but her quiet, self-possessed, dignified demeanor always gave the impression of being in complete control. "She made you feel that everything was running smoothly for the WAACs—that there were no problems in the Army," recalls a Navy woman who often attended joint meetings of the line directors. Nothing could have been farther from the truth. Had Hobby had any inkling of what lay ahead when she agreed to take the job of Director, WAAC, she might have had second thoughts and gone back to Texas.

Being first, the WAAC director had no precedents to fall back on so had to chart her own course. Although she was the youngest of the four, the other directors leaned heavily on Hobby's advice and experience. However, the WAAC's position outside the Army created problems unique to the War Department and placed Hobby in a position that differed from those of the three other directors. Hobby, by law, was designated "commander" of the Corps. As such, she was burdened with legal responsibilities for command without authority or control of policy or procedures. It was an untenable position in a military organization and could only lead to frustration, conflict, and confusion.

The location of the WAAC director's headquarters within the Army organization also created special obstacles. At the time she accepted the job, Hobby's office was slated to be in the General Staff, providing direct access to the Chief of Staff, General Marshall, who was her mentor. She would also have access to the policy guidance of the General Staff and therefore have the clout necessary to get the program rolling.

However, immediately after she was sworn in, the Army was reorganized and the General Staff streamlined. All operating functions were removed from the purview of the General Staff, leaving only policy and planning. Because of her dubious role as a "commander" with direct command over units, Hobby's office was moved out and down. A rumor abounded that there had been a contest among the chiefs of various agencies to see who would get stuck with the women's program and the Chief of Administrative Services of the Services of Supply lost. This arrangement proved to be a near fatal mistake. The Commander of Services of Supply (SOS), Lt. Gen. Brehon B. Somervell, was not supportive and had no appreciation for the unique problems of the WAAC and its director, who, three echelons removed from the Chief of Staff and isolated from the General Staff, had lost her chief power base.

Marshall had made it clear that Hobby could come to him should she encounter problems she could not resolve; but, as a practical matter, no one could circumvent the military chain of command without grave risks. Only when a situation grew desperate, and Marshall got wind of it, did he get involved.

Hobby was expected to command a corps administered and supervised by the SOS headquarters. She lacked the rank or authority to effect necessary action and could be vetoed by any other agency of the SOS headquarters. Yet her office was expected to do the work of each agency and submit it to them for their approval, compelling the hard-pressed WAAC staff to duplicate each agency's work without the agency's expertise. For example, Hobby was forced to prepare the annual budget for the Corps for submittal to Congress because the staff agency who prepared the Army budget said it was not its responsibility since the WAAC was not part of the Army. The same was true in housing, uniforms, supply, etc. This "catch 22" situation continued through the crucial first eighteen months of the women in the Army: the technical work of the WAAC was done by an office that knew little of the method, and the policy approval was given to agencies that knew little of the WAAC's overall needs. Staff conflicts were inevitable, confusion unavoidable.

By March 1944, Hobby's position within the SOS headquarters had become so difficult that Marshall directed that the Office of Director, WAC, be elevated to the General Staff within the office of the Chief of Army Personnel. At that point, her job and location in the staff closely paralleled those of the three other women directors. She was only an advisor, coordinator, catalyst, and titular head of the Corps. Although following the conversion to WAC, the WAC director had ceased to be a commander and became a staff officer, this distinction was never to be fully understood. The public in general and most people in the Army continued to look upon the director as the WAC "commander," a misconception often applied to the directors in the other services as well.

After three hectic and frustrating but nonetheless successful years as director, Hobby resigned in a state of ill health, probably brought on by exhaustion, overwork, and not a little exasperation with the U.S. Army. A glimpse of what she had endured was revealed in a statement she made shortly after resigning in 1945: "It was my feeling [at the time of appointment] that any woman who brought a Corps through its early difficulties had to fight so many battles and antagonize so many individuals that she must eventually destroy her usefulness to the Corps."[3]

Probably the most colorful of the first line directors was Mildred McAfee of the WAVES, who became something of a legend in her own time and remains one to this day. Fondly referred to as "Captain Mac," she was regarded by those who knew her as a brilliant, articulate person with a marvelous sense of humor and no phony affectations. She could disarm everyone from the lowliest yeoman to the top brass of the Navy, and did.

From the beginning, the WAVE director's office was established in the Bureau of Naval Personnel with direct access to the Bureau chief, Rear Adm. Randall Jacobs. McAfee was told to "run" the women's program and should she encounter problems to go directly to the Bureau chief. She had to make enough noise so that things got done. "But I really had no authority . . . except the authority of influence with Admiral Jacobs."[4] Whether she used this prerogative or not was not as significant as the impression it made on the rest of the staff. The admiral probably assumed that the mantle of his prestige would give McAfee the clout needed to deal with a reluctant staff, which, of course, it did. As a lieutenant commander, she would otherwise have been almost powerless in her dealings with agencies headed by senior, career naval officers. Naturally, this arrangement generated a certain amount of mistrust and resentment toward McAfee's office and often produced confusion and conflicting actions. But, on the whole, it was effective in getting the job done with a minimum of hassle.

Although Navy agencies often expected the WAVE office to do all of the staff work required by the women's program, McAfee's small staff with a handful of officers clearly made that impractical. So, the various offices had to cope with the needs of the women's program or default on their responsibilities.

After an initial shakedown period, McAfee was given the title of Special Assistant to the Chief of Naval Personnel for Women. In that position, she performed the role of innovator, coordinator, catalyst, front woman, and all-around "gadfly." By nature a direct person, she believed that if there was a problem you fixed it. She soon discovered the hard way that as a neophyte to Navy ways and as a lieutenant commander you do not get things done that way, particularly if you are only a woman with blue stripes on your sleeve. Being devious was against her better nature, but as a pragmatist she soon discovered how to get what she wanted and found out that meeting the issue head-on was often not the best way.

McAfee had female officers planted in each staff agency of the Bureau of Personnel. Each morning she had an informal coffee mess, known as Captain Mac's coffee klatsch, to which they were all invited whenever they could make it. Here they openly exchanged information, discussed problems, and explored ways to solve them. As one participant described it, "Nobody had any axes to grind, no turf to protect, like the men have, no concern for who got credit for anything. We just laid it all out on the table and decided how best to solve it." Each would then return to her own office and try to convince whomever was responsible for taking some action that it was his own idea. "It worked like a charm. Captain Mac usually got what she wanted and the men never knew what had hit them. It made them look good because they had solved this problem for the ladies."

Even though the four women's line components competed with one another for the available resources, the rivalry was always a friendly one, and their relationship was cooperative. They eventually formalized this relationship as a special subcommittee of the Joint Army/Navy Personnel Board and met regularly to discuss matters of mutual concern. A major policy affecting women was seldom adopted by one of the services until all had had the opportunity to consider it. Through the cooperation of this group, identical policies were usually developed and announced jointly. This spirit of cooperation and friendship existed until the directors' offices were abolished in the mid-1970s, although by that time there were growing disagreements on policy issues.

THE UNIFORMS

The design, development, and procurement of uniforms was a classic example of the bureaucratic bungling that characterized the women's programs during their first year, especially in the Army. In what may have been one of the greatest miscalculations of the war, the Quartermaster General in 1942 anticipated "no unusual difficulties" with WAAC clothing. In the end, whatever could go wrong did.

Several agencies within the Army General Staff, the Services of Supply, and the Quartermaster Corps with no expertise in women's clothing decided upon designs, materials, colors, and items to be issued. The WAAC director acted as an advisor only, had no final decision-making authority, and was often not consulted at all. When consulted, she was often overruled by the agencies.

From the beginning there was bickering over designs, materials, colors, and what items should be issued. Decisions were often made by ludicrous comparisons between male and female clothing items. For example, there was much discussion about whether women should be issued "foundation garments" since men were not. Yet it was generally agreed that women should be required to wear them to "present a neat and military appearance." It was also considered discriminatory to issue pajamas and bathrobes to women when they were not issued to men, but it was reluctantly agreed that it would not be appropriate to have women running nude around the barracks and to the latrines (gang bathrooms), which were often in separate buildings.

The Quartermaster Corps, which was responsible for design, had had some, though limited, experience in the development and procurement of the Army nurse uniform, but the numbers were very small and the uniform was something less than a total success. While it had seemed to photograph well on male dress forms, it had always looked a little peculiar on the female nurses.

Despite a somewhat masculine appearance, the basic design of the WAAC uniform was not all that bad considering how little precedent there was to go on. The end product, however, could not have been worse from any standpoint—cut, fit, color, tailoring, material, quality.

To begin with, the supply depot had failed to make graded designers' models in the various women's sizes, so the manufacturers had to develop their own. The contracts were let to manufacturers of men's wear because the women's garment manufacturers could not make them at the price the Army would pay. As might be expected, the end product looked and fit as though it had been intended for men rather than for women. The jackets were heavily padded in the shoulders and flat chested, and the skirts were too narrow for women's hips. Moreover, the materials used were generally unsatisfactory for women's clothes, and the colors of the skirts and jackets rarely matched. The general cut of the uniform plus the low-heeled, laced oxfords, men's shirts, and neckties combined to create a generally unfeminine appearance that did not enhance the WAAC's public image.

The supply system was a bureaucratic nightmare: the Army was unable to issue one complete set of authorized uniform items to its first groups of female recruits. During the first winter, half the women in some training centers graduated without uniforms. One center opened in Massachusetts in March 1943 with no uniforms at all. Thousands of women had to endure training, often in the snow, wearing the same single civilian outfit they were allowed to bring from home. The Army had simply failed to let the contracts in time, or in sufficient quantities, to meet the recruit accession schedules. Moreover, the supply system got fouled up by

a requirement to disperse the stocks on hand to five different training centers to support the unprogrammed expansion of WAAC
recruiting. In one instance, a supply depot shipped clothing items
needed at one training center to another center and vice versa, and
the depot commander refused to exchange them because it would
confuse his records. Even when supplies arrived, the depots soon
ran out of small sizes. Said one dismayed trainee, "It looks like
those clothes were intended for a race of giants." An enormous
amount of time and effort was expended cutting size 18L to fit
size 10S.

By the time the supply began to catch up with the demand in
mid-1943, the bottom had fallen out of the recruiting program,
and the Army was stuck with an enormous surplus of uniforms. By
then the gross deficiencies in quality and fit were evident, but,
because of the surplus of stocks, new improved uniforms could not
be procured. The women were stuck with them. Not until the
Army realized the negative effect the sorry state of uniforms was
having on morale and recruiting was the decision made to get rid
of the surplus and introduce a decent uniform. Meanwhile, right
in the middle of the clothing crisis, Director Hobby's office was
reorganized on the orders of General Somervell, and her supply
division was abolished on the premise that the functions were not
of sufficient importance to justify a separate division.

The Navy avoided the Army's problems by going to a well-
known women's fashion designer, Mainbocher of New York, for
the original design and then contracting with the women's fashion
industry to make the uniforms. WAVE Director McAfee recalled
that she became involved in the design of the WAVE uniform
almost by accident when she was told quite casually by a young
male staff officer who was handling WAVE uniform matters:
"We're having a showing this morning." She had known nothing
about it. With some reluctance, he told her she could come and
look at the uniforms if she wanted to. According to McAfee, the
original design "looked like a comic opera costume" with red,
white, and blue stripes to denote grade. The Navy did not want its
women in gold stripes so, at McAfee's insistence, light blue braid
was used. She later recalled that this was "a terrible slap in the
face" but that she did not know enough about the Navy to realize
it at the time.[5] It was not until the women achieved permanent
status after the war that the Navy reluctantly gave in and allowed
women to wear the gold. Despite these difficulties, the final design

of the WAVE uniform proved to be excellent and popular, and, with minor modifications, it survives to this day.

Another major controversy had to do with hose. Since men did not have to wear them, there was no precedent to fall back upon, and civilian custom required that women wear hose. Decisions on the matter were dictated to a large extent by wartime shortages. Japanese silk was no longer available, and the new nylon had immediately disappeared from lingerie and hosiery shelves, to reappear as parachutes. The only material left for stockings was cotton—either heavy weight or the finer lisle—and rayon. The Army had settled for the cotton in tan shades, which soon turned a dingy greenish yellow; but the Navy would not hear of cotton.

McAfee termed the ensuing conflict, which was resolved by a high-level decision, as the "battle of the black stockings." The Chief of Naval Operations, after visiting Canada and being impressed with the Women's Royal Naval Service members in black stockings, insisted that the WAVES should wear them, even though they strongly objected. American women did not wear black hose except in the evening hours, and the only ones available on the market were sheer rayon—very fragile and inappropriate for daytime wear. But the CNO would not be dissuaded; not even his wife or daughter could convince him. Only when he was told by a man during a dinner party that the dye used for black stockings was also needed in the manufacture of gunpowder and that it was in short supply did he back down. Because he did not want to jeopardize the war effort, Navy women could wear the tan rayon hose they preferred.

In another fortunate decision, the Navy avoided the Army's procurement and distribution problems by contracting with several local department stores in New York to do the issuing and final fitting of the uniforms. Within ten days of the opening of boot training at Hunter College campus, the stores were capable of outfitting seventy women an hour. Also, since it did not embark upon an unprogrammed expansion as the Army had, the Navy was never faced with monumental supply problems. Because the SPARs and women marines initially trained with the WAVES, they too benefitted from the Navy system.

Despite the confusion, bureaucratic bungling, and SNAFUs (Situation Normal—All Fouled Up), the women's programs moved forward at a pace that was nothing short of miraculous considering that each was starting from scratch—literally. Public attitudes were generally favorable, recruiting was far better than expected, and the requests from the field for women far exceeded the numbers available. That things went so well was a tribute to the services' abilities to adjust to new realities, however reluctantly. In fact, it was the Army's own newfound enthusiasm that nearly killed the goose that laid the golden egg.

NOTES

1. U.S. Marine Corps, *Marine Corps Women's Reserve in World War II* (Washington, D.C.: HQ U.S. Marine Corps, historical reference pamphlet printed 1964, revised 1968), p. 3.
2. Mildred McAfee Horton [Capt., USNR (Ret.)], *Recollections* . . . (Annapolis: Naval Institute Press, 1971), p. 17.
3. Treadwell, p. 720.
4. Horton, p. 17.
5. *Ibid.*, p. 52.

CHAPTER 5

THE BIG PUSH

By THE SUMMER of 1942, when the WAAC program was getting under way, six months had elapsed since the Japanese attack on Pearl Harbor had jolted the United States into the war that was to become the most stupendous military struggle in recorded history, costing twenty million casualties and another ten million deaths. One hundred million men and women would become engaged in the fighting forces of the belligerent nations. The great wealth and resources of the world would be concentrated on destruction in what was generally regarded as a "war of survival." By mid-1942, much of continental Europe had fallen to Hitler. Rommel's Africa Corps was sweeping unchecked through North Africa, and a million German troops were moving toward the oil fields of the Caucasus as the Eastern Front crumbled. British forces were largely pinned down to the defense of the home islands. Moreover, Britain's war effort had created severe strains on her manpower, and only by resorting to conscription of women had she been able to meet her commitments and to maintain herself precariously in her far-flung empire.[1] Meanwhile, America's Pacific frontier had been pushed back to the Hawaiian Islands. Gen. Douglas MacArthur had left the Philippines for Australia, which was itself jeopardized, Maj. Gen. Jonathan Wainwright had surrendered Corregidor, and Guam had fallen.

RECRUITMENT

The human resources of the United States were being mobilized as never before in history. Four million Americans were in uniform, and millions more were directly involved in vital war work. The War Manpower Commission, created to marshal this enormous effort, had been given near dictatorial powers over the allocation of human resources.

As late as May 1942, the only U.S. military women being mobilized were the nurses. From a peacetime strength of 940, the Army Nurse Corps had expanded to nearly 12,500 by June 1942, and the Navy Nurse strength had gone from 430 to just under 1,800. Twenty-one Army nurses had escaped from Corregidor before it fell in May, but sixty-six of them and eleven Navy nurses remained in Japanese prison camps in the Philippines for thirty-seven months. Another five Navy nurses, captured at Guam, were interned in a military prison in Japan.

It was becoming increasingly apparent that the choices the nation faced were to draft eighteen-year-olds, fathers, and men engaged in vital defense work, or to recruit women on a scale never envisioned during the abortive planning in the 1920s or during the preliminary planning for the WAAC in 1941–42.

The Army chose to beef up radically its recruitment of women —a decision so poorly conceived and ineptly executed that it was to place an excruciating burden on the frail WAAC organizational structure and eventually contribute to the restructuring of the Corps. Less than a month after the WAAC bill was signed, General Marshall informed his staff of his concern about the growing Army personnel shortages and told them he wanted every effort made to organize and train WAACs at the earliest possible date and to speed up the existing plans. Having received the order of their chief to charge, the General Staff finally got out of low gear and, in a bureaucratic scramble to produce results, succeeded in making a series of near-fatal blunders.

The first mistake was establishing unrealistic strength goals. War Department studies had indicated that the Army could easily employ as many as 1.5 million women. Of the military occupational specialties, only one in three was identified as "unsuitable" for women. These included combat jobs, jobs requiring considerable physical strength or working conditions or environment "improper for women," and jobs requiring a long training time. However, all supervisory positions were automatically declared unsuitable for women, as were certain types of personnel jobs such as classification specialist, personnel consultant, or psychological assistant since in these jobs women might be called upon to classify recruits for combat duty and "men would resent it."

The 1.5 million figure had also been validated by a survey of field commanders. It must have come as a shock to many old-timers when it was revealed that so many soldiers' jobs in their modern Army were "suitable" for women. Clearly, this revelation required a major change in thinking and some new policy decisions as to how many the Army would attempt to get, how they would get them, and how they would allocate them to using commands and agencies.

However, it seemed not to occur to anyone except Director Hobby at that point that it might not be possible to recruit that many women volunteers, particularly in a period of record employment opportunities for women in the private sector. Hobby expressed the view that the Army could probably not recruit even 150,000, much less ten times that number, without some sort of national service or conscription.

In November, Lt. Gen. Brehon B. Somervell, Commander, Services and Supply (later to become the Army Services Forces, or ASF), recommended to the War Department that legislation be sought to draft 500,000 women annually through regular induction facilities. Estimates projected that there were between 25 and 26 million women of service age, 13 million of whom should be available for the war effort. He reasoned that the Army could take 10 percent of the pool and leave the rest for other essential war work. Preliminary "feelers" to the Hill, however, indicated that Congress would not be receptive to legislation to draft women; so the subject was shelved.

Despite Hobby's warnings, after several months of vacillation the War Department decided in February 1943 to recruit 150,000 women by June of that year. With 34,000 on board at that point, this would amount to more than quadrupling the strength in four months. This decision was to have a calamitous impact on every aspect of the WAAC program—on recruiting, training, clothing, and administration.

The Army launched a crash recruiting drive unsurpassed in Army history. It pulled out all the stops: huge rallies, nationwide publicity, thousands of recruiters, door-to-door searches for prospective recruits. The drive was an unmitigated disaster. The number of qualified applicants actually fell off dramatically.

By the time the decision had finally been made to step up recruitment, it was already February, and that month, for the first time, recruiters had failed to meet their goal. Only 12,000 were recruited against a goal of 18,000. The bubble had burst, but the message was ignored. The goal for March was set at 27,000; only 11,500 were recruited. From then on it was downhill to 2,400 recruits in July and 839 in August.

In the final six weeks before the June 30 deadline, a last-ditch, all-out drive was launched—described as the most intensive recruiting effort it was possible to make. One aspect that involved a door-to-door search in which over 73,000 families were contacted produced only 168 recruits. The entire effort was a miserable failure.

Army planners were baffled. How could a program starting with such promise eight months earlier so suddenly turn around and be totally resistant to the Army's best efforts? In retrospect, the reasons are plain enough to see. Some were built in from the start and others developed over time. The initial post–Pearl Harbor surge was like the opening of the floodgates and it had soon to run its course; the WAAC's ambiguous auxiliary status was a handicap; growing competition from the other services eventually cut into Army recruiting; competition came from the war industry with its high-paying jobs; the organization and philosophy of the Army recruiters were obstacles; and the negative attitudes of the male G.I.s, coupled with the public disapprobation that produced a slander campaign chiefly targeting the WAACs, created a hostile environment. All these factors brought the recruiting drive to a grinding halt.

When the Marine Corps started recruiting women beginning that February, all four services found themselves competing for essentially the same resources. The WAAC was at a considerable disadvantage. First, it could not offer full military status: all the others could. Second, all of the other services offered better training facilities and housing. Third, the other services had superior recruiting personnel and facilities. And finally, the other services had more attractive, more feminine, better quality uniforms—not an insignificant consideration in appealing to women volunteers.

The Navy, recognizing the difficulty in recruiting WAVES, wisely gave direct appointments in high ranks to well-known advertising experts and authorities on sales methods to set up and run its program. Realizing that recruiting women was more selective than drafting men, it separated entirely the recruitment of enlisted women from the agencies that inducted enlisted men and placed it in the Office of Naval Officer Procurement.

WAAC recruiting, on the other hand, had been turned over to the same Army recruiting system that inducted male draftees on the mistaken assumption that no intensive recruiting effort for women would be required or advisable. The task of recruiting 150,000 volunteers in a matter of months was simply beyond a system that had never been organized or equipped to muster a volunteer recruiting effort of that magnitude. It was organized and staffed to recruit a modest number of men for a peacetime army of only 120,000 during a depression with high male unemployment, and since in wartime Congress had always instituted conscription, the Army had no first-rate sales organization.

The recruiting service hadn't the faintest idea how to recruit women and did not have the facilities to do so. Staffed by men with a "draft mentality" and a macho attitude, the recruiting service's offices were usually in the worst part of town, often on "skid row." Typical comments from enlisted women, as reported by Treadwell, were: "The recruiting station was in the dirtiest place I ever saw." "It was in the post office basement next to the men's toilets." "Everyone in the room turned to look as the captain bawled out 'Are you one of them Wackies?' " To turn WAAC recruiting over to an organization so poorly equipped to handle it, and then to impose impossible goals, made failure inevitable. In the first months of WAAC recruiting, when the numbers of applicants far exceeded the quota, the recruiters were able to cope. When the pressures generated by the massive expansion were imposed, the system quickly began to buckle under the strain.

Meanwhile, four additional WAAC training centers had been opened and prepared to receive tens of thousands of recruits who did not materialize. Three centers had to be closed within a few months. In addition, hundreds of officers and enlisted women who had been scheduled for the first assignments to Army stations were diverted to staff the new centers, to the annoyance of the station commanders who had prepared to receive them. Besides that, uniforms of bad quality were procured on a crash basis only to sit rotting on the shelves. In the words of one exasperated commander, "No one seemed to know what he was doing."

As WAAC recruiting plummeted, the Adjutant General, in charge of all Army recruiting, made the unilateral decision to lower female enlistment standards and to slacken controls on selection procedures. This action dramatically lowered the quality of the recruits and thus further aggravated the recruiting problem by giving the public the impression that the Army was scraping the bottom of the barrel for WAACs. In fact, it was reduced to recruiting its own previous rejects and the rejects of the other services. Yet, the quotas were raised again as the recruiters fell farther behind.

Within weeks, the previously high quality of the WAAC recruits had been seriously compromised. Hobby discovered the trend only after receiving complaints from the training centers and the field. She became so alarmed that she made a bold attempt to get WAAC recruiting transferred to her control so that she could restore the quality standards. It was her view that if low quality personnel constituted the majority of the volunteers, higher quality personnel would not volunteer.

By sacrificing quality for quantity, the Army, she felt, was not only destroying the recruiting climate but also seriously damaging the positive image that highly skilled women had created within the Army. Many male leaders felt that there was simply no place in the military for unskilled women of limited capacity or with tendencies to become administrative liabilities. Such women were considered unassignable. Men of that caliber were relegated to menial tasks generally involving heavy labor, i.e., stoking coal furnaces, road work, and the like—jobs for which women were not acceptable.

Because of her efforts to restore quality standards, Hobby came to be regarded as the villain in the Army's failure to meet its WAAC goals. A civilian male consultant charged with evaluating the WAAC problem complained:

> The root of the whole matter is that Mrs. Hobby feels that deterioration of standards would result from any mass recruiting technique, yet, whether she admits it or not, she has to have 385,000 WAACs by 1 July 44 . . . consideration [should] be given to appointment of a new WAAC Director capable of mass organization.

When the matter came to Marshall's attention, he sided with Hobby, and recruiting was transferred to her control. From then on the emphasis was on quality, but a great deal of damage had already been done. Regaining the lost momentum and the confidence in the quality of the women in the Corps was an uphill battle. In some respects it would be a losing one.

From the beginning, the primary emphasis of the women's programs had been on quality. In every case, the selection criteria for female officers and enlisted personnel were higher than those for men in the same service. Women were on the average better educated, of higher intellect, older, and more carefully selected in terms of character and personal backgrounds. Also, by design, the vast majority brought with them work experience of value to the services. While the services might have preferred a comparable quality among male recruits, the need for greater numbers of men, reliance on the draft, and the lower minimum age for men made this impractical. In fact, it soon became apparent that quality was a key factor in successful recruitment of women volunteers and in their acceptance by the services.

There can be little doubt that the women proved their value early on. The record of World War II is replete with testimonials attesting to the excellence of the women's contributions, their disciplined characters, and their overall positive effect on all the services. If there was one complaint common to all of the services, it was that there were not enough women. Commanders who in 1942 had cried, "Over my dead body will I take military women," were soon asking for their "fair share."

Nonetheless, the attitudes of military men continued to be the dominant factor influencing the acceptance and morale of the women individually and collectively. There was a constant, all-pervasive awareness that women had invaded a male preserve.

The attitude of each unit commander and how he communicated it to his men played a decisive role in how women were received in his command. But even when he projected a positive attitude, each woman found that in her immediate working environment she was pretty much on her own. In the words of a SPAR officer, "Reception by the men ranged from enthusiasm through amused condescension to open hostility." Each found that she had to prove herself each time she went to a new job or had a change in supervisors. Whereas a man was accepted immediately at face value and was assumed to be competent at his job, a woman was always regarded with suspicion. Because it was considered unnatural for a woman to join the military, she was often considered a deviate of some sort. And although she might have the technical skills for the job, there was something inherently and mysteriously different about doing any job the military way that women were supposed not to comprehend, whether the job was clerk-typist or gunnery instructor.

Men's attitudes were also determined by their desires or fears about going to sea or into combat. The recruiting themes for all the women's components were variations of "release a man for sea" or ". . . to fight." Early in the war, the military naively assumed that all able-bodied military men wanted to see action. In reality, many preferred the relative safety of stateside noncombat jobs and bitterly resented the idea of being replaced by a woman to go off to fight. Their resentment naturally focused upon those responsible—the military women.

Once a woman was on the job and proved that she was not only competent but that she did not expect special favors, the men usually came around even though deep down they may have held serious reservations about her invasion of their male world. More often than not, acceptance was an individual thing: "I don't approve of women in the service but she's O.K. . . . She's an exception." Collectively, however, the attitudes of male peers were rife with an antagonism that took its toll on the morale of the women and was soon communicated to the public at large.

The general public's attitude toward military women was for the most part favorable despite the reluctance of the press to treat the subject seriously. Reporters were accustomed to treating women in a cavalier, titillating manner. And women in uniform were fair game. Starting with Hobby's first press conference, reporters focused on either the trivial or the sensational—underwear, makeup, whether women would salute, whether enlisted women could date male officers and vice versa. Some of the stories were snide or mean, with titles like the "Petticoat Army," "Wackies," and "Latter-day Amazons." Cartoonists had a field day over bras and bosoms.

Nevertheless, the women seemed to weather the media attention well, at least initially. Things were going so well in the early months that it seemed the smears and gossip about military women that had sprung up following the establishment of all the previous women's groups might be avoided. The Nurse Corps had been subject to vicious attacks forty years earlier, as had all the British women's auxiliaries in both world wars. The attacks on the morals of the women in the British and Canadian armed forces had been so violent and widespread that they had nearly ruined recruiting. Contrary to early optimism, American women were not spared. In 1943, a campaign of slander descended upon the U.S. military women that was of unexpected viciousness and scope. Unfounded gossip and rumors were circulated within the military and the national media. Dirty jokes, snide remarks, obscenities, and cartoons became commonplace. It was a humiliating and demoralizing experience for the thousands of women who had responded to what they had perceived as their patriotic duty.

The campaign reached such extravagant proportions that the President, First Lady, and Secretaries of the services themselves attempted to squelch it. The President accused the press of a "deliberate newspaper job." The First Lady claimed that the rumors were Nazi propaganda and that "Americans fall for Axis-inspired propaganda like children." The Secretary of War stated that "sinister rumors aimed at destroying the reputation of the WAACs are absolutely and completely false. Anything which would interfere with their recruiting or destroy the reputation of the corps, and by so doing interfere with increase in combat strength of our Army, would be of value to the enemy."[2]

A full-scale investigation by Army Intelligence with the assistance and cooperation of the FBI produced no evidence of enemy involvement. After exhaustively running down spurious rumors to their sources, investigators found not enemy agents but American G.I.s. In the machismo world of barracks humor, where women and sex are a primary topic, military women had become fair game. Having joined what was a masculine domain, the women were "asking for it." The underlying motive was to degrade military women and to drive them out of the "man's world." In the words of one WAAC leader, "Men have for centuries used slander against morals as a weapon to keep women out of public life." It is as true in 1982 as it was in 1943. But it is not as effective now as it was then because women are less willing to play the role of victim today. Nonetheless, military leaders are still not adequately sensitized to their responsibilities for the well-being of the women in their charge.

While the Army women took the brunt of the attack in 1943, the other women's services were not impervious. The Commandant of the Marine Corps, Lt. Gen. Thomas Holcomb, felt compelled to send a letter to all commanding officers of posts and stations on 14 August 1943, reminding them of their responsibility for the behavior of men toward women marines.

Information reaching this Headquarters indicates that in some posts and stations officers and men of the Marine Corps treat members of the Women's Reserve with disrespect. . . . In some cases, coarse or even obscene remarks are being made without restraint by male marines . . . in the hearing of members of the Women's Reserve. . . . This conduct . . . indicates a laxity in discipline which will not be tolerated. . . . Commanding officers will be held responsible to this Headquarters.

To remedy attitudes within the Army, Hobby proposed a campaign to reeducate male personnel. Her suggestion never got past General Somervell. Months later General Marshall was outraged when he saw some of the material being circulated about WAACs, including literature mimeographed and circulated by soldiers to every Army installation, cartoons from soldier publications, and G.I. crank letters. The most unexpected were anti-WAAC statements made by general officers who had little or no experience in the employment of WAACs. Marshall was moved to write a letter to all Army commanders reminding them of their leadership responsibilities for the attitudes of the men in their commands and reminding them that "all commanders . . . are charged with the duty of seeing that the dignity and importance of the work which women are performing are recognized and that the policy of the War Department is supported by strong affirmative action."[3]

Even after the slander campaign had peaked and begun to play itself out, the attitudes of the male G.I. continued to have a dampening effect on morale and recruiting. In early 1944, Army recruiters reported that their number one problem in recruiting enlisted women was the attitude of enlisted men. According to one prospective recruit, "The trouble lies with the U.S. men. The average serviceman absolutely forbids his wife, sweetheart or sister to join a military organization, and nearly all U.S. women are in one of these categories." In that period, and to a certain but lesser extent today, a major constraint on the lives of women was their subservience to the opinions of the men in their lives. Parental attitudes toward daughters were shaped by this same social disapprobation.

The heavy public relations and advertising campaigns for military women that were designed to enhance public acceptance and thus to help recruiting produced a backlash that further inflamed the men's already negative attitudes. Since men were subject to draft, no massive recruiting campaign was required to enlist them. But they resented the fact that the women were getting all the attention while the men were doing the fighting and dying.

Conversion from an auxiliary corps (WAAC) to full military status as the Women's Army Corps in the late summer of 1943 removed one of the principal impediments to recruiting and morale. It also resolved much of the internal confusion.

The WAC was integrated into the normal Army command channels. But because the "corps" concept was retained, many people were unaware that any change had taken place and continued to view the WAC as a separate command and the women as auxiliaries. For the women, however, integration was a real shot in the arm. Coming right in the middle of the slander campaign, the conversion gave them the official message that they were wanted and needed by the Army.

When offered the option of converting to WAC, most of the officers and three out of four of the enlisted women elected to stay on. WAAC "relative ranks" were converted to Army ranks: thus 1st, 2nd, and 3rd officers WAAC became 1st and 2nd lieutenants and captains; auxiliaries became privates, and so on. For the first time, Army women were entitled to equal pay and most of the benefits normal to military status, which had been enjoyed by the women in the other services for over a year.

The relationship between the Director, WAC, and the Army Service Forces (ASF) (formerly Services of Supply) staff was not much improved by the new status, however. Even though she was no longer in command of the Corps, Hobby's position within the ASF headquarters remained essentially unchanged and, if anything, had become more untenable. Although officially designated advisor to the Chief of Staff, General Marshall, and to the Air and Ground Forces, she remained, for all practical purposes, boxed in by the ASF staff and lacked the support of her commander, General Somervell. The situation was best described by a prominent civilian advisor to the ASF staff who was asked to diagnose the problems of the WAAC at the time of the conversion. In blunt terms, he accused Somervell's headquarters of killing the WAAC with its left hand while publicly supporting it with its right:

> Does the Army really want the [new] WAC to succeed? I am not at all convinced that the answer is "yes." . . . I have seen no real evidence of such a desire. . . . Are civilians really convinced that the WAC is an important organization? Civilians will be convinced of this only when the Army is convinced of it.

Finally, after six more months of SNAFUs and confrontations

within the ASF headquarters, General Marshall in exasperation interceded and in March 1944 had the director's office moved up to the General Staff in Personnel, where it remained until it was discontinued thirty-four years later. With that transfer, more of the director's recommendations on major issues were approved in two weeks than had been in the previous two years in ASF.

NOTES

1. In December 1941, the National Service Act No. 2 made British women subject to conscription. One significant difference existed between men and women, however, in that no woman called up for service could be required to use—or touch—any lethal weapon without her written consent. The first women conscripts were called up in March 1942. During the three-year period in which conscription was used, 74,000 British women were inducted into the Army.
2. Treadwell, p. 205.
3. *Ibid.*, p. 275.

CHAPTER 6

CONSOLIDATION

B Y THE BEGINNING of 1944, it was possible for a woman to walk down a public street in uniform without being stared at like some kind of freak. With 120,000 women in uniform and most of them stationed in the United States, the novelty had worn off. Considering the long tradition of machismo associated with the military image and the instinctive resistance to radical social change, the integration of women into the services had gone remarkably well. The programs had outgrown their status as dubious experiments, and the women were fitting into the previously all-male environment better than most people had expected. They were serving in a far wider range of jobs and at more locations than had originally been anticipated.

The first twelve to eighteen months proved that in the absence of a female draft, the numbers of women the services could employ were limited only by the ability to recruit them. By 1944, recruiting had leveled off to a point where a gradual growth in strength was assured, but it became clear that the supply of volunteers would never meet the demand. Women volunteers would never exceed more than 2.3 percent of the total military strength during the war, but what they lacked in quantity they generally made up for in quality. Moreover, for every woman volunteer recruited one less man had to be drafted.

The War Department had estimated in the fall of 1943 that it would have to draft an additional two million men in the coming year. It was not what the public wanted to hear. The "war of survival" had been going on for nearly two years, and public enthusiasm for it was growing thin. Moreover, most Americans naively believed that victory was just around the corner. Roosevelt and Churchill had demanded unconditional surrender. The Allied forces under Eisenhower had pushed the German and Italian forces out of North Africa, had taken Sicily, and were fighting their way up the boot of Italy. The German eastern offensive had been broken, and the enemy forces were being pushed back, sustaining appalling losses. In Europe, Eisenhower had been selected as Supreme Commander to direct the Allied invasion. In the Pacific, MacArthur's forces were closing the ring around Japan, fighting bloody battles from island to island. Casualties in both areas were mounting. Some eleven million Americans were in uniform, and the manpower pool was just about drained of eligible men.

The irony of the situation was that the Army had earlier estimated that some 600,000 military jobs could be done *better by women*. Presumably, since the women had not been recruited, the jobs were being filled by men who might otherwise have been available for combat assignments.

The War Department estimated that some 446,000 fathers would have to be drafted unless enough women could be recruited in their stead. But the experience of 1943 left no doubts that recruiting that many women volunteers was totally out of the question. Although public attitudes toward the women had become more positive, there was a general feeling that if the women were really needed they would be drafted. In fact, the Army seriously considered urging just that.

Hobby had told General Marshall in September 1943 that the Army could not obtain an adequate supply of women to meet its needs through volunteer means. Gallup polls conducted in late 1943 showed that a surprising 78 percent of the public had concluded that single women should be drafted before any more fathers were taken. Of the single women of draft age, three out of four endorsed the idea but stated they would not volunteer as long as the government did not feel it was important enough to draft them.

A proposal was prepared by the War Department on selective service for women, stating that "an obligation rests upon women as well as men . . . to render such personal service in aid of the war effort as they may be deemed best fitted to perform." Population data indicated that there were roughly five million women who could qualify by WAC standards. Only 631,000 of them would have to be inducted to satisfy the Army requirements for WACs and nurses.

Nonetheless, without serious military reversals, the prospect of drafting American women was remote at best. With her usual perceptiveness, Hobby observed that "what happens on the question of Selective Service [for women] depends on how long the war lasts. I do not think there is any thought of it in Congress at this time."[1] In January 1944, a bill that would have provided for conscription was actively considered by Congress but was defeated in committee.

In the winter of 1943–44, with preparations for the invasions of Normandy and New Guinea, all of the services were stripping their stateside bases of physically fit men and shipping them to combat theaters and the fleets. Requests for military women as replacements soared. Requests for WACs from overseas theaters also rocketed.

In March 1944, Marshall stated publicly that for American women, aside from urgent family obligations, enlistment in the military should take precedence over any other responsibility. "It is important," he said, "that the general public understand the Army's urgent need for women to enable the military effort to go forward according to the schedule of operations in prospect."[2]

Unfortunately, the War Manpower Commission, the supreme national arbiter in the allocation of human resources, never seemed to get the message. Throughout the war, the services were competing not only with one another but with the war industry and agriculture as well. In the process, they were locked in a continuing battle with the War Manpower Commission, which was imposing restrictions on where the services could recruit and on whom they would be allowed to take.

In February 1943, the Commission had compelled the services to accept sweeping limitations on enlistments of women. In effect, the Commission took the remarkable position that the requirements of the armed forces were secondary to those of the Civil Service, war industries, or agriculture. It also placed most major population areas off limits to the recruitment of women, even those not classified as "labor-tight areas." It ruled that the armed forces should limit their recruitment to unskilled women from low mental categories, the exact opposite of the services' needs. Despite the protestations of the armed forces, the Commission continued to put up obstacles to the recruitment of women throughout the war under the apparent assumption that there were no legitimate requirements for women in the military anyway.

By mid-1944, the services were really scraping the bottom of the barrel for men. Although nearly at peak strength, all of the services needed to recruit replacements for losses in order to sustain their strengths. A suggestion was made that the Army should recruit 4-F men (physically unqualified) instead of women as replacements. The Secretary of War replied that he would prefer a good, capable WAC any day. "We need women because they have the skills we are looking for," he said. "It is not economy to take men from their families and from jobs in essential industry to do work in the Army which women . . . could do with less training." The Chief of Staff said that the Army needed fighting men as combat replacements, not 4-Fs, and WACs qualified for those jobs requiring the technical and administrative training commonly found among women.

As a result of Army efforts to revive WAC recruiting, enlistments improved somewhat, despite the obstructionist tactics of the War Manpower Commission. All of the services held the line on quality, which they believed continued to pay off in efficiency and acceptance.

During this period of consolidation, the occupations of military women expanded far beyond the limited range initially prescribed for them. Whereas it had been assumed in 1942 that they would be employed in only three or four skills, personnel shortages and operational necessity soon dictated otherwise. By 1944, women were performing a wide range of military jobs.

Earlier, it had been assumed that there must be some finite number of military women that could be used in each service and that each service, by identifying the "women's jobs" and surveying commanders to determine their requirements, could come up with at least a ballpark figure. But it never worked that way. Women began to move out of the stereotype jobs into nontraditional fields, and the services soon revised their "requirements" upwards as the manpower pinch got worse. The only real controlling factor continued to be how many women could be recruited. It was a matter of deciding how to utilize and allocate the resources available.

For the women, job satisfaction was probably the single most important element in their daily lives. Morale was best when women worked in jobs that matched their skills and training and when they felt they were contributing directly to the war effort.

Unfortunately, by modern standards the personnel systems were still in the horse-and-buggy stage. The services were used to bulk allotments of manpower furnished by the draft and were notorious for what seemed to be a total (sometimes deliberate) disregard for matching individual skills and abilities to job requirements. In this respect, the women may have fared a little better than the men because the skills many of them possessed were in critically short supply—namely, typing and other clerical skills, i.e., the so-called women's skills. Their most common complaint still was not being assigned to jobs that used the skills they brought from civilian experience or for which they had been trained by the services.

However, as more men were being shipped overseas, demands increased for women to replace them in jobs previously considered unsuitable or marginal for women. Before long, women were serving in virtually every occupation outside of direct combat—as control tower operators, Link-trainer instructors, radio operators and repairmen, parachute riggers, gunner instructors, naval air navigators, engine mechanics, celestial navigation instructors, aerophotographers, and the like.

Highly classified projects, previously off limits, were opened to women. For example, both the Navy and Coast Guard employed women in LORAN (Long-Range Aid to Navigation) stations, at that time the most sophisticated and highly classified navigation system. One Coast Guard LORAN station was staffed entirely by SPARs. WACs were assigned to the super-secret Manhattan Project, code name for the atomic bomb project, and WAVES participated in a highly secret night-fighter training project.

The men were astonished to see that the women were good workers and could do things the "Army way" or the "Navy way" or the "Marine way." Initially there was grave concern that women would resist the regimentation of military life, particularly the marching. Much to everyone's surprise, the women adapted very well, probably because they were highly motivated. They took to drill like ducks to water, their parades and ceremonies were spectacular, and whenever they competed with men, they invariably marched off with the honors.

The women never quite adjusted to some things, and the services were forced to make concessions. For example, the women did not like heavy military food. They especially disliked beans with brown bread and creamed chipped beef on toast (referred to as SOS) for breakfast. They also frowned on heavy lunches. So, at the insistence of the women, salads began to appear and, to the surprise of many an old mess sergeant, the men began to eat them, too.

Women had an insatiable need to know the *why* of what they were doing, a characteristic disconcerting to the male military mind, which had been imbued with the philosophy "Ours not to reason why—ours but to do or die." A later WAVE director, Jean Palmer, recalled that at the Navy secret communications center in Washington, women spent long, dull hours staring at screens, watching for "blips" which were to be immediately reported. It was boring, sense-numbing work. No one had bothered to tell the women why they had to do it. When they were told that each blip represented one of our ships being sunk, the jobs took on more meaning and morale improved.

Also, women insisted on privacy almost to the point of obsession. They abhorred gang showers and open toilet areas. It was almost unthinkable to a woman to use a commode in open view of others or to strip naked and shower in front of other women. Thus, the first thing they did upon moving into military barracks built for men (which most were) was to hang curtains and build partitions in the latrines and heads from whatever materials they could lay their hands on.

The next thing they did was to ask for laundry tubs, ironing boards, and electrical outlets. Men used base laundry facilities, but women's clothing would not have survived the brutal process. The women preferred to do their own laundry anyway and demanded the facilities for it. In the meantime, they did their ironing on their G.I. bunks or footlockers, blowing fuses as they went.

Women were used to entertaining men in their homes. This meant providing a place to entertain their dates in a wholesome, familylike atmosphere without invading the privacy of the women who wanted to sit around reading, sewing, or just rapping. The result was often two dayrooms instead of one—one for the dates, the other for relaxing and letting their hair down. Each organization had "unit funds," which were allocated per capita from profits made at base concessions and exchanges. The men generally used their money for an occasional "beer bust." The women used theirs to fix up the dormitories with drapes, furniture, sewing machines, and kitchen equipment.

Although they would rarely admit it, many of the young

enlisted women liked having a curfew at night because it gave them an excuse to get home from a date at a reasonable hour when they were tired and had to get up early to go to work. For the men, it was part of the military masculine mystique to stay up half the night partying and go to work hung over, behavior not tolerated in women.

It was difficult for most military men to comprehend or accept the possibility that most jobs in the military were not inherently masculine. Like the male Marine Corps office clerks in World War I who estimated it would take two women to replace one male marine at a desk, most men genuinely believed the masculine mythology of the military world.

Throughout the war, the services conducted studies to determine exactly what kinds of jobs women could and should do. The subject is still being debated four decades later. The Army in 1942 and the Marines in 1943 conducted two of the earliest and most extensive studies.

The Army classified all MOSs (military occupational specialties) as either "unsuitable" or "suitable" for women. The unsuitable category included any specialty involving combat, specialties requiring considerable physical strength or placing women where conditions or environments were "improper," and specialties requiring long training time. After discovering that nearly four million Army jobs fell in the "suitable" category under those criteria, the Army decided to take another cut at it. It declared as unsuitable all supervisory jobs over men and certain personnel jobs such as classification specialists and personnel consultants, on the assumption that male recruits would resent having a woman classify them for combat duty. After applying these and other subjective criteria, the Army revised the number of "suitable" jobs from 4 million to a more palatable 1.3 million.

The Marine Corps classified all MOSs in varying degrees of "appropriateness" for women based on "innate female capabilities" to perform work in contrast to the men they were to replace. Their four categories were:

Class I: Jobs in which women are better, more efficient than men. Examples: all clerical jobs, especially those involving typing or requiring fairly routine tasks but coupled with a high degree of accuracy in the work; administrative jobs connected with organization and administration of the Women's Reserve; and instructional jobs of all types.

Class II: Jobs in which women are as good as men, and replaced men on a one-to-one basis. Examples: some clerical jobs in which men are especially good, such as accounting; some relatively unskilled service or clerical jobs, such as messengers or Post Exchange clerks; some of the mechanical and skilled jobs, such as watch repairman, fire control instrument repairman, tailor, sewing machine operator—especially those jobs requiring a high degree of finger dexterity.

Class III: Jobs in which women are not as good as men, but can be used effectively when need is great, such as wartime. Examples: most of the jobs in motor transport—men are better as motor mechanics and even as drivers when the equipment is heavy and the job demands loading and unloading as well as driving, as it often does; most of the "mechanical" and "skilled" jobs; supervisory and administrative jobs, such as first-sergeant (except in WR units) where maximum proficiency depends on years of experience in the Marine Corps, and also some supervisory jobs where part of the personnel being supervised is male; strenuous and physically tiring jobs, such as mess duty where experience showed that more women had to be assigned to cover the same amount of work because they could not endure the long hours and physical strain without relief as well as men.

Class IV: Jobs in which women cannot or should not be used at all. Examples: jobs demanding excessive physical strength, such as driving extremely heavy equipment, stock handling in warehouses, heavy lifting in mess halls; jobs totally inappropriate, such as battle duty or jobs requiring that personnel be engaged at particularly unfavorable hours, jobs protected by special civil service regulations for civilians, such as librarians.

The primary constraint on the utilization and assignment of women in the three naval components during the war was the law prohibiting them from serving at stations outside the continental United States. The restriction to the U.S. bases was later modified to allow assignments to specific territories of the United States but not to foreign countries. No similar geographic restrictions applied to WACs or nurses.

Initially, all Navy ratings (specialties) were assumed open to women, at least in theory. Decisions on women's jobs were made on a decentralized basis depending on the needs of the naval stations. However, some enlisted ratings, such as control tower operator, soon became so suffused with WAVES that the Navy became concerned those jobs might be taken over entirely by women. To preclude this, the Navy began to control centrally the proportions of women who could enter certain ratings.

Probably the most progressive and innovative military units in the employment of military women throughout the war were the aviation components of all the services. Not only were they the first to show enthusiasm for the women, but they used more. Military women were in great demand at air stations and were generally received well and made to feel needed. This favorable climate in all probability was a direct reflection of the positive attitudes projected by the aviation leaders at that time. Less tradition bound in attitude, most of these leaders made no bones about their support of women and their views that the women were an essential, integral part of their organizations., For this reason, the aviation components usually were more willing to open technical fields and to integrate the women more fully into their organization.

In the Army Air Forces (AAF) under the leadership of Gen. Henry H. "Hap" Arnold and his staff, no measure was neglected that might impress upon the public and his commanders the AAF's real need for "Air-WACs" and its cordiality toward them. Lt. Gen. Ira Eaker, Air Commander in Chief in Europe, and Lt. Gen. George C. Kenney in the Pacific had similar views. No AAF schools were closed to women, except combat and flying schools, and no noncombat jobs for which they could qualify were closed. Approximately 40,000 women served as Air-WACs at bases all over the world—they included nearly half of all the women in the Army.

Another thousand women known as the WASPs (Women's Airforce Service Pilots) were hired as pilots in Civil Service status to ferry military aircraft, tow air gunnery targets, and teach flying to AAF flying cadets. The group logged nearly 300,000 flying hours during its three years of existence. During much of that time, its leader was Jacqueline Cochran, Director of Women Pilots, who had already flown almost everything with wings. As General Arnold pointed out, she "several times had won air races from men who are now general officers of the Air Force."

By the time they were disbanded in 1944, the WASPs had flown nearly every aircraft in the AAF inventory, including bombers and fighters, and thirty-eight lost their lives doing it. Their primary role was to release male pilots for combat duty; they were not permitted to fly combat missions.

The WASPs as a group were never granted full military status.[3] A number of them later received commissions in the armed forces, but not as pilots. The peacetime Air Force was not ready to take that step until 1976, and then only reluctantly.

In the Navy more than one in four WAVES—more than 23,000—served in naval aviation. Some were noncombat crew members, but none were pilots although a thousand taught instrument flying. Others taught aircraft gunnery and celestial navigation. Some one hundred female officers were trained as navigation instructors. Although they received fifty hours in flight, none were used as air crew members.

Nearly a third of the Women Marines served in aviation at Marine Corps air commands and stations in the United States and Hawaii. At Cherry Point Marine Air Station, 90 percent of the parachute packing, repair, and inspection and 80 percent of the air control tower operations were handled by women.

The services differed considerably in their treatment of women officers. The WAC officers faced a unique set of circumstances that stemmed from their auxiliary status in the first year. Where the other services started off with the idea of employing female line officers in staff assignments as replacements for male officers, the Army did not.

The Navy and Coast Guard recruited women officers for the primary purpose of releasing male officers for sea duty. Although the first women commissioned were mostly assigned to administration and communications, as more male officers were pulled out, WAVES and SPAR officers moved into the more technical jobs —finance, chemical warfare, aviation ordnance, aerological engineering, navigation instruction, aviation gunner instruction, etc.

During the auxiliary phase, the Army recruited women officers only to administer the enlisted women. Not only were there no provisions for WAAC officers to replace male officers in staff, technical, or command positions, but they were specifically prohibited by law from commanding male personnel, unless ordered to do so.

In mid-1943, after the expansion of the enlisted program failed to materialize, the Army ended up with a large surplus of unassignable WAAC officers. So, at the time of the conversion to WAC, provisions were made for WAC officers to move into staff and technical jobs, which many of them welcomed. But the women officers were about as welcome in their new roles as a school of piranha. They often complained of not being given responsibilities commensurate with their rank and abilities. They were sometimes used in jobs appropriate to enlisted personnel, such as secretary, aide, or even chauffeur, usually to general officers. Nonetheless, WAC officers were soon serving in all of the Army branches and arms except the combat arms. WAC troop duty came to be regarded as "glorified housemother," to be avoided at all costs.

In late 1943, the Army arbitrarily reduced WAC Officer Candidate School (OCS) to 200 per year. The reason given was that there was a surplus of male Army officers; however, no similar reduction was made in male OCS. The War Department set the ratio of female officers to enlisted women at one to twenty. The ratio of male officers to enlisted men was one to ten. The net effect was to impose an arbitrary ceiling on WAC officers and to almost close off opportunities for women to gain commissions in the Army.

Requests from commands to allow qualified women to attend male OCS in the various branches and commands were refused. For example, the Army Air Force had 300 highly qualified enlisted women whom it wanted to commission and for whom there was an urgent need, but the War Department refused to allow the women to attend either the small WAC OCS or the AAF School. There can be little doubt that the primary motivation behind the Army's decision in this case was a strong general reluctance to accept female officers in any jobs other than ones in support of the women's programs.

The whole thrust behind the Army's desire for military women was to provide *enlisted skills*, not officers. When the WAC officer strength became surplus to the requirements of the WAC enlisted program, the Army simply did not know what to do with WAC officers; thus the overall surplus of Army officers was used as the excuse to cut off the flow.

THE AAA EXPERIENCE

The Army in December 1942, on orders from General Marshall, launched an experiment to determine what AAA (antiaircraft artillery) duties could be performed by women and with what degree of success. This brief test was to be the only American experience in using women in more or less tactical combat roles until modern times. It was conducted on the East Coast partly in response to genuine concern of possible air attacks, particularly on the nation's capital. The experiment was kept secret because of the highly classified equipment, and because the Army feared bad publicity since the women were integrated into a mixed male/female tactical unit. Women were employed in over half of the jobs in two mixed batteries in the vicinity of Washington, D.C. They were not assigned to actually fire the guns nor were they given training in small weapons.

At the completion of the test, it was concluded that WAAC personnel could be used to perform many tasks of the AAA; they were superior to men in all functions involving delicacy of manual dexterity (such as operation at the director, height finder, radar, and searchlight control systems); and they performed routine repetitive tasks in a manner superior to that of men. Morale was generally high because they felt they were making a direct contribution to the successful prosecution of the war.

How much of the report's observations reflected preconceived notions about women's manual dexterity and performance of dull, repetitive work can only be surmised. However, of the experiment's success there can be no doubt since at its end the AAA Command requested to retain the WAAC they had and be authorized ten times more. The Army General Staff agreed with the conclusions but would not agree to allocate women for that purpose because the need for AAA protection on the East Coast had subsided and it felt the women could be better used elsewhere.

Over the years the experience would be forgotten, buried in Army files. Another thirty-five years would pass before the use of women in any form of combat in the U.S. armed forces would be seriously considered again.

NOTES

1. Treadwell, p. 247.
2. *Ibid.*, p. 250.
3. U.S. Congress, 23 November 1977: granted military veteran status to women who served in the WASP during World War II.

CHAPTER 7

ATTITUDES AND
CHANGING CUSTOMS

THE INFLUX OF women into the previously all-male military challenged both the outlook of the armed forces and their deeply entrenched customs. In many respects the women did not fit into the highly structured, tradition-bound military society. For the most part, the women were forced to adapt to institutional social values, rules, and modes of life. However, the services, although they resisted, eventually succumbed to some adjustments in the organization, particularly in matters of social conduct and policies unique to women.

Concurrently, the services had to deal with a different set of problems arising from the recruitment of larger numbers of black men and, ultimately, some four thousand black women. Segregation, which was deeply ingrained in policies and attitudes, came under increasing pressures for reform. Although officially established racial segregation survived the war, its days were numbered. However, racial prejudices, like sexist ones, were not eradicated by official adoption of integration and continued to plague the military for years to come.

From the outset, all of the services tended to treat enlisted women like immature girls in a boarding school, away from home for the first time. In part, this was a reflection of the military's traditional attitudes toward enlisted personnel, which was by habit paternalistic, and in part a reflection of our cultural attitudes toward women in the 1930s.

The male recruit before the war was a teenager, sometimes as young as seventeen. Even during the war, when older men were inducted, a large proportion of the enlisted men were under twenty. The enlisted women, by contrast, were relatively mature women, all twenty years or older, with an average age running in the mid-twenties. Many were married, some had children, and a few even had grandchildren. Yet, the services persisted in thinking of adult mature women as girls in the literal sense. The female leadership was particularly prone to this, probably because so many of the senior officers were from the academic community where they were used to dealing with schoolgirls. The cultural value system imposed upon the women in the services was that which prevailed in the American society of the 1930s. It was not far removed from Victorian, the influence of the 1920s sexual revolution notwithstanding.

While genuine concern for the moral welfare and reputations of the women was an important factor here, the primary motivation was the overwhelming desire for acceptance by both the military and the public at large.

But whatever the motivation, there was an ever present, almost prudish concern for protecting military women's virtue, chastity, and reputation—individually and collectively. Each woman was made responsible not just for her own conduct but for the collective reputation of the entire group, indeed, of all women in the services. As Hobby admonished her officers, "I want you to impress on each [woman] that she is not one person being judged by the public, but the Corps is being judged by the things she does."[1]

For a member of the WAAC, being charged with "conduct bringing discredit upon the Corps" was grounds for discharge, and there was no legal recourse. One concerned Judge Advocate complained to Hobby: "For goodness sake, treat these girls like the enlisted men of the Army and do not try to chaperone and shelter them in too exacting a fashion . . . their lives should be more or less left to their own guiding." While he had a point, he could hardly have been in a position to understand the pressures the director and the women were under, particularly during the slander campaign and its aftermath. The women hardly needed to be reminded by their directors that they were subject to public curiosity and scrutiny.

Because of their societal backgrounds and their overwhelming desire for acceptance and approval, particularly by the men of their services, the women in general were most intolerant of any misconduct in their groups. The peer pressure to conform to the prevailing standards of conduct for women was considerable and effective. In this context the women's dormitory or barracks played an important role.

Unlike the men's dormitory where men spent very little time except to sleep, the women's dormitory represented a home away from home. It was the one place the women could retreat to from constant outside pressures. It was the one place the enlisted women could let their hair down and relax, be themselves. It was particularly true in overseas areas where social activities off base were limited or nonexistent. With the single exception of the movies, social and recreational activities on military bases were designed by and for the men. Women often felt conspicuous and out of place, even at the service clubs.

Moreover, the men could always go off base "on the town" either singly or in groups. The women had less freedom of movement than today. As a result, the women spent much more time in their dormitories than the men did.

The dormitory served as a refuge from the whole gamut of sexual harassment that military women were subject to, which ranged from verbal abuse to outright propositioning and created at its least a hassle and at its worst a climate of hostility and fear. "You can't even go into the chow hall without running the gauntlet," complained a corporal. "You feel naked and you want to hide. It doesn't do any good to complain to your boss about it. He just shrugs it off as a joke. And, you can't complain to the women officers because they are powerless to do anything about it, besides they get the same hassle from the guys—sometimes worse."

Most women did not have to worry about getting dates, however. In fact, the reverse was usually the problem, particularly overseas. The problem was to choose the kind of men one wanted to go out with and to turn down others without being labeled a lesbian—a difficult situation under the best of circumstances. As most women discovered at one time or another, a man's ego is a very fragile thing, especially when he feels rejected.

The record shows that, contrary to the rumors circulated about military women, neither homosexuality nor promiscuity were serious problems. The incidences were probably much less than in the general female population. Also, heavy drinking and foul language among the women were relatively rare. There can be no doubt that the strong identification with the group and its code of behavior was an important factor here. But just as important was the influence of the protected, middle-class backgrounds of the majority of women who entered the services during the war. As relatively mature women, they brought with them fairly fixed value systems that were not easily shaken by the pressures of the military community. But the conflict between the values they were raised with and the pressures of the male-dominated community could produce considerable anxiety.

All of the services' women directors were of the view that "moral offenders" should be discharged on the grounds that other members of the unit had the right to "decent surroundings as defined by American religious and social customs." Local discharge boards required to discharge women for undesirable "habits and traits of character" often felt that the double standards of conduct applied to women were unjust but were powerless to do anything about it.

Illegitimate pregnancy was not stigmatized, but many thought it should be since in American society at that time unwed maternity was generally tantamount to moral degeneracy. Prior to the war, the Army Nurse Corps made a sharp distinction between married and unmarried pregnancy. Pregnant unmarried nurses were given dishonorable discharges, which were otherwise reserved for convicted criminals. In fact, the whole subject was so abhorrent to the Nurse Corps that losses for this cause were not officially published and the word cyesis was used in lieu of pregnancy.

Although the services were opposed to retaining any pregnant women, they were just as opposed to abortion. If an Army medical officer could prove an illegal abortion, a woman could be discharged for misconduct since she had committed an illegal act. Hobby believed that a woman guilty of deliberate abortion, married or unmarried, should be promptly discharged, both for the sake of the other women in the corps and for the good of the individual herself, who would ordinarily be emotionally and physically unfitted for exacting military duty for some months. In this matter Hobby reflected societal disapprobation of abortion and probably the consensus of all the directors—nurses as well as line.

In the Army Nurse Corps before the war, even marriage was grounds for dishonorable discharge. Not only were married women ineligible to join, but they were not permitted to marry while serving in the Corps. In the line services, marriage was neither a cause for disqualification nor a reason for discharge. The nurses came around to the same policy but forbade married couples from being assigned to the same station. The rationale apparently was that marital bliss was incompatible with a nurse's duty, and that she would not be available to pull night or weekend shifts.

The services had no tolerance for female offenders. When it came to dealing with those convicted of crimes, a double standard of treatment was applied as much for practical reasons as for any concept of dual justice, particularly where sentences to confinement were adjudged. There were few serious offenders in the first place, and, since there were so few, it was neither practical nor economical to maintain confinement facilities for women.

Also, the services reasoned that, since women were all volunteers, service for them was a privilege that if taken away was punishment in itself. So most women offenders were conveniently discharged as quickly and quietly as possible. Those who were convicted of serious civil crimes could be discharged and sent to the Federal Women's Reformatory at Alderson, West Virginia, for confinement.

THE SOCIAL CASTE SYSTEM

The very presence of the women tended to impinge upon the social traditions of the armed forces, which had evolved for generations around an all-male social structure. Many of the resulting conflicts were fairly well resolved by compromise during the first year or so. Satisfactory solutions to others have yet to be found.

Rules of a social nature were rarely published in official regulations but were understood as part of the quasi-official code under the title of "customs and courtesies" of the services. They included such precepts as: enlisted personnel salute and call an officer "Sir," and never by his first name; officers never carry packages or push baby carriages; and military members never carry umbrellas—but never.

In some cases the services made minor concessions—female officers were called "Ma'am" instead of "Sir" and were allowed to wear their hats indoors on social occasions, unlike their male compatriots. In other situations, individual men and women had to solve on a case-by-case basis such problems as who holds the door, the male officer or the female enlisted person. Most women in such circumstances "played it by ear," relying on their common sense to avoid sticky situations. On some issues the military would not bend: there would be no umbrellas!

The most troublesome issue was that of fraternization between officers and enlisted personnel of the opposite sex. The services were never able satisfactorily to come to grips with this sticky social problem.

The military social caste system is probably as old as the military itself. That which has been a part of the U.S. armed forces probably has its roots in European custom, from which the early American military borrowed most of its traditions. By custom, an officer was a "gentleman," presumably of good family, who either inherited or could afford to buy his officer's commission. The enlisted personnel or "other ranks" were "the men," presumably from the lower classes. Gentlemen did not socialize with the lower classes. Custom, not law, dictated social activities and preserved the class distinctions.

The American Revolution did not change the social order in the armed forces. Although established to defend our democratic institutions, the U.S. military is not itself a democratic institution by either intent or design, as anyone who has ever served can attest. The class distinction between officers and enlisted personnel survived two world wars despite the large number of officers who came from the enlisted ranks, the infusion into the enlisted ranks of men from the upper socio-economic levels, and the interjection of women into the officer and enlisted ranks.

The subject surfaced at Colonel Hobby's first press conference upon being sworn in as director. She was asked by a reporter if WAAC officers would be permitted to date male privates. Being new to the military, Hobby deferred to a general to explain Army tradition on officer/enlisted association. He did his best but was not sure how it would apply to women.

Subsequently, over Hobby's objections, the Army took a hard line: there would be no fraternization irrespective of the sex of the people involved. But nothing was officially published, again over Hobby's objections. She felt if there was a policy it should be published so as to avoid misunderstanding.

The Officer's Guide, which was the military encyclopedia for officers, explained simply that

officers and men have not generally associated together in mutual social activities. No officer could violate this ancient custom with one or two men

> of his command and convince the others of his unswerving impartiality.
> The soldier does not need nor desire the social companionship of officers.

The rule did not simply apply to men within the officer's command, however; it applied across the board to all officers and enlisted men and even men of other services. It made no allowances for friends, dates, relatives, or even spouses.

Since during the war military members were required to wear uniforms in public at all times, some difficult situations arose. Brothers and sisters, if one was an officer and the other not, could not eat together in a restaurant. Neither could parent and child if one were an officer and the other an enlisted person. For example, in 1944, a WAC trainee requested a letter authorizing her to have dinner with her father in public, to avoid apprehension by the military police for "socializing" with an officer. She was the daughter of Lt. Gen. Brehon Somervell, Commander of the Army Service Forces responsible for the WAC program. Had her father been a mere second lieutenant, she would probably have dined alone.

Since the rule was not published in any official directive, enforcement was not uniform among the services or even within each service. At the local base level, male officers took a somewhat cavalier attitude toward male officers dating enlisted women, but not the reverse. Any female line officer who socialized with enlisted men was considered a traitor to her class; but, interestingly, a nurse was not. Moreover, the burden of complying with the rule was placed mainly on the woman in each case. If caught in the act of fraternizing, it was she who was disciplined, rarely the man.

In general, female line officers strongly disapproved of any officer/enlisted fraternization. WAC commanders were particularly sensitive to male officers dating enlisted women in their companies, believing that it was corrosive to unit discipline and morale, especially if the officer was of high rank—and he frequently was.

Where it was condoned, mixed dating in itself rarely caused problems except where officers dated subordinates or brought their enlisted dates to officers' clubs where other officers felt uncomfortable about it or strongly disapproved. Enlisted men often bitterly resented enlisted women dating officers but also resented being told they could not date female officers. It was a no-win situation for them.

The Navy Department took a somewhat different tack and, as it turned out, a more practical one. Publicly, they took the position that officers and enlisted personnel of the opposite sex might attend social functions together so long as they "conduct themselves in accordance with the general rules of conduct applicable to ladies and gentlemen," whatever that was supposed to mean. Thus, the Navy avoided the public relations problems of the Army. However, there was little doubt in the minds of most Navy women after their initial training that mixed dating was off limits.

Few aspects of military life caused so much dissension among military women as this social caste system. Enlisted women were especially resentful during the war, not only because most of them were qualified to be officers, but also because by American social custom, women tend to date and marry up while men tend to marry down. American women do not take lightly the suggestion that they are not socially good enough to associate with whomever they please.

Because the whole issue was incomprehensible to the average civilian, it was a public relations nightmare throughout the war for the Army. Being very democratic, Colonel Hobby never agreed with the rule though publicly she was obliged to defend it. In fact, she consistently attempted to get the Army to adopt a more relaxed policy to permit enlisted women to associate with male officers. Eisenhower too was one of many male officers who did not agree with the application of the rule to members of the opposite sex. He thought it was silly and said so. General Somervell and the Chief of Personnel, however, were set against any revisions. In the view of the latter, "The traditional relationship between officers and enlisted personnel is a strongly entrenched custom of the service, and any exception which is made for WACs will be a step in the direction of its complete elimination." When a proposal to liberalize Army policies reached General Marshall, he was inclined to agree with Hobby: "The situation between sexes is very different from that in the male Army."[2] The issue was shelved in the preparation for demobilization but would rise again in the peacetime services and would not go away.

With the integration of women into the Regular, peacetime services in 1948, the subject surfaced again as a public relations problem having a negative effect on the recruitment of enlisted women. As in the war, enforcement varied among and within the services. It was generally conceded that a joint policy of some kind was needed at least to settle some of the confusion, but nothing was done. The issue was a public relations hot potato no one wanted to touch. Meanwhile, men and women continued to do what came naturally. By then, civilian clothes were worn off duty, so mixed couples were less obvious. If they married, however, they were headed for all kinds of problems. They could not occupy government housing because enlisted personnel could not live in officers' quarters and vice versa. Socially, they were outcasts because the officers' club was off limits to enlisted personnel, and officers were not always welcome at enlisted social activities. Neither spouse was entitled to the status of a dependent for any family entitlements.

As recently as 1978, a captain, a graduate of West Point with a promising career ahead, was forced to resign because he had married an enlisted woman, and the Army could not cope with it. In a valiant effort to clarify and justify its position, the Army subsequently announced its policy:

> Relationships between service members of different rank which involve, or give the appearance of, partial preferential treatment or the improper use of rank or position for personal gain, are prejudicial to good order, discipline, and high unit morale. Such relationships will be avoided if relationships between service members of different rank cause actual or perceived partiality or unfairness, involve the improper use of rank or position for personal gain or can otherwise reasonably be expected to undermine discipline, authority or morale. Commanders and supervisors will counsel those involved or take other action as appropriate.[3]

THE BLACK WOMAN'S EXPERIENCE

The situation of the black woman was the most difficult. Congresswoman Shirley Chisholm once said that she had been discriminated against more because of her sex than because of her color. The position of black women in American society has always been one of double jeopardy. The black woman in the armed forces during the war found herself in triple jeopardy.

Until President Truman issued an Executive Order in 1948 calling for "equality of treatment and opportunity in the armed forces," racial segregation and discrimination were official policy. In the Army, black men had traditionally been assigned to segregated "Negro" combat and noncombat units commanded by white officers. In many cases, they were relegated to lower status jobs duplicating their "place" in civilian life.

At the outset of the war, Marshall declared that "the settlement of vexing racial problems cannot be permitted to complicate the tremendous task of the War Department." Consequently, nothing was done to solve the racial problems of the Army during the war.

The Army set a goal of 10 percent black men that it had little difficulty filling with the draft. With the establishment of the WAAC in 1942, the same proportion was applied to the women. And with the help of Dr. Mary McLeod Bethune, Army officers attempted to recruit WAAC officer candidates at black colleges. The Navy, which restricted black males to mess stewards and similar jobs, refused to open its doors to black women until near the end of the war. (The Marine Corps held out until 1949.)

Ironically, the only service to accept black women, the WAACs, came under attack by the National Association for the Advancement of Colored People and other Negro organizations. They had hoped to use the volunteer women's corps as the wedge to crack the Army's segregation policies. But the Army held fast. The WAACs, even though at that time a separate corps, were required to follow the Army policy. And there the situation remained throughout the war.

Starting with the first OCS class, segregation became the rule. The forty black women candidates were segregated in one platoon in a separate area of the dormitory. The only concession made was a decision to integrate the officer housing and messing at the Des Moines training center. Black enlisted women lived in separate barracks, ate at separate tables in mess halls, sat in separate sections of theaters, and participated only in segregated social and sport functions. Off base, they had to conform to the racial customs of the civilian community. Needless to say, the blacks who had migrated north to escape Jim Crow were not eager to volunteer to join the Army and be faced with the likely prospect of an assignment to a military base in the Southeast.

Black enlisted women could only be assigned to segregated units commanded by black female officers. They were stationed only at bases where they had been specifically requested, usually where there were black male troops or a sizable black population in the local community. This naturally created complex administrative problems, malassignments and low morale. Some commands refused to accept black female units unless the War Department would relax a ban on their use as replacements for civilian women in kitchens, dining halls, and cafeterias, or other menial jobs, which the Department refused to do.

It was not uncommon for white male commanders to request black WAACs for the "morale" of the black troops. Although not usually stated openly in so many words, the ulterior motive was often implicit in the request. It was clearly the motive behind the first overseas requisitions. Sensing this, Hobby refused to permit their deployment until early 1945, at which time an entire battalion was sent to Europe to staff half of a central postal directory. The battalion was under the command of Maj. Charity Adams, who was later promoted to lieutenant colonel, the highest rank authorized for women outside of the directors.

The female black officers had special problems. It was the policy that black WAC units have black female officers. Yet most black male units had white officers. Thus, the women were often the only black officers on a station. In the highly segregated Army community, they were frequently totally isolated, and they could not go to the officers' club or social functions.

Black civilian leaders expressed the view that the Army policies of segregation and discrimination would deter recruiting of black women as volunteers, particularly under the higher quality standards set for women. They were right, of course. In spite of a great deal of effort, the goal of 10 percent was never even approached for the WAAC/WAC. With the draft, the Army was able to reach the goal for black men and, in truth, the 10 percent may very well have served as a ceiling in that case. Only 4,000 black women were recruited during the war, representing 4 percent of the WAC strength.

The first major step toward integration came in 1946 when the Secretary of the Navy ordered all naval ratings (specialties) opened to all sailors regardless of race. For the first time, black women were enlisted in the Navy, albeit only a highly selected few. Seventy enlisted women were recruited on the basis of high aptitudes and skills and attractiveness. They were integrated directly into the WAVES assignment system and dormitories. Because of their small numbers, doing otherwise would have been impossible.

Toward the end of the war, the Army had taken steps to integrate male combat units in the European theater, but that is as far as they were willing to go at that point.

In 1948, President Truman issued an Executive Order directing the integration of the armed forces. The Air Force decided to integrate immediately, over the objections of many commanders who were adamantly opposed to the whole idea. Many agreed with the wing commander at a base in Germany who stated emphatically to his senior staff, "It will never work." It did work, of course.

The Army continued to drag its feet, however. "You shouldn't move too fast in these kinds of things," said more than one commander.

An official policy of integration did not solve the problems of discrimination against blacks nor end institutional racism any more than integration would solve the problem of discrimination against women or end sexism in the armed forces. The chief difference between the two, however, is that segregation and discrimination based on race are officially banned while that which is based on sex remains institutionalized in laws and official policies. Officially, racism is no longer tolerated. Sexism remains alive and well.

NOTES

1. Treadwell, p. 499.
2. *Ibid.*, p. 724.
3. Army Regulation 600-20, 31 November 1978, para. 5–7.

CHAPTER 8

OVERSEAS

THREE DAYS BEFORE Christmas in 1942, five WAAC officers arrived in North Africa aboard a British destroyer. Their troopship, bound from England and one day out of port, had been torpedoed and sunk with a loss of all equipment and many lives. Dirty and bedraggled, the WAACs had lost everything but their lives. Two of the officers had been plucked from the burning ship, the other three from a lifeboat along with five or six men and one violently seasick crewman they had helped fish out of the water.

As the first WAACs to arrive in any overseas theater, they were greeted at dockside by the local military brass. They had been sent on priority shipment orders at the urgent request of General Eisenhower. The WAACs were not, however, the first American military women to arrive in North Africa. Army nurses had landed on the day of the invasion with a surgical hospital.

Hobby had originally intended that the WAACs not go overseas during the first "experimental" year. She felt that the women should have time to adjust to the Army, and vice versa, before being thrown into the overseas environment. Moreover, the whole idea behind the establishment of the Corps in the first place had been to release men from stateside jobs for duty overseas. The trouble was that not enough men could type or take dictation.

However, General Marshall overruled Hobby and promised Eisenhower to ship WAACs to his headquarters. After visiting London and seeing a male colonel hunting and pecking through his own correspondence, Hobby became convinced that the need was urgent; so, plans were made to start shipping women. By the time the first group was ready to go, Eisenhower had moved his headquarters to North Africa. The shortage of skilled personnel was even more critical than it had been in England, where local civilians and members of the British women's services were available.

The Army desperately needed stenographers, typists, and telephone operators. There were nowhere near enough military men with the required training and experience. Qualified local nationals with adequate facilities in English were scarce outside of Great Britain and the Commonwealth countries, and the Army had to arrange security clearances to hire them. So, once the initial resistance to the idea of American women in uniform was overcome, servicewomen came to be viewed as the solution to filling these "women's jobs." However, the military was reluctant to ship women overseas for jobs requiring less traditional skills for fear that women might not be able to replace men on a one-for-one basis.

For the first two years, the only service legally authorized to send female personnel other than nurses overseas was the Army, despite the dubious legal status of the WAAC as an auxiliary. By the time the WAACs were converted to WACs with full military status in 1943 and they received the same rights and protection as men, more than 1,000 of them were already serving overseas. Not so the other services. Throughout most of the war the WAVES, SPARs, and Women Marines were restricted by law to assignments within the continental United States, much to their frustration. Only in the final months of the war was this ban lifted and then only partially.

The possibility of being selected for an overseas assignment was a great morale booster for those stuck in stateside jobs. Whereas the men generally wanted to avoid it if possible, the women viewed overseas duty as a real prize, and the closer to the actual fighting the better.

NORTH AFRICA AND MEDITERRANEAN THEATER

The first group of enlisted women to be deployed in North Africa arrived in Algiers in January 1943, a month after the five WAAC officers. Dubbed as the "first American Women's Expeditionary Force in history," they were for the most part experienced stenographers, typists, telephone operators, drivers, cooks, and bakers. In addition, almost all were linguists, and most were eligible for Officer Candidate School. The first group was so well received that there were not enough women to meet the demands, and additional personnel requests were fired off to Army headquarters.

Much of the credit for the success of the first overseas WAAC deployment can be attributed to General Eisenhower, then Commander of the North African Theater of Operations. In his book *Crusade in Europe*, Eisenhower says that he had been opposed to the use of women in uniform until his experience in London. After seeing the British service women perform "so magnificently" in various jobs including service in antiaircraft artillery batteries, he was converted. In North Africa, many of his officers, particularly his older commanders, were skeptical and filled with misgivings. But Eisenhower felt that it was "scarcely less than criminal" to recruit needed manpower to do jobs that highly qualified women were available to perform. "From the day they first reached us," he says, "their reputation as an efficient, effective corps continued to grow. Toward the end of the war the most stubborn die-hards had become convinced and demanded them in increasing numbers."[1]

Eisenhower's initial conversion may have been influenced by Maj. Gen. Everett S. Hughes, who fifteen years earlier, as a major in the War Department, had prepared the study on "Participation of Women in War." In the fall of 1942, Hughes was Eisenhower's Deputy Commander in North Africa.

EUROPE

Many of the women in the first groups to arrive in North Africa in early 1943 continued to serve with the Allied forces throughout the war. Some were assigned to the 12th Air Force, the Signal Corps, and Gen. Mark Clark's 5th Army. The WAACs moved with the advancing forces into Sicily and Italy, to within twelve miles of the front. They lived in whatever billets were available—tents, requisitioned apartments, school buildings, whatever. Their average stay in one place was two weeks. They were provided no more in facilities or comforts than the noncombat men with whom they worked. In fact, in some ways they were worse off. Their clothing was inadequate for wear in the field and for the climate, and the men's clothing, which they had resorted to wearing, did not fit. Shoes were a particular and ever present problem. The ones they were issued were totally unsuitable for field duty. This was the first real inkling of the horrendous problems the Army would soon face with women's clothing overseas, problems that would not be resolved during the war; nor for that matter would they ever be fully resolved.

Despite discomforts, hardships, lack of supplies, lack of promotions, and problems of administration, the morale overseas was high because the women felt that they were needed and that they were contributing directly to the war effort. Male commanders were amazed to discover that there were few disciplinary problems, that the women's time lost from work was less than noncombat men's in the theater (2.7 per hundred versus 3.6 per hundred), that venereal disease rates for women were practically nonexistent although the disease was endemic with men, and that there were few pregnancies (fewer than in comparable civilian populations).

By far the largest overseas deployment of women was to the European Theater of Operations (ETO). At the insistence of Lt. Gen. Ira C. Eaker, commander of the theater's Air Forces, an entire WAAC battalion was shipped there under priority orders. Eaker later recalled, "Shortly after I arrived in England the problem was presented to me. . . . The commanding officer counseled me against bringing WAACs over . . . he said I would be held responsible."[2] The battalion arrived in July 1943 and was commanded by Capt. Mary A. Hallaren, later to become the Director, WAC, and one of the giants among military women (although she was only five feet tall, if that).

Although it had been anticipated that special facilities and housing would be required, there were no particular problems. The women found that with the exception of the inadequacies of the uniforms and the German bombing raids, there was very little difference from stateside assignment. The proximity of the war had little effect on morale except to improve it. Once they became accustomed to the bombing, the women stopped seeking out the protection of the air raid shelters and continued to work. Eaker commented later, "One of the factors in their success was courageousness. I saw this demonstrated when German planes came over . . . they keep more calm than the men in emergencies." Sixteen WACs received Purple Hearts for injuries. As in North Africa, after the first arrivals commanders were motivated to requisition more. "Their work has improved the efficiency of my office tremendously," exclaimed one supervisor. "Their attitude, discipline, and efficiency are of such value that not only enlisted men but some officers have been released to perform other duties."

Less than a year after the first group arrived in Europe,

WAACs moved into France aboard LSTs (landing ships, tank) during the invasion of Normandy. They followed closely behind the fighting forces, slept in the field under shelter halves or in tents on Army cots, ate field rations, and washed in their helmets with cold water. Despite bad weather and inadequate clothing, only one WAAC returned to England sick during the first six months after the landing in Normandy. Moving on to Paris with an advance party a few days after the city was liberated, they later went to Germany.

Contrary to what had been feared, there was no indication that the men's efficiency was impaired by the presence of women. In fact, the men seemed glad to have American women along. The parity in living and working conditions may have put a damper on the normal male griping.

When it came to WAAC assignments, the overseas areas got the cream of the crop. Of those in the ETO, 99 percent were skilled in their jobs, and more than half had the mental test scores required of officers. Army and WAAC leaders believed that the quality made them easier to assign and less likely to become disciplinary problems, suffer low morale, or develop health problems. Eight out of ten were either stenographers, clerk-typists, or telephone operators. Only 8 percent were employed in the less traditional skills, and women in technical jobs regarded as unfeminine, such as mechanics, were often reassigned to "more appropriate" desk jobs.

The ETO's demands for skilled clerical WAAC/WACs were insatiable. Filling all requests would have absorbed the entire recruiting intake and would have required replacing women with men at stateside bases. Such replacements were considered, but stateside commanders protested that it would be embarrassing to have men releasing women for duty in combat zones. Even so, the theater felt that it should get first priority over U.S. bases, since in their view one WAC typist could replace two men while eating half as much.

As was the case in the North African and Mediterranean areas, the morale of the women who served in the ETO remained high throughout the war. The attrition rate for women remained the same as for male noncombatants overall. The hospitalization rates, on average, were lower, even though pregnant women were hospitalized whether or not they were ill. Gynecological complaints accounted for almost one-fourth of the WAC hospitalization; however, the time lost from duty for this reason was exactly offset by the time lost by men for venereal disease, which among the women remained conspicuous by its almost total absence. The pregnancy rate was negligible likewise, as were disciplinary problems. The official history shows that men were 89 times more likely to go AWOL, 85 times more apt to get drunk, and 150 times more apt to commit offenses. The differences may have been due at least in part to greater off-duty supervision of the women and in part to the constant pressure exerted by the female peer group to uphold group standards of conduct.

The chief sources of the morale problems that did surface in Europe were: antagonism between the Army men and women; the misconduct of female civilians authorized to wear WAC uniforms, which often reflected on the military women; the theater policy of keeping married couples apart; and the Army-wide rule of non-fraternization between officers and enlisted personnel of the opposite sex.

Antagonisms between the women and men were exacerbated by the women's feelings that they were being hassled and that many men treated them as if they were prostitutes. And indeed, the first requests for WAACs from the theater had implied that they were needed for "morale purposes." This was probably the chief reason that Hobby was reluctant initially to allow the women to deploy overseas—the notion of some commanders and their men that, whatever skills the women might possess, their primary value would be in "servicing the troops." Although it was made abundantly clear that this was not the case, the problem was ever present and the women deeply resented it.

The command policy that forbade married couples to cohabitate was also a source of great annoyance. The logic behind it remains an enigma to this day. It applied only to couples in which the wife was military; if she were a civilian, there was no hassle. This situation was aggravated by the common knowledge that many men had taken to living openly with local women.

The policy's results were both ludicrous and predictable. For example, one Army captain married to a military woman was admonished by his commander in a letter saying, "It has come to the attention of this headquarters that you are living with your wife. This must cease at once." Because of the rule, engaged couples sometimes lived together without being married to avoid being separated.

Incredibly, the Air Force established a similar policy in Southeast Asia thirty years later. The reason given then was that if military couples were allowed to live together it would affect the morale of men there without their wives. Misery loves company!

THE SOUTHWEST PACIFIC AREA

The second largest deployment of WACs overseas was to the Southwest Pacific Area (SWPA), where some 5,500 served under much less favorable conditions and with far less positive results than in the other combat theaters. It was also something less than a happy experience for the women involved.

Not until 1944 did the SWPA get around to requesting women. The major headquarters were located in Australia, where there had been no problems in staffing since thousands of qualified local civilians were available. However, once preparations got under way to move out to forward bases, the clerical personnel situation suddenly became critical. The Army could not take the civilians with them, and there simply were nowhere near enough military men with the required skills. Because military women seemed to be the logical solution to this almost insurmountable personnel problem, the decision was made to request some ten thousand WACs. By then, however, the full WAC strength had long since been allocated to other commands. In desperation, the SWPA successfully negotiated with a stateside command for an allocation of military women in exchange for civilian authorizations.

The first WACs arrived in Australia in May 1944. From there they would move to New Guinea, Hollandia, and on to the Philippines, arriving in Manila just four days after organized enemy resistance had ended, with dead enemy soldiers still littered in the streets and fighting still going on in the nearby hills.

Things got off to a bad start. To begin with, the theater failed to make adequate preparations for housing, clothing, and general administration for the enlisted women, having little appreciation for what was required. Then, before the first enlisted women set foot in Australia, rumors were circulating among the men that the WACs were being imported to provide "companionship" for the officers. When the women arrived and heard the rumor, they were angry and disillusioned. Nonetheless, everything went fairly smoothly until the move to New Guinea.

At Port Moresby, New Guinea, enlisted women were housed within a barbed wire compound and subjected to unexpected and unprecedented restrictions on their personal freedom. For the next eighteen months, they lived like virtual prisoners. Allowed out only to go to work or to officially sanctioned social functions, they were under armed guard. They could go nowhere without an armed guard, not even with a date (who had to be approved twenty-four hours in advance). Even then, they had to be in by 11 P.M. They were not permitted to board ships, boats, or aircraft, possibly out of fear they might escape.

Their confinement was compounded by the total lack of any approved recreational facilities for enlisted women in the area. Even the R&R (rest and rehabilitation) centers in Australia operated by the Red Cross refused to accept them. Regular military flights set up to take men on leave to Australia, "the leave shuttle," were off limits, even though the aircraft often flew half empty.

During their entire stay in New Guinea, the enlisted women were permitted no leaves or passes because there was no place they were allowed to go. This concentration-camp policy followed the women wherever they moved in the theater, all the way to Manila.

It is not clear just what the underlying motive behind the restrictions was—whether it was to protect the virtues of the women or to protect the men from the possible "corrupting influence" of military women. The official explanations were that the women required protection from U.S. troops, many of whom had not seen a white woman for eighteen months, and that the restrictions were needed to prevent "regrettable incidents and unwholesome impressions of any nature," a possible reference to the slander campaign going on in the States. Historian Treadwell hints at a more plausible explanation: the deeply rooted fear that white women would be raped by black troops.

Whatever the motive, the women bitterly resented being treated like children or, worse, like criminals, and the men resented the extra trouble of providing the protection and complained of the expense of it. One male officer protested: "They require special quarters, special handling, and so many damned military police to guard them that it more than eats up the manpower relieved." The negative attitude this situation generated among the men made life much more difficult for the women, who faced enough problems of peer acceptance under the best of circumstances.

There were a number of other factors that affected the women's morale—among them, lower than normal promotion rates and a lack of adequate medical care, especially for female problems. Also, the long work days—which were generally between ten and fifteen hours, six or seven days a week, without any break or leave or passes—produced a chronic state of exhaustion.

Deficiencies in clothing, which plagued WACs worldwide, were especially bad in the SWPA and further aggravated women's medical and psychological problems. The field uniforms were totally unsuited to the climate. They were too hot, irritating to the skin, and conducive to "jungle rot." Their shirts were too thin to provide protection from insects. The single pair of field shoes each had brought with her soon rotted from the constant moisture, and there were no replacements. Clothing supplies shipped from the United States never caught up. A WAC officer upon arriving in Manila reported in frustration, "No supply has been available for WACs where I have been stationed since our departure from Australia." While supply problems for the men were severe in the area throughout the war, they were mild compared to what the women endured, and the Army seemed unwilling or unable to correct the situation.

In spite of all their problems, morale remained relatively good at most locations. As in Europe, those women in the most forward areas sustained the best morale. Even where they were not near actual combat, the presence of combat-wounded men and released POWs gave them a sense of purpose. General MacArthur later recalled,

> I moved my WACs forward early after occupation of recaptured territory because they were needed and they were soldiers in the same manner that my men were soldiers. Furthermore, if I had not moved my WACs when I did, I would have had mutiny . . . as they were so eager to carry on where needed.[3]

The WACs coped with 100-degree, humid weather and insect-infested camp sites. They turned yellow from atabrine tablets. They endured the blowing mud of New Guinea and the hub-deep mire of Leyte. They lived in tents with dirt floors and mission schools recently deserted by Japanese. They ducked for shelter from enemy air raids and sniper fire. They scrounged for boxes to make improvised furniture and discarded parachutes to make drapes. They conned their men friends into helping with the manual labor to improve living conditions in exchange for laundry services or a decent meal in the WAC mess.

There was and, to some extent, still is a popular notion that the tropical environment, per se, leads to greater moral disintegration than other environments. The record of the WACs in the SWPA does not bear this out. By the traditional standards used in the military to measure such trends—disciplinary rates, venereal disease rates, and, in the case of women, pregnancy rates—the women who served in that area showed no unusual signs of such a moral disintegration. Although these rates were slightly higher than in other commands, despite the tight restrictions (or because of them), they were not significantly out of line with the typically low norm for women.

As far as discipline was concerned, there were few offenses of any kind. The one minor offense most often reported concerned violations of the Army ban on the socializing of officers and enlisted personnel. For a time at some bases, even husbands or blood relatives were off limits. Resentment toward the policy was widespread in the Pacific and violations were commonplace, as in other commands. However, there is no evidence that discipline broke down as a result.

Although morals and discipline did not present problems, health—both mental and physical—did, as the medical evacuation rates from the area revealed soon after the WACs arrived in Manila. During the first year, the number of WACs evacuated from the theater for medical reasons was unexpectedly low, much lower than for the nurses who had been in the area since the beginning of the war. But after the WACs reached Manila the second year, fatigue and exhaustion, the lack of proper clothing, inadequate medical care, and the long-term effects of the confinement policies all combined to take their toll. With the war reaching its final phase and the inevitable letdown, medical evacuation rates for WACs began to soar and remained high until the end of the war. At that point, the rate was running three times that of the men. Brig. Gen. Guy B. Denit, the Chief Surgeon in the area, believed that the abnormal losses for the women had no medical or geographic cause. He thought that a white woman could live in the area for any length of time as easily as a white man and considered the command policies affecting women the primary cause for the losses. A WAC inspector, after touring the area, came to the same conclusion: the high losses were not environmentally based but were the result of theater policies toward women that were not applicable to men.

This contention is borne out by the lower evacuation rates in other combat theaters. WACs served in all of the theaters of war including the Southeast Asia Command, the China-Burma-India Theater, the China Theater, and the Middle East Theater, as well as in Hawaii, Alaska, New Caledonia, Puerto Rico, and other miscellaneous locations. In no other theater were WACs subject to the demoralizing treatment endured by those in the Southwest Pacific. And in no other instance were the losses so abnormally high.

When the war was over, most SWPA authorities rated the deployment of WACs to their theater an unqualified success. Lt. Gen. George C. Kenney, Commanding General of the Allied Air Forces, praised the caliber of his women and stated that each had "better than replaced a soldier."[4] Other commanders expressed similar views. One commanding general called them "courageous soldiers" who from Australia to Manila "more than carried their own." Even MacArthur, the theater commander, praised the women as "my best soldiers" and claimed they worked harder and were better disciplined than his men and complained less.[5]

One wonders whether MacArthur was fully aware of how his "best soldiers" were treated in his command. Although he had a reputation for aloofness, he must have had more than an inkling of the WACs' problems toward the end of the war. At that point, Marshall, alarmed at the numerous press and congressional inquiries, pointedly requested from MacArthur a full confidential report on the condition of the WACs in his command. Marshall never received a satisfactory reply.

Not everyone shared the enthusiasm of the area's commanders on the success of the WAC deployment. One general officer close to the program commented, "I cannot truthfully say that their contribution, great as it was, outweighed the difficulties." He concluded that the hardships, isolation, and privation of jungle theaters are conditions to be endured only by men, and that women should only be employed there as a last resort. The Director, WAC, Col. Westrey Battle Boyce, also expressed doubts about the wisdom of assigning women to the area.

Some questioned whether it was economical to employ WACs in an area where losses were so much higher for women than for men in similar skills. This argument, of course, missed the point. The reason for sending the women in the first place was that men with the necessary skills were not available. Economy was not the issue. Getting the job done was. As one personnel chief put it, "[The headquarters] could not possibly have moved from Australia without the WACs. . . . Except for the WACs, I had only a few clerically skilled men . . . plus a few malarials and other men sent back from combat, naturally not very useful at exacting office work."

Some WAC leaders felt that the greater sacrifices of the combat soldier made it impertinent even to question whether women should be sent to any combat area in which men are required to fight. Which was even more to the point.

The real question should not have been whether the women should have served in the Pacific but under what policies they should have been administered—what should have been done to provide adequately for their welfare to ensure maximum effectiveness of a critical resource. It is worth noting that some 565 of these women received combat decorations.

THE NURSES

Of the women who served overseas during the war, the nurses deserve special recognition. Wherever the U.S. forces could be found, there were nurses. By the time the first WAACs had landed in North Africa, Army and Navy nurses had seen action in Bataan and Corregidor and would see more. Five Navy nurse POWs in Japan were repatriated on the exchange ship *Gripsholm* early in the war, but the eleven Navy and sixty-six Army nurses interned in Santo Tomas prison in the Philippines would remain POWs for thirty-seven months. Although they were not permitted to care for military patients, they continued to care for the sick in the camp hospital during their entire internment.

After landing in North Africa, Army nurses followed closely in support of the fighting men. They waded ashore on Anzio beachhead in Italy five days after the invasion, and four days after the invasion at Normandy, the nurses arrived with the field and evacuation hospitals. They endured relentless bombing and strafing on land, torpedoing at sea, and antiaircraft fire in the air. They assisted in the development of a new concept of recovery wards for immediate post-operative care that would save countless lives. As flight nurses, they provided care on air evacuation flights, a concept employed for the first time in World War II.

Navy nurses were serving at sea aboard twelve hospital ships, in air evacuation, and in naval activities in Alaska, Australia, the islands of the Pacific, Africa, England, Italy, and a number of other locations.

Of all the U.S. women's components, the Army Nurse Corps took the heaviest casualties, losing over two hundred, seventeen of whom are buried in U.S. cemeteries overseas. Moreover, 1,600 received decorations including Distinguished Service Medals, Silver Stars, Distinguished Flying Crosses, Soldier's Medals, Bronze Stars, Air Medals, Legions of Merit, Commendation Medals, and Purple Hearts.

Of those who lost their lives, six were on Anzio beachhead when the Germans bombed the hospital. On that occasion, Army officials on the scene applied a strange convoluted logic. It was February 1944 and a German counter-offensive was in full swing. When conditions on the beach were at their worst, an evacuation of the nurses was considered but abandoned because to have removed them in the thick of action, it was reasoned, would have been interpreted as an admission of defeat in the eyes of the American combat troops, which would have devastated morale. So the nurses remained—six of them never to depart. Of those who survived, four wore the Silver Star, the first women ever to receive that decoration.

The attitude of the men overseas toward the nurses was expressed in a letter signed by hundreds of G.I.s and published in the *Stars and Stripes* newspaper in Europe on 21 October 1944:

> To all Army nurses overseas: We men were not given the choice of working in the battlefield or the home front. We cannot take any credit for being here. We are here because we have to be. You are here because you felt you were needed. So, when an injured man opens his eyes to see one of you . . . concerned with his welfare, he can't but be overcome by the very thought that you are doing it because you want to. . . . you endure whatever hardships you must to be where you can do us the most good.

Because of the legal restrictions, the experiences of the WAVES, SPARs and Women Marines with overseas deployment was on an entirely different scale. The impetus for sending the women in the line of the naval services overseas came from the need to rotate men to the continental United States from overseas stations and the fleet, largely as a morale factor. Requests coming in from bases in the Pacific area and England prompted the Navy's Bureau of Personnel in 1944 to urge amending the law that prohibited the stationing of women other than nurses outside the continental limits of the United States. A survey by the Bureau of Aeronautics of its overseas stations came up with the startling conclusion that WAVES could replace large numbers of men. It estimated, for example, that women could replace 90 percent of the control tower operators, 85 percent of the yeomen, 70 percent of the parachute riggers, 65 percent of the Link-trainer instructors, 50 percent of the gunnery specialists, and 30 percent of the seamen.

But it was not until November 1944 that the law was modified to permit women to serve overseas, and then only in certain U.S. territories, not on foreign soil. So by the time the Navy, Marine Corps, and Coast Guard got around to deploying their women overseas, the war in Europe had ended and victory in the Pacific was only seven months away. Nonetheless, the women were eager to go. When they joined the services they had expected to travel. Instead, most of them had been stuck in one place in the States in the same job, while the men were shipping out and the WACs and nurses were on duty all over the world. The WAVES sang a parody on a popular song that expressed their frustration over not going overseas: "We joined the Navy to see the world and what did we see? We saw D.C."

From the care with which the WAVES, SPARs, and Women Marines were selected for duty overseas and the elaborate indoctrination they received in preparation for shipment, one would have thought that the women were going to some far-off combat zone instead of the Hawaiian Islands, a United States territory where many Americans lived. Only volunteers were selected and then only after careful screening for excellent records of performance, conduct, maturity, emotional stability, and health. They also were required to have a minimum of six months' stateside service and a "real desire for service."

Although they were twenty years old and over, there was considerable concern over how the women would react to the overseas environment and apprehension that, because they were volunteers, they might be looking for excitement. Women marines were warned, for example, that it would not be glamorous, "just hard work," that they would be under more restrictions than at home, and that their working and living conditions might not be as good. They were also cautioned gravely that they would see ships damaged in combat and meet many men who had recently been in combat. These warnings were typical examples of the services' penchant for treating enlisted women like not-too-bright children rather than as the mature adults they were. Servicewomen who had originally enlisted from Hawaii must have found the whole thing pretty ridiculous.

Naturally, having been prepared psychologically for the worst, the women were astonished to be met at dockside by bands playing "Aloha," crowds of well-wishers with leis, and a clamoring press. Thousands of military men turned out to get their first look at female sailors, coast guardsmen, and marines. And, contrary to what they had been led to expect, the women found that living and working conditions were much like those stateside. A hardship post it clearly was not. Jean Palmer, who succeeded McAfee as WAVE director, recalls that the Marine Corps built a stockade around their women's quarters but that the men were scaling it and causing a lot of trouble—it was a challenge to be met by any good, tough marine. The Navy commander, on the other hand, built a white, two-foot picket fence around the WAVE quarters. He had no problem with the men invading the area.

Although the majority of the WAVES, SPARs, and Women Marines deployed were in the clerical, stenographic, and communications skill areas, many were in the less traditional jobs. For example, one entire Marine Corps motor transport section was staffed with women.

THE ASSESSMENT

At peak strength, some 17,000 WACs were overseas serving in every combat theater. Most were there voluntarily, but when not enough volunteers with the right skills could be found to meet the needs of the overseas commands, nonvolunteers had been shipped. It was Hobby's view that, once they joined the Army, WACs were soldiers and would go where they were needed.

By the close of the war, roughly 4,000 WAVES, 1,000 Women Marines, and 200 SPARs were serving in Hawaii; another 200 SPARs were in Alaska. So far as is known, all were volunteers.

Despite the hardships, inconveniences, and even physical dangers, the women's morale overseas, almost without exception, remained high and their esprit de corps intact. Whether they served in Europe, the Pacific, Asia, or in the U.S. territories of Hawaii and Alaska, these women generally considered their overseas tours as the high point of their wartime service. A typical group of WACs upon disbanding at Leyte, Philippines—generally regarded as one of the worst bases in the war—wrote in their scrapbook sentimentally about the tents, candles, lack of supplies, mud, foxholes, air alerts, and rain: "We'll never have a detachment so ideal and so perfect again."

Clearly, the World War II experience overseas of the services, more particularly the Army, shows that, by and large, the American woman can cope with and function effectively in combat zones under conditions of severe hardship for extended periods, and that she functions best when she feels her job is contributing to the mission and when she is treated like a mature, responsible adult. Also, her morale and feeling of self-worth are directly related to the attitudes of male leaders and her male peers.

Acceptance of women in the combat zones hinged in large measure on whether the men perceived that the women were receiving equal or preferential treatment. Wherever they perceived that the women had better housing, better food, or shorter hours, etc.—which was rarely the case—the men resented it. The women, on the other hand, resented it when the noncombat men in the same units were given greater personal freedom and more time off for R&R, passes, and leaves, as happened in the Southwest Pacific. The interrelationships were best and morale was the highest for both men and women when they felt they were treated equally and fairly.

This is not to say that there were no special problems encountered by the women overseas, all other things being equal. A consultant to the Army Surgeon General on women's health and welfare, Maj. Margaret D. Craighill, M.D., concluded, after touring overseas theaters, that the women had special problems serving in combat zones. Although spared the strain of actual combat, the women faced a type of combat that men did not, namely the defense of their character and the double standard of morality. Dr. Craighill observed that, because of their scarcity in the overseas areas, the women were under abnormal pressures from the men and that, because there was a more radical change in the patterns of their lives, the women were under greater emotional strain.

Most military people who have served overseas agree that there tends to be a change in standards of conduct and social value systems in both sexes, particularly in a combat area. After talking to personnel in all overseas theaters, Craighill observed that their future lives become vague and unreal so that only the present is of importance. She concluded that men are apparently better able to partition off their lives adequately so that they do not as readily become deeply or permanently involved emotionally, and that men are therefore less liable to psychic trauma from transient attachments.

NOTES

1. Dwight D. Eisenhower, *Crusade in Europe* (Garden City, NY: Doubleday, 1948), p. 132.
2. Address given to the sixtieth WAC OCS graduation class, 17 November 1945. *See* Treadwell, p. 380.
3. Treadwell, p. 423.
4. *Ibid.*, p. 460.
5. *Ibid.*

CHAPTER 9

WAR'S END

TO HATTIE R. Brantley and the other military nurses, the dirty, war-wearied soldiers of the 1st Cavalry Division of the 6th Army were the best looking men they had ever seen. After three long years as POWs in Santo Tomas and Los Banos prison camps in the Philippines, these survivors of Bataan and Corregidor were to be liberated at last.

It was February 1945. The five thousand prisoners had known for months that America was gaining in the war because the more our forces advanced, the more pressure the Japanese brought to bear on their prisoners. The food rations had stopped in December and for the last two months they had subsisted on about five hundred calories a day. The older and weaker prisoners began dying. "We ate anything edible and some things that were not," Brantley recalled.[1]

Three months earlier, the war had ended in Europe with the defeat of Germany. Six months later, on 2 September, General MacArthur, with the Japanese Premier and representatives of the Allied nations, signed the surrender document on board the U.S.S. *Missouri* in Tokyo Bay.

Hostilities had ceased, and ten million American men and women were like the nurses at Santo Tomas and Los Banos prison camps—ready, willing, and *anxious* to go home. Yet, the process of returning home was to be not a simple one but one that required thousands of people, reams of paper, and two long years. Concurrently, it evoked a second look at the role of women in the line. Had they been successful? Should they in fact remain as a permanent part of America's military forces?

97

The suddenness of the Japanese surrender had caught everyone by surprise. Some called it a "sneak surrender." The services were almost totally unprepared for the end of the war and were without acceptable plans for the instant demobilization demanded by the public and the Congress.

Once the V-J Day celebrations were over, there was a tremendous letdown in morale. The vast majority of the men and all of the women were committed only for "the duration of the emergency and six months." When the Japanese surrendered, both the men and women expected to go home. But the emergency did not automatically end with the war, as most thought it would. It would end when the President declared it and not before. The question in most people's minds was not whether to get out but when. This was particularly true in the case of women since, with the exception of the nurses, there were no provisions for them in the peacetime military. Moreover, many women were eager to reestablish homes with their returning husbands, and others wanted to find good civilian jobs before returning servicemen — who would probably get first priority — glutted the civilian job market.

In the summer of 1945 there were nearly 100,000 WACs, 86,000 WAVES, 18,000 Women Marines, 11,000 SPARs, plus 57,000 nurses in the Army and another 11,000 in the Navy. It was assumed that all but a few hundred nurses would have to be separated from the services and that the women's line components would be completely disbanded. Although the drafting of men continued, recruiting for women came to a grinding halt, except for those with critical skills, so the numbers of enlisted women began to decline rapidly through attrition even before demobilization policies affected them. Then decisions were made to allow all married women to leave, and an exodus began.

However, in the panic to get organized for the massive demobilization, the services began to have second thoughts about letting all of the women go. The women had skills required to staff the ports processing personnel returning from overseas, to assist the new separation centers springing up all over the country, and to provide medical care for convalescing wounded men in service hospitals. At that point, military leaders began to doubt seriously the wisdom of complete demobilization of the women. In fact, some military leaders began asking for more enlisted women. The

Army Service Forces, for example, asked for 5,000 more WACs in order to maintain its separation centers.

When the war ended in Europe, there were over 8,000 women in the ETO, mostly with the Air Force. Theater authorities decided that 50,000 would be needed for the Army of Occupation. In view of the overall size of the Corps, however, the request submitted to the Pentagon was scaled down to 10,000 (over and above the 6,000 assigned to the Air Forces in Europe).

The War Department did not want to send them because the women were needed in the States for demobilization work. The theater was told that male combat returnees would not be substituted for returning WACs because the men lacked the skills and were "temperamentally unsuited for the work." A compromise was reached and the ETO received an authorization for an additional 2,000 women.

Unfortunately for the ETO, the war ended in the Pacific and shipments of WACs were curtailed in order to staff the new stateside separation centers. Personnel eligible for rotation, male and female, who were not absolutely essential were to be sent home. Declaring the women indispensable, the theater froze all clerical WACs in their jobs on the basis of "military necessity." They would not be allowed to leave without acceptable replacements, and men were not considered acceptable as replacements for WACs. The War Department thereupon forbade any theater to retain discharge-eligibles, male or female, on the grounds of "military necessity"; those who wanted to leave were finally allowed to go home. This was a blow to the theater authorities who considered the WACs a primary source of critically needed skills for the Army of Occupation. Many WACs did stay on as volunteers until they were eligible for discharge rather than go home to temporary jobs. A few moved on to Germany with the occupation forces.

One of the factors that weighed heavily in the War Department's firm stand against retaining the WACs in Europe was a rumor circulating among the ETO women, which had reached the Pentagon, that behind the insistence on having so many WACs with the occupation forces was the desire to discourage U.S. troops from fraternizing with German women. The WACs resented it.

Perhaps the ultimate recognition of the contribution of America's women to the war was paid by Albert Speer, Hitler's weapons' production chief:

> How wise you were to bring your women into your military and into your labor force. Had we done that initially, as you did, it could well have affected the whole course of the war. We would have found out, as you did, that women were equally effective, and for some skills, superior to males.[2]

At war's end, of the 12 million people in the U.S. Armed Forces, nearly 280,000 were women. All together, 350,000 women had actually served in the military. They were all volunteers and, with the exception of the nurses, had served in programs literally started from scratch three years earlier. In spite of their problems and frustrations, most of the women who served during the war felt satisfied that they had meaningfully contributed to winning the war. Having gained a self-confidence and maturity beyond their expectations, most would look back on the experience as one of the high points of their lives.

The women were generally regarded as eager beavers and quick learners, even by those who had initially been skeptical about the whole idea. Most of the anticipated problems either failed to materialize or were soon resolved by common sense and goodwill. Commanders and supervisors who had once said, "We want them but we don't have the facilities," soon found the facilities. For example, at one naval air station in a hangar with only one "head," the chief petty officer in charge solved a facilities problem by putting a peg on the outside of the door below a sign: "Before entering hang up your hat here."

Leaders in all of the services commented openly and often on the positive effect the women had on their units. Service chaplains often noted that their chapel facilities had to be doubled and tripled to accommodate not just the women but the increasing numbers of men. Commanders often commented that the women had brought an air of refinement to their units. The men just acted differently with the women around. They worked harder, dressed better, goofed off less, and in general behaved better.

The WAVES, which had begun operating only in 1942, by 1945 comprised over half of the naval personnel of the Navy Department headquarters in Washington, D.C., 70 percent of the Bureau of Naval Personnel, and two-thirds of the enlisted personnel in the office of the Chief of Naval Operations; 18 percent of the total naval personnel of the stateside shore establishments were women. Adm. Ernest J. King, Chief of Naval Operations, praised the WAVES for their competence, hard work, and enthusiasm and stated that "they have become an inspiration to all hands in naval uniform." The Navy estimated that the WAVES had made available enough men to man the ships of a major task force including a battleship, two large aircraft carriers, two heavy cruisers, four light cruisers, and fifteen destroyers.

The Marine Corps, in 1942, was the last service to accept the concept of military women. Two years later, the Commandant, Gen. A. A. Vandegrift, gave his women credit for putting an entire marine division in the field. Without the women to fill 19,000 jobs throughout the Corps, there would not have been sufficient men available to form the division. By the end of the war, the women were filling 87 percent of the enlisted jobs at Corps headquarters and comprised one-third to one-half of the post troops at many Marine stations.

Even the Army Ground Forces (AGF), which had been the most resistant of Army major commands, had come to accept the value of women in the military. It had been the view of Lt. Gen. Lesley J. McNair, the AGF commander, that the educational, occupational, and physical training of the average American woman would make it extremely difficult to adapt women to military duties. But the manpower shortages of 1943 and 1944 had made a convert of him. By the close of the war, the AGF had decided that the services of the women had proved of direct assistance in winning the war, and that a far greater number could have been effectively employed. A study concluded that "economical, efficient, and spirited results are achieved in military installations where both male and female personnel are on duty." The once reluctant AGF subsequently took the lead in urging a permanent place for women in the Regular Army.

Unfortunately, no one has ever done an unbiased assessment of the cost and worth of the women's programs during the war. The end came too suddenly; in the haste to demobilize and disarm, no one seemed to see the need to compile any useful data on costs and effectiveness—probably because most people thought that once the war ended there would be no need for women as the services disbanded to a small peacetime force. Besides, cost was never a factor in mounting the war effort, and it certainly was never a factor in the decisions to employ women. Had it been, there would have been little choice but to draft them.

In subsequent years, however, the cost of the women's programs became a recurring theme, the underlying assumption being that women cost more than men. In fact, the reverse has always been the case, as every study of the subject has revealed.

In its postwar planning, the Army General Staff compiled estimated relative costs of male and female soldiers which clearly showed that one on-board woman had cost less primarily because of the higher costs associated with dependents of men. The Army estimated that in the future it could save the taxpayers $7.7 million a year for each 100,000 women substituted for an equal number of male noncombatants.

If the estimates of the ETO were correct, the savings could have been doubled by the use of only 50,000 women to replace 100,000 men for jobs in which women appeared to excel. These savings would be offset, it was believed, if women were used to replace men for jobs in which they are not able to perform as well as men, such as those requiring physical strength beyond their capabilities, or those well below their intellectual skill levels, which destroy motivation and morale.

If, indeed, the enlisted women were a lot of trouble, as many men perceived them to be, it was due in part to the tendency to segregate and overprotect them. The situation in the SWPA was an exaggerated case in point. But, even under what might be considered normal circumstances, the tendency was to segregate the women by separate housing and administrative procedures and by a combination of sexist and paternalistic attitudes.

Interestingly, the wartime directors of the WACs, WAVES, SPARs, and Women Marines were not to be among those urging a permanent place for women. All believed from the very beginning that the women should serve only during the war, and that they should be disbanded as fast as possible after the war. The directors themselves set the example.

In July 1945, Col. Oveta Culp Hobby resigned as Director, WAC. Although she had planned to stay to the bitter end, ill health and repeated periods of hospitalization forced her to leave. It was not the last Washington would see of her, however. Several years later, she would return to serve in President Eisenhower's cabinet as the first Secretary of Health, Education, and Welfare, the second woman to serve as a cabinet officer. Col. Westrey Battle Boyce, her replacement as director, shared her views on the rapid demobilization of WACs.

Col. Ruth Cheney Streeter resigned as Director of the Marine Corps Women's Reserve in December 1945. Early in 1946, Capt. Mildred McAfee left the Navy to return to her position as president of Wellesley College. Capt. Dorothy C. Stratton left the Coast Guard and joined the federal Retraining and Reemployment Administration with the job of ensuring that women were not overlooked in its mission of guiding civilian communities in reintegrating veterans.

It has always been something of a mystery why the wartime women's leaders did not support the permanent retention of women in the armed forces or even their retention in the immediate postwar interim force. The directors did not appear before congressional committees during the 1947–48 hearings on the Integration Act, presumably to avoid undercutting the women who favored the legislation. There are indications that the wartime directors had deep reservations about the long-term utilization of women in the armed forces, which they were reluctant to express publicly for fear of seeming to deride the women's wartime efforts. Their views, however, are revealed to some degree in the report of the Commission on the Organization of the Executive Branch of Government, known as the Hoover Commission since it was chaired by the former President. The wartime directors were called to testify before the Commission in mid-1948.

One of the major conclusions of the report, which Treadwell calls the "Corps' greatest single dilemma," was that there was a need for the services to protect more fully the women's well-being. Whereas industry had long since recognized and accommodated the needs of both sexes in setting up work standards, the armed forces' rules and operations had been designed over the years for men only and the services tended to look at any modification as favoritism or special privilege. Because of the unbending male orientation and the ratio of women to the total strength, the women were almost without exception expected to make the entire adjustment to men's standards of dress, privacy, cleanliness, and recreation.

The early directors were worried over the possible long-term effects of women's attempts to adjust to the rigid male environment and did not care to assume the responsibility for what they apparently feared would be a masculinizing experience for the young women involved. Moreover, having fought the early battles in the highest echelons of the services to wrest concessions to what they perceived as legitimate differences in women's needs, the wartime directors were all too familiar with the built-in intransigence of the military bureaucracy, in which uniformity is next to godliness and tradition acquires the status of religious orthodoxy.

Having been through the mill and having butted heads with and been intimidated by officers much higher in rank, with years of service experience, the directors were understandably dubious about the services' ability and willingness to adjust adequately to the long-term "coeducationalization" of the armed forces. Their worries were not groundless. There was, and continued to be, a general reluctance at all service levels to accept as valid, or equally compelling, the special needs and concerns of women, accompanied by a tendency to treat those needs as frivolous or not worth the bother. The women are expected to adjust and to conform to the rules laid down *by men for men.* The women seldom complain because they feel powerless and fear reprisal.

Another issue that emerged from the Hoover Commission report and that contributed to the directors' concerns was that the place of women in the services was "not completely secure": their morale relied greatly on the opinions of the public and the soldiers. These opinions needed to be improved.

The generally negative attitude toward military women in the aftermath of the slander campaign must have been a major source of anxiety and frustration for the directors. Not only did it have a pronounced depressing effect upon recruiting for years, but it was devastating to the morale of the women. Hobby in particular was compelled throughout her tenure to spend an enormous amount of time and effort fighting off the allegations and attempting to turn public opinion around with facts.

Although in frequent visits to the field the directors heard praise from commanders about what good soldiers, sailors, and marines their women were, the directors must have been aware of, and dismayed by, the real state of affairs. At the working level, things were not all that rosy. Even by the end of the war, acceptance of military women by the men was at best marginal, tentative, and usually grudging despite all the lavish praise from military leaders. The women were taught that acceptance, like respect, is something they must earn; and in the military, they learned that it had to be earned over and over and over again. Many women who served in the war also concluded that as long as they did not share in combat, women would never be full-fledged military citizens.

Full-fledged or not, there were men and women who felt there was a useful role for women to perform in the armed forces after the war. One of these was General Eisenhower, who, at war's end, became the Army's Chief of Staff. Faced with severe shortages of skilled personnel for the postwar "interim Army," Eisenhower decided to keep the WAC beyond the scheduled demobilization date. As demobilization continued to decimate the ranks of skilled people, the Army's Personnel Chief, Maj. Gen. W. S. Paul, over the objections of the WAC director but with the blessings of the Chief, authorized retention of women who volunteered to remain on active duty and a re-entry program for women already separated. "General Eisenhower is calling upon the Women's Army Corps to remain in operation," the women were told. "The Army is turning to the WAC for help in the manpower emergency."

In January 1946, Paul told a Senate committee that the Army fully expected to have a small permanent group of women. "The women have done a very outstanding job in this war and in line with getting more men out of the Army [in the demobilization] we should use every available replacement we can get."

At Eisenhower's direction, the following month legislation was drafted to establish a Women's Army Corps in the Regular and Reserve of the peacetime Army. This legislation was introduced a year later as the WAC Integration Act. It was approved unanimously by the Senate. That is as far as it got. The hate mail started. According to the *Congressional Record* of 6 April 1948, Congresswoman Margaret Chase Smith said that the opposition stemmed from off-the-record statements made to members of the House Armed Services Committee by "duly authorized officer representatives of the Navy Department."

The Navy was moving in the same direction as the Army. Vice Adm. Louis Denfeld, Chief of Naval Personnel, announced plans to keep women in the Naval Reserve beyond the demobilization target date, and the Marine Corps soon followed suit. Thus, of the four services, only the Coast Guard proceeded totally to disband its women's component on schedule. The SPARs were all demobilized by 30 June 1946.

Some WACs with scarce skills were retained on active duty

involuntarily, but many of them, along with several thousand women in the other services, stayed on voluntarily in the hope that a permanent place might be found for them in the peacetime services.

The decisions to retain the Army and Navy women beyond the scheduled demobilization date were made over the strong objections of the two directors. Colonel Boyce stated emphatically that it was "not practical to contemplate an Interim WAC." Both directors thus found themselves at cross-purposes to the desires of many of their own women and out of the mainstream of service planning insofar as the future status of women was concerned. They must have found their positions almost untenable. Leadership soon passed to a new generation of officers who favored the retention of women over the long term; among them were Joy Bright Hancock and Mary Hallaren. Hancock became Assistant Chief of Naval Personnel for Women in July 1946 and Hallaren the Director, WAC, in May 1947.

In the Army, Lt. Col. Mary A. Hallaren led the charge for integration. A feisty, bright woman known affectionately as the "little colonel," Hallaren had been a schoolteacher and lecturer for women's groups before the war. After receiving her commission as a 3rd officer in the first WAAC officer candidate class, she had moved up quickly to become a lieutenant colonel. Having led the first group of enlisted women into the ETO, she became the WAC staff director of the Air Forces in Europe and the leader in the movement for a permanent, peacetime corps. At war's end, she became deputy to Colonel Boyce, whom she eventually replaced as director. With a reputation for quick wit and straight talk, she always remained a generation ahead of her time on matters pertaining to military women.

Joy Bright Hancock's background was unique in that as a young woman she had enlisted as a yeoman (F) during the First World War. Between the wars, she was twice married to naval aviators and was twice widowed. During the early days of the Second World War, as a civilian in the Bureau of Aeronautics, she had been a strong advocate of the legislation to permit women to become members of the Naval Reserve; she was subsequently among the first officers commissioned by the Navy in 1942. She continued to serve in the Bureau of Aeronautics as the women's representative until the end of the war, when she was assigned to the Bureau of Naval Personnel to plan for the peacetime use of women in the Navy. At that point, it was a foregone conclusion that Hancock would become the WAVE director after the brief interregnum of Jean Palmer, who had stepped in when McAfee resigned. Palmer had not intended to remain beyond the wartime demobilization.

Hancock believed that women should become an integral part of the Navy because they were needed not only to carry out the publicly demanded rapid demobilization but also to continue some of its peacetime programs. For example, because of the heavy loss of skilled men through demobilization, WAVES were needed to "man" GCA (ground controlled approach) equipment then in its early experimental stage, and they were needed in the hospital corps for the rehabilitation programs. Hancock drew up plans for a permanent complement of women integrated into the existing structure of the Navy—both Regular and Reserve.

Meanwhile, in March 1946, Congressman Carl Vinson introduced a bill (H.R. 5919) to amend the Naval Reserve Act to authorize establishment of a Women's Reserve on a permanent basis. The Department of the Navy, not content with merely Reserve status, proposed that any legislation include authority to commission and enlist women in the Regular Navy and that the Marine Corps also be included. After hearings in the Naval Affairs Committee, the legislation failed to pass before adjournment, and the bill died. But the seeds had been sown, and—chiefly because of the efforts of Admiral Denfeld and Congresswoman Margaret Chase Smith, a member of the House Naval Affairs Committee—both the Navy and Congress were interested, albeit mildly.

Despite the actions of the Army and the Navy, the Marine Corps wanted no part of a peacetime women's program. "The opinion generally held by the Marine Corps is that women have no proper place or function in the regular service in peacetime," declared Brig. Gen. Gerald C. Thomas, Director of Plans and Policies in October 1945. "The American tradition is that a woman's place is in the home . . . women do not take kindly to military regimentation," he added. "During the war they have accepted the regulations imposed on them, but hereafter the problem of enforcing discipline alone would be a headache."[3]

Marine women tended to agree with this view. The wartime director, Col. Ruth Streeter, expressed the opinion that there would be a noticeable difference in the women who enlisted during the war and those who enlisted after the G.I. bill was passed,

granting educational benefits to discharged service personnel—
the former being motivated by patriotism and the latter by self-
interest. The same observation could have been made about men
who volunteered; those who were drafted were hardly moved by
patriotic impulses. Nonetheless, the female leadership for the most
part eschewed any notions of peacetime service and had worked
actively to phase out the active force the moment hostilities ended.

The Marine Corps was unconcerned that it was out of step
with the other service chiefs and the Secretary of the Navy concerning an active force of women in peacetime. It was soon persuaded, however, of the need for a permanent organized reserve
and set about organizing one. Later, with the momentum generated by the other services for women in the Regular establishment,
the commandant caved in to the inevitable and supported the
existence of women in the Regular Marines.

Efforts to grant permanent status to the Nurse Corps were
more successful. The Army–Navy Nurse Act (P.L. 36-80C) was
enacted in April 1947, establishing the Nurse Corps as permanent
staff corps of the two services. The legislation provided for integration of female nurses into the officer ranks of the Regular Army
and Navy in grades up to lieutenant colonel/commander. The
Chief of the Corps could serve in the rank of temporary colonel/
captain so long as she occupied that position. Later, in 1949, the
Air Force established the Air Force Nurses Corps, the nucleus of
which was formed by nurses who had served in the Army Nurse
Corps during the war.

There never had been a question, however, of whether nurses
would remain after the war. It was a foregone conclusion that
their skills would be essential in the peacetime armed forces. For
the nurses, the central issue was whether they would receive full
membership in the Regular Officer Corps.

Critical shortages of registered nurses throughout the war had
already prompted Congress to establish a training program for
nurses in 1943, to grant them full military status in 1944, and to
even consider drafting them in 1945. Congress in July 1943 had
established and funded the U.S. Cadet Nurse Corps under the
Public Health Service. Some 125,000 women eventually graduated from the program with a pledge to serve either with the military or with other essential governmental or civilian services for
the duration of the war. Although the pledge was more a statement
of good intentions than a binding agreement, it was an enormous

assistance to the services in meeting their requirements for nurses.

Yet, by early January 1945, the shortage of nurses was so critical that the President, in his State of the Union address, requested legislation to draft nurses. A bill was passed by the House; but before the Senate acted, the war ended in Europe, and the shortage vanished. There were enough nurses on duty and enough new volunteers to meet the needs of the war in the Pacific.

In 1949, two new women's components were established—the Army Medical Specialists Corps and the Air Force Medical Specialists Corps—bringing the total number of women's components to nine. They included: the four line components (WACs, WAVES, WAF, and Women Marines), three Nurse Corps (Army, Navy, and Air Force), and two women's medical specialist corps (Army and Air Force)—a confusing array of women's military categories.

Of the line components, only the WAC was established by law as a female organizational entity, and within a few years the all-female nurse and medical specialist corps became "coeducational."

NOTES

1. Barbara Davis, "POW Nurses: So Proudly We Hail," *The Retired Officer* magazine, March 1974, p. 18.
2. As reported by Ira C. Eaker [Lt. Gen., USAF (Ret.)], *Air Force Times* magazine, 6 December 1976.
3. Mary V. Stremlow [Col., USMCR], *A History of Women Marines: 1946–77*, working draft (Washington, D.C.: HQ USMC, March 1979), p. 1.

PART II
INTEGRATION THROUGH VIETNAM

CHAPTER 10

INTEGRATION: 1948

O N 2 JUNE 1948, by a vote of 206 to 133, Congress passed the Women's Armed Services Act of 1948 (P.L. 625—80th Congress), ending more than a year of bitter, sometimes ludicrous, and often acrimonious debate. On 12 June, President Truman signed the measure that finally established a permanent place for women in the Army, Navy, Air Force, and Marine Corps.[1]

The act was many things to many people: to feminists, a leap forward for women's rights; to most women veterans, recognition of their contribution and vindication of their service; and to the military women who worked for its passage, sweet victory.

To the generals and admirals who actively supported it, the law was a vehicle for mobilizing women's skills in the event of a future national emergency and for meeting the military's more immediate requirement for volunteers, especially for those needed to fill clerical and other so-called women's jobs.

The new law provided limited opportunities for peacetime service for women in the regular establishment of the four services plus the framework to mobilize womanpower in the event of a national emergency without going through the confusing, time-consuming process of organizing women's programs and developing policies as had had to be done in 1942 and 1943. In Col. Mary Hallaren's words,

> It would be tragic if, in another emergency, a new generation had to start from scratch; had to duplicate effort; make the same mistakes twice. . . . It would be foolhardy to wait for another war to find out how and where women could best be used in the national defense. To write, "finis" to women's contribution . . . would be turning back time.

Capt. Joy Bright Hancock expressed much the same view during hearings in the Senate: "It would appear to me that any national defense weapon known to be of value should be developed and kept in good working order and not allowed to rust or to be abolished."

The Integration Act did not slip through the Congress easily. Its final passage was due more to the prevailing military manpower philosophy than to concerns about women's right to serve. The United States had emerged from the war as a superpower with global military commitments and risks. U.S. troops remained deployed all over the world and carried the major burden of the occupation of Germany and Japan. Nevertheless, Americans were war weary and in no mood to support a large military establishment. With the precipitous postwar demobilization, active forces had shrunk from 12 million to 1.4 million in the short span of two years.

Most military strategists subscribed to the view that, since the United States had a monopoly on the atomic bomb and the means to deliver it, conventional wars were obsolete; hence, large conventional forces were unnecessary. With the implied threat of nuclear retaliation, the United States could impose a sort of Pax Americana on the rest of the world without the expense of maintaining a large manpower-intensive force. This concept, although attractive at the time, was soon to be proven unrealistic.

The first ominous signs of the tenor of the fifties and the skirmishes of the Cold War were the communist-inspired civil war in Greece and the communist coup in Czechoslovakia. Then, in April 1948, Russian troops cut off access to Berlin, and, to prevent a communist takeover of the city, the United States and Great Britain embarked on the largest airlift in history.

These events made American military leaders reexamine their manpower requirements. With fresh memories of the personnel crises of the recent war, they became increasingly concerned about meeting manpower requirements if a new major mobilization were required to meet the growing threat. For the first time in history, consideration was given to a peacetime draft for men and to providing a permanent place for women in the Regular and Reserve components of the armed forces as a base for rapid mobilization of the nation's womanpower for war.

Nearly a year before the crisis in Berlin, Congress had passed the Armed Forces Unification Act, creating the Department of Defense (DOD), an umbrella structure encompassing the Departments of the Army and Navy and a new Department of the Air Force. From then on, all legislation for the services was handled jointly through the DOD rather than via individual service bills. The Army and Navy Departments' bills for women, already on Capitol Hill, were thus combined into Senate Bill 1641, entitled "The Women's Armed Services Integration Act," with separate titles for the services: Title I dealt with the Army; Title II, the Navy and Marine Corps. In November, the Air Force got into the act with Title III.

In 1947, the existence of a permanent place for women in the armed forces, other than for those in the health professions, was by no means a foregone conclusion. According to a future WAF director, Maj. Emma Jane Riley, the general supposition was that the Integration Act would not pass. Therefore, the Air Staff put the least possible effort into drafting Title III, which was to establish the women in the Air Force. Riley recalls the frustration of the officer who worked on drafting Title III, Lt. Col. Frances "Sue" Cornick, who was told by the male staffers not to worry about the wording of the title since the bill was not going anywhere anyway.

During the legislation's early stages, the only people who had seemed interested in pushing it were women—Hallaren, Hancock, Margaret Chase Smith, and Edith Nourse Rogers (the mother of the WAAC Bill of 1942). With the exception of leaders like Eisenhower, Denfeld, and Eaker, most military men did not take the legislation seriously; many men and some women were flatly against it but were reluctant to say so publicly since their chiefs supported it. Privately, they were more outspoken and their hostility forestalled the bill's passage in the House of Representatives. Nevertheless, after a brief series of hearings, the bill sailed through the Senate.

Its course provided some interesting moments. One was a congressional discussion on menopause, recalled by Hancock. After some members of the Armed Services Committee expressed concern over the prospect of large numbers of military women retiring for physical disability because of "menopausal symptoms," the Navy Surgeon General astonished the senators by stating that there was very little difference between male and female officers in retirement for physical disability:

> The commonly held idea that women are invalided in their middle years
> by the onset of the menopause is largely a popular fallacy. It is well known
> that men pass through the same physiological change with symptomatol-
> ogy closely resembling that of women.[2]

That laid the subject to rest.

The House of Representatives was less receptive than the Senate to the idea of having women as permanent members of the armed forces. Although a Gallup poll revealed that a majority of the American public favored peacetime service for women, the House bill came under sharp attack from the same sources that had perpetuated slander during the war years: military men and veterans who wrote articles in soldier magazines and letters to members of Congress.

Margaret Chase Smith hinted that opposition to the legislation came in the form of off-the-record statements made to members of the Armed Services Committee by Navy men who were secretly out to scuttle the legislation.[3] One member commented, "There are several aspects to this bill that I do not care to discuss here publicly," to which another member exclaimed, "If we could only discuss publicly on the floor of the House those things we discuss behind closed doors!"[4] The anonymous opposition became so vicious and intense that the House, at the recommendation of the Armed Services Committee, passed only the Reserve portion of the bill. The proponents of the full Integration Act were stunned, and a battle ensued for passage of the Senate version, which included Regular as well as Reserve status.

Secretary of Defense James V. Forrestal; Generals Eisenhower and Bradley of the Army; Admirals Denfeld, Nimitz, and Radford of the Navy; Air Force Generals Spaatz, Vandenberg, and Eaker; Marine Corps General Vandegrift, and others either testified personally or came out in strong public support of the legislation. Eisenhower made the point that, in the event of another war, which he believed would be even more global than the last in its effects upon the entire population, everybody in the country would serve under some form of call to duty: "I look upon this measure as a 'must.'" Fleet Adm. Chester Nimitz, then Chief of Naval Operations, testified that it was the considered opinion of the Navy Department and his own personal belief that the services of women were needed:

Their skills are as important to the efficient operation of the Naval establishment during peacetime as they were during the war years. . . . The Navy's request for the retention of women is not made as a tribute to their past performance. We have learned that women can contribute to a more efficient Navy. Therefore, we would be remiss if we did not make every effort to utilize their abilities.

Gen. A. A. Vandegrift, Commandant of the Marine Corps, ultimately, but not initially, took much the same view. The Marine Corps originally had taken the official position that women were not needed in their Regular peacetime forces since such forces would be composed almost entirely of combat-qualified marines available for deployment to trouble spots anywhere in the world on a moment's notice. Vandegrift reasoned that, since the Corps relied upon the Navy for most of its noncombat support, there would be few jobs in its Regular peacetime structure that women could fill. The need, as the Marine Corps saw it, was for an organized, highly trained Women's Reserve available to augment the Regular active forces in the shore establishments should combat marines be deployed for an emergency. Maj. Julia Hamblet, who had left active duty at war's end, was called back to organize this new Women's Reserve and to serve as its director. Later, the commandant changed his mind and joined the other services' chiefs in support of the Regular legislation.

Once again, as in 1942, national women's organizations and thousands of concerned women rallied to the cause, sending letters and telegrams to the House Armed Services Committee urging support of the Senate version of the legislation.

At the time of the hearings, there was much speculation about why the women's wartime military leaders did not testify for or come out in public support of the legislation. Treadwell says,

The wartime WAC leaders . . . were not asked to testify or to submit statements; the same was true of the wartime heads of the WAVES, SPARs, and Women Marines. When privately approached by members of Congress to inquire whether such an invitation should not be issued by the armed forces, the wartime WAC leaders discouraged such action. While personally uninterested in peacetime service, most did not feel justified in barring it for any women who wished to remain. More importantly, they feared that their opposition to peacetime service might mistakenly be construed as a condemnation of the WAC's wartime record, or of future service by women in national emergencies.[5]

A main point of anonymous opposition on the Hill turned out to be a general fear that women would command men. In the words of one congressman, a Navy veteran, "There is not a member of the House Committee on Armed Services who has not received a telephone call or a call in person from an enlisted man objecting to the idea of having to take orders from WAVES officers." To allay these fears, language was inserted to give the service Secretaries the prerogative of prescribing "the military authority which female persons . . . may exercise and the kind of military duty to which they may be assigned," thus allowing the services the latitude to deal with this particular problem.

Another subject of debate was women in combat. The issue was not whether women should be allowed to serve in combat; that was never seriously considered. It was instead how best to ensure that women would not be employed as combatants.

Delineating women's noncombatant position in the Navy and Air Force was a simple matter—just ban them from combat ships and aircraft. During the hearings in the Senate, over the Navy's objections, a section prohibiting women from serving aboard ships was inserted. The Navy representative stated at the time that while the Navy did not presently intend to assign women to general shipboard duties, it "did not feel . . . that it was necessary to write that into law." But the committee insisted that the question not be left to Secretarial discretion. The rationale behind the committee's action was never clear. Judge John Sirica concluded in 1978 that it was based on the notion "that duty at sea is part of an essentially masculine tradition."[6]

The Army's problem was different because defining combat was not as simple, as Hallaren pointed out at the hearing:

> It is possible for us to exclude the use of women in combat, that is on either aircraft or ships, and while it is up to the War Department to limit the utilization of women in the Army to noncombat jobs, it is impossible for the War Department to outline combat areas in the future since the experts advise that modern warfare makes the entire United States vulnerable as a combat area in the future.

Because the Army was unable to come up with an adequate, acceptable definition of combat, Congress elected to leave this matter to be sorted out by the Secretary of the Army so long as he clearly understood the intent of the Congress, which was *no com-*

bat for women. The Secretary got the message and complied, as did all his successors.

Thus, after numerous amendments and much debate, Senate Bill 1641 became law on 12 June 1948. Women had won an important battle in their fight for the opportunity to serve in the United States armed forces; there was still a long way to go.

THE INTEGRATION ACT

The primary purpose of P.L. 625 was to provide a means of mobilizing womanpower in the event of general war. Its specific objectives were:

- To assist in filling current personnel requirements and lessen the need for a peacetime draft.
- To provide a trained nucleus, a basic reservoir for future expansion, in time of national emergency.
- To find out how and where women could best be used before an emergency arises—to catalog skills, to develop abilities, and to find what types of training were needed for women.
- To provide for greater economy in the use of all personnel by using women in the jobs for which they were better suited than men.

Lofty as some of these objectives were, their realization was another matter. From the beginning, implementation became bogged down by changes in military conditions and strategies, societal attitudes about women's roles, and mistaken assumptions about the future. For example, one of the act's stated objectives— to lessen the need for a peacetime draft—was the first to fall by the wayside since the draft was reinstated on 24 June, twelve days after the Integration Act was signed.

Moreover, the act had certain inherent barriers which hindered its objectives and prevented, except in the case of the new Air Force, any greater integration of women in the services than existed in World War II.

In its specific provisions, Public Law 625:

- Gave permanent status to women in all the armed forces—Regular and Reserve.
- Gave permanent status to the Women's Army Corps as a separate organization within the Army "which shall perform such services as may be prescribed by the Secretary of the Army" and required all women *not* members of the Nurse or Women's Medical Specialist Corps, to be

members of the WAC. No similar organizational entities were established in the other services.

- Authorized the appointment of female commissioned officers and warrant officers and the enlistment of women in the Regular and Reserve components of the four services.

- Imposed a 2-percent ceiling on the proportion of women on duty in the Regular establishment of each service.

- Limited each service to only one line full colonel or Navy captain. (No generals or admirals were allowed at all.) This senior grade could be held for only a temporary period of four years unless extended by the service Secretary. The Army colonel had to be "the Director of the Women's Army Corps"; the Navy captain was required to be "an assistant to the Chief of Naval Personnel" (presumably for women); and the Marine Corps colonel was assigned to assist the Commandant in the "administration of women's affairs." Only the Air Force was unconstrained in the assignment of the one authorized full colonel.

- Set a 10-percent limit of the female officers who could serve as permanent Regular lieutenant colonels and Navy commanders. In the case of the Navy, a 20-percent limit was imposed on the number of lieutenant commanders.

- Established separate female officer promotion lists for women in the Army, Navy, and Marine Corps in each grade. Only Air Force women were integrated into the male promotion lists in all grades below colonel.

- Set the minimum enlistment age at eighteen, with parental consent required under twenty-one (as compared to seventeen for men, with parental consent required under eighteen).

- Provided that officers and enlisted women could claim husbands and/or children as dependents *only* if it could be proven that they were in fact dependent upon the women for "their chief support." Wives and children of male members were automatically considered dependents.

- Authorized the service Secretaries to prescribe the military authority that women might exercise and the kind of military duty to which they might be assigned *provided*, in the case of the Navy and Air Force, that they "may not be assigned to duty in aircraft while such aircraft are engaged in combat missions"; nor, in the case of the Navy, "may they be assigned to duty on vessels of the Navy except hospital ships and naval transports."

- Authorized the service Secretaries to terminate the Regular commission or enlistment of any female member "under circumstances and in accordance with regulations proscribed by the President." No such blanket authority existed for discharging men.

Even a cursory examination of these provisions, from the vantage point of the 1980s, reveals barriers to full integration and the accomplishment of the act's objectives. Some were to prove bigger hurdles than others, and the effects of each were somewhat dependent on the interpretation each service placed on the act.

Also, the inconsistencies in organization and treatment are striking. For example, the organizational patterns of women varied considerably, depending on the service. The Air Force women were the most fully absorbed into organizational structure, and the Army women the least. The Army made no pretext of integrating its women. There is no indication that the Army even considered giving up the Corps in favor of a system more in line with the other services. As individuals, WACs could serve side by side with male personnel and would be considered interchangeable on a one-for-one basis, but the women's primary identification —their first loyalty—must remain with the WAC. The helmeted head of Pallas Athena (Greek goddess of victory, womanly virtue, and the arts of war), which had been adopted in 1942 as the official WAAC/WAC insignia, continued to grace WAC uniform lapels to identify WAC's separate status. The Corps would continue to train, house, administer, promote, and monitor the women's careers.

The Army's persistence in maintaining a separate identity for women is not clear except perhaps because it maintained the status quo. The system had worked during the war. So why change it? One explanation, given by a senior WAC officer, was that the Army would never have accepted the women on any other basis.

Whatever the rationale, and however logical it seemed at the time, the women's corps was always something of an anachronism, even for the Army. In the vernacular of the 1970s, it was often defined as a "women's ghetto." However, in its time the Corps served a useful purpose and for the most part the women themselves had an emotional attachment to it. The Corps survived intact for another thirty years and many bemoaned its passing.

There were never any similar organizations in any of the other services, although it was commonly believed that there were. The use of acronyms like WAVES and WAF, although perhaps convenient tools for communication, lent credence to this misconception and to incorrect assumptions about the structural positions of women in the services. There were, nonetheless, women's support systems in all of the services that exercised varying degrees of control and influence over the women's programs; although the formal corps structure was absent, there were similarities in functions.

The WAF was the least formalized of the four. The Air Force was new, literally born of the Army, having been created lock, stock, and barrel out of the Army Air Force. Many of the child's concepts and traditions came from the parent, but its organizational philosophies did not. The fledgling Air Force, in fact, rejected most strongly the parent service's notions about how to integrate women. It would have no part of an all-female corps. Its reason was not that the Air Force had an aversion to a women's corps; the Air Force had a deep aversion to *any* corps. When it became a separate service, it made sure that the Unification Act would not set up Army-type organizations: there would be no Signal Corps, no Quartermaster Corps, no Chemical Corps, no Medical Corps, and no Women's Corps. Although the acronym WAF was adopted because it seemed appropriate, it stood for Women *in* the Air Force, not Women's Air Force, as was commonly thought. As one director was fond of saying in order to emphasize the point, "We don't have our own Air Force . . . yet!"

STRENGTH CEILINGS

The law's 2-percent ceiling on Regular strengths was designed for one purpose: to keep the numbers small. It was imposed to allay fears that, if their numbers were not controlled, too many women might join. As it turned out, the military with its masculine trappings, traditional restrictions, and low pay was not all that attractive to young American women of the 1950s. At no time, not even during the buildup for the Korean War, was the 2-percent limit ever reached. Until the late 1960s, women rarely exceeded even *1 percent* of the services' strengths.

LID ON PROMOTIONS

While the strength ceilings had no practical effect on the women's programs, the grade ceilings did. The sole purpose of the grade ceilings was to prevent the possibility of women becoming top-level policy or decision makers in the military, except on women's matters, and even there the authority and responsibilities of the directors were carefully circumscribed.

Because the grade of colonel and captain were only temporary and only one such position was authorized for a woman in each component, when the woman occupying the position of director completed her assignment, she either had to step down or leave active duty. If not yet eligible to retire, she would revert to the next lower grade in order to complete the service tenure required for retirement. A number of directors did just that.

Because the only opportunity for promotion to colonel or captain was to be selected for the director's job, promotions to these grades were few and far between. Therefore, for all practical purposes, lieutenant colonel or commander was the highest grade a woman could aspire to, and even there the 10-percent restriction limited promotion opportunities. Navy women were limited still further by the 20-percent ceiling on lieutenant commanders.

Of course, the fact that women could not be promoted to permanent colonel or Navy captain and could not even be considered for general or admiral meant that they faced mandatory retirement at an earlier age than many men. In the Navy and Marine Corps, the maximum retirement age was set at fifty-five, and in the Army and Air Force, at fifty-three years. This applied only to permanent lieutenant colonels and commanders. The maximum age for major and lieutenant commander was lower.

The requirement for having separate promotion lists for the WACs, WAVES, and Women Marines meant that women would not compete for promotion with male officers in these services. The rationale behind it was that women could not or should not compete with men who would most likely have combat and command experience and, in the case of the Navy, duty at sea.

With the integration of women into the Air Force promotion system, female and male officers competed with one another in all grades up through lieutenant colonel, where the women encountered the legal ceiling. At that point, a female officer's career was at a standstill as her male contemporaries, often her own male subordinates, began to pass her by. The fact that Air Force women were in competition with men for promotion did not mean they fared any better in promotions than did their sisters in the other services. In fact, the reverse was often true. Their chief handicap was their exclusion from all pilot and navigator jobs, which were heavily favored in determining promotions and other career-enhancing opportunities.

THE PROBLEM OF DEPENDENTS

The law's provision on dependents created especially galling problems for women. P.L. 625 and all previous laws dealing with the subject of military dependents were based on deeply ingrained cultural assumptions: first, that women when they married would leave the service and, hence, all married personnel would be male and all spouses would be female civilians; and second, that husbands are the breadwinners and heads of the households. Even in the face of conflicting circumstances, assumptions such as these die hard. Their eradication has been especially difficult in the tradition-bound military.

Under the husband-as-breadwinner concept, the civilian wife was, and still is, presumed to be the dependent of her military spouse irrespective of her own financial or economic status. She could be making more money than her husband, even be a multimillionaire, and it would make no difference. A marriage license is the only proof required to establish her dependency. On the other hand, until 1973 the military woman who was also a wife was neither fish nor fowl as far as military entitlements were concerned. If her husband were a civilian, to claim him as a dependent she had to prove that he was dependent on her for over half his support, which meant that he had to be unemployed and unemployable for physical or mental reasons. If she were married to a military man, neither she nor her husband could claim the other as a dependent. They did not qualify for government on-base family quarters or for family housing allowances if they lived together off base. As far as the law and the services were concerned, they were both single. This "catch 22" situation was a constant source of irritation and financial hardship for the couples involved and resulted in the early loss of many women who might otherwise have made successful careers in the armed forces.

Dependent children were another matter. Even though the law provided that a woman might claim children as dependents if they were in fact dependent upon her for their chief support, the services would not accept women with children nor permit women to stay if they acquired children by birth, adoption, marriage, or other circumstances. The policy was very arbitrary, and there were no exceptions.

UNPRECEDENTED DISCHARGE AUTHORITY

By today's standards, probably the most odious and legally indefensible aspect of P.L. 625 was the authority vested in the service Secretaries to discharge Regular female officers and enlisted personnel for unspecified reasons and without the normal safeguards that protected male personnel from arbitrary administrative actions of this nature.

By law, a male member of the Regular services could be discharged involuntarily only for moral dereliction, professional dereliction, or because his retention was not clearly consistent with the interests of national security; and then he could be discharged only by action of a duly constituted board of officers. This provision applied also to female personnel, but, in addition, the blanket authority contained in P.L. 625 gave the Secretaries the authority to terminate commissions and enlistments of women subject only to "regulations prescribed by the President." The purpose of this provision was to facilitate terminating the service of women who were pregnant or who had minor children; and subsequent to passage of the law, Executive Order 10240* was issued on 27 April 1951 to provide the official authority to expel women for those reasons. Once again, the rationale used was that a woman's maternal responsibilities were incompatible with, and should take precedence over, her military career. She had no choice in the matter.

There was never any question that pregnant women, married or unmarried, should be automatically discharged. This was accepted practice during the war, and most women agreed with it. At that time, the idea of having pregnant women in the military—in uniform—was abhorrent to many men and women alike. Moreover, without child care facilities, it would be impossible to care for an infant and remain in the services. The low military pay scales at that time would have made remaining out of the question, since the cost of paying for the services of a full-time baby-sitter would have been prohibitive.

Minor children were another matter since pregnancy was not involved and the children were rarely infants. The arbitrariness of discharging women with minor children was inexplicable and totally unjustified. The rule applied to stepchildren, foster children, siblings—any child living in the home for thirty days a year. The circumstances other than that were irrelevant. The most common situation was that of the woman who married a man with children by a previous marriage. The children might have been motherless for years, but it never would have occurred to the services to discharge their father on that account. Yet, if a military woman married the father and the children lived at home, she was summarily discharged without regard to her personal desires, her

*See Appendix #1.

investment in her career, the taxpayers' investment in her training, or the criticality of her skills to the service. Incomprehensible as such a policy seems by today's standards, at the time it all seemed perfectly logical and proper, even to the directors.

THE QUESTION OF COMBAT

Despite P.L. 625's seeming ambiguity concerning women in combat and the discretion it allowed the service Secretaries as to women's roles in combat situations, none of the services seriously contemplated placing women in anything even remotely associated with combat roles. The law provided the services with a convenient crutch for excluding women from any skill, position, or organization merely by declaring it combat or combat-related.

Restrictions on sea duty not only had a serious impact on individual careers, since sea duty is an essential part of a naval career for both officers and enlisted personnel, but also became the primary justification for limiting the number of women who would be allowed to serve in the Navy, even in shore assignments. The Navy argued that if women were permitted to fill a large number of shore-based positions, fewer men could be assigned ashore, and they would have to spend a longer time at sea. To guard against this, a large number of shore billets were set aside for men to ensure that every sailor returning from a prescribed tour at sea had a shore job available.

The prohibition from duty in "combat aircraft engaged in combat missions" was interpreted by all the services to mean that *all* pilot jobs should be closed to women on the theory that a pilot was a pilot was a pilot, and that a pilot should be available for duty in any type of aircraft on any type of mission at any time. On the same grounds, women were also excluded from serving as navigators and in most other flight crew positions.

The impact of the aircraft restrictions on Navy and Marine Corps women was small compared with that of the shipboard restrictions. Its effect on women in the Air Force was a different matter. Career opportunities for female line officers were severely handicapped since the rated officers (pilots and navigators) are the Air Force elite: they get the best jobs and preferential consideration in promotions, school selections, and selection for Regular status.

Prohibited by law and, more pertinently, by the services' restrictive interpretation of the law from all forms of combat and combat-related assignments, women were, for all practical purposes, automatically excluded from participation in the primary mission of the armed forces, and their second-class status was thus assured.

OPPORTUNITY WITHOUT EQUALITY

Viewed in the context of the 1980s, P.L. 625 would be classified as a classic example of sexist legislation. While it allowed the services to take women, there was no mandate to do so. Also, many of the special provisions included in the law made full integration into any of the services virtually impossible and put equal opportunity out of reach. But that would be an unfair judgment based on hindsight. This law accurately reflected the prevailing cultural attitudes of the postwar period concerning women's roles and legal status. To have completely integrated them into the armed forces in 1948 with fully equal status would have been totally out of character with that stage in the evolution of women's roles in American society. It would simply never have occurred to those who were most directly involved.

Thus, P.L. 625 was never intended to plow new ground or to give women greater status in the peacetime forces than they had "enjoyed" during the war, but rather to consolidate the ground gained during the war and to prepare for the mobilization of the nation's womanpower in the event of another. Indeed, had it not been for the growing threat of another major war and the assumption that women would again be needed, it is doubtful that P.L. 625 would ever have seen the light of day.

GEARING UP FOR PEACETIME

The Integration Act's passage in June 1948 ended the two-year hiatus of waiting and wondering by experienced female veterans who wished to remain in the military. During all that time, the recruitment of enlisted women and line officers had been closed. With the signing of P.L. 625, each of the services had begun preparing for an expected buildup, limited by law in the first two years to a total of 18,000 women excluding those in the health professions (nurses and medical specialists).

The directors had already been chosen. Col. Mary A. Hallaren, serving as the Director, WAC, since May 1947, led the Regular Women's Army Corps. Capt. Joy Bright Hancock, assistant to the Chief of Naval Personnel for Women since July 1946, continued in that capacity in the Regular Navy using the quasi-official title of Director, WAVES. Col. Katherine Towle, former director of Marine Corps Women's Reserve, returned to active duty as the Director of Regular Women Marines. Col. Geraldine P. May, a graduate of the first WAAC officer candidate class in 1942, became the first Director, Women in the Air Force (WAF), on 15 June 1948.

To gear up, the services notified women on active duty of their option to join the Reserve or Regular components of the services in which they were serving, to enter the new Air Force, or to be discharged. Consequently, by late June the cores of the women's components were established. The record shows 1,296 line and staff officers and 6,476 enlisted women in the four services.

WOMEN IN THE LINE: JUNE 1948

	Officers	Enlisted
Army	676	3,266
Navy	444	1,618
Air Force	168	1,433
Marine Corps	8	159

Next, the services engaged in disappointing efforts to attract both neophytes and female veterans who had left active duty during the general demobilization and who were now given the same option as those women still on active duty. But women only trickled in; there had been no need to batten down the floodgates and place limits on women's service strengths.

The lukewarm enthusiasm of female veterans was unexpected but understandable. Most female veterans and most male veterans had never seriously considered a career in the military. They had returned to civilian life to establish or reestablish homes, to raise families, to get jobs, or to go to school on the G.I. Bill of Rights.

Unlike the male veterans, who had been welcomed home as heroes, most women had found to their surprise and chagrin that their military service, however patriotically motivated, was not universally applauded by family and friends or the community at large and was in fact often derided. Consequently, many women veterans concluded that the less said about their military service the better. Moreover, many local offices or agencies responsible for assisting returning veterans, including the Veterans Administration, were either unsympathetic to the needs of female veterans or unaware that women were entitled to the same benefits as male veterans.

The poor response to the initial buildup of the women's components was exacerbated by the draft's reinstatement. The nation, having grown accustomed to drafting its young men to meet the services' manpower needs in an emergency, turned once again to conscription as tensions grew in Europe with the Russian blockade of Berlin and the ensuing airlift. Within two weeks of the signing of the Integration Act, the President signed the Selective Service Act of 1948, authorizing the first peacetime draft in U.S. history. It would be another thirty-five years and two more wars before the nation would again be free from conscription.

With the males-only draft back in business, the gray shadow of a manpower crisis disappeared along with any real motivation to employ military women. However, in view of the strong public stand taken by the service Chiefs and the Secretary of Defense in support of the legislation, there was an implied obligation to follow through with some type of peacetime utilization, even if only token programs were established. Thus, recruiting goals were set, but those goals for enlisted women with no prior service were limited to only 650 per month for all the services combined. Officer procurement goals were so low as to barely offset normal attrition.

In August 1949, the Joint Chiefs of Staff directed the services to use military womanpower "to the maximum extent practicable," but then the Berlin airlift ended, and the matter of women was soon on the back burner again, awaiting a new manpower crisis. It came in 1950 in the form of the Korean War.

NOTES

1. Coast Guard reverted to the Treasury Department after the war (and later to the Department of Transportation) so was not included in the DOD-sponsored Integration Act of 1948. All SPARs were demobilized. During the Korean War a few officers and noncommissioned officers were recalled to active duty but only as reservists. U.S. Coast Guard did not begin to recruit women again until 1974 under a new law that authorized Regular and Reserve status for women.
2. Hancock, p. 227.
3. U.S. Congress, *Congressional Record*, 6 April 1948, p. A2241.
4. *Ibid.*, 21 April 1948, p. 4831.
5. Treadwell, p. 748.
6. *Owens v. Brown*, 455 F. Supp. 291 (D.D.C. 1978).

CHAPTER 11

THE FLEDGLING
AIR FORCE

NINE MONTHS AFTER the Air Force gained its independence from the Army, the WAF (Women in the Air Force) was born with passage of the Integration Act. Air Force leaders perceived their service as the new military elite and, in keeping with that philosophy, its women would be the best in every respect—the WAF would be the elite of the women in the services. Air Force leaders also were intent on avoiding what they considered to be the most serious mistake of the Army, namely, a separate women's corps. As reflected in the designation Women in the Air Force (WAF), they were to be integrated into the organization. These concepts— elitism and integration—while deeply held, were only vaguely understood even by the top leaders and had to be implemented by people imbued with the Army's traditions and ways of doing things. Conflict and confusion were inevitable.

There was every reason to believe in 1948 that the Air Force would lead the way in the utilization of women in the peacetime armed forces. After all, the AAF had been both the most enthusiastic supporter of women during the war and the most innovative in their utilization. There were few jobs Air-WACs were not allowed to do or technical schools they could not attend. They might even have attended pilot training schools had politics not gotten in the way. Certainly, enlisted flying jobs, such as airborne radio operators on B-17s (during training flights), aerial photography, and aircraft mechanics, were open to WACs. Several women received Air Medals, an award reserved for combat missions. These included one Air-WAC who mapped the Hump in India and another (posthumously) who died in the crash of an aerial broadcasting aircraft.

The principal complaint about the Air-WACs was that they could not be absorbed fully into the AAF. Given the chance, AAF leaders would have done it differently. In 1947–48, as the USAF, they got that chance when it came time to draft Title III of the Women's Armed Services Integration Act. In matters of organization and administration, Title III was intentionally vague so the Air Force would not be locked into any prescribed structure like the Army's WAC. The Air Force was free to go its own way without cumbersome legal constraints.

It is one thing to know what you *do not* want; it is quite another to know what you *do* want. Full "integration" was the Air Force's theoretical goal, but the degree to which women should, or could, actually be integrated into an overwhelmingly male organization was only vaguely perceived and, as it turned out, soon became a major area of controversy. To complicate matters, the Air Force in 1948 was itself experiencing growing pains. As one Pentagon staffer recalls, "It seemed like there was a new organization every week."

Most male officers, and many female officers, saw no need for, and inherently distrusted, anything resembling a women's corps or "petticoat channel." But faced with the day-to-day decisions, those trained in Army traditions found old habits hard to break. Instinctively, they thought of the women as a separate category of people. More often than not, the women were referred to as the "WAF Corps" or the "Women's Air Force." Female officers were referred to as "WAF officers" rather than USAF officers, and enlisted women were "WAF airmen."

True to this tradition, the Air Force was quick to establish a Director, WAF, although the law did not require one. On 16 June 1948, the Deputy Chief of Staff for Personnel and Administration[1] published a memorandum announcing the establishment of an Office of Director, WAF, and designating Geraldine P. May as the director with the grade of colonel.

A graduate of the first WAAC Officer Candidate class at Des Moines in 1942, May was a widow and former social worker. During the war years she had served in the AAF as Air-WAC Staff

Advisor for the Air Transport Command. Over the maximum age for appointment in the Regular Air Force, May was commissioned in the active Reserve. A tiny, gentle-mannered, soft-spoken woman known by her friends as Gerry, May was not the sort of person one would expect as the director of a military women's program. She would more easily have passed for a mother superior than an Air Force colonel. She will readily admit with a wry chuckle that at the time of her appointment, Secretary of the Air Force Stuart Symington told her, "I think you should know, you were not my first choice."[2] She was, however, the choice of the military. Little Gerry May's low-key demeanor disguised a strong will and an iron determination. Nobody's "yes-woman," she was not given to compromise on matters of principle.

Officially, May was responsible for advising the Chief of Staff and the air staff in the formulation of plans and policies pertaining to WAF and for advising commanders in the field on matters pertaining to the utilization, training, administration, and well-being of the women in their commands.

Direct communication between the director's office and other agencies of the air staff was authorized, and the staff was instructed that all matters pertaining to formulation or interpretation of policy concerning WAF were to be referred directly to that office. The concept was fine in theory but not in practice. The director had no authority to "direct" anything or anyone outside of her own tiny staff, and she was outside of the normal chain of command and the mainstream of decision making. She was, in Capt. Mildred McAfee's words, "the dangling link in the chain of command." Giving advice was her job, but outside of the personnel staff there was no requirement for others to seek her advice, since the directive establishing her office was binding only on the agencies within the Deputy Chief of Staff for Personnel and Administration. Coordination with the director was, therefore, a sometime thing, a matter of courtesy when the spirit moved. She could be ignored with impunity in the decision-making process, even in the matters vital to the WAF, and frequently was. She was regarded more as a "front woman" and titular head than a person with an important staff function.

Actually, there was no desire to create a strong office to direct women's affairs because, for one thing, with integration it was considered unnecessary and, for another, there was a natural reluctance to have a woman meddling in the normal activities of the staff, even on women's matters.

However artificial her status, the director nevertheless enjoyed a unique prestige both within and outside the Air Force, a prestige greater than her grade as a colonel and position as an advisor would otherwise have inferred. Her ability to actually influence policy and the course of events in her own small program depended on perceptions of her relationship to the power structure. There the winds could shift very quickly, depending on who had the ear of the Chief and/or the Secretary, as May soon discovered to her dismay.

Organizing the WAF got off to a slow start. With enactment of P.L. 625, Air-WACs still on active duty were required either to go back to the Army (WAC), transfer to the USAF, or revert to civilian status. By the end of June 1948, a meager 168 officers and 1,433 enlisted women had signed on with the new Air Force.

According to Title III, 300 officers, 40 warrant officers, and 4,000 enlisted women could be integrated into the Regular Air Force during the first two years. After that, the 2-percent ceiling applied. No limits were imposed on the Reserve, either on active or inactive duty status.

Even before the law was enacted, notices had been sent to the women who had served honorably in the other armed services to apply to join the new Air Force in either the Regular or Reserve components. An individual's grade was to be determined by age, length of active service, and the highest grade held while on active duty.

Of the thousands of officer veterans of World War II contacted (WACs, WAVES, SPARs, and Women Marines), only about 400 applied for commissions in the Regular Air Force; of those, 211 were actually tendered appointments. Because the majority of them were in their mid-thirties or over, they were appointed as senior captains and majors with dates of rank back-dated, based on age rather than actual service, thus making them immediately eligible for promotion to higher grades. As it turned out, those women constituted the largest—in fact, the *only*—significant influx of Regular female line officers in the history of the WAF and, as such, they would comprise the senior ranks of the WAF program for the next fifteen years.

The enlisted women who signed on were NCOs, also in their thirties and older, most of whom had considerable wartime experience both in the United States and overseas. These "old-timers" would form the cadre for the influx of young women who were expected soon to fill the enlisted ranks. Because the new legal minimum-age limit was eighteen, as compared with twenty for the wartime WAC, and because of the cessation of recruiting between 1946 and 1948, there would be a considerable age gap between the older NCOs and the new recruits. The vast majority of both the officers and NCOs were former WACs. Only small numbers of women came from the other services.

With unification, a joint Army–Air Force Recruiting Service was established under the supervision of the Army. (The Navy and Marine Corps remained independent.) From an Air Force point of view, the joint operation was never satisfactory, particularly for recruiting women. Eventually, the Air Force pulled out and went its own way.

But, in September 1948, the joint Recruiting Service opened its doors to young women. With high expectations that attractive, bright, high school graduates would come flocking to the offices to join the WAC and WAF, the services assumed they could afford to be selective. Instructions to the field described the qualities they wanted:

a. Good moral character and reputation
b. Ability to get along with people
c. Sufficient intelligence to assimilate training
d. An educational background which will be at least that of the average high school graduate
e. A desire to become a part of the Army and Air Force

WAF authorizations of from 250 to 350 per month were given to the recruiting service. The Air Force emphasized that these were "ceilings" not "quotas" on the naive assumption that this would somehow ensure high quality.

The WAF was to be a small, elite group of women—the best—which in the eyes of most Air Force leaders meant being superior to the WAVES. Comparing the WAF with the WAVES became almost an obsession with Air Force leaders. However, rather than adopt the Navy's practice of segregated procurement and commissioning programs and its insistence on a college degree for its officers, the Air Force elected to integrate women into its Officer Candidate School (OCS) at Lackland Training Center, San Antonio, Texas. It would be the first major coed officer-commissioning program in any service, but since its purpose was to provide commissioning opportunities for enlisted personnel, a college degree was not required. Also, because there had been no recruiting for enlisted women since World War II, there were very few in the active force that could qualify for the program.

Although the entrance of women into the formerly all-male OCS program was a major breakthrough in terms of integrated training, it was totally inadequate for building the WAF officer strength and would not provide an input of college graduates who would have the best chance of competing in an integrated officer system for Regular appointments, promotions and other career-enhancing opportunities against men commissioned from other sources, particularly college ROTC and the service academies.[3] The concept of integration would not be extended to these institutions for many years.

In January 1949, the Air Force enrolled nineteen women in OCS, and the first sixteen women commissioned as second lieutenants in the U.S. Air Force graduated in July. In general, integrated training worked well despite early misgivings. According to Colonel May: "Although the co-educational training of officer candidates was viewed with some trepidation by the faculty of the school, it soon became apparent that the young candidates regarded such training as a normal condition of accepted American public school practices."

Men and women met the same scholastic requirements and received the same instruction except for physical training and field exercises. While the men participated in field exercises, the women studied the administration of enlisted women—a job to which most of them were expected to be assigned at some point in their careers.

It should have been apparent at the outset that OCS would never produce the numbers anticipated. It was expected that sixty women would graduate each year, but the first year produced only thirty-four women and the second year, 1950, only thirty-nine. Thus for all practical purposes there was no effective female officer-commissioning program even to meet the modest goals and no source of college graduates to enhance the overall quality of the WAF officer force during the formative years.

Not until the Korean War buildup did Air Force officials recognize the need for additional sources of WAF officers and then the solutions were only temporary during the emergency. In June 1950 there were only 310 WAF officers on active duty. With the onset of the war, women in the reserves were recalled to active duty on the same basis as men and direct appointments were offered to women college graduates in the grades of second lieutenant through captain. At war's end, as WAF officer strength peaked at 1,023, both programs were discontinued and it was soon back to business as usual. In the whole of 1954, for example, only fifteen women were commissioned into the Air Force.

During the initial planning phase the Army and Air Force had agreed that WAC and WAF basic training would be consolidated at the WAC Basic Training Center, Camp Lee, Virginia. However, after her appointment as WAF director, May convinced the Air Staff that the Air Force should train its own women, and a basic training operation was set up at Kelly Air Force Base outside of San Antonio, Texas. It was soon moved to nearby Lackland and incorporated into the men's training wing. The women remained in a separate WAF basic training squadron and received segregated instruction as the only exception to the coeducational rule. That is not to say that all other training was coeducational, only that all instruction *open* to women was integrated such as courses in military intelligence, supply, meteorology, procurement, camera repair, air traffic control, cryptography, finance, electronics, etc. At one point coeducational basic training had been considered, but because of the women's higher mental and educational standards, they required a shorter training time than the men (eleven versus thirteen weeks, both later shortened during the Korean emergency for lack of space). Moreover, male basic training was heavily involved in body building, following the Army philosophy of "making men out of boys." Everyone agreed such a program was hardly appropriate for "the ladies" (they were not called women). Except for the differences in emphasis and lengths of training, the two programs were otherwise the same and were both conducted as an integral part of the Basic Training Wing at Lackland rather than at separate locations as was the practice of the other services.

Probably no subject connected with the WAF program caused more discussion and disagreement than that of how the enlisted women should be administered at base level. Before becoming a separate service the enlisted women were assigned to Air-WAC squadrons but performed duty in other units, e.g., the base hospital, supply squadron or communications squadron. Except for job performance rating, the Air-WAC unit commander had complete authority and responsibility for the women's administration and management.

This arrangement, however, was incompatible with the new Air Force's organizational philosophies and counter to the concept of integration. The majority of the air staff and most field commanders vigorously advocated the total integration of the women into their duty organizations (except for housing) and the elimination of any supervision of enlisted women by WAF commissioned officers. Colonel May could not go along. Although fully committed to the goals of integration, she believed this carried things too far.

May and most WAF officer veterans of the wartime WAC insisted that some kind of formalized structure of supervision and control was essential to ensure that the women were properly supervised and cared for and that their problems did not get lost in the overwhelmingly male organization. They also felt that young women needed to be able to identify with role models to sustain and reinforce their feminine orientation. There was never a question over housing women separately from the men; that was a foregone conclusion. The women working in many organizations on one base were housed in an all-female dormitory. The main unanswered question was: Who should be responsible for the women when they were not on the job?

Many male commanders insisted that full-time, twenty-four-hour control of *all* their people was essential to mission accomplishment: "If the women are going to work for me, they must belong to my unit just like my men." They wanted no part of dual control or divided loyalties. Some insisted that women were much more willing to discuss personal problems with a man, who represented a father figure: "Girls are used to going to their fathers for advice." Some male commanders even insisted on the prerogative of inspecting the women's dormitory, which, of course, created problems for the shift workers trying to sleep during the day. Others preferred to leave the women's off-duty supervision, administration, and welfare to a female officer on the assumption that she would be better equipped to deal with "women's problems."

Among the enlisted women themselves, there was also sharp division of opinion. The old-timers, NCO veterans of the World War II WAC, tended to feel the need to identify with a WAF unit; some even longed for a return to the esprit de corps they fondly associated with the Women's Army Corps. Others, while conceding a need for a WAF squadron to supervise the younger women, wanted no part of it for themselves. As mature adults in their thirties and forties, they had outgrown the organization and in fact resented its intrusion into their personal lives. Most NCOs abhorred living in a dormitory with normal, active, usually noisy, younger women but felt that "young girls need the supervision, guidance and discipline" that could only be provided by a WAF squadron with a full-time, dedicated, female commander.

A compromise system was settled on by 1949 whereby the enlisted women would be assigned to their duty organizations and attached to a WAF squadron for guidance, counseling, and off-duty supervision. The compromise satisfied no one but was the best the air staff could come up with under the circumstances. Dual responsibilities and authority and divided loyalties plagued the organization. Other systems were tried but all came up against the same inevitable dilemma: all else being equal, the sex of the individuals is an artificial basis for segregating members of organizations.

Sex is also a suspect basis for job classification, particularly in the Air Force, which by its own admission resembled a large industrial organization more than did its sister military services. Nonetheless, the Air Force found itself emulating the older services when it came to sex-stereotyping jobs.

Soon after achieving its independence, the Air Force designed its own job classification system. It established a total of 43 career fields, comprised of 349 separate specialties within career ladders for enlisted personnel, and 23 career fields with 216 separate specialties were established for officers.

Although Colonel May wanted a broad utilization of women within the career fields, the air staff decided that it was "unnecessary and uneconomical to train WAF in all Air Force specialties [because] effective utilization of women is not dependent solely on the ability to learn and effectively perform a job but also on the circumstances under which the job will be performed." In 1949, a study was undertaken to determine how best to utilize enlisted women. Four criteria were developed:

1. **Physical demands.** Each specialty was rated on a scale of five, ranging from "little or no physical effort," such as in "strictly clerical jobs," to the "very heavy demands of a construction job." Whether these determinations were based on actual, scientifically acquired data or purely subjective analysis is not clear, but it was most likely the latter.

2. **Psychological and environmental.** "To place a woman in a job where she would be the only one in a group of men, or in a job where she would be obliged to work alone for extended periods of time, or in a job in a mobile unit, would adversely affect the worker as well as unit efficiency." To measure jobs against this criterion, the type of unit using the specialty and its probable geographical location and mission were considered. For example, a specialty that might otherwise have been considered suitable for women would be classified as unsuitable if it were used primarily in tactical units that would deploy to locations "not necessarily equipped with adequate quarters and facilities for women."

3. **Career opportunities.** If for any reason women could not progress to the top of the career ladder, all specialties in that career field were closed to them.

4. **Opinion poll.** After consideration of all other criteria, if any factor was questionable or obscured because of lack of basic data, experts in the particular field were consulted for professional advice and recommendations as to the suitability of the specialty for women. This left room for men who had never worked with women in a given field to express their personal opinions on whether it might be "suitable" for women.

Of the 43 enlisted career fields, the Air Force determined, by using these four criteria, that only 13 were "fully suitable" for women; 14 were "partially suitable," and 16 were "unsuitable." By this unscientific process, the Air Force rationalized closing 158 of its 349 enlisted specialties in peacetime. Under mobilization, additional jobs would be open. In effect, the Air Force rejected its affirmed goal to experiment in peacetime to find out how women could be employed in wartime. No experimentation was planned, none was conducted, and none was contemplated.

On 12 June 1950, the two-year initial integration phase of the WAF officially ended with mixed results. Instead of 300 Regular officers, 40 warrant officers, and 4,000 enlisted women as allowed by P.L. 625, there were only about 200 Regular officers (plus 90 Reservists), 7 warrant officers, and 3,800 enlisted women on active duty. This failure to meet the modest initial goals took the Air Force by complete surprise. After the success of the wartime AAF in recruiting Air-WACs, it had simply not occurred to Air Force leaders that women would not flock to the new, glamorous service. The situation must have been especially perplexing to the Chief of Staff. Gen. Hoyt S. Vandenberg personified the image of the new Air Force. At a youthful forty-nine, the tall, quiet, and exceptionally handsome general could have passed for a movie star. Both as Chief and earlier as Vice Chief of Staff, he had shown interest in the WAF. But, in 1950, when one would have thought he would be preoccupied with concerns about the Korean War and the looming prospect of another general war, Vandenberg involved himself to an extraordinary degree in the details of the tiny WAF program.

Evidently the Chief was not satisfied with the way the program was progressing but, for reasons that remain obscure to this day, rather than discuss his concerns with the WAF director, Geraldine May, Vandenberg chose instead to go to an outside source for advice and counsel—a decision that dismayed many on his own staff, generated havoc among Air Force women and, in the end, cost Geraldine May her job.

THE COCHRAN EPISODE

In most respects Jacqueline Cochran was the exact opposite of Geraldine May. A tough-minded, competitive, outspoken woman, Cochran had strong convictions and powerful connections in Washington in 1950. Having pulled herself up from abject poverty to a position of considerable affluence and international fame, she was well known in political Washington and greatly respected in aviation circles. In the words of more than one respectful Air Force flyer, "Jackie was one helluva pilot."

Having served briefly as AAF Director of Women Pilots during the Second World War, Cochran was a familiar figure around the new Air Force and a personal friend of most of its top officials, including Secretary of the Air Force, Stuart Symington, and the Chief of Staff, General Vandenberg. When the Integration Act was passed, she personally urged Symington and Vandenberg to recognize the wartime service of the WASPs by offering ex-WASPs commissions in the Regular Air Force as pilots. She was told that their time in the WASPs could not legally be counted for Regular commissions since it was not "Federal Military Service" but that it would be a consideration for appointment as an officer in the Reserves. She was also told that the Air Force did not intend "for the time being" to utilize women as pilots in either the Regular Air Force or Reserves. Cochran herself accepted appointment on those terms as a Reserve lieutenant colonel and personally contacted ex-WASPs, encouraging them "to avail yourself of the privilege" of applying for commissions as Reserve second lieutenants in the expectation that at a later date they might be put on a flying status.

Ironically, had the women pilots been included under the WAC law, as had been suggested in 1943, their wartime service would have qualified them for Regular appointments in 1948. It was Cochran who had blocked the move, preferring instead to gamble on separate legislation to give her pilots military status as a separate organization under her control. She lost the gamble and the WASPs were disbanded a year later.

This brief exposure had given Cochran a certain credibility on women's matters in Air Force circles, and in 1950 she had some definite ideas about what kinds of women should be in the Air Force and how the program should be run.

Exactly what precipitated Cochran's involvement in the WAF program in the winter of 1950–51 is not altogether clear. Some say it all started during a conversation with Vandenberg at a football game. In any case, on 25 October 1950, Vandenberg wrote to Cochran expressing his appreciation at "your generosity as a public-spirited citizen in accepting this assignment" as a "Special Consultant to me" on matters pertaining to Air Force women. He assured her that the commanders of all Air Force activities would render her every assistance in this undertaking. The air staff was thereupon informed of her assignment: to advise him specifically on

> whether our current programs for women form a sound basis for expansion in wartime and what additional actions than those now in progress should be taken by this Headquarters to bring all programs to the highest possible state of effectiveness both for peace and for war.

The staff was to furnish "such assistance as she may require, both for work in this Headquarters and for field trips."

Despite the Air Force's glowing public pronouncements and statements before Congress, Colonel May was under no illusions that the WAF program was popular in air staff. ("It was forced down the Air Force's throat by Eisenhower in 1948.")[4] Getting things done in an atmosphere of indifference had not always been easy, and in late 1950 she knew there were still problems to be ironed out. However, the director was not aware up to that point that the Chief of Staff was anything but satisfied at the way things had been going. But then she did not have frequent access to the front office. So May was taken aback by this sudden interest in her program from topside and in particular by Cochran's involvement.

Once Cochran entered the WAF picture as a personal representative of the Chief, conflict was inevitable. Most people perceived it as a personal confrontation between two women, and in
some respects it was. However, it was chiefly a struggle between
Cochran and the air staff. Nonetheless, as director, May would
become the focal point and ultimately pay the price (some called
her the "scapegoat") for what were perceived as the failures of the
program, despite the fact that she had little authority and no direct
control over it. A colonel buried under layers of generals was no
match for a special consultant to the Chief of Staff. Few generals
were a match for the powerful, flamboyant aviatrix.

Cochran was the kind of person who could sweep into George
Air Force Base at the controls of her own C47 with a perfect three-
point landing, toss her fur coat to the nearest colonel to hold, talk
over old times with the commanding general, meet a few military
women, and be off again—all in the space of an hour. It must have
been a rather awesome and intimidating show.

Cochran's formal, ten-page report to Vandenberg, dated
6 December 1950, landed like a small missile on the fourth floor,
E-Ring of the Pentagon. If she found anything to praise about the
WAF in the course of her six weeks of travel, briefings, and discussions, it was not included in the report. Her numerous recommendations, she said, were concurred with by several generals,
including Curtis LeMay, then commander of the Strategic Air
Command. The report was critical of most aspects of the WAF
program (uniforms, assignments, housing, training, etc.) but particularly acerbic about the quality of the women and the way the
program was being run: "The WAFS [sic] should be equal to the
best among the women's service. It should be the aim to make
them the best. They are not so now." Without supporting data or
comparative analysis, Cochran charged that "about one-third of
all enlisted personnel that have been indoctrinated at Lackland
are not fit material for the nucleus that the Air Force is trying to
establish."

She charged that the Surgeon General had not established
adequate physical standards or operating procedures for recruits
and that the Army–Air Force Recruiting Service was attempting
to fill quotas and bringing in "misfits." The term was not fully
defined but the examples given painted a graphic picture of what
she had in mind:

I personally came across a WAF (and I was informed during my conversations at Lackland that this type of error has been duplicated many times) who was approximately 4 feet 9 inches tall and who admittedly weighed 134 pounds. This is far too much weight for the height but, what is even worse, she is very much out of proportion as to bodily profile and in addition she is cross-eyed. A person with these physical defects or handicaps should never have been taken at the recruiting level in the first place, but if these cases slip through the recruiting officers, then the Air Force's own medical examiners should turn such girls down.

Cochran claimed that the Training Center at Lackland was responsible for not eliminating recruits who "appear to be emotionally or hormonally maladjusted," an apparent reference to lesbians, though the term never appears in the report.

Officer Candidate School did not fare much better: "I met and talked with approximately 30 OCS trainees and was certainly not impressed, either with their physical appearance or grooming. In fact, 3 or 4 women in this group seemed out of balance, weight for height."

Beyond the various examples, Cochran offered no corroborating evidence or comparative data on quality between Air Force men and women or between WAF and women in the other services to support her conclusions, and she also did not discuss job performance or productivity. The issue rested almost solely on the women's physical appearance, which apparently was not up to the standards of the Air Force.

To solve the quality problem, Cochran believed that the Air Force should pull WAF recruiting out of the joint Army–Air Force Recruiting Service, adapt the Navy's recruiting system for WAVES, train the recruiters better, eliminate quotas, and change the physical standards and procedures. She also felt that the Air Force should emulate the Navy by training its WAF at women's college campuses rather than at the Lackland Training Center.

Cochran's other major criticism was leveled at what she believed to be a lack of overall supervision of the program from the top. Because the level of the director's office was buried so low in the staff, "this tends to place the whole organization—psychologically at least—on a lower level than is proper to achieve results." In consequence, she said, "the program gets lost sight of, at least in its major policy and planning phases." The solution, she believed, was a strong WAF organization headed by a woman "in a position of dignity" as a permanent Special Assistant to the Chief of Staff or as an Assistant Secretary of the Air Force with top-level responsibility for the women's program to "ride herd" on it. Because the highest rank authorized by the law was colonel ("the law seems wrong in this respect"), the position would most probably have to be a civilian one. Some in the air staff thought they saw more than a glimmer of ambition in the lady's eye.

A number of recommendations in the report strongly suggest that Cochran either did not fully understand the implications of the Air Force's philosophy of integrating women into the organizational and personnel structures or, if she did understand, she did not fully agree. It was clear that she felt the program needed to be strengthened and made more autonomous.

This was fully consistent with her views earlier in connection with the WASPs. In 1942, when it had appeared that the AAF might recruit women pilots for integration into the Ferry Command, Cochran fired off an angry note to General Arnold expressing the view that women pilots should not be integrated but should be in a separate corps commanded by a woman. "Hiring women on the same basis as men, individually and without any organization," she warned, "will bring disrepute on the services before very long and injure the interest of the women themselves."[5] During the brief life of the WASP program, there was never any doubt about who was in charge or who made the rules—the Director of Women Pilots sitting at the right hand of the Commanding General of the AAF. Cochran ran the show with a firm hand. Her WASPs were a small, hand-picked, elite group living by a strict code of conduct. They were "Cochran's girls." The restrictions and isolation imposed on the training program at Avenger Field, Sweetwater, Texas, quickly earned it the nickname of "Cochran's Convent." Cochran's reactions to the WAF program and the way it was being run in 1950 clearly reflect this same conservative view.

Had any woman other than Jacqueline Cochran produced the report, it would most probably have been referred to the air staff "for appropriate action" and, after a brief flurry of feigned activity, would have been buried in the files to gather dust. And had the report not been so overtly critical of the quality and appearance of the women, alleging that the Air Force was recruiting less than the best, it might not have caused such a furor. But personnel quality was a matter of service pride, and Cochran had touched a nerve.

Within days after Vandenberg received the report, a message was fired off to commanding generals informing them that the Chief of Staff had observed that "the appearance of some members of the WAF is not up to the required standards of the USAF" and that he desired all commanders "to take prompt action to insure that all members of the WAF reflect credit upon themselves, their uniforms and the United States Air Force."

The commander of the Air Training Command got a letter expressing the Chief of Staff's personal dissatisfaction with "the failure of the screening process . . . to eliminate those who will be a discredit to the Air Force" and informing him that those failing to meet the standards in morality, cleanliness, neatness, appearance, and intelligence be screened out and returned to their homes as undesirables.

The commander dutifully responded that the Training Command would continue to discharge women who did not meet Air Force requirements and that every effort was being made to assist the WAF members who needed improvement in personal appearance. He pointed out, however, that there was no regulation that permitted the discharge of any individual solely on the basis of personal appearance. The Training Command would need help in getting the Recruiting Service to stop accepting "individuals whose physical appearance does not meet Air Force standards."

The head of the Army–Air Force Recruiting Service was told of the Air Force Chief's displeasure with the quality of the WAF enlistees and reminded once again that the figures from USAF headquarters for monthly WAF inputs were ceilings and not quotas. He was told to develop better procedures to ensure higher quality recruits.

The Recruiting Service promptly asked for more WAF recruiters, opened a training program for recruiters, and set up a new system for processing WAF applicants whereby final selections were made by female officers rather than male NCOs.

Meanwhile, the press was having a field day with the story of America's foremost woman pilot and former head of the WASPs calling WAF "misfits." They especially enjoyed quoting the part about the woman with "cross-eyes."

Air Force women were outraged and demoralized, particularly the senior officers and NCOs who felt that the WAF were being singled out for an unwarranted attack by someone whom they felt had little understanding of their role in the Air Force or the jobs they were doing. They took it very personally. Typical was the reaction of an embittered, middle-aged supply NCO at Wiesbaden, Germany: "So Betty Grable I'm not. But I do my job the best I know how and I did it during the last war. I earn my stripes every day while she's flying around with the brass. Where does she get off calling me and my friends 'misfits'?"

The air staff's instinctive reaction to the whole affair was to go into a deep defensive crouch. Maj. Gen. R. E. Nugent, the Deputy Chief of Staff, Personnel, who was responsible for monitoring and directing all Air Force personnel programs, set up an ad hoc committee of his own people to review and evaluate Cochran's recommendations. While taking exception to most of them, the committee nonetheless conceded that certain deficiencies in the WAF program existed but pointed out that they "have already been recognized and have been or are in the process of correction." For example, new recruiting procedures were being developed, and additional WAF officers were being assigned to recruiting duties; new height-weight charts (the Navy's) were about to be published; additional screening had been initiated at Lackland; and actions were underway to improve the clothing situation, including the procurement of a new blue uniform. In short, everything was under control.

The most troublesome aspect of the report, as the committee saw it, was that it pointed in the direction of "placing WAF in a separate category subject to special rules and regulations," which was in effect a suggestion that the Air Force step back from its commitment to integration. The idea of a strong semiautonomous WAF organization with a permanent female special assistant— probably a Jackie Cochran, sitting at the right hand of the Chief of Staff or Secretary and "riding herd" on women's matters—sent shivers down the backs of the air staff. The committee lamely suggested that "to establish such a position for a minority sex group might well lead to demands for similar positions for other minority groups."

SECOND THOUGHTS ON INTEGRATION

Armed with his committee's evaluation of Cochran's report, General Nugent met with Vandenberg to decide future courses of action. Many of Nugent's recommendations coincided with Cochran's, others did not. The most important conclusion to come out of this meeting was that the extent to which women had been integrated into the Air Force had been "faulty" in that women "could not and should not be treated in the same way as the men." The two generals agreed that the program should be reoriented to treat WAF more as a "separate personnel component" on the theory that it "would raise the quality of the WAF, would encourage improved relations between male and female members of the Air Force and would attract more desirable women into the WAF."

Nugent told Vandenberg at that time of the Director, WAF's "unalterable opposition" to such a change. This undoubtedly helped to seal May's future.

Although the Chief was soon persuaded by an apprehensive staff to back off the idea of a separate WAF structure, actions were taken aimed at ensuring that WAF problems received the appropriate attention in the future. The director's position was strengthened by giving her direct, frequent access to the Secretary and the Chief. Her duties and responsibilities were published for the entire air staff and the field commanders. WAF staff directors were set up in each major command headquarters to monitor the program in the field, and WAF officers were installed in most air staff agencies to keep track of women's matters (as an additional duty) and to keep the WAF director abreast of matters that could have an impact on women—a system not unlike that developed by the Navy in World War II. In fact, the Navy's WAVES continued to be the Air Force's ideal, and it was to the Navy that the fledgling Air Force would soon turn for new leadership for the women's program to replace Geraldine May as director.

NOTES

1. The title subsequently dropped "and Administration."
2. Geraldine May, interview with author, 20 June 1973.
3. In the early days of the Air Force, men were commissioned through four sources: ROTC; OCS, later replaced with Officer Training School (OTS); aviation cadet training for pilots, which was soon discontinued; and the service academies at West Point and Annapolis. In 1955, the Air Force established its own academy in Colorado.
4. May interview, op. cit.
5. Sally Van Wagenen Keil, *Those Wonderful Women in Their Flying Machines* (New York: Rawson, Wade Publishers, 1979), p. 102.

CHAPTER 12

THE FIFTIES: KOREA AND THE COLD WAR

KOREA, AS MANY later acknowledged, was not the kind of war the United States had expected to wage in an age of nuclear deterrence; it was what many later acknowledged: "the wrong war, in the wrong place, at the wrong time." Most Americans believed that Russia was the real enemy and thought that Europe would be the site of the next conflagration. Moreover, military planning, dominated by World War II thinking, assumed the next war would be a global war much like the last, but one which relied on nuclear weapons. In this World War III scenario, the onset of hostilities would be followed by a general, phased buildup of personnel and materiel over a period of many months.

During 1948 and 1949 the United States had withdrawn its troops from Korea after the Joint Chiefs of Staff had declared the country had no strategic value. However, on 25 June 1950 the communist troops of North Korea marched across the 39th parallel into the Republic of Korea — an ally of the United States — and two days later President Harry S. Truman ordered United States air and naval forces into South Korea. On 1 July, the first United States Army combat troops landed, and Americans found themselves at war again less than five short years after World War II's end.

President Truman perceived events in Korea as another Soviet probe of United States' and United Nations' intentions. He believed that if a firm stand was taken in Korea, the chances of Soviet expansion in Europe leading to another general war would be lessened. Preoccupied with the prospect of being dragged into a larger conflict, the administration was leery of committing full military power in Asia. Korea was, thus, to be a limited war with limited objectives. Gen. Omar Bradley described it during the MacArthur hearings as "a preventive limited war aimed at avoiding World War III." Therefore, when hostilities broke out, the DOD was confronted with the unhappy prospect of expanding the military services without a formal declaration of war, while at the same time gearing up for the increasingly possible contingency of a general war.

To prepare for the larger conflict and to cope with the immediate crisis, the DOD announced that the services would require three million men in uniform. This meant doubling the size of the armed forces. To provide the additional manpower, the services called up selected reserves and increased draft calls.

Shortly thereafter, the National Security Resources Board's subcommittee on manpower warned that if a force in excess of three million was required, Congress might need to change the draft law to provide for the registration and military liability of all men *and women* between the ages of eighteen and forty-five. The women "should be inducted for noncombat assignments only." The situation never required such desperate action.

When war broke out in Korea, there were only 22,000 women on active duty, and a third of these were in the health professions. The roughly 15,000 in the line (WACs, WAVES, WAF, and Women Marines) actually comprised less than 1 percent of America's total military force, or less than half the legal strength.

As before, the most immediately perceived need was for nurses. Within four days after the first U.S. troops landed in Korea, fifty-seven Army nurses arrived at Pusan to help set up a hospital. The next day they were caring for battle casualties. Two days later, twelve nurses moved forward with a mobile Army surgical hospital to Taejon on the war zone's perimeter; within less than a month, there were over one hundred nurses on duty in South Korea.

Within a year the Army Nurse Corps had grown from 3,500 to nearly 5,400; between 500 and 600 of them would serve in the war zone, supporting the combat troops during amphibious landings on the east coast, as forces pushed toward the Yalu River, and during the disastrous retreat before the driving force of the Chinese. Most of these nurses were veterans of World War II. Many had joined the Reserves after the war, never thinking that they would be called to active duty again so soon.

For the nurses, Reserve status was well established; there was never any question that they were essential. Not so with women in the line. There was little incentive for women in the line to become affiliated with the Reserves; so, only a few were available for active duty when war broke out in Korea.

Meanwhile, requisitions for women with a wide variety of skills poured into the Pentagon. But, because of the fluid nature of the fighting, the services refused to assign women other than nurses to the combat zone. Nevertheless, WACs and WAF did serve at a number of bases in the Far East in direct support of the war: in Japan, Okinawa, Iwo Jima, and the Philippines. Women in all the services also replaced men in the United States for service in the combat area and filled new positions generated by the buildup.

At the beginning of hostilities, all the services doubled or tripled their tiny recruiting programs for women. However, after an initial surge, the response was disappointing, and only insubstantial gains in the women's strengths were achieved during the first year. The Army and Air Force, with the largest goals, did not even come near them. But there was no sense of urgency since, with the draft, the services were able to get enough men to meet overall strength requirements. Hence, the limited success in recruiting women was of little concern.

By June 1951, the line components had grown to 28,000, still just over 1 percent of the total strength of the armed forces. At that point, in response to an earlier request from an optimistic Assistant Secretary of Defense for Manpower, Anna Rosenberg, Congress removed temporarily the 2-percent ceiling on the line, apparently under the naive expectation that young women would flock to the colors.

Meanwhile, interest in the employment of military women was coming at the DOD from several directions. For example, Sen. Margaret Chase Smith wrote to George Marshall, then Secretary of Defense, inquiring about plans for the utilization of military and civilian women in the war effort, "not only in the event of all-out war but in the event of a limited emergency, a full emergency, or the period which you refer to as months of tension." She asked, "Do you have any actual plans, if so, what are they?"[1] The

Munitions Board and National Security Resources Board were raising similar questions.[2] Under growing pressure from the outside, and faced with mounting resistance to the draft and a critical manpower situation in the offing, the DOD became concerned about the services' inability to meet their recruiting goals for women volunteers.

At Rosenberg's suggestion, Marshall formed a committee of fifty prominent women—the Defense Advisory Committee on Women in the Services (DACOWITS)—to advise and assist in the project. The committee's membership included former wartime women directors, well-known academicians, and other professional women from business, the legal profession, the arts, and politics. It was chaired by Mrs. Oswald Lord, who had previously chaired a similar Army women's advisory committee. DACOWITS members were asked to help collectively and individually: (1) to inform the public of recruiting needs; (2) to reassure parents as to the administration and supervision of young women in the military services; (3) to convey to young women the career opportunities in the service; and (4) to raise the prestige of military women in the public mind.

At the first meeting of the committee, on 18 September 1951, Colonel Hallaren, speaking for the line directors, explained the services' needs for more women and the current difficulties in meeting their goals. She stressed that "every woman volunteer means one less draftee" but added, "There's just one objective to keep in mind above all others . . . the services cannot sacrifice quality to fill a quota, for these women will be the framework of any future [general war] expansion."[3]

The committee suggested a nationwide, heavily publicized DOD-sponsored joint campaign to accomplish collectively what the services seemed unable to do individually. Whereupon, in October, more than two years into the war, Rosenberg announced a Defense Department nationwide program to recruit an additional 72,000 women for the armed forces by July 1952. It would be the biggest drive of its kind since World War II and, if successful, would build the numbers of military women from 40,000 to 112,000 within the short span of ten months. After the announcement, a rumor circulated on the Washington grapevine that, if the big push did not entice enough women to join, a woman's draft might be considered.

Although part of the expansion would be in the critical area of the health professions, the lion's share would be in the line components to help offset draft calls. The Army and Air Force planned the largest increases, with the WAC strength expected to build from 12,000 to 32,000 and the WAF to leap from 8,200 to a whopping 50,000. The Navy and Marine Corps typically were more conservative, projecting increases in the WAVES from 6,300 to 11,000 and in the Women Marines from 2,250 to 3,000.

Prior to the campaign's kickoff in November, recruiting staffs were beefed up, and enormous funds were expended on public relations and advertising. On 11 November 1951, President Truman personally launched the drive, and all the stops were pulled. An appeal was made to women's patriotism with slogans like "Share Service for Freedom" and "America's Finest Women Stand Beside Her Finest Men."

However, despite all the effort and ballyhoo, the campaign never really got off the ground. In fact, it was a near disaster. Not only was it ill-conceived and very poorly timed, but the drive had been launched without any real assessment of its chances for success. Recruiters were consistently unable to meet their goals; the higher the goals, the greater the short-falls. The Air Force and Army were in the deepest trouble. For example, the Air Force, which increased its monthly recruiting quota for enlisted women from 400 to 1,200, actually leveled off at roughly 500 recruits per month. Each month, frustrated recruiters faced certain failure, only to be rewarded with higher quotas the next month because planners in the Pentagon simply would not face up to the reality of the situation.

Of greater concern to the directors was that the gains consisted mostly of the least qualified women. It was apparent that zealous and overburdened recruiters had begun to cheat on quality. Evidence of falsification of test scores, educational records, and references was mounting and unauthorized enlistments for all causes were on the increase: under age, fraudulent papers, police records, etc.

Alarmed at this trend, and as a result of complaints from the field, the Director, WAF, Col. Mary J. Shelly, recommended that sharp restraints be imposed on the Recruiting Service. WAF enlistment criteria, already high, were raised even farther, and female officers were given responsibility for all final selections. The tightened controls had the desired effect of halting the quality slide but reduced the small intake by half. The demoralized recruiters fell still farther behind.

Finally, at Shelly's request, enlistment quotas were cut back drastically to bring them more in line with the supply of qualified applicants. Later they were removed entirely. The intake of new recruits leveled off to about where it had been before the expansion. The strength declined further, however, as losses by attrition overtook accessions. The net effect of these new losses on all of the services was that a significant part of the gains from the expanded recruiting effort was wiped out, and, in the case of the WAC, gains were entirely eradicated.

By early spring of 1952, the expansion had fizzled, with only fractional numerical gains overall. Minute gains had materially lowered the overall quality of the enlisted force. Instead of the planned 112,000 women, there were only 46,000—still less than 1 percent of the total force. The Navy and Marine Corps, having taken the most conservative approach in the beginning, came within 25 percent and 18 percent of their goals, respectively, with a modest 8,000 WAVES and 2,400 Women Marines.

For the Army, and more especially the Air Force, the recruitment drive was a disaster on several fronts. Instead of reaching its planned goal of 50,000 members, the WAF strength peaked at only 13,000. The WAC, with a planned strength of 32,000, actually lost ground during the campaign and slipped from 12,000 to less than 10,000. Training and housing facilities, uniforms, and support activities had all been grossly overprogrammed: again, uniforms were rotting in the warehouses. More importantly, most of the objectives of the Women's Armed Services Integration Act had not been met. The idea that women would play a significant role as a supplemental "manpower" resource in either peace or war had lost credibility.

In retrospect, it is easy to see the reasons for the expansion's failure. First, the services and the DOD completely misread the lessons of World War II. Having recruited more than 300,000 women during the previous war, they simply assumed there would be no difficulty in recruiting a third that many for a much smaller war. They had failed to take into account the fact that the two situations and the national mood were entirely different.

World War II had fired the patriotism of the American people, but in its aftermath most Americans were weary of war, of crises, and of the military. They were anxious to get back to a state of normalcy—to get on with their lives. Korea was an unwelcome intrusion into that impetus.

Second, the public's attitude toward women serving in the

armed forces had not mellowed since World War II. If anything, the frantic recruiting campaigns of 1951–52 had reawakened the old accusations of immorality and masculinity as attributes of women who joined the services. While public disapprobation was probably no more prevalent during the 1950s than during the 1940s, powerful patriotic incentives did not counter the negative social pressures being applied to young women.

Third, their timing was all wrong. By the summer of 1951, when the DOD made the decision to recruit more women, the pace of the war had already begun to slacken, as had public interest. Although initially supportive of the President's decision to commit American troops to Korea, public attitudes turned sour as U.S. objectives became fuzzy. The concept of limited war without clear-cut military objectives and without victory in the field, which had emerged from the MacArthur hearings, was little understood and did not sit well with most Americans (as it would not a decade later). They wanted an end to it: "Bring the boys home!" By the spring of 1952, when the recruiting campaign for women should have been in full swing, the military situation in Korea was stalemated and the services were actually reducing manpower through the release of Reserves and lower draft calls.

Fourth, given their poverty-level pay scales and low standards of living, the services could not compete in the labor market for good people, and the demand for young women was soon outstripping available resources. The manager of a Long Island employment bureau reported, "I've got more orders for qualified women workers than I can possibly fill." Moreover, both the military and the civilian sector were recruiting from an ever diminishing pool of potential workers, since, due to the low birthrate during the Depression years, there were fewer young women in the population in their late teens and early twenties than there had been ten years earlier during World War II. They estimated that the reserve of unmarried women ages eighteen to twenty-four who were not at school or working was only 500,000. Thus, for the services to have met their goals, they would have had to recruit one out of four in the eligible age group.

Finally, the issue of quality figured heavily in the services' failure to meet numerical goals. Not only were the women required to meet higher educational, mental, and physical standards than the men, but they were subjected to special additional processing which included an investigation of the records of local police, mental hospitals, schools, former employers, and personal references to detect "personality problems" or an inability of the applicant to deal with people or "conform to the requirements of community living." To ensure that applicants with personality problems and psychoneuroses were screened out, the Air Force further required all female applicants to receive a psychiatric examination, preferably by a military psychiatrist.

The stated intent of these cumbersome, time-consuming, and expensive procedures was to weed out possible "misfits"—those of questionable character and "poorly motivated" women whose usefulness to the service would be limited or who had a high potential for becoming early losses or administrative nuisances. Its net effect was to impose heavy demands upon the already over-burdened recruiters and to make it extraordinarily difficult to recruit women at all.

In support of maintaining a double standard for women, the directors argued then, as Hobby had ten years earlier, that high standards enhanced the ability to recruit volunteers in the long term by sustaining the "prestige" of the program in the eyes of the public. Even more important from the directors' point of view was that quality enhanced acceptance of the program by the men, and acceptance was the name of the game. The presence of the double standards can in retrospect be traced not so much to legitimate requirements for high quality as to cultural biases toward women, which required that they be more qualified than men for the same jobs, particularly in male-dominated fields.

The question this conflict between quality and quantity raises, of course, is: Where do you draw the line? When does insistence upon higher and higher standards defeat the whole purpose of a program whose purpose is in the first place to provide manpower for national defense?

Whatever the rationale, there can be little doubt that double standards and the systems for processing female applicants contributed to the expansion campaign's failure; how much is unclear. The record shows, however, that when the Air Force tightened the screws on the Recruiting Service in early 1952, the small WAF recruiting intake was halved.

One of the most serious miscalculations of the war was the impact that changing the marriage policies would have on retention. Incredibly, the services were taken completely by surprise when, as a result of a seemingly innocuous decision to let married women leave before completing their contracts, losses by attrition skyrocketed.

Prior to the Korean War, attrition rates for enlisted women had been running roughly the same as those for men. Most of the women then on duty were veterans of World War II, hence older and mostly single. In 1948, the legal minimum age was lowered from twenty to eighteen, and an entirely new group of young women became eligible for enlistment. The younger age of this group was to play a significant role in higher attrition rates for years to come.

The Army and Air Force immediately adopted the lower age limits but the Navy and Marines held out until the Korean War. At that point, in 1950, the average age of women in the services dropped significantly as the incoming eighteen- and nineteen-year-olds began to outnumber "old-timers" many times over. The vast majority of the new recruits were right at the most vulnerable marriage ages—eighteen, nineteen, and twenty—an entirely new phenomenon for the armed forces.

Also, at the onset of hostilities in Korea in June, a ban had been imposed on voluntary discharge of women for reasons of marriage. At about the time the expansion was announced a year later, the ban was lifted, loosing an unexpected landslide of separations. While some women remained after marriage to complete their contracts or until they became pregnant, most did not. They left in droves.

Another failure of the Korean War period was the secret mobilization planning done by the services in the early days of the war. On the assumption that a major mobilization might be in the offing, each of the services hastily updated its general war plans. Fortunately, they were never tested because there were gross deficiencies insofar as their reliance on the use of women was concerned.

Each was based on two major assumptions that proved to be faulty: first, that in the event of a major war, women would volunteer in large numbers even though men had to be drafted; and second, that a mobilization nucleus of women could be developed in peacetime as a basis for rapid expansion. World War II had proven the first assumption to be incorrect, and the experience of the fifties would prove the second to be invalid as well.

Despite the record of the forties when women constituted no more than 2 percent of the wartime forces, the Army and Air

Force plans called for at least 10 percent of their mobilized wartime strength to be women. The Navy estimated that 15 percent of its officers and 12 percent of its enlisted force could be women, and the Marine Corps projected a 7-percent female force. All told, these plans combined called for the mobilization of one-half to one million women by volunteer means alone.

Only the Army had some reservations about its ability to meet its requirements without drafting women. In a memo to the DOD Personnel Policy Board in January 1951, the Army Secretary said, "To obtain the large number [of women] required for full mobilization, some form of induction is required." He informed the board that the Army was drafting a bill to make standby Selective Service legislation applicable to women as well as to men in time of full mobilization. No such proposal ever came forth, however, probably because the WAC director expressed the belief that the American public would be against it.

The Korean War experience reinforced the lesson that should have been taken from World War II: the mobilization of large numbers of women through volunteer means is not possible.

During the phase-down from Korea, the numbers of Americans in uniform were reduced from 3.7 to 2.9 million, and once again the nation attempted to return to some degree of normalcy. For the next decade, the military forces would be sustained at their highest levels in U.S. peacetime history—ranging between 2.5 and 2.8 million—as they rose and fell with each new crisis in Berlin, Cuba, and Asia until the one in Southeast Asia escalated into another hot but "limited" war.

After peaking at 48,700 in October 1952, the women's total strength dropped off to just over 35,000 by June 1955. The line strengths dropped from 3,400 officers and 33,500 enlisted women to 2,600 officers and 23,800 enlisted women. For the women of the line, the next ten to twelve years would be a period of survival in an unwelcome environment.

Emerging from the Korean experience was the first clear picture of what the women's line programs would be for the balance of the 1950s and the first half of the 1960s. That picture was of a small token force of young women with low career potential but with the mental and educational capacity for making a contribution out of proportion to their numbers, provided they were properly trained, motivated, and employed.

The Korean experience and subsequent events, however,

raised serious doubts about the value of women's programs to the peacetime defense forces. Attitudes toward military women in the decade following Korea were influenced by disillusionment stemming from the expansion's failure; the changing military strategy of the Cold War; the continuation of the peacetime all-male draft; societal attitudes toward women's roles; the abnormally high turnover; and the almost total absence of any pressures to use women.

Indeed, given this combination of negative factors, it is remarkable that the women's programs survived the Cold War years at all. That they did was due more to bureaucratic inertia and political expediency than to any conviction on the part of military leaders that women were necessary to the national defense. Had it been politically expedient to do so, some would gladly have scuttled the peacetime programs.

The women leaders were fully conscious of the tenuousness of their programs. All of the directors harbored deep misgivings about the future and a constant fear, seldom expressed openly, that "if we rock the boat, if we create too many waves, they will get rid of us." Their fears were not groundless.

The precipitous decline of the women's programs beginning in 1952 was the death knell of two more of the objectives of the Integration Act: the development of the women's programs as mobilization nuclei and the experimental roles for women. The women's peacetime forces had been slated to be nuclei to provide the leadership, training cadre, management expertise, and utilization patterns needed as a basis for explosively expanding women's forces according to wartime mobilization plans. The peacetime 2 percent was to have been a miniature model of the wartime distribution of needed skills and resources and a vehicle for experimentation to see what types of jobs women could perform and what training they required.

The weakness in these concepts began to appear during the Korean War period with the failure to meet even the 2-percent strength. By 1955, women comprised less than 1 percent of the force and did so for the next ten years, and none of the services made any attempt to achieve the legal ceiling.

The accepted wisdom of all the services was that, because of normal patterns of women's lives and general public disapproval of military careers for women, recruiting women in peacetime in significant numbers was not feasible, except at prohibitive recruiting costs and at an unacceptable sacrifice of quality.

Dr. Eli Ginzberg, a nationally known manpower expert who had completed a series of studies on women in the work force for the National Manpower Council, painted a gloomy picture for the services in 1956. He told the DACOWITS and the directors, "This country has still . . . not accepted the military as a normal part of its life. Your problems [in recruiting women], therefore, may have more to do with uniforms than with women." Recruiting women in the absence of compulsory service would be difficult and costly, he warned: "One cannot turn the country on its head in order to get a few more women into the uniformed services of the United States."[4]

In any case, Korea had convinced the directors that no amount of money would produce additional women volunteers without sacrificing quality, a trade-off they were unwilling to make. The only other alternative would have been to draft them, an idea abhorrent to the directors.

By the mid-1950s, as unpleasant memories of the Korean War faded, the recruiting climate improved somewhat. However, administrative ceilings that were about half the legal limit continued to be routinely applied to female recruiting and/or to the strengths. On the rare occasion when they were asked why they did not take more women, or why the standards were higher than for men, the services gave stock responses: "requirements" for women were small, and they could afford to be "selective." The services also contended that they needed to limit the numbers of women because of the requirement to provide stateside and shore assignments for men rotating from overseas and sea duty. There was, however, no reason other than service policy to limit overseas assignments for women so that, in effect, they could have constituted their own rotation base. Both the Army and Air Force were maintaining huge overseas base complexes, and women were serving at many of them. The number of women that could have been absorbed at those installations was almost unlimited.

Indeed, the demand for women overseas exceeded the supply. Although the Navy and Marine Corps had fewer shore establishments overseas, most were in locations where women could easily have served (the Philippines; Naples, Italy; London, England); but with the exception of Hawaii, Navy and Marine Corps policies generally confined women to stateside installations for reasons never adequately explained. Although the Navy and Marines had the unique problem of legal restrictions on duty aboard combat ships, there were transports and hospital ships aboard which women could legally serve. For a time, a few WAVES were allowed to serve on this type of vessel but never on a routine basis or in significant numbers.

In truth, the real reasons the services kept the lid on the women's programs was that they were perfectly comfortable with the peacetime draft of men, which provided the motivation for men to serve, and which they had every reason to believe would go on indefinitely (it very nearly did); and short of an all-out emergency on the scale of World War II, they saw no real need for women except as nurses. In the absence of any compelling reason to do otherwise, the services were happy to keep the women's role small, feeling no compulsion to achieve the 2 percent authorized by law—not even as a mobilization base. Women represented a token force and nothing more.

The mobilization nucleus concept was undermined on other grounds as well. The composition of the small female force that emerged from the Korean phase-down turned out to be disproportionally noncareerist and nonexperimental. Because of the small numbers of line officers commissioned in the Regular services and the inordinately high turnover of enlisted women, the cadre of careerists remained very small—hardly the cadre of professionals to provide wartime leadership and experience in the event of a major mobilization.

Also, instead of cataloging skills, developing abilities, and finding what type of training would be needed for women in the event of an emergency as envisioned in P.L. 625, the services concentrated women in jobs they do "as well as or better than men," thus merely duplicating the stereotyping of civilian employment. An important difference, however, between the civilian and military distributions of male and female employees was that, even though women were concentrated in the traditionally female jobs in the military community, those fields remained overwhelmingly staffed by men (the only exceptions being the nurses and medical specialists, who remained exclusively female until 1955).

Female line officers gravitated to administration, personnel, communications, club management, protocol, etc. It became popular for generals and admirals to have attractive young female junior officers as administrative assistants and protocol officers. The enlisted women continued to gravitate to the clerk-typist and administrative jobs and to the medical wards to assist in the care of dependents. At one point, it was even suggested that all enlisted women entering the Navy be given typing classes during recruit training.

Despite the obvious deficiencies in the mobilization nucleus concept, all of the services and the directors of the women's programs continued to use it as the principal rationale for peacetime utilization of women in the absence of any other compelling justification. They were on slippery ground indeed because concepts of mobilization were changing.

In January 1954, John Foster Dulles, President Eisenhower's Secretary of State, in a speech before the Council on Foreign Relations, announced the "New Look" policy of defense strategy. Based on the doctrine of massive retaliation, it placed military dependence "primarily upon a great capacity to retaliate, instantly, by means and at places of our own choosing," thereby gaining "more basic security at less cost" or, as some critics characterized it, "a bigger bang for a buck." Air power advocates argued that the nation only needed to prepare for general war, and, since general war with a nuclear exchange would be of limited duration, the ultimate outcome would be decided in the first exchange.

Dr. Henry Kissinger described this new twist of military strategy in his book *Nuclear Weapons and Foreign Policy:* "We can no longer afford to count on a more or less prolonged period of mobilization. An all-out war will be primarily an air war, or at least a war of strategic striking forces, and it will be decided by the forces in being."[5] The nation's dollar and manpower resources should be invested in the active *forces in being* who would bear the brunt of the conflict—by implication the Air Force.

Carried to its logical conclusion, this new concept would make obsolete war plans based on massive, protracted mobilization of bulk, untrained manpower. Without manpower mobilization, the peacetime women's programs were in danger of being set adrift without a raison d'etre.

As might be expected, the Air Force—being its principal architect and primary beneficiary—fully embraced the doctrine of massive retaliation and the forces-in-being strategy. The other services were naturally less enthusiastic, since they stood to lose in the battle for defense dollars and resources. Nonetheless, from about 1953 until 1960, the forces-in-being concept held sway over

DOD personnel planning and policy. It was the Air Force's official dogma, and very early on the WAF program was in deep trouble. While the other women's components were not openly challenged, their positions in the services were not entirely secure either.

In August 1959, a rumor circulated in Washington that there was a move afoot on Capitol Hill to eliminate women from the armed services. Service newspapers worldwide reported that there was to be a "searching inquiry" into the need for military women in the peacetime forces. Although emphatically denied by the Chairman of the House Armed Services Committee, Carl Vincent, who stated that the women in uniform were making a notable contribution to national defense, the rumor was not lightly dismissed by servicewomen who suspected that where there was smoke there must surely be fire.

The women's programs during the Cold War period were also threatened by internal factors, namely, the high attrition of first-term enlisted women that continued unabated throughout the 1950s and early 1960s. Most young people who entered the services did not contemplate full military careers, but the men were obligated to complete their initial contracts whereas it was assumed that women would marry and then leave the service.

During the hearings on the Integration Act, retention was discussed. Eisenhower in a matter-of-fact fashion acknowledged that women's retention would naturally be lower than men's: "Ordinarily the enlisted individual will come in and, after an enlistment or two, they will ordinarily—and thank heaven—get married." He considered it a normal thing, as did everyone else, but worth the price in view of the contribution the women could make to the military. According to societal standards of the period, a woman's obligations as wife and mother superseded all other responsibilities and were assumed to be inherently incompatible with military service. Ginzberg said in 1956 that if the services were to insist on keeping their sights primarily on women in their late teens and early twenties, "you are going to have some difficult problems. If you snare them, you can't keep them, because the number of women who marry is at an all-time high."[6]

That attitude, which was shared by all military leaders, male and female alike, became a self-fulfilling prophecy—marry and get out they did. Some used marriage as a convenient way out of their enlistment contracts when they became disenchanted with their jobs or service life: "It beats getting pregnant or seeing the 'shrink.'"

Of enlisted women, 70 to 80 percent left the service before their first enlistments were up. The services were replacing from 40 to 50 percent of the strength each year just to sustain their programs. This was approximately two and one-half times the replacement rate for men. There was only one group with higher turnover rates than the enlisted women—the male draftees with a minimum tour of only two years which many failed to complete.

Understandably, the turnover of the enlisted ranks raised serious questions about the cost effectiveness of the women's programs and was a constant source of agitation among military leaders, even some who were favorably disposed to them. The basic hypocrisy in the services' hand-wringing over female attrition, however, was that those who viewed the losses with the most alarm often were those most reluctant to change the policies that generated the losses, by, for example, requiring married women to fulfill their contracts. It was easier to say, "If we *have* to have women, that is the price we must pay." It was the cost of doing business. It then logically followed: "Why bother with women when we can get all the able-bodied men we need?" No matter that the men available were less well educated, less intelligent, or that as draftees they were even less likely to complete their tours than women. No matter that men actually cost more in the long term.

It was from the General Accounting Office (GAO) that the first important challenge to the programs came on the basis of the high turnover. As the investigative arm of Congress, the GAO, in about 1963 made a study of the losses of enlisted women. Their study was shallow in the extreme, but as a result of the investigation, the GAO concluded that, because of discharges for marriage, pregnancy, and "unsuitability" for military service, the armed forces were spending $12 million annually to replace enlisted women who failed to complete their first enlistments. They recommended that the Secretary of Defense and the services take "appropriate action" to materially reduce the high turnover rates or consider filling such positions through the federal Civil Service.

The GAO investigators assumed, without any cost comparison data, that because the turnover was higher, the women must cost more than men—which was not the case. The principal disparity in costs between male and female enlisted personnel was in the number of dependents. Enlisted men had more dependents: in the Army, 36 percent of enlisted men had dependents, compared to less than 4 percent of WACs; and in the Air Force, 60 percent of the enlisted men and only 7 percent of the women had dependents. Considering the costs of housing, medical care, and allowances for dependents, the cost factor heavily favored the enlisted women.

Incredibly, the GAO even failed to include in its analysis a comparative cost analysis between military women and the Civil Service employees suggested as replacements. Had it done such an analysis, the GAO would have been unable to justify its conclusion, since the federal employment data clearly showed that the turnover rates of civilians in lower-grade positions were similar in every respect to those of military women in the same grades. And the higher civilian salaries would have more than wiped out any possible savings in military recruitment and training costs.

The DOD and the services all came to the defense of their women's programs, challenging the GAO's data and analyses (or lack thereof). While acknowledging that losses were high, the services pointed out the steps being taken to reduce them (initiated after the GAO investigators arrived on the scene). The DOD acknowledged that action should be taken "to materially reduce the high turnover rate for enlisted women" but did not agree that replacing them with civilians would be either more efficient or economical.

Had the GAO report been published five or six years earlier, it might well have scuttled the women's programs. But as it turned out, the report was published in May 1966 at the very time the DOD was groping for alternative sources of manpower to offset rising draft calls necessitated by the Vietnam buildup. The DOD was on the verge of rediscovering womanpower. So the GAO effort was soon gathering dust in the Pentagon files.

An interesting insight into the mind-set of the agency at the time of its investigation is provided by a paragraph in the 31 May 1966 cover letter from Comptroller General Elmer B. Staats to the Secretary of Defense:

> We believe that military service imposes unusual demands on enlisted women, particularly first-term enlistees in the 18-to-21-year-old age group, in terms of meeting physical standards and qualifications, undergoing military training and discipline, and adjusting to the regimentation inherent in military life. Thus many conditions that might disqualify women for military service probably would not seriously impair their performance in, or bring about their discharge from, civilian positions.

NOTES

1. Letter from Sen. Margaret Chase Smith to Secretary of Defense George C. Marshall, 11 December 1950.
2. Interagency Manpower Mobilization Committee of the National Security Resources Board, Report of Registration Subcommittee, 11 August 1950.
3. Briefing given by Col. Mary Hallaren to the Defense Advisory Committee on Women in the Services, 18 September 1951.
4. Ginzberg briefing to the DACOWITS, spring meeting, April 1956.
5. Published for the Council on Foreign Relations (New York: Harper & Brothers, 1957), p. 93.
6. Ginzberg, *op. cit.*

CHAPTER 13

WAF: AN ENDANGERED SPECIES

OF THE FOUR women's line components, the WAF was in the most vulnerable position in the Cold War period. With no overall plan or fixed long-range objectives, and operating under an integration concept that was selectively applied at the whims of a passing parade of policymakers, the WAF program lurched from one crisis to another. On more than one occasion its very survival was at stake.

Despite the Air Force's reputation for being the most modern, forward-looking of the services, its male leadership persisted in viewing women in stereotypical ways. Moreover, just below the surface there existed considerable skepticism about the validity of having women in the peacetime establishment at all. As the most favored service, the Air Force could obtain all the high-quality men it needed from the ranks of those eager to avoid being drafted into the Army. The most compelling rationale for having women in peacetime was the need to provide a base for rapid expansion in the event it became necessary to mobilize the nation's woman-power for war. But this rationale was soon challenged: first by the failure of the Korean War expansion and then by the forces-in-being concept to which the Air Force committed itself in the 1950s.

It is evident from the Cochran episode and the ensuing events that Air Force leaders did not comprehend the forces driving the WAF program, much less how to deal with them. They assumed that by replacing the WAF director the problems could be resolved and the program put back on the track.

In the spring of 1951, Secretary of the Air Force Thomas Finletter contacted Mary Josephine Shelly and asked her to be the Director of the WAF. Fortunately, she had a keen sense of humor; she would need it for the next thirty months. As far as the WAF officers and NCOs were concerned, the new director started out with three strikes against her: first, they assumed that Cochran had been involved in her selection as the replacement for Geraldine May, whom the WAF felt had been railroaded; second, Shelly was an outsider rather than one of their own, a Regular Air Force officer; and, third, she had served in the Navy rather than the Army during the war.

Shelly had been among the first women commissioned in the Navy in 1942 and, involved chiefly in setting up WAVE training, had risen rapidly to the grade of commander. She was highly regarded as a brilliant, hard-working staff officer. At the time she was approached by Finletter, she was assistant to the president of Bennington College. Like May, she had not been the Secretary's first choice: Jean Palmer, who had briefly headed the WAVE program toward the end of the war, was approached first but turned down the job, recommending her friend Shelly instead.

For her part, Shelly always protested that she had not wanted the job: "One hitch in the military was enough," she said. "Besides, I can't stand uniforms." She claimed to have been "shanghied" at lunch in the Pentagon by no less than the Secretary of the Air Force, the Chief of Staff, and the Assistant Secretary of Defense, Anna Rosenberg. She was told that she was badly needed because after becoming a separate service the Air Force had taken "any women from the Army Air Forces mostly with no screening whatsoever" and that they were having "every problem in the book."

"I really don't want to do this," she protested. "Isn't there someone else?"

Finletter responded sympathetically, "None of us who is here wants to be here. There is a war on, and we do not know where it's going. We cannot afford this inefficiency."[1] Vandenberg assured her that the day that she could file her recommendations and name a successor, she would be free to leave.

Shelly had a knack for cutting through the extraneous to the heart of an issue. Having accepted the appointment only at the insistence of the Secretary and the Chief, and with personal assurances of their full support, Shelly as a colonel carried unusual clout in the air staff. Also, since she had no career aspirations or emotional stake in the outcome, she was in a unique position to be objective and pragmatic about the WAF program; in fact, some senior WAF officers felt she tended to be too pragmatic and lacked emotional commitment.

Nonetheless, Shelly quickly zeroed in on the basic anomalies of the WAF program and, because of the new organization and obvious support of the Secretary and the Chief, she was in a better position than her predecessor to force decisions and get action on long-smoldering problems created by staff indifference and inaction. She soon realized that there were limits to what could be accomplished—that, just below the surface, the Air Force had not fully accepted women as full members.

Less than a year after taking office, Shelly reported to the Chief of Personnel that even though full military membership of women had existed in law for four years, it had still only been partially achieved. The cause was not due to shortcomings in doctrine, policy, or specific regulations, but to limits in acceptance and implementation of those directives.

> The evolutionary process by which women are to be accepted into a domain preempted by men is not to be hurried by orders to do so. The burden of proof remains with the women, but equitable opportunity to demonstrate ability to do the job must be provided by the organization that admitted them in the first place.

In her view, that opportunity was not yet being provided by the Air Force.

But the Air Force was faced with larger problems: managing a buildup for an undeclared war and preparing for a larger conflict that it believed to be almost inevitable.

THE WAF STRUGGLE

The Air Force emerged from the Korean War with renewed confidence in its ability to recruit and retain the cream of the draft-eligible men to meet its quality and quantity manpower requirements. In this respect, it was the most uniquely favored of the four services. On the other hand, having set the most ambitious goals for the recruitment of women, it experienced the greatest shortfall in the 1951–52 expansion program. Whereas only months before the Air Force had viewed women as a potential source of thousands of high quality personnel to supplement their forces, the need and the high expectations died with Korea. Whereupon the Air Force simply lost interest in the matter. In opting to sacrifice quantity for quality, the Air Force in effect settled for tokenism in the WAF program, and a token program had little to offer the peacetime forces in being to which the airmen were committed.

As early as April 1952, Colonel Shelly sensed that the program emerging in the aftermath of the abortive Korean expansion would be of questionable value as either a supplemental resource of military personnel or as a peacetime nucleus for wartime mobilization. She also perceived the Air Force's lack of interest in the success of the program, at least below the Chief and Secretarial level.

At that time, she reported to Lt. Gen. Laurence S. Kuter (then Deputy Chief of Staff, Personnel) that the program had been drifting from one requirement to another in search of a mission—"it is more a matter of discovery than design"—and that a "token force" was emerging. She felt that, in view of the commitments already made to Congress and the public as to the need for women, it was incumbent upon the Air Force to put the program on a sound basis as soon as possible and to do so by conscious decisions, not by drift and neglect.

It had been clear to Shelly when she took the job of Director, WAF, that the Air Force's first priority insofar as its women were concerned was quality. If there had been any doubts on that score, they would have been laid to rest in December 1952 when she briefed the Chief of Staff and Secretary on the actions she had recently initiated to shore up the sagging quality of the new recruits. She told them that, as a result of lower recruiting goals, rather than achieving the planned goal of 46,000 enlisted women, the strength would probably level off at around 12,000 (an overly optimistic estimate, as it turned out).

She had concluded that since the WAF could not carry more than a very small fraction of the Air Force workload, it was important to draw out the maximum capability "to look not for significant numbers, but for better than average performance per person." In that case, they should be an asset out of proportion to their numbers.

Shelly was told she was on the right track: an "elite Corps" was what must be established, and no pressures should be placed on the recruiters "to accept other than people the Air Force can be glad to have." The Secretary discussed with her the relative caliber of the women in the various services and expressed his dissatisfaction that the Navy's women seemed to be of higher quality than the Air Force's. He wanted the situation reversed.

Although Shelly fully agreed with that philosophy, she was worried about the future viability of the program, given the trends and the attitudes of the air staff. She had told Kuter in April that it was critical to develop a new approach rather than to let events control what happened. The Air Force needed to decide how to get the most out of the program given its size and composition. "A positive attitude aimed at developing an optimum program with the resources at hand is the only tenable one in view of the commitments already made by the Air Force to grant women full military membership." The only alternative, she said, would be to terminate the program.

> It is not an acceptable alternative to undermine the program by a fundamental disbelief in it, expressed in delays rather than actions, in permitting events deemed more important constantly to overtake considerations necessary to it . . .

But the enlisted program would not hold still long enough to get a firm handle on it. Rather than leveling off, it kept sliding downward as losses by attrition and completion of first-term enlistments continued to decimate the ranks. By mid-1953, it had become clear that the strength at which the gains would offset losses would be closer to 6,000 than the 12,000 Shelly had predicted.

In October 1953, the new Deputy Chief of Staff for Personnel, Lt. Gen. Emmett "Rosie" O'Donnell, raised the question of maintaining a force of enlisted women at all during periods short of full mobilization. Shelly gave him the pros and cons of retaining the program.

The pros were: the Air Force's public commitment to having women, the fact that women do some jobs better than men, that they augmented mental categories I and II personnel, and that continued experience in the management and utilization of women was indispensable if the demands for women in full mobilization were to be efficiently met. The cons were: the abnormally high turnover, "indifferent morale," "a measure of nuisance value," and the fact that "men and/or civilians could do the same work." Shelly asserted that in her view "the case for retention outweighed, though it did not cancel, the negative." O'Donnell agreed, and the program survived its first hurdle.

Others were not persuaded, however. In April 1954, an Air Force colonel, James Bearley, then a student at the Air War College of the Air University, submitted his thesis, entitled "Why WAF?" In it he concluded:

Women occupy a special place in the United States, and a large majority of our people are still opposed to women-in-uniform. The proper utilization of women elsewhere than in the armed services can undoubtedly aid military efficiency and the national effort. *But to continue the use of women as members of the Air Force cannot be justified.* [emphasis added]

He had reached this conclusion using all the arguments made by Shelly earlier in her case for and against retention but with one major addition. Having just been imbued at the Air War College with the latest Air Force strategic doctrine, Bearley argued that with the announcement by the President of the "New Look" in defense,

the last crutch for advocates of women-in-uniform was taken away. There will not be time to cope with WAF when D-Day comes with all its fury and destruction of fission and fusion weapons. Only the forces in being will be able to participate in the decisive phase. To maintain that force in being the manpower potential of the United States is adequate to provide an all-male Air Force.

It seemed not to matter that those men would have to be motivated by the peacetime draft.

Although Bearley's thesis was circulated around the air staff, nothing came of it. But it remained in the Air University Library and it was often cited as an authoritative reference work on the WAF.

The WAF faced its most difficult tests in the late 1950s with the arrival of Gen. Curtis LeMay in the Pentagon to become Vice Chief of Staff. It was a foregone conclusion that he would be the next Chief.

LeMay was a world symbol of air power, having almost single-handedly rejuvenated and built the Strategic Air Command (SAC) as its commander from 1947 to 1957. He was popularly regarded as a man of strong views and autocratic ways who inspired respect and fear.

It was popularly believed that the laconic LeMay was anti-

WAF. Others claimed that he was a great supporter of the women officers, but not the enlisted women. Shelly recounted that when she called upon him at SAC headquarters, he told her straight out, "I'm not supposed to want to have WAF. That's not the point. I don't want a bunch of green kids here. You send me people who can run that switchboard out there and who can do the job ready-made and I'll take any number of them. I don't care whether they're men, women, or children. I've just got a job to do here at SAC."[2]

Col. Emma Jane Riley, then the Director, WAF, later recalled that LeMay had been known to disapprove of WAF control tower operators. The best operator at Maxwell Air Force Base was a WAF, and her commanding officers refused to reassign her to another job. Whenever LeMay was scheduled to land at Maxwell, she was replaced by a man because of fear of his reaction to a woman's voice over the headset.

Whether or not LeMay actually disapproved of WAF, the air staff was under the impression that he did and acted accordingly. Within months of his arrival in the Pentagon, Riley was directed to reevaluate the WAF airmen program "to determine whether or not the Air Force should continue a WAF airmen program considering operational concepts, availability of personnel, and the high rate of attrition among first-term enlistees."

At that point, the administrative ceiling on the program was set at 8,000. Actually, because of recent early releases applicable to men and women, there were only 7,200 women on active duty against a total enlisted force of over 734,000. But in the spring of 1958, the Air Force was in the throes of a small but painful manpower reduction. The Director of Personnel Plans, Maj. Gen. J. J. Nazzaro, reasoned that the reduction "made it mandatory that all possible measures be taken to improve upon the quality of personnel and to reduce the rate of turnover."

It was popularly but erroneously believed that manpower authorizations were designated as male and female—"his" and "hers"—as was the case in the Army. The theory was that if you eliminated the WAF program, you could eliminate 8,000 manpower spaces.

Riley completed her study in May, recommending the program be retained and continue to be pegged at 8,000 since reducing or abolishing it would save only about 155 manpower spaces used in the administration of the program. Also, she pointed out that since the women occupied validated manpower spaces, they would have to be replaced with men, that men were in short supply, that women constituted an essential part of the national "manpower pool," that they did some jobs better than men and many others as well as men, and that the Air Force "needs to draw both men and women from the country's manpower pool to fill its qualifications requirements."

While she acknowledged that the turnover was higher than for men, she did not agree that women cost more—quite the reverse. She pointed out that because of dependents (60 percent for men versus 7 percent for women) the men were more costly. That may have been a tactical blunder on her part. As Riley said later, "It was very unpopular to ever suggest that dependents cost too much."

As might have been expected, Riley was sent back to the drawing board to come up with more acceptable answers. Seeing the handwriting on the wall and with a little guidance from above, she prepared another version of her study in June with a different approach.

That June study called attention to a recent survey of commanders that revealed their desires for from 6,500 to 9,100 enlisted women and their preference for women in certain jobs in air defense combat control centers and passenger air transport operations, statistical analysis and data processing, as well as in the usual clerical, stenographic, and medical fields. This, in her view, justified continuation of the program. However, in recognition of the overall airman reduction, she conceded that the WAF ceiling might be reduced to 5,000 by 1960. That amounted to a reduction of over 30 percent in the WAF strength while the overall Air Force airman reduction was proportionally less than half that. Nonetheless, the figure was accepted and programmed. (It is interesting to note that the previous year the Air Force strength had been increased, but the increase had not been applied to the WAF program. It was a one-way street.)

The Air Force also decided at that point to phase women out of nontraditional fields and any other fields where their numbers were small. They were to be employed only on those jobs "women do better than men." The Air Force also closed more bases to enlisted women.

In the spring of 1961, an obscure colonel (Lewis Turner) in the office of the Director of Personnel Plans did a superficial study of the WAF airman force "to determine the optimum enlisted WAF strength." His study concluded that, since there were no positions that specifically required WAF personnel and because attrition was high, the "best interests of the USAF will be served" by phasing out the WAF airman program—by discontinuing recruiting and allowing attrition and retirements to do the rest. Upon touching base with the Armed Services Committees on Capitol Hill, however, the Air Force was told in no uncertain terms that Chairman Carl Vincent would never hold still for it. Whereupon the personnel staff recommended reducing the WAF enlisted program to approximately 1,500. Those remaining would be confined to serving as switchboard operators, hospital orderlies, and flight attendants. However, the personnel staff later decided that 3,800 would be a better figure. At that point, someone reminded the military staff that, by law, the strength of the WAF was controlled by the civilian Secretary, not the military staff.

When the proposal was presented to Secretary Eugene Zuckert, he told the staff that, in view of the growing public concern over the involuntary recall of reservists to meet the most recent international crises, he was not about to reduce a volunteer program. The figure 5,000, agreed to in 1958, remained the enlisted strength goal for the immediate future. But with little enthusiasm for the program in the air staff, the strength was allowed to slide below that goal until it hit its all-time low of 4,700 in 1965.

NOTES

1. Interview with Lt. Cmdr. Mary Josephine Shelly, USNR (Ret.), about her service in World War II with the WAVES (Annapolis: U.S. Naval Institute, 1970), pp. 51–53.
2. *Ibid.*, p. 56.

CHAPTER 14

THE SİXTIES:
TYPEWRITER SOLDIERS

IN JANUARY 1966, as America braced for another war in Asia, a *Washington Post* article by columnist Jack Anderson charged, in effect, that America's military women were unprepared to go to war because they had gone soft. Anderson claimed that instead of being the "soldiers in skirts" of World War II, the WACs, WAVES, WAF, and Women Marines had been transformed into "typewriter soldiers" more concerned with the arts of makeup than the arts of war. He asserted that "more attention is paid [in training] to the rise and fall of hemlines than to the ebb and flow of battle lines."[1] There was more than a grain of truth in Anderson's allegation.

Paradoxically, women who in the forties had fought for status in the most masculine of professions found themselves in the mid-sixties excluded from the mainstream of the military for all practical purposes—tolerated, but not to be taken too seriously. By 1966, the women's programs had indeed evolved into something quite different from those of World War II or those envisioned at the time of the Integration Act. Moreover, they did not encompass the ideals of the new feminist movement. As if caught in a time warp from which they could not or would not escape, the women's programs remained wedded to the dead-ended, outmoded philosophies of women's roles devised in the fifties.

With the change of administration in 1961, a new military strategy—the strategy of flexible response—emerged and gradually took precedence over the massive retaliation concept espoused in the fifties.

The doctrine of massive retaliation, which held sway over military planning and force structures during the Eisenhower/Dulles years, had always had its detractors, especially in the Army and Navy. Massive retaliation placed almost total reliance on the strategic forces to deter war and, if war came, to win it decisively at the outset through the overwhelming might of superior U.S. air power.

Many military experts had consistently argued that in placing so much reliance on massive retaliation, America was putting all its eggs in one basket; that while postured for all-out nuclear confrontation, the United States could find itself outflanked by local conflicts below the nuclear threshold because it did not have adequate conventional forces to respond effectively. Thus, the security of the noncommunist world could be nibbled away by limited wars such as Korea unless the balance between U.S. nuclear and conventional forces was restored.

The Chief of Staff of the Army, Gen. Maxwell Taylor, became one of the most articulate of the dissenters to the strategy of massive retaliation. After retiring in 1959, Taylor stated his views in his best seller, *The Uncertain Trumpet:*

> It is my belief that Massive Retaliation as a guiding strategic concept has reached a dead end and that there is an urgent need for a reappraisal of our strategic needs. . . . The strategic doctrine which I would propose to replace Massive Retaliation is called herein the Strategy of Flexible Response.[2]

Taylor's book was read with great interest by John F. Kennedy and Robert McNamara. "Flexible response" became the doctrine of the next administration.

The new administration shared with the old an essentially common view of the world and of America's place in it. Both believed, after twelve years of cold war, in the existence of a supposedly monolithic communist bloc under Russian control that was determined to attack and defeat the forces of freedom, wherever they existed. Both saw the Soviet Union and America locked in a global struggle for the soul of the free world.

Almost from the moment of taking office, Kennedy was faced with a series of overlapping crises—Berlin, Cuba, Laos, Southeast

Asia—all demanding attention, all beckoning for deeper U.S. military involvement, all seemingly orchestrated from the Kremlin to test the mettle of the young President.

Following the humiliation of the Bay of Pigs and the confrontation with Khruschev in Vienna, Kennedy decided to expand U.S. military forces to meet communist probes wherever and whenever necessary to show America's resolve to stand firm. In June 1961, he ordered a limited call-up of reserves, boosted the defense budget, deployed several thousand troops to West Berlin, and moved toward his fateful decision to commit U.S. forces to Southeast Asia. By 1965, just prior to Lyndon Johnson's escalation of our involvement in Vietnam, there were already over 2,655,000 Americans in uniform—up 190,000 from the 1960 post–Korean War figure.

The services' expansion in the early sixties did not generate a proportional growth in the women's programs. In fact, all of the women's programs continued to decline during this period. Despite an unexpected turnabout in the recruiting climate beginning in 1960, the women's strengths receded to their lowest levels since before the Korean War. By 1965, there were only 30,600 women in the line in all of the armed forces.

Instead of looking to women to swell its ranks, the military as usual relied on the Selective Service System to provide men. The draft was still generally accepted as a necessary means of military manpower procurement; there had been virtually no debate or opposition to the extension of the Universal Military Service and Training Act in 1955, 1959, or 1963.

Relatively small draft calls and a surplus of young men removed any incentives to use more women, despite avowed policies of both Presidents Kennedy and Johnson to encourage greater utilization of the nation's womanpower in all areas.

On 14 December 1961, when he established the Commission on the Status of Women, Kennedy said:

> If our nation is to be successful in the critical period ahead, we must rely upon the skills and devotion of all our people. In every time of crisis women have served our country in difficult and hazardous ways. They will do so now, in the home and at work. . . . Women should not be considered a marginal group to be employed periodically only to be denied opportunity to satisfy their needs and aspirations when unemployment rises or a war ends.

Later, Johnson stated that "the under-utilization of American women continues to be the most tragic and most senseless waste of this century. It is a waste we can no longer afford."

Although President Johnson told the DACOWITS in April 1964, during a ceremonial meeting, that he thought there should be more women in the armed forces "to play even more important roles," there is no indication that this was taken as anything more than presidential rhetoric. No one present was pressing for an expanded role for military women except in the health professions, where additional nurses and medical specialists were required. For their part, the line directors were in no position to make demands for changes in their programs even if they had been inclined to do so, particularly in view of the GAO investigation of enlisted losses that would soon threaten the future of the enlisted women's programs.

Even as the forces began to expand to meet the insatiable demands of the military as the U.S. sank into the quicksand of Southeast Asia, women were never considered as a factor. Nor were there yet any pressures to expand women's roles from the new women's movement, whose leaders had not yet discovered military women. If they were aware of the women who served in World War II at all, it was as relics of another age like "Rosie the Riveter." Feminists were still fighting the battle for equal pay and other benefits long since taken for granted by military women.

When Betty Friedan wrote *The Feminine Mystique*[3] in 1963, few feminists knew or cared of the battles that had been fought for a woman's right to serve her country. Had they bothered to take a closer look, they would have been dismayed at the degree to which women's position in the armed forces had retreated since enactment of the 1948 Integration Act. Instead of serving as a springboard to further integration and equality for women, the act had become the base of a system of institutional segregation and unequal treatment that would shock modern-day civil libertarians.

Even when Congress modified the provisions of the act in 1967, it left no doubt as to the continued unequal status of women in the military. In its report in support of H.R. 5894, which removed certain grade ceilings, the House Armed Services Committee said that there could not be complete equality between men and women in the matter of military careers.

The women directors seldom questioned this concept, both because they recognized that women in the service received a better break than those in many other professions dominated by men and because they believed in the fundamental rightness of this second-class role. Col. Barbara J. Bishop, Director of Women Marines, explained it in May 1967 when she said that military women should really not try to make comparisons with men because much more is asked of the men: "It behooves every woman to remember she is not going to be asked to put her life at stake as the men are."[4]

But service policies of the sixties transcended the restrictions in the law and the congressional intent relative to combat. They mirrored the stereotypical thinking of the fifties concerning women's proper roles in society and in the workplace. They also reflected the attitudes of the women's military leadership, which was still strongly influenced by the struggle for survival and acceptance and by the search for identity in the masculine world of the military.

Two general themes characterized the thrust of the women's programs in this period. The first was the continued commitment to the concept of "elitism," manifested by double standards in recruitment, assignments, and other policies. The second was an almost obsessive emphasis on preserving femininity and projecting a "ladylike image."

THE GOAL: ACCEPTANCE, NOT EQUALITY

The double standard for women, developed in the aftermath of the Korea debacle, remained relatively unchanged but became increasingly difficult to defend in the climate of civil rights agitation of the mid- and late sixties. The official justification for the continued use of higher standards for women was that, because relatively few women were required, the services could be more selective and thus attract more capable women. Yet the services consistently failed to meet their recruiting goals for women in the fifties, and, even when recruiting improved in the early sixties, they made no attempt to reach the 2-percent ceiling authorized by law. The services also continued to insist that recruiting higher quality enlisted women was desirable because it resulted in fewer personnel problems. This argument was not used, however, to raise standards for the men, who comprised more than 99 percent of the force.

Finally, the services contended that the jobs in which women were used were of a skilled or semiskilled level and that, therefore, women of higher educational attainment and mental capacity were required to absorb the training and perform effectively on the job. As it turned out, most of the jobs to which women were assigned did not require above-average intellect or educational ability. In many cases the women were overqualified for their jobs. Consequently, boredom, job dissatisfaction, and low morale ensued—all militating against retention.

The directors themselves were the principal defenders of the double standards because of their deep fears of repeating the mistakes of World War II and Korea. In many respects, they were still suffering from the image crises of those periods. Quality not quantity must remain the chief goal even if it meant that men would have to be drafted to do jobs women could do.

For example, in 1961–62 when the Army was in the throes of an expansion, WAC recruiting took an unexpected upswing. For the first time in years, recruiters were coming in well ahead of their goals for WAC recruits. The Army then decided on a modest increase in the WAC program that would have allowed for a corresponding reduction in draft calls. The WAC leadership, however, saw this as an opportunity to improve the quality of the recruits (already much higher than for the men but arguably lower than for women entering the Navy and Air Force). Monthly ceilings were imposed on WAC recruiting and selection standards tightened, with the net result that the planned expansion never got off the ground. This at a time when draft calls were being increased to meet the Army's manpower requirements, and reserves were being called up involuntarily.

The directors were able to stick to the double standards with the full knowledge that they had the active, decisive support of their respective military chiefs, who seemed to view the women's programs more as a ladies' auxiliary than as a serious personnel resource. The women also were viewed as pawns in the continuing game of interservice one-upmanship.

In 1964, for example, when the Marine Corps was expanding, a board of senior officers was appointed by the Commandant to plan a small increase in the Women Marines program. The board determined that the principal objective must be *quality*, not quantity. In competing with the sister services, the study group reported,

> Women Marines must always be the smallest group of women in the military service. In accordance with the Commandant's desire, they must also

be the most *attractive and useful women in the four line services.* Within a [small] group of . . . enlisted women, there is room for none but the *truly elite.* [emphasis added]

To achieve that goal, the Marine Corps raised minimum standards for enlistment of Women Marines to match or to be more stringent than those of the other services; "procurement expediencies" would not be permitted to compromise a program designed to select "only the best."

Two years later, the Air Force Chief of Staff admonished the commander of the Recruiting Service to get "better looking WAF." Physical appearance became the chief criterion in the selection process; each applicant was required to pose for four photographs: front, side, back, and full-face. Civil rights leaders assumed the photographs' purpose was to determine race, but this was not the case—it was a beauty contest, and the commander of the Recruiting Service was the final judge.

This obsession with appearance carried over to all aspects of the women's programs. For example, except for the uniforms and the marching, the indoctrination programs more closely resembled ladies' finishing schools than military programs. Military aspects of training considered too masculine were played down or eliminated, and subjects designed to enhance femininity and women's proper role in the military were emphasized. WACs no longer underwent bivouac training, in which they had learned how to live in the field, to rig tents, to read maps and compasses, and to move noiselessly in the night. Nor were they allowed any longer to take weapons familiarization courses or to fire small arms, even voluntarily, because these were considered a waste of training time and would detract from the image the Army wanted to project.

All basic training programs were heavily sprinkled with courses to enhance feminine appearance and bearing. Service women were taught how to apply makeup correctly and appropriately. WAF recruits were told lipstick and nail polish were to be of a "natural shade"—not too bright, but not too light either. Lady marines, on the other hand, were told their lipstick and nail polish had to match the braid on their uniform hats, which was Marine Corps scarlet.

Hair styles had to be fashionable but "conservative" and "appropriate" to the uniform. Elaborate beehives and large bouffants were frowned upon but were preferable to very short "mannish" styles (there must be no appearance of lesbianism). According to Navy regulation, "Hair shall be arranged and shaped to present a conservative, feminine appearance."

In fact, in all the services, anything that detracted from the "neat, feminine appearance" was frowned upon or forbidden. Gone were the field packs and the high-top field shoes—the "Li'l Abners" of World War II; gone were the grease monkey coveralls. If fatigues were issued, they were seldom worn. The women were allowed to wear their issued low, quarter-lace oxfords only for marching and when absolutely necessary on the job. Otherwise, pumps were generally mandatory because they were considered more feminine.

Even in the combat zone, where they were regularly diving for shelter in bunkers, the women were expected to uphold the image: "I am aware that conditions are bad and it must be difficult to maintain a neat and feminine appearance," the Director, WAC, wrote to a senior WAC officer in Vietnam in 1967. "Boots and field clothing certainly will not help this. . . . I know our women are doing a fine job and I do not want anything to spoil their image or standing as women. The matter of proper dress is very important to me." The other directors generally shared that view.

Trainees were taught that hats and gloves were the hallmark of the service lady and as such must be worn on social occasions indoors and always out-of-doors. In 1968, when the women showed a tendency to emulate the changing civilian trends and to stop wearing hats, the WAVES' fastidious director reminded them that "WAVES are ladies first and always. . . . Taking off the hat in public is strictly a man's gesture; it is not ladylike."

Skirt lengths were the grounds of constant skirmishes as the young women attempted to follow the extremes of civilian fashion and the directors attempted to hold to a more conservative hemline—with the directors always losing the battle. Regardless of what the regulations said, the women found ways around them, especially when lengths were going up. Women simply rolled up their skirts at the waist when their female commander or advisor was not in sight. Male commanders and supervisors for the most part approved of or—being ignorant of the women's uniform regulations—ignored the infractions.

The services regarded physical training and fitness as a means to keep the ladies "fit and trim" and to improve posture, instead of as a method to build endurance, strength, or coordination or to prepare women to live in the field. As one old-timer put it, "I've known Campfire Girls more rugged than we are." Ruggedness was certainly not the name of the game—good health and appearance were.

Considering the roles set out for women, their physical training was adequate. While recruiting literature promised "challenging jobs with unlimited opportunities," the range of suitable jobs open to women kept shrinking. Unlike their predecessors in World War II and Korea, American servicewomen were no longer to be found driving trucks, taxiing aircraft, teaching aerial gunnery, running motor pools, staffing post offices, repairing engines, manning airborne radios, or aiming aerial cameras. Most of the truly challenging technical jobs were closed to them, and the grimy ones were off limits—unsuitable for "ladies." The Pentagon's official attitude was that women would not be employed at jobs that "are not in conformance with the present cultural pattern of utilizing women's services in this country." The work had to be "psychologically, physiologically and sociologically suitable." Also, fields that required extensive training investment were closed to new recruits and junior officers on the grounds that women's high attrition rates did not warrant the expense.

All the services assigned the most attractive women to front-office jobs as receptionists, secretaries, and protocol officers. They, of course, were handpicked and carefully screened. More than one attractive officer highly trained in some technical field such as intelligence or communications found herself as a protocol officer in the Pentagon or at a major command headquarters, and more than one attractive technically trained enlisted woman found herself decorating the outer office of a general or admiral with nothing more challenging to do than to look pretty, answer the telephone, and be pleasant to visitors.

Old-timers who had served in responsible jobs, which had included the supervision of men, in World War II and Korea were incredulous at the narrow attitudes that emerged in peacetime. Many were prevented from assuming new positions with responsibilities concomitant to their old ones. For example, M. Sgt. Ruth Ryan in 1960 was ordered to the Marine Corps reserve district in Atlanta as the logistics chief. But when it was discovered she was a woman, she was subjected to the unusual procedure of being interviewed by the officer in charge. She was eventually allowed to go, but as the fiscal chief rather than as the logistics chief because the officer deemed it a more appropriate position for a woman. In another case, Marine 1st Sgt. Frances A. Curwen Bilski—who had been a mail clerk in the fleet post office in San Francisco during World War II, the postmaster at the Montford Point branch of Camp Lejeune during the Korean War, an instructor at the Marine Corps Postal School, and postmaster at Parris Island—was rejected for similar duty in Hawaii in the early 1960s because the command refused absolutely to have a woman in the job, parlaying the excuse that mail bags were too heavy for a female.

The "integrated" Air Force was perhaps more systematic and up-front about discriminating against women. Beginning in 1958, on instructions from the front office, enlisted women were phased out of fields where their representation had been small on the theory that they could better be used in jobs "women do better than men." Women were no longer allowed to enter fields like intelligence, information, weather, flight attendance, intricate equipment maintenance, and control tower operation. Women already trained and experienced in technical skills were retrained for one of the increasingly limited jobs open to them. Flight attendants were taken off flying status and shunted into desk jobs; information specialists were transformed into personnel specialists. Even though only about 4 percent of the total enlisted force was directly affected, the price in terms of low morale was reflected in the highest turnover rates in the history of the WAF program. The waste of talent and experience, to say nothing of the dollars invested, was incalculable.

By 1965, enlisted women could be found in only thirty-six of sixty-one noncombat occupational groups of all the services. Nearly 70 percent were performing clerical and administrative work. Another 23 percent were in medical facilities. The ratios varied from service to service, but the pattern in all was much the same. Opportunities were likewise limited for officers. Of the forty-six noncombat officer occupational areas defined by the DOD, women could be found in only thirty-five. More than 75 percent of the women line officers were in administration, personnel, information, and similar desk jobs.

As their roles became more and more circumscribed, women were increasingly isolated and segregated from the military mainstream. Although they added to the overall quality of the force, numerically they contributed little to the services' personnel requirements, even in the fields of their highest concentration. They had, for all practical purposes, become a token force.

NOTES

1. Jack Anderson, "Should We Send Our Women Soldiers to Vietnam?" *Parade* magazine, *Washington Post*, 2 January 1966.
2. Maxwell D. Taylor [Gen., USA (Ret.)], *The Uncertain Trumpet* (New York: Harper & Brothers, 1960), pp. 5, 6.
3. Betty Friedan, *The Feminine Mystique* (New York: Dell, 1963).
4. Ruth Chandler, "Our Military Women," *Family* magazine, *Air Force Times*, 17 May 1967.

CHAPTER 15

A NEW BEGINNING

Events in the last half of the sixties and early seventies combined to end the long period of stagnation and regression in the women's line programs. Converging with the military's manpower problems generated by the war in Vietnam were other pressures growing out of the expanding role of women in the labor force and a new, more aggressive tide of feminism to which the military could not remain indefinitely immune. The synergistic effect of these forces challenged the services' traditional attitudes toward women and forced change upon a reluctant military establishment. The result was a gradual shift in the role and status of women, which accelerated in the seventies with the congressional passage of the Equal Rights Amendment and the drive for an all-volunteer force.

As in the past, interest in military women was generated by a military manpower crisis precipitated by a war. But in the mid-sixties, the services' problems stemmed not from a shortage of men but from a national reluctance by men to volunteer when faced with the prospect of fighting in the jungles of Vietnam.

As hostilities and casualties mounted, so did opposition to the draft. With the authority for induction due to expire in June 1967 and support for it eroding in Congress, President Johnson appointed a National Advisory Commission on Selective Service, chaired by Burke Marshall, to study the antiquated Selective Service System and to examine alternatives to it. In its report in February of the following year, the commission recommended that the draft be continued "to provide the nation with a flexible system of manpower procurement which will assure the Armed

Forces' ability to meet their national security commitments under all foreseeable circumstances."

In May 1967, President Johnson told Congress that extension of the Selective Service Act was essential to national security. To make this more palatable, every effort would be made to hold down the numbers of men to be inducted—to use the draft "only as a residual source of manpower." To encourage volunteerism, Johnson called for raises in military pay, more G.I. education benefits, and increased medical services for dependents and pointed out the need to take other actions designed to make service life attractive to young men.

In an effort to hold down requirements for additional military personnel, the Secretary of Defense ordered the services to convert more than 114,000 military positions in support-type activities to civilian positions. The DOD also mandated that the services lower enlistment standards for men and accept over 100,000 men who would not have qualified under the previous standards, because it was estimated that about half of these lower quality men would enter as volunteers. Although the services were outraged at this assault on their quality standards, they were told by the DOD that "Project 100,000," as it was called, was a continuing program. In 1967, the services actually took in over 150,000 mental category IV men and in 1968 another 180,000. In the Army, one in every four recruits fell into this category, and in the other services nearly one in five.

The DOD also announced, almost as an afterthought, plans to augment the number of military women by just over 6,500 in 1968. This would be the first increase in the women's line programs since the Korean War; and its implementation marked the end of their decline and the beginning of a new trend that gathered momentum in the years ahead.

It was symptomatic of the military mind-set that the decision to use more women came after all other options had been considered. Moreover, unlike the civilian substitution program and Project 100,000, which the DOD imposed without consulting the services, the 6,500 expansion in the women's forces was undertaken only after exhaustive study followed by months of negotiation between the DOD and each of the services. One is reminded of the observation in 1941 that they would probably have preferred "dogs, ducks or monkeys" to women if they could have used them.

The Marine Corps had always contended that it had a lower capacity than the other services to absorb women because of its relatively high ratio of combat to support troops. However, the Corps was the first of the services to move toward expansion. In August 1964, the Commandant, Gen. Wallace M. Greene, Jr., appointed retired Lt. Gen. Robert H. Pepper to chair a group charged with studying the Women Marines program. After receiving the group's report, the Commandant decided to expand the strength by 70 percent during the coming fiscal year, to open to women some skills previously closed to them, and to assign women to additional bases. Ostensibly, this would improve the mobilization base in the event of an emergency and "render the peacetime services of Women Marines of optimum benefit to the Marine Corps." This expansion plan was geared only to bring the tiny program up to a full 1 percent of the Corps' strength (2,750) but included increased job and assignment opportunities and important policy changes to improve enlistments and retention.

Meanwhile, as a result of an inquiry from Secretary of the Air Force Eugene Zuckert, a debate of growing intensity over the future of the WAF program was under way. In November 1964, the Secretary asked the air staff for a study:

> In connection with studies relative to eliminating, or at least reducing, use of the draft, the utilization of civilians and increased use of women in uniform are obviously of great interest. I want to be sure that our own studies will provide a basis for justification of our real requirements for male enlistees.

Having only three years earlier seriously considered abolishing the WAF airmen program, or reducing it to near extinction, the air staff was hardly favorably disposed to any suggestion of expansion. It informed Zuckert that the WAF airmen program was being held at 5,000, under a "highly selective minimum-force concept." Yes, it was "feasible" to expand the strength if selection standards were lowered, but to project the extent of a possible expansion would be "too speculative at this time."

However, some months later the Director for Manpower and Organization, Maj. Gen. Bertrum C. Harrison, ordered a study of the matter and concluded that the WAF strength could and should be doubled to 1,500 officers and 10,000 enlisted women as soon as possible in order to "help meet the military force buildup and to release men for combat and combat-related duty." Moreover, this could be accomplished without lowering quality; rather, the increased use of women would improve the overall quality of the Air Force by increasing the proportion of mental categories I and II, high school graduates. Harrison also recommended changes in personnel policies aimed at improving recruitment, retention, utilization, and assignments and at bringing Air Force policies on military women more in line with those in effect in the civilian sector.

However, the Director of Personnel Planning and others in the Office of the Deputy Chief of Staff for Personnel did not agree. They contended that there was no advantage to recruiting volunteer WAF personnel as an offset to the draft when the Air Force was having no difficulty recruiting male volunteers. This parochial service view, of course, ignored the larger manpower pressures encroaching on the defense establishment and the President's official commitment to fuller utilization of the nation's womanpower. The Director of Personnel Planning also argued that because of high losses, women were more costly than men—a contention already disproven by cost studies done in his own office —and that, because WAF were assigned to only a few designated locations overseas, any increase in total numbers would impose greater burdens on male airmen to fill overseas rotation requirements.

The WAF director, Col. Jeanne M. Holm, supported Harrison's point of view and in May 1966 advised the Deputy Chief of Staff for Personnel that, because of the growing national manpower shortages,

> it is incumbent upon the military services to concentrate their male military resources in those jobs most closely associated with combat and combat support roles [and that] the increased use of women in military positions in support roles could contribute to meeting the Air Force's overall military manning requirements.

The higher losses and assignment constraints could be corrected or at least ameliorated by a few simple policy changes, all of which were within the purview of the personnel people. Holm believed that the Air Force should take whatever steps were necessary to equalize the retention rates of enlisted men and women and to create greater assignment flexibility by opening more specialties and more bases to women. She stressed particularly the importance of removing the unwritten existing ban on the assignment of WAF to Southeast Asia.

These policies pushed by Harrison and Holm were eventually

adopted, but in 1966 the Air Force staff remained unable to resolve the conflict between the proponents of change and the defenders of the status quo, a conflict that at one point degenerated into a face-to-face confrontation of generals accompanied by an emotional exchange of personal invectives.

The turning point came in the spring of 1966. At the April DACOWITS meeting, the DOD had briefed the committee on the growing demands for manpower to support the escalating war in Vietnam and other troop deployments. DACOWITS members were aghast to hear that thousands of qualified women volunteers were being turned away and that many recruits, once signed on, were being delayed for months in reporting for duty because of artificial ceilings on recruits.

Following the meeting, the chairman of DACOWITS, Agnes O'Brian Smith, briefed the Deputy Secretary of Defense, Cyrus Vance, and the new Assistant Secretary for Manpower and Reserve Affairs, Thomas D. Morris, on the results. She stressed a committee's consensus that the DOD should more rationally define policy and objectives about the use of military women. Vance and Morris agreed. This was the first evidence of DOD interest in the matter since the days of Anna Rosenberg.

On May 14, the DOD notified the services that an interservice working group, chaired by the Director, WAF, was being set up to study the utilization of women in the armed services. The group's charge was to examine: the current and planned use of women by military occupational fields; the policies and practices relative to their assignment; and the potential for greater employment, recruitment, and retention, especially in relation to current skill requirements of the buildup for Southeast Asia and other deployments. The goal of the study was to increase the use of women in the line to the legal 2-percent ceiling if practical.

Uncharacteristically, the line directors disagreed among themselves about this action. Some felt it unwise to have their programs studied on a joint basis under the sponsorship of the DOD, that these were matters of service prerogative and, as such, outside the purview of the DOD. They feared that expanding the women's programs could jeopardize their quality and that scrutiny of service policies might open them to unwarranted meddling by the new militant feminists.

The working group nevertheless reported to Morris in August 1966 that the women's line components could be increased by

73 percent—from 20,000 to 35,000—within two years and that the legal ceiling of 2 percent could be reached within three to five years. The services could accomplish these goals by merely expanding recruiting efforts and initiating a public information program to inform the public on the role and need for military women. Lowering quality standards would not be necessary.

In November 1966, Morris asked each of the services for their comments on the study, telling them they should give serious consideration, as a means of broadening the volunteer manpower supply, to the recruiting objectives and strengths for military women outlined in the study.

The Army, Navy, and Air Force agreed to a small expansion in their women's programs; the Marine Corps had already made a similar commitment. Although the aggregate numerical increase —6,500—programmed for fiscal year 1968 was relatively modest in the overall, for the women's programs this was the first major break with the status quo since Korea and the beginning of an expansion that continued through the 1970s.

The decision to use more military women was reinforced in February 1967 by the report of the President's Commission on the Selective Service, chaired by Burke Marshall, which recommended extension of the draft. The commission emphatically stated that the services could take certain actions on their own to encourage more voluntary enlistments, thereby reducing the number of draftees required. Specifically mentioned was the possibility of opening more military positions to women:

> Particularly at a time when manpower demands are great—such as the present—there is a disturbing paradox in this circumstance: Women willing to volunteer for military duty exist in far greater numbers than the services will accommodate; but at the same time there are undoubtedly military tasks suitable for women which are being filled by men who have to be involuntarily inducted.

Noting that the DOD was currently reviewing the utilization of women in uniform, the commission expressed the hope that out of that review would come "decisions which will benefit young men and women alike and increase the effectiveness of the military services." It recommended that "opportunities should be made available for more women to serve in the Armed Forces, thus reducing the number of men who must be involuntarily called to duty."

The Marshall Commission provided the first important linkage from a prestigious outside source between women and the draft. Although three years later another presidential commission to study an all-volunteer force failed to make a similar connection, the future course of the women's programs inevitably rested on the fate of the draft.

Eventually, opposition to conscription would force the services to find alternative resources, inexorably leading to an expanded role for women. However, for women to make anything more than a token contribution, the laws would have to be changed to remove arbitrary constraints. Efforts were already under way to do just that.

REMOVING THE CEILINGS

On 8 November 1967, with the strokes of several pens, President Lyndon B. Johnson signed Public Law 90–130, "to amend titles 10, 32 and 27, United States Code, to remove restrictions on the careers of female officers in the Army, Navy, Air Force, and Marine Corps, and for other purposes."

Flanked on his right by the uniformed women directors, DACOWITS members, and women leaders, and on his left by the Vice President, members of the Cabinet and Congress, and the Joint Chiefs of Staff, the President spoke solemnly of the war and of the contribution the women were making to that effort. Then, referring to the law he was about to sign and with a mischievous glance at the stiff row of beribboned male service chiefs, he said, "There is no reason why we should not some day have a female Chief of Staff or even a female Commander-in-Chief." General laughter at the chiefs' expense broke out. A civilian lady with a wry smile whispered to anyone within range, "You can bet we'll see a woman President long before we have a female Chief of Staff."

The new law was the first major policy change affecting servicewomen since the enactment of the Army–Navy Nurse Act in 1947 and the Women's Armed Services Integration Act in 1948. Others would follow in succeeding years as the barriers came down one by one.

Many people, especially those in the media, saw P.L. 90–130 as a woman's promotion law, promulgated for the specific purpose of creating female generals and admirals. But that was neither the primary intent of the act nor its principal effect. Although in 1966 and 1967 public attention was focused on the prospect of female generals and admirals, the new law was aimed at curing some very serious problems in the lower officer ranks.

The 1947 and 1948 laws had been modified from time to time during the intervening years, but most of the original sex-based provisions of the Integration Act and the Nurse Act had remained intact, codified in the U.S. Code. With the passage of time, laws that had seemed logical and equitable in the climate of the postwar period had come to be viewed as obstacles to individual careers and to the services' ability to effectively manage the women's programs.

Officers commissioned during World War II and later integrated into the Regular services faced particularly severe problems. The arbitrary ceilings on upper grades and the percentages within certain middle grades had as early as the mid-fifties created promotion bottlenecks, career stagnation, and, for many, early retirement at what should have been an officer's most productive years.

As the World War II "hump" of officers rose to meet artificial grade restrictions, the top of the grade pyramids bulged. For example, in 1949, a year after the Integration Act was passed, only 2 WAC lieutenant colonels and 108 majors were on active duty in the Army. In 1966, there were 77 lieutenant colonels and 237 majors. Of the lieutenant colonels, 39 were in the promotion zone for colonel but, because they were women, could not even be considered. The Army estimated that, had the limit of one temporary colonel not been in effect, 13 percent, or five, would probably have been promoted that year.

Similar situations existed in all the women's components. For the older women officers, time was running out, and, without a change in the rules, the senior ranks would soon be decimated as the wartime hump passed through the force to premature retirement. Many of these officers occupied responsible positions calling for grades higher than they were permitted by law to hold; they were being denied promotions solely on the basis of their sex and without regard to their individual levels of competence or experience. For example, Lt. Col. Emma H. Clowers served for seven years as Head, Personnel Affairs Branch of the Personnel Department at Marine Corps Headquarters, a position previously held by male colonels. Upon completion of her assignment, she was replaced by a male colonel.

Moreover, only those few line officers selected to serve as directors could retire as colonels or Navy captains, and no less than eight of those had had to accept temporary demotions to a lower grade in order to serve out their active duty time to be eligible for full retirement. For example, Louise Wilde reverted to commander after serving four years as a captain in the Navy. Emma Jane Riley of the Air Force, Julia Hamblet of the Marine Corps, and Mary Hallaren of the WAC all reverted to lieutenant colonels after serving as colonels. All eventually retired in the highest grade they held on active duty—colonel/captain.

It was especially irksome for women to have to step aside when male contemporaries with the same or less experience (sometimes their own subordinates) passed them by on the way to the senior ranks or were selected to attend senior professional schools that were closed to women because attendance was reserved for potential generals and admirals. "I was really frosted," a forty-three-year-old WAF lieutenant colonel said, "when I was told I could not attend the Air War College because, as a woman I had no future career potential in the Air Force so there was no point in wasting a good school quota on a woman."

Navy women faced a crisis unique to the WAVES. Because of a percentage limit on the numbers who could serve on active duty above the grade of lieutenant, promotion vacancies had been reduced to a point that forced the discharge of most female line officers as they reached their thirteenth year. Because they could not serve out twenty years, these officers had no retirement option. In 1966, the Navy estimated that without legislative relief, forced attrition among WAVE lieutenants would average 50 percent or more over the next five years and that promotions to commander for the next four or five years would have to be suspended. Augmentation into the Regular Navy came to a standstill since qualified women reservists would think twice before applying for appointment in the Regular Navy—there was no future in it. Some legislative relief was obtained, but the problem could not be resolved without a major change in the law.

Judging why these problems were allowed to reach so critical a stage is difficult. The answers can only be found in the services' general attitude of indifference to the seriousness of the problems and in the women's powerlessness to effect change. Also, any overt effort by the directors to open promotions to the senior grades would inevitably have been construed as self-serving—an attempt on their part to improve their own status by gaining star rank.

In point of fact, most male officers and many female officers sincerely believed that lieutenant colonel/commander was as much rank as women deserved and could handle, given the fact that they were noncombatants in the profession of arms. But there was another more subtle reason for maintaining the ceilings on promotions.

As much as anything, the services were reluctant to tamper with the women's promotion laws out of fears of opening a Pandora's box. Any attempt to remove grade ceilings inevitably would lead to pressures to promote women to general and admiral, a prospect regarded in some circles as unthinkable and as a threat to national security. Most military men simply could not picture themselves serving under a woman general; this attitude stemmed from the prevailing concept of women's role, which had stymied military women on every front. Changing it would be difficult but necessary if women were to gain equal military status. Changing it would involve a basic reevaluation of fundamental belief. Army psychiatrists at the end of World War II noted that "in order for women to gain an active participation in military activities it was necessary for man to change his basic concept of the feminine role: to overcome his fear of 'women generals.' " The women directors not only were sensitive to the attitude of military men, but to a large extent agreed with them.

The issue of women generals first surfaced during the 1942 hearings on the WAAC bill and then again some months later when vain attempts were made to promote Oveta Culp Hobby to brigadier general (some reasoned that the number of personnel under her control justified two-star major general rank).

It bobbed up again during the 1947 and 1948 hearings on the Integration Act. During these hearings and those held two years later on proposed legislation to upgrade the line directors to general/flag grades, the women directors staunchly opposed star rank. It was the line directors themselves who argued most forcefully against star rank on the grounds that the Nurse Corps chiefs were colonels/captains, as were all the wartime line directors, when women's strengths were many times those of the peacetime components. One factor behind the directors' opposition at that time was their conviction that the idea would never sell and could jeopardize passage of the Integration Act.

The directors objected to star rank again in 1950. "When we heard about it, we tried to stop the bill from going in at this time," Colonel Hallaren told a conference of civilian women leaders.[1]

"We have been under way [in the Regular service] for just two years, and are getting along just fine, thanks, but if the bill passed we would have a strong feeling among the men that we were just grasping for more constantly." The Marine Corps' Col. Katherine Towle agreed, stressing that it had been difficult gaining acceptance even in the grade of colonel, and that "there has been a feeling that women should not have even that much rank."

The nurses did not share the line directors' reluctance. As Col. Mary G. Phillips, Chief of the Army Nurse Corps, pointed out, the nurses, unlike the younger line components, had been around for fifty years and, in her view, it was time they were recognized. Noting that the Public Health Service was headed by a woman brigadier general, Phillips added, "I think the time is not far off when the military Nurse Corps will have to have that rank if they are going to be able to compete [for nurses]."

With the advent of the sixties and the rising national concern for equality, many laws that discriminated on the basis of sex came under the sharp scrutiny of civil libertarians and Congress. Congress passed both the Equal Pay Act of 1963 and the Civil Rights Act of 1964; both focused on the problems of wage inequities and discrimination in employment. In addition, Presidents Kennedy and Johnson put the White House solidly behind the drive to eradicate sex discrimination in federal employment. In March 1965, Johnson admonished his cabinet:

> Where there is an office or an officer of the Government, there must be equal treatment, equal respect, equal service—equal support—for all American citizens, regardless of race, or sex, or region, or religion.

Military laws were obviously incompatible with these goals, and in this climate the idea of women wearing stars no longer seemed so farfetched. This possibility, if anything, heightened the fears of the military. Apprehensions were exacerbated by Senate-mandated ceilings on the total number of generals or admirals each service could have on active duty. Hence, the promotion of any woman would deny a man that coveted opportunity, a prospect considered untenable by most senior male officers.

In August 1964, under constant and growing pressure from the DACOWITS, Norman Paul, then Assistant Secretary of Defense for Manpower, queried the departments on their views concerning the eligibility of women officers for promotion to general or flag grade. All the services were firmly against promotion of the directors on the grounds that their positions did not warrant it. The services were not unified on the question of whether the statutory bars should be removed entirely, thus allowing women to serve in other positions that authorized star rank: the Navy was unopposed to lifting the barriers while the Air Force strongly opposed it. The Army was divided, with the civilian leadership for and the military against.

It was generally acknowledged that without the statutory bar, it would be difficult to justify *not* promoting a woman who might otherwise qualify in her own right unless the promotion eligibility criteria could be couched in terms that would exclude *all* women without appearing to do so. A memorandum to Paul in October 1964 from a member of his staff revealed the dilemma:

> Justification for the eligibility rule is rather hard to put into language that would be acceptable to the DACOWITS members. Simply stated, the reason for eliminating women from eligibility for promotion to general officer grade is the conviction that none ever will be qualified for a job justifying star grade and that there should be a wall to hold off pressures to promote some as a token. This reason not only is impolitic as a forthright statement, but it also has a built-in weakness. The departments have been able to withstand pressures, at least sometimes, for other honorary-type promotions [of men] to star grades without the benefit of statutory prohibitions. . . .

The memo acknowledged the inappropriateness of the DOD's insistence on maintaining the legal prohibition but emphasized the importance of stressing that if the prohibition were removed, it would not guarantee promotion to star grades:

> For one thing, the most senior women now have not more than 22 years of service. More importantly, the inherent restrictions in the operational utilization of women mean that they probably never would qualify for star grade in the command line. Instead, it is likely that if a woman officer were to be promoted to star grade it would be based on her capacity for executive work in a technical field. We do not have such women officers now; perhaps some day we will.

Given the prevailing military attitudes, the almost seven-year effort to secure legislative relief for promotions is understandable. Had it not been for the DACOWITS, the struggle might have taken another seven.

DACOWITS committee members had sought to improve the position of military women in the fifties even though they had received little or no encouragement from the directors. By 1960, when the situation had reached crisis proportions, the DACOWITS advised the Secretary of Defense, presumably with the acquiescence of the directors:

> For some time DACOWITS has been concerned over the inconsistency and inequity of the laws affecting women's services. The structure prescribed for them, at the time they were originally created as part of the permanent military organization, appeared to be adequate. However, the women's line components have now reached a maturity which calls for reexamination of the structure with respect to the maximum career potential afforded new recruits, and of the full utilization of outstanding women officers now on duty.

At that time, the DOD was preparing a legislative proposal to revamp the thirteen-year-old Officer Personnel Act to establish uniform promotion and retirement rules for career officers of the four services. At the DACOWITS' insistence, provisions were incorporated in this proposal to correct the inequities in the laws affecting women. However, the DACOWITS had hitched its wagon to the wrong star: the proposal was doomed from the beginning. But while it languished on Capitol Hill, the DOD used it as an excuse for not considering separate legislation for women. Fifteen years later, an almost identical impasse would develop between the DACOWITS and the DOD over residual discriminatory laws.

In growing exasperation with DOD foot-dragging, the DACOWITS recommended in October 1965 that separate legislation be prepared, and the DOD finally bowed to the inevitable. Thomas Morris, Assistant Secretary for Manpower, ordered legislation to be drafted.

Morris' decision may have been influenced by knowledge that Congressman Otis G. Pike was introducing legislation relating to women's promotion and retirement policies. Chances for the success of Pike's bills, however, seemed slim at best: insiders speculated privately that Pike had been chosen by the DOD to sponsor this proposal because he was anathema to Congressman Mendel Rivers, whose support was essential. It was generally believed that Rivers would "oppose to the death" anything Pike proposed. It was not until Senator Richard S. Schweiker was persuaded to introduce a bill identical to Pike's that Rivers got behind the idea and things began to move.

The DOD advised Congress that, while they had no objection to the Pike bills, a detailed proposal was being drafted in-house that would effectively remove the restrictions on women officers. This proposal was introduced by Mendel Rivers as H.R. 16000. With his sponsorship, chances of success noticeably brightened.

Hearings were held in September and October 1966 by the House Armed Services Committee, with Morris as the principal witness for the Defense Department, backed by the nine directors. Noticeably absent was the spectacular array of military brass present at the 1947 and 1948 hearings on the Integration Act.

To allay fears that H.R. 16000 was a promotion bill for "lady" generals and admirals, Morris carefully explained that the primary intent of the bill was

> to eliminate insofar as possible any distinction between men and women officers in regard to ceilings on grades, limitations on numbers who can occupy certain grades, as well as those mandatory retirement and separation practices. There is no objective . . . to establish any quotas as between men and women in each of the officer grades. We seek parity only in respect to recognizing merit and performance.

The hearings were unexpectedly brief and devoid of controversy. The bill was reported out favorably on 5 October, with the recommendation that it be passed, but it was too late in the session for the bill to clear the Eighty-ninth Congress.

By the time the Ninetieth Congress got itself organized, the campaign for the legislation was in high gear. Support was coming in from all over the country, much of it generated by current and former members of DACOWITS. From the time the DOD proposal was finally drafted until its enactment on 27 October 1967, committee members pulled out all the stops—soliciting support from women's groups, encouraging letter-writing campaigns, focusing media interest, and individually lobbying Congress. Chairman Agnes O'Brian Smith held regular strategy planning sessions with military women; after each DACOWITS meeting, the members fanned out over Capitol Hill, paying court to whomever they knew, gaining support for the legislation. Many had political connections in the White House and on the Hill, others direct access to the media, which they used.

Active duty personnel were not permitted to lobby openly, but they could, and did, write letters to members of Congress by the thousands. Retirees and reservists, being free agents, lobbied directly and indirectly. Col. Emily Gorman, retired Director, WAC, was especially active and effective working behind the scenes on the Hill, drafting bills and educating anyone and everyone who would listen on the need for the legislation. She also worked with the White House staff to acquire its support.

In February 1967, Rivers reintroduced his bill (H.R. 5894), and other members of both houses introduced companion bills to show their support. In April, the Armed Services Committee reported the bill out favorably and on 1 May it passed the House.

The most important support in the Senate came from Strom Thurmond of South Carolina, a powerful member of the Armed Services Committee and a major general in the Army Reserve. After perfunctory hearings, the bill cleared the Senate and went to the White House, where it was signed on 8 November 1967 to become Public Law 90–130.

As with previous legislation dealing with military women, while P.L. 90–130 constituted an important step forward, the new law was a sign of its time and in no way signaled a major break with the conservative traditions of the military.

Throughout the hearings and in the report of the House Armed Services Committee to accompany H.R. 5894, it was made abundantly clear that it was not the intent of the DOD, the services, or Congress to alter in any substantive way the unequal status or circumscribed roles of women in the armed forces. The purpose was purely and simply to provide a greater degree of career parity for women than was possible under the old laws—nothing more. Specifically, the new law: unlocked the doors for promotion to general/flag grades (but with important caveats); opened promotions to colonel/captain; removed the 10-percent ceiling on the numbers of regular officers who could serve as permanent lieutenant colonel and commander and the 30-percent limit on Navy line officers in the grades above lieutenant; equalized retirement rules for men and women in most cases; and removed the 2-percent ceilings on the regular line officer and enlisted strengths.

The essentially masculine character of the military profession and the unequal status of women within it were never challenged. Indeed, both were reinforced by the DOD testimony and House Armed Services Committee's report on H.R. 5894. During his testimony, Morris explained what the DOD had in mind:

> I should like to dispel any apprehension that H.R. 16000 is intended to remove restrictions on the kinds of duties women will be expected to per-

form. We believe that the Nation still adheres to the concept that combat, combat support, and the direction of our operating forces are responsibilities of male officers. The utilization of women for duties which they can perform, as well or better than men, is fully compatible with this reality.

The Armed Services Committee was of the same mind:

The Committee of the Armed Services is aware that there cannot be complete equality between men and women in the matter of military careers. The stern demands of combat, sea duty, and other types of assignments directly related to combat are not placed upon women in our society. The Defense Department assured the Committee that there would be no attempt to remove restrictions on the kind of military duties women will be expected to perform.

Within the framework of this understanding, the Committee believes that women officers should be given equality of promotion opportunity consistent with the needs of the service.

The Committee's report went on to say:

It is recognized that a male officer in arriving at the point where he may be considered for general and flag rank passes through a crucible to which the woman officer is not subjected—such as combat, long tours at sea, and other dangers and isolations.

But the new law had some inexplicable inconsistencies. Under it, the Army and Air Force could promote women to any general officer grade on both a temporary and permanent basis, while the Navy and Marine Corps were limited to only temporary "spot" promotions to rear admiral lower half (equivalent to one star) and brigadier general. The net effect was to deny anything close to promotion parity for senior women in those two services.

The rationale behind the disparity is not clear. A DOD official tried to explain it away: "Any effort to make the Navy and Marine Corps provisions even superficially equivalent to the Army and Air Force provisions would require some changes to the male officer laws that would raise broader issues," presumably duty at sea. Ten years later, with Air Force and Army women serving as permanent brigadier generals and as major generals, the DACOWITS was once again recommending legislation to equalize promotion opportunities for women in the Navy and Marine Corps.

Among the other issues left unresolved by the 1967 law were:

- The separate promotion systems for men and women in the Army, Navy, and Marine Corps (the Air Force still retained its integrated system)

- The segregation of women in the Army line in their separate WAC Corps
- The arbitrary authority maintained by the service Secretaries to discharge women for unspecified reasons (used in cases of pregnancy and minor children)
- The unequal status of the dependents of military women
- The prohibition of women from service academies
- The statutory restrictions on women serving aboard aircraft engaged in combat missions and ships of the Navy (except hospital ships and transports).

Most of these issues later became targets of litigation and/or legislative action.

The most immediate result of the new law was the long overdue promotion of women to colonel and Navy captain. The Air Force was the first to act but also, as it turned out, was the most conservative. In 1968, with forty-one WAF lieutenant colonels on active duty, more than half of whom were eligible for promotion, it selected only one for promotion to colonel. Later that same year, the other services moved: the Army promoted seven WACs, the Navy six line and staff officers, and the Marine Corps eight. Under the new law, all the services but the Air Force set up systems whereby women on their segregated promotion lists would be assured of essentially the same selection ratios as the men in the same categories up to colonel and captain. For example, in the Navy the selection board to captain was authorized a 60-percent selection opportunity from among the eligibles in the promotion zone; hence, of twelve eligibles, seven were selected and promoted. At that point, Air Force women began to wonder if they could expect a fair deal under the integrated system when it came to promotions to senior grades. Their concerns were not without foundation, as would become apparent in the succeeding years when women's promotions to senior grades consistently fell short of the men's selection rates even when compared with officers in the same nonpilot skills.

THE FIRST STARS

Once the law was enacted permitting promotion to general and admiral, it was only a matter of time before women would wear stars. Two and a half years after P.L. 90–130 was signed, the Army promoted two women to brigadier general.

It was probably altogether fitting that the distinction of being first went to the oldest of the women's components, the Army Nurse Corps. In Anna Mae Hays the Army had an ideal candidate. A veteran of twenty-eight years who had served in three wars, Hays, as chief of the Corps, was then marshaling a force of some five thousand military nurses to care for Vietnam war casualties. On 11 June 1970, Gen. William Westmoreland pinned the stars of a brigadier general on Hays and then, to her surprise and the delight of the press, bussed her squarely on the mouth. Moments later, after pinning a star on Elizabeth P. Hoisington, the Army Chief of Staff said solemnly, "And now, in accordance with a new Army custom . . ." and he kissed the Director, WAC. With that, the United States had it first women generals in history.

The next two years brought three more promotions. In 1971, the Air Force promoted Jeanne Holm, then WAF director, to brigadier general. A few months later, E. Ann Hoefly, the Chief of the Nurse Corps, became the fourth woman general. In July 1972, Alene B. Duerk, Chief of the Navy Nurse Corps, received a spot promotion to become the first female rear admiral (lower half), the Navy's equivalent to brigadier general.

When it came to the line, the Navy and Marine Corps acted more slowly. Because of the "spot" promotion aspects of the law as it applied to the Navy Department, the Navy took eight years to get around to promoting a female line officer, Fran McKee, to flag rank. Ten years were to pass before the Marine Corps promoted Margaret Brewer to become its first woman brigadier general. By that time, the Air Force and Army were promoting women to major general.[2] It would take another act of Congress to equalize promotions in the Navy and Marine Corps, but neither service showed any inclination in this direction despite continuous pressure from the DACOWITS.

The sleeper in P.L. 90–130 was the removal of the 2-percent ceiling on regular strengths, which had been incorporated in the DOD legislation proposal at the suggestion of the Air Force. At the time it was proposed, none of the services contemplated that the 2-percent limit would ever be reached. But then it had not yet seriously occurred to the military that the draft would end and that women would become an important alternative to draftees in an all-volunteer force.

NOTES

1. This conference of civilian leaders was held on 21–22 June 1950 in the Pentagon under the auspices of the Personnel Policy Board of the DOD to discuss future utilization of women in defense. It was chaired by Mrs. Mary Lord, who had chaired the Civilian Advisory Committee appointed by General Marshall in World War II to advise on the WAC. Out of this 1950 conference came a recommendation that a similar committee be set up to advise Secretary of Defense Marshall on women in all the armed forces. That was the genesis of the DACOWITS.

2. Until 1981 the Navy used the rank of rear admiral with two stars to cover two flag officer grades: "lower half" to denote an O-7, which is comparable to one star brigadier general in the other services; and "upper half" to denote an O-8, which is comparable to major general with two stars. Unlike the other services, where promotion to O-8 was by selection of a board, being upgraded in the Navy was automatic, for all practical purposes, except in the case of women.

CHAPTER 16

VIETNAM

As THE LIGHTS dimmed, a color film clip flashed on the screen. The film visually depicted air fire power in action while the narrator described the key air strikes of the previous thirty-six hours to the handful of generals and staff at 7th Air Force headquarters who directed air operations in Southeast Asia.

"A WAF had never briefed air strikes before and I fully expected to be thrown out," recalled Maj. Norma A. Archer. "But the briefing couldn't have gone more smoothly. They fully accepted my presence and listened to my narration." From that day forward, the daily briefing became part of her other duties as Operations Officer for the 600th Photographic Squadron at Tan Son Nhut. She also monitored other facets of the photo mission conducted by the 600th's sixteen subordinate units in Southeast Asia —including base still-photo labs, armament recording, motion-picture laboratories, base film libraries, and combat documentation.[1]

With an outstanding record and a degree in motion-picture technology, Major Archer was eminently qualified for her job. But had the officials in the 7th Air Force headquarters during 1966 and 1967 had their way, she would not have been allowed to come to Vietnam, much less give a briefing to senior officers. Except for nurses in Korea, U.S. women had not served in a combat theater since World War II, and there were strong sentiments in some circles that they did not belong in Vietnam.

Many military men and some women contended that a combat area, especially in Southeast Asia, was no place for American women used to their creature comforts and protected environment. While some commanders would have given anything for a top-notch military woman secretary, others believed any military woman in a combat zone would be more trouble than she was worth. Out of necessity, the nurses were the one exception to the rule, the anomaly. But even here some questions were raised as to the advisability of having female nurses exposed to combat.

By the time the U.S. forces were withdrawn, some 7,500 military women had served in Southeast Asia. Many of them returned with combat decorations, some with wounds inflicted by the enemy, others with psychological wounds inflicted by dealing firsthand with the horrors wrought by modern warfare. Hundreds more could have been deployed to noncombat positions—thus freeing men for combat assignments—had the services adopted more realistic policies and made the necessary arrangements earlier.

Unlike previous wars, Vietnam had no dramatic beginning—no Pearl Harbor attack, no North Korean march across a border—just a gradual escalation of the U.S. involvement. In fact, the war in Southeast Asia had been going on for a long time before the United States stepped into the quicksand, seemingly oblivious to the dangers and the possible repercussions.

In December 1961, there were about 1,000 U.S. military advisors in South Vietnam. A year later, there were ten times that many. But 1965 was the year when U.S. involvement really accelerated; in March, two battalions of combat-ready marines landed at Da Nang; by October, nearly 150,000 troops were in country; and by the following March, 215,000. By June 1967, 463,000 Americans were bogged down in Vietnam, and more were on the way.

As the United States was drawn into the new Asian war, the armed forces would build to over 3.5 million; about one in five of the new recruits would be conscripts, and at least that many more would be directly motivated by the draft. In 1964–65, monthly draft calls had been running only 5,000–10,000. With deployments to Vietnam, inductions jumped to 20,000–30,000. Before the forces were pulled out, Vietnam would be the longest and one of the most divisive wars in U.S. history.

In retrospect, it is difficult to realize that in the beginning the public in general supported the President and believed the U.S. involvement to be a just cause. Not until the casualties mounted with no end in sight and the objectives became obscured in official obfuscation did public support dissolve into rancor, frustration, and often violence.

But whatever the public attitude at any given point, the military's job was to prosecute the war under guidelines set down by civilian authority. Each individual was trained to perform a specific role as part of the whole; each was expected to do his or her job irrespective of their private views of the war.

The women who were assigned to jobs in Southeast Asia during the war proved that, contrary to popular mythology and the image so carefully cultivated for them during the post–World War II period, the modern American woman is fully capable of functioning effectively in a military role in a combat environment, even under direct hostile fire. The fact that a disproportionate number of the women serving were nurses in no way diminishes the reality of the women in the line's performance. It instead highlights the inconsistency and irrational nature of the service policies. The dangers and inconveniences routinely endured by the nurses in the field, for instance, were generally greater than those experienced by the clerks, personnel specialists, intelligence officers, stenographers, and others, *male and female*, assigned to the headquarters in Saigon, Long Binh, or other major installations.

The reluctance on the part of the military to assign women to the Southeast Asia theater (SEA) was curious considering the history of this country and the courage and endurance demonstrated by American women over and over again—in wars and on the frontier. As a sergeant who upon being denied an assignment to Vietnam in 1966 told the WAF director, "If American women were half as fragile as the brass seem to think they are, we never would have conquered the West."

One needed only to look back a generation to disprove the theory that American women are weak and fainthearted and to see that they could cope with hardships and dangers as well as anyone else, even in Asia. As early as October 1943, members of the WAC served with Adm. Louis Mountbatten's Southeast Asia Command, first in New Delhi and later in Ceylon, and with Maj. Gen. George E. Stratemeyer's Air Force headquarters in the China-Burma-India theater (CBI).

The WACs were initially on trial in India because many Army officials, including the CBI Commander, Gen. Joseph W. ("Vinegar Joe") Stilwell, believed that American women would not be able to withstand for long the climate and diseases found in Asian countries. They were wrong, as Stratemeyer soon reported to Gen. Henry H. Arnold, Chief of the Army Air Forces, from Calcutta:

> Experience of the past several months has proven any doubts concerning the propriety of the experiment to be false. It is with enthusiasm that the Headquarters reports the substantial over-all improvement in efficiency as a result of the placement of the Wacs. . . . Officers and enlisted women alike have quickly adjusted themselves to the climate, food, and somewhat rugged living conditions.[2]

Later when Stratemeyer moved his headquarters to Chungking, China, in July 1945, he insisted that the Air-WACs go with him despite the official decision of the theater commander that no WACs would be brought into the China theater on the basis that they could not be properly housed. But the Air Force commander insisted, and in August the first WAC contingent flew the Hump, soon to be followed by others.

In comparison to conditions on most bases in Vietnam and Thailand twenty years later, those in India and China were primitive indeed. In Ceylon, for example, the enlisted women were quartered with the British WRENs in minimal facilities with bucket-latrines and no hot water. They ate in messes without cold storage, thus having very little fresh meat, vegetables, or dairy products. They boiled drinking water and stored it in Lyster bags. The WACs soon discovered firsthand the ailment theater veterans designated "Delhi Belly," as well as a few other local ailments, but after they had spent eighteen months in the theater, medical inspectors found their general health and mental outlook to be excellent.

In those days, a tour in a combat theater was for the "duration" and the only way to cut it short was to be medically evacuated or worse. And there were no periodic, jet-assisted R&R trips to exotic places to relieve the tedium and the strain.

The total number of WACs to serve in the area, between 350 and 400, was small by World War II standards; but contrary to expectations, the WACs adapted readily to the environment, morale remained high, medical evacuation rates were low, and many volunteered to stay on indefinitely after the war. Treadwell records: "The employment of WACs in India and China, although on a small scale, had done much to counteract the impression that women could not be successfully employed in a tropical or disease-ridden area."[3] This was a lesson soon forgotten, however.

When U.S. forces deployed to Korea a few years later, military women, with the exception of nurses, were left behind, even though civilian women (Red Cross workers, USO girls, etc.) were routinely present. The nearest the WACs and WAF would get to the fighting was Japan and Okinawa. The nearest women in the other services got was Hawaii.

THE LINE COMPONENTS IN SOUTHEAST ASIA

For a time, it appeared that those opposed to the assignment of military women to Vietnam would prevail, as they had during the Korean conflict. Indeed, had it not been for the commander of the U.S. forces in the country, Gen. William Westmoreland, Vietnam might well have been a males-only war as far as the U.S. forces were concerned. However, Westmoreland soon found, as Pershing, Eisenhower, and Stratemeyer had discovered before him, that he had two wars on his hands: the fighting war and the paper war. While men were necessary for the former, women were preferred for the latter. Within months after his arrival, he made arrangements for a few WACs to be assigned to his headquarters to help keep the paper flowing.

As for the women themselves, many were raring to go and were volunteering in ever increasing numbers—to little avail. As more and more women in all the services witnessed their male counterparts—many with families and many with the same or lesser qualifications—going off to the war theater, women who would never have considered themselves feminists began to agitate and to question why they were exempt. Some interpreted the assignment policies as a direct reflection on their abilities and their patriotism; others were simply itching to get as close to the action as possible and could see no reason why they could not go. On occasion, the women's discontent boiled over: "What kind of delicate creatures do the brass think we are?" a WAC lieutenant complained to columnist Jack Anderson.[4] "There's a war going on in Vietnam, but you have to be a civilian to get assigned there. Women are fighting in the jungles with the Vietcong. Yet we aren't allowed to dirty our dainty hands." A WAC major described as "gray and grandmotherly" echoed the lieutenant's words: "Women fought as hard as the men to build this country and shot as many Indians . . . you'd think we were a bunch of sissies."

Air Force women were voicing similar complaints. In early 1966, a plainspoken master sergeant, a veteran of World War II, demanded to know why she had been told by a "fresh-faced" lieutenant in the base personnel office that he would not accept her request for duty in Southeast Asia. "He wouldn't know one end of an M-16 from the other," she exclaimed in exasperation, pointing to her triple rows of ribbons. "I served in North Africa and Italy—I can sure as hell serve in Vietnam."

An Air Force lieutenant colonel wrote that she was astonished and outraged when, after she had successfully completed a highly classified counterintelligence course in preparation for assignment to Vietnam, her orders had suddenly been canceled. In this case, the officer was not sure whether the rejection was based on race or sex. She was not comforted to learn that there were no racial implications; that would have been illegal.

A young sergeant clerk-typist in the Pentagon was more philosophical about having her request for assignment to SEA turned down until she learned to her chagrin that a civilian typist who worked across the hall had volunteered and was soon on her way to Saigon. "Why not me?" she wondered aloud.

Why indeed! By March 1966, an estimated 650 American women, mostly nurses and civilians, were already living and working in Vietnam. Only a few WAC officers and a dozen or so enlisted women, all seasoned troops, had found their way to desk jobs in Saigon in response to Westmoreland's efforts. The enlisted women were all handpicked and served as secretaries to ranking officials in the MACV headquarters (Military Assistance Command, Vietnam). Also, at the request of the Vietnamese, a WAC major and a noncommissioned officer were on loan to help organize and train the Vietnamese Women's Armed Forces Corps, to be patterned after the U.S. WACs.

Beyond that, the services had no plans to deploy women in Vietnam even though there were literally hundreds of jobs in the Saigon area alone that could be performed by qualified military women, thereby releasing men for duty in combat units. All of the military headquarters—Army, Air Force, and Navy—were teeming with male secretaries, clerks, personnel staffs, information specialists, intelligence officers, communications specialists, and logisticians, to name only a few. Even the telephone switchboards were operated by men.

A similar situation existed at U.S. installations all over the area. Air Force Maj. Gen. Bertrum Harrison, after touring Air Force installations in Vietnam and Thailand in August 1966, reported to the Chief of Staff that the wing headquarters he visited needed secretarial help and would welcome WAF: "The paper war has not diminished. Male airmen are not good secretaries.

Civilians are not readily available." He went on to point out that at almost every base there were nurses, Red Cross workers, and other women working and that every field commander agreed that he could provide adequate accommodations for WAF and needed their skills.

Actually, the initial reluctance to assign women to the area seems to have been more an absence of specific policy rather than an overt decision to exclude them. Not to have sent them to a combat theater would have been entirely consistent with the overall thrust of the women's programs at that time: the programs were not designed to send women to war. They were developed to release *men* for duty in the combat area. As mentioned earlier, everything even remotely suggestive of living and working in a combat environment overseas had been systematically expunged during the post-Korean period. The women in the line had not the training, conditioning, clothing, or equipment to prepare them for deployment to a combat theater.

For example, although for many years the WAC training program had included a weapons familiarization course, the course was discontinued some time in the early sixties because, according to the WAC director, Col. Elizabeth P. Hoisington, it was regarded as "a waste of time" and "failed to contribute to the image we want to project." Later, when the question of issuing arms to the women in Vietnam arose, the director turned thumbs down:

> The possibilities for unfavorable publicity about our WACs over there are sufficient without adding this to them. Daily I am reminded of how parents feel about their young daughters being sent to Vietnam and I do not want to add to their disfavor by introducing the subject of weapons.[5]

The two services with the heaviest commitments and largest installations in SEA were the Army and the Air Force. They could easily have accommodated many women had service policy been clearly defined in advance. Although the Army had constructed no official barrier against WACs going to Vietnam and was accepting volunteer statements, it was quietly acknowledged in the Pentagon that such service was being "discouraged." In the Air Force, wartime planning guidance provided for WAF to be assigned anywhere in the world; but when war came in Southeast Asia, no specific policy guidance was forthcoming from Washington. Instead, the decision on assigning women was left by default to the whim of the two major field commanders, and they were not prone to accepting women when they could get men.

The primary reasons for excluding military women from SEA included the stereotypical attitudes toward servicewomen, which bordered on paternalism (or maternalism)—the desire not to expose them to the harsh realities of the combat area environment —and the disinclination of many field commanders to be bothered. These commanders found it easier to deal with men even though there were some jobs for which they would have preferred to have women.

In addition to the plethora of jobs that women could perform in the war zone, there were other ethical and practical reasons why military women should serve in Vietnam. Service by military women would help alleviate the burdens on military men and would also enhance the careers of military women.

On the assumption that Vietnam would be a limited U.S. involvement of short duration, the Pentagon had established a one-year rotation policy. This policy served two purposes: first, short tours distributed the burdens of combat theater service and the hardships of family separation over the widest possible military population; second, they exposed the maximum number of military personnel to combat and combat-related experience, enhancing the overall combat readiness of the U.S. armed forces worldwide.

The exclusion of women from this rotation imposed an additional burden on men to meet the rotation requirements and at the same time reduced the comparative level of the women's experience as well as their professional value to the services. Moreover, as U.S. forces in Vietnam expanded tenfold between 1965 and 1967—to a half million, with no end in sight—this rotation policy generated unprecedented turbulence in the personnel systems of all the services, and soon many men were facing second tours.

To compensate for the dangers and hardships and to encourage volunteers, monetary and career incentives were devised. Each person was entitled to hostile fire pay ($65 a month), cost of living allowances (roughly $2.40 a day), and tax exemptions (100 percent of enlisted pay and $500 of officer pay). It was not uncommon for an individual to accumulate a sizable nest egg during a year's tour. Even more attractive were the added career incentives associated with such a tour: choice of follow-on assignments, education and training opportunities, and accelerated promotions. Thus, anyone who did not serve a tour in SEA carried a permanent handicap. Women already suffered from a number of career handicaps and needed all the credits they could get. This was especially significant for Air Force women who, alone among the women's line components, competed with men in all career respects, most importantly for promotions. Lack of SEA experience could and often did spell the difference between selection and nonselection for a rank increase.

By the time the first contingent of enlisted WACs arrived in Saigon for duty in Westmoreland's headquarters, nearly two years had passed since the marines landed at Da Nang.

"You will initially be somewhat of a novelty," the general felt compelled to tell the WACs on their arrival. He was right. According to a story filed by a UPI reporter on the scene, the men walking by craned their necks so hard to get a peek at the women that they walked blindly into parked cars, palm trees, and garbage cans. In another instance, one company of G.I.s that had been exercising each evening in dirty fatigue trousers and T-shirts suddenly blossomed out in sharp-looking track suits, faces suddenly clean-shaven, hair combed, boots shined.

A young captain said his men just could not believe there were American women in Vietnam. "With women," he said, "it's bearable over here. If I can just sit down and talk with an American woman once a month I can get through."

Capt. Peggy E. Ready, the WAC detachment commander, was willing to concede that her women had done a lot for morale just by coming to Vietnam, but she let it be known that was not their purpose for being there. They were there to do a job.

As the war escalated in the field, the paper battle mounted. In April 1966, Westmoreland had requested a detachment of WACs, complete with commander and staff, to provide 50 clerk-typists for duty in the U.S. Army Headquarters (USARV) in Saigon. The request was soon upped to 120. These were to be in addition to those already on duty in the joint MACV headquarters.

With the arrival of Captain Ready's contingent, false rumors began circulating that 8,000 WACs would be coming. Actually, there were barely that many in the entire corps, and there appears to have been no intention of sending very many of them to Vietnam. "There will be no escalation of the war as far as the WACs are concerned," a WACs personnel officer said flatly and assured that they would only be used in "appropriate" jobs in Vietnam.

As it turned out, the detachment assigned to USARV headquarters was the only one formed, and, when the headquarters moved to the giant new Army base at Long Binh, the detachment went with it. The few WACs serving in MACV remained in the Saigon area and moved with the headquarters to the more protected location on Tan Son Nhut Air Base on the outskirts of the city.

By mid-1967, the total number of WACs in Vietnam had leveled off at about 160 officers and enlisted personnel in Saigon and Long Binh, the only two locations where enlisted women were allowed to serve. Requests were made for small contingents of enlisted women at other locations, but the Director, WAC, who controlled their assignments, did not want them scattered in small groups.

On one occasion, a request was made for seventy additional WACs with data processing skills to alleviate a severe shortage of qualified men to fill critical requirements. These WACs were to handle new, sophisticated data processing equipment in the Saigon area, thereby releasing men with those skills for assignments to similar jobs in the combat divisions. Because of a dearth of women with these skills, only twenty were available.

On another occasion, MACV urgently requested Washington to send twenty WAC stenographers. Because of an Army-wide shortage of male stenos, the Saigon headquarters had nineteen unfilled positions, one-third of the command's total authorization in that specialty. The Pentagon agreed to provide only six WACs. Presumably, either the rest of the openings remained vacant, or civilians were sent over to fill the jobs.

Despite the difficulties and seeming lack of enthusiasm in the Pentagon for assigning women to Vietnam, the Army estimates that a total of approximately five hundred WACs served tours there as both volunteers and nonvolunteers; from all accounts, they were exceptionally well received. In addition, their morale was high, and they adapted extremely well to the combat theater.

"This has been one of the most challenging assignments in my entire Army career and I've never worked as hard in all my life," Staff Sgt. Betty Reid wrote to her director in January 1967. "This is one of those jobs where I have left an office with a feeling of self-satisfaction and accomplishment and a feeling that I have been taxed to the extent of my capabilities."[6]

More WACs would have served in Vietnam had they had the skills and grades in demand. But the Army's system of identifying positions on manpower authorization documents as "his" and "hers" and the need to requisition WACs specifically for upcoming vacancies proved to be too cumbersome. As a result, when replacement requests arrived, if WAC replacements were not specified, a man would often be sent instead. Assigning a man in a position designated as female was permissible, but not the reverse. Consequently, men who could have been assigned to fill positions in front-line units ended up in headquarters jobs that women were supposed to fill.

"It's hard to believe that there is a war going on around me," Capt. Vera M. Jones wrote to the Women Marines director from Saigon during the Tet Offensive. "I'm here calmly writing this letter and yet can get up, walk to the window, and watch the helicopters making machine gun and rocket strikes in the area of the golf course which is about three blocks away. At night, I lie in bed and listen to the mortar rounds going off."[7] This was a new experience for female "leathernecks" who had never before been allowed to serve in a combat theater.

With increased deployments of combat troops to Vietnam, the Marine Corps wanted to release men for duty with the Fleet Marine Force in the Pacific area by replacing as many as possible of those in noncombat jobs with women. Also, the decision to expand the size of the Women Marines spurred efforts to provide greater opportunities for women to serve overseas in order to help recruiting and improve retention.

Until 1966, only about sixty women marines were permitted to serve overseas, and all but seven of these were assigned to Hawaii. Col. Barbara Bishop, Director, Women Marines, had selected three locations in the western Pacific as suitable for women marines: Saigon, Okinawa, and Iwakuni (Japan). All the commands had been queried as to the numbers of jobs suitable for women marines and the availability of accommodations. Their responses were disheartening. For example, MACV identified the availability of only one officer (later increased to two) and nine enlisted marine positions. Unexpectedly, resistance to the plan to assign women marines to the Pacific area increased with the distance from actual combat: there was some objection at Okinawa, but in Iwakuni there was outright opposition.

The usual imagined problems were cited as reasons for not assigning women, i.e., inadequate housing and on-base facilities

and lack of off-base liberty areas. When asked by the Chief of Staff
to comment on the subject, the director wrote:

> Verbal and written objections expressed to date concerning the assignment
> of enlisted women to Iwakuni imply either that the prime consideration is
> the women's enjoyment of their tour or that their presence constitutes a
> serious threat to the good order and discipline of their masculine asso-
> ciates.[8]

She advocated that the Corps weigh the adequacy of liberty facilities against the chance for the women to make a meaningful contribution to the personnel needs of the Corps under conditions of
minor hardships. "This response was not beyond their capabilities
in the past," she wrote. As for the problem of female presence:

> Presumably, the command has been able to maintain sufficient discipli-
> nary control over the masculine element to avoid undue unpleasantness for
> Navy nurses, dependents of the other services, and civilian school teachers
> aboard the base.[9]

After making a personal visit to see the situation for herself,
during which she was dragged around to the local bars and "what
nots" and presented with a fan by an aging "proprietress" who
wanted to show "she bore no ill will to the women," Bishop had
her way. The women marines were assigned to all three locations
as planned and were welcomed with good grace, even in Iwakuni.

The first woman marine to serve in a combat theater, Sgt.
Barbara J. Dulinsky, stepped off the plane at Bien Hoa Air Force
Base on 18 March 1967. The next morning, she journeyed by bus
with the usual armed escort through thirty miles of enemy-infested
area to Saigon to take up her new duties at MACV headquarters.

Like Dulinsky, most of the female leathernecks were generally
confined to the Saigon area with the Marine Corps Personnel Section on the staff of the Commander, Naval Forces, Vietnam, providing administrative support to marines assigned as far north as
the Demilitarized Zone. On occasion, duty took them to the field
to conduct on-the-spot audits of the service records of the widely
scattered men in the north. Capt. Elaine E. Filkins described one
such occasion when she and an enlisted woman went to Da Nang:
"It was obvious that the men enjoyed the unfamiliar click of the
female high-heeled shoes. The weather was on our side so we were
able to wear the dress pumps the entire visit."[10] When the weather
was bad, or when an area was under attack, the women had to

wear their utility uniforms and oxfords. The effect was not the same.

By the end of the U.S. involvement, some thirty-six women marines had served in the combat theater. Theoretically, all were volunteers: all had expressed a willingness to go, and none had objected when she received orders. When asked why she had volunteered, Sgt. Bridget V. Connally said, "Who volunteered? I received my orders in the guard mail."[11] But she did volunteer to extend her tour for an additional six months.

Like the WACs, even though they were confined to desk jobs, the women marines acquired, from their closeness to the war, both a sense of the mission and a conception of what it meant to be a marine. They could have experienced these in no other way.

When the Navy announced that Lt. Elizabeth G. Wylie was being assigned to the staff of the Commander, Naval Forces in Saigon in June 1967, Capt. Rita Lenihan, the WAVES director, felt compelled to inform the WAVES not to get their hopes up. The Chief of Naval Personnel had decided that women would not be assigned to Southeast Asia "in significant numbers . . . because of the small comparative ratio between the numbers of WAVES and the total strength of the Navy." Accordingly, "requests for duty in Southeast Asia are not being solicited at this time." WAVES were advised that any officer or enlisted woman who wished to have on record her request for Vietnam duty should "submit such request in the usual manner." The director was gratified to know that women in the Navy "have a deep sense of patriotism and are willing to do their share in the cause of peace."[12]

Actually, the proportion of women to men in the Navy was approximately the same as in the other services. However, the Navy's total strength ashore in Vietnam was much smaller. Just how many women decided to submit volunteer statements is unclear, but no more than one or two officers were there at any one time, and no enlisted women were permitted to go although there were undoubtedly jobs they could have filled.

There were also, as Harrison pointed out, many jobs that Air Force women could have filled and eventually did fill, over the objections of many in high places. It would have been logical to expect that the Air Force—the service that had pioneered in the use of military women in combat theaters in World War II—would lead the way in deploying women in Vietnam. This did not happen even though the Air Force had the best facilities in SEA and possessed the greatest capacity to employ women.

Units of the 7th and 13th Air Forces conducted operations from large, modern fixed bases in Vietnam and Thailand that were in most respects identical to air bases in the States. Their personnel requirements cut across the full spectrum of officer and enlisted specialties: technical and clerical, combat and noncombat. Though by stateside standards living conditions were austere, the manning levels were not. SEA enjoyed top priority for people, and its demands on the worldwide resource pool were insatiable because of the one-year rotation policy.

WAF were an integral part of this pool, at least in theory, and as such should have shared the burdens and benefits of combat theater duty. This was fundamental to the whole concept of integration. If, after their training at government expense, military women could not be employed in their specialties whenever and wherever there was a military requirement, then the legitimacy of the continued existence of the women's programs, even on a token basis, would be in doubt. The military must be able to deploy its people, otherwise it might as well use civilians.

As the GAO correctly pointed out in its 1966 report, most military women were in jobs identical to those occupied by Civil Service employees. But as the DOD and the services insisted in rebuttal, *the essential difference between the military and the civilian is the ability of the former to deploy on short notice to any location where they might be needed.* Air Force wartime planning guidance clearly stated that WAF could be assigned to any geographical location. Southeast Asia was therefore a crucial test.

However, as the forces deployed, the WAF stayed behind, and, when replacements were assigned, men were routinely sent. In effect, when it came to manning units in the combat area, some six thousand people were excluded from the personnel pool— irrespective of their qualifications or the abilities of the theater units to employ them effectively.

As the war dragged into its second year and newspaper and magazine articles featuring other service women and civilians serving in Vietnam began to appear with increasing frequency, Air Force line officers and enlisted women began to realize that they were being excluded from the combat theater not because they were women, but because they were WAF. The WAF director's office received growing numbers of complaints from rejected volunteers. In April 1966, for example, a first lieutenant administrative officer on duty with a combat support group in Japan wrote of her frustration. In an effort to persuade the Personnel Center that she should go, the lieutenant listed all of her numerous qualifications (including experience as a mortuary officer), took note of the fact that nurses were serving there, and offered the opinion that WAF officers had the ability to perform in Vietnam in the same capacity as their male counterparts in noncombatant positions. She was sure other WAF felt the same way. Her application had been turned down with a cryptic "It is Air Force policy that WAF's [sic] will not be assigned" in Southeast Asia. The only reason female nurses were going, she was told, was that there was "an insufficient number of male nurses to meet the requirements." Her interest in serving there was "appreciated."

"Perhaps the only alternative," the discouraged lieutenant wrote to the director, "is to continue to volunteer again and again until our worth is recognized by those in a position to take positive action in our behalf."

Actually, no such Air Force policy existed. The WAF lieutenant was rejected because of an ad hoc Personnel Center policy that was based on a "gentleman's agreement" between the Center and the commands in the theater.

Not everyone at the Center condoned the agreement. One harassed assignment officer complained privately to the Director, WAF: "I've got jobs to fill over there and a pile of volunteer statements from WAF who could fill them," he said. "Something has got to give."

Slowly, the bastions of resistance were breached. General Harrison's August 1966 trip report observed that WAF skills were needed at bases in SEA and that wing commanders had said they could accommodate them. This provided the opening wedge but was not sufficient to force the issue. Col. Jeanne Holm, the Director, WAF, agreed with Harrison but had no firsthand knowledge of the situation. In January 1967, she visited bases in Vietnam and Thailand and the various headquarters in Saigon, Bangkok, and Hawaii. Her subsequent report verified Harrison's conclusions.

It had been commonly held that the commander of the 7th Air Force in Saigon was the obstacle to employing military women, and certainly he was a likely suspect. A laconic and doctrinaire commander with a no-nonsense personality, Gen. William Momyer had a reputation—much like Gen. Curtis LeMay—of not liking WAF, and no one wanted to beard the lion in his den. However, when the WAF director did, she was pleased and surprised to find the general cordial and open-minded. In fact, he related how he had requested a WAF secretary but had been told by his personnel director that WAF could not be assigned to Vietnam, so he had been given a U.S. civilian secretary (female) instead.

Momyer agreed that WAF officers could be immediately assigned to some locations in Vietnam and that later, when the critical enlisted housing situation had eased, probably in about six months, enlisted women might be assigned. Similar agreements were reached with the deputy commander of the 13th Air Force, in Thailand, and the commander of the Pacific Air Force (PACAF), in Hawaii. There was therefore room for cautious optimism that the logjam had been, if not broken, at least partially bridged. WAF officers were soon on their way to Southeast Asia.

Ironically, it was the Army that first broke the ice for Air Force enlisted women. Brig. Gen. Donald H. McGovern, the Assistant Chief of Staff (J-1, personnel) at MACV, moved first by requesting a WAF officer and nine enlisted women to fill Air Force positions in the joint MACV staff, thus making the WAF representation on the staff roughly comparable to that of the WAC and women marines. Likewise, Maj. Gen. Richard G. Stilwell, Commander of the Military Assistance Command in Thailand (MACTHAI), did the same in his headquarters in Bangkok. In January 1967, McGovern submitted his request; in May, Stilwell identified about twenty-three Air Force positions in his headquarters as being "amenable to the assignment of WAF airmen." Senior Air Force members of his staff were aghast and attempted to block the move to no avail.

In June 1967, Lt. Col. June H. Hilton, accompanied by five enlisted women, walked down the steps of a commercial airline ramp onto the tarmac of Tan Son Nhut for duty in MACV. Other officers were on their way to the 7th Air Force headquarters in Saigon and to bases in Thailand, and enlisted women were being selected to fill the remaining positions at MACV and in MACTHAI. But the two Air Force commands continued to resist the assignment of enlisted women. At one point, the 7th Air Force, out of fear of being inundated with female officers, even managed to get the Personnel Center to agree to a ceiling of twenty WAF officers and to restrict their assignments to the Saigon area although female officers' quarters were available elsewhere, including the large complex at Cam Ranh Bay.

Moreover, several attempts were made to veto individual assignments, some successfully, others not, depending on the Personnel Center's willingness to acquiesce. For example, in September 1967, PACAF attempted to cancel the orders of a lieutenant information officer to the 7th Air Force Headquarters Office of Information. PACAF clearly viewed this as a test case, which had as its ultimate objective the closing of all information officer positions in Southeast Asia to women. The Pacific Air Force personnel office contended that "performance requirements peculiar to the combat environment dictate employment of a male information force." Information officers had to be capable of performing escort duty for newsmen "at any hour day or night, to any geographic point in the theater of operations, traveling by any available mode of transportation." They would be required to "fly on combat aircraft for generating news material and for escorting newsmen reporting on battle activity." An escort officer was expected to provide "physical assistance" for the newsmen, such as "carrying camera equipment, recorders, and other equipment of the trade," which could not be expected of WAF personnel. Instead of assisting the reporter, the WAF escort "would handicap the working newsman and thus be unacceptable to him." As if to clinch the case, PACAF explained: "Aggressive newsmen of the caliber reporting the Air Force effort in Southeast Asia will not consider the WAF Information Officer as a credible and authoritative spokesman for an air combat unit engaged in battle."

Brig. Gen. Robert Dixon, the new commander of the Air Force Personnel Center, found all this too much to swallow; he declined to cancel the lieutenant's orders. She was a "well-qualified information officer," he wrote to the PACAF personnel officer, and "should be able to perform all the duties normally expected of an information officer," adding parenthetically, "I have some reservations about the female-can't-carry-equipment line—men are available. . . . Further, I seem to remember some female photographers and reporters who carried their own—don't you?" The personnel objective, he said, was to assign the officer and "to utilize her as befits her training, capabilities, and rank."

Holm's attempts to open assignments to enlisted women in other than the two joint headquarters failed, despite earlier verbal commitments from the commanders. PACAF, for example, persisted in claiming lack of "appropriate facilities" without making plans to provide housing for women as part of base construction and expansion programs. The commands continued to contend that WAF could not be accommodated on bases despite the fact that they normally housed thousands of men as well as nurses and civilian women. They insisted that funds required to modify existing enlisted quarters could not be expended for this purpose, yet huge sums could always be found for tennis courts, swimming pools, photo labs, libraries, hobby shops, bowling alleys, air conditioning, clubs, well-stocked exchanges, etc.

In exasperation, Holm wrote to the Personnel Center in December 1967: "I have no desire to impose unnecessary additional burdens on the forces serving in Southeast Asia, however, I feel we must identify the real constraints on the assignment of WAF and not be misled by imaginary problems." The real constraint, she contended, was obviously not facilities as claimed:

> WAF airmen continually ask me why they are not allowed to "pull their share of the burden" in Southeast Asia when men who have families must go involuntarily, and some may now be threatened with second tours. These women know that nurses, civil service employees, WACs, and Red Cross women are serving in Southeast Asia and they can find no logical reason why enlisted women in the Air Force should be considered unacceptable by their own Service. While lack of adequate housing may have been a good excuse initially, it becomes less and less acceptable as time goes on.

WAF had somewhat better luck in acquiring assignments with the 13th Air Force in Thailand than they had with the 7th Air Force in Vietnam. By late 1969, no less than seventy WAF officers were in SEA, fifty of whom were in Thailand distributed among all seven 13th Air Force bases in the country. An attempt by PACAF to impose a ceiling on the number of WAF officers in the 13th Air Force was turned down with the strongest articulation of policy on the subject to come out of the Personnel Center thus far:

> Air Force shortages throughout the support skills require the full use of those qualified and available for assignment to Thailand, whether male or female. The contribution of WAF officers is currently delaying the advent of second involuntary SEA tours for many of their male contemporaries. Housing shortages do not invalidate the importance of their efforts any more than it serves to restrict the women of the Red Cross, USO, and nursing staff from going to many of these same bases where they are needed and quartered.

The WAF Director has recommended, and we concur, that no action should be taken at this time to limit the assignment of WAF officers to Thailand, either by location or by AFSC.

Unfortunately, a similar position was not forthcoming on the assignment of enlisted women. The openings for them in the two joint headquarters in Saigon and Bangkok were too few in number and too limited in specialties (mostly clerical) to provide the openings necessary to accommodate the hundreds of women qualified and volunteering to serve in Southeast Asia. Only assignments at base level could accomplish that objective, and the major installations in Thailand were ideally situated to that purpose.

A 1968 PACAF survey to determine the probability of employing enlisted women and the availability of accommodations for them revealed that between 483 and 518 could be assigned using existing facilities by the simple expedient of redesignating existing male dormitories or portions of them. However, it was not until August 1969, well into the fourth year of U.S. involvement, that plans were finalized to send a total of seventy enlisted women to two bases in Thailand—Korat and Takhli. In January 1970, over fifty were in place, and others were on the way. The key to the final resolution of this issue was the positive attitude of Lt. Gen. Francis C. Gideon, the new commander of the 13th Air Force, who could see no reason why women could not serve at his bases in Thailand.

Meanwhile, a change in command and key staff in 7th Air Force in Saigon had also softened attitudes in that headquarters. The ceiling on officers was relaxed, and a few enlisted women were assigned to Tan Son Nhut beginning in 1970. But, by then, the "Vietnamization" phase of the war was well under way, and the U.S. forces were phasing down.

Too little was done too late for enlisted women to make a contribution proportional to their total number in the Air Force. The proportion of WAF officers, on the other hand, despite the 7th Air Force ceiling, had reached a level nearly comparable to that of the male officers; 7 percent of all female officers were serving in SEA by 1970 as compared to 8 percent of all male officers. In fact, the proportion of WAF officers then overseas surpassed that of the men, with 28 percent of the WAF overseas versus 26 percent of the men.

In all, between 500 and 600 WAF served in Southeast Asia

during the U.S. involvement there, more than half of them officers. Several times that number could have served there had the Air Force gotten its act together earlier, had they given more than lip service to the concept of integration.

Permeating decisions on the deployment of women—especially enlisted women—to the combat area was the services' habit of overprotectiveness, based on the notion that the women would not be able to cope with the slightest inconvenience without loss of morale and efficiency. In 1968, for example, when the Air Force was constructing a huge new air base at U-Tapao on the coast of Thailand to conduct SAC bomber operations, the WAF director recommended the base as an ideal location for the assignment of enlisted women. Since it was in the process of construction, including provisions for women would be a simple matter. However, a WAF captain assigned to the base recommended that enlisted women not be assigned there because the climate, working conditions, and facilities were "undesirable for WAF airmen: They are hot, dusty, and dirty. This is compounded by the lack of appropriate latrine facilities." She also considered the lack of off-base recreation and entertainment facilities as a "determining factor for not assigning WAF to this station" since it "could create a morale problem." Applying similar criteria to the assignment of men would never have occurred to anyone. But it was just this kind of thinking that was continually interjected into the decision-making process when it came to enlisted women, who were often treated as though they were not-too-bright children.

Understandably, when tours in SEA were opened to women, many of those volunteering had husbands either in the area or on orders to go. Some commanders took a dim view of husband and wife combinations in a combat zone for two reasons: first, men with civilian wives complained that they were being discriminated against since they were not allowed to have their wives with them (the old misery-loves-company theory); and, second, once a husband and wife were in the same theater, they often made requests for assignments to the same base and, once co-located, expected to have quarters together. Housing in a combat theater was not designed or designated for this purpose; it was based on the assumption that all personnel would be housed as "bachelors."

In August 1968, after receiving complaints from commanders,

the Army established the policy that married enlisted women would *not* be assigned to Vietnam. The reason given was "lack of appropriate housing for couples." A request from MACV for the assignment of the WAC wife of an enlisted man in Saigon in 1970 was firmly rejected in the WAC director's office even though the command stated that housing for the couple could be provided. At about that same time, the Air Force commands in the area requested that joint assignments to SEA be discontinued for the same reasons. As might be expected, married couples thought this was unreasonable since their numbers were so small and particularly since it was common knowledge that many of the U.S. troops (married and single) solved their morale problems by cohabitating with local women. A male sergeant married to an enlisted woman observed, "They make it easier for a guy to take up with a local gal than to live with his own wife." (Shades of World War II!) A compromise of sorts was reached whereby joint assignments per se were banned, but in the event a husband and wife should end up at the same base, it was understood that the local base commander was under no obligation to provide joint accommodations. If they found them on their own, nothing would be said.

THE NURSES

Of the American military women who served in the war in Southeast Asia, the majority by far were nurses. They were there first and always in the largest numbers, especially the Army nurses. Nothing in the training or experience of military nurses could have preconditioned them for the casualties encountered in the Vietnam War. "The injuries they handle are unprecedented," said Maj. Gen. Byron Ludwig Steger, the Army Chief Surgeon in the Pacific area in 1967, "because this war is fought largely with small arms—booby traps, punji sticks, claymore mines, high-velocity bullets. Nearly all inflict multiple wounds of the most vicious mutilating kind."[13]

Dedication, patience, courage, and the willingness to do difficult, often dangerous tasks were the words most often used to describe the military nurses in Southeast Asia.

Unlike the women in the line, the nurses always knew that in an emergency or war they would see action, and their training reflected this. They learned to select camp sites, pitch tents, and read maps and compasses. They were instructed in the rudiments of field sanitation, the use of field equipment, and planning for disaster situations. They practiced field problems, road marching, and disaster exercises.

Even in peacetime, military nurses often used these skills. During the Lebanon crisis of 1958, military nurses were assigned to the staffs of the hospitals deployed to support over 10,000 American troops in Lebanon; in 1962, they accompanied a hospital unit airlifted to Iran to aid the victims of a disastrous earthquake; in 1962 they were also dispatched with medical teams during the Cuban missile crisis to participate in medical support operations worldwide; in 1963 and in 1964, they participated in earthquake relief operations in Yugoslavia and Alaska; and in 1965, they were with the military forces sent to the Dominican Republic. In 1961, Navy nurses had been assigned aboard combat ships assisting in hurricane disaster relief missions in Texas; the following year, they were dispatched with a special naval medical mission to the Republic of Honduras to assist local health personnel in combating an epidemic of gastroenteritis.

As the forces deployed for Southeast Asia, the nurses packed their bags again. Before 1965, Army and Navy nurses had served on a small scale in SEA at Saigon, Nha Trang, and Soc Trang, Vietnam, and in Korat, Thailand, acting as advisors to help train local nationals in nursing care techniques in addition to providing patient care for U.S. personnel in the area. With the rapid buildup of American forces, the nurses began to deploy. In 1965, Army nurses were dispatched with medical units to support the fighting forces. The 8th Field Hospital in Nha Trang was joined in country by the 3rd Field Hospital in Saigon with Maj. Edith M. Nuttall as chief nurse. Air Force flight nurses of the 9th Aeromedical Evacuation Group also arrived in Saigon to coordinate the airlift of patients, and clinical nurses were assigned to the new Air Force hospital at Cam Ranh Bay and other Air Force posts in Vietnam and Thailand. In October 1965, the hospital ship USS *Repose* was commissioned and twenty-nine Navy nurses assigned for duty. A year later, the USS *Sanctuary* was recommissioned, also with a complement of twenty-nine nurses, to handle casualties offshore.

By February 1966, some three hundred Army, Navy, and Air Force nurses were serving in Vietnam and Thailand in field hospitals, mobile surgical hospitals, evacuation hospitals, and aboard hospital ships. Countless others were flying as members of air evacuation crews, carrying the sick and wounded to U.S. hospitals in Japan, Okinawa, the Philippines, and the States.

Because the corps were now accepting men, attempts were made initially to assign only male nurses to the combat area. However, these attempts failed both because there were not enough male nurses and because female nurses were usually preferred. "There is nowhere else in the world where the American woman is such a great morale booster," said Maj. Henry Voegele, head nurse of two wards at the 3rd Field Hospital. Although they worked twelve hard hours a day, six days a week, they cheerfully accepted invitations to go to a firebase or on a MEDCAP (Medical Civil Action Program). "That's above and beyond the call of duty," said Voegele.[14]

The women themselves saw the need for female nurses in Vietnam: "It's really something to see a lonely and hospitalized G.I. perk up when he looks up and sees that his nurse is a woman," remarked Capt. Louise T. Nichols, one of the first female nurses to be assigned to the Aeromedical Evacuation Squadron at Tan Son Nhut, which previously had had only male nurses. "I have even had them take my picture while I was on ward rounds."[15]

"I think it's a little easier for a woman here," said 1st Lt. Margaret LaBarbera, staff nurse in the emergency room of the 71st Evacuation Hospital in Pleiku. "Everyone tries to make you feel more important because there are so few women in Vietnam." The patients and hospital personnel testified that they received a morale boost every time LaBarbera made an appearance. But each time a chopper called reporting a litter was on its way, her heart beat a little faster. "I just don't know what will be coming in, so I just pray that the injured will make it and . . . put my full effort into making things ready for their arrival. . . . I have found no greater satisfaction in my life than to help young men who are giving a portion of their lives to defend our country."[16]

Cmdr. Mary F. Cannon at the Navy hospital in Da Nang reported the patients' surprise at finding Navy nurses so close to the battlefield. "When they discover us here," she added, "it seems to give the men a sense of security and a tie-in with a more pleasant, normal way of life than they have just experienced." Cannon felt that regardless of what her special training might be, a nurse's biggest job in Vietnam was to influence the morale of the patients.[17]

In addition to caring for casualties and attending to the routine illnesses of service personnel, some of the nurses in all three services also worked with their Vietnamese counterparts in providing medical care to civilians, setting up medical care units, training personnel, and providing casualty care to South Vietnamese troops. They also served in provincial health assistance teams, developing village-level health and sanitation programs.

The Chief Nurse at Cam Ranh Bay described the work with the U.S. MEDCAP:

> Twice a week a team goes out to local villages to perform "sick-call" type of work. Much soap and water, Bacitracin ointment, and many, many bandaids are used. The team consists of one physician, one dentist, one nurse and two [medical technicians]. I have rotated the nurses in this program and they all love it.

By the time the American forces were pulled out, between 5,000 and 6,000 nurses and medical specialists had seen duty in the combat area, and many more had participated in evacuation of the sick and wounded or served at hospitals in the Pacific area in direct support of the troops.

NOTES

1. "WAF Major Had Unique Job of Air Strike Briefer," *Command Post* (Norton Air Force Base, CA), 15 August 1969.
2. Treadwell, p. 470.
3. *Ibid.*, p. 473.
4. Anderson, *op. cit.*
5. Letter from the Director, WAC to the WAC Staff Advisor, HQ USAPAC, 20 March 1967.
6. Historical files of the WAC director's office.
7. Stremlow, p. 93.
8. *Ibid.*, p. 88.
9. *Ibid.*
10. *Ibid.*, p. 93.
11. *Ibid.*, p. 92.
12. Rita Lenihan [Capt., USN], bulletin from the Assistant Chief of Navy Personnel for Women, No. 13, April 1967.

13. Katharine Drake, "Our Flying Nightingales in Vietnam," *Reader's Digest,* December 1967, p. 75.
14. "Nurses Meet Challenge With Determination," *The Observer* (newspaper published by MACV, Saigon), 1 January 1969.
15. U.S. Air Force news release, No. 6-67-18, "First Female Flight Nurses Assigned to 903rd AMES in Vietnam" (Directorate of Information, Tachikawa, Japan), 13 September 1967.
16. "Army Nurse Devoted to 4th Division," *The Observer,* 1 January 1969.
17. "Navy Nurse Thankful for Chance to Serve," *The Observer,* 1 January 1969.

CHAPTER 17

TET OFFENSIVE:
THE TEST

If ANY PROOF was needed that American women of the sixties were as capable of performing under fire as their predecessors, the Tet Offensive provided it.

For most Americans in Saigon during the first two and a half years of the war, life had a surrealistic quality. Except for the distant sound of artillery and the occasional *whump* of a mortar round or crack of sniper fire, it was difficult to realize there was a war going on. "Where else could you sit with a date in a hotel roof garden cocktail lounge, drink in hand, listening to a Vietnamese girl singing 'Moonlight in Vermont' and look across the river where flares and munitions are being dropped less than eight miles away?" wrote a lieutenant colonel from Saigon. "The men in combat operations near the city say it's quite a war—to be under battle conditions all day and then come back to Saigon for an evening on the town."

All that changed in the early morning hours of 31 January 1968, when the Viet Cong launched the first coordinated attack on Saigon, catching the American command completely off guard and changing the entire character of the war. This was the first time since World War II that U.S. military women, other than nurses, were put to the test of enemy fire in a combat theater.

The first attack hit downtown Saigon. "We were awakened at 0400 on 31 January to spend the night behind rows of sandbags that surrounded the male BOQ (bachelor officers' quarters) next door," Maj. Lillian Lewis recalled.

> Dragon ships, helicopters and jets were firing from the skies; fire and smoke from the ground was all over the place. We even had a number of snipers in the immediate area. One shot out of the side of one of our [women's] bedrooms and must have continued down the hall—luckily none of us was in the hall at the time. Throughout, our reaction has been one of caution rather than fear. . . . I guess most of us weren't really frightened until the mortar attack early Sunday morning.[1]

The second attack hit at between 1:00 and 1:20 A.M. on Sunday. Lt. Col. June Hilton described it to the WAF director:

> I was asleep, but that loud flat WHAP! WHAP! sound when the first mortars hit the base jolted me awake immediately. In only a minute or two, all of Tan Son Nhut looked ablaze. I've never seen that much fire and it was terrifyingly close. There were over 100 rounds of mortars and rockets within a fifteen minute period. The chapel took a direct hit and burned to the ground, six aircraft were hit, base operations was damaged and two fuel trucks burned, not to mention various smaller targets. That's enough for quite a fire![2]

"We are still on a 24-hour curfew, with all hands in utilities. . . . MACV personnel (women included) were bussed down to Koeppler compound and issued 3 pair of jungle fatigues and a pair of jungle boots," Master Sergeant Dulinsky wrote to Colonel Bishop in February 1968. "Right now, most of us don't look the picture of the New Image. Whew! Hardly! I can't determine at night, if I'm pooped from the work day or from carrying around these anvils tied to my feet called combat boots." She added, as though to reassure her worried director, "Our young-uns (and me too inside) were scared; but you'd have been proud of them. They turned to in the mess, cashiering, washing dishes, serving, and clearing tables."[3]

In the midst of it all, the leathernecks—men and women— found time to celebrate the silver anniversary of women in the U.S. Marine Corps.

Far more than other noncombatants, the nurses were exposed to the realities that were Vietnam—the pain, ugliness, and too often, death. "Sometimes it's depressing," said Lt. Lynn Laabs, a twenty-two-year-old from Green Bay, Wisconsin, on duty at the 3rd Field Hospital. "The wounded soldiers are all too young and they suffer such horrible pain. But I want to be here. I want to work hard for these men. And at the end of my day, I know I've done something, or at least I've tried."[4]

The twelve-hour day was standard for the nurses and medical corpsmen, but if there was a push on, they could be working for twenty-four to seventy-two hours without ever stopping. "You stayed until you either dropped or until it stopped."

The morning Tet began, Cissy Shellabarger was reminded of a scene from *Gone With the Wind* wherein all the wounded were lined up for miles around the train station. "I've never seen so many wounded in my life," she recalls. Working in the emergency room of an evacuation hospital in Cuchi, she probably saw more action than most. There were mortar and rocket attacks on the hospital, food was rationed, and medical supplies were scarce. The nurses would reach the end of one twelve-hour tour only to hear the helicopters bringing in more wounded. It was a gruesome, painful, and exhausting experience that would stay with most of the nurses for the rest of their lives. "Nothing," says Shellabarger, "really prepares you for it. . . . I never got to a point where mutilated bodies didn't bother me."[5]

At Pleiku, the Army nurses were upholding the tradition of their corps in a repeat of the Anzio situation of World War II. When the attacks came, the Army decided to move the nurses out of the area, but the women said no. They were there to do a job, and they were going to stick it out. They had been through many other rocket and mortar and sapper attacks, and they were not about to leave.

"In the beginning I could hardly move during a rocket attack," recalls a nurse who was only twenty-three at the time. "I was so frightened I could hardly breathe. But you get used to it in a way—to your own fears—and you soon begin to cope and to function—you had to. There was too much to do most of the time to dwell on it anyway." Was the women's reaction any different from the men's? "I don't think so. Anyone who wasn't scared during an attack was either a liar or didn't understand the problem."

As medical personnel, nurses were legally noncombatants, but that was small comfort when the enemy rounds came in. "The Viet Cong seemed to think the cross on top of the tent was a target to aim on," said an operating-room nurse who served at Pleiku in 1969. Lynda Van Devanter described what it was like during an attack:

> We were responsible to protect all our patients. We had to go around dragging guys off the beds and getting them under the beds or bringing the mattresses up and covering them over. We were the ones who were protecting the men who were the patients. In the operating room, if the attack was bad, we would lower the operating tables as low as possible so we could operate on our knees, but you had to keep going and you did.[6]

Van Devanter believes the nurses showed far more strength than anyone else expected of them. "We had several guys come in with live grenades still in their bellies. We operated with sand bags around the table. If you allowed your own fears to show through, you could lose the person in front of you on the operating table. You couldn't do that, so you blocked it out."[7]

During the monsoon season, the attacks might let up, but they might be operating with three inches of mud under their feet. "What are you going to do? Quit? You shovel it out, it comes back in. You just go on. You operated in the mud and blood knowing full well that Vietnam is just going to suck you all down."

Because of the capability for rapidly evacuating casualties directly from the battlefield, by air, to medical facilities, and the extraordinary care and dedication of the military nurses at every step of the way, the record of the Vietnam War in terms of saving the lives of the wounded was unparalleled in the history of warfare. Less than 2 percent of the casualties treated died as a result of their wounds. Having the hospital ships operating just off the coast, only a few minutes from the battlefield, was a major factor in the high recovery rate of the marine casualties in Vietnam. Also, the seriously wounded or ill could be airlifted out of the war zone to hospitals in Japan or the United States, staging through the Philippines on Air Force air evacuation flights that were jet cargo aircraft converted to winged hospitals.

The airlift covered roughly six million square miles, mostly over water. The nurses' duty in air evacuation was challenging and often risky. For example, on one occasion when the C-141 med-evac plane landed at Da Nang to pick up battle casualties, the base was under enemy attack. As flight nurse, 1st Lt. Jane A. Lombardi was responsible for enplaning thirty-eight patients, twenty-six of whom were on litters. Despite extreme danger from small-arms fire, Lombardi got them all safely on board in a minimum of time and the flight departed. For her "extraordinary and outstanding professional skill and personal calm," she was awarded the Bronze Star Medal.

Fifty-four Air Force flight nurses were assigned to PACAF aircraft operated exclusively in the SEA theater, picking up casualties in Vietnam and Thailand and delivering them to medical centers in the Philippines, Japan, and Okinawa. From there, the Military Airlift Command evacuation flights with sixty-seven flight nurses took over to return the wounded to the United States in C-141 Starlifters outfitted like hospital wards.

Flight nurses stationed at Clark Air Force Base in the Philippines regularly donned their flight uniforms at 4:30 A.M. and headed for the flight line, where they would be briefed on the day's pickup in Vietnam, stow the needed medications, and instruct their medical technicians. By 7 A.M. the C-130, camouflaged like overcooked spinach, would take to the air. In four hours, the nurses would be on the ground in Vietnam, taking aboard some sixty casualties for the return flight. If the pickup point was in an unsecured area, the nurses wore side arms, which they had been trained to use. They also knew how to handle an M-16 rifle. The aircraft was due back at Clark at 4 P.M., where the ambulances waited to whisk patients to the hospital. Not until the last of the patients was on his way would the exhausted air evac nurses leave the ramp. It was a grueling schedule with little margin for error.

The toughest part was always the return flight. While in flight, the air evac nurses were prepared to and did perform the work of doctors as well as that of nurses, because doctors were normally not present, and the patients often teetered on the thin edge between life and death. In their constant battle to buy time for sinking patients, nurses gave blood transfusions, performed emergency tracheotomies, and administered intravenous feedings.

Almost any case could turn into an emergency in flight. When that happened, the nurse could declare a "Medical Emergency"— the air evac's equivalent of "Mayday"—and in effect assume command of the aircraft. She could instruct the pilot to change altitude or cabin pressure, turn back, or make an unscheduled landing at the nearest medical facility. Despite the dangers and responsibilities, or maybe because of them, nurses considered flight duty the most prestigious in the Air Force.

With Tet came a new anti-WAF offensive. Up to that point, no one had seriously suggested that the possibility of exposure to hostile fire might serve as justification for keeping women WAF out of Vietnam; the emphasis had always been on bathrooms, not bullets.

In March, at the request of the 7th Air Force, PACAF sent an urgent message to the Personnel Center:

> Combat situation presents risks and hardships for WAF personnel well beyond that contemplated by current WAF assignment and utilization policies. Terrorist activities and repeated rocket/mortar attacks against TSN [Tan Son Nhut] Saigon complex have caused critical reexamination of policy allowing assignment of WAF in active combat zone. Advantages of assigning token WAF in order to allow more flexibility in management of male resource totally negated by associated increased requirements for their support and security in current environment.

The message requested authority to take immediate action to preclude further WAF assignments to units of the 7th Air Force, to cancel women already on orders, and to replace them with men with the same skills from Thailand and the United States.

There is no evidence that the 7th Air Force contemplated evacuating its female civilian employees; yet, had they been injured or killed, neither they nor their survivors would have been entitled to any medical or survivor benefits. Had they been taken prisoner, they would have had none of the protections of the Geneva Convention normally accorded to military personnel in a combat area.

Investigation revealed that *no* increased requirements for WAF support or security had been requested or provided. In fact, the WAF/Nurse barracks, which was one of a series of four barracks, was the only one without the protection of either revetments or an accessible bunker. Also, when flak vests were being issued, the women were not at first entitled to them.

Meanwhile, a similar effort to replace the WAF was brewing among Air Force officials in the joint MACV headquarters, supported by the senior WAF officer present. This same officer six months earlier had written in glowing terms of her experiences and joked about the dangers from frequent sniper attacks: "Maybe we'll all get purple hearts or something." After Tet she had second thoughts. Vietnam, she wrote the WAF director, was "very definitely no place for a woman now." It was fine for nurses, since they were "indispensable" and had to be there, but WAF did not have to be there. Even though they were doing excellent work and were highly praised, none were, in her view, actually essential. "The living conditions are arduous, the hours are excessive, the tension is cumulative, and the situation is dangerous. All of this would be acceptable," she concluded, "if the contributions were significant." Since WAF were in "soft core jobs," she did not regard their contributions as significant. Of course, the same could have been said of the thousands of men required to serve in Vietnam in exactly the same kinds of jobs and of the men who would be sent as replacements if the women were withdrawn.

As rumors circulated in Saigon that a move was afoot to evacuate the WAF, a flood of letters arrived in the Pentagon office of the WAF director from women protesting that they did not want to leave. An officer wrote on 25 February, "I, and several others with whom I've spoken, want to stay. Most of us volunteered for this assignment, some for selfish reasons, others for patriotic reasons." After describing in detail the dangers and fears endured in the Viet Cong attacks, she wrote,

> We're all scared to death when those rockets come bouncing in around us, who isn't? The men readily admit they are scared too. . . . I would like to stay here and finish my tour. I'm not a fool and am not saying this because I'm patriotic. I feel we have a job to do—it's here to be done and we'd best get with it.

Male staff officers also interceded, declaring that the women were performing in a fine manner and should not be sent home. They stated emphatically that no special security measures had been taken in the women's behalf and none had been requested.

In Washington, checks with the WAC and Women Marines directors, the chiefs of the Nurse Corps, the Red Cross, and the director of Air Force Civilian Personnel revealed no plans to evacuate their women or to change policies with respect to assignments.

As far as the Director, WAF, was concerned, the WAF must stay. If a decision were made to evacuate *all* U.S. women from the area, the WAF would be the last to leave. They were there to do a job; the risks came with the territory and were no greater than those Air Force men similarly situated were expected to endure.

General Dixon agreed and took a firm stand informing PACAF of Air Force policy in unequivocal terms:

> WAF are fully integrated into the Air Force personnel structure and are considered to be equally capable of performing support duty as male counterparts. . . . The basis for the return or evacuation of WAF personnel from overseas commands will be the same as for male military personnel performing duty in support functions.

A male senior master sergeant confirmed the correctness of this policy. In a letter to the Chief Master Sergeant of the Air Force in April, he wrote his unsolicited comments on the conduct of the women under fire in the combat zone during the final assaults of the Viet Cong in the area in February 1968:

> One would expect the male members of the military to remain as calm as could be expected and that they would exert that little extra during a crisis such as was occurring here during the Tet Offensive—and they did just that. I guess what impressed me most was the calm that the female service members went about their duties (WAF, WAC, WAVES and Marine). That belief that the frail (or fair) sex will tremble at the first sign of trouble is not true. During February the MACV building would shake from US/RVN bombings in the nearby area, quite frequently and there is little difference in this noise and that made on the impact of a Viet Cong mortar round striking nearby. Yet, I observed the female military members, in various offices of MACV, performing their duties no different than anyone else. If they had fears, which I am sure were no different than any male members, then they did a terrific job of concealing them. My final comment is "the WAF are doing an outstanding job for which they were assigned here to do."[8]

The Tet Offensive had a profound effect on the U.S. attitude toward the war. For the first time, it became clear that a military victory was not in the cards, that another solution had to be found. In April, the North Vietnamese accepted President Johnson's offer of a partial bombing halt in exchange for peace talks; in May, delegates sat down together in Paris; and in November, Richard Nixon was elected President with a campaign commitment to "Vietnamize" the war. The gradual, painful winching down of the war began, but the fighting continued.

Lt. Col. Eleanor Jeanne McCallum described to the WAF director the situation in Saigon in July 1969.

Life at Tan Son Nhut for the most part is routine. The jobs really don't differ too much from those back in the states. Some of us don't have much to do but neither do the men. We do however have our moments of excitement in the form of sporadic rocket attacks. These happen just often enough to keep the blood circulating and the adrenalin glands alive. The VC always choose the hours of darkness for these attacks since they must infiltrate into friendly territory to get close enough to reach us. Thank God they can't aim any better than they have so far.

As for several recent rocket attacks, "you instinctively recognize the sound." Then she added reassuringly,

After this tale you are probably having doubts as to whether we should be here—DON'T! There's not a WAF soul who would want to trade her experiences here for stateside until her tour is finished. There's a lot of satisfaction in knowing we are sharing the duty here with our male counterparts and these fellows appreciate this fact.[9]

UNIFORMS AGAIN

One would have thought, given the problems of uniforms endured by the WACs overseas during World War II, that by the 1960s they would have been resolved. Not so. Military women in Southeast Asia encountered the same old problems. Their issued clothing was not designed for wear in combat in the hot, muggy climate and would not hold up to the wear and tear of repeated washings; they did not have adequate shoes for field wear; the field gear in general was inadequate; and the clothing stores seemed unable or unwilling to supply adequate stocks. As a result, the women had to order uniforms from the States. Often they resorted to wearing the men's fatigues and jungle boots, especially when outside Saigon.

With the onset of the Tet Offensive, everyone was ordered into jungle fatigues or field uniforms. The Army women's jungle fatigues consisted of olive green trousers; a man's-style shirt worn open at the neck, outside the trousers, with sleeves rolled up; high-top laced boots; and a baseball-style cap. Neat, feminine, and attractive this ensemble was not. Before long, the WAC director was in a long-distance, running battle with the command in Vietnam over the wearing of fatigues in lieu of the two-piece, green cord uniform with skirt and pumps.

The matter of wearing fatigues might have been less troublesome had it not been for the occasional photograph appearing in newspapers of women "roughing it" in the war zone. In the director's view, the parents of young girls did not like to envision their daughters in the rough, tough environment conveyed by the field uniforms; it lowered the desirability of military service for women and the prestige of the Army as contrasted with the other services, namely the Air Force, whose women had more feminine work uniforms.

Air Force women were issued a three-piece work uniform consisting of a light blue overblouse, navy blue wrap-around skirt, and navy slacks to be worn with sneakers and without any hat. By comparison to the Army's, it was attractive yet functional—except when diving for cover in a bunker, and then it was a mess.

The WAC director insisted that the women in Vietnam wear the green cords and pumps in order to make "a neat and feminine appearance," but a WAC major advised that she was meeting with resistance from the women. "You'll be interested to know," she informed the director in Washington,

> that the resistance stems from the feeling that the WACs are in Vietnam to do a job and not to improve the morale of the male troops. The enlisted women feel that their morale will suffer if forced to wear the green cord. Hopefully we can sell the optional wear and in time, more and more women will don the cords for duty. Conditions have improved to the extent that the uniform can be worn comfortably in the headquarters; however, there are still women working in areas where the green cord would be most inappropriate.

To which the director replied flatly, "I shall expect that an order be issued by the Headquarters and the WAC commander that the women will wear green cords on duty in the Headquarters. . . . In my opinion, this is not a matter for discussion or for a vote of all hands."

But field commanders, not the Pentagon, decide what their troops will wear. An order was issued by the local commander that was permissive rather than mandatory: they "may wear the women's Army Green Cord uniform. If desired, WACs may continue to wear the tropical Field Uniform."

"You must know that I am still waging war to get our women out of those awful field uniforms and into the Army Green Cords," the frustrated director wrote to the major in Long Binh in June 1969. And in what may have been the last word on the subject, the exasperated major informed the director:

> We all realize that you want us out of fatigues and we know that we look much better in skirts. Maintaining a wardrobe in a reasonable state of repair, particularly shoes, is still difficult at best. I'm afraid that the only

way you'll win your uniform war is to end this one over here and bring us all home.

THE HOMECOMING

For those Americans who served this country in Southeast Asia, coming home was an unexpectedly painful experience. In some respects, it was especially difficult for the returning women.

Like most of the returning vets, Charlotte Miller found it was hard to talk about her experiences to anyone who had not been there. "If I say I was in Vietnam, people say (incredulously) 'you were in Vietnam?' . . . People don't know what to say." She recalls that as the plane settled down for a landing in Seattle, she and the other returning G.I.s howled for joy at being home. They kissed the ground as they got off the plane. Their euphoria faded quickly in the airport though, when people greeted them by throwing fruit and yelling obscenities. "It really made you wonder why the hell did I go?" she says. "If I had the choice right then I would have gone right back to Vietnam."

Miller, like all the other young women, had gone into the military voluntarily. "I requested Vietnam," she explains, because "it seemed the humanitarian thing to do. If our men were over there, the least I could do is go over there and help. I'm proud of my accomplishments," she says without apology. "If I had to do it over again, I'd go again." [10]

Cissy Shellabarger had similar experiences. When she stepped off the plane in the States wearing her combat fatigues and boots, the Army advised her to change into civilian clothes before leaving the base. "I guess they were trying to protect me." She had served as a medical floor nurse at the 8th Field Hospital in Nha Trang and was surprised and annoyed at the indifference to the war that she found back in the States. "It was hard for me to believe that the world was going on here while that was going on over there." A year after her return, Shellabarger found herself at the University of Pennsylvania, where the Army had sent her to get a bachelor of science degree in nursing. It was a time of campus unrest, and the war was unpopular. "I didn't dare wear my uniform or tell people I was an Army nurse or that I had served in Vietnam," she recalls. "My professors were taking digs at the military establishment." [11]

Lynda Van Devanter believes that the returning woman faced a greater sense of alienation than the man. While he was told he was a "fool" or a "real sucker" for going to Vietnam, she was met with degrading, unfounded innuendos about her morals. Since the average nonveteran could not understand why any woman volunteered to serve in the military, much less go to Vietnam, many assumed that those women who went must have had other motives, that they must have been there to "service the troops."

As director of the women's unit of the Vietnam Veterans of America (VVA), Van Devanter found that in the eight years following the fall of Saigon, although much was written about the problems of the returned veteran—the aftereffects of the war, the delayed shock, the psychological wounds—nothing was done to ascertain the war's effect on women. A Veterans Administration-sponsored study of the war's multiple impacts on 1,340 veterans, published in 1981, failed to include a single woman. Perhaps it was based on the assumption that either the reactions of the women would be the same as the men's or that because they were noncombatants their reactions were not important enough to warrant study.

Van Devanter says, based on personal experience and correspondence she has received, that some nurses who had been stationed in Vietnam came home and went into a closet, unable or unwilling to accept that they might be suffering from symptoms of delayed shock. They tended to blame themselves for adjustment and psychological problems that the male returnees properly blamed on the war. Hence, they were reluctant to seek professional help when they needed it, and the V.A. counseling programs did not reach out to them as they did to the men.

The V.A. officials deny that women were ignored, but contend that the number of female compared to the number of male Vietnam veterans was so small that the women did not warrant special programs. Although the V.A. hospitals might not have facilities for women, they would be sent to private clinics and the V.A. would pick up the tab.

Although information compiled by the author indicates that 7,500 served in SEA, actually, neither the V.A. nor the DOD has reliable data on how many women were there, what they did, how many were decorated, or what special problems they might be experiencing as a result of that service. "It's almost as if they think we didn't exist," says Van Devanter. "The government has almost a vested interest in not displaying us as vets because for so many years they have been saying that women will never serve in combat."[13] These feelings of being forgotten were reinforced on 15 March 1981 when President Ronald Reagan spoke of the Vietnam veterans at a Medal of Honor ceremony in the courtyard of the Pentagon:

> Several years ago, we brought home a group of American fighting men who had obeyed their country's call and who had fought as bravely and as well as any Americans in our history. They came home without a victory, not because they'd been defeated, but because they'd been denied permission to win. They were greeted by no parades, no bands, no waving of the flag they had so nobly served. There's been no thank-you for their sacrifice. There's been no effort to honor and, thus, give pride to the families of more than 57,000 young men who gave their lives in that faraway war. . . . There's been little or no recognition of the gratitude we owe to the more than 300,000 men who suffered wounds in that war.

Apparently, no one had informed the new President that women had also answered their country's call with no obligation, real or implied, to do so. All received combat pay, many received combat decorations, some were injured, and others died. Even though data have not been compiled, it is known that in January 1965, four Navy nurses injured during a Viet Cong terrorist bombing became the first women in the Vietnam War to be awarded the Purple Heart. Army nurses, because of the nature of their mission and their larger numbers, suffered the heaviest casualties. Eight died, most from air crashes, but 1st Lt. Sharon A. Lane died of shrapnel wounds during an enemy rocket attack on an evacuation hospital. An Air Force nurse, Capt. Mary T. Klinker, was killed on 4 April 1975 while serving as a flight nurse on a giant C-5A Galaxy that crashed on takeoff while evacuating a load of Vietnamese orphans prior to the Saigon government's fall.

NOTES

1. "History of the WAF Directorate: 1 January–30 June 1968" (on file at the Air University, Maxwell Air Force Base, AL).
2. *Ibid.*

3. Stremlow, p. 94.

4. Kurate Kazickas, "300 to One: A Wonderful, Wacky Ratio," *Washington Post*, 28 July 1968.

5. Marcia Smith, "Wartime Experiences Change Nurses' Lives," *Dallas Times Herald*, 25 January 1981.

6. Lynda Van Devanter, interview with author, 22 April 1981.

7. *Ibid.*

8. "History of the WAF Directorate," *op. cit.*

9. *Ibid.*

10. Kathy Kafer, "Vietnam Aftershock," *The News American* (Baltimore), 26 January 1982.

11. Smith, *op. cit.*

12. Van Devanter interview, *op. cit.*

13. Rosalind Rossi, "Women Viet Vets Fight Memories," *Chicago Sun-Times*, 29 March 1981.

PART III

EXPANDING SEVENTIES TO UNCERTAIN EIGHTIES

CHAPTER 18

THE SEVENTIES:
A DECADE OF EXPANSION

On 17 OCTOBER 1968, presidential candidate Richard M. Nixon told the American people that it was time to take a new look at the draft—"at the question of permanent conscription in a free society"—and that if other means could be found to meet the peacetime manpower needs, then "we should prepare for the day when the draft can be phased out of American life." Less than five years later, with the signing of the peace agreement in Paris, Secretary of Defense Melvin Laird announced that the armed forces henceforth would depend exclusively on volunteer soldiers, sailors, airmen, and marines. The use of the draft had ended. This decision, more than any other factor during the seventies, produced an expansion of women's participation in the armed forces that was of unexpected and unprecedented proportions. Well before the end of the decade, the United States emerged as the world leader in the use of military womanpower both in total numbers and in proportion to the total force.

Other factors were also at work, chief among them the congressional passage of the Equal Rights Amendment. However, the arrival of the all-volunteer force provided the irresistible incentive to reevaluate both the role of military women and the contribution they could make to the difficult task that lay ahead: that of fielding a military force of two million volunteers.

Even before Richard Nixon assumed the presidency, disenchantment with the draft was running so high that it was threatening the renewal of statutory authority for the conscription of young men, which expired in June 1971. A variety of student and other deferments had seriously undermined public confidence in the fairness of the system. Moreover, with the winding down of the unpopular Vietnam War and the rapid growth in the population of military-age youths in the 1960s and 1970s, an end to conscription became a true and attractive possibility.

Shortly after taking office, President Nixon appointed a Commission on an All-Volunteer Force (AVF) with Thomas S. Gates, Jr., former Secretary of Defense, as its chairman. The commission was chartered to develop a comprehensive plan for eliminating conscription and moving toward an all-volunteer force. It was instructed to study a broad range of possibilities for increasing the supply of volunteers, including "increased pay, benefits, recruitment incentives and other practicable measures to make military careers more attractive to young men."

The Gates Commission examined at length the virtues, in a free society, of a force comprised entirely of volunteers, the various alternatives to conscription, and the methods needed to encourage enough men of the necessary quality to make careers in the military. Its analysis of the potential resource of qualified men and the trends in the labor market through the seventies led it to conclude that, with the right incentives to attract and retain them, a force of volunteers was within reach and that the draft could be allowed to expire. Its report, submitted to the President in February 1970, stated:

> We unanimously believe that the nation's interests will be better served by an all-volunteer force. . . . We have satisfied ourselves that a volunteer force will not jeopardize national security, and we believe it will have a beneficial effect on the military as well as the rest of society.

Nowhere in its report did the commission discuss the subject of military women as a potential military resource. This omission is especially puzzling since references were made to the earlier Marshall Commission report, in which a strong recommendation was made on the subject. But while it made no direct references to women, the Gates Commission report included a number of observations on the qualitative characteristics of a future military force that had important implications insofar as the use of women is concerned. The most significant of these related to the occupational mix of enlisted men, particularly in the Army:

In 1953, 18 percent of all enlisted men were assigned to ground combat occupations that require comparatively little technical skill. The proportion of enlisted men in these relatively unskilled occupations has declined over time. Indeed, the projections of the force structure in a post-Vietnam environment show only 11 percent will be in the ground combat forces. The declining importance of the ground combat forces cannot be attributed to a relative reduction in the size of the Army. In the Army occupational structure, the percentage of enlisted men in the ground combat occupations is projected to fall from 29 percent in [fiscal year] 1963 to 21 percent in the forces of tomorrow. The services' demands for highly skilled men to staff electronics and other technical occupations has climbed over time.

The report added:

Various estimates suggest that 20 to 30 percent of active duty billets are directly related to combat missions. The remaining positions are required for logistical support, administration, maintenance and training.

Although these comments were intended to suggest the use of greater numbers of civilians to meet the services' needs, they obviously bore on the popular contention that expanding the proportion of women would necessarily impinge on combat effectiveness.

Thus the commission reinforced the services' requirements for people with more education, higher general intelligence, and greater technical skills. The first two of these qualities were found in equal proportions in the male and female population. And, although proportionally fewer women showed aptitudes in some of the technical skills, a significant segment of the female population did have the aptitudes, and the proportion was increasing.

Generally accepting the commission's recommendations, but not its timetable, the Nixon administration sought and the Congress approved a two-year extension of the induction authority, to 1 July 1973. However, the administration eliminated the draft six months earlier than anticipated because the phasing down of U.S. involvement in Southeast Asia diminished military manpower needs. Also, intensified recruitment campaigns attracted greater numbers of applicants than had been anticipated.

Despite the unanticipated high number of recruits, the DOD was not certain that the supply of male volunteers would continue to meet the services' requirements. The all-volunteer force was a new venture, and many unknowns remained. Thus, to evaluate various options for maintaining personnel strengths, the DOD set up a Central All-Volunteer Task Force. Sometime around the end of 1971, the task force was ordered to study the use of military women and to prepare alternative utilization plans. The study was designed to "provide a contingency option for meeting all-volunteer force objectives by increasing use of women to offset any shortage of men." It was to focus on the critical transition period, fiscal years 1973–77, "when male accessions may not meet requirements or male recruiting costs may increase because of tight supply of men having requisite quality." The study was headed by George A. Daoust, Jr., Deputy Assistant Secretary of Defense (Manpower Research and Utilization).

Meanwhile, the role of women in the military had become an important element of the debate in Congress on the Equal Rights Amendment (ERA). Two amendments had been proposed that would specifically exclude women from the draft and from combat. The rejection of these proposed amendments suggested that Congress may have anticipated a larger role for women in the armed forces at a future date. When the ERA cleared Congress on 22 March 1972, it focused the nation on the issue of equal rights for women and spurred a new awareness within the DOD and the services of the problems of sex discrimination within the military. At that point, the services believed that the ERA would be ratified by the states and that its impact on their personnel policies would be profound.

On 6 March, a special subcommittee examined the utilization of military manpower. Chaired by Representative Otis Pike, the subcommittee held hearings on the role of military women. The chief witnesses for the services were the line directors, Brig. Gen. Mildred C. Bailey (Army), Capt. Robin L. Quigley (Navy), Col. Jeanette I. Sustad (Marine Corps), and Brig. Gen. Jeanne M. Holm (Air Force). George A. Daoust, Jr., testified for DOD.

Throughout the hearings and in the subcommittee's final report, published in June 1972, the chairman and members of the subcommittee were highly critical of the policies and attitudes of the services and the DOD concerning the status of, and opportunities available to, military women. At the conclusion of its brief report, the subcommittee stated:

> We are concerned that the Department of Defense and each of the military services are guilty of "tokenism" in the recruitment and utilization of

women in the Armed Forces. We are convinced that in the atmosphere of a zero draft environment or an all-volunteer military force, women could and should play a more important role. We strongly urge the Secretary of Defense and the service secretaries to develop a program which will permit women to take their rightful place in serving in our Armed Forces.

Following the hearings, Daoust, as head of the AVF Task Force study of the utilization of women, tasked the services to develop contingency plans to increase the use of military women. He specified that the Army, Navy, and Air Force should plan to double their women's programs by the end of fiscal year 1977, and that the Marine Corps should plan a 40-percent increase during the same period.

The requirement to develop contingency plans had unexpected results, apparently forcing the services to cave in to the inevitable. Their contingency plans suddenly became "plans of action." Even before the study was completed, the Navy and Air Force decided to increase their programs far beyond the goals set for them by the task force, and the Army reported that it expected to reach the goal set for it by 1978. Only the Marine Corps felt meeting its goal would not be feasible. However, the task force expressed confidence that the Corps' goal could be met, and it proved to be right.

The combined service plans projected a total increase in the line officer and enlisted strengths of nearly 170 percent, with the Navy and Air Force programs more than tripled in size. Ambitious as the plans seemed at the time, as it turned out, they were conservative. By the June 1977 target date, more than 110,000 line officers and enlisted women were on active duty, and the numbers were still climbing even in the face of overall military force level reductions. Consistent with the growth in strength was a marked increase in the number of women entering the services. In contrast with 1972, when one in every thirty enlisted recruits was a woman, by 1976 one in every thirteen was a woman.

In 1976, however, it appeared the major expansion phase would be ending in the near future. Service plans for the second half of the seventies showed a marked leveling off of the growth rate. Where in the first phase of the buildup the growth had averaged about 20 percent annually, estimates showed a slowdown in 1976 to a 5-percent growth rate which would remain constant through fiscal year 1982, when some 147,000 women were expected to be on board and would constitute about 7 percent of the

total military force. As one observer put it, "The prevailing attitude was 'we have all these women so let's move more cautiously
until we see how they work out.' "

THE BROOKINGS STUDIES

But, just when it appeared the heat was off, pressures again
began to build both from without and within the DOD. In 1976,
the Brookings Institution, an independent organization that spe-
cializes in research on national policy issues, was in the process of
completing a two-year study on women in the military. The study
was being done by Martin Binkin, a senior Brookings fellow, formerly with the DOD, and Dr. Shirley J. Bach, an Air Force lieutenant colonel and an executive fellow with the Institution.

Three years earlier, Binkin had coauthored a report for the
Senate Committee on the Armed Services, *All-Volunteer Forces:
Progress, Problems and Prospects*, which suggested that the services might conceivably move toward a 20-percent-female force in
order to reduce their requirements to attract men. "In addition,"
the report said, "accepting a greater proportion of women might
also raise the average mental capability of the military since a
high proportion of female high school graduates of above average
intelligence have not been recruited." The report also recommended promptly addressing two questions: "What are the relative merits of using women and civilians in jobs traditionally filled
by military men?" and "To what extent can such substitution take
place?"

The subsequent Brookings study attempted to answer these
questions insofar as women were concerned. After assessing the
services' current rationale in developing their goals for women,
the legal and policy restrictions, the need to set aside additional
positions for men to allow them assignment and career development opportunities, and other "management" adjustments (housing, etc.), Binkin and Bach concluded that "by any reckoning, the
goals for the female work force appear inordinately small."

In their report *Women and the Military*, published in June
1977, Binkin and Bach estimated that, without radically departing
from current policies and practices and without disrupting the
rotation or career opportunities for men, close to 600,000 military
enlisted jobs—or 33.3 percent of those performed by the enlisted
force—could *potentially* be filled by women. Because of the
missions and ratios of combat versus noncombat and support-type

positions, the estimates varied from service to service, with the Marine Corps at 8.8 percent, the Navy at 9.2 percent, the Army at 25.9 percent, and the Air Force reaching a whopping 76.1 percent.

Although they did not say so, the authors must have recognized that there was not the remotest possibility that three out of four enlisted positions in the Air Force would be filled by women (though it is an intriguing thought). Also, recruiting experience would indicate that nowhere near that number of qualified women (600,000) would find the military an attractive career option in the best of circumstances. So Binkin and Bach took a stab at a more realistic but nonetheless significant estimate. They concluded that if the services better publicized available opportunities, encouraged women to enter the specialties offered, and developed sex-neutral standards, "it is conceivable that the number of military enlisted women could eventually reach 400,000 or 22 percent of the force." Beyond this range, however, they believed that "further expansion would depend on a resolution of the combat issue."

Even before the Binkin/Bach study was published, its contents were generally known. Understandably, the revelation by the prestigious Brookings Institution that the number of women the services could realistically expect to employ was more than double the planned expansion sent shock waves through the Pentagon.

With the 1976 elections over and the prospect of a change of administration, a wait-and-see attitude settled over the service staffs. Many in the Pentagon continued to harbor genuine misgivings about the efficacy of the AVF and the wisdom of expanding roles for women. Some viewed both as serious threats to military preparedness. But if they held any notions that the new administration might back off on either score, they were in for disappointments on both counts. The administration of Jimmy Carter seemed as determined as those of Nixon and Ford to ensure the continued success of the AVF and to demonstrate a strong commitment to women's issues.

Within a week of taking office, Secretary of Defense Harold Brown waded into the manpower area with a request for a priority analysis of military manpower to include yet another study on the use of women. A number of women were also appointed to key sensitive civilian positions within the DOD and the services' staffs; some of these appointees had been deeply involved in feminist

issues or litigation. Brown's request and these appointments signaled the new administration's decision not to back off the
women's issues.

The new study's purpose was to provide background data to
evaluate the services' growth plans for their women's programs
and to form a basis for future policy decisions. The officer charged
with the project was a Navy commander, Dr. Richard W. Hunter,
who had been working at Brookings as a research fellow with
Binkin and Bach.

The central issue of Hunter's paper was the DOD's ability to
meet enlisted manpower requirements: "this is where the all-
volunteer force will succeed or fail, and this is where most of our
recruiting money and effort are aimed." Officer recruitment was
not seen as a problem. However, the services were already experiencing some difficulty in meeting their goals for high quality
enlisted men, and projections of a declining youth population in
the eighties signaled a worsening situation. In that context, the
slower growth in the number of enlisted women the services had
programmed for 1979 through 1983 was out of sync. With 1.8 million enlisted positions to fill, the question was: How many could or
should be filled by women?

Hunter's conclusion: "The recruiting of more high school
graduate women for active duty in the all-volunteer force can have
two effects: (1) to improve quality or (2) save money."

Contrary to what had been feared at the outset of the AVF, the
quality of new recruits—as measured by such indicators as mental
aptitude and educational attainment—had actually increased following the removal of the draft. One factor contributing to this
qualitative increase was the expanded recruitment of women who
were required to meet higher standards. More than 91 percent of
all female recruits were high school graduates as compared with
less than 67 percent of the men, and all the female recruits were
average or above average in intelligence.

Hunter's analysis revealed that high quality women and low
quality men were cheaper to recruit than additional high quality
men. According to Hunter, the recruiting and advertising effort
and expense that had to be put out in order to attract enough high
quality men (i.e., high school graduates, upper mental categories)
to meet the services' requirements for new recruits also attracted
more women high school graduates, top mental categories, than
the services planned to accept. It also attracted more lower quality

men than the services wanted. In other words, it would have been cheaper to put out less effort and take more high quality women and lower quality men than to go to all that trouble and expense to go after a larger share of the cream of the male crop.

Because of the relative attractiveness of the services, the cost differentials varied from service to service, but the pattern was the same. For example, based on the services' own data, the Army spent about $3,700 to recruit a high quality man versus $150 for a comparable quality woman or a lower quality man. The Air Force, with the smallest differential of the four services, estimated its costs at $870 and $150, respectively. Hunter concluded that if the services were to attempt to sustain their quality level of male accessions as the number of available men declined, the costs would go up. By substituting women, the services could save in excess of $1 billion annually by 1982 (Binkin and Bach estimated the figure at $6 billion)—an attractive option to any budget-conscious administration.

Thus, while the 1972 decision to expand the use of women had been based on the AVF's personnel needs, these new data, the first based on a volunteer recruiting environment, strongly suggested that budgetary factors supported the correctness of that decision. While the draft existed, it had always been contended that women were more expensive to recruit—and they were. Without the draft, the tables were turned. The law of supply and demand was at work: the demands of the services for female recruits, though greater than ever, continued to fall far short of the supply of quali-fied young female applicants. As opportunities for women ex-panded, so did the supply.

However, as Binkin and Bach pointed out, the services' plans for utilizing women were tapering off. While just over 113,400 women were on active duty (including the health professions), future plans called for comparatively small increases to 157,000 by 1982. Whether this modest increase represented a real chal-lenge to their recruiting capabilities was unknown, and none of the services cared enough to do market research on the subject to find out.

The services did not even have a fix on their potential for using women, since they had never contemplated that their outer limits would ever be tested. It was this question that the Binkin and Bach study raised and that Hunter tackled head on: What were the limits?

The services were asked to submit to the DOD data from their own manpower programs to be used to evaluate their potential for utilizing women. In that evaluation, the overriding issue was not *cost* effectiveness but *combat* effectiveness. And in that context, other factors came into play. First, women tend to be physically weaker than men, which limits some of the work they can do; second, women were excluded by law and/or policy from combat units and positions calling for combat skills. These two factors reduced utilization and assignment flexibility. Hunter found most of the other arguments favoring both more and fewer women in the military to be "centered on emotionalism" and "supported by unsubstantiated generalities, or isolated examples."

Because there were so many unknowns, many people cautioned against moving too fast in expanding the roles and numbers of women: "We should err on the side of national security," cautioned the Army, "until such time as we have confidence that the basic mission of the Army can be accomplished with significantly more female content in the active force." In other words, men had proven themselves in combat for centuries and, therefore, we know the Army will fight effectively with men; we do not *know* that it will with women.

The services' own manpower data, however, revealed that the margin for such error was much greater than had been supposed, and that many more women could be used. Service submissions to the DOD indicated that, out of a total of 1.5 million enlisted and 244,500 officer positions, only 638,400 enlisted and 95,000 officer positions could be identified as either combat or combat support. This left a staggering 863,000 enlisted and nearly 150,000 officer positions as theoretically available to women— again, with wide variations among the services.

The obvious conclusions were that the services could utilize far more women than they had planned to (more than twice as many) without disturbing combat effectiveness, and that significant economies and force quality improvements would result. This was thoroughly consistent with Binkin and Bach's study.

However, the services used a variety of techniques for reducing these "available" positions to levels more acceptable to their leadership. For example, the Navy and Marine Corps insisted that, because of shipboard assignments, the rotation base requirements should apply to 55–75 percent of the otherwise available enlisted positions. The Air Force, with very little justification for rotation base, determined that lack of "adequate facilities" for women was a problem. It had been decided, for example, that for single enlisted men and women sharing the same hallway in a dormitory was unacceptable.

The Army's system of limiting the number of positions available was the most elaborate and the most dubious of all. DOD estimates would have allowed the Army to double the number of enlisted women and to triple WAC officer strength. But the Army contended that it should not be forced to increase the number of enlisted women above the 50,400 planned for 1979 and beyond until it had evaluated the impact of such increases upon mission effectiveness. After all, the Army reasoned, it had already taken the brunt of the expansion in both numbers and percentages of women in the last five years and had devoted considerable study effort to the use of additional women.

In its 8 March 1977 submission to the DOD, the Army insisted on the need for "systematic study of the effectiveness of women in Army units and their impact on mission performance under conditions of deployment or in time of war." In addition, it stressed "data must be collected and analyzed to determine the cost effectiveness of women soldiers." The DOD was informed that when the results of these studies became sufficiently clear, "the Army will adjust its female force accordingly."

The Army's own data identified no less than 53,000 officer and 217,000 enlisted positions that were neither combat or combat support nor required as a rotation base (nearly 33 percent of the officer and 38 percent of the enlisted positions).

This was fully consistent with Army estimates made as far back as 1942. However, in order to justify holding the numbers of enlisted women to the planned figure of 50,400, the Army applied an arbitrary system of percentages to its units based on each unit's expected distance from front-line or forward combat areas in wartime. Percentages ranged from zero, in units operating forward of brigade level near the enemy contact boundary, to as high as — but not to exceed — 50 percent, in units not expected to leave the continental United States in an emergency. The Army limited the maximum number of women it could use by applying these percentages to all units.

Moreover, claiming the necessity to provide acceptable "promotion, rotation, and management flexibility," the Army set up additional constraints through an exquisitely complex and biased system of analyses, published under the innocuous title "Women Enlisted Expansion Model" or WEEM. For example, all E-3 (private first class) clerk-typist positions in Army *combat* units were reserved for men. But in major command headquarters and in the Pentagon, E-4 (corporal) and E-5 (sergeant) positions could be filled by women or men. So, to provide promotion opportunity for male clerk-typists in combat units, many headquarters positions were set aside for men.

By this and similar one-sided rationales, the number of positions available to women was systematically reduced until the total reached 50,400, a number more acceptable to the Army leadership. An exercise designed to come up with a preconceived tolerable strength level, this was a classic example of a decision in search of a rationale.

The Army submitted a report entitled *Women in the Army Study*, dated December 1976, to support its arguments against further increases in women. This document was patently biased. For example, to prove that women were uneconomical, it devoted an entire chapter to lost time problems associated with pregnancy and sole-parent dependency of women but made no mention of areas where lost time rates favored women, e.g., disciplinary absences, AWOL, drug use, and alcohol abuse. In reality, overall, lost time for women, even including pregnancy, was lower than that for Army men. Women also scored higher than men in retention rates.

In the final analysis, the Army was hoist by its own petard with a series of studies and tests called *The Women Content in the Army*, which examined the performance of individual units with women in the field under simulated combat conditions. Two tests were conducted in connection with this study: MAX-WAC and REFWAC. The first tested women in three-day field exercises with the units' female content ranging from zero to 35 percent. The second studied women in sustained combat-related exercises in 1977 during the NATO annual "REFORGER" exercises in Europe.

The explicit purpose of the MAX-WAC experiment was to assess the effect on unit performance of varying proportions of women soldiers in Army companies, with the implicit purpose of providing guidance in the formulation of policies regarding the use of women in the ranks. In theory, the test was expected to reveal what proportion of women in a unit would produce a deterioration in unit performance, on the assumption that there is an upper limit to the proportion of women that even a noncombat company could contain and still function effectively. The decision to set the maximum proportion at 35 percent is instructive in that it implies that the designers of the test presumed that the critical mass whereat women would draw down unit effectiveness must be somewhere between zero and 35 percent. The REFORGER exercise provided a thirty-day test of the same concept in a situation as close to simulated combat conditions as possible.

The tests proved, to the surprise of many and the consternation of others, that women in support and combat-support units and in combat unit headquarters above battalion level did not adversely impact unit performance. "When properly trained and led," the Army found, "women are proving to be good soldiers in the field, as well as in garrison." This was a lesson it could have learned from a review of the WAC record in World War II.

After examining all the available evidence, Hunter drew his own conclusions:

> The tradeoff in today's recruiting market is between a high quality female and a low quality male. The average woman available to be recruited is smaller, weighs less, and is physically weaker than the vast majority of male recruits. She is also much brighter, better educated (a high school graduate), scores much higher on the aptitude tests and is much less likely to become a disciplinary problem.
>
> To put the question bluntly: Is recruiting a male high school dropout in preference to a smaller, weaker, but higher quality female erring on the side of national security, in view of the kinds of jobs which must be done in today's military? The answer to that question is central to the decision on how many women should be used in the various Services. Sometimes the answer will be yes, and sometimes it will be no, but the question continues to be relevant.[1]

Hunter made no recommendations as to what the services numerical goals should be, but with all the facts laid out the direction seemed obvious. Consequently, after a review and discussion with service leaders, Harold Brown directed that the number of enlisted women be doubled by 1983.

Subsequently, the goals were raised to over a quarter of a million by 1985. By that point, women would represent over 12 percent of the forces, as shown on the accompanying chart. However, these plans would be challenged in 1981 by a new administration.

TOTAL NUMBER OF WOMEN ON ACTIVE DUTY *

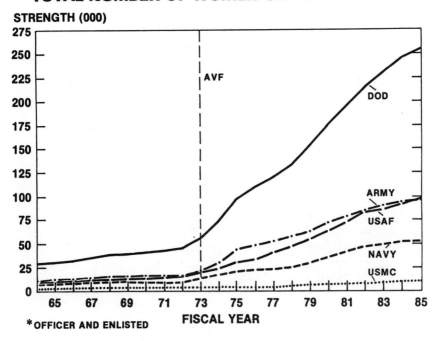

STRENGTH (000)

*OFFICER AND ENLISTED   FISCAL YEAR

NOTE

1. "Use of Women in the Military," Office of the Assistant Secretary of Defense (Manpower, Reserve Affairs and Logistics) (background study), May 1977.

CHAPTER 19

POLICIES CATCHING UP
WITH REALITIES

The pursuit of these two goals, equal opportunity and greater utilization, may well bring about the most revolutionary policy changes experienced in the history of military women.

Report on the Utilization of Military Women, by the All-Volunteer Task Force, December 1972

THE NEED TO expand the numbers of women for the all-volunteer force in the seventies coincided accidentally, but fortunately, with the national drive for women's legal and economic equality. This convergence precipitated the first major overhaul of service laws and regulations since the creation of the WAAC in World War II. It resulted in stunning reversals of policies long regarded as inviolable. It swept away the majority of those sex discriminating rules that prevented women from being assimilated into the military mainstream, and although significant barriers were still in place at the end of the decade, integration progressed faster and farther than even the most visionary military planner would have thought possible. Gradually, the selection criteria were equalized; most all-female procurement/training programs were combined with previously all-male programs; assignments to most non-combat and many combat units were handled on an interchangeable basis; promotion lists and career monitoring for women were incorporated with men's; family policies were revised; and the women's support systems were abolished.

In the end, the services' own personnel management needs

propelled many of the changes. The need to recruit ever growing numbers of people and to absorb them into the military work force required greater flexibility in selection, training, and utilization. Separate, dual systems simply were too wasteful and cumbersome to meet the services' needs.

Economist John Maynard Keynes once observed, "The difficulty lies not in new ideas, but in escaping from old ones." In the conservative world of the military, this is especially difficult. By 1970, the rules governing women in the services for the better part of three decades were entrenched traditions. Despite the obvious benefits to be gained in eliminating dual personnel systems, many men and women firmly resisted the change, often highly emotionally and occasionally irrationally. Many were sincerely convinced that relaxing the restrictions on women and further integrating them into the services would undermine the military's ability to perform its primary functions.

Military women themselves, both active and retired, were split on many of the issues and on whether a fundamental change in their status would benefit or harm them and the armed forces. Even the directors often found themselves marching to different drummers. Some service policies were revised with a director's active participation, others over her strong objections. The DACOWITS membership was also pulled in opposite directions; in the end, committee consensus usually came down on the side of change.

1970–72: THE PRESSURES BUILD

Before 1970, the defense establishment was incredibly insensitive to the presence of military women. Rarely in any public statement by top-level officials or in published materials were references made to the women who served in the armed forces. Except for the brief flurries in 1966 and 1967 over lifting the grade ceilings and modestly increasing strength, the services largely ignored women even in matters that directly affected them—it was as though women did not exist or did not count.

This myopia was dramatically demonstrated with the publication in August 1969 of the "Department of Defense Human Goals." Promulgated in response to civil rights (i.e., racial) pressures, the document was distributed worldwide for prominent display in offices and shops throughout the armed forces. Ostentatiously lettered in calligraphy on parchment in full color with the official DOD seal, the Goals bore the signatures of the Secretary and Deputy Secretary of Defense, the three service Secretaries, the Chairman of the Joint Chiefs of Staff, and the four service Chiefs. The Goals spoke eloquently of the need to show respect for the "service man" as a person, recognizing "his individual needs, aspirations, and capabilities," and of the need to make military and civilian service in the department "a model of equal opportunity for all regardless of race, creed, or national origin." Incredibly, even for that time, the Goals did not mention women.

Only after an incredulous DACOWITS took DOD officials to task during the committee's spring 1970 meeting did the DOD hastily revise the statement to include women. The new version carried the same date as the original even though several signatures had changed, apparently to avoid calling attention to the original error. (See Appendix #4.)

A year later, when the DOD published its new directive entitled "Equal Opportunity Within the Department of Defense" (Directive No. 1100.15, December 1970), it did not repeat its earlier mistake. Much had happened in the intervening months to make the Pentagon more aware of women's presence. Indeed, 1970 can be seen as the watershed year for women in the armed forces, the year in which important national events converged to force the issue: President Nixon decided to go for the all-volunteer force and Congress debated the Equal Rights Amendment. This was also the year when women began to attack military sex discrimination in the courts for the first time. During the next decade, Congress, the courts, and a succession of administrations constantly pressured the services to bring policies and regulations into line with contemporary concepts of equal opportunity and personnel management.

IMPACT OF THE EQUAL RIGHTS AMENDMENT

Most legal experts concurred that a ratified ERA would profoundly affect military personnel policy. As it turned out, the mere fact that Congress passed the amendment provoked a strong reaction in the Pentagon because some of the most heated debates evolved around issues of women's relationship to the military— namely, to the draft and to combat.

Although Congress had constitutional authority to draft women and to permit them to serve in combat, it had always chosen not to do the former and to discourage, though not to ban outright, the latter. Under the ERA, the question became whether the Constitution would *require* either or both. Experts disagreed. According to Congresswoman Martha Griffiths, the principal sponsor in the House, the ERA would require women to serve under a draft though, as men do, only in positions for which they were fit, implying that women found "fit" could be assigned to combat roles. Senator Birch Bayh, a cosponsor in the Senate, argued that the amendment would allow Congress to exempt women from military service on the grounds of "compelling reasons" of public policy.

During the House Judiciary Committee hearings on the amendment in April 1971, William H. Rehnquist, then the Assistant Attorney General of the United States (later appointed to the U.S. Supreme Court), was asked to provide a legal opinion on the amendment's probable effects on various matters, including the military draft. He presented the Department of Justice's legal opinion:

> The question here is whether Congress would be required either to draft both men and women or to draft no one. A closely related question is whether Congress must permit women to volunteer on an equal basis for all sorts of military service, including combat duty. We believe that the likely result of passage of the equal rights amendment is to require both of those results. . . . [T]hat would not require or permit women any more than men to undertake duties for which they are physically unqualified under some generally applied standard.[1]

The Senate report on the amendment clearly showed the Congressional intent on women and the draft. It stated:

> It seems likely . . . that the ERA will require Congress to treat men and women equally with respect to the draft. This means that, if there is a draft at all, both men and women who meet the physical and other requirements, and who are not exempt or deferred by law, will be subject to conscription. . . .
>
> Of course, the ERA will not require that all women serve in the military any more than all men are now required to serve. Those women who are physically or mentally unqualified, or who are conscientious objectors, or who are exempt because of their responsibilities (e.g., certain public officials; or those with dependents) will not have to serve, just as men who are unqualified or exempt do not serve today. Thus the fear that mothers will be conscripted from their children into military service if the Equal Rights Amendment is ratified is totally and completely unfounded. Congress will retain ample power to create legitimate sex-neutral exemptions

from compulsory service. For example, Congress might well decide to exempt all parents of children under 18 from the draft.[2]

Sen. Sam Ervin, leading the charge against the ERA on Capitol Hill had proposed an amendment to the bill to specifically exempt women from the draft, knowing full well it would kill chances to enact the ERA. The ploy succeeded in the Ninety-first Congress, but a similar maneuver two years later was foiled by a seventy-three to eighteen margin. Ervin's companion amendment to exempt women from serving in combat units suffered the same fate. In this case, the senator pulled out all the emotional stops, arguing passionately to "prevent sending the daughters of America into combat to be slaughtered or maimed by the bayonets, the bombs, the bullets, the grenades, the mines, the napalm, the poison gas, and the shells of the enemy." The vote went seventy-one to eighteen against him, and Congress enacted the unamended ERA on 22 March 1972 by an overwhelming majority, signaling to women that equal responsibility as a citizen accompanied equal opportunity. The message beamed to the armed forces was that they would not be exempt from the mandate of the ERA if and when it became part of the Constitution.

In the early seventies, Pentagon leaders believed that the ERA would very likely be ratified by the states. The conviction provided the first clear mandate for the services to review their laws and policies to determine the ERA's full impact. The question of drafting women was sidestepped when President Nixon decided to let induction authority expire and to stop drafting men; but other issues could not be put off.

While Congress debated the ERA, the White House pressured all governmental agencies to improve the utilization and status of women in federal employment. On 1 March 1972, not satisfied with the Defense Department's progress, the director of the Office of Management and Budget (OMB) sent a letter to Secretary of Defense Melvin R. Laird concerning the "less than full compliance toward the President's objective of full employment opportunity for women in many Federal departments." The OMB expected DOD, as the largest employer in the government, to play a "lead-the-way" role. Accordingly, it asked Laird to evaluate the current recruiting, training, and assignment practices of the department as they affected "minority groups and civilian women, and women as members of the military services."

On 6 April 1972, Roger T. Kelley, the Assistant Secretary of

Defense for Manpower and Reserve Affairs, in a letter to the military departments, cited considerable variation in the treatment of men and women and between women in different services. He said that "while certain restrictions in assignment and physical standards are justified, there is little apparent need for many discriminatory regulations." Kelley, who instructed the services to take action to eliminate unnecessary distinctions and, where appropriate, to recommend legislation to strike out inequities, stated:

> The effective utilization of women in the Armed Forces can be greatly improved by the elimination of regulations which create distinctions which are burdensome. Separate organizations and restricted assignments do not provide adequate career opportunity for women even though pay and promotion potential are equal to that of men.

No doubt the Pike subcommittee's biting criticism during its 6 March hearings on the use of military women gave the DOD incentive to interject itself in an unprecedented fashion into service personnel policy. The subcommittee insisted that the military could rely less on the draft if it made more vigorous efforts to recruit women and if it provided better job opportunities for them. The subcommittee recommended, as a first step, that Congress eliminate any and all discriminatory laws.

Although no evidence suggests that Congress took the subcommittee's recommendation immediately to heart, George Daoust, then heading up the DOD AVF Task Force, did. The AVF Task Force's study of the utilization of military women, published in 1972, identified several policies that prevented the maximum use of women in support of the AVF goals. It contended, for example, that higher enlistment standards and policies that denied enlistment to married women and those with dependents reduced the pool of qualified women, and that "until the discriminatory restrictions are removed, the pool of qualified women is unnecessarily constricted to the detriment of the Services and in a manner inconsistent with the Human Goals of the Department of Defense." It correctly pointed out that restrictive assignment policies had two main negative effects on increased use of women:

> First, large numbers of women will not be attracted to volunteer for military service unless interesting, challenging, and rewarding occupations are open to them. Second, the maximum number of women who can be effectively used in the military service is directly related to the number of occupations open to them.

The task force believed that "as assignment policies for women and men become more standardized, men and women will become much more interchangeable in military assignments."[3]

The task force labeled the notorious enlisted attrition rates as "the most powerful argument used against increasing the use of military women," contending that the higher attrition rates appeared to result from service policies and were not inherent in the women who volunteer for military service. Noting that the Air Force had managed to effect a remarkable decline in annual loss rates—from 48 percent in 1960 to 26 percent in 1972—by changing some of its policies, the report suggested that by adopting similar changes the other services could do the same.

Unexpectedly, the ultimate catalyst in revising discriminatory policies was not the Congress, the White House, or the DOD —it was the federal courts. Beginning in 1970, the services were hit with a series of lawsuits brought by military women who challenged the constitutionality of policies on equal protection grounds. Traditionally, the courts had deferred to Congress and the executive branch in issues involving military personnel policy on the grounds that such matters were best left to those charged with national defense and with special expertise in military affairs. Moreover, the Supreme Court had, as yet, never found a sex classification in law to be in violation of the equal protection clause of the Constitution. The Court required only that the government show that such a classification have some "rational" reason for treating men and women differently for a statute to be upheld. Needless to say, meeting so loose a test—especially when the vagaries of "national security" could be invoked—was not difficult.

The situation changed dramatically in 1971 when the Supreme Court struck down a statute drawing a sex-based classification, ruling that such a classification "must be reasonable, not arbitrary, and must rest upon some ground of difference having a fair and substantial relation to the objective of the [law] so that all persons similarly circumstanced shall be treated alike." Thus, laws challenged on the basis of sex discrimination would now be required to meet a more rigid test to be found constitutional.

By that time, military women were already challenging service policies on constitutional grounds, much to the services' astonishment and concern. Although most of these early suits were unsuccessful, the services feared defending their policies in courts that were already showing marked inclinations in the direction of civil rights and that were in the shadow of the ERA debates. The services also recognized that because the policies in litigation were rooted in social stereotypes rapidly falling into disrepute, they were extremely vulnerable to challenge by civil rights groups, most particularly the American Civil Liberties Union. Clearly, the military had to update policies, find better justifications for them, or risk having the courts strike them down.

The last thing the services wanted was outside interference in military personnel policy. Faced with these pressures, each military department embarked on its own extensive review of sex-discrimination rules. These reviews were the first real steps toward reform. Initially, the studies inclined toward labored justifications for retaining the status quo, but it is safe to say that, in the process, all the services were surprised to learn, really for the first time, the extent of the problem. Certainly the Air Force, which had always so proudly proclaimed that its women were "integrated," was surprised to find no less than thirty-two laws and policies that treated Air Force men and women differently.

One by one over the ensuing ten years, the barriers toppled over, sometimes catapulted by sweeping decisions, more often downed by the laborious process of studies, tests, hearings, and litigation.

As a first step to absorb large numbers of women and to afford them equal career opportunities, the services had to take a hard look at segregated women's programs and double standards for entrance and, wherever possible, to "coeducationalize" previously all-male programs. Up to this point, the only officer commissioning program conducted on a coeducational basis was the Air Force's Officer Training School.

While most public speculation focused on women in the prestigious service academies, the preliminary skirmishes were fought over the Reserve Officers Training Corps (ROTC). Contrary to a popular misconception that most officers in the armed forces are academy graduates, the vast majority, nine out of ten, actually receive their commissions through either ROTC or officer candidate school–type programs. Conducting these programs on a coeducational basis was therefore essential to expanding career roles for military women. In 1969, the Air Force made the first move. It somewhat reluctantly opened its ROTC to women on a test basis. This venture's unexpected and extraordinary success led to the eventual abandonment of all separate women's commissioning programs and ultimately spurred the enrollment of women in the service academies.

Historically, one of the major shortcomings of the Air Force integration concept had been its lack of a firm, consistent system of WAF officer procurement or strength objectives; the program simply drifted, the victim of benign (often malign) neglect. Following the Korean War, the Air Force had cut off sources of WAF officer procurement by terminating direct appointments and phasing down enrollments in coeducational OCS. OCS, which was chiefly a means of providing commissioning of enlisted personnel, was gradually replaced by Officer Training School (OTS), which was designed to commission college graduates who had not participated in ROTC.

Although OTS was coeducational, its yearly "objectives" on the number of women participating were in fact ceilings on the number of women who could be commissioned as line officers. The Air Force adjusted the WAF ceilings downward each time it reduced overall officer year-end strengths—but never upward when it increased them. The net effect was to curtail or close off entirely WAF officer commissioning in the second half of nearly every fiscal year: in 1955, for example, only fifteen WAF officers were commissioned. This process produced instability in the WAF officer accessions and a declining strength. In the late 1950s, as the result of a study done by then Maj. Jeanne Holm, the Air Force had embarked on a test of coeducational AFROTC at a few selected colleges; but interest was minimal, and the program was jettisoned before it really got off the ground.

By 1969, however, coeducational AFROTC was made to order. There was no logical reason not to allow women to obtain commissions through this program, which was attractive to college students since it offered scholarships to those seeking degrees in skills critical to the services (e.g., engineering, science, and so forth) in exchange for military commitments. In effect, young women had been denied these educational benefits; and in excluding women, the services had been denying themselves a valuable source of needed skills.

The final impetus came from Dr. Theodore C. Marrs, Deputy Secretary for Reserve Affairs. He telephoned WAF Director Holm: "Do you or don't you want women in ROTC?" drawled Marrs.

"Yes, I do," she replied, "but, as you know, my boss is dead set against it; so my hands are tied."

Marrs well knew that the Chief of Personnel, Lt. Gen. John W. Carpenter III, was not amenable to having women in the program. He also knew that Lt. Gen. Albert P. Clark, who was in charge of AFROTC, was against it. "I just wanted to know how you felt," Marrs said. "Sit tight and I'll see what I can do."

In July 1968, Marrs requested the air staff's views on the matter. After four months of study and debate, the staff reluctantly submitted a compromise proposal to test the enrollment of women at four colleges in the two-year program (junior/senior years) only, beginning in 1970. In January 1969, Assistant Secretary for Manpower and Reserve Affairs J. William Doolittle approved the plan but specified that it begin that fall in at least four campuses, to be expanded to ten by the following year.

Doolittle more than anyone else seemed to understand the problems of the WAF program. He also saw the inevitability of an increased role for women in the military in the future. Not only did he set the ball rolling on their participation in AFROTC, but he also approved a plan submitted by the WAF director to stabilize officer accessions through OTS at 225 per year, and, much to the surprise and dismay of the personnel staff, specified that any production from AFROTC would be in *addition* to and *not in lieu* of OTS accessions. Thus, for the first time a fixed floor was set for WAF officer accessions, with no ceiling, and a second source of women officers began to materialize.

Because the decision on AFROTC came so late in the academic year, only seven women were able to get into the 1969 summer field training, a prerequisite to enrollment as juniors in the fall. However, the program's success was immediately apparent to everyone involved. The women were of exceptionally high quality, and they performed far beyond anyone's expectations. Moreover, and of far greater importance, the air science professors were reporting that the women's presence had enhanced acceptance of AFROTC on campus, a phenomenon significant to the Army and Navy as well as the Air Force.

Before the academic year was half over, the Air Force extended the program, including four-year as well as the two-year courses, to all interested host campuses. That fall, eighty-one campuses offered coed AFROTC, and over five hundred women enrolled. Moreover, in at least one instance, the women in the program outnumbered the men. At Ohio State, which had been the first to lobby for coed AFROTC, the commander of cadets was a woman, Sue Orkins. The following spring, the first women received commissions as second lieutenants through AFROTC; and by the fall of 1971, 154 campuses offered the program and enrollments had doubled.

Meanwhile, Army and Navy professors of military and naval sciences, witnessing the Air Force program's phenomenal success, were unsuccessfully pushing to enroll women in their ROTC programs. Much of the resistance was coming from the offices of the WAC and WAVE directors, who preferred separate women's programs as a means of controlling the training and the quality of women officers and who feared that a coeducational ROTC would jeopardize them. They also believed that the ROTC curricula were not suitable to women officers' needs.

In 1972, however, the Army moved out on an experimental basis at ten campuses, and the Navy tested the program on five campuses. Both were a success. By 1979, a total of 20,000 women were enrolled in ROTC, 2,100 of whom were on scholarships. One in four of the Army ROTC enrollees was a woman, one in five of the Air Force's, and one in twenty of the Navy's. By then, ROTC had become a primary source of women officers.

Women were also gaining ground in Officer Candidate Schools. Navy women were being exposed to the mysteries of the deep at Newport, where they joined male officer candidates in the study of seamanship, navigation, and damage control, in addition to the usual courses in naval orientation, leadership, management, and administration. In 1973, the first coed class in the history of the Naval Officer Candidate School was graduated.

In 1975, a congressional mandate decreed that the service academies would admit women in the fall of 1976, thus wiping out any justification for the services to continue any separate commissioning programs for women. In November 1976, WAC officer candidates began attending integrated OCS at Fort Benning, Georgia, and in 1977 the separate WAC commissioning programs were discontinued.

The macho Marine Corps was the last to succumb, and then only temporarily. In no service did a coeducational officer training program seem more unlikely. Yet in 1976, the Commandant, Gen. Louis H. Wilson, mandated a review of the requirement for separate women's units and training. The new commander of the women's company of the Marine Corps Basic School, Maj. Barbara E. Dolyak, was questioning the differences in training given to male and female officers. At that time, the twelve-week Women Officer Basic Course for newly commissioned women marine second lieutenants was geared to prepare women for the limited duties prescribed for a female officer. The longer, more demanding twenty-six-week men's course was designed to educate all young male officers in the standards of professional knowledge, esprit de corps, and leadership traditional to the Marines Corps, with special emphasis on the duties and responsibilities of the infantry platoon officer.

However, despite the popular image of the Corps, not all new marine officers became infantry officers. Only 18 percent were assigned to the infantry in 1976, and that was projected to decrease to 12 percent in 1977. Thus, 82 percent of the men commissioned were assigned to other fields—aviation, support, and services; in 1977, the proportion would reach 88 percent. Why, then, the heavy emphasis on infantry training? So that all could share a common education and have a greater appreciation for and understanding of the role and needs of the infantryman, who was, after all, the heart and soul of the Corps' mission. All would share this experience except newly commissioned women officers, even though their jobs and responsibilities would be identical to those of many men officers.

"Why can't the women do it?" Dolyak wondered. If ever the time was ripe for change, it was now. "If it is essential that male lawyers and supply officers share this commonality of experience with the infantryman, why isn't it important for the women?" Dolyak asked officials almost rhetorically, knowing there was no logical answer.[4]

As for the women themselves, by the mid-seventies many of the new marine second lieutenants were products of the recently integrated naval ROTC rather than the all-women OCS program. "These women are ready to go," said Dolyak. They expected more integrated military training and were not placated by the official explanation for the abbreviated course for women. They were especially incensed when issued rubber rifles for a combined field exercise.

After much study and debate, in January 1977 twenty-two female second lieutenants entered the twenty-one-week Basic Course as members of Charlie Company, and the women's twelve-week course was discontinued. Although assigned to an all-female platoon, soon dubbed "Charlie's Angels," the women were attached in small groups to the other platoons. Coeducation had finally arrived, but not for long. The next Commandant had second thoughts and partially resegregated the program. The explanation of this turnabout given by Brig. Gen. Margaret Brewer was that extensive press coverage of women successfully completing the course raised charges in some circles that the Marine Corps officer training had gone soft.

However, in all the services, women officers were gradually integrated into the faculties and staff and some progressed into top command positions. Even the senior joint and service staff colleges, the National War College and the Industrial College of the Armed Forces, soon had female students, staff, and faculty members. The Joint Armed Forces Staff College admitted women from each service for the first time in 1969, and the first woman to attend the Air War College entered in 1970. Women had at last secured these important milestones in the careers of professional military officers that had so long been denied to them.

Meanwhile, dual standards for enlistment and segregated basic and boot training programs also came under scrutiny—with mixed results. The Air Force went to single enlistment standards for men and women—except for those based on legitimate physical differences such as height and weight, which were adjusted to compensate for the difference in body structure between the sexes—and consolidated basic training at Lackland.

There was no consistent pattern among the other services, however. The Army consolidated male and female basic training but was reluctant to lower female enlistment standards to those of the men's, which were much lower than the Air Force's. It eventually did so in 1978 but was unhappy with the results and reverted to higher standards for women. The Navy and Marine Corps, on the other hand, continued to insist that the mental and educational requirements for women should remain higher since they were able to meet their recruiting objectives, and saw no reason not to accept the highest quality recruits possible. Both contended that if in the future they were unable to meet their numerical goals, they would adjust the criteria to ensure meeting the objectives. Combined, the two services were recruiting fewer women than either the Army or Air Force and were thus able to stick with the double standards.

The Navy consolidated boot training for men and women, but the Marines stood firm and continued to train enlisted recruits in segregated units, on the theory that male boot training was designed to produce combat-ready marines, with heavy emphasis on infantry skills. All other training courses attended by women were conducted on a coeducational basis, the women being segregated only for housing and for classes where sex differences warranted segregation, such as courses in personal hygiene, grooming, and some physical training. As women progressed up the promotion ladder, they attended coeducational NCO academies and leadership courses, were assigned as faculty and staff members, and served as drill instructors and in training positions previously held only by men.

But while women readily accepted men as drill instructors, the reverse was less successful. Many men resisted that type of instruction from enlisted women essentially because they perceived women as less convincing in the role of the tough drill sergeant. The fact that women were excluded from combat specialties also tended to detract from their credibility.

Women also suffered from role identification problems when put through military training programs designed traditionally "to make men out of boys"—the thrust of male basic and boot training. Much of the traditional male training has more to do with the rites of manhood than the requirements of service jobs. While women often gained a sense of pride in accomplishing training (or surviving it), there was (and is) a concern for loss of feminine identity. More than a few have expressed the belief that the training was designed to make "little men" out of them; having to wear men's fatigues reinforced this belief. This may have been a factor in the decision of Gen. Robert H. Barrow, the Marine Corps' Commandant, to indoctrinate men and women marines separately. On more than one occasion, he said that while he wanted his men to be men, he wanted his women marines to remain women.

WEAPONS TRAINING

Weapons training, once taboo for women, became de rigueur. Beginning in 1975, the Army required all women to participate in individual weapons training. Enlisted women took to the firing range to learn basic rifle marksmanship and, during advanced individual training, learned to handle whatever weapon was required to meet the prerequisites of their specialties. Those assigned to combat support units learned to use light antitank weapons, M-16 rifles, grenade launchers, claymore mines, and M-60 machine guns. In the other services also, women were soon to be found on the firing ranges alongside their male counterparts.

BREAKING WITH PATTERNS OF JOB STEREOTYPING

Even before consolidation of procurement and indoctrination programs, utilization patterns began to shift as fields previously closed to women gradually opened up. Then, almost overnight, the entire philosophy of the services in the employment of women flipped from one of deliberate exclusion from all but the "women's jobs" to one of programmed inclusion in all but combat and direct combat–support jobs. Even there, some assignments crossed over that fuzzy line into what could properly be classified as combat.

The metamorphosis from "typewriter soldiers" to mainstream military personnel began in the late sixties with the gradual opening of occupations choked off during the post–Korean War period. This was followed by service decisions in 1970–72 to allow women to work in all fields except: those beyond the physical capabilities of most women, those few still considered "socially undesirable," and those closed because of combat restrictions. Soon the services permitted women to serve in essentially all noncombat jobs. However, women were actually being assigned to only 44 percent of the jobs open in the Marine Corps, 63 percent in the Army, 70 percent in the Air Force, and 72 percent in the Navy. Most women were still in administrative and medical slots because recruiters failed to explain women's new options. Also, many women preferred the more traditional jobs in which they knew they could perform and would be accepted, and for which future civilian job opportunities seemed better.

Clearly, the services needed a more aggressive approach to show a good-faith effort to counter charges of sex stereotyping and discrimination and to avoid saturating the traditional fields with women. Thus, beginning in 1972–73, the military designed programs to force a more balanced representation of women across the board in all but the combat and direct combat–support fields. These established numerical or percentage female objectives for accessions into each occupation, based upon best assessments of the potential pool of available, qualified recruits; and recruiters were assigned the often difficult task of filling these quotas. These were purely and simply sex-based affirmative-action quota systems, which established mandatory quotas on the hard-to-fill nontraditional occupations (e.g., mechanical, electronic, crafts, etc.) and caps on the easy-to-fill traditional white-collar occupations (e.g., administration, medical, dental, personnel, etc.).

Adherence to these quotas produced somewhat of a more balanced distribution of women across the board and some important breakthroughs. In 1972, some 90 percent of enlisted women were concentrated in traditional occupations; by 1980, the percentage dropped to 54.

The services could justifiably point with pride at their gains. Officers were flying huge jets and helicopters, teaching flying skills, sitting at the launch controls of ICBMs, standing watch on quarterdecks, and commanding large training centers and Coast Guard cutters. Enlisted women were maintaining fighter aircraft, trucks, missiles, tanks, helicopters, and computers; operating construction equipment, small craft, forklifts, and ships' stores; refueling aircraft on the ground and in flight; and controlling motor vehicle traffic, air traffic, and harbor traffic. There was scarcely a skill open to them in which women could not be found.

However, before long, some disquieting trends became evident, especially in the enlisted force. Because of the services' overly ambitious recruiting goals for women to serve in the nontraditional occupations, many otherwise qualified women were being denied entry or delayed for extended periods because the female ceilings in traditional fields were met. Consequently, many accepted fields they did not want and were often only marginally qualified for, simply to get in with the idea of cross-training into something else later. Also, because the services had not established standards for measuring strength, stamina, and other physical requirements for jobs, some women were assigned to jobs that they could not perform or that required them to work to the outer limits of their capabilities. On the other hand, men were in jobs that used only a fraction of their physical capabilities—jobs that women normally performed with ease.

As evidence of misclassification mounted, the services built in greater flexibility to allow adjustments in the ratios of men and women into the occupational areas and back-filling to ensure meeting overall accession objectives. Even so, troublesome patterns of migration were becoming evident. As early as 1975, the WAF director, Col. Billie M. Bobbitt, expressed serious concern about poor utilization and low morale of women in nontraditional fields. Evidence soon mounted in all the services that a pattern was developing of migration out of the nontraditional back into the traditional fields on the part of both men and women. DOD data showed, for example, that 76 percent of the women trained in electronics equipment repair in 1973 had left the field by 1976, compared with 51 percent of the men. In the maintenance fields, the rates were running as high as 90 percent for women and 53 percent for men.

The rates for both men and women were shocking, but the bureaucracy's gut reaction was: "This is a woman's problem." It also chose to ignore a reverse situation in fields nontraditional to men. The data showed, for example, that some 60 percent of the men left the administration field, as compared to only 30 percent of the women; in medical/dental specialties, the rates were 54 percent for men and 25 percent for women. One should therefore conclude the fault lay not with the women, but with the classification system operating on artificial, sex-based quotas.

Although migration is unquestionably a personnel management problem of both men and women, with enormous retraining cost implications, the services continue to view it as a problem inherent with women per se and therefore uncorrectable, a price of doing business when they have women.

INTEGRATING OFFICER PROMOTIONS

One of the most important developments during this period was the consolidation of the officer promotion systems. Although this was an essential, inevitable step, it was not accomplished without a degree of trepidation on the part of the women involved, and its full impact would not be known for many years.

Until the late 1970s, the only service to maintain integrated officer promotions was the Air Force. In 1973, the DOD developed a comprehensive legislative package to provide, for the first time, uniform laws for managing the officer structures of the separate services. It was called the Defense Officer Personnel Management Act (DOPMA). Included in DOPMA were provisions to abolish separate female promotion lists in the Army, Navy, and Marine Corps and to integrate the women into the men's lists.

Because of its complexities and sheer volume, DOPMA did not fare well on Capitol Hill and by the late 1970s was given up for dead by most congressional experts. The Army, meanwhile, decided to disestablish the Women's Army Corps. It proposed, and got, separate legislation to authorize this and to integrate women into its male promotion lists. This left the Navy and Marine Corps women as the only segregated groups. In the last moments of the Carter administration, DOPMA was suddenly revived and, on 12 December 1980, enacted. It would take effect in September 1981, and at that point, the Navy and Marine Corps promotion lists would include women.

Military women viewed this development with mixed emotions. They wanted the full status that integrated promotions offered yet were apprehensive about whether they would be able to compete successfully. The older officers who had grown up under the old rules and who had been so long denied equal career opportunities felt especially handicapped in a competitive situation. The only legitimate comparison these officers had to go by was the experience of the Air Force, where promotions had been integrated for thirty years.

Unfortunately, women could take little comfort from the Air Force—quite the reverse. Historically, of the four services, Air Force women had fared the poorest in the promotion process. This could be graphically demonstrated: In 1978, for example, of the forty-eight women line colonels/captains in the four services, only three were in the integrated Air Force. This dearth of line full colonels has its roots in the integrated system and in naive assumptions about the inherent unbiased fairness of the military promotion process. The most crucial career points for an officer are selection for Regular augmentation and for promotion to major. Failure on either score can be fatal to a career. Historically, at both junctures, Air Force women's selection rates were less than half the selection rates scored by men. Also, checks by the WAF director clearly showed a consistent pattern of discrimination in the selection process wherein women with outstanding records were being passed over while some men with much lower ratings were selected.

The Air Force was quick to point out that it promotes not just on effectiveness ratings but on what it calls the "whole-man" concept. The proceedings of the selection boards are secret, but it is common knowledge that the system is weighted to favor the rated officer, the academy graduate, the unit commander, the officer with combat service, the professional school graduate, and the Regular officer. In each category, women have been either entirely excluded or at a disadvantage over the years. Also, a review by the Personnel Center found that even the effectiveness reports, which were supposed to be reflections of an individual's performance and future potential, were tainted with bias and laced with sexist remarks: for example, "In spite of the fact that she is a WAF officer, I can rate her as outstanding in the best of conscience," or "although she thinks like a man, she is always a lady and never too aggressive." Imagine the deleterious effect of such remarks on selection boards meeting in secret session where women are competing with men for a finite number of vacancies!

In recent years, many of these problems have been corrected, opportunities have improved, and attitudes have changed. However, in a closed personnel system, the mistakes of the past cast long shadows. Only the survivors of the past system made it to the twenty-one-year point to be considered for full colonel. In 1976, no female line officers were selected for colonel; only three were selected in 1977, and four in 1978. The Air Force looked so bad in comparison to the other services that, in an effort to make a better showing, it resorted to what one senior official referred to as "a bit of chicanery." In 1978, some of the best field grade nurses were offered transfers to the line. Understandably, the Surgeon General, Lt. Gen. George E. Schafer, was not happy about this: "We can ill afford to lose top quality nurses. . . . We must consider too that these women chose the nursing profession first, then elected to practice that profession in the Air Force." He need not have worried. There were no takers. As one savvy nurse put it, "You needn't think I'm going to give up my professional status to jump into that lion's den."

Despite the often discouraging results, however, Air Force women line officers always rejected suggestions of separate promotion quotas for women as a means of assuring parity of opportunity. "I don't want to have to apologize to anyone for any promotion I receive" was the usual comment. But, given the Air Force experience with integrated promotions, the women in the other services have reason to fear that they may indeed be stepping into a lion's den. This is especially true of older officers who were reared in the separate systems with built-in parity. Younger officers with a wider range of career opportunities may see things differently. However, it would be unrealistic to believe that a system still so heavily weighted toward operational experience of the kind as yet available on only a limited basis for women will be able to operate in an unbiased fashion.

END OF THE SUPPORT STRUCTURE: END OF AN ERA

The question in many women's minds was: Who will be watching to see that we receive a fair shake? The women's support structures set up in the wake of the Integration Act had traditionally kept an eye on such things and had survived almost intact until the early seventies. But by 1978, few vestiges remained. Even the acronyms—WAC, WAVES, and WAF—had been unceremoniously stamped out in the name of equality and integration. For better or worse, the women were on their own for the first time since 1942.

There can be little doubt that the continued existence of the women's support structures and the use of artificial acronyms perpetuated the notions of separateness, of uniqueness, of a special category within the service. With the decisions to end discrimination and to effect integration, these structures had to go. The only remaining questions were: When? and How?

The process started at the bottom with the gradual elimination of separate housing and administration of enlisted women, thus ending the cumbersome, often confusing system of dual command and divided loyalties. It was made possible in large part by the gradual replacement of the old World War II–type barracks and their common hallways, lack of privacy, and gang latrines with more modern, motel-like dormitories with semiprivate rooms and bath facilities. This new type of housing made it easier to accommodate a mixed population with the necessary privacy and protection. For the first time, integrating women into their duty organizations became practical. In the process, male commanders learned, often for the first time, that they could deal with "women's problems." Moreover, women officers were gradually given command of mixed units, something that had rarely happened before, and the services learned that women could indeed command men. By 1974, for example, twenty-one women in the Air Force were commanding predominantly male organizations (support groups, recruiting groups, communications squadrons, weather detachments, etc.). By the end of the seventies, two female major generals were commanding huge training installations: Air Force Maj. Gen. Norma Brown ran Chanute Technical Training Center, and Maj. Gen. Mary E. Clarke was in charge at Fort McClellan, Alabama, where the Army's military police and chemical warfare schools are located, along with coed basic training.

The first service to abolish the women's support structure was the Navy. Capt. Robin L. Quigley often referred to herself laconically as the "Great Mother of All Women" because she believed that was how Navy people had come to view the woman who occupied the position of Assistant Chief of Naval Personnel for Women (popularly known as the WAVE director). It was based on the belief that she controlled the fate of all Navy women, which she did not. Quigley referred to the acronym "WAVES" as "that cute little designator."

On 23 February 1972, Quigley published a memorandum to Navy women that produced what she described as an "unbelievable" and "violent" reaction from Navy men and women of all ranks. Simply entitled "Memorandum . . . #5" (which she said would probably be her last such communication), it announced, in effect, that the WAVES were being consigned to Davy Jones' locker, and implied that the women's support system would probably soon follow. "My intent is to make it quite clear that the unofficial title which has been attached to this billet . . . Director of the WAVES . . . is just that, unofficial, and I have stopped using it," she wrote. "It is gravely misleading in two ways. For one thing there is no such thing as 'THE WAVES'—for another, I do not *direct* it or anything else." She explained that the continued use of the term implied that women were members of a "ladies auxiliary" rather than of the U.S. Navy. "There IS an organization called the NAVY—you are in it—you can use its professional titles." No modifiers were required. Henceforth, she noted, women should refer to themselves simply as "officers," "petty officers," and so forth rather than as "WAVE officers" and "WAVE petty officers" if they expected to be recognized as full-fledged Navy professionals.

Having made that point, Quigley reminded them that under Adm. Elmo R. Zumwalt, the Chief of Naval Operations (CNO), "good things" were happening for women; and she announced that they would soon be taking one more step into the personnel system.[5] The desks that had traditionally handled women's actions in the Bureau of Naval Personnel were being absorbed into the appropriate offices, and the functions of the women's communications and advisory system in the Navy's command structure—

the Women's Representatives and Assistants for Women—were being suspended on a pilot basis.

Quigley correctly perceived that some women would believe the move to be disastrously wrong, that enlisted women would be thrown down the drain or to the dogs and that others would fault the timing: "Later, perhaps, but we are not ready for it yet." But Quigley said she had faith in the system and believed that with the changes wrought by Zumwalt, the stage was never better set. "If we women fail to shoulder the Challenge of Change as it affects us, to turn the corner with the rest of the Navy," she concluded, "then we will be relegated—and rightly so—to the perimeters of this profession tomorrow and forever."

Having said that, it was Quigley herself who in the end was unable to turn some of the most important corners of all—sending women to sea, to the air, and to the Naval Academy. In fact, many widely believed that her haste to abolish the support structure was motivated by her inability or unwillingness to get along with the CNO and the new challenges he proposed for women.

In January 1971, Quigley had been "deep selected" for the line director's position over a number of women much senior to her. She was young, bright, articulate, and attractive, and many anticipated that she would be the first woman admiral in the Navy. As it turned out, however, Quigley soon found herself at considerable odds with the CNO and a large segment of the Navy's women over the women's issues and how to deal with them. Her fall from grace was formalized in July 1972 when Zumwalt set up an ad hoc committee on equal rights for women in the Navy to study all the programs and come up with recommendations to the CNO. The committee was comprised of senior- and middle-grade male and female officers and chaired by Rear Adm. Charles F. Rausch. The senior woman on it was Capt. Fran McKee; Quigley was not included and had every reason to believe that it had been set up to circumvent her as the Assistant for Women because she had lost credibility with the CNO. She refused to attend its meetings.

Z-GRAM 116 (see Appendix #2), on the subject of equal rights for women, was the product of this committee. Because Quigley strongly disapproved of the message and disagreed with many of its tenets, she could not support it, much less participate in its implementation. She informed Zumwalt of her position, requested to be relieved from the job, and recommended her position be abolished.

Many Navy people, men as well as women, believed the time was not right to eliminate the office of the Assistant for Women. Now more than ever there was a need to have someone to ride herd on the new programs and coordinate actions. While Quigley was unable to take this on, there were other senior Navy women who believed in what Zumwalt was trying to do and would have welcomed the challenge.

In March 1973, Captain Quigley was reassigned to San Diego, California, as Commander of the Service School Command. The office established by Mildred McAfee in 1942 with much fanfare was quietly and unceremoniously consigned to the deep.

When Zumwalt retired the following year, many Navy traditionalists assumed the pressures on women's equality would let up. That proved to be premature. The issues of women's attendance at the Naval Academy and duty at sea were still very much alive in Congress and the federal courts. Also, a long list of inequities contained in the DOPMA package remained, the most important being the elimination of the separate promotion system and the limits on promotion to admiral.

The long survival of the WAF director's office is remarkable considering its peculiar status within the air staff in a position anomalous to the fundamental concept of integration. Its monitoring and oversight functions made it a constant burr under the saddle of other personnel agencies when it was doing its job and a nonentity to be ignored with impunity when it was not. From 1970 to 1974, Lt. Gen. Robert Dixon was Deputy Chief of Staff for Air Force Personnel. He set up a new management system to coordinate and monitor the entire personnel program. Issues affecting women were incorporated into each life cycle of the system from procurement to retirement. Theoretically, after all the issues were identified and staff agencies were assigned responsibility for follow-through actions, phasing out the WAF director's office would be possible.

When Col. Billie M. Bobbitt became director in March 1973, she had high hopes for the new system to take over monitoring women's issues. By the time she decided to retire two years later, her optimism had faded. She expressed her concerns in her end-of-tour report of April 1975 to Lt. Gen. John Roberts, who by then had replaced Dixon as the Head of Air Force Personnel. Bobbitt cited a number of pressing problems that she felt were not being adequately addressed by the Personnel staff, such as problems in nontraditional fields, officer promotions and effectiveness reports, and the issues of opening the Air Force Academy and flying jobs. Of particular concern to her was the existence within the Personnel staff of what she believed to be false assumptions that all the problems and issues concerning women were being dealt with effectively by the staff agencies, and that because "total integration" had already been achieved, there was really no longer a need for a WAF director. In reality, she contended, the workload of her office, rather than declining as it was supposed to, had steadily increased to the point that her staff could hardly cope.

Soon after Col. Bianca Trimeloni succeeded Bobbitt as director, she too realized she was in an untenable position. The WAF strength was exploding in record numbers and demands on the director were more than she and her tiny staff could deal with effectively. The air staff, on the other hand, was undergoing manpower reductions and she would be expected to cough up her share of positions. Trimeloni concluded that phasing out the office would be preferable to maintaining a skeleton staff totally incapable of coping with what was expected of it.

In June 1976, Trimeloni retired. At her suggestion, the office was unceremoniously dissolved. "I thought the timing was bad. It was too soon because the Air Force had a lot of problems yet," she said, "but there was really no other practical solution under the circumstances."

The Army's WAC Director was another matter. Because the director was required by statute (Sec. 3071, Title 10, USC), it was a more complicated problem. On 21 August 1972, the Chief of Staff directed that an ad hoc committee study the ERA's impact on the Army. The most serious implication involved the continued existence of the Women's Army Corps. At the outset, the committee assumed that the ERA would force the discontinuance of the separate women's corps; its studies, however, led them in the opposite direction. Its December 1972 report contended that "the existence of the Women's Army Corps does not in itself deny equal opportunity for women; conversely, the nonexistence of a women's corps does not insure equal opportunity." The committee's conclusion was:

> That the Women's Army Corps should be continued as a separate organi-
> zation for the primary purpose of providing privacy between the sexes by
> maintaining women's units, conducting women's basic training, and pro-
> viding officers trained to receive, administer and train large numbers of
> women in the event of mobilization.

It recommended that the Corps be retained for those purposes. In essence, the committee rationalized the Corps' continuation on the separate-but-equal philosophy used to defend racially segregated schools in earlier days but rejected by the federal courts. Six years later, the ERA remained unratified (and probably unratifiable) but the Women's Army Corps had ceased to exist.

In drafting DOPMA, the statutory requirements for a separate women's corps with the stipulation that all women commissioned in the Army (other than nurses and medical specialists) be appointed in the Corps was seen as inconsistent with the laws governing the other services. The DOD proposed that DOPMA include provisions to eliminate the WAC. The then Deputy Chief of Staff for Personnel, Lt. Gen. Bernard W. Rogers, agreed with repeal of Section 3071 but did not perceive this action as a signal for the immediate disestablishment of the Corps; he expected that the Corps would continue under Secretarial authority unless, or until, further study indicated otherwise. With repeal, the Army would then have the flexibility to move as it saw fit with respect to organizational structure for its womanpower. On 26 September 1973, Rogers asked his staff for recommendations on whether the WAC should be disestablished and, if so, on what timetable.

WAC Director Mildred Bailey, on the other hand, believed that if the Corps' statutory requirement were repealed, there would be no assurance that the Army would not take precipitous action to eliminate the key women's advisor positions, and that the positions themselves would lose authority and prestige. She also feared that abolishing the Corps would deny opportunity for women to be promoted to general officer rank. (To date, the only two line officers selected had been her and her predecessor, Hoisington.) On 18 October, Bailey apprised Chief of Staff Gen. Creighton W. Abrams of her views; and following this meeting, the provision to repeal Section 3071 was deleted from DOPMA.

The subject was by no means dead, however. A year later, on

7 October 1974, Army Secretary Howard H. Callaway resuscitated it in a memorandum to the Director of the Army Staff: "The time has come when we should consider elimination of the Women's Army Corps as a separate identified entity. The increasing role being assumed by women and their integration into practically every aspect of the Army, less combat units, would seem to support this idea." Bailey reacted immediately, insisting that before doing away with the Corps, a "detailed study" should be made and that this would take time. She believed that "precipitous actions" would be unwise, and important actions needed to be taken before any phase-out of the WAC. "Radical, overnight changes will promote 'women's lib in uniform,' thereby, in all probability, forcing actions which would not be desirable," she wrote to the Director of Personnel Management.

Six months later, during hearings on DOPMA, the DOD unsuccessfully attempted to justify the Army's decision to retain the WAC as a separate corps. Noting that the Army did not have a separate "Black Corps" or "Texas Corps," the committee's chairman saw retention of the women's corps "as a cover to provide the opportunity for continued discrimination." Consequently, the DOD recommended to the Army that Section 3071 be repealed and the WAC structure disestablished, leaving only a senior officer to serve as advisor to the Secretary and Chief of Staff and as spokeswoman for women in the Army. The Army approved this recommendation on 18 June 1975, and its provisions were incorporated in DOPMA.

On 1 August 1975, Brig. Gen. Mary E. Clarke became the last Director, WAC, replacing Bailey when she retired. Knowing the impending fate of the Corps, Clarke began making plans "to self-destruct." Meanwhile, with the Army committed to phase out the WAC by October 1977, the vehicle for accomplishing it, DOPMA, was in deep trouble on Capitol Hill. In May, the Army sought separate legislation to repeal Section 3071, but Congress failed to act on it.

At this juncture, the DOD tried another tack, relying on the Secretary of Defense's authority to reorganize the department subject to the congressional notification. On 7 March 1978, the DOD published a reorganization order, Section 1 of which abolished the Office of the Director, Women's Army Corps. After Congress was notified, the curtain came down on the Corps on 28 April 1978 in a brief ceremony in the Pentagon and General Clarke was reassigned to Fort McClellan as commander.

Subsequent legislation legally disestablished the Women's Army Corps on 20 October 1978. Under the new law, women officers who previously could only be detailed to other Army branches could now be permanently assigned to them, with the exception of the combat arms (infantry, armor, field artillery, and air defense artillery).

The Army's Chief of Staff, Gen. Bernard W. Rogers, recognized that for integration to work it would have to have support from the top to the very bottom of the organization. In March 1978, he sent a message to his commanders emphasizing the Army's commitment to integration of women and to accomplishing it "smoothly and rapidly." Rogers called attention to the triple expansion in numbers and their entrance in nontraditional skills and the obligations of commanders to provide women with whatever additional training was required for the full participation in field exercises and unit duties. His message read, in part:

> Qualified women now have the opportunity to serve in all but a few specific combat units and combat specialties. In availing themselves of that opportunity women, like their male counterparts, must accept the responsibility for sharing all risks and enduring all hardships inherent in their specialty. Some people believe that women soldiers will not be deployed in the event of hostilities: that they are only to be part-time soldiers—here in peace, gone in war. Some women are being used in skills other than those for which they were trained and some are being excused from performance of unit duties. The Army cannot operate effectively in this manner. Women are an essential part of the force; they will deploy with their units and they will serve in the skills in which they have been trained. . . .
> The first considerations in the assignment of women in the Army have been, and will continue to be, the mission of the Army itself, and the uniquely demanding nature of Army service in wartime. Within that context, women can make many important contributions; indeed, they are doing so now. The burden which rests on leaders at every level is to provide knowledgeable, understanding, affirmative and even-handed leadership to all our soldiers.*

Meanwhile, the Marine Corps quietly abolished its director. Legend has it that when Gen. Thomas A. Holcomb authorized women to serve in the Marine Corps, the portrait of Archibald Henderson, a mid-nineteenth-century occupant of the Commandant's Quarters, had fallen off the wall. When the twenty-sixth Commandant, Gen. Louis H. Wilson, disbanded the office of the

*See Appendix 3 for full text.

Director, Women Marines, he said that if at some future time the announcement should be made that there would no longer be women in the Marines, he hoped his portrait, too, would fall off the wall.

Because the Marine Corps was smaller than the other services and because the Director's office was located within the office of the Commandant, the Director of Women Marines had from the early days exercised more control over the women's program than her rank would warrant. More than her counterparts in either the Navy or Air Force, she was directly involved in recruiting, training, uniforming, and assigning the small cadre of women in the Marine Corps. However, over the years her function gradually evolved into an essentially advisory one, more on the model of the WAF director.

In October 1973, as a result of a major reorganization of the Marine Corps' headquarters, the director position was moved down to the control of the Manpower Division, and Wilson directed that women were to be treated more truly as marines: recruited, trained, and assigned as members of a single corps. Col. Margaret A. Brewer, the director since February of that year, devoted the remainder of her tenure working her way out of a job by gradually transferring the functions of the director to the appropriate agencies in the headquarters. Finally, in June 1977, as the women's strength was rapidly expanding, the director's office was abolished and Brewer was reassigned as the Deputy Director of the Division of Information. She later became the director of the division and was promoted to brigadier general.

It remained something of a paradox that the services were eliminating the women's support system at a time when they were creating new structures to deal with racial issues in response to exploding tensions that arose from continued inequities for blacks twenty years after the President had declared that blacks would be integrated into the services and accorded equal treatment. As in the case of blacks, the services would find that integration of women would be harder to achieve than originally thought. Moreover, so long as the combat issue remains unresolved, total integration will remain an elusive goal.

NOTES

1. U.S. Congress, *Congressional Record*, Vol. 118, S. 4403 (Daily Edition, 21 March 1972).

2. "Equal Rights for Men and Women," 92nd Congress, 2nd session, Report 92-689, p. 13.

3. "Utilization of Military Women," U.S. Department of Defense, Central All-Volunteer Task Force Report, December 1972, p. 23.

4. Stremlow, p. 137.

5. Soon after his appointment in 1970 as Chief of Naval Operations, Adm. Elmo R. Zumwalt electrified the U.S. Navy with a series of controversial reforms announced in "Z-Gram" messages to the field. At the time, he said these were meant "to bring the Navy into the twentieth century." His Z-Gram 116, "Equal Rights and Opportunities for Women in the Navy," was one of the most controversial (see Appendix #3).

CHAPTER 20

FAMILY POLICY

THE FAMILY POLICY arena became the site of some of the most emotional policy battles of the seventies, and the one in which court action, or the threat of it, had the greatest impact. The body of family policy that had evolved quite naturally in the post–World War II social climate had survived almost intact for nearly two decades. It rested on the simple assumptions that a woman's natural responsibilities as wife/mother were inherently incompatible with her military duties, and that wherever these two came into conflict, the former must take precedence, irrespective of her professional value to the service and often in total disregard for her own desires or best interests.

The first policy to get the ax was one of the few that discriminated against men: the practice of allowing women, but not men, to leave voluntarily solely because they were married, after having served specified minimum periods following training or reassignment. In 1964, motivated by a desire to reduce losses in the wake of the GAO investigations, Col. Barbara Bishop had led the fight in the Marine Corps to tighten the rules by introducing the logical requirement that when a woman was stationed close enough to her husband to establish a joint household, she would be required to fulfill her contract; all the services soon followed with similar policies. Subsequently, the bans on married women entering the services were lifted. Later, the services discontinued marriage separations for women entirely, except in documented cases of hardship.

These policy revisions immediately reduced attritional losses and rapidly increased the numbers and proportions of married women in the services, producing new demands for joint assignments of husband-wife teams. The services then simplified procedures to enable a husband or wife to request an assignment at or near the same base as his or her spouse with the chief requirement being that jobs must be available for both at the joint location. The major exceptions were joint assignments to the Southeast Asia war zone and to certain isolated locations where family accommodations were not available. Even with these exceptions, the system worked so well that roughly 90 percent of married couples were able to establish joint homes.

The growing numbers of married women spurred increased demands to eliminate discrimination in dependency entitlements whereby a woman was required to prove that her spouse and/or children were in fact dependent upon her for more than one-half of their support to be entitled to dependency allowances, family housing, and other benefits normally available to military personnel.

Based on the Integration Act and a 1952 Comptroller General decision, the dependency entitlement rules were a source of great inconvenience, irritation, and financial hardship for service women and as such negatively affected their morale and retention. For many years, the directors and the DACOWITS had tried to get them revised, and Congresswoman Martha Griffiths had introduced corrective legislation, all without success. The issue was finally settled in the courts.

In December 1970, twenty-three-year-old 1st Lt. Sharron Frontiero filed a class action suit in federal court contending that the denial of equal benefits for women amounted to unreasonable sex discrimination under the equal protection provisions of the Constitution. Sharron had joined the Air Force as a physical therapist in 1968 and had married Joseph Frontiero the following year. While she worked at the Maxwell Air Force Base hospital, he attended college on the G.I. Bill, for which he received $205 a month. Although on-base family housing was available for married men, because Lieutenant Frontiero was a woman she was required to live off base at her own expense since her husband was not recognized as a dependent. For all official entitlement purposes, she was classified as a single officer. Nor was her husband entitled to medical facilities routinely available to the spouses of male members under the same circumstances.

A three-judge court rejected Frontiero's argument, but she appealed to the higher court and won. On 14 May 1973, the

Supreme Court declared that it was unconstitutional to require a female member of the armed forces to prove civilian spouse and/or unmarried minor children to be in fact dependent upon her for over one-half of their support unless the same rules were required of male members.[1] The services would either have to provide the same entitlements to women or revise the rules to require men to prove dependency of their wives and children. This the services would never have done.

Subsequently, the DOD revised its directives: women were now to be treated equally with men in all matters of dependency and entitlements, and the word "spouse" was to replace "wife" and "husband." The DOD also authorized back pay for women who had been denied these benefits in the past. The drive for equal treatment had inched forward one notch.

The next step was to allow women to raise families and remain in the military, and here again the courts played a pivotal role. This was more than the services had bargained for and farther than they were willing to go voluntarily.

The idea was not new, however. In 1949, Rear Adm. Clifford A. Swanson had suggested that women should be allowed to have families and remain in the services. As Chief of the Navy's Bureau of Medicine and Surgery, Swanson noted that pregnancy "is a normal biological phenomenon in women in the military age group." He wrote:

> It cannot be presumed to be the policy of the military service to regard either the institution of marriage or the raising of a family with disfavor. However, it is recognized that if such personal interests seriously interfere with military duties, or if female military personnel desire to give up their military career voluntarily in order to raise a family . . . it would be desirable to have means available whereby such personnel can be expeditiously separated from the service. Aside from these considerations there would appear to this Bureau to be no reason for terminating the service of personnel who are pregnant but physically able to perform their duties.[2]

The admiral made specific recommendations about time off during pregnancy, maternity leave, and discharge—radical ideas not even espoused by most military women.

Apparently unpersuaded by the admiral's logic, the study group developing the postwar policies on the subject wrote:

> It is believed that a woman who is pregnant or a mother should not be a member of the armed forces and should devote herself to the responsibilities which she has assumed, remaining with her husband and child as a family unit.

True to that philosophy, Executive Order 10240, signed by President Truman on 27 April 1951, permitted the services to terminate, regardless of rank, grade, or length of service, the commission, warrant, or enlistment of any woman (Regular or Reserve) if or when it was established that she:

a. Is the parent, by birth or adoption, of a child under such minimum age as the Secretary concerned shall determine [eighteen was the minimum established by all services]
b. Has personal custody of a child under such minimum age
c. Is the stepparent of a child under such minimum age and the child is within the household of the woman for a period of more than thirty days a year
d. Is pregnant, or
e. Has, while serving . . . given birth to a living child.

Such women could be totally separated from the service by administrative action, by termination of commission, termination of appointment, revocation of commission, discharge, or otherwise. Although the order was permissive, the services chose to regard it as a mandate for the next twenty years.

Of the two circumstances involved, the one dealing with minor children was the more inexplicable by far. Unlike being pregnant, there is nothing uniquely female about having a minor child in the home. The military's standard justification for treating women differently from men in these cases was based on the concept that child care places greater and different responsibilities on a mother than it does on a father, even when the father is the natural parent of the child and the mother the stepparent.

During the fifties, the services rarely granted waivers to this policy except in cases where a woman was approaching twenty-year retirement. In the late sixties, however, with the rise in civil rights litigation and growing criticism of attrition rates, the military more liberally allowed waivers, albeit often grudgingly and after agonizing delays. To obtain one, a woman had to prove that she could provide for a child without interfering with her official responsibilities. Approval of her case rested with a faceless bureaucracy where the decision was made, Solomon-like, as to what was in the best interests of the child and/or the service. Decisions could be, and often were, subject to the biases and whims of reviewing officials; and a negative decision could be based on flimsy rationale, as Col. Eleanor L. Skinner recalls.

In late 1967, Skinner, then a major in the Regular Air Force with twelve years' service, and her civilian husband, Earl, arranged to adopt a beautiful little boy, Bobby. However, what should have been a routine waiver case turned into a "catch 22." The adoption agency told the Skinners that it was withholding final approval pending the outcome of Eleanor Skinner's request for a waiver from the Air Force. When Skinner applied for the waiver, the Air Force denied her request, contending that the basis of the waiver—e.g., custody of a child—did not yet exist, and that there were therefore no grounds for granting it. Thus, the Air Force told Skinner that she should first adopt the child and *then* resubmit her request, but it gave her no assurance that a waiver would be granted. In effect, the adoption hinged on the waiver, consideration of the waiver on the adoption, and her career as a Regular officer was at risk. Only after WAF Director Holm learned of the situation and pleaded Skinner's cause was the waiver granted, and even then over the objections of other personnel offices.

On several previous occasions, the director had recommended the Air Force rescind the automatic discharge policy for women with minor children—to no avail. Outraged at the decision in the Skinner case, Holm fired off a memo to the Deputy Assistant Secretary of the Air Force for Personnel Policy, James P. Goode, pointing out the untenable position the Air Force had put Skinner in and urging reconsideration:

> I cannot believe that the decision in this case, which jeopardizes the career of an outstanding field grade officer simply because she and her husband wish to adopt a child, is in fact in the best interest of the Air Force. . . . The ultimate responsibility for the care and welfare of children rests with the parent, not, we submit, with the Air Force. For the Air Force to become overly involved in evaluating the capability of a parent to care for his or her children constitutes unwarranted meddling into their private affairs. We do not meddle in this fashion in the personal affairs of male military personnel. There are many male military personnel in the Air Force without spouses but with minor dependents. So far as we know, the Air Force never questions their capability for providing adequately for their children.

At that time two cases in the national press dramatized the inconsistency in the policies applied to men and women with minor children. In one, a sergeant was lauded for accepting an assignment to Vietnam even though, as a result of the death of his wife, he had become the sole parent of several children. In the other, an unmarried male chaplain (captain) was praised for adopting two Vietnamese boys. No policy required the discharge of either of those men even though they had assumed full responsibility for raising children. Conversely, if either ever married a military woman, *her* career—not his—would be in jeopardy.

Skinner got her waiver and her son without interrupting her career and even served a tour in Vietnam. The odious policy, however, survived for another two years despite Holm's persistent efforts to have it rescinded. In January 1970, she requested the Judge Advocate General's office (JAG) to provide a legal opinion on the policy. The JAG advised her that, although the policy was legal under the laws passed in 1947 and 1948, subsequent legislation (i.e., the Civil Rights Act of 1964) and recent executive orders dealing with equal opportunity on the basis of sex cast a shadow over it. The JAG stated, "It is our opinion that the signs of the times and the demands of justice require that discriminatory rules which are essentially based on sex must be discarded; and, accordingly, we concur with the [WAF Director's] proposal" to eliminate the policy.

James P. Goode, a civilian lawyer with more Pentagon Secretarial-level experience than most military men, became another important ally. Goode's job was to review involuntary discharge actions in which the individual appealed for an exception to policy and to render final decisions in the name of the Secretary. In March 1970, Goode asked the air staff to review the minor-children policy. Unfortunately, those charged with the review in the Directorate of Personnel Planning were the people most opposed to changing the policy. The Directorate surveyed air staff agencies, including the offices of the JAG, WAF, and Surgeon General, and found a clear consensus that the policy should be rescinded. The Directorate, not satisfied with these results, and in what must have been a first for the Air Force, solicited the opinions of the WAC and WAVES directors with the obvious intent of canceling out those of the WAF director—to pit woman against woman, as it were.

The effort was well rewarded. The WAC director did not mince words. Not only did Col. Elizabeth P. Hoisington oppose any change to the policy, but she was "displeased" with the current practice of granting waivers. She had not fought it because the Army Nurse Corps and Medical Specialist Corps appeared to favor it. In her view, however, the day would come when the Army would be required to eliminate the waiver provision because it restricted the Army's ability to assign its women. Also, she contended that such women were inhibited from pursuing "a normal career-enhancing program, from furthering their education, and from accepting assignments which would advance their promotional potential." The fact that once these women were discharged they would neither be assignable nor promotable seemed not to enter into the equation. Hoisington insisted that if a proposal to rescind the discharge policy were in Army channels, she would "vehemently oppose it." She concluded:

> Finally, in my opinion, no basis exists to consider equalizing Army policy for male and female members concerning parenthood through adoption or other means. A valid comparison cannot be made between the civilian wife of a male member and the military wife of a male member. The interests of the Army will best be served by women who are free to travel. The interests of the children will best be served by women who have no military obligation.[3]

The Navy's Capt. Rita Lenihan characteristically was less strident. She liked the current waiver policy: "[It] is operating very satisfactorily and the number of waivers requested . . . is so small that a change is not warranted. Furthermore, a change in the [child] custody policy certainly would have an impact on policies governing related matters," she said in a veiled reference to pregnancy, concluding that "it is considered that there will always be in the Navy certain differing policies for men and women and, although such policies may differ, it does not follow that they are necessarily discriminatory."[4]

The official air staff position, signed by Maj. Gen. John L. Locke, the Assistant Deputy Chief of Staff for Personnel, on 13 July 1970—over the WAF director's strong objections—was that the policy not be changed. The rationale included: the old "our mission is to fly and fight" theme—that is, since women with minor children were presumed to be immobile, the mission would be jeopardized (even though the numbers requesting such waivers in any one year never approached twenty and none were permitted to fly or fight); the contention that other problems or discriminations could arise that would have more far-reaching effects; and the argument that it was really in the women's best interests for the Air Force to discharge them involuntarily to meet their family responsibilities so that they did not have to show hardship, as the men did.

There matters stood until Lt. Gen. Robert J. Dixon stepped into the fray. As the new, dynamic Deputy Chief of Staff for Personnel, Dixon operated from a simple straightforward philosophy: "We should be doing things FOR people, not TO them." On 7 August, he ordered his staff to rescind the minor-children discharge policy. Unfortunately, the unenthused staff did not get around to finalizing the change until 29 September, the day after a suit seeking to block enforcement of the regulation was filed in a U.S. District Court.

Capt. Tommie Sue Smith, a judge advocate (lawyer) assigned to Andrews Air Force Base, near Washington, D.C., had no way of knowing that the policy was about to be overturned. As far as she knew, the Air Force was forcing her to choose between her eight-year-old son, Miller, and her Air Force career, and she was not about to take it lying down. Smith, a member of the bar in Tennessee and admitted to practice before the U.S. Court of Appeals and the Supreme Court, as well as a divorcee of two years, had joined the Air Force in 1966 because of "feelings of loyalty and duty to my country." The recruiter, she recalled, said that she would have to give up legal custody of her son but made no mention of personal custody. After her appointment, she learned of the rule against having a child in the home for more than thirty days a year; so she requested a waiver, which was denied. Because she wished to lose neither her new career nor her son, she sent young Miller off to military school in nearby Virginia, within weekend commuting distance.

Then, in 1969, Smith received orders for reassignment to the Philippines. Even though men routinely took their families, she was told that Miller could not go with her because of the thirty-day rule. She could either go without her son or leave the service, even though she was an expert in military law and an outstanding JAG officer. That did it—Smith decided to fight back.

Calling the regulation "blatantly inequitable," she filed suit in U.S. District Court on 28 September, maintaining that since no such regulation applied to men, the policy violated her equal protection rights under the Constitution's Fourteenth Amendment. "We have a general right here on base with eight kids and his wife isn't with him," she told a reporter to dramatize how ridiculously unfair the regulation was.[5] The following day, the Air Force announced that she could stay because it was changing its policy.

The implication was that the policy was being rescinded because of Smith's suit, much to Dixon's great annoyance and the staff's chagrin.

Meanwhile, the other services were having their own problems with strong-willed mothers. Maj. Lorraine R. Johnson, a forty-three-year-old Army Nurse Corps officer since 1958, was suing in federal court to retain her commission in the Reserve. Johnson lived in Cypress, California, worked as a nurse in the local school district, and attended monthly weekend drills at the U.S. Army's Reserve Training Center in Santa Ana. In 1967, she married a teacher in the same district and a year later gave birth to a son, Thomas. The Army notified her that she would have to resign her commission because of the minor-child regulation. Denying her request for a waiver, the Army then initiated discharge proceedings.

Consequently, Johnson filed suit in the U.S. District Court, claiming that she was being discriminated against in violation of federal law. The suit pointed out that she only had eight years remaining for her twenty-year retirement, and that she was "ready, willing, and able" to perform her duties. If she was discharged, not only would she lose twelve years vested in retirement and $16,000 in lost reserve pay, but the Army would lose a highly qualified nurse who was devoting 2,000 hours a year instructing medical corpsmen in intensive care.[6] The court issued a preliminary injunction ordering the Army to refrain from discharging Johnson in order to give the Army time to prepare its case. The Army, however, opted to drop its discharge action rather than try the case in court.

Nevertheless, the Army continued to require waivers until the mid-seventies even though nearly all were routinely approved and those serving on waivers presented no assignment problems. The DOD ordered the practice discontinued in 1975 as part of its attack on all the policies provided for by the 1952 executive order.

One might wonder why there was so much resistance to the retention of women with minor children. So few people were involved that the possibility of their affecting the military mission adversely was nonexistent. The root cause was a deep-seated fear, not unfounded, that allowing women with adopted children or stepchildren to remain would also lead to demands to permit retention of women with their own children, and this would open up the whole question of pregnancy. Here the services would be dealing not with a few dozen women, but with thousands.

During the seventies, the services' fears were realized, making the battle over minor children seem a minor skirmish compared with the one that ensued over pregnancy. Even most military women tended to draw the equal opportunity line when it came to pregnancy. Yet change would come, and a few like Col. Jeanette I. Sustad, the Director of Women Marines, saw it coming and eased its way. Sustad astounded those attending the 1970 Women Marines Association convention in Philadelphia by suggesting the possibility of natural mothers being allowed to remain on active duty. Within a year, her projection came true with the help of the federal courts and a few determined women.

Anna Flores was a twenty-three-year-old seaman at a U.S. naval air station in Florida when she became pregnant in the spring of 1970. Before she and her fiance, a Navy enlisted man, could be married as they had planned, she miscarried at the base dispensary. Although Flores was no longer pregnant, her commanding officer nonetheless took action to have her discharged as provided for in Navy regulations. "To do otherwise," he said, "would imply that unwed pregnancy is condoned and would eventually result in a dilution of the moral standards set for women in the Navy."[7]

The Navy, however, had underestimated Flores' determination to stay. On 24 August, she asked the U.S. District Court in Pensacola, Florida, to prohibit the Navy from discharging her on the grounds that the Navy was unconstitutionally discriminating against women by discharging them for becoming pregnant while not discharging the sailors who got them pregnant. The complaint, drawn up by the American Civil Liberties Union, became a class-action suit attacking all service policies that discriminated on the basis of sex, maintaining that all military women were being deprived of due process and equal protection of the laws, and their rights of privacy under the Constitution of the United States. Faced with a barrage of press inquiries sympathetic to the seaman and the prospect of a damaging court suit, the Navy allowed Flores to stay and let it be known that there were no hard feelings: "This incident should not affect her future eligibility for duty assignments, promotions or reenlistment for which she is qualified," said an official spokesman.

Meanwhile, the Air Force was also drawn into litigation. Capt. Susan R. Struck, a pregnant twenty-six-year-old nurse at McChord Air Force Base in Washington, like Johnson and Flores, refused to leave quietly. Much to the Pentagon's relief, the lower court decided against her. But Struck appealed. Despite Dixon's own misgivings, the Air Force was determined to see the case through—all the way to the Supreme Court if necessary—hoping that the justices would see the wisdom of the policy and would not require the military to retain pregnant women.

The Solicitor General, however, concluded that the case could not be won and recommended that the Air Force retain Struck rather than press the case. The three service Judge Advocates General discussed the ramifications that an adverse decision could have on all their policies on pregnancy and agreed that the Air Force should back off rather than risk losing everything. Struck was allowed to remain on active duty.

Although the Struck and Flores cases were moot, the services had their thumbs in a dike. From then on, they were almost continuously swamped with litigation that required them to defend their actions in courts and to explain to an increasingly incredulous, unsympathetic press that they were not against motherhood per se. "It's a touchy subject," explained one harassed official. "It would be rather hard to carry out the Air Force's mission with a girl that's eight months pregnant," said another, reminding a reporter that "the mission of the Air Force is to fly and fight."

"Pregnancy would certainly affect her status of duty in the later stages," said a WAC major, by way of explaining the Army's position. "Many women are company commanders in parades and you couldn't have a pregnant woman leading a parade."

"We're expected to be in tip-top shape, on our toes, ready any minute," said a woman marine major; "it's called readiness posture."

Capt. Rita Lenihan, a single veteran of twenty-seven years' naval service, offered the observation that women did not want to make the service a career anyway: "A little seaman wants to be with her husband who makes more money. That's what WAVES want to do. They want to have families."[8] As far as all the directors were concerned, maternity uniforms were definitely not on the drawing boards.

But growing numbers of women wanted to stay *and* raise a family and saw no reason why they should not. "I am a mature, responsible adult, capable of making my own decisions and of taking care of a family and my Air Force duties," Staff Sgt. Lora Singer told the WAF director. "I resent having to choose between my career and a family. Men don't, so why should I?" Why indeed!

As Air Force Personnel Chief, Dixon believed that some women should be given the opportunity to remain; and, pragmatically, he felt sure that if some compromise were not found, the arbitrary discharge policy would probably be shot down in the courts. Although the lower courts' rulings were favorable to the policy, one adverse decision could bring down the whole house of cards. Thus, in March 1971, the Air Force announced a new policy that provided for waivers of discharge, reentry within twelve months for women who were discharged, and cancellation of discharge action when a pregnancy was terminated by miscarriage or abortion. The Air Force also changed recruiting rules so that they no longer excluded women with children from entering.

The Marine Corps followed suit, largely due to the efforts of Colonel Sustad. Gunnery Sgt. Frances I. Gonzales and Maj. Carolyn Auldridge Walsh became the first women marines to retain their military status while pregnant. Soon, all four services had adopted policies similar to that of the Air Force. For the first time in history, military women were granted waivers to permit them to start raising families with reasonable assurance that they would be allowed to continue their service careers.

By 1973, the services were approving from 60 to 86 percent of the waiver requests, but were still losing on an average of nearly 6 percent of their enlisted women (roughly 3,000 annually) to pregnancy and parenthood. Therefore, the DOD considered seeking total repeal of the statute and executive order that authorized the involuntary discharges. On 1 June 1974, it told the services that policies permitting involuntary separation of women for pregnancy and parenthood were no longer "viable" and that separations would be voluntary. The services objected, but the DOD stuck to its guns and told them to develop joint policies to carry out this concept. The date set for the new rules to take effect was 15 May 1975.

The Army resisted to the bitter end. "No matter what you say about equal opportunity, you cannot deal with the situation of an expectant father and an expectant mother in the same way," Brig. Gen. Mildred C. Bailey, the Director, WAC, explained in November 1974. "Mothers have a role in child rearing that is different from fathers and we have to think about what effect this has on mission readiness and our ability to be available for world-wide assignment." Bailey believed that the chief problem came from single women who regarded the Army "as a haven for their needs inasmuch as the security, protection, and entitlements are unequalled elsewhere." Expressing a view held by most military women, Bailey wrote: "It is unthinkable that a pregnant woman should continue to live in troop billets, sharing rooms and facilities with her peers during the advanced stages of pregnancy; yet should she be put out in the civilian community without an adequate capability of caring for herself?" All the line directors shared this dilemma: they felt compassion for individuals who became pregnant but were reluctant to subject the rest of the women to the stigma that would come from sharing dormitories with those bearing illegitimate children. Bailey recommended that the Army hang tough in the face of litigation, taking encouragement from a recent lower court decision upholding the Marine Corps' policy on pregnancy discharge (a case later reversed).

One of Bailey's and the Army's chief concerns was the widely held belief that mothers were being given special, i.e., preferred, treatment in assignments, additionally burdening other personnel. Yet the Army's own data did not support this. Although several hundred women with children were on active duty, the Directorate of Enlisted Personnel identified in a period of six months only thirty-nine cases of Army enlisted women seeking to be taken off assignments due to parenthood. Only sixteen of those requests were approved, and the enlisted women involved received no special consideration. It was contended that an enlisted woman with dependents was provided the same assistance that would be provided any soldier. No more, no less. It was also pointed out that the Army had no available data on how many enlisted men were deleted or deferred from assignments because of dependent problems. The Army did know, however, that some five hundred men a year were given twelve-week deferments from overseas assignments because their civilian wives were in an advanced stage of pregnancy (a practice common to all the services). By comparison, the average time lost by military women during pregnancy was only eleven weeks.

The services were told to implement the new policy by 15 May 1975. The Air Force complied, the Navy Department (whose policy included the Marines) followed shortly, but the Army made a last-ditch appeal. With no data to substantiate the Army's fears, the Secretary, Howard H. "Bo" Callaway, strongly appealed to the Assistant Secretary of Defense, William K. Brehm, to postpone the new policy implementation until Callaway could discuss it further. He believed that the "far-reaching impacts" had not been assessed. His chief concern was that motherhood limited assignment mobility and interfered with an individual's ability to perform all military duties. "I am concerned that we are overreacting to special interest social pressures and are failing to recognize Army/Defense requirements," Callaway wrote. He was sure that the courts would see the wisdom of the current mandatory discharge-with-waiver policy.

Brehm was not persuaded. He informed Callaway that he would be happy to discuss the matter further but that the determination "that we will not separate women for pregnancy or parenthood is one which we have accepted in order to best apply the concepts of equal opportunity for our people." Brehm requested that the Army get out the new policy as soon as possible, and in November instructions finally went to the field.

Meanwhile, the courts were still processing pregnancy suits and in 1976 the ax fell. The Second Circuit Court held, in *Crawford* v. *Cushman*, that the Marine Corps' regulation requiring the discharge of a pregnant marine as soon as pregnancy is discovered violated the Fifth Amendment.[9] The court deemed the regulation irrational because no other temporary disabilities also resulted in mandatory discharge and because no individual determination was made of a pregnant woman's fitness to serve. The court found that the regulation violated the Fifth Amendment's due process aspects because it established an irrefutable presumption that any pregnant marine was permanently unfit for duty. The regulation penalized the decision to bear a child by those marines whose mobility and readiness would not be reduced during most months of pregnancy preceding birth or during their careers after giving birth.

For all practical purposes, the court's decision should have settled the issue. It did not. The services, especially the Army, continued to chafe under the policy and made several attempts to prove that pregnant women and women with children were problems. "It's no way to run an Army," complained a male warrant officer. However, the record did not substantiate the military's expressed concern that women would lose an inordinate amount of time away from their duties for pregnancy and child care. In 1977, a comprehensive DOD study of lost time for service members concluded that the differences in lost time for men and women were not significant because men lost much more duty time on an average than did women for absence without leave, desertion, alcohol/drug abuse, and confinement.

The Director of Women Marines put the subject of the new retention policy into perspective. When asked if she anticipated its causing problems for the Marine Corps, Col. (later Brig. Gen.) Margaret Brewer noted that as far as the Corps was concerned, women's pregnancy was a management problem. She believed the Corps should explain the ramifications of remaining on active duty to pregnant women who chose to do so and indicate that they could not expect special favors. If a woman later found that she could not cope with both her job and her small child, she could request hardship discharge.

In 1978, when the Army was staffing a recommendation to go back to the involuntary discharge policy or to give pregnant women periods of absence without pay, Brig. Gen. Mary E. Clarke, the WAC director, took a position diametrically opposite to her two immediate predecessors. Calling the recommendations "discriminatory," she said that they failed to recognize pregnancy as a temporary disability and violated the principle that the Army takes care of its own.

The subjects of pregnancy and parenthood could not be laid to rest, however. They continued to surface as the major concerns of the services with respect to women; by 1981, the services were considering the possibility of going back to the waiver policy in the case of pregnancy and discharging single parents. Just how they planned to get around *Crawford* v. *Cushman* was not clear.

NOTES

1. This very nearly became a landmark decision. Four of the five justices declared sex to be a "suspect classification," thus triggering a requirement that the governmental policy be supported by a "compelling governmental purpose" rather than a mere rationale relative to a permissible objective. In a subsequent case, however, the court did not regard sex as a suspect classification, at least when dealing with the armed forces. (*Schlesinger* v. *Ballard*, 419 U.S. 498, 1975).

2. Stremlow, p. 156.

3. "Policy Concerning Release of Women Members of the Armed Forces for Reasons of Child Custody (with statement of Director, WAC)," memo to Directorate of Personnel Planning, Department of Air Force; from Chief of Promotion, Separation and Transition Div., Department of Army; 23 April 1970.

4. "Policy Concerning Release of Women Members of the Armed Forces for Reasons of Child Custody," letter to Chief of Policy Division, Directorate of Personnel Planning, Department of Air Force; from Chief of Naval Personnel; 23 April 1970.

5. "Air Force Captain Battles Ban," *The Evening Star* (Washington, D.C.), 29 September 1970.

6. "Sues for Ouster Attempt," *Los Angeles Times*, 12 July 1970.

7. "A Double Standard in the Navy," *Washington Post*, 25 August 1970.

8. "Military Women Making Waves Over Sexist Rules," *Washington Daily News*, 5 October 1970.

9. *Crawford v. Cushman*, 531 F. 2nd 114 (2nd Cir., 1976).

CHAPTER 21

THE SERVICE ACADEMIES

ON 7 OCTOBER 1975, President Gerald Ford signed Public Law 94–106, thus settling one of the most controversial issues surrounding women in the military in the 1970s. This law, which had passed the House by a vote of 303 to 96, and the Senate by a voice vote, required the services to admit women into their sacrosanct academies the following year. In the fall of 1976, women enrolled at West Point, Annapolis, and Colorado Springs, and the classes of 1980 became the first coeducational classes in the history of the academies.

The doors of these prestigious institutions might have remained barred to women had Congress not pried them open. Senator Jacob Javits inserted the first wedge in 1972: when the Naval Academy refused to consider a woman he had nominated, he made a public issue of her rejection. Sensing the need for action of some sort, the Navy then opened up the NROTC program to women in what may have been an effort to stave off attempts to integrate the Naval Academy. But Congress became interested in integrating the service academies and began to pursue it.

The line directors were split on the question of women attending the service academies, with the Navy and Army on one side and the Air Force and Marine Corps on the other. Their divergent views came out during the 1972 Pike hearings: "The (Naval) Academy exists for one viable reason, to train seagoing naval officers and also to give the Marine Corps a hard core of career Regular officers," explained Capt. Robin Quigley of the Navy. "There is no room, no need, for a woman to be trained in this mode, since by law and by sociological practicalities, we would not have women in those seagoing or warfare specialties." The Army and Brig. Gen. Mildred Bailey agreed, adding, "We don't need to send women to the Academy to get sufficient qualified women into our officers' program. We get all we need at no expense to the Government. Why should we spend money to train them?" She also asserted that the armed services should be given more time to concern themselves with national defense and should spend less time on "items like this that we don't need and that would not really serve a useful purpose."

As for the Director, WAF, Holm stated, "In my personal opinion, I would like to see women in the Academy in the not too distant future." Although the Air Force still officially opposed women's entrance into the academy at Colorado Springs, Secretary Robert Seamons had recently said that the Air Force would accept women nominated by the members of Congress if funds for facilities were provided. Actually, the Air Force had been quietly considering this possibility for some time and Maj. Gen. Oliver Lewis (Director of Procurement and Training), with Dixon's concurrence, had prepared a study supporting the idea.

Although the women directors continued to disagree, events were happily conspiring against the all-male traditions. In September 1973, suits were brought against the Air Force and the Navy by two women who desired to enter those academies and by four members of Congress who objected to being required to discriminate on the basis of sex in making nominations for the academies.

As these cases began their arduous trail through the courts, Congress began pursuing the issue with increased vigor. In 1972, Javits and Congressman Jack H. McDonald introduced a concurrent resolution to the effect that a woman duly nominated to a military service academy should not be denied admission solely on the basis of sex. The Senate passed this resolution with little debate, but it died in the House within the Armed Services Committee, chaired by F. Edward Hébert, who clearly had no intention that it see the light of day. Then, on 20 December 1973, the Senate accepted by voice vote an amendment introduced by Senator William D. Hathaway and cosponsored by Senators Mike Mansfield, John Stennis, Jacob Javits, and Strom Thurmond to permit women to enter the service academies. Early in 1974, however, the House, with much internal dispute, struck the amendment from the bill. On the House side, Hébert promised to hold hearings on the issue, and the Senate agreed to drop the amendment.

The promised hearings began late in May 1974, but by that time the services' positions had coalesced and hardened. They had received their marching orders from the Deputy Secretary of Defense, William P. Clements, Jr. Whether Clements was personally against having women in the academies or whether he was bowing to the wishes of Chairman Hébert remains unclear; but, whatever his motivation, he moved like a zealot, and from then on the defense establishment spoke as one.

Early in April, in an extraordinary show of unanimity and as if on cue, the three military departments simultaneously promulgated almost identical official statements totally opposing admitting women to their respective service academies. Each was signed by the service Secretary and military chief. On 15 April, Clements capped this with a statement of the official DOD position and a week later got President Nixon's endorsement, despite contrary advice from the White House staff, including Anne Armstrong, Counselor to the President. The party line, according to Clements, was:

> The primary responsibility of the Department of Defense is to provide for the National Defense. The Service Academies, in providing officers to fill combat roles in the Armed Forces, are essential ingredients of that national defense. Training cadets at the Academies is expensive, and it is imperative that these opportunities be reserved for those with potential for combat roles.

As the hearings approached, Clements urged each of the services to "continue to refine the rationale and appropriate data to support the proposition that the Service Academies are institutions focused on producing leadership for combat." This theme, with variations and elaborations, was the DOD position for the hearings, which lasted into August 1974.

During the hearings, service witnesses testified as one. Navy Secretary J. William Middendorf II set the tone: "Simply stated, unless the American people reverse their position on women in combat roles, it would be economically unwise and not in the national interest to utilize the expensive education and facilities of the Naval Academy to develop women officers." Air Force Academy Superintendent Lt. Gen. Albert P. Clark dramatized the issue:

> The environment of the Air Force Academy is designed around these stark realities [of combat]. The cadet's day is filled with constant pressure. His life is filled with competition, combative and contact sports, rugged field

training, use of weapons, flying and parachuting, strict discipline and demands to perform to the limit of endurance mentally, physically, and emotionally. It is this type of training that brings victory in battle. It is my considered judgment that the introduction of female cadets will inevitably erode this vital atmosphere.

Army Secretary Howard H. Callaway agreed: "Admitting women to West Point will irrevocably change the Academy. The Spartan atmosphere—which is so important to producing the final product [combat leaders]—would surely be diluted."

One of the more interesting twists of the hearings came from Jacqueline Cochran, then a retired colonel in the Air Force Reserve. "It is my firm considered opinion that women should not be permitted to enroll in the Air Force Academy," she said. "The basic reason . . . is that the Academies are for the purpose of teaching combat to their students. . . . Women should not go into combat and therefore they should not receive this specialized training." As far as she was concerned, any idea that women should go into combat was "ridiculous."

Some members of Congress took a strong, opposite stand. Congressman Donald Fraser, who had nominated a woman sailplane pilot to the Air Force Academy, only to have her application returned unconsidered, was particularly vehement: "How cynical that while we make an effort to recruit women into the forces—to quadruple their number by 1977—we are denying them access to the best educational program of their profession. We are squandering our human resources."

Congressman Fortney H. (Pete) Stark, Jr., had also nominated a qualified woman to the Naval Academy. "In short," he testified, "women should, with haste and without question, receive appointments to the academies. The fact is that we need them there—with their talents and skills and perspective—far more than they need the academies."

Congresswoman Patricia Schroeder noted the passage of the Equal Rights Amendment by Congress and stated that admission of women to the service academies was inevitable and she wondered why the DOD was fighting it. She observed that bureaucracies are often not responsive to changing circumstances. Women should go to the academies for the same reasons men go, she said—to pursue a military career, to be pilots, to get a good education.

It is noteworthy that during the 1974 hearings, none of the

services' senior women were invited to testify. Military witnesses who did knew full well they were skating on thin ice, that in reality the service academies did not exist for the *exclusive* purpose of producing leaders for combat. Air Force witnesses were especially hard pressed to defend that line, since the academy at Colorado Springs knowingly, and by design, accepted men who were not qualified to fly and could therefore never qualify as Air Force combat leaders. The record shows that of the graduates from that academy between 1964 and 1973, fewer than 40 percent participated in combat jobs and that of the twenty-four career fields open to academy graduates, all but three were open to women. Moreover, being a noncombatant did not exclude an officer from assignment to combat areas. The 1,170 Air Force women officers who served in Southeast Asia during the war were subject to the same combat risks as the men in the same units and skills.

The question then was one of equity. The academy man has always been a member of the "elite," the favored few "ring-knockers" who are traditionally singled out for the choice opportunities: faster promotions, attendance at senior schools, and command assignments. Also, in the Air Force, only the academy graduates received regular commissions upon graduation; all others (products of OTS and ROTC) received commissions in the Reserves. Thus, by being denied admittance to the academies, women were being denied equal opportunity for successful careers commensurate with other officers.

During the hearings, each of the services was asked: If required, was integration of women into the academies possible? Each service agreed, with varying degrees of reluctance, that if Congress so ordered, the academies could—and would—be integrated.

The House hearings ended with the issue unresolved, but it would not go away. On 3 June, Senators Hathaway, Mansfield, Thurmond, and Javits again introduced legislation in the Senate. Then, on 12 August, the Commandant of the Coast Guard announced that in July of the following year, the Coast Guard Academy would accept women, ending the hundred-year tradition of a male-only Coast Guard school. The Merchant Marine Academy had already done so.

Meanwhile, lawsuits on behalf of women applicants were grinding away in the courts. Seeing the handwriting on the wall, yet still hoping that somehow the threat of women at the academies would go away, each of the services began planning for what appeared to be the inevitable. Each made plans regarding curricula, uniforms, facilities, and physical training requirements. It was not in vain.

Evidence began to mount against the DOD position. On 16 April 1975, Congressman Samuel S. Stratton revealed in a press release that, according to a new GAO report, of the 8,880 graduates of the Air Force Academy on active duty as of October 1974, 29 percent had never had a career combat assignment. In fact, a total of 3,777 of the 30,576 graduates of the nation's three top service academies then on active duty had never had a combat assignment. "The GAO figures," Stratton said, "give the lie to the academies' claims that they are in the business of training combat officers exclusively."

At that point, the House added an amendment to a DOD appropriation authorization bill that would authorize women at the service academies. After a flurry of unsuccessful counterproposals, including one for a study to determine the possibility of a separate women's military academy and another to exclude West Point from integration, the amendment passed 303 to 96. In the Senate, Senator Hathaway introduced the same amendment during the debate on military procurement; it was accepted without a roll call vote. Left totally unaddressed was the issue of women's exclusion from combat, and the effect this could have on the academies and on the women who would attend.

With the signing of P.L. 94–106, directing that women be admitted to all three academies, the time had come.

The services took their marching orders from Congress manfully. While the Army was perhaps less enthusiastic than the others, sending rather discouraging brochures to women who wrote for information, the Air Force took the most active role in bringing women into its academy. Letters were sent out to every high school in the nation, expressing an interest in bringing in bright women students. Key to the Air Force's program was the use of fifteen women lieutenants who were given an abbreviated version of the academy training and then served as surrogate upperclassmen to the incoming class of women. Significantly, at the end of the first summer of training ("Beast"), the highest level of attrition was at West Point; the lowest was at the Air Force Academy, where the attrition rate of women was even lower than that of men.

In the first class entering in 1976, women represented 6 percent of the fourth (freshman) class at Annapolis, 8 percent at West

Point, and 10 percent at the Air Force Academy. The academies reported that, except for physical qualifications, all the women compared favorably with the male appointees.

Perhaps the easiest of the changes required of the academies was the reconfiguration of the facilities for women. The academies modified cadet barracks and dormitories primarily to provide rest room facilities for women. They also revamped gymnasiums to include women's locker rooms.

Much debate had raged over the effect of women on the curricula, basically because of the combat exclusion for women. Yet, significant changes in curricula were actually required only in the area of physical training: for example, women at West Point carry lighter rifles; pugil stick training, in which cadets practice hand-to-hand combat with padded sticks, pits only women against women; and parts of obstacle courses have been adjusted to accommodate shorter people. Other adjustments in physical training reflect the relative difference in upper body strength between men and women.

Other aspects of the curricula, however, remain basically unaffected by the women's presence. The Navy alone adopted a "two-track" system, as statutory restrictions on women serving aboard ships initially precluded women from the summer cruises onboard such ships. A subsequent modification of the law partially resolved this problem.

The greatest obstacle the academies encountered in integrating women was, and continues to be, the attitudes of men—faculty members and students. At the Air Force Academy, the presence of the women upperclass surrogates prior to the arrival of the first group of women cadets helped alleviate some of the prejudice because the men who had to train the women officers were surprised and favorably impressed at their stamina and skills. Nevertheless, upperclassmen in all three academies strongly resented women's intrusion. For example, at the Naval Academy, the class of 1979, the last class to graduate without women, chose as their class motto "Omni Vir": all male.

The services hoped that as increased numbers of women entered the academies, the resentment and harassment would decrease significantly. Much of this resentment centered not just around preconceived notions of what a woman is for, but around the perception that women are not fully a part of the team and, hence, do not really belong at the academies. The women are still excluded from combat, which remains in the minds of most at the academies and throughout the services the primary purpose of an academy education. Until this issue is resolved, women at the academies will continue to be regarded, to some degree, as less than fully participating members of their military society.

The first classes with women graduated in June 1980. Of the 327 women who entered, 217—over 66 percent—remained to graduate; of the men entrants, 70 percent graduated. At the Air Force Academy, the retention rate for women exceeded that for men. It came as a surprise to many that the attrition resulting from academic failure was twice as high for men (one in five) as for women (one in ten). Although women provided a variety of reasons for their resignations, most cited a change in career goals—the same reason cited by most men who resigned.

With the first graduates entering the officer ranks, the concern of the eighties shifts to a new front: What will happen to these female graduates of the prestigious academies? What kinds of career opportunities will they have? Will they remain proscribed by law and policy from the types of assignments for which their professional training has prepared them? Will they, the military, and the nation reap the benefits of their academy education, and the potential of each of these women to make a professional contribution? Admiral Zumwalt had said that he could see no reason why a woman could not some day be Chief of Naval Operations; perhaps the first female service chief was a member of the class of '80.

Air Force 2nd Lt. Marianne Owens expressed the sentiments of the first women graduates:

> Needless to say, it's been no picnic here. Yet many of us have made it through under the same conditions as the men. Therefore, we say: Don't point us out; don't applaud us, or you'll be ruining what we've been trying to establish. We've come so far in fighting the hard feelings. . . . It is the goal . . . for us, to simply leave this institution, not as the first women graduates, but as deserving, hard-working graduates to enter the Air Force.[1]

NOTE

1. Cynthia Little [Lt. Col., USAF], "A Look at Women Cadets after Four Years," U.S. Air Force Academy, Colorado Springs, CO, spring 1980.

CHAPTER 22

TAKING TO THE AIR
AND THE SEA

There is an eternal dispute between those who imagine the world to suit their policy and those who correct their policy to suit the realities of the world.

Albert Sorel

DURING THE SEVENTIES, women also inched closer to the essence of the military as flying jobs, missile duty, and seagoing assignments were gradually, if grudgingly, opened up. In each instance, the services arrived at halfway measures that allowed women limited access without directly encroaching on the combat restrictions imposed by law and service policy.

Limited as the new opportunities were, women were for the first time allowed into the core activities of the armed forces. This would lead inevitably to demands to remove the legal barriers to their serving in combat aircraft and ships.

During the hearings on the admission of women to the academies, an Air Force lieutenant general command pilot made the incredible statement that the nature of warfare had not changed in a thousand years. Such an utterance from the mouth of a man of his experience is especially ironic since, more than any other single factor, the airplane and associated development of air power characterizes the changes technology has wrought on the requirements, techniques, and organization of warfare.

Flying is an integral, indispensable element of all the services, but it is the heart of the Air Force—its raison d'etre: "We live in fame or go down in flame, nothing will stop the U.S. Air Force." It is this aura, this mystique, as much as anything rational that kept women out of the cockpit—the only identifiable minority totally excluded.

The services employed two basic rationales for excluding women: the availability of qualified men and the exclusion of women from air combat. With the burgeoning airline industry's insatiable demands for experienced pilots, plus pressures of the draft, military flying training was a very attractive option for young men. Moreover, since the law prohibited women from flying in combat, they would have constituted a special category of limited-duty pilots (had they been allowed to fly) which the services did not need or want. The services argued that all pilots must be available to fly aircraft in combat, yet there were huge requirements for noncombat flying. In reality, thousands of military pilots never touched the controls of a combat aircraft from the day they earned their wings until the day they either left the service to take on more lucrative commercial flying or retired. Nevertheless, from the services' point of view there were no "requirements" to open this prestigious field to women. Additionally, many service personnel believed that women could not cope with the difficulties and hazards of military flying, despite substantial historical and contemporary evidence to the contrary.

In 1941, when Jacqueline Cochran first proposed that the Army Air Corps (later Army Air Force) establish a division of women pilots, she was turned down. As far as the AAC's commanding general, "Hap" Arnold, was concerned, "The use of women pilots serves no military purpose in a country which [has] adequate manpower at this time." He noted that there were so many male pilots in America and so few female pilots that he saw no reason why men could not fill all the AAC's needs. Furthermore, he added, housing and feeding women pilots presented a "difficult situation" on air bases. He later confessed his real reason: "Frankly, I didn't know in 1941 whether a slip of a young girl could fight the controls of a B-17 in the heavy weather they would naturally encounter in operational flying."[1]

Arnold soon changed his mind and discovered that women could not only handle B-17s but could fly anything in the Army's inventory from the smallest trainers and hottest fighters (P-51s, P-38s, P-47s, P-39s) to the biggest bombers, the B-29 "Superfortress" atomic bomb carrier. Some 25,000 women applied for the limited openings in the WASP program, 1,830 were selected, and 1,074 completed the program before the Army Air Force abruptly cancelled it. Many were seasoned pilots and eligible except for one criterion: they were not male. These women flew 60 million miles, ferried 12,650 aircraft, towed countless gunnery targets, and instructed hundreds of Air Force pilots. They flew as regularly and as long as male pilots in the same jobs and showed no difference in physical, mental, or psychological capabilities. Although thirty-eight lost their lives, the record shows that the women's accident rate was about the same as the men's.

Had the women pilots been integrated into the AAF from the beginning as military planners had wanted, rather than organized as a separate women's group as Cochran insisted they be, the story of women as military pilots might have been different. But when the determined Cochran decided to hold out for a separate organization of women pilots under her personal control, which required new legislation, she lost the gamble. Nevertheless, the record of these WASPs during their brief existence should have left no doubts about the ability and willingness of American women to fly military aircraft.

The Russians also had demonstrated that women not only could fly military aircraft but were also quite capable of performing in combat. The USSR formed three all-female air regiments during World War II. All saw action: a fighter regiment flew cover for Soviet combat units from the Volga River to Vienna; a short-range dive-bomber regiment saw service in the Baltic States, at Stalingrad, and other front areas; and a night bomber unit carried out missions as far afield as Berlin.

The fighter regiment alone carried out 4,419 combat missions and fought 125 air battles that downed thirty-eight enemy aircraft and damaged forty-two more. Its pilots were described as "cool, resourceful, and fearless"; two became aces, bagging eleven and twelve enemy aircraft, respectively. One German ace could not believe he had been shot down by a twenty-three-year-old girl until he met his attacker, Lily Litvak, and heard her describe the dogfight in detail. In one battle over the Don River, two women flying fighters took on forty-two enemy bombers, shot down four, and forced the others to turn back without hitting their targets.

Both bomber regiments were also highly successful. The night bombers flew some 25,000 combat sorties—day and night—and dropped 3 million kilograms of bombs on railroad junctions, river crossings, ammunition dumps, and artillery positions, often against heavy enemy fighters and antiaircraft defenses.

Few pilots in any armed force can match the combat records

of many of those Soviet women. One flight commander, Irina Sibrova, racked up a total of 1,008 operational sorties. Another woman commanded an otherwise all-male air regiment that flew important bombing missions behind enemy lines.

There is no reason to believe that American women would have behaved any differently under the same circumstances. But at the time, the circumstances were different. The USSR faced a monumental manpower shortage due to staggering battle losses. Although the United States had a severe pilot shortage for a while, it managed to squeak through by using thousands of civilian men who had been disqualified for military service and by relying on the WASPs to do noncombat flying.

During the postwar hearings on the Integration Act, General Vandenberg testified emphatically that the new Air Force, while it wanted women, had no intention of using them as pilots. Congress clearly did not intend to foreclose on that possibility, however. By providing very specifically that they would not be used in "aircraft engaged in combat missions," Congress left the door wide open for women to engage in noncombat flying, even in combat aircraft—the kind of flying the WASPs had done very successfully during the war. The legislators incorporated the same provisions in the Navy's law.

Thus, the subsequent decision to exclude women from *any* flying duties was a policy one that denied the opportunity to fly even to those women who had logged thousands of wartime hours in military aircraft. Cochran encouraged former WASPs to apply for commissions as lieutenants in the Reserves, and some did in the hope that in some future emergency their skills would be needed, and that they would be allowed to fly again. The services simply wrote off their training and experience, while actively recruiting green young male candidates into their pilot training programs. When the Berlin Airlift came, World War II pilots in the Reserves were ordered up to fly coal and other supplies into the beleaguered city, but the former WASPs, Reserve and active duty, remained grounded.

The same thing happened two years later when war came again. Mobilization plans in effect in early 1950 called for a small number of women pilots to be mobilized, but General Vandenberg decided that the determination on the use of women pilots in a future emergency would be made at the time of mobilization "depending on the circumstances." Apparently, Korea did not meet that criterion. When the war broke out in June 1950, the services again ordered male Reserve pilots to active duty. At that point, much to the chagrin of Air Force leaders, some pilots refused to fly, claiming a "fear of flying." Yet the military continued to ground women who were ready, able, and willing to fly, their training and experience withering away. Even Cochran, a lieutenant colonel in the Air Force Reserve, who was universally regarded as one of the finest pilots in the world and who was still able to set records in military jets, was not even put on rated (flying) status or called to active duty in the emergency.

The subject of women pilots did not surface seriously again until the early seventies and then in the context of equal opportunity, not as a matter of military requirement. Although the draft had ended, the services still anticipated no difficulty in recruiting enough men to meet their needs for rated officers for the all-volunteer force. During the hearings of the Pike subcommittee in March 1972, Congress questioned the Air Force on why it did not use women pilots. The services' studies on equal career opportunities for women and their known large requirements for noncombat flying made it increasingly difficult to defend the total exclusion of women from the field.

THE NAVY TAKES OFF

In March 1972, following the Pike subcommittee hearings, WAF Director Holm briefed the Air Force Secretary and Chief of Staff on the committee's criticism of policies on women and suggested that the Air Force open flying training to women—that the Air Force "step out front" as it had on other policy issues on women and lead the way. "If we don't," she said, "the Navy under Zumwalt will, the Army will then jump on the bandwagon and the Air Force will be running to catch up." Both smiled graciously, but remained noncommittal. In August, Admiral Zumwalt came out with Z-Gram 116 on the expanded role of women in the Navy; and in 1973, six Navy women became the first to win their wings and to be designated naval aviators.

One of the early Navy pilots, Barbara Habedank, said she had no idea what she was getting into when she signed up for the Navy's flight program or what she would be allowed to fly if she got through the course. She had no doubts about her ability to fly, since she was already a licensed pilot with an instructor's rating and had been teaching flying for some time. She recalls that when she first inquired about entering the services as a pilot, "the recruiters had laughed at me." "Don't call us, we'll call you" was their attitude. Later, the Navy recruiter tracked her down—he was no longer laughing. Explaining that the Navy was recruiting a few women for pilot training, he asked if she was still interested. She was. Along with seven other women, Habedank entered the previously male-only Naval Aviation OCS. She recalls that the Navy did not know whether the women should be treated differently or exactly the same as the men. It opted for the latter with one exception: their heads were not shaved, although their hair was unceremoniously chopped very short. All eight made it through OCS with flying colors and went on to flight training.[2]

By 1980, Lieutenant Habedank was flying out of the Naval Air Station at Norfolk, Virginia, as commander of a T-39 jet Sabreliner with VIPs aboard. She was looking forward to her new assignment to fly C-1 aircraft where she would be delivering passengers and freight to aircraft carriers. Carrier landings were made possible by a modification to the Navy's law, but a woman still cannot be assigned permanently as a member of the ship's aviation complement.

If that day ever comes, it will probably be too late for Habedank: the Navy shows no signs of moving in that direction in the foreseeable future. Meanwhile, because there are only some forty-five women pilots on active duty (as of mid-1981) and only twenty to thirty pilots and ten navigators programmed for training annually over a five-year period, women do not constitute a serious threat to the ship/shore rotation of their male colleagues. Just how long the women will be willing to endure their double standard, however, remains to be seen.

Lt. Barbara Allen Rainey faced these realities in 1977. "Navy flying isn't a viable career for a woman," she said. "It is too limited." A jet pilot from the first coed class, assigned to fly passenger/cargo transports, she often found herself watching male pilots in her squadron fly missions that should have been hers but for her sex. "Flying the mail to a ship," she said, "meant you had to be assigned to the ship, and a pilot assigned to a ship is a combat role, so I couldn't do it." She found that she was falling behind in flying time. After three years, she had logged between 1,100 and 1,200 hours in the air, compared to the 1,500 to 1,600 hours accrued by most of the men who had graduated with her.

When she became pregnant, Rainey had a choice to make: she could continue with her Navy career by taking maternity leave and then return to her flying duties, or she could get out. She opted to resign and to join her husband, a Navy flight instructor at Whiting Field in Florida. "If all things had been equal," she said, "it would have been a much harder decision. I might have taken leave and gone back on active duty if I had felt the opportunity for career advancement was there." But as far as she could see it was not, and the situation was not likely to be changed soon. "The patterns of male pilots to advance as naval officers are established, but with us, it hasn't really been worked out yet." She reluctantly decided to hang up her Navy uniform and maybe fly with the Reserve when she was able.[3]

THE ARMY FOLLOWS SUIT

The Army followed closely on the Navy's heels. In April 1973, the Chief of Staff, acting on the recommendation of an ad hoc committee that had studied the feasibility of opening the aviation program to women, approved the idea. The first coed flight training class graduated in June 1974, and Lt. Sally Murphy became the first female helicopter pilot in the U.S. Army.

Unlike its sister services, the Army was not restricted by the law on the use of women in either combat or noncombat missions. Army policy permitted women to be assigned to combat support and combat service support units, and there appeared to be no major problems that would mitigate against training and utilizing women as Army aviators.

Army pilots come in two varieties: officers and warrant officers. By 1978, some sixteen female officers and twenty-five warrant officers had entered flight training, and all but six got their wings; two had been named honor graduates of their classes.

The use of women as Army pilots, particularly in helicopters, raised the inevitable question of their role in the combat area. Helicopter pilots' duties, even in support capabilities, bring them into the combat environment. Women helicopter pilots will almost certainly find themselves in combat situations.

The women have had mixed views about this possibility. First Lt. Deborah Rideout, who received her wings in 1977, thought having women in a combat situation could be a serious problem "because deep down inside, I think every woman—even the toughest Tug Boat Annie—wants to be protected."[4]

Nancy K. Carter took the opposite view. Raised as an Air Force dependent with a stepfather who was a World War II flying ace, she had developed an intense interest in aviation and wanted to fly. By the time she entered Army helicopter training at the age of twenty-six, Carter was already a civilian fixed-wing pilot and had served in the Army as a medic on a helicopter ambulance. She was the first woman to become a full-fledged member of the mountain rescue team as a chief medic and the first woman to rappel from a CH-47 Chinook helicopter.

Unlike Rideout, Carter believed that the day was coming when Army women would see combat. She acknowledged that, while society was changing, men still wanted to protect women. "But as far as combat is concerned, I'm very proud of my country, and if Congress said 'You're going to combat,' fine, let's go, right along with my male counterparts," she said. As for men wanting to protect her, she didn't want it: "I can hold my own."[5]

THE AIR FORCE TEST

As predicted, the Air Force lagged behind the Navy and the Army in providing opportunities for women to fly. Because flying is the essence of their service's mission, those admitted into the rated ranks are accorded preferential treatment over nonrated officers throughout their careers. This preferred status is clearly demonstrated by the fact that while rated officers constitute 46 percent of the officers, they constitute 70 percent of the colonels, and 83 percent of the generals. They also enjoy substantially higher pay. So, exclusion from rated programs has more than symbolic implications.

In April 1975, when Col. Billie M. Bobbitt retired as Director, WAF, she urged the Air Force to reevaluate its policy of excluding women and to consider entering them in pilot and navigator training:

> I urge the Air Force to take a more practical view toward the possibility of entering women in flying training. The pressure to make this move is not going to slow down. Women perceive that as long as they are prohibited from serving in this capacity solely because they are women, it can only be viewed as a policy of containment, and they must continue in the role of second class citizens of the Air Force. That is particularly true when the Army and Navy allow women in rated positions, regardless of how limited. Should all pilots fly combat missions? What is so offensive about a two-track system if it would save training time, manhours, and money? If such a program would adversely impact on combat mission accomplishment, then we need better rationale and facts than are presently being given.

The Air Force finally made its move in 1975 when the Chief of Staff announced a test program for women pilots and navigators to be used in noncombat flying. The purpose of the test was unclear because women had already proven that they could fly all types of airplanes, even modern jets. What was being tested? Ostensibly, the test program's purpose was "to identify training or utilization problems associated with women in previously all-male careers." Some thought that, as in the case of the AFROTC test, the Air Force was seeking a way to forestall the inevitable.

In August 1976, the first ten women arrived at Lackland Air Force Base for flight screening; ten more followed, and from Lackland all twenty went to Williams Air Force Base in Arizona for the forty-nine-week undergraduate pilot training (UPT) program. In March 1977, six additional women were scheduled into navigator training. All twenty-six participants were already commissioned officers. As they had in the other services, these aviators would participate on the same basis as the men in all phases of the training and meet the same demanding requirements.

Capt. Connie Engel knew that when a pilot trainee soloed in the T-37 Tweet jet trainer, tradition required that he be unceremoniously tossed fully clothed into a tank of water by classmates. Engel made quite a splash as the first woman accorded this honor. One by one, the other nine women in the first coed group followed her into the solo tank and moved up to the supersonic T-38 Talon. "A lot of people had a lot of ideas that women wouldn't be able to hack it because of their lack of physical strength, because of their inadaptability to stress, because of this, because of that," said Lt. Col. C. T. Davis, the operations officer of the Flying Training Squadron, as the first class was completing its training. "So far, our experience has been that it hasn't changed things at all. The women are going through exactly the same training as the men and are hacking it just as well."[6]

According to 1st Lt. Shirley Popper, a former Air Force weapons loader, the first group of women were accepted well in the UPT program. They got "jumped on" just as hard as the men when they did something wrong and got as much praise as anyone else. Male students agreed. "The whole program is structured and we all meet the same standards," said male classmate Capt. Bob Boltzer.[7]

Despite the acceptance of their colleagues, the new breed of women pilots soon had experiences similar to those of World War II WASPs: seeing the astonishment on people's faces when they climbed out of the cockpit of an Air Force airplane after a smooth, uneventful landing. "When you step out of the airplane and take off your helmet, the transient maintenance guys almost fall over backwards," said Capt. Kathy La Sauce. "That sort of keeps us going." Keep going they did—all of the first ten graduated in September, put on the silver wings of the Air Force pilot, and went on to flying jobs. La Sauce's greatest desire had been to become a C-141 pilot. Before entering pilot training, she had been a maintenance officer on the giant Starlifter. "I feel at home there." She got her wish.[8]

First Lt. Christine E. Schott's wishes, however, were not so easily fulfilled. The first to solo in the supersonic T-38 Talon, Schott was described by a classmate as having "a fighter pilot's personality." A former communications officer, she had always wanted to be an astronaut and had even completed her degree in physics with that in mind. She had to settle for flying C-9 "Nightingales" with the Aeromedical Airlift Squadron at Scott Air Force Base, Illinois.

Others of their group went on to fly WC-130 weather reconnaissance aircraft and KC-135 jet refueling tankers. Capt. Connie Engel would remain at Williams as an instructor pilot in T-38s.

The Air Force soon declared the test program a success and decided to enter 150 women in flying training annually. The Air Force would evaluate the women's performance and assess their attrition and retention rates, utilization, and career progress through 1982.

There is no reason to believe that the women pilots' performance will be any different from that of their male peers, assuming they are given the same opportunities to use their skills. They will nonetheless continue to be something of a novelty as long as their numbers remain so small, and their performance will continue to be subject to scrutiny from all sides, even from their subordinates.

"As a fellow crew member, I found she encountered no problems with the flight," observed a male master sergeant after making the flight from Frankfurt, West Germany, to Charleston, South Carolina, with Capt. Charlotte Greene at the controls of the C-141. "The most unusual occurrence was the 'stares' the lady pilot received when we landed at Kuwait, an Arab country where women have little status." As with La Sauce, it had been Greene's goal to fly C-141s when she graduated from pilot training in August 1976. "Women are in the pilot business to stay," says Greene. "I'm proud to be among the first."[9]

A lot of old-timers would have loved to be in Greene's place.

"I was so happy when the military finally opened up flying careers for today's women," exuded Lt. Col. Yvonne C. Pateman (USAF, Ret.). She had logged 700 hours as a test and ferry pilot with the WASP and later served a full and distinguished career in the Air Force as an intelligence officer. Her only real regret was that she was never allowed to use her flying skills as an officer.[10]

Even with the combat restriction, the Air Force identified some 30 percent of the pilot and 18 percent of the navigator positions as "available to women"; and the major air commands labeled as "women acceptable" no less than twenty different types of aircraft—totaling roughly 2,400 planes, none of which are combat aircraft. In that light, the Air Force plans to train only 150 women each year were called tokenism by some. Others viewed it as a major breakthrough for women since it opened the way for opportunities never before available: operational flying, command of operational units, and important staff positions reserved for rated officers.

The goal was subsequently lowered to 125, and in 1981 the original figure of 150 was inexplicably halved, thus conveying the distinct impression that the Air Force did not consider the training of women pilots to be a serious commitment. Just how much the prohibition against women flying combat aircraft will affect their futures remains to be seen. However, the women themselves, while they don't necessarily agree with the combat aircraft restrictions, think they would see combat in a future war irrespective of the law. In 1981, Capt. Kathy La Sauce Arlington said she believed that her C-141 would be among the first to see war action because it would drop Army paratroopers into combat. "You're an American, female or not," she said. "I'm perfectly willing to do what I've been trained to do—to pilot aircraft into combat."[11]

When Capt. Susan Regele, the pilot of a C-9 Nightingale flying hospital, was asked what her reaction would be to being told she was going into combat the next morning, she said, "I probably wouldn't sleep all night but I'd go. I wear the uniform. I take the pay, and it comes with the territory."[12]

THE ICBMS

A related issue for the Air Force was whether women should be allowed to launch intercontinental ballistic missiles (ICBMs). Launch officers are classified in the rated categories and are considered combat positions. But when the Integration Act was written, ICBMs were only in the rough development stages and hence not even considered for the air combat exclusion contained in what became Section 8549. Within a decade, they would become an important element of the strategic forces, and by the early seventies whole generations of missiles had been phased in and out of Air Force inventories. By 1980, the Minuteman solid-fuel system had become the backbone of the land-based ICBM force consisting of over one thousand weapons. In addition, some fifty-four aging Titan II liquid-fueled missiles were still in the inventory but with uncertain futures.

In the early seventies, the Air Force opened missile maintenance and other support positions to women in both Minuteman and Titan systems. However, it kept the operational launch crew positions closed. The Air Force reasoned that the latter were classified as combat crews; while they were not specifically covered by the letter of the law, the Air Force believed its policy was consistent with the law's spirit. An underlying reason, however, was the Air Force's mistrust of mixed crews in situations where men and women in pairs would be isolated for long periods in underground silos. Minuteman launch crews consisted of only two members on long shifts—each holding a key to launch the most devastating weapons.

In 1974, as hearings were coming up on women's admission to the service academies, considerable interest was generated on the subject of women serving on missile crews. The commander of Strategic Air Command was requested to furnish the Air Force Chief of Staff with an "impact statement" on women serving as launch officers (1) on mixed male/female crews and (2) on all-female crews. SAC's reply stated that mixed crews "would probably produce undesirable morale and social considerations for crew members, both within the operational [silo] and family environment." Also, facilities would have to be modified to provide privacy, and this would break security policy, which required that crew members be in view of one another at all times—even while on the toilet. Mixed crews were therefore, in SAC's view, "undesirable and unfeasible." All-female crews could be formed without these complications, provided the numbers were large enough to allow normal assignment progression. SAC concluded that "if social and political moods require, SAC can assign women to missile combat crews." SAC exhibited, however, a noticeable lack of enthusiasm.

In April 1975, in her final report as WAF director, Bobbitt raised the issue of women in missile operations:

Based on duties performed, there is truly no defensible rationale to continue to exclude women from these duties based on law regarding women
in combat or because of assumptions regarding facilities and cultural
attitudes.

The break came in 1977 when Secretary of Defense Harold
Brown ordered the services to examine ways to increase the utilization of women. At that point, the Director of Air Force Personnel Plans, Maj. Gen. Bennie L. Davis, asked the SAC Personnel
Chief, Maj. Gen. Earl G. Peck, to justify the keeping of missile
launch officer and enlisted crew positions closed to women. Peck
replied that opening the field was feasible. Some women had volunteered and believed they should have the opportunity to compete in the operations environment. There were no physical or
mental limitations, he said, that would preclude them from performing the functions, but there were problems to be considered:
all-female crews were not practical, and mixed crews would cause
concern among the wives of male crew members. "Many wives
find mixed crews acceptable," Peck wrote, "but the percentage
who object are highly vocal and emotional." He concluded, "It
does not appear propitious to open missile operations to women at
this time."

The Secretary of the Air Force, John C. Stetson, decided on a
compromise measure, one that would partially open the missile
field without posing a real threat to nervous wives and without
requiring the facilities to be remodeled. He opened the Titan II to
women on a test basis, but not the Minuteman.

Unlike the Minuteman, with its two-member crew, cramped
quarters, and open toilet area, the older Titan has larger crews, its
on-site accommodations are relatively spacious, and bathrooms
have doors with latches.

Of the thirteen women officers who entered the Titan missile
training, all completed it. By mid-1979, four were assigned as
combat crew commanders, and nine were deputy commanders.
Moreover, of the twenty-one enlisted women who entered the
program, seventeen completed it. But the Minuteman remained
off limits.

Capt. Patricia Fornes, who was the first to qualify, recalls that
after five months of learning the "nitty-gritty" of the Titan system,
they spent another eight weeks learning how to "get to war," what
to do when the President sends you a message. As the first woman
assigned to a crew position, "I get all the 'flak,' " she says. "There
were still some reservations among the men I worked for. They

weren't sure if I'd get raped the first week or whether I'd rape someone," she recalls with a laugh.[13] Apparently, all survived uncompromised. Fornes went on to become a crew commander and loved it. Her career goals? To become a missile wing commander. Presumably, by then she will no longer have to worry about the availability of "facilities."

The Titan II experience was an unqualified success, and by 1980 the Air Force had "normalized" women in the system. Now the Air Force faced a real dilemma: women were virtually everywhere throughout the missile operations and support fields—in positions such as maintenance officers, munitions officers, and security police—with one exception: Minuteman launch control officers. SAC was still insisting that this position required study.

By now, no one was seriously pretending that Minuteman facilities were the problem; minor modifications were feasible. So the rationale (or blame) for women's continued exclusion now shifted to the wives. The Air Force had conducted a survey to determine the extent of their objections. This revealed that of the 1,200 Minuteman officers, 841 were married; and 67 percent of their wives disapproved of the idea of their husbands serving with a woman. In the eyes of the air staff, this was a vindication of the 1977 decision not to open the field to women. "What they are saying," observed a woman officer, "is that the Air Force is more concerned about the morale of the wives than the morale and careers of female officers."

Meanwhile, the Titan II system, plagued with mechanical problems, was under constant threat of elimination. In that event, what would become of the women trained as launch officers? The Air Force insists that the new systems coming on line, the ground launch cruise missile planned for deployment to Europe and the controversial MX, will be designed to accommodate mixed crews.

GOING TO SEA

If flying is the heart of the Air Force, duty at sea is the soul of the Navy. But whereas Air Force flying directly involves only a relatively small proportion of its personnel (mostly officers), duty at sea affects nearly the entire population of naval personnel. Hence, the key to deployment of personnel and to a successful career in the Navy has always been at the business end of the gangplank. All other considerations are secondary.

On 1 November 1978, eight young women ensigns reported aboard ships on the Atlantic and Pacific coasts. "Permission to come aboard, sir," said Ens. Mary Carrol, of Roanoke, Virginia, the first to join the ship's company of the USS *Vulcan*, a 530-foot repair ship home-ported at Norfolk. "Permission granted," came the reply as salutes were smartly exchanged. This was the beginning of the first wave of 55 officers and 375 enlisted women to be permanently assigned to Navy ships under a new law.[14]

Navy women had waited a long time for this moment. Most of those who had waited the longest and worked the hardest for it would never be able to participate now that the time had come to go to sea—they were too senior in rank.

The author recalls that in 1971, shortly after Adm. Elmo Zumwalt had become CNO, he was reportedly asked if he had ever thought about having women aboard ships. "When I was younger I thought about it a lot," was the handsome CNO's offhanded response. But he was not to get off the hook so easily.

Later, he faced a far more formidable and persistent audience. In May 1971, the DACOWITS pinned him down on the same question. Zumwalt admitted that he had not given serious thought to the question but felt it was not beyond the realm of possibility. Indeed, he did not see why women should not be able to do just about anything on a ship, and even allowed that an all-female crew might not be a bad idea.[15]

His Assistant Chief of Naval Personnel for Women, Capt. Robin Quigley, strongly disagreed. She later wrote:

> The key point here is that we are talking about *our* young women—out of our American societal structure. . . . The uncommodious, spartan, unrelieved, and physically demanding life of months aboard a destroyer or a fleet oiler might be tolerable for various reasons to women from other societal structures, where different sociological and political factors pertain, but it seems to me most unlikely that the comfort, convenience, and glamour-oriented young American woman would view such life as her golden opportunity and the basis for which to volunteer![16]

In 1948, when the law was written, the powerful chairman of the Armed Services Committee would have agreed with Quigley, as would nearly everyone else at the time. "Just fix it so that they cannot go to sea at all," Chairman Carl Vinson had told the Navy witnesses during hearings on the Integration Act. Fix it they did; Section 6015 of Title 10 stated:

The Secretary may prescribe the kind of military duty to which such women members may be assigned and the military authority which they may exercise. However, women may not be assigned to duty in aircraft that are engaged in combat missions nor may they be assigned to duty on vessels of the Navy other than hospital ships and transports.

So worded, the law was an accurate reflection of not only the spirit of the postwar period with regard to women's roles in the military, but the desires of the Navy itself. For although the Navy leaders would have preferred that the provision not be spelled out in the law, it in no way conflicted with their intentions for the assignment of women.

The Navy could well afford the restriction in 1948. The law had also placed a 2-percent ceiling on the number of women serving in the Navy, and women had minimal impact on the overall sea–shore rotation policies for naval personnel. As time would show, however, the Navy found it increasingly difficult to live with Carl Vinson's legacy.

In 1953, Congress allowed hospital corpswomen to serve aboard the Military Sea Transportation Service ships, which transported military dependents to overseas duty stations. Navy women onboard MSTS ships and hospital ships were not, however, filling positions that involved running the ships; rather, they remained in health care areas. In 1961, a woman line officer was assigned to a transport ship as an assistant transportation officer, which was a significant first.

But even these limited opportunities for sea duty dwindled away. In the early years of the Vietnam conflict, the transport ships were diverted from carrying dependents to carrying troops, and eventually the use of MSTS ships to transport dependents was discontinued entirely. Over three hundred nurses served aboard hospital ships off the coast of Vietnam, but when the last ship was decommissioned in 1971, even the nurses were landlocked.

When the legal 2-percent strength ceiling was lifted in 1967 and the number of women in the Navy began to increase, fears arose in the ranks of the Navy's old salts who felt that the ties that had so neatly secured the lid on Pandora's box were beginning to unravel at an alarming rate. The arrival of Admiral Zumwalt on the scene heightened these fears—justifiably, as it turned out. His Z-Gram 116 sent shock waves through the Navy, especially because it implied a future role for women afloat. With the opening of seagoing ratings such as boatswain's mates, signalmen, hull technicians, and many other seagoing specialists, women would for the first time begin to encroach on the rotation base—that magic number of billets the Navy sets aside to ensure that men at sea can have a job to which to come ashore. Yet, even as the women in those seagoing ratings filled those shore billets, there was no place for them to use the seagoing skills they had learned. To remedy this, the Navy needed a grand experiment.

In 1972, the hospital ship USS *Sanctuary* was taken out of mothballs, refurbished, and manned with an integrated male/female crew. Initially, all crew members were volunteers. Approximately fifty-three enlisted women and twenty women officers went onboard. Most of the women were assigned to the hospital; the others held jobs in the deck, supply, operations, resale, and administrative departments. No women were assigned to the engineering department, which remained an all-male stronghold.

The *Sanctuary* was to have been used primarily to provide medical care for Navy dependents home-ported overseas, but this role never materialized. Instead, after transiting from Alameda, California, through the Panama Canal, she tied up at Mayport, Florida, where she served chiefly as a dispensary for military personnel in the area. After that, she was only under way quarterly for training; for the disappointed crew, she became little more than a floating token. In 1975, the *Sanctuary* was again decommissioned, and the women went ashore.

The experiment, although limited, did give some firsthand indication of how women could perform at sea. The skipper reported that

> women can perform every shipboard task with equal ease, expertise and dedication as men do. Significant in this regard was the success of women on general quarters repair parties, and on general emergency teams, performance on which is considered a good gauge of general naval ability.

The end of the *Sanctuary* experiment, the continued expansion of the numbers of women, and the increasing pressure from women with seagoing rates to go to sea all pushed the Navy to find a solution. One possibility was assignment to Navy units aboard civilian-operated USNS (U.S. Naval Survey) ships. Because civilian women scientists were frequently assigned aboard, these ships had facilities for women. In 1974, the USNS *Michaelson* needed an

Interior Communications electrician (the IC rating), and there were no male ICs whose shore duty tour was completed. There was, however, a woman IC, Yona Owens, who had made inquiries about such an assignment. A recommendation that she be given the assignment was forwarded up the chain of command, but the Navy Judge Advocate General rendered an opinion that it would violate Section 6015 and recommended disapproval. Owen's orders were canceled, thus laying the groundwork for a critical court challenge.

While not favoring women on oceangoing survey ships, the Navy JAG did decide that women could serve on non-oceangoing tugs and harbor craft; in early 1975, as the *Sanctuary* was being decommissioned, Navy women began to arrive at the Service Craft Division of the naval station at San Diego. Unfortunately, any knowledge gained on the *Sanctuary* concerning the use of women onboard ships was apparently not passed on to the people in charge at San Diego.

The San Diego experience illustrates all that could be done to ensure the failure of a mixed crew. First, the women were sent there without the required special seamen apprenticeship training because it was available only to men. Next, the supervisors aboard the service craft were given no preparatory training and were uncertain as to how to supervise women or mixed crews. Consequently, they tended to grant the women special favors of the most damaging kind: women stood no watches, due to fear for their safety, and men had to pick up the slack; women were given the best assignments, bypassing the men who had been working their way up to those assignments; single women were allowed to live in off-base housing, while the men lived in the barracks or onboard the tugs. Such obvious and offensive double standards had predictable results. Eventually, the Navy called in a consultant to help resolve the difficulties. The majority of the inequities were corrected and training was provided for the men, the women, and the supervisors.

As this small source of shipboard duty was being developed, a new requirement arose for seagoing billets for women. With the passage of P.L. 94–106 allowing women into the service academies, the Navy had to provide opportunities for female midshipmen to participate in summer training cruises. Midshipmen, of course, generally trained on combat ships. The first group of women was slated for summers on the service craft, but this was in no way comparable to the training and experience the men received on the combat ships.

Meanwhile, Yona Owens had met three other Navy women who had felt the impact of Section 6015 in a very personal way. They decided to bring a class-action suit *(Owens v. Brown)* against the Navy, charging sex discrimination in that Section 6015 unconstitutionally denied Navy women equal protection under the law.

On several occasions the DACOWITS had recommended that the DOD propose legislation to rescind both Sections 6015 and 8549 so that the Secretaries of the Navy and Air Force would have the same latitude in the assignment of their personnel as did the Secretary of the Army (who had no legal constraints). However, such a sweeping change was the last thing the Navy had in mind at that point. Its leaders saw the law as a convenient hedge against the inroads of the more militant women (several of whom held important positions in the Pentagon during the Carter administration) and against the machinations of mavericks like Zumwalt (whose retirement had produced audible sighs of relief among Navy traditionalists).

Yet, the Navy was finding itself in increasingly intolerable situations under the law as written, or, more precisely, under the Navy JAG's strict interpretation of the law. For example:

- Navy women trained to repair complex shipboard electronic equipment could not go onboard the ship to make repairs; yet, similarly trained civilian women could, and did.
- Navy women could not be transported on a Navy ship, while Air Force and Army women could be, and indeed, on occasion, were.
- Navy women pilots could not land on aircraft carriers, or make deliveries to ships if such delivery required landing on or *hovering over* a ship; women pilots of the other services and civilian women pilots were not so restricted.
- Women at the Naval Academy were restricted by one law from obtaining the sea-duty training mandated by another law.
- Enlisted women in seagoing ratings were taking up shore billets with no hope of ever using their skills and training at sea.

While *Owens v. Brown* was in the courts, the Navy went to Congress for legislative relief. But its proposal was for half a loaf: rather than seeking outright repeal of Section 6015, the Navy proposed an amendment that, while allowing for the assignment of women to certain noncombat ships, would still leave the pride of the Navy—the combat fleet—pure and untainted by the intrusion of women.

During 1977 and 1978, Navy officials went before Congress to present their case for modification of Section 6015. Secretary of the Navy W. Graham Claytor, Jr., calling the existing law "incredibly archaic," argued for an amendment that would allow women to serve onboard auxiliary ships such as tenders, repair ships, research ships, and rescue ships.

> This [proposed] relaxation of the prohibition [against women going to sea] would open for assignment of women a significant number of billets, even though relatively few in the overall Navy Register, on non-combatant ships for permanent assignment of women, some 49 ships in our present Navy. Even more important than this ability to give permanent assignments to women on non-combatant ships, this statute would permit us to assign women to temporary duty in peacetime to any ship for training, indoctrination, repair and the like. . . . This change would open up more sea billets for enlisted women than we are likely to be able to fill with qualified people within the next few years.

On 27 July 1978, while Congress was considering these modifications, Judge John J. Sirica ruled on *Owens* v. *Brown*.[17] Noting that "whatever problems might arise from integrating shipboard crews are matters that can be dealt with through appropriate training and planning," Sirica ruled that Section 6015 "unconstitutionally denies plaintiffs and the class of Navy women whom they represent their right to the equal protection of the laws as guaranteed by the fifth amendment of the Constitution."

Judge Sirica did not require the Navy to assign women to ships immediately; he left that decision to the Secretary of the Navy:

> As the court has noted . . . there remain many unanswered questions about the effects of full sexual integration that may well convince military authorities that women members should be excluded from shipboard combat assignments, or even from permanent assignment to some noncombat positions, or for that matter, from all shipboard duties until such time as the vessels are properly equipped and crew members properly trained to accommodate their female counterparts. Those are essentially military decisions.

Sirica ordered the Navy to proceed with "measured steps" in a nondiscriminatory manner, making *individualized* decisions regarding women's capabilities with respect to their roles in the Navy. Although Sirica left to the Navy the decisions on how to proceed and how far to go, the ruling served notice that blanket exclusions would no longer be tolerated by the courts; the proposed amendment to the statute would meet this mandate. Congress approved the proposed modifications to Section 6015, and, after P.L. 95–485 was signed into law by President Jimmy Carter in fall 1978, the Navy began at last to send its women down to the sea in ships, but on noncombat vessels only—except for temporary duty on combat ships not to exceed 180 days.

During the hearings that eventually led to the opening of sea duty for women, much ado was made over restricting women from permanent duty on ships with combat missions. "What we're trying to do," Secretary of the Navy Claytor testified in March 1978, "is avoid having them as part of the combat team." However, he was never clear on precisely why they should not be a part of the team. Indeed, with regard to combat, he noted, "There is no hand-to-hand combat in the Navy. There just is none. You don't board enemy ships with a cutlass in your teeth any more. This is all done by electronics and long-range missiles and that sort of thing." Rather than a combat issue, according to Secretary Claytor, "the problem is whether or not we really can have women permanently assigned to ships that are on these long-range missions mixed with men, doing this type of thing in the kind of living conditions and environment that you have."

While the mighty Navy anguished over female sailors, the little Coast Guard pulled out of the harbor with mixed crews. In May 1977, more than a year before Judge Sirica ruled on *Owens* v. *Brown*, two high endurance cutters, the USCGC *Morgenthau* and the USCGC *Gallantin*, were selected as the first Coast Guard ships to operate with women assigned as permanent crew. Male crew members were briefed on the various aspects of a mixed crew, including the kind of conduct that would be expected and required. A newsletter was sent to families explaining the program and the command policy regarding the women's coming; and a "passive cooperation" policy was established with the ever curious media. The women arrived on board in late 1977. Each ship received ten enlisted women and two women officers representing about 13 percent of each crew. The women received the same briefing on conduct as had the men; this same presentation was then again given to the combined crew. The emphasis was on adult, professional behavior and proved a successful approach.

The experience of the Coast Guard should have given considerable comfort to those in the Navy who feared that women at sea would adversely affect combat readiness. Capt. Alan D. Breed, commanding officer of the *Gallantin,* summarized the situation briefly in 1978: "There have been no major problems to date." He conceded that several at least of his male crew members suffered "apprehensions, reservations, concerns, and in some cases frustrations," when the decision was announced that women would serve at sea. When the first female crew members reported aboard, two male seamen were standing on the fantail watching the women come across the gangway. One turned to the other and said, "There goes the neighborhood." Despite the initial opposition of some of his men, Breed adds, "Today I doubt that there are over two or three who retain such hard core opposition." The reasons for the changed attitudes: (1) that no favoritism has been shown in any assignments; and (2) that *Gallantin's* female crew members— officer and enlisted—had from the beginning carried out all assigned duties fully and professionally and their performance had not significantly differed from the men's.[18]

Indeed, the Coast Guard's success onboard these two first-line ships encouraged the service to employ mixed crews on many of its ships and, in August 1978, to remove all assignment restrictions based on sex. Soon afterward, two women were selected to command ninety-five-foot cutters.

The Navy soon discovered, as had the Coast Guard, that with proper planning and preparation, mixed crews were no big deal. Contrary to a widespread supposition, no major structural modifications were required for integrating crews. All that was required was to close off berthing compartments, reroute traffic that would have gone through those spaces, and modify some of the plumbing in a "head." Navy personnel policies required a bit more work. The Navy made it a policy from the beginning that *all* women would be eligible for sea duty. Other policy decisions included:

- Husbands and wives would not be assigned to the same ship or mobile unit. If two members of a crew were to marry, one member, usually the junior member, would be reassigned.
- Pregnant women would not be assigned to sea duty. A woman who became pregnant while serving aboard ship would be reassigned to shore duty.
- Women with dependents would be eligible for sea duty, as were their male counterparts.

Many of the older enlisted women had mixed feelings about going to sea. Unlike their male peers, they had not been trained for it and had not had the experience of serving at sea as youngsters.

"I'm no volunteer," said a woman who described herself as a "former WAVE" who had grown up in the old school. Because she was a single person when she came aboard, she had had to dispose of her household goods. Giving up the personal things she had acquired over the years and moving into the cramped quarters pained her. "This is for the younger kids. I'll do my time and then retire soon."

The older officers and NCOs, on the other hand, had too much rank to go to sea because the jobs they would have been assigned to required some previous experience at sea as junior officers and sailors—experience that had been denied them.

Most of the young women—officers and enlisted personnel— seemed in favor of the idea of going to sea. Ens. Jo Anne Carlton was "pretty thrilled about it." So was Christine Berringer, who had asked herself, "If the guys can go, why can't I?" "It was harder for the men to get used to us than for us to get used to them," said a female seaman assigned to the ship's galley as a cook. She found life at sea not as exciting as she had expected, but "O.K."[19]

Once the "guinea pig," "fishbowl" effect had worn off, life aboard soon became routine. The men and women seemed to adjust to the new situation after some initial uneasiness. As expected, the men's first reactions varied from "Hell, no, it'll never work" to a wait-and-see attitude. "They told us to get rid of our girlie magazines and clean up our language," said one skeptical seaman. "The Navy's changed a lot," said Petty Officer Larry Brown. "I used to be a line handler like that—but it was never like this."

"I wasn't sure what to expect," said Electronics Technician 3rd Class Mary Hazelton, but she was not bothered by the men's initial reactions "because I knew the novelty would wear off." It did.[20]

Christine Berringer's boss, Machinist's Mate 2nd Class Frank McKay allowed that "she does a damn good job. I'd like to have four more like her." He admitted he did not think much of having women at sea at first, but conceded that "I don't think that way now." As far as he was concerned, Berringer "worked as hard as any man." Finishing a twenty-hour shift overhauling the *Vulcan's* evaporators prior to a sea voyage, the nineteen-year-old female "grease monkey" said she enjoyed the work; it was what she had asked for when she joined the Navy.[21]

The people serving on the ships with mixed crews soon wished they would be left alone to get on with their jobs. They were tired of the official scrutiny, of living in a goldfish bowl, of having their every action observed and recorded, and of having their thoughts probed. They were fed up with constant media attention—the women were embarrassed by it and the men often resentful. The women were especially annoyed at the constant speculation about dating, socializing, and sex, much of which had been fueled by the much-publicized reaction of some Navy wives to the idea of having women aboard the ships with their lonely, deprived husbands. Early on, a letter from an angry wife appeared in the *Navy Times*, protesting that allowing women on ships was creating a "floating brothel" for lonely husbands. "Ban the broads," she demanded. Some women aboard ship thought the media attention was "disgusting," others that the press was playing up the issue of the wives to pit women against women. The question had come up earlier when women were put aboard the *Sanctuary* but Capt. James F. Kelly aptly pointed out, "Wives cannot seek to protect their husbands against temptation at the expense of other women's rights."[22] A female lieutenant put the issue more bluntly: "Navy wives who don't like the idea of women going to sea don't trust their husbands. If they really think it's easier for men to be straight arrows ashore, they're only kidding themselves." A female member of the crew of the USS *Vulcan* did not understand what all the fuss was about. "I'm married so I'm also a Navy wife," she said. "I have a nine-year-old son and I don't have room to think about the wives' resentment. My husband doesn't have any at this point."

The women all agreed that sex was just not a problem aboard ship, and most seemed to believe that becoming too involved with the people they worked with every day was inadvisable. "Besides," said one, "the Captain laid the law down—there'll be no fooling around aboard ship. What we do on our own time ashore is our own business. But when we're aboard, we have a job to do."

Within a short period, it was obvious that the women in ships program was an impressive success. Ongoing studies conducted by the Naval Personnel Research and Development Center and periodic reports of ships' commanders show that, with a few minor problems, the women have adapted well to shipboard life and are routinely performing in both traditional and nontraditional areas with skill, dedication and confidence; that, overall, they have proven they can handle shipboard tasks, including the long and hard work. Commanders report that the women's professional performance is at least equal to that of their male counterparts and have often commented that, if anything, women hold a slight edge over men in completing assigned tasks. They tend to be more thorough and determined to do a job well. They have demonstrated professionalism during deployments, even to isolated places like the Indian Ocean and Diego Garcia. They have significantly fewer disciplinary problems than the men, and one commander expressed that his men should follow the example set by the women for good behavior.

In 1981, Rear Adm. J. R. Hogg (the Director of Military Personnel Training), said that ships' commanders were asking for more women and that the Navy planned to have over 5,000 women on fifty-five ships by 1985, 1,200 over what had been originally planned. To go beyond that will require a change in the law to remove the combat ship restriction, he said.

DEBATE OVER THE "COMBAT" LAWS

In his 1978 decision against the Navy, Judge Sirica said of Section 6015 that the legislative background of the law "tends to suggest a statutory purpose more related to the traditional way of thinking of women than to the demands of military preparedness."

When the DOD drafted DOPMA in 1973, it included provisions for repeal of Sections 8549 and 6015. However, at the services' suggestion, the DOD dropped these provisions because they raised the issue of women in combat, which was considered too controversial and which, therefore, could delay DOPMA's passage. The subject's controversy was abundantly clear during the debates over women's enrollment in the service academies. The issues were clouded by the fact that each service had its own definition of what constituted combat.

Following the DOPMA hearings, Congress told DOD to come up with an agreed-upon definition of "combat" together with recommendations on expanding job classifications to which female members of the armed services may be assigned, and recommendations on any changes in law necessary to implement these recommendations. In February 1978, the DOD responded:

Definition of Combat. The term "combat" refers to "engaging an enemy or being engaged by an enemy in armed conflict." Under current practices, a person is considered to be "in combat" when he or she is in a geographic area designated as a combat/hostile fire zone by the Secretary of Defense. Members of the armed forces, not in a designated combat/hostile fire zone, may be designated as being "in combat" by the Secretary of Defense based on specific circumstances and events. These definitions apply to men and women of all the services.

A service member in combat is authorized to receive combat/hostile fire pay and earn combat awards. Women have received hostile fire pay and combat awards in past conflicts. Women have served in combat in many skills during World War II, Korea, and Vietnam. Army nurses have served in combat for over a hundred years, although they and other medical personnel are considered noncombatants. *Since the word "combat" has historically been used to include such a broad range of activities, the Department of Defense does not believe that the term provides a useful basis for expanding the opportunities for women in the service.* [Emphasis added]

At that time, the DOD described the limiting effects of Sections 6015 and 8549 on the Navy and Air Force personnel policies and suggested that the sections be repealed. In May 1979, the DOD sent a proposal for repeal to Capitol Hill.

Meanwhile, Section 6015 had been modified at the request of the Navy in the wake of the Sirica decision, and women were already serving at sea on noncombat vessels. Also, the Army, unencumbered by statutory constraints, had redefined its combat restrictions and was allowing commanders to employ women soldiers throughout the battlefield, though not as combatants. The Army nonetheless recognized that women would be deployed in combat zones as an inevitable consequence of their assignments, even though they would not be assigned to units where they would regularly engage in close eyeball-to-eyeball combat as part of their primary duties. They could be assigned to all units except the infantry, armor, cannon field artillery, combat engineer, and low altitude air defense artillery units of battalion/squadron size or smaller. Army women could work in all military occupational specialties except those concentrated in such units and could be assigned to combat support and combat service support units including signal battalions, maintenance battalions, brigade level headquarters, and certain artillery units.

In November 1979, the Military Personnel Subcommittee of the House Armed Services Committee held hearings on the DOD proposal to rescind Sections 6015 and 8549. But rather than being a debate on the merits of secretarial prerogatives and the need for flexibility in the utilization of personnel, the hearings turned into four days of heated, often emotional debate over women in combat with emphasis on ground combat and the horrors of war in general.

The lead-off witness was Maj. Gen. Jeanne Holm (Ret.), who favored repeal. Arguing that the services should have the widest possible flexibility, particularly in time of war, to make personnel policy "consistent with our national goals," Holm noted that the restrictive laws enacted in the post–World War II period had outlived their usefulness and had become counterproductive to the development of an optimum fighting force in the event of war:

> Whether or not the services expect to assign women permanently aboard combat ships or combat aircraft in peacetime is not the most crucial consideration here. That they may have to do so some day in the event of a national emergency is the point. The service secretaries should not be hamstrung in peacetime by laws they may not be able to live with in wartime.

Responding to the subcommittee's questions, Holm asserted that women could fly combat jets, serve on combat ships, fire missiles and artillery, and do any job that requires skill rather than muscle. Could they handle the stress of combat as well as men? Yes, if they had the same training. But "I have great difficulty with ground combat where the number one concern is physical strength," she said. "Every member of a ground combat team must support the team effort to come out with minimum casualties."

Assistant Secretary of Defense Robert B. Pirie also favored repeal to "allow the secretaries of the Navy and Air Force to set policy for, monitor, and review the assignment of women . . . just as the Army does now." The DACOWITS chairman, Sally K. Richardson, took the same position.

But the services were not unanimous in their support. Although official witnesses of the Air Force, Navy, and Coast Guard supported repeal, their reasons and degree of enthusiasm varied. Moreover, many retired military personnel and the Marine Corps representatives testified against the repeal.

Air Force Undersecretary Antonia Handler Chayes testified in support of repeal because it would allow greater flexibility and provide greater opportunity for Air Force women. "Moreover, there is the question of equity—of equal opportunity to fight and die for country as opposed to the risk of death women have always faced in roles as nurses and other support functions during wartime," she said. "It is also a matter of equity for men who should not be forced into greater danger than the women who take the same oath and wear the same uniform." There should be no concern, she insisted, that the services would rush out and do anything drastic if the law were repealed. "There is an innate conservatism that will operate as a brake on hasty action," Chayes reassured the committee. But she had no illusions about the risk factor or the women's ability to function:

> In any future war, I have no doubt women will face more severe risks of injury, just as United States civilians will. What we achieve by barring women from combat roles is an obstacle to career advancement, and little enhancement in protection.

Vice Adm. Robert B. Baldwin, Chief of Naval Personnel, testified to the DOD position in support of repeal, but he made it clear in response to questions that he did not personally favor the idea of women serving on combat ships. The admiral later told reporters the whole idea of repealing the restriction was the Defense Department's, not the Navy's.

The Marine Corps' witness pulled no punches. Lt. Gen. Edward J. Bronars, the Corps' Deputy Chief of Staff for Manpower, stunned DOD representatives by stating bluntly that the Marine Corps did *not* support repeal. While women had an important contribution to make to the Corps, "I do not subscribe to their participation in the combat role." He also had "a feeling that the nation is not ready to see their women participate actively in a combat role." This was flatly in contradiction to the official Navy Department and DOD position in support of the repeal.

The most meaningful testimony from military witnesses came from a young Air Force pilot and a Coast Guard admiral. Capt. Stephanie Wells, an instructor pilot, when asked if she could fly combat aircraft, affirmed that she had no doubt about it. She said she had flown in the back seat of an F-15 and had no problems. What about emergencies? She could handle them as well as anyone else. If the aircraft lost hydraulic fluid, "no one could fly it— not even a man," she said coolly. Could she handle the emotional problems associated with combat, strafing, and killing? "I haven't experienced it, but I think I could cope as well as a man," adding, "the other women pilots feel the same way."

As for women on combat ships, Rear Adm. William H. Steward, Chief of Personnel for the Coast Guard, saw no difficulties. The Coast Guard's experiences had convinced him. How were the women doing aboard its ships? How had they performed in fire-fighting details, on rescue operations that involve a good deal of physical requirements? Were there any limitations? Did women perform exactly the same duties as men? The admiral's reply was firm and to the point:

> There are always going to be some limitations on our people because no two people come of the same size and strength, generally speaking. This has not been a problem to us. Our women perform the duties as do our men. . . . There are times when obviously a 200-pound pump cannot be lifted by women; however, that same pump may not be able to be lifted by all of the male population of a particular unit as well. We have exposed the women to the gamut of our missions: law enforcement; marine environmental protection; aids to navigations; all of the other missions that we have. I can categorically state, sir, that their performance has been outstanding.

Significantly, when asked if he would have hesitation about taking a vessel with women crew members into a combat situation, Admiral Steward was positive: "As a commanding officer who has served under combat conditions, and given the performance of our women officers and enlisted women, I personally, sir, would have no hesitation in having them with me."

Retired Gen. William Westmoreland set the tone for much of the testimony in direct opposition to repeal and was clearly convinced that the Army had already gone too far in assigning women battle area jobs. "The political administration is trying to use the military as a vehicle to further social change in our society . . . in utter disregard for potential fighting effectiveness," he said, adding that "no man with gumption wants a woman to fight his battles." Acknowledging that his testimony really pertained to Army ground combat, he stated that he did not object to women ferrying bombers as they did in World War II or to their firing intercontinental ballistic missiles, where they are "subject to an environment that is perhaps no more hazardous than living in a [U.S.] city if you are going to have nuclear war" but that he opposed women serving on antisubmarine missions or aboard aircraft carriers in time of war.

Retired Brig. Gen. Elizabeth P. Hoisington agreed with her former chief: "I want my name on record as having stood up to oppose women being trained or assigned to combat units . . . such as riflemen, driving a tank, firing an artillery piece, piloting a fighter plane or serving aboard a naval ship." She admitted that she had no personal experience in a combat unit, but explained that "my male colleagues tell me—and I believe it—war is hell. Heads are blown off; arms and legs are maimed; suffering is so intolerable it affects a man for years," adding, "it is bad enough that our young men have to endure this. But do we want our women to suffer it too?" She believed that in a protracted engagement against an enemy, women would be "weak links in our armor. We cannot build a winning army if the soldiers in it have no confidence in the long-term mental and physical stamina of their comrades." She also felt that mixing men and women in units in close situations gave rise to "man-woman relationships" problems that could cause "costly distractions" in combat. "In my whole lifetime," she said, "I have never known ten women whom I thought could endure three months under actual combat conditions."

Concurring with Hoisington, retired Navy Rear Adm. Jeremiah Denton, a prisoner of war in North Vietnam for seven years, said that it would be moral and social insanity to subject women to war. He believed that women should be used to free men to fight.

Like the military witnesses (active and retired), the civilians who asked to testify came down on both sides of the issue. Carol Parr, executive director of the Women's Equity Action League, avoiding the emotional arguments, said that there is "absolutely no reason women can't make a full contribution to the nation's defense." Military jobs should be assigned "on the basis of skills not sex." The American Civil Liberties Union saw the question of combat as an equal rights issue: "The exclusion of women from combat causes severe injustice to women who are qualified and eager to serve in the military," said lawyer Diana A. Steele. "Men do not have a monopoly on patriotism, physical ability, desire for adventure or willingness to risk their lives." Until both share in the rights and responsibilities of citizenship, she contended, "women will continue to be considered less than full-fledged citizens." Other civilian witnesses did not agree. "Leadership and authority are male attributes ordained by God," proclaimed the director of the Moral Majority. "Women in combat roles violates the order of creation, will of God."

After four days of hearings, nothing was resolved. If anything, the case for repeal had suffered a strategic setback by the conflicting testimony from official service witnesses, which had prompted the chairman, Congressman Richard C. White, to observe that the DOD should "get its act together."

Upon learning of Bronars' testimony in opposition to repeal, the Undersecretary of Defense, W. Graham Claytor, Jr. (who had previously served as Secretary of the Navy when the official position was established), discussed the conflicting testimony with the Navy Secretary and sent a letter to Chairman White "to clear up any possible misunderstanding about the Department of the Navy's position." Claytor reiterated the Department's support for repeal.

The rift between the uniformed Navy and its civilian superiors on this subject widened. On 11 December 1979, the CNO, Adm. T. B. Hayward, sent a memorandum to the new Navy Secretary, Edward Hidalgo, "to provide you with my professional judgment on the issues involved." Hayward pointed out that the official position had been established prior to his becoming CNO and that he was not consulted prior to the decision to send the legislative proposal forward. "Had I been, I would not have concurred in the proposal, or in its rationale." Hayward's position was that:

> There is currently no requirement to assign women to combatant vessels. Such ships can be adequately manned in war without resort to so fundamental a change in policy.

Further, the admiral stated:

> There are a number of practical considerations which lead me to believe that men as a group can better cope with extreme combat situations involving extrication of themselves and their shipmates from battle damage while maintaining the combatant capability of damaged ships and aircraft under the severe physical stresses of battle.

Unfortunately, the admiral did not define what he meant by "practical considerations." If women were a danger to themselves and the ships, as Hayward implies, they should not be onboard any vessels. Indeed, it would seem that the questions regarding women on ships with combat missions are, at heart, the same as those which should concern us regarding women on any ships. The degree of concern may be greater during combat, due to the increased stress and likelihood of battle damage. But if it has been determined by the Coast Guard and the Merchant Marine and the Navy itself that women onboard can serve effectively and safely, then the restriction against women serving on ships with combat missions would seem to be unrelated to women's abilities. One suspects that the reasons are rooted more in the tradition of the sea than in the realities of modern naval combat.

In January 1980, the split between the Navy's civilian and uniformed leaders came out into the open. During the hearings before the House Armed Services Committee, the Secretary testified, "I support repeal of 6015," adding, "that does not mean I go to the next step saying women should go into combat." In his view, that decision should be left to the service. But the CNO could not agree and this time stated his position publicly. Repeal would give the public "the wrong signal," implying that women should go into combat. Hayward told the committee, "Let the country decide whether we want women in combat."

The Coast Guard had reason to be concerned about the Navy's attitude. In the event of an emergency, the operational control of Coast Guard vessels could be transferred from the Department of Transportation to the Navy. If the Navy decided to impose its restrictions on women at sea in the Coast Guard, it could mean that the women would have to be removed from the cutters right when they were most needed. The Coast Guard indicated that it had no intention of doing so.

The hearings were adjourned with no decision on repeal of Sections 6015 and 8549, but both Chairman White and the ranking minority leader, Congresswoman Marjorie Holt, indicated that the repeal was not a likely prospect, and indeed there were hints that the committee might consider proposing restrictions on the Army's use of women.

To those who sat in on the hearings, it was apparent that the DOD officials did not have their act together and that they had misread the depth of resistance in the military ranks to repeal. They were taken by surprise when the Marine Corps jumped ship and the Navy seemed to be treading water. Capitol Hill and the media gained the impression that the proposal was being pushed by civilian feminists within the administration who, rightly or wrongly, were perceived as being more concerned with women's rights and "social experimentation" than with legitimate personnel requirements or the needs of national defense.

The danger in the aftermath of this abortive attempt to secure repeal is that Sections 6015 and 8549 might have become symbols of the larger, more emotional issue of women in combat, and the opportunity may have already been lost for ever arguing successfully for repeal on its own merits. There may be no way to argue for repeal as a matter of principle, either from the standpoint of Secretarial management prerogative or as a matter of equity without conveying the strong impression of an immediate, practical purpose—that of placing women in *all* forms of military combat. Though that was not the intention of the DOD or the services, it was clearly on the agenda of some women's rights activists and was the underlying fear of many military leaders and extreme conservative elements of society. Unfortunately, the subject has become so emotionally charged that Congress may not be able to deal with it at all. In that case, it will undoubtedly end up in the courts once again. Litigation on constitutional grounds could come from either men or women. It will be a tough one to decide.

But so long as Section 6015 remains on the books, the ability of the Navy to absorb and effectively employ the talents of women will always be severely limited. The constraints of Section 8549 are less dramatic since they chiefly involve the officer force, and the Air Force still has a great deal of latitude under the law if it chooses to use it.

NOTES

1. Keil, p. 99.
2. Lt. Barbara Habedank, interview with author, 24 April 1980.
3. "Limits on Career, Not Pregnancy, Moved Female Pilot to Quit Navy," *The Ledger Star* (Norfolk, VA), 26 November 1977.
4. Eve Miller, " 'Ladybirds' Are Making History in Army Aviation," *Recruiting and Reenlistment Journal* (U.S. Department of Army, Washington, D.C.), May 1978.
5. *Ibid.*
6. T. A. Arnold [Maj., USAF], "Baptizing the New Breed," *Airman* magazine (USAF, Washington, D.C.), October 1977, p. 2.
7. *Ibid.*
8. *Ibid.*

9. M. N. Stanton, " 'Old' and 'New' Fly Together," *The Airlift Dispatch* (Scott Air Force Base, IL),.15 June 1979.

10. *Ibid.*

11. Donald Robinson, "Trained as Combat Pilots: Should U.S. Women Kill?" *Parade* magazine, *Washington Post*, 25 January 1981.

12. *Ibid.*

13. Capt. Patricia Fornes (panelist) before the DACOWITS, 22 April 1980.

14. "Navy Ships Get First Female Ensigns," *Washington Post*, 2 November 1978.

15. "Women Aboard Ships Is No Joke," *Washington Post*, 15 May 1971, p. E-1.

16. Robin Quigley [Capt., USN (Ret.)], "Women Aboard Ships: A Few Observations," *Seapower* magazine (Navy League), Washington, D.C., May 1977, p. 17.

17. *Owens v. Brown*, 455 F. Supp. 291 (D.D.C. 1978).

18. "The Gallantin Experience: 'No Major Problems to Date,' " *Seapower* magazine, September 1978.

19. "Women at Sea: Navy Traditions Being Rewritten," *Washington Post*, 25 February 1979, p. 1.

20. *Ibid.*

21. *Ibid.*

22. James F. Kelly [Capt., USN], "Women in Warships: A Right to Serve," *U.S. Naval Institute Proceedings*, October 1978, p. 47.

CHAPTER 23

REGISTRATION
AND THE DRAFT

ON FRIDAY, 8 FEBRUARY 1980, Commander-in-Chief Jimmy Carter boarded the presidential helicopter for a weekend at Camp David, leaving behind a written statement announcing his decision to request congressional authority to register women as well as men for the draft. "My decision to register women," the President explained, "is a recognition of the reality that both women and men are working members of our society. It confirms what is already obvious throughout our society—that women are now providing all types of skills in every profession. The military should be no exception." Pointing to the 150,000 women already serving in the armed forces and performing well while also raising the level of skills in every branch, he added, "There is no distinction possible, on the basis of ability or performance, that would allow me to exclude women from an obligation to register."[1]

The announcement ended more than two weeks of suspense following the 23 January 1980 State of the Union message in which the President enunciated a shift in U.S. foreign policy and a decision to reinstate registration for the draft to back it up. He had later indicated that he was considering requesting authority to include women and would decide by 9 February, when plans for registration were to be unveiled. Few doubted what Carter's final decision would be: to exclude women from registration would be inconsistent with his advocacy of the ERA and other measures aimed at enhancing the equality of the sexes.

Under existing Selective Service law, the President has the authority to register young men but not to draft them. In 1975, President Gerald Ford terminated peacetime registration and put the system in "deep standby" with a small staff. To put the system back in working order, Congress would have to provide additional funds; but to include women would require an amendment to the Selective Service Act. Actually to induct anyone would require a separate act of Congress. Carter carefully pointed out that he had no intention of drafting anyone and that he was not abandoning the all-volunteer force; registration was simply a time-saving device to help mobilize troops in case of an emergency.

In the end, the President obtained funds to register men, but Congress could not bring itself to shatter 204 years of tradition by including women. That omission threatened to bring down the entire system in the courts. On Friday, 18 July 1980, a three-judge federal court—the Third U.S. Circuit Court of Appeals in Philadelphia—ruled in *Goldberg* v. *Rostker* that draft registration that excludes women is unconstitutional and ordered the government not to begin registering nineteen- and twenty-year-old men, which was to commence the following Monday. On Saturday, Supreme Court Justice William J. Brennan, Jr., ended the legal confusion, at least temporarily, by granting a government request to block the lower court ruling. Registration of men could proceed pending a final ruling by the Supreme Court. Until that time, the system remained under a heavy legal cloud.

The President's decision to revive peacetime registration came as a stunning surprise to members of Congress and to officials in his own administration who only months before had been locked in battle on this very subject.

In 1979, powerful members of the Armed Services Committees of both houses of Congress made serious efforts to replace the AVF with another peacetime draft. When they failed, they attempted to force the President to use his authority to reinstate registration. Two bills came up for floor debates. Neither made it through Congress, and credit for their defeat was laid at the door of the Oval Office.

The White House and top officials, ranging from Secretary of Defense Harold Brown to the Acting Director (later Director) of the Selective Service System, Dr. Bernard D. Rostker, argued repeatedly and persuasively that there was no need to resume registration for the draft. "We do not believe it is necessary to impose this burden on our nation and its youth at this time," White House domestic affairs advisor Stuart E. Eizenstat wrote to members of Congress in July 1979, "when there are effective ways to improve the capabilities of the Selective Service System so it can respond quickly in time of emergency."

Defense officials insisted that a premobilization registration would not meet the services' needs since their requirements during the initial phase of a war would be for *pretrained* individuals, not for untrained conscripts. "We believe that peacetime registration is not needed from an operational point of view," the Assistant Secretary of Defense for Manpower, Reserve Affairs, and Logistics, Robert B. Pirie, Jr., wrote to Sen. William S. Cohen in September 1979. "We are going to need pretrained individuals for the first 90 or 120 days . . . regardless of the status of registration or a draft. Peacetime registration cannot meet our pretrained individual manpower needs." Moreover, Rostker testified that if adequate funds were provided by Congress to revitalize it, the Selective Service System would be able to develop the capability to meet DOD wartime requirements. The collective view of these two agencies and all their studies suggested that the premobilization collection of names was not necessary for improving the ability to prepare for an emergency mobilization.

The administration's arguments were persuasive enough to kill efforts on Capitol Hill to force registration. One factor that helped cool Congress's ardor for peacetime registration was Defense Secretary Brown's suggestion in early 1979 that if registration were resumed by congressional order, it should include women. If Brown had wanted to throw a monkey wrench into the bring-back-the-draft effort on Capitol Hill, he could not have chosen a more effective way. The issue of whether women should register became a dominant part of the discussion and, as far as the pro-registration/pro-draft people were concerned, confused "the real military issues."

In its report of 19 June 1979 on the bill seeking to require registration "of certain persons," the Senate Armed Services Committee stated emphatically:

The committee feels strongly that it is not in the best interest of our national defense to register women for the Military Selective Service Act, which would provide needed military personnel upon mobilization in the event of a peacetime draft for the armed forces.

However, members of Congress were unsure at that point as to whether an all-male registration would be constitutional. If not, litigation could tie up the whole system in the courts, possibly for years. Faced with this prospect, other unanswered questions, and the strong resistance of the administration, the pro-draft forces on Capitol Hill capitulated.

The only legislation to come out of these debates was a law, passed in November 1979 (P.L. 96–107), requiring the President to prepare and transmit to Congress a plan for reform of the existing Selective Service System. The plan was to include recommendations on a number of specific issues, among them: whether resuming registration was desirable and feasible; whether the President should be given authority to induct previously registered persons during periods when he determines it to be required in the interest of national defense; and *whether women should be subject to registration and induction.*

Before that report was finished, the President preempted its conclusions and recommendations by announcing on 23 January 1980 his decision to register men and, on 8 February, his decision to request authority to include women. Ostensibly, the reason for this sudden reversal was the new international crisis in the Middle East precipitated by the Soviets' bold move into neighboring Afghanistan, which was perceived as a threat to the area's vital oil fields. The reinstatement of draft registration was to be a signal to the Soviets that Americans were ready to make the necessary sacrifices to meet aggression and to protect their vital interests abroad —a show of national resolve, as it were.

Understandably, the President's road-to-Damascus conversion on registration in January 1980 not only surprised Congress but stunned key members of his own administration, who confessed privately that they had not been informed of the President's decision until a few hours before the State of the Union address.

With no prior warning of the President's decision, key officials in the Pentagon also were caught flat-footed. "We had no inkling of this," lamented one harassed official. "The press is all over us and we don't even have officially approved answers on the questions yet." The mail was pouring in, some on the registration of men but a high percentage addressing the registration of women, much of it negative.

Predictably, antifeminists rose to the bait. "President Carter has stabbed American womanhood in the back in a cowardly surrender to women's lib," exclaimed the leader of the anti-ERA movement to the press. She claimed to have gathered more than 100,000 signatures on petitions to Congress. "We are not going to send our daughters to do a man's job."

A crude, hand-drawn poster arrived at the offices of the House Armed Services Committee, depicting a young woman in uniform, missing a leg, a hand, and an eye. She is supported by a crutch on one side and her mother on the other. "This is what the Equal Rights Amendment did for my daughter," sobs the distraught mother.

Unlike the antifeminists, who knew where they stood, feminists were thrown into confusion. If, by including women, the President had expected to woo feminist support of registration, he had seriously misjudged the women's movement in America. As those familiar with it know, the feminist movement has its roots in pacifism and many of the current leaders are veterans of the antiwar, antidraft protests of the sixties and early seventies. Carter's sudden decision to call for registration of men and women put feminists on the spot; they were torn between their abhorrence of war and the combat mission of the military profession, on one hand, and their desire that women enjoy the many benefits and advantages bestowed by military service—training, education, and G.I. and veteran's benefits—on the other.

The registration was especially troublesome to ERA advocates because the draft had always been a main emotional stumbling block to the ratification process. If there was one thing on which the pro- and anti-ERA people could agree, it was that if the ERA were ratified, women would have to be included in any future draft. Because of its negative impact on the ratification, most of the "pro" people preferred to avoid the issue. Once it had been made a subject of national debate, however, feminists had no choice but to support the President—he had made them an offer they could not refuse.

Nonetheless, many ERA supporters were clearly uncomfortable. "It is ironic," lamented one proponent, "that women might be drafted before they have even gained their constitutional rights." Some suggested that women should refuse to register until the ERA was ratified. "When American women have equality of opportunity," said Bella Abzug, "it will be time enough to talk about equality of sacrifice."[2] Others believed that it would help ratification by putting women in a stronger position to insist on equal protection of the Constitution they would be required to defend: "Equal obligations deserve equal rights." The National Organization for Women took the position against registration of young people "because it is a response which stimulates an environment of preparation for war. . . . War is senseless. Neither the lives of young men nor young women should be wasted. But, if we cannot stop the killing, we know we cannot choose between our sons or daughters."[3] Carol Parr of the Women's Equity Action League, on the other hand, saw registration as an opportunity to show that women mean business and will take on responsibilities.

Those on Capitol Hill who had fought for a return to registration were overjoyed at the President's decision on that score but annoyed that he wanted to include women. That was excess baggage they did not want. The Manpower and Personnel Subcommittee of the Senate Armed Services Committee (the Nunn subcommittee) accused the President of "confusing the real military issues" by interjecting the question of women into the 1980 registration debate.

Those who had supported the administration's previous position against registration felt Carter had pulled the rug out from under them. Congresswoman Patricia Schroeder, member of the House Armed Services Committee and the Congresswoman's Caucus, had reason to feel especially betrayed, having earlier led the administration's successful fight in the House against registration. "I was a little ticked," she told reporters, "to find Carter changed his mind." Then a White House lobbyist told her, "Don't worry, you can carry the part about women." She was outraged.[4]

House Speaker Thomas P. "Tip" O'Neill warned the President not to propose registration of women—that it would never make it through Congress. "As I read the Congress," the Speaker told reporters, "it wouldn't go. . . . It would be anathema around here." O'Neill believed that the White House would be better off dropping it. But as for himself, he said, he favored the idea of registering both men and women.[5] Chairman Richard C. White of the Military Personnel Subcommittee of the House Armed Services Committee concurred with O'Neill's estimate of the proposal's success but not with his views on women. He also prophesied that it would be stopped in its tracks.[6]

The differing reactions of young people were assessed in varying polls. A Gallup poll of eighteen- to twenty-four-year-olds showed that overall they favored registration for women as well as men but were against a return to the draft. If a draft were to become necessary, most men said women should be included (61 percent to 35 percent), but most women said they should not (58 percent to 39 percent). Overall, the young people surveyed favored drafting women as well as men by 50 percent to 47 percent. A healthy majority thought that if the draft were put into effect, young people would protest or evade it. Surprisingly, by a hefty margin—two out of three—both men and women believed that women should serve in combat but only if they *volunteered* to do so. Only one in five were against it. On 25 February, *U.S. News and World Report* reported that the question of including women in any registration drew a "cautious 'yes' " from most students. A poll taken at Ohio State indicated that two-thirds of the men felt women should register, but that women were against it by 52 to 48 percent.

The question of drafting women has always been and is still regarded on Capitol Hill as an emotional minefield on a par with abortion and sex education in the schools, and Congress clearly did not relish having to deal with it in 1980, an election year. Congress was in no mood to mandate registration of men, far less women, White told reporters, because the White House "fought us tooth and nail last year" on the proposal to register men. As far as he was concerned, the proposal to register women eroded the message of strength the President was trying to send to the Soviets.[7]

Women in Congress were divided on the issue. In the House, Congresswoman Marjorie Holt, influential ranking minority member of the Military Personnel Subcommittee, remained firm in her conviction that as long as women were not to be used in combat, there was no need to register them for the draft. Her fellow Marylander, Barbara Mikulski, predicted "a terrible backlash" if women were not registered. "I come from a working class neighborhood," she said. "We've told the guys in the unions and on the construction sites to move over and make room for sisterhood. If the women aren't registered, the guys will say, 'Jesus, you want to be equal on the assembly line.' It could cause a lot of anger and resentment."[8]

Schroeder believed that registration would not provide "one iota of improvement in our defense posture," but "if the country needs registration to defend this country and the draft, then of course women will have to go."[9]

The Senate's only woman, Nancy Landon Kassebaum, wrote the President on 31 January 1980 that "both equity and national resolve would be best advanced by including women in the registration requirement." If the registration system were not equally applied to both men and women, the plainspoken senator cautioned, "I fear we will lose the cooperation of both."

The principal reason that American women have not been drafted before is not, as some believe, because there has never been a need to do so. Neither is it, as others believe, because the American public has always been against drafting women. Women have not been drafted because the United States has never faced a manpower crisis of the magnitude of those that confronted the USSR and Great Britain during World War II or Israel in its fight for independence in the late forties. In the absence of such a crisis, the U.S. Congress has been able to sidestep the issue rather than deal with it finally and objectively on its own merits even in times of severe military manpower shortages.

The nearest this nation ever came to inducting women was during World War II. Had the conflict in Europe not ended when it did, the United States would probably have experienced its first draft of women.

When the Army discovered, after a survey of commanders in 1942, that it could use 1.5 million WAACs, serious consideration was given to seek legislation to draft some 500,000 women annually over a three-year period. However, in anticipation of public and congressional opposition, the idea was shelved in favor of an all-out volunteer WAAC recruiting program. Director Hobby warned then that "I don't believe we are going to get even 150,000 volunteer women unless there is some move . . . requiring national registration or compulsory service."[10] Her advice was ignored, and the Army embarked on the disastrous recruiting effort that almost destroyed the infant WAAC before its first year was out. When it soon became obvious to the Army that recruiting 1.5 million women volunteers was not in the cards, the goal was lowered to 150,000, and draft calls for men were increased to make up the deficit.

By 1944, with 12 million Americans in uniform, the draft scraping the bottom of the manpower barrel, and the Women's Army Corps nowhere near its planned strength despite enormous recruiting effort and expense, the subject of drafting women once more surfaced. At that time, Hobby advised the Chief of Staff that "a year's experience indicates the improbability of attaining, through voluntary enlistments, an adequate supply of woman-power to perform essential military services." To a military conference she stated, "I believe it is as fair to ask volunteers for service as to ask volunteers to pay taxes. . . . When people are asked, 'Why aren't you in the Service?' they remark, 'Oh come now, if the Government really needs us they will draft us.' "[11]

The choice at that point, as the Army saw it, was between drafting older men with children or single, unemployed young women. The British were already registering women and had the power to direct them into the armed forces. There were an estimated 5 million American women who could meet WAC selection standards, and only 631,000 would have to be drafted to meet the Army's requirements.

Congressman Emmanuel Cellar of New York put the case clearly before Congress when he introduced legislation to draft single, unemployed women between the ages of twenty and thirty-five, arguing that it was more logical to draft these women than to "wrench" married men away from their families and away from needed civilian war production:

> In so drafting older and married men, women will necessarily have to replace them and we have the double time waste of training women to do the man's work in civilian life and training men for jobs in the Army for which women already have the prerequisite skills. Able-bodied enlisted men are cooks, hospital aides, clerks, telephone operators, typists, draftsmen, optometrists, stenographers, bookkeepers, laundry workers, storekeepers, teletype operators, dental mechanics, pharmacists, laboratory technicians, and so forth. A half million unmarried idle women could replace these men without upsetting the economy, without withdrawing much needed manpower from essential jobs and without destroying the family unit.[12]

Congress remained unmoved even though the American public seemed solidly behind the idea. Gallup polls showed that 78 percent of Americans believed that single women should be drafted before any more fathers were taken. Even single women agreed by a three-to-one majority, but stated that they would not volunteer as long as the government did not believe the matter important enough to warrant a draft. This was no doubt the reason why, in three years of herculean effort and at enormous expense, the Army WAC achieved its peak wartime strength of just under 100,000.

Drafting fathers would not solve the growing nurse shortage, however. A bill to draft nurses was introduced on 7 March 1945 by the chairman of the House Military Affairs Committee with the backing of the Secretary of War and the Surgeon General.[13] The Nurses Selective Service Bill of 1945 passed the House and cleared the Senate Committee on 28 March but was never enacted because the war's termination in Europe in May eliminated the shortage of nurses.

Thus the war ended without women being drafted—with the nation still relying on a conscription system for men in the armed forces and a voluntary one for women. The effects of the juxtaposition of these approaches were clearly obvious to WAC historian Treadwell:

> Without a draft, the armed forces could not expect . . . to plan on a women's corps of any great size. Greater expansion plans founded on voluntary recruiting had not only failed in World War II, but had involved the [Women's Army] Corps in expensive miscalculations in clothing, housing, officer strength, and other allotments. The competitive expense of recruiting had also become so high that it appeared unthinkable for the armed forces and industry to enter another such contest against each other, with each spending tremendous sums on recruiting and advertising.[14]

However, despite the historical evidence, a popular myth emerged after the war, which persists to this day: that is, that in the event of a national emergency, there will be no need to draft women because they will rise to the colors in sufficient numbers to meet the services' needs "as they have in the past." This notion simply is not supported by the facts.

In the postwar era, one of the purposes for making women a permanent part of the peacetime services in 1948 had been to provide an additional source of volunteers and thus avoid the need for a peacetime draft. But, when the draft was reenacted two weeks after the Integration Act, it applied to men only.

Congresswoman Frances Bolton, a key figure in the Integration Act enactment, then stated her continued belief that women should be included in the draft: "Women should not be in the position of serving their country on sufferance," she wrote in a national magazine.

> They should serve as men do . . . because their country needs them. . . . [It] boils down to a very simple choice: Either we need women in our armed forces or we do not. The hard-won lessons of the war prove that we do and that there is only one way to get them—by a general registration and selective service.[15]

As U.S. forces expanded to meet deployments to Korea, plans to expand the women's programs once again foundered on the rocks of volunteerism. The strength goal of 112,000 fell disastrously short, at enormous cost, and a shortfall of nearly 70,000 women had to be made up by increasing recruiting and draft calls for men—to perform jobs that the armed forces had slated for women.

The lessons of history, then, are simple. First, in peacetime the nation should have, in place, a means to mobilize the vast resource of talents and skills that women possess. Second, the nation cannot rely on women to volunteer in significant numbers while men are being drafted. And third, unless there is a way to draft women in an emergency, the nation will have to conscript many thousands of men to do jobs that women can do as well or, in many cases, better, and for which many women already have the required skills.

Administration officials who in 1979 had so successfully fought off the earlier attempts to reinstate registration found themselves the following year in the difficult and embarrassing position of making the case *for* it. Especially embarrassing was the fact that the presidential recommendations to Congress on Selective Service reform had already been drafted supporting the 1979 administration position against registration, and copies of that draft, dated 15 January, had been leaked to members of Congress. With the President's change of heart, the report had to be revised to support the latest official position *for* registration.

The report's position on women, however, remained constant. The final report, published on 11 February 1980, concluded:

> In order to expand the potential personnel pool available during a national emergency, women as well as men should be subject by law to registration, induction and training for service in the Armed Forces. Women should constitute a part of the personnel inventory from which the Services could draw to meet requirements as needed. The utilization of women would be determined in accordance with the needs and mission of each Service.

Its recommendation was:

> The Military Selective Service Act (50 U.S.C. App. 451, *et seq.*) should be amended to provide Presidential authority to register, classify and examine women for service in the Armed Forces. At such time as Congress authorizes the conscription of men, authority should also be extended to provide for the conscription of women.

The report also emphasized that the ability of the all-volunteer force to meet its military personnel requirements could be enhanced by the recruitment of more women, thereby reducing reliance on the pool of young men.

Hearings were held in both the Senate and the House by subcommittees of the Armed Services Committees. However, it was clear from the outset that key members had already made up their minds on the question of registering women. In the Senate, the powerful chairman of the Armed Services Committee, Sen. John Stennis, announced on the floor of the Senate on 21 April his opposition to the registration of women. Sen. Sam Nunn, chairman of the Subcommittee on Manpower and Personnel, which would hold hearings, let it be known that although he had introduced the legislation, he did so only as a matter of convenience for the administration and that he personally was against it. On the House side, in announcing hearings of the Military Personnel Subcommittee, Representatives Richard White and Marjorie Holt, Chairman and ranking minority member, stated jointly that many members opposed the proposal to register women but that "the subcommittee is obligated to provide a forum for representatives of varied views to present their views to the Congress on the issue."

Given the attitude of the leaders of the key committees, the hearings turned into a search for justification *not* to register women instead of an objective analysis of whether women *should* be included. The results were predictable.

On Thursday, 17 April, the Manpower and Personnel Subcommittee of the Senate Armed Services Committee rejected by a vote of five to two the proposal to register women but voted to authorize the funds for registration of men. In its report, the subcommittee listed the following "specific findings":

1. Article I, section 8 of the Constitution commits exclusively to Congress the powers to raise and support armies, provide and maintain a Navy, and make rules for government and regulation of the land and naval forces, and pursuant to these powers it lies within the discretion of the Congress to determine the occasions for expansion of our armed forces, and the means best suited to such expansion should it prove necessary.

2. An ability to mobilize rapidly is essential to the preservation of our national security.

3. A functioning registration system is a vital part of any mobilization plan.

4. Women make an important contribution to our national defense, and are volunteering in increasing numbers for our armed services.

5. Women should not be intentionally or routinely placed in combat positions in our military services.
6. There is no military need to include women in a Selective Service system.
7. Present manpower deficiencies under the All-Volunteer Force are concentrated in the combat arms–infantry, armor, combat engineers, field artillery and air defense.
8. If mobilization were to be ordered in a wartime scenario, the primary manpower need would be for combat replacements.
9. The need to rotate troops and the possibility that close support units could come under enemy fire also limits the use of women in non-combat jobs.
10. If the law required women to be drafted in equal numbers with men, mobilization would be severely impaired because of strains on training facilities and administrative services.
11. Under the Administration's proposal there is no proposal for exemption of mothers of young children. The Administration has given insufficient attention to necessary changes in Selective Service rules, such as those governing the induction of young mothers, and to the strains on family life that would result from the registration and possible induction of women.
12. A registration and induction system which excludes women is constitutional.

Sen. William S. Cohen, one of the two dissenters, filed separate views in which he took issue with most of the subcommittee's findings and said, "If we are to have registration at some point, whether in a pre- or post-mobilization plan, there is no rational basis for excluding women." He called the subcommittee's findings

> fatally flawed because they erroneously focus on the assignment of women to combat and fail to address approved plans for the use of women to meet "non-combat mobilization requirements." The assignment of women to combat roles is an issue that unnecessarily clouds the central issue of how the nation can best meet its personnel requirements in time of mobilization.

Cohen also took the subcommittee to task for addressing the wrong question:

> The question should be why women should not be registered, rather than why they should be. The burden of proof falls on those who would exclude women from this obligation. No convincing case for such an exclusion has been made thus far.

In coming to these conclusions, the committee had to ignore the historical evidence and gloss over factual testimony by numerous expert witnesses and the Defense Department's and White House's insistence that there was no intention of using women in combat. This testimony, however, was of paramount importance in that it became a permanent part of the legislative history of the all-male Selective Service Act and as such would serve as the basis for future court decisions on the issue.

By a voice vote, the measure was rejected by the Senate. A last-ditch effort by Senator Kassebaum to prohibit use of funds for registration unless women were included was also defeated.[16] On 25 June 1980, the House voted 234 to 168 authorizing funds for the registration of men.

OTHER COUNTRIES

Perhaps the most convoluted reactions to the 1980 proposal to register women for the draft was that to do so would send the wrong message to the Kremlin—that it would be a demonstration of weakness rather than one of strength and resolve, showing that America was so weak it needed its women to fight. This argument flies in the face of fact: Soviet law has long provided for the conscription of women on the presumption that large numbers of them might be needed in the event of war, as they were in World War II, when the Soviet armed forces drafted a million women.

One cannot effectively contend that the Soviets and the British were less resolute during the war because they conscripted women or that the Soviets showed greater weakness because they used women to fight. To the contrary, these actions have been regarded as heroic demonstrations of the will to mobilize all of a nation's human resources in an emergency—something the United States has so far been unwilling to do. It is more likely that the Soviets view the United States' historic reluctance to register and draft women as a sign that the nation does not really take women seriously as a viable, valuable resource in an emergency, despite their growing importance to the readiness of the peacetime forces.

Of the other major nations in the free world, only Great Britain, Canada, and Japan require neither registration nor conscription as of this writing. However, of the some seventy-five other countries that register and/or conscript persons into armed services, the Defense Intelligence Agency reports that nine include women: Algeria, Chile, Israel, North and South Korea, Peru, Romania, Vietnam, and the USSR.

West Germany conscripts men at age nineteen, who then serve for fifteen months and become members of the reserve. France requires compulsory service of men at age nineteen for one year, but fathers of two or more children are exempt. Italy imposes compulsory service on men only at age eighteen; they must serve one year in the army or air force or eighteen months in the navy.

Israel requires that at age seventeen, all men and women register for service. Starting at age eighteen, men serve for three years, women for two. Women married by eighteen serve in reserves only; mothers and pregnant women are exempt.

The USSR has continued to rely on compulsory military service for men to provide the resources to sustain its force of over 3.5 million. It tends to regard the role of women in the peacetime armed forces as an auxiliary one, much as the United States did during the peacetime draft. The USSR emphasizes women's immense potential for large-scale mobilization in the event of war. The Universal Military Service Law of 1967 (amended in 1977) subjects women to conscription during wartime; and, in anticipation of a widespread call-up for women, the Soviets have instituted preparation procedures on a large scale. All women must take part in preinduction military training programs for youth. All women with specialist skills, especially in the field of medicine, must register with their local draft boards. Reservist status is compulsory for all discharged servicewomen and all women who have completed reserve officer training in institutions of higher learning.

Viewed in the context of Soviet preparedness, one must conclude that the registration of American women for the draft would most likely enhance the U.S. posture rather than weaken it. It would seem that if this nation is to be truly prepared to meet a potential threat from the Soviet Union, it should be prepared to make a comparable commitment by providing for the mobilization of all its human resources. If the enemy anticipates placing the burden of wartime service on all its people, can the United States afford to do less? Apparently, Congress in 1980 believed we can.

NOTES

1. Statement by President Jimmy Carter released by the White House Press Office on 8 February 1980.
2. Margot Hornblower, "Women's Dilemma: Equality v. Pacifism," *Washington Post*, 9 February 1980.
3. National Organization for Women, "The Registration and Drafting of Women in 1980," position paper, 6 February 1980.
4. Hornblower, *op. cit.*
5. Michael Getter, "O'Neill: Congress Will Not Pass Registration of Women for Draft," *Washington Post*, 1 February 1980.
6. George C. Wilson, "Registration of Women Held Unlikely," *Washington Post*, 20 February 1980.
7. *Ibid.*
8. Hornblower, *op. cit.*
9. Testimony before a subcommittee of the Committee on Appropriations of the House of Representatives. Hearings on Selective Service System, 27 February 1980, pp. 145, 194.
10. Treadwell, p. 122.
11. *Ibid.*, p. 246.
12. H.R. 4906, *Congressional Record*, 1 June 1944, p. 5151.
13. H.R. 2277.
14. Treadwell, p. 760.
15. The Hon. Frances P. Bolton, "Women Should Be Drafted," *The American* magazine, June 1949. Entered in the *Congressional Record* by Sen. Margaret Chase Smith on 20 June 1949, p. A4002–4.
16. Rejected by a vote of 51 to 4; *Congressional Record* (U.S. Senate), 10 June 1980, p. S6527–49.

CHAPTER 24

ISSUES AND DECISIONS

SEVERAL OVERLAPPING ISSUES emerged from the debates over the registration of women for the draft. The most important of these were:

- Whether the exclusion of women from combat justified their total exemption from registration;
- Whether there was a "military requirement" to draft women in the event of mobilization;
- Questions of equity; and
- The constitutionality of any system that does not include women.

Throughout the 1979 and 1980 debates, the main argument against registering women was that women cannot fill *all* positions in the armed services, especially combat positions. Opponents of registration argued that women should be excluded from the Selective Service System because in times of mobilization the primary need will be for manpower in the combat arms and in support positions which may have to deploy into combat.

The Armed Services Committees in both houses of Congress rejected women's inclusion in registration primarily on that basis. In 1979, the Senate committee's report stated, "The policy precluding the use of women in combat is, in the committee's view, the most important reason for not including women in a registration system." In 1980, the subcommittee report reiterated this position: "The starting point for any discussion of the appropriateness of registering women for the draft is the question of the proper role of women in combat."

On the House side, Chairman Richard White of the Military

Personnel Subcommittee said, "If they are not going to be used in combat, then registration is just a gesture." Marjorie Holt, the senior minority member, agreed: "If we're not using them in combat arms I don't see the point [in registering them]."

The problem with this argument is that it fails to recognize that since 1940 the draft has not been used merely to provide combat personnel, rather it has been used in war and peace to augment the active duty strength when voluntary enlistments of men *and women* fell below that required to maintain authorized strength levels. Most men drafted in the nearly two decades following World War II saw no combat service, nor were they even nominally assigned to combat roles. Many of them did the same jobs that women were, and are, doing in the military: serving as clerks, drivers, radio operators, dental technicians, personnel specialists, and in other general support skill areas of a modern military organization.

Moreover, over 70 percent of the men drafted into the Army during a wartime draft were not assigned to combat positions. Of all the men eligible for the draft in 1971, only 1 percent were actually inducted and subsequently assigned to combat units. Even in 1967, at the height of the U.S. involvement in Southeast Asia, only about half the annual draftees were serving in Vietnam, and over half of those were in noncombat roles.

The reason for this low combat exposure is, of course, the combat-to-support troop ("tooth-to-tail") ratio of a modern fighting force. Bureau of Census data in 1960, for example, revealed that only 15 percent of the military personnel were classified as combatants, and the Gates Commission ten years later made the same point. The Senate Armed Services Committee has said in its own reports that "fully 42 percent of all billets filled by enlisted personnel in the Army are in specialties, skills or units not available to women." It glosses over the obvious fact that 58 percent of them are in specialties, skills, and organizations that are *not* closed to women.

Defense witnesses pointed out during the hearings that the work women were doing in a wide variety of jobs was essential to the readiness of the forces, active and reserve. Some 20,000 (or 35 percent) of the women then on active duty in the Air Force, for example, served in nontraditional jobs, many of which related directly to the care and maintenance of the fighter aircraft and missile operations vitally important to the Air Force's readiness.

Thus, the reasoning that women should be exempted from registration requirements because they are excluded from combat simply is not sound.

The logic of the combat argument is further undermined by the congressional decision that *all* men in the age cohort must register, even men clearly unsuited for military duty, much less for combat duty—the blind, the dumb, the mentally unfit, and the otherwise handicapped. It matters not if he cannot find his own way to the post office and, having gotten there, is unable to sign his own name—a man must register.

As explained by administration witnesses, the purpose of the peacetime registration is to equip us with information so that if we had a national mobilization, we could move quickly to achieve our wartime personnel requirements with greater effectiveness. While some of those requirements have to be filled by men, many could be filled by women as well as men—a fact members of the congressional committees were unable or unwilling to recognize.

Repeatedly, witnesses were asked: Is there a military requirement for registering women for the draft? Repeatedly, they answered that out of the total manpower authorization of the armed forces, a certain number had to be filled by men because of the combat restrictions and policies that limited the use of women. The rest required qualified *people*—either men or women—and the same would be true in the event of mobilization. At one point, Richard Danzig patiently explained, "If you said to me does the military require people with brown eyes to serve, I would have to tell you no, because people with blue eyes could do the job." The committee chose to interpret this to mean that there was no "military requirement" for women, hence, no "need" to register them for the draft. The committee's conclusions, thus, were not derived from inadequate communications but from faulty perceptions in the set minds of the members.

Part of the mind-set of some committee members seemed to be rooted in their inability to take women seriously as military professionals. While acknowledging that women were making a contribution to the military in peacetime, some committee members nonetheless tended to view women's expanded role in the armed forces as a "social experiment" rather than as a resource of value to the overall defense effort. They reasoned that while such experiments might be commendable in peacetime, they had no place in a mobilization scenario.

A more logical question for Congress to address would have been: Is there a requirement to draft *only* men in the event of mobilization? In that case, the answer would have to be an unqualified NO.

In addition to the 150,000 women serving in the active forces in 1980, another 60,000 military women were in selected Reserve units and would be called to active duty if their units were mobilized. DOD projections call for 250,000 women in the active forces and 100,000 in selected Reserve units by 1985. In addition, in the event of war, the Coast Guard would be transferred to the Navy from the Department of Transportation, adding further thousands of women to the active naval forces. If mobilization were ordered, the military would require 650,000 additional people in the first six months. Defense witnesses testified that at least 80,000 of these are expected to be women. Further, if not enough women volunteered, and there were no provisions to draft women, the services would need to draft men to fill that requirement.

By registering women for the draft, the pool of registrants would be doubled, and twice as much high quality talent would be available from which to select personnel for induction. Registering women would also provide a pool of skills that would not otherwise be available—people trained in the so-called "traditional women's jobs," which are essential to an effective fighting force. As Robert B. Pirie, Assistant Secretary of Defense, explained it,

> It would make far greater sense to include women in a draft call and thereby gain many of these skills than to draft only males who would not only require training in these fields but would be drafted for employment in jobs traditionally held by females. A further advantage would be to release males currently holding non-combatant jobs for reassignment to combat jobs.

The case of the health professions is especially compelling. In an editorial in July 1979, Sen. Sam Nunn, arguing the case for reinstitution of registration, predicted that in a major conflict the military would not be able to ensure adequate medical support because of grave shortages of surgeons, nurses, and enlisted medical manpower: "Thousands of unnecessary deaths would occur for lack of medical treatment."[2] Yet, he adamantly opposed the registration or drafting of women, many of whom would serve in the health professions, which are recognized by international law as noncombatant fields.

Moreover, according to Department of Labor data, the enrollment of women in medical schools has been steadily increasing. In 1969–70, only 9 percent of first-year students were women. In just four years, the figure had jumped to 20 percent, at which time 15 percent of all medical students were women. There can be no rational justification for excluding women in the event it becomes necessary to reinstitute a draft of doctors.

The case for drafting nurses and enlisted medical personnel is even stronger. Some 98 percent of all nurses in this country are women. Recruitment by the armed services in the peacetime environment has become increasingly difficult as the demands in civilian institutions, offering higher pay, continue to outstrip the supply. If the services were to substantially expand medical personnel requirements, as in the case of mobilization, there is no way they could meet their nurse needs without a draft of female nurses. The experience of World War II proves that. It is absurd to assume that the services would draft only male nurses; not only are there not enough of them, but the inequity of such a procedure would be too obvious to be ignored.

The situation in the enlisted medical and dental technical fields closely parallels that of the health professions. In the civilian work force, women hold 84 percent of the jobs in these fields. In the armed forces, women now fill only 17 percent of available positions, but the numbers and proportions are climbing. If the services require a large influx of medical and dental personnel, they will need to tap the already existing civilian resource, which is overwhelmingly female.

In 1980, the administration concluded that an all-male registration would be inequitable and legally indefensible because there was no rational basis to exclude women. As Rostker has testified,

> It was the job of the Selective Service System to ask young people to serve their country in the most fair and equitable way. It is our determination that excluding a majority of the population that could serve, for reasons that were apparently not sufficient, given the substantial contribution that women make in the defense effort of this country today, is not consistent with the equity that we hope to strive for in the Selective Service System.

Since World War II, the pool of young men has exceeded several times the numbers the services would need in the event of mobilization. This has always raised the questions: Who should serve when not all serve? On what basis does a fair and equitable system select those who will have to serve against their wills and those who will be exempt? In that context, the issue is not whether there is a requirement to register women, but whether the burden of any registration can justifiably be imposed on men alone. The simple truth of the matter is that there is no military justification for drafting only men, and, that being the case, equity demands that the burden be shared.

Turning the equity issue around, the opponents to registering women contend that if women must register for the draft, then equity dictates they be drafted in equal numbers. This is like saying that because the law calls for drafting men between the ages of eighteen and twenty-six, each age group would have to be drafted in equal numbers, or that since blacks and other minorities are subject to registration, they should be drafted in proportion to their representation in the national population. It is nonsense. Decisions on who will actually be drafted will be made at the time Congress authorizes inductions.

Pirie very emphatically stated, and Rostker confirmed, that if women were subject to the draft, the DOD would determine the number that could be used in the armed forces, subject to existing constraints on combat and the need of the services. If not enough women volunteered to meet the programmed requirement, then they would be conscripted to make up the deficit.

To the contention that this would not be "equitable," Defense Department and Selective Service witnesses replied that, in their view, equity is achieved when both men and women are asked to serve in proportion to the ability of the armed forces to use them effectively under existing constraints of law and policy. At the time of mobilization, attainment of military efficiency will determine how many women will be used. The rate of induction for both women and men will depend upon the need.

Would this be legal? Larry L. Simms, Deputy Assistant Attorney General in the Office of Legal Counsel at the Justice Department, testified that it would be. He noted that when legislation was considered by Congress to authorize the actual induction of individuals, the power to induct selectively on the basis of sex would be spelled out. He expressed the view that the induction of women based on a current assessment of the number of women the military could use, rather than on a broad generalization, would be the kind of determination the courts would be reluctant to disturb.

One of the reasons given by the administration for requesting authority to register women for the draft in 1980 was to avoid the risk of having the male-only system overturned by the courts in response to an equal protection suit based upon the Constitution. The issue of constitutionality became a major subject of controversy throughout the congressional hearings.

At one point, a witness suggested that it is not the administration's or Congress's business to attempt to second-guess what the courts will eventually rule. Rather, it is Congress's business to do what is right under its interpretation of the constitutional requirement, regardless of what the courts may decide. Sen. John W. Warner disagreed: "I think it is a responsibility of the Congress to try to anticipate how the Federal Court system would deal with this issue. And in large measure, my ultimate decision on this problem will be guided by that."

There was sharp division among legal scholars and those expert witnesses who testified at the Senate hearings on what the courts would decide in the event male-only registration were put into effect. For example, the general counsel of the Selective Service argued that to meet "correct constitutional law requirements of equal protection, any system of registration for an induction into the armed forces must include both men and women." On the other hand, on 31 January 1980, the Justice Department, in a memorandum to the deputy director of the Office of Management and Budget, expressed the belief that the male-only draft was "constitutionally defensible," and that the linchpin of the successful argument supporting constitutionality is that Congress has the power to prohibit the use of women in combat based on either "generalization regarding their physical characteristics or on psychological factors."

In a letter to Nunn of 2 May 1980, submitted during the hearings, three professors of law at the Yale Law School considered whether or not recent judicial rulings on equality between the sexes under the Constitution or under the possible ratification of the ERA would prevent Congress from drafting men for the armed forces without also drafting women. They concluded that

> it is and will continue to be possible for Congress to conscript men or women, or both men and women, in exercise of its constitutional discretion to raise and support the armed forces it deems necessary and proper to defend the interests of the nation. If Congress should decide that the conscription of men is an appropriate way to create the kind of armed forces

> the United States requires to deal with threats to its security, as Congress
> perceives those threats, no court could challenge its decision.

Some legal experts, however, contended that under current interpretations of law, male-only registration cannot withstand constitutional scrutiny and would not survive a Fifth or Fourteenth Amendment challenge on equal protection and due process grounds. For example, the American Civil Liberties Union (ACLU) stressed in its testimony that when evidence of women's participation in the military since the last draft is measured against new heightened review standards used by the courts in sex-based classifications, their exclusion from a draft registration requirement will not adequately relate to the maintenance of national security. While admitting that there is judicial support for the proposition that involuntary conscription may be necessary to satisfy a vital governmental objective in maintaining the national security, the ACLU contended it does not follow that the imposition of this obligation on men alone is "closely and substantially" related to the accomplishment of that objective, as would be required by the court.

The Air Force General Counsel, in a detailed analysis of the issue completed in May 1979 and updated on 7 February 1980, concluded that

> the exclusion of females from the draft is not substantially related to the
> national defense or the fair distribution of compulsory military service.
> Rather, the legislative histories of the various selective service laws suggest
> that the exclusion was based on outmoded notions of military service and
> stereotypic conclusions about the role of women. Therefore, we believe
> that any future law which would continue this total exclusion for similar
> reasons would fail to survive constitutional review under the current
> standards.

Both the ACLU and the Air Force General Counsel refuted the contention that women's exclusion from combat had any bearing on the issue of constitutionality. The question of whether women should be assigned to combat units, in their view, was not central to determining whether a male-only draft registration furthers the objective of maintaining the national security with a combat-ready military. They also contended that the current and planned utilization of women shows that whether or not they are assigned to combat, it is clear that they are qualified for a full range of non-combat jobs. Therefore, it was argued, the constitutional issue does not turn on what role draftees will assume once inducted, but rather on the blanket exclusion of women, which arises out of social and political considerations instead of military requirements.

The committee majority voted to continue the exclusion of women on the assumption that it would be upheld by the courts. On a motion by Senator Warner, the Senate Manpower and Personnel Subcommittee rejected the bill by a vote of five to two. Senator Cohen disagreed, however, and said:

> Contrary to the conclusion of the subcommittee majority, I believe that the constitutionality of excluding women remains to be resolved. No one who has addressed the issue of constitutionality has adequately addressed the following question: If the Department of Defense stated it can accept 250,000 women by 1985, if mobilization occurs at that time, and if we have an insufficient number of women volunteers for those positions, what is the rational basis for drafting men for those noncombat positions?

He might also have asked: What if the additional 80,000 women planned to be added to the active strength in mobilization do not volunteer? What is the rationale for drafting men for those noncombat positions as well?

THE CONSTITUTIONAL CHALLENGE

The Justice Department, while stating that, in its view, the Selective Service Act was "constitutionally defensible," nonetheless acknowledged that, if the provisions were put into effect, the constitutional issues raised by it "are generally ripe for a thorough review." The court challenge was not long in coming—in fact, it had been in the making for nine years.

Within sixteen days after the President's order for resumption of registration, the U.S. District Court for the Eastern District of Pennsylvania ruled on a case that had been pending since 1973. In *Goldberg* v. *Rostker* (Civil Action No. 71-1480), the court ruled:

> The Military Selective Service Act, 50 U.S.C. App. Secs. 451 *et seq.*, is declared to be in violation of the Fifth Amendment to the United States Constitution for the reasons set forth in the accompanying opinion.
>
> Defendants are hereby permanently enjoined from requiring the registration under the Military Selective Service Act of any member of the plaintiff class.

Justice Brennan's subsequent stay of execution only permitted the registration to proceed as planned pending review by the Supreme Court.

The case that threatened to bring down the all-male Selective Service System was decided as much by luck and timing as by the three judges hearing it. When a group of draft-eligible war protesters filed a class-action suit in the U.S. District Court in Philadelphia in June 1971, their intent was to end the war, not to end sex discrimination in the draft. The male plaintiffs alleged that the draft law was involuntary servitude, a violation of several of their constitutional rights, one of which is the right to the equal protection of the laws guaranteed by the Fifth Amendment. They accused the draft law of abridging that right because women were not included. The court dismissed the case in July, an action that went largely unnoticed as just another in a long string of antiwar protests.

On review, however, the Third Circuit Court of Appeals upheld the dismissal of all of the claims except the one claiming discrimination based on the failure to conscript women. Whereupon, in 1973, the case was sent back to the lower court, where a three-judge panel was convened to hear the sex discrimination challenge. Had the case been tried at that point, the outcome would probably have been different. The constitutionality of the all-male draft had recently been upheld in several cases and the Supreme Court had never yet made it illegal to distinguish between men and women in the law.

In 1973, the draft ended, and two years later registration was discontinued. Without registration, the case languished untried, hanging by a thin legal thread, waiting like a time bomb for the facts and the law to change—which they did. With Carter's decision to reinstate registration, the fuse was set.

Oddly, those who write the laws are not called upon to justify them when their constitutionality is challenged. The courts must rely on the legislative history to determine the rationale used by Congress in writing a law.

Unfortunately, up to 1979, the history of the forty-year-old Selective Service Act is silent on reasons for excluding women. From the time the law was passed in 1940 up to the recent debates, Congress did not explain why it singled out young men and men alone to bear the burden of compulsory military service. The law was to be a "fair and just system," it specifically prohibited "discrimination against any person on account of race or color," but no mention was made of women—not in 1948 when the present law was written, nor in 1951 or 1967 when Congress amended it.

On the last occasion (1967), President Johnson's message to Congress stressed that

fairness has always been one of the goals of the Selective Service System. When the present Act was passed in 1948, one of its underlying assumptions was that the obligations and benefits of military service would be equitably borne.

Notwithstanding the rhetoric about sharing the obligations and benefits of military service equitably, the only reference to women in the legislative history of the 1967 Act was in the President's message: "The Secretary of Defense is taking steps to expand opportunities for women in the services, thus further reducing the number of men who must be called involuntarily for duty." Those "expanded opportunities" consisted of raising the female recruitment ceilings to add 6,500 women volunteers while at the same time 300,000 men were to be drafted.

Thus, the 1979 and 1980 hearings provide the first detailed insight into Congress's reasons for continuing the exclusion of women. The chief support for the belief in the law's constitutionality comes from legal precedent, which is in itself impressive, albeit outdated. Beginning in 1968, a total of twelve district and circuit courts considered the issue. In each case, litigation was brought by a man claiming, in effect, that the exclusion of women from the statute was arbitrary and unreasonable and violated his equal protection rights under the Constitution. No less than eleven courts upheld the law.

In all decisions where the draft was held constitutional, the courts relied upon the "minimum rationality" test. This was the traditional standard applied by the Supreme Court for equal-protection claims. In this test, it was only necessary for the government to show that there was a "reasonable" basis or justification for the sex discrimination in the statute for it to be judged constitutional. Needless to say, few laws failed to meet so loose a test. If any of the facts in the case could reasonably be conceived to justify it, the statute would be upheld.

So it was with the draft cases. Here the justification for excluding women fell under the general headings of "national security," which is related to military necessity and preparedness, or "maximum efficiency and minimum expense." In such matters, the courts have traditionally shown a special deference to Congress on the basis of its constitutionally mandated responsibility to raise and maintain armed forces and to decide who will serve.

In 1969, for example, the Seventh Circuit Court of Appeals ruled:

> We hold such classifications and deferments are reasonably related to the purposes of the Selective Service Act. Congress was entitled to consider factors which would both maximize the efficiency and minimize the expense of raising an Army and minimize the disruption of what were considered important civilian functions.[3]

The court emphasized the inappropriateness of judicial involvement in issues that are the proper jurisdiction of Congress to determine.

In the one instance where a district court found the statute unconstitutional, it was overruled by the circuit court. In that case, the government argued that the gender-based classification was essential to "national security" mainly because of the combat requirement:

> Only a limited number of women would be as suited as men for combat assignments, and in order to assure that sufficient numbers of combat qualified soldiers were members of the armed forces, Congress would have to send most of the women of eligible age through the induction process in order to find the qualified few, and it would be unreasonable to disrupt the lives of millions in order to find a very few.[4]

The district court rejected this argument, reasoning that sex was a "suspect classification," and found there was no compelling state interest in justifying the exclusion of women. Had this been allowed to stand, it would have been a landmark decision in sex discrimination; but the Ninth Court of Appeals rejected it and found instead "a clear rational relationship between the government's legitimate interests, as expressed in the [Selective Service] Act, and the classification by sex."

Inherent in all of the earlier draft cases was a presumption of the correctness of excluding women, based either on women's special role in society or on the need of certain physical characteristics required for military service, such as strength and endurance, which presumably are possessed by men only. The courts' decisions were laced with stereotypes and archaic notions about women's place as the center of the home and family. In a 1968 case, for example, the court said:

> In providing for involuntary service for men and voluntary service for women, Congress followed the teachings of history that if a nation is to survive, men must provide the first line of defense while women keep the home fires burning.[5]

In another case, the court stated:

> As they are born so they are created and no amount of legislation or "modernization" will change their distinguishing and distinctive physical characteristics. While each of the sexes has its own innate characteristics, for the most part physical strength is a male characteristic, and so long as this is so, the United States will be compelled to establish and maintain armed forces of males which may at least physically be equal to the armed forces of other nations, likewise composed of males, with which it must compete.[6]

In 1980, most legal experts agreed that many of the arguments used to justify the all-male draft in the past would no longer be acceptable by the legal standards that emerged in the aftermath of the ERA's enactment and in the light of recent Supreme Court decisions in equal-protection cases. In the years between the time the last draft case was decided and *Goldberg* v. *Rostker* was tried, the new stricter standard to be applied to sex discrimination cases had emerged from the Supreme Court. It requires that the law further an important governmental interest and that the sex-based classification be substantially related to the purpose of the legislation.

In *Goldberg* v. *Rostker* the court had first to decide which standard of review to apply—the traditional "rational basis" test as eleven previous courts had applied in draft cases, or the new stricter standard. It chose the latter. Thus, the government was required to show that the total exclusion of women served an "important governmental objective." It could not do so, at least not to the satisfaction of the court.

It is one of the paradoxes of our system that a government official can one moment forcefully urge Congress to amend a law he believes to be unconstitutional and the next find himself the defendant in a case challenging the constitutionality of the same law. That is the strange position Bernard Rostker found himself in in the summer of 1980. His testimony before Congress, along with that of other witnesses from the White House, the DOD, and the Justice Department, became the basis for the district court's decision to find the law unconstitutional.

Contrary to Congress's expectation and the Armed Services Committees' insistence, the district court did not see the combat exclusion as the issue:

> The issue before us is the constitutionality of the total exclusion of women from the [Selective Service Act], not the extent to which the military services must utilize women. The imposition of the burden to register upon any class of citizens must be justified. The justification here should relate to the governmental need to raise military forces by conscription.

The court went on to point out that:

> Congress could not constitutionally require registration of only black citizens or only white citizens, or single out any political or religious group simply because those groups contain sufficient persons to fill the needs of the Selective Service System. It is not enough to show that their inclusion was needed; it would have to be shown that their exclusion was needed.

"We need only decide if there is a substantial relationship between the exclusion of women and the raising of effective armed forces," the court explained. There was no need to decide if women must serve in all roles in the military, including combat, or if women must be conscripted in equal numbers with men; these were military matters inappropriate for the court to deal with.

The court noted that Congress generally analyzed the problem in terms of the *need* for women rather than the *need to exclude* women and found that many of the arguments put forth by Congress in its reports did not justify the total exclusion of women.

The court also had difficulty accepting what it called "the inconsistent positions of Congress" in that it had continuously allocated funds to increase the numbers of women in the armed forces, both in absolute terms and as a percentage of the total force. "There can be no doubt," said the court, "that the experience of women in the all-volunteer army has been a success story." The court found it "incongruous," then, that Congress believe on the one hand that constantly expanding the utilization of women in the military "substantially enhances our national defense" and on the other hand endorse legislation excluding women from the pool of registrants available for induction.

Congress allocates funds so that the military can use and actively seek more female recruits but nonetheless asserts that there is justification for excluding females from selective service, despite the shortfall in the recruitment of women. Congress rejects the current opinion of each of the military services and asserts that women can contribute to the military effectively only as volunteers and not as inductees.

The judges went on to point out that the President, the Director of the Selective Service System, and representatives of the Department of Defense informed Congress during the hearings that including women in the pool of people eligible for induction would increase military flexibility. The record revealed "that in almost any conceivable military crisis the armed forces could utilize skills now almost entirely concentrated in the female population of the nation." Noting that there was already an extensive utilization of women and planned increases, the judges said that "the die is already cast for substantial female involvement in the military."

Because the Selective Service creates a gender-based classification, the court contended that the burden of justifying that classification fell to the government. The principal justification offered by the government for men-only registration was that it provides "military flexibility." The court reasoned that, though military flexibility might call for fewer female than male inductees in a given crisis situation, induction calls for women could be made according to the military needs as they accrue in the future. The record reveals that women do serve a useful role in the military and provide important skills, thus "flexibility is not enhanced, but is in fact limited by the complete exclusion of women."

The court therefore held that: The complete exclusion of women from the pool of registrants does not serve "important governmental objectives" and is not "substantially related" . . . to any alleged government interest. Thus the [Selective Service Act] unconstitutionally discriminates between males and females.

THE DECISION: HEALTHY DEFERENCE

On 25 June 1981, the Supreme Court, voting six to three, overturned the lower court's decision and ruled that Congress had the constitutional authority to exclude women from the military draft. In so doing, the Court reaffirmed the concept that ordinary tests of equality do not apply when Congress is considering national defense. In this area, unlike all others where the Court has struck down distinctions based on sex, Congress may discriminate between men and women. The Court should not "substitute" its own judgment by requiring Congress to "engage in gestures of superficial equality," Justice William H. Rehnquist wrote for the Court. "The decision," he said, "shows the Court's 'healthy deference' to the other branches of government." So, barring a change of heart by Congress, which seems unlikely, or the ratification of the ERA, which seems equally unlikely, the Court has said that the obligation to register and be drafted if called upon, will continue to rest on men alone for the foreseeable future. The tradition that women should serve their country only on sufferance, and not as a matter of right or obligation of citizenship, survived the test—this time.

The decision's full effect on future military policy is unclear, but it seems reasonable to expect that the services will interpret this "healthy deference" to allow greater discretion in differentiating on the basis of sex; and, on that basis, they may be more willing to risk litigation than they were in the seventies. It could also have a chilling effect on women (and men) seeking to challenge, in the courts, actions or policies of the military that discriminate on the basis of sex.

Another development cast light in a counter direction, however. Within two weeks of this decision, conservative Ronald Reagan confounded experts by nominating Sandra Day O'Connor to the Supreme Court. It would be intriguing to speculate how the Court might have ruled in the draft registration case had a "sister" been seated among the "brethren." It goes without saying that her presence will be felt in all future cases on sex discrimination. Irrespective of how she may vote, just by her being there, the continuation of sexual barriers in lesser circumstances becomes more difficult to justify—even in the armed forces. It is worth noting here that Justice O'Connor is no novice to the subject of military women, having served as a member of the DACOWITS from 1974 through 1976.

NOTES

1. Wilson, *op. cit.*
2. Sen. Sam Nunn, "The Case for Peacetime Registration," *Washington Post*, 27 July 1979 (op-ed).
3. *United States v. Follon*, 407 F. 2nd 621 (7th Cir., 1969).
4. *United States v. Reiser*, 532 F. 2nd 673 (9th Cir., 1976).
5. *United States v. St. Clair*, 291 F. Supp. 122 (S.D.N.Y., 1968).
6. *United States v. Cook*, 311 F. Supp. 618 (W.D.Pa., 1970).

PART IV

BLAZING NEW TRAILS

CHAPTER 25

THE EIGHTIES: A NEW PERIOD OF UNCERTAINTY

IN 1984, GEN. John W. Vessey, Jr., Chairman of the Joint Chiefs of Staff, was moved to say:

> The greatest change that has come about in the U.S. Armed Forces in the time that I have been in the military service is in the extensive use of women ... I am not against it. We have wonderful service-women doing extraordinary things and doing very well, but we have taken a male institution ... and turned it into a coed institution, and it has been a traumatic exercise for us .[1]

That an institution the size of the U.S. armed forces could be so traumatized by a few women speaks volumes about the military mind-set of the time. General Vessey was expressing a widespread apprehension that the military services were in the process of being "feminized" for reasons associated more with a national liberal agenda than the requirements of national defense. The services were never convinced of the necessity for expanding the utilization of women since the advent of the all-volunteer force. They were especially traumatized by the forced integration of women into operational areas and the sacrosanct service academies.

Although the growth in the proportions of women admitted had been dramatic, by the early 1980s, women still constituted fewer than one in ten military members and still were concentrated overwhelmingly in the jobs considered traditional to their gender.

But what kept military traditionalists in a defensive mode was the fact that women had succeeded in breaking out of the parameters set for them over the years and were demanding more. Most disconcerting was the fact that they were demonstrating the ability to perform many military roles previously reserved for men. This influx of women, this feminization, could only be seen as an additional threat to a military already under siege by its critics as a "hollow" force.

The military community continued to believe that reliance on women was a temporary condition that would pass with the demise of a misguided Carter administration. It didn't turn out that way. Despite the continued opposition of the military leadership, the trends continued throughout the 1980s, albeit at a slower pace. By the end of the decade women would constitute nearly 12 percent of the force and would be integrated into the armed services to an extent never before envisioned or thought possible. They would become so essential to the armed forces, including combat support operations, that the United States would be unable to deploy forces for war without them and during deployments to hot spots around the world, women would be exposed to and even become involved in combat situations.

Throughout the 1980s, the issue of military women continued to generate tensions and open conflict between appointed civilian officials and military leaders. On the one hand, civilian officials, committed to strengthening the armed forces in a period of shrinking resources, sought to expand the utilization of women as a means for meeting overall military personnel requirements while resisting pressures to restore the peacetime draft. As in previous administrations, they felt the necessity for a political mandate to assure fair treatment and equity for women within the constraints of the law and the dictates of force readiness.

The tradition-bound military leadership, on the other hand, mistrusted the motives of political appointees, especially in matters of military personnel policy. When it came to women, the military instinctively defended the status quo, and on numerous occasions even sought to reverse the trends. The closer women got to the services' primary mission elements, the stiffer the resistance of the generals and admirals.

Congress was often drawn into the middle of the debates

between the military and the civilian leadership and found itself split along the same lines on the issues as the Pentagon.

For their part, women were caught in the middle of the debates, feeling like pawns in a political game played by giants, with no say in the outcome. Since they were now fully integrated into units open to them, women often found themselves isolated in predominantly male organizations, without female friends or role models. At most installations, female networking was either frowned upon or overtly discouraged. Male commanders were usually so preoccupied with the problems of their larger male constituency and their dependents that the women were often reluctant to seek them out for counsel and advice. The sense of isolation could sometimes be overwhelming, especially for the young first-term enlisted women. And women of all ranks, from private to general, often felt frustrated and angered by their own powerlessness to influence policies and decisions affecting their status, quality of life, and careers.

It was chiefly through the Defense Advisory Committee on Women in the Services (DACOWITS) that servicewomen were able to communicate their concerns to the top levels of the power structure that controlled the quality of their lives and their futures. Without the committee the senior officials in the Pentagon would have remained oblivious to the women's needs and concerns that were not being addressed. They would have remained unaware of potentially explosive problems such as sexual harassment brewing below the surface within each of the services. Understandably, the services resented this intrusion into affairs that they thought best left to military experts. The military leaders tended to regard members of the committee as a group of busybodies, meddling in things they could not possibly understand. The services deeply resented the committee's direct access to the Secretary of Defense.

THE "HOLLOW" MILITARY

As in the past, the primary impetus for the employment of women in the armed forces during the 1980s was the overall military manpower situation. By the late 1970s, as the Carter administration was nearing the end of its term, many at home and abroad were questioning the war-deterring and war-fighting capabilities of the U.S. armed forces. The Iranian hostage seizure, followed by a botched rescue attempt, had conveyed a message of military incompetence; and with the Soviet invasion of Afghanistan, the public perceived a growing disparity in defense expenditures between the United States and the Soviet Union. These events raised serious questions about the readiness of U.S. forces. The growing public sentiment was that the U.S. military had become a "hollow" force—neglected to the point that its ability to defend the nation's interest was in jeopardy. It was contended that the services were undermanned, underequipped, and underpaid. Many experts concluded that the solution was a lot more money and a revival of the draft. These same experts tended to see women as a symptom of the services' personnel problems rather than as a partial solution.

In reality, by the late 1970s women were literally keeping the All-Volunteer Force (AVF) afloat. All the services, even the never-fail Air Force, were struggling to meet male enlistment goals. As had been predicted in the early studies of the AVF, the trade-off was between low-quality men and high-quality women. The Army, in particular, was having great difficulty meeting its requirements, even with lower quality standards. In 1979, all four services had failed to meet their recruiting goals. Had they not enlisted some 42,000 women that year, the recruiting shortfalls would have been even larger.

The following year the services met their numerical recruiting goals, due in large part to the enlistment of 50,000 women. It was also due to the acceptance of large numbers of minimally qualified men. More than half the Army's male recruits, for example, were high school dropouts in the lowest acceptable mental category (Category IV). By contrast, most of the women were high school graduates and scored in the top mental categories.

Reports from field commanders and numerous studies revealed that the services were paying dearly for the poor quality of male recruits in terms of soaring disciplinary problems and training failure rates.

An article in the 19 April 1982 U.S. News and World Report described the concerns being expressed by many within the Army's ranks. It posed the question: "Can GI's in Europe Answer a Call to Combat?" From Kaiserslautern, West Germany, they reported serious doubts among military leaders and career soldiers about the quality and readiness of U.S. forces to fight a shooting war in Europe against the huge Soviet Army. There was concern that "use of drugs and alcohol, plus poor morale, may take their toll when the chips are down." The main gripe among career soldiers was that the young male recruits couldn't read. "We're taking guys who really can't read or write and putting them into a tank, a 2-million-dollar piece of equipment," complained a sergeant in an armored unit. "There's a big, fat manual for operating it. But what good is that to an illiterate?"

Widespread complaints about the quality of male recruits prompted Congress to set limits on the numbers of marginal quality recruits the services could accept. But male recruiting difficulties were further aggravated by a shrinking youth population, which was projected to get smaller until well into the 1990s.

Even as the AVF faltered and the quality of the force plummeted, the services refused to acknowledge that women were making positive contributions and continued to resist OSD plans to increase their numbers. Some military experts believed that dependence on women for defense had gone too far, too fast—that it was more the product of liberal social experimentation than of military need and that it was undermining military readiness. With the transition from the Carter to the Reagan administration in 1981, the prevailing wisdom within the military was that expanding the roles of women in defense would end and might even be reversed. This was a major miscalculation on the part of the military—the first of many.

THE REAGAN BUILDUP

Even before Caspar W. Weinberger settled into his spacious Pentagon offices overlooking the nation's capital, the military forced him into a DOD-wide reappraisal of women's strength goals and policies. The timing could not have been worse for the newly named Secretary of Defense, who had more pressing issues on his mind than military women.

The Reagan administration planned to expand the military by 200,000 (about 10 percent) as early as 1985. It would be the largest defense buildup since the Vietnam War and it was to be achieved, if possible, with all volunteers. To shore up the AVF, the administration came in with plans to increase service pay, expand benefits, enhance the quality of service life, and restore public confidence in the armed forces. But even with these incentives, the new administration faced the same formidable set of manpower realities that had confronted its three predecessors.

First: the demographics of the youth population. The pool of age-eligible males was declining and was projected to continue downward through the eighties into the mid-1990s. This pool was further limited by the quality constraints mandated by Congress on male recruits.

Second: the available market of age-eligible women. Although women followed the same demographic trends as men, their numbers still far exceeded the services' recruiting demands. Although marketing studies clearly showed that women's interest in seeking military service was less than half that of men, the military was nowhere close to exhausting the potential market. In fact, the main rationale cited by the Army, Navy, and Marine Corps for continuing to require women to meet higher standards for enlistment than men was that the supply of female applicants far exceeded service "requirements" and "vacancies," both of which were artificially set.

And *third*: the impact of modern technology on military jobs. As technology replaced brawn at an escalating pace, the scales tipped farther in favor of women, a reality that the military continued to resist.

The manpower challenge of the eighties would be to recruit and retain enough people of sufficient education and intellect to "man" the high-tech forces of the future without costs going through the roof. By increasing military pay and other benefits to enhance service life, the male recruiting picture improved measurably and there was growing optimism that the immediate recruiting crisis might be at an end. But the planned force buildup loomed as a new and daunting challenge, especially for the Army. Some elements of the Army's leadership believed that what really was needed was a good dose of conscripts to solve the recruiting problem. Here again, they seriously misjudged Ronald Reagan.

Paradoxically, as the military was about to enter a new period of public support, the drive for women's rights seemed to be running out of steam and the influence of women activists over public policy was on the decline. The resounding defeat of Jimmy Carter, an unabashed proponent of women's rights and the ERA, by Ronald Reagan, an equally unabashed supporter of the conservative social agenda, was popularly perceived on both sides of the issues as a blow to women's rights. Although Reagan repeatedly proclaimed his belief in legal and economic equity for women, even many in his own party did not believe he was seriously committed.

The military determined to test this perception early on in a move that surprised and angered military women, not so much for the fact that it occurred but they sensed they were being set up as scapegoats for the low state of military readiness. It was a bum rap—led by the Army.

WOMANPAUSE 1981

Shortly after the November 1980 election, the Army and Air Force secretly submitted to the Reagan transition team proposals to scrap the Carter administration's strength goals for enlisted women until women's impact on force readiness could be determined. Both services asked permission to hold recruitment numbers for 1981 and 1982 to the minimum needed to ensure meeting overall recruiting goals. There was no indication that the Navy or Marine Corps participated in this proposal, but, in response to press inquiries, they indicated that they shared some of their sister services' concerns.

Under the Carter administration the numbers of women on active duty had grown to 173,450, and plans called for adding another 91,000 by 1986. Because the overall military strength was projected to remain constant, the proportion of women would rise from 8.5 percent to 12 percent of the total. With Carter's defeat, the military decided that the time was right to challenge these plans. Many military women feared that an anti-women campaign was in the making—a form of backlash in reaction to the gains made during the seventies. They feared that if given the opportunity, the services would turn back the clock. Their fears were not unfounded.

It was no secret that, just below the surface of the military ranks at all levels, there persisted a deep well of resistance and even resentment toward women and their growing incursions into previously all-male preserves. Many military leaders, including some senior women, believed that military policy decisions were being made by well-meaning amateurs, with little or no service experience, who were motivated more by political expediency and misguided desires for social equity than by the requirements of national defense. Some agreed with retired Gen. William Westmoreland, who charged that the services had already gone too far in relying on women and that a halt should be called before combat readiness was irreparably undermined.

Some senior women officers and noncommissioned officers agreed that a reassessment might be in order of where the women's programs were headed and the effect of new policies. They were concerned that recruiting ever larger numbers from a diminishing pool of young women would undercut the image of quality that women leaders had carefully cultivated over the years, and that enlisted attrition rates would climb again to unacceptable levels. They saw evidence that the overemphasis on assigning women to nontraditional fields had backfired—that it was hurting recruiting, reducing acceptance, lowering retention rates, and contributing to growing problems of sexual harassment. Furthermore, the services still had not adequately worked out the pregnancy and child care policies and, until they did so, a cloud would continue to hang over women's participation in the military.

Before the Reagan team had a chance to evaluate the entire manpower situation and formulate plans for the buildup, and before key members of the manpower/personnel team were in place in the Pentagon, the Army forced the administration to take action. On 26 February 1981, testifying before the Senate Armed Services Manpower Subcommittee, the Army's acting Assistant Secretary for Manpower and Reserve Affairs, William D. Clark, and Deputy Chief of Staff for Personnel, Lt. Gen. Robert G. Yerks, stated that the Army was taking a new look at the entire issue of women soldiers and that, meanwhile, it planned to cut back on recruitment of enlisted women. It was not that the women were not doing their jobs, Clark was careful to explain: "Most of them are doing a really fine job . . . they are valuable and productive soldiers." Nor was it a question of their being exposed to combat: "The Army has accepted the fundamental premise that women will be killed and wounded and captured in the event of the next war"; that was a "societal problem." The issue, as the Army saw it, was "the combat effectiveness of the organizations as you have large numbers of women in them." The Army had no hard data to prove these contentions, only "feelings" of field commanders. An extensive study was under way, Yerks said, to look at how pregnancy, sole parenthood, lost time, and "physical problems" impact on readiness.

He didn't know, for example, whether 40 percent of women in an organization such as a medical unit was too high, but had a "gut feeling" that it was. In any case the Army had decided to "idle our motors" with its then current numbers of about 65,000 enlisted women until the new study was completed.

The Army's testimony caught the fledgling Reagan administration flat-footed, kicked up a flap on Capitol Hill and in the press, and enraged Army women. Some members of the armed services committees were gratified at the Army's decision. Sen. Roger W. Jepsen, Chairman of the Senate Manpower Subcommittee, seemed especially pleased. "I would suggest," he observed helpfully, "that our armed services are in being to provide national security . . . and not to provide the foundation for any social experimentation."

Sen. William Proxmire immediately picked up the challenge. In a press release on 4 March he blasted the Army, charging that its decision "is counter to sound military policy as well as an infringement on the rights and obligations of citizenship." Taking Clark to task over his implied criticism of women's abilities to do military jobs, the senator said: "We now have proof . . . that women can operate sophisticated aircraft, command the latest missile silo centers, repair vehicles, fire small arms accurately and carry out the vast majority of military functions." As for General Yerks' worries over lost time for pregnancy, "Well he should take a good look at the amount of time lost by the average woman in uniform compared to that of the average man." Senator Proxmire noted that the GAO had testified that men lose more time as a result of drug and alcohol abuse than women do for pregnancy and substance abuse combined, "But do you hear the Army saying they should stop recruiting men for their drug and booze problems? Hardly. It wouldn't make sense," he said. "At the very least women in the military mean that they can displace men for the front lines. This improves readiness and greatly enhances our mobilization base. At the best," he added, "women can compete for and accomplish just about every job in the military including actual combat."

Many Army women and men shared Proxmire's indignation and agreed with his assessment. "If the Army has readiness problems," insisted a colonel, "women are the least of them." Instead of studying the effect of a few pregnancies on unit performance, she felt that the time might be better spent assessing the impact on readiness of the thousands of male high-school dropouts the Army had recruited, many of whom were unable to read the training manuals, or the effect on readiness of what could be described as "men's problems," for example, substance abuse and being AWOL.

The problems concerning women that were raised by the Army and echoed in some degree by the other services were, in reality, routine personnel management matters that, with the exception of pregnancy, applied to men as well as women but on a much larger scale. They were framed as "women's problems" to create doubts in the new administration about the wisdom of relying on women for defense. Similar tactics had been used at the beginning of the Carter administration, only to backfire, resulting in a 60 percent expansion. In neither instance was there any evidence to support service contentions that, because of these so-called "women's problems," their presence degraded readiness.

By raising doubts about the effect of women on readiness in 1981, the services hoped that the Reagan administration, out of conservative conviction or simple naivete, would rise to the bait and call a moratorium on expanding women's recruitment—in essence, to allow the services to call their own shots.

Given the precarious state of the AVF and considering the new administration's announced intent to expand the armed forces, why would the services decide to hold the line on recruiting enlisted women? Accepting the basic fact that the military was inherently biased against the use of women, there was also a more compelling hidden agenda—to force a return to the draft by undercutting the AVF.

Many leaders and manpower experts both within and outside the military community, and even on Capitol Hill, sincerely believed that the AVF had been a serious mistake. The recruiting problems of the late seventies only reinforced that view. A return to the draft was seen as the only way to restore a strong military. Senator Proxmire spelled out the game plan:

> Women have made the All-Volunteer Force successful to date. So maybe what lies behind the Army's change of policy is the simple decision to restrict women recruits, accept the inevitable shortfalls in manpower levels, and then justify a return to the draft.[2]

Indeed, what better way to undermine the AVF than to denigrate the contribution of a group capable of making a sizable impact on its success?

Civilian Pentagon officials denied the possibility. "No way we would ever leave a spot vacant rather than taking a woman," protested Dr. Lawrence J. Korb, the just-appointed Assistant Secretary of Defense for Manpower, Reserve Affairs, and Logistics. He would soon learn to be more skeptical of services' motives in these matters. Subsequent Army actions confirmed the "hidden agenda" theory.

Whatever the Army's motives in announcing the "pause," the decision had not been cleared with the DOD beforehand, as policy dictated; thus, the move had all the earmarks of an end-run power play between the Army and the Senate Armed Services Committee. The reaction of the new Defense officials, as described by one insider, was "incredulous."

The Air Force's motives in 1981 for proposing a moratorium on recruiting women were more difficult to discern. Upon learning of the Army's plan to hold the line on female enlistments, Air Staff planners feared that OSD might look to them to take up the slack by recruiting additional women, thus leaving more men to the hard-pressed Army. To forestall this possibility, the Air Staff set out to convince the Reagan transition team that the Air Force had as many women as it could take. But if the Army's case was weak, the Air Force's was weaker. Vague, unsubstantiated assertions about women having a negative impact on readiness and claims of having "too many" women in traditional fields were unconvincing, even to unseasoned Defense manpower officials. To its credit, the Air Staff did not take the case to Congress.

Although the new Defense manpower officials had more important things on their minds at that moment, they were forced to deal with the military women's issues because of the readiness implications and because any reductions in planned female access-ions could impact on the total manpower program for the planned buildup.

On 19 March 1981 Deputy Defense Secretary Frank C. Carlucci ordered a joint assessment of female officer and enlisted accession and retention policies, which was undertaken under the aegis of Lawrence Korb. The review was to address two questions: (1) How is readiness and mission capability affected by existing or proposed levels of women in each service? and (2) If the goals are lowered, what will be the costs of recruiting additional males to meet the required end strengths? The services were told that the review represented "an excellent forum" for them to express and document concerns about the impact of women on mission capability and to consider the implications of revising existing accessions programs.

In effect, the services were invited to make their case for reducing female recruitment in the context of the overall manpower requirements and budget considerations. It also conveyed the message that final decisions would rest with the OSD, not the individual services. However, Korb let it be known that OSD was opposed to "artificial goals" on the numbers of women the services should have by a given year: "We wouldn't take a woman for the sake of taking a woman," he said. "We would take women who we felt would contribute to the overall effectiveness of the force in quality and quantity."

The military read this to mean that the heat was off in recruiting women and immediately cut back female enlistments. During the first seven months of fiscal year 1981, enlistments dropped 4,900 below the same period of the previous year. When the services presented their five-year budget programs to OSD, they had slashed a total of 60,000 from the female enlisted strength goals set for 1986 by the previous administration.

Thus, after more than ten years of continuous expansion, the services abruptly suspended the forward momentum of military women's programs. It turned out to be only a temporary hiatus, however, as the new administration began to come to grips with the realities of the manpower situation they faced.

As with earlier studies of military women, the new joint OSD/service assessment ordered by Carlucci focused on enlisted women, since it was they who were the source of services' discontent and it was they who bore directly on the manpower problems of the AVF. Also, the services expressed no major female officer management concerns. They were having no problems in attracting well-qualified women into the officer ranks. Coeducational ROTC and the other officer commissioning programs (that is, OCS and OTS), combined with the service academies (which began graduating women in 1980), were producing an unprecedented growth in the numbers of female officers in all the services. The same training was being provided for male and female officers in all occupations to which both sexes were assigned. Despite an influx of women into operational specialties and fields that had been traditionally off-limits to them, none of the services were contending that the women officers might degrade missions or readiness. In fact, their integration into the forces was considered an unqualified success story, at least from the services' point of view—if not always from the women officers' perspective.

The DOD *Background Review: Women in the Military,* published in October 1981, added little to what was already known on the subject. However, its major conclusions were essentially what the services had hoped for. The principal one took an indirect swipe at the previous administration:

> Goals for recruitment and representation appear to have become the main objective in the management of women in the military. OSD's setting of goals has been based on equal opportunity considerations and, particularly for the Army, the utilization of women in the recruiting market to offset potential male non-prior service shortfalls.

In fact, the report had it backwards. The principal objective of the Carter administration, born of pragmatism, was to meet the overall manpower needs of the military, both qualitatively and quantitatively, without resorting to some form of conscription or driving personnel costs out of sight. However, couching decisions to expand the use of women in equal opportunity terms was the politically correct public posture to project during the seventies for an administration committed to the ERA. It happened to conveniently coincide with the military's manpower situation.

The conclusion in the report was exactly what the military services wanted the new Reagan officials to buy into—that the armed forces had been used to satisfy the liberal agenda of the Democratic party at the expense of readiness. The services' motive in portraying the expansion in these terms was to raise serious doubts about the wisdom of relying on women for defense. The services' objective was larger budgets for recruiting men and, failing that, a return to conscription.

Another significant conclusion of the report pleasing to the services: "Each service has created detailed program development methodologies designed to accommodate its own mission and management considerations. *These methodologies appear to be reasonable means to determine end-strength and accession programs . . ."* (Italics added for emphasis.)

It was exactly the message that the services had intended to convey—that they could be trusted to set their own strength and accession goals. Their objective, of course, was to get OSD out of the business of managing their women's programs. In reality, the services' methodologies were essentially elaborate data manipulations designed as rationale for supporting predetermined female ceilings and for keeping women out of mainline operational functions.

Based on data submitted by the services, the review also concluded that continually expanding the recruitment of women to offset shortfalls in male recruiting might be approaching a point of diminishing returns. At female accession rates of from 45,000 to 50,000 annually, women were becoming more difficult to recruit and the quality gap between male and female recruits was narrowing, especially in the Army and Air Force. It was noted, however, that part of the growing difficulty in recruiting women stemmed from affirmative action goals imposed on recruiters by the services. They consisted of quotas for women recruited into nontraditional blue-collar fields that most women did not want (for example, mechanical, crafts, and electrical); and caps on traditional white-collar fields that most women preferred (clerical, administrative, medical, and dental).

The report noted that affirmative action goals for female representation in nontraditional fields, although producing larger numbers of women in these fields, contributed to problems of job migration and attrition, both of which increased training costs. The report recommended that the assignment constraints be loosened to allow the supply of female recruits to "free-flow" against service totals for each field, but set aside enough quotas to accommodate needs for men, for example, to fill combat and sea/shore rotation base requirements.

Probably the most revealing and to-the-point finding of the DOD review was that the services failed to document what effects military women had on readiness or mission accomplishment. The Army continued to insist that a complete policy review was needed before such a judgment could be made and reiterated its contention that OSD-imposed female strength objectives should be suspended until its own new study was completed. The report recommended that the Army be allowed to hold female enlistments at current levels until its study of women's impact on readiness was completed in December. But there was an important caveat: "*Should the Army fail to meet its total recruiting, end strength, or quality goals . . . it will be necessary for them to demonstrate why female accessions should not be increased.*" (Italics provided.) In other words, the Army was still on the hook to produce rationale to support its "womanpause."

With the completion and publication of the review, OSD negotiated new five-year enlisted female accession goals with each service, resulting in a leveling off at roughly 40,000 new female enlistments annually. OSD officials were quick to point out that the goals were neither ceilings nor floors but flexible "objectives." There were no planned year-end strength objectives.

Despite evidence to the contrary, the Army's General Staff continued to harbor the misguided notion that, once shown the evidence, the Reagan administration would see the wisdom of a new draft. When they submitted the Army's manpower requirements to meet the President's new military strategy, they requested an additional 96,000 soldiers (presumably all men) by 1987. To achieve this growth, they said, "will require extraordinary manpower policies to include significant augmentation to the volunteer concept." Terms such as "draft" and "conscription" were not used, but the meaning was clear—to force a return to the draft.[3]

The Army's proposal landed like a live grenade on the third floor of the Pentagon. One Defense official described the Secretary's reaction as livid. "The draft is not anything anybody is considering," Weinberger said through a spokesman. There were many Washington old hands who saw the probability of collusion between the Army and members of the Senate Armed Services Committee who had long espoused a return to the draft.

On 8 July 1981 the President announced the establishment of a Military Manpower Task Force to be chaired by the Secretary of Defense to evaluate the total manpower situation and make recommendations to the President "to increase the effectiveness of the active and reserve all-volunteer services." The Task Force was to evaluate various options. Although a draft was not ruled out, the thrust of the Task Force was clearly aimed at the volunteer concept.

In a speech in New York City, Weinberger gave examples of alternative methods for holding down the demand for military men, such as using civilians to do nonmilitary tasks, thus releasing men for military work such as manning combat units. He also said that he hoped to use more women in noncombat jobs.[4]

Any residual expectations on the part of the military services that, under a Reagan administration, there would be a moratorium or backtracking on women's roles in the armed forces were shattered on 14 January 1982. Out of concern that the military and even some appointed Pentagon officials were misreading the administration's intentions, Secretary Weinberger set the record straight in a memorandum to the service secretaries:

> Military women are a very important part of our total force capability. Qualified women are essential to obtaining the numbers of quality people required to maintain the readiness of our forces. This administration desires to increase the role of women in the military, and I expect the Service Secretaries actively to support that policy.
>
> While we have made progress, some institutional barriers still exist. I ask that you personally review your service policies to ensure that women are not subject to discrimination in recruiting or career opportunities. This Department must aggressively break down those remaining barriers that prevent us from making the fullest use of the capabilities of women in providing for our national defense.

Deputy Secretary Carlucci followed up with instructions to the service secretaries to report on actions to remove institutional barriers and their assessments of how women's career paths were affected by their exclusion from combat. Where career paths were restricted by the exclusion, the Secretary was to specify whether the limitations existed because of law, policy, or by definition of combat.

At this point the discussions on women in the military began to shift from how many women should serve and focused instead on their roles in operational areas and, in particular, on the services' applications of the combat exclusion laws. It was rarely a question of whether women should *be* combatants—it was still generally assumed that they would not. The issues usually revolved around definitions of combat in the context of service missions and organization, which varied greatly. Also at issue was how to provide equity of career opportunities for women while excluding them from the core operations of the military.

*   *   *

In March 1982, Assistant Secretary Korb officially ended the "womanpause" by announcing that the numbers of women in the armed forces would continue to increase in the years ahead.[5] Although specific numerical goals were not set, by 1990 there were 223,000 women on active duty in the DOD services, constituting nearly 12 percent of the total active forces. Numbers by service were as follows:

Army	83,200	(11.5%)
Navy	57,100	(10%)
Air Force	73,580	(14%)
Marine Corps	9,320	(5%)

Source: Department of Defense

In addition, there were 151,000 women in the selected reserve and guard, constituting more than 13 percent of the reserve forces. The Coast Guard, under the Department of Transportation, had another 2,700 women in its active units, plus 1,200 in its reserves.

Altogether, there were nearly 378,000 women in uniform, the largest number in the history of the U.S. armed forces.

NOTES

1. Testimony before the House Armed Services Committee, February 1984.
2. Robert S. Dudney, "Fresh Doubts About Women in the Armed Forces," *U.S. News and World Report*, 20 July 1981, p. 44.
3. George C. Wilson, "Army Hints Draft May Be Required," *Washington Post*, 9 July 1981, p. 1.
4. Weinberger speech reported in *Air Force Policy Letter For Commanders*, 1 July 1981.
5. Dr. Lawrence Korb left the administration in mid-term and joined the Brookings Institution, but he continued to speak out frequently and forcefully on military manpower issues. He became one of the severest critics of the armed services' policies and attitudes on military women and a major spokesman in support of women's roles in the armed forces.

CHAPTER 26

COMBAT AND THE HUMPTY DUMPTY FACTOR

MANY OF THE services' decisions on military women since 1948 were analogous to Humpty Dumpty's admonitions to Alice in *Through the Looking Glass.* When Alice pressed him to explain himself on some obscure point, Humpty Dumpty grandly asserted: "When I use a word it means just what I choose it to mean, neither more nor less."

"The question is," protested Alice, "whether you can make words mean so many different things."

"The question is," replied Humpty Dumpty, "which is to be master—that's all."

When it comes to women in the military, the all-purpose word is *combat*—it means whatever the services choose it to mean. The meaning of *combat exclusion* was the common element driving decisions on military women in all the DOD services during the 1980s. The one sure-fire justification for barring women from any job, unit, ship, aircraft, or mission was to designate it "combat" or "combat related" no matter how tenuous the connection. Although the laws remained unchanged and unchallenged, the definitions of what constituted combat or a combat mission differed from service to service, producing some strange contradictions. The definitions were revised from time to time, even reversed, in response to political pressures, changing missions, and changes in service leadership.

At the heart of the services' power to impose combat exclusion rules was the deeply ingrained popular myth that there was a blanket law excluding *all* women from *all forms of combat*. In reality, no such law ever existed. Belief in the myth was nonetheless widely held both within and outside the armed forces. Not until nationwide media coverage of women's participation in the U.S. military operations in Panama at the end of 1989 was the myth finally exposed, and the public saw for the first time just how unclear and confusing the issue really was.

Sections 6015 and 8549 of Title 10 U.S. Code, which provided the bases for the combat exclusion policies, were the last remaining provisions of the 1948 Women's Armed Services Integration Act. Even though the so-called combat exclusion laws applied specifically only to Navy ships and to Navy and Air Force aircraft "engaged in combat missions," the widest possible interpretations of the laws were used by the four DOD services in establishing limits on women. Where the statutes did not specifically apply, as in the case of ground combat, the "intent of the Congress" was invoked in its place. Conveniently, Congress did not state its intent when it enacted the original law. It wasn't necessary in 1948. At that time, laws to protect women in the workplace from work that could be considered dangerous or "unsuitable" to their delicate natures were common. For their own "protection" women were routinely barred from being police officers, fire fighters, railroad workers, and the like. The combat exclusion statutes were among the last examples of this archaic concept. They would be regarded today as quaint reminders of a bygone age were it not for their continuing impact on military policy.

In the absence of a clear statement of congressional intent, there was always confusion over what ought to be the objective of a combat exclusion policy: whether it should be to prevent women from performing actual combat roles or to keep them from harm's way. So, like Humpty Dumpty, each service devised its own definitions and rules, often on the flimsiest pretexts. The result was that many noncombat positions, units, ships, aircraft, and missions were routinely declared combat or combat related and therefore off-limits to women.

During both the Carter and Reagan administrations, attempts were made to devise standard definitions of combat that could be applied to all the services. They inevitably foundered on the differences in service missions and organizations. Also, many policymakers continued to focus on the issue of women's competence to perform combat roles, an argument that was continually undermined by the increasing technology of weapons systems and by the performance of women serving in combat support roles in ever larger numbers. Increasingly, Pentagon policymakers shifted from questions of competency to blaming Congress and the American public for the continued existence of the combat restrictions. The Navy's CNO, Adm. James D. Watkins, used this line in January 1985. Speaking to the Women Officers Professional Association, he said: "Our position has been . . . that repeal . . . or changes to the laws are going to have to emanate from the grass-roots of this country." If public support for repeal is there, they will "quickly escalate to the Congress . . . and they will be responsive to them." In discussing future opportunities for women in the Navy, Watkins said, "The issue of combat will always be there," but added, "The [question] is can you do combat as well as we can? The answer is yes. Can you fly the planes as well and as effectively, and the answer is yes. That is really not the issue, in my opinion, out there with the American public."

Five years later the Air Force personnel chief made the same point testifying before Congress on the question of women flying combat aircraft. Furthermore, as late as 1991, DOD officials were arguing that it was up to Congress and the American people to decide the issue—not the Pentagon or the services.

BE ALL YOU CAN BE—IN THE ARMY

For women, the Army's recruiting slogan meant: "Be All We'll Let You Be." In the absence of combat exclusion statutes directed at ground forces, Army policymakers were free for many years to make their own exclusion rules without outside interference. Beginning in the mid-1970s, however, Army policies came under the increasing scrutiny of OSD, members of Congress, and women's rights groups. In defending the policies, Army leaders often found themselves in no-win situations. If a new policy broadened opportunities for women, it would be attacked by conservatives and military traditionalists with charges that the Army was going too far—catering to feminists at the expense of readiness. If a policy reduced opportunities, it was challenged by OSD, the DACOWITS, and the press as being regressive and anti-woman. The Army found no middle ground.

In 1981, having convinced the DOD staff that they should be allowed to hold female enlisted strength at the current 65,000 level pending completion of its policy review of women's impact on readiness, the Army was committed to producing yet another report on women. The target date for submitting the report was December 1981. Only four years earlier the Army had conducted a series of studies and field tests on women's impact on unit performance (MAXWAC and REFWAC). It was found then that women generally performed their tasks as well as men and that any unit degradation was negligible or statistically insignificant. That was not what the Army had expected to find.

The new Women in the Army Study (WITA) would focus on combat exclusion. It turned out to be much more difficult than expected and stirred up a fire storm of criticism in the process. The study dragged past its target date with no end in sight. Meanwhile, qualified women were being denied entry into the Army because of arbitrary ceilings imposed on female enlisted accessions, and questionable decisions on assignment policies were being implemented. Also, new mandatory physical standards were imposed on all enlisted jobs. Many Army officials said that it was to give the Army a "legitimate means" of controlling the number of women in each skill.

Understandably, most female soldiers were becoming increasingly suspicious of the Army's motives. They felt that they were being studied to death and suspected that the Army was being less than honest—that the generals were merely looking to justify decisions already made to hold the line against further expanding opportunities for women and to turn back the clock on previously hard-won gains.

Maj. Gen. Mary Clarke, who had retired as the top-ranking female soldier after thirty-six years of service, shared the women's concerns. In June 1982, Clarke published an open letter to Army women. "The duty performance of the average woman soldier is a solid, quality performance—too good ever to return to an all-male force, or a force with only a few token women," she asserted. The heart of Clarke's message, however, was clearly intended for the Army's leadership rather than its women:

The bottom line for the Army is the mission. Do women really contribute to mission readiness? Anyone who asks that question seriously, man or woman, needs to question his or her assumptions and prejudices, and instead face the facts. It is the quality of women's service which gives an affirmative answer to the readiness question.[1]

Clarke was well aware that the Army had already announced that it was returning to "gender pure" basic training. This was a retreat from coeducational basic training, which she had pioneered as commanding general of Fort McClellan, Alabama.

In September, with the study still in progress, it was announced that twenty-three additional military occupational specialties (MOSs) were to be closed to women, bringing the total MOSs closed to 52 percent of all Army jobs. The reason given was "exposure to direct combat." Many of the closed jobs were in fields where the relationship to combat was remote to nonexistent, for example, carpenters and masons, interior electricians, and plumbers. The data to support these decisions were to be in the WITA report, as yet unpublished.

The long-awaited report was finally released on 12 November 1982, but only after DACOWITS had vigorously pressed the issue with the Army and DOD. In the report the rationale for utilizing women was built around combat exclusion and physical demands of jobs. The DACOWITS was highly critical of the Army's handling of the entire matter and with the report's findings, which they felt were not adequately substantiated by the data. Within a week of its release, Army Secretary John O. Marsh, Jr., threw cold water on it by announcing that although he approved some aspects of the report, others required "further validation"—a euphemism meaning more studies. He also announced a planned strength increase to about 70,000 enlisted women, emphasizing that this number was a planning guide and that, "No qualified woman will be turned away for [want of] available vacancies."

Subsequently, thirteen of the twenty-three MOSs that had been closed were reopened and it was decided that the new physical standards for men and women would be used only as a "counseling tool" at the time of enlistment.

But by this time the morale of female soldiers had sunk to a new low, as had the Army's credibility when it came to women. In a personal letter to Secretary Weinberger, in July 1983, DACOWITS

Chair Dr. Mary Huey outlined the serious morale problems the Army was creating for itself and questioned its motives:

> We [DACOWITS] have serious questions regarding the merit of continual studying of women's military participation. As a study reaffirms the positive performance and contribution by [women] . . . a new one seems to be ordered. This finally raises the question of whether objectivity or the "right answers" is the purpose.

The centerpiece of the Army's new assignment system was Direct Combat Probability Coding—DCPC. The system was based on the Army's then current interpretation of the "intent" of the combat exclusion laws imposed on the Navy and Air Force. It had always been a foregone conclusion that Congress never intended for women to serve in the ground combat arms—infantry, armor, and artillery. Popular mythology to the contrary, however, the majority of soldiers are not in the combat arms. Most serve in the enormous network of support operations essential to supply and sustain the combat troops in battle. In wartime, some operate with the frontline units, some even in advance of them. Most operate in the rear areas. But advances in the technology of warfare increasingly blurred the lines between direct combat and combat support.

Also, with the demise of the separate Women's Army Corps (WAC) in 1978, and the subsequent integration of women into previously all-male Army units, women increasingly infiltrated the combat support areas. In 1977, then Secretary of the Army Clifford L. Alexander had revised the Army's combat exclusion policy permitting women to serve on crews at long-range missile and rocket sites (Pershing, Hawk, Hercules) and in nuclear security duties. For the first time, women officers could be commissioned in the Field Artillery and Air Defense Artillery branches. The Army also opened assignments in the 82nd Airborne Division, and women began to receive parachute training. Many Army leaders believed that these assignments crossed the line into combat, thus setting a dangerous precedent.

The DCPC, put into effect in 1983, attempted to profile the battle area from high probability of enemy contact to low probability and to assign women accordingly. It established a complex system of coding all positions and units in relation to their probability of being involved in direct combat. The theory was to preclude assignments of women in skills and positions that, through doctrine, mission, or battlefield location, invite the highest probability of direct combat action.

To many Army women and outside observers, including the DACOWITS, DCPC was an elaborate scheme for putting a lid on total numbers of women in the Army rather than a legitimate means of reducing women's exposure to combat. As feared, the immediate impact of the coding system was to remove thousands of women from jobs and units where they were performing successfully. In the ensuing uproar and under pressure from the OSD, the Army "refined" its criteria and some of the positions were reopened. The system, however, remained intact as the Army's bible on the utilization of women even though it was a personnel management nightmare.

The first real-world test of the Army's combat probability coding system came in October 1983 when integrated Army units deployed to Grenada on Operation Urgent Fury. Some 170 female soldiers served in the operation, the majority of whom were with units out of Fort Bragg, North Carolina. The most visible were the military police who rode armed jeep patrols throughout the island, on roadblock and checkpoint duty and perimeter guards. They also guarded the prisoner of war and detainee camps. At one point, two of four military police platoon leaders were women. Other female soldiers were helicopter pilots, crew chiefs and maintenance personnel, intelligence specialists who were prisoner of war interrogators, signal and communications specialists, truck drivers, and medical personnel with a MASH unit. Twenty-six were stevedores of a transportation company out of Fort Eustis, who loaded captured weapons and ammunition on ships and aircraft. One ordnance captain was responsible for detonating unexploded ammunition.[2]

Privates Rebecca Church and Pauline Farrell were stevedores with the 7th Transportation Group tasked to load captured ammunition and equipment aboard cargo planes destined for the United States. They acknowledged being "a little bit scared" the first night as they walked around the equipment at the airfield. But they took comfort from the presence of the 82nd Airborne troops in the hills around the field. Both said gender was not a problem. As Farrell put it: "They [the men] don't treat us like females—'Don't do this; don't do that.' It was all just working together."[3]

MP E-4 Julie Escude, who was accustomed to carrying her M-60 machine gun, made a similar point about the men's reactions. "The guys always come up and shake my hand."[4]

Pfc Kelly Chagnon was only twenty years old but she found herself in her helmet and flak jacket cradling an M-16 automatic rifle, riding around the island on patrol. "I didn't know what to expect," she told an inquisitive reporter, "but I like it; it's a challenge."[5]

Considering that this was the first time that integrated Army units had been deployed, it went remarkably well. There were some glitches, however, that could be traced to confusion over the DCPC. Initially, some military policewomen were returned to Fort Bragg because of high risk of direct combat exposure. The units lost trained members of their teams, and the women were furious that they were not being permitted to do the jobs for which they had been trained. They took it as a personal affront to their professionalism. After the commanding general of the 82nd Airborne overruled the action, the women were returned to Grenada.

Similar situations occurred when troops deployed to Panama on Operation Just Cause in 1989. In one well-publicized instance, a female Army intelligence analyst, whose expertise was in Panamanian affairs, was left behind at Fort Bragg when her unit of the XVIII Airborne Corps was deployed. She was replaced by a man with no knowledge of the area.

These incidents and others that surfaced in the Persian Gulf War revealed the confusion in the field over application of the coding system. And, more importantly, they revealed the basic contradiction in the Army's policy. "One does not join the military to lead a sheltered and protected life," said Maj. Ann Wright after serving in Grenada for three months as part of the XVIII Airborne Corps's International Law Team. "A soldier knows the potential dangers of military life." In Wright's opinion, shared by many Army women and men: "The bottom line for the United States Army [is] a successful mission due to the dedication of trained soldiers, men and women, who, when given the chance, prove what professional soldiering is all about."[6]

During a worldwide inspection of soldier assignment policies in 1987, the Army's Office of the Inspector General found DCPC to be unworkable. The team conducting the investigation recommended that the policy be rescinded. However, the Army Chief of Staff chose *not* to do so. The report was then "sanitized" in the Pentagon to omit problems reported by field commanders, and word went out from Army Headquarters to the field, forcing full compliance with DCPC.

In 1987, in what was billed as a "fine tuning" of DCPC coding, nearly 12,000 positions were opened to women in the forward support battalions of the Army's combat divisions. The Army leadership finally realized that, given the large number of women in supply and service jobs, the readiness of combat units would be hampered if women were excluded from these forward support battalions. So, in a departure from their own DCPC, women were moved forward where they were needed.

The next year the Army announced that it was opening 3,128 additional jobs to women in the active forces to include electrician jobs and positions in headquarters units of the infantry and armor divisions, air defense artillery battalions, signal battalions, and some light infantry divisions. While these adjustments were being made, DCPC remained a prime target for criticism—not just in the active establishment but also in the reserve components where the system was creating the same problems.

A GAO report in 1988 cited the Army's system as an example of service policies that "unnecessarily restrict" the numbers of women. The report pointed out that, although 40 percent of its enlisted positions could be opened to women, only about one third of those were held by women. It concluded that the Army's recruiting limits "prevented women from competing for all available unrestricted jobs."[7]

One of combat probability coding system's most knowledgeable and outspoken critics was Brig. Gen. Evelyn "Pat" Foote, commanding general of Fort Belvoir, Virginia. At the time of her retirement in 1989, Foote expressed her views in a letter to Army Chief of Staff Gen. Carl E. Vuono.

I know of no more dysfunctional military policy in effect today than the much-despised and unquestionably inoperable [DCPC] system which places gender-based restrictions on the assignments of highly trained Army Women . . . [N]o amount of factual, authenticated data from the field attesting to its unworkability has dented the iron wall of resistance dictating its perpetuation by those who lead the Army.[8]

DCPC's critics continue to contend that it is not possible to manage an organization the size of the U.S. Army by gender—that it creates readiness problems in combat units by understaffing many MOSs having high concentrations of women. For example, combat units are routinely below acceptable manning levels in the medical, clerical, food service, and military intelligence fields. In many cases, frustrated field commanders arrange for the assignment of women to fill vacancies in their units in direct violation of DCPC.

In spite of the many problems and complaints from field commanders, the Army's top leadership remains committed to DCPC at this writing. To abandon it would raise the obvious question of what policies would replace the system given the Army's determination to limit the numbers of women and the ambiguous state of existing law.

NAVY NAVIGATES ROUGH SEAS

While the other services were making waves for the new Pentagon officials over military women, the Navy seemed to be sailing tranquil seas. It was only a matter of time, however, before Navy leaders found themselves on a collision course with civilian officials over the numbers and roles of women in the Navy. As with the other DOD services, there was strong resistance at all levels of the Navy to the growing incursions of women, particularly in the seagoing elements. While there was a grudging admission that the women in ships program was going better than expected, a this-far-but-no-farther attitude nevertheless permeated all levels of the Navy.

Manpower requirements of the Navy are largely determined by the needs of the fleet. As its part of the Reagan buildup, the Navy under its ambitious new secretary, John F. Lehman, Jr., planned for a fleet of 600 ships. It called for adding 120 ships to the fleet, as well as the resources to crew them. Although the goal soon foundered over budgets, it was the centerpiece of Navy personnel programs for much of the 1980s. Considering the demographics of the male youth population, logic would argue that additional ships be opened to women. Instead, like the Army earlier, the Navy chose the opposite course.

With women now going to sea, the key factors in determining the numbers of women the Navy planned to utilize were the combat exclusion statute and the sea/shore rotation formula for men. Some of the ad hoc decisions and actions taken by the Navy, however, gave the distinct impression, at least to skeptics, that its leaders were motivated more by the desire to protect the traditions of men and the sea than by law or rotation requirements.

Under the law as it existed during the eighties (Title 10 U.S. Code Section 6015), women could be assigned permanent duty aboard noncombat ships and temporary duty aboard combat ships "not expected to be assigned to combat missions." It was left to the Navy to designate which ships, aircraft, and missions would be classified as combat and to select among the rest those to have mixed male/female crews. Once women began going to sea in the late 1970s, the total numbers of women in the Navy and the annual recruiting goals (or ceilings) were closely tied to the number of ships selected for mixed male/female crews and the proportions of women allotted to each. A noncombat ship's allocation was determined by accommodations designated for female occupancy.

Also factored in planning female recruiting ceilings was the sea/shore rotation formula for men, which meant reserving for men enough positions ashore in each skill to allow for time ashore between tours at sea. The formula could be easily manipulated to provide a comfortable cushion.

In designating which vessels would remain closed, the Navy applied the broadest possible interpretation of the combat exclusion law, resulting in many ships that would normally be considered noncombatants being off-limits to women. Prior to the mid-1980s, this practice was seldom challenged by civilian authority.

In the initial phase of the women in ships program, women were assigned to designated auxiliary ships—primarily repair ships, tenders, tugs, and research vessels. By 1981 ship commanders were asking for more women and the Navy was identifying additional ships for mixed crews. During the joint DOD Background Review, the Navy reported that the women in ships program had been an impressive success: "Navy women are routinely performing in both traditional and non-traditional areas with skill, confidence, and dedication and are contributing to the general operational effectiveness." Commanding officers often commented that, if anything, the women held a slight edge over the men in completing tasks, that they tended to be more thorough and go farther to research a problem than their male counterparts, and that they tended "to produce better results when given undesirable, tedious or dirty work." Also, "the women have demonstrated professionalism during deployments, even to isolated areas like the Indian Ocean and Diego Garcia."[9]

Skippers discovered what World War II military leaders had found—that women were generally better behaved and had significantly fewer disciplinary problems than men. One commanding officer commented that he wished the men would follow the example set by his women for good behavior.

Given the obvious success of the women in ships program and the demographic trends, and considering congressional pressures to improve the quality of recruits, it would have been logical for the Navy to expand the recruitment of women and open more billets at sea. Even a cursory evaluation would have revealed that there were still many ships closed to women that did not meet the combat mission criteria, and that additional accommodations could be provided on those already available. The obvious examples were the underway replenishment ships of the Mobile Logistics Support Force (MLSF), which resupplied the battle groups. Civilian women were already serving on the civilian counterpart vessels of the Military Sealift Command (MSC) and, in 1984, OSD made the decision to assign Navy women to the small military detachments aboard these same ships. However, the MLSF vessels, which included oilers, stores ships, and ammunition ships, remained off-limits. Applying the combat exclusion law to such ships defied logic.

The first inkling that the Navy was about to dig in its heels on women came in June 1986 when the retiring CNO, Admiral Watkins, warned in a press conference that the Navy might have reached its limit on recruiting women without affecting readiness. The issue, as he defined it, was equity for Navy men in sea/shore rotation. Watkins claimed that women had eaten into some of the more desirable shore billets for male sailors. Even though there were enough shore billets available for men, they were not in the areas the men always wanted. Those billets, said the admiral, had become "chock-a-block" with women.[10]

Exactly what precipitated Watkins' outburst on women was never clear. Some believed it was an attempt to forestall pressures from Congress and DOD to expand the recruitment of women to meet the manpower requirements of the growing number of ships coming on line. Whatever his motives, Navy women felt betrayed by a leader they had thought was a friend. While CNO, Watkins often admitted that they performed as well or better than men and bragged that both officers and enlisted women were being promoted at faster rates than men. In a letter published in *Navy Times*, one woman expressed the reaction of most Navy women to Watkins' parting shot:

> I was outraged at the comments apparently made by the CNO during his "outgoing interview" concerning women in the Navy. It seems to me that energies of this nature would be better directed toward legislation to allow us to serve on combat units and within the ranks that are now "men only" rather than to continue to limit when and where we can serve our country, then put us down for those very limitations.

Kathrine A. Goodwin, a second class builder in the Seabees, who had just returned stateside from a two-and-a-half-year tour in Adak, Alaska, wrote in more pithy, personal terms:

> I bust my butt for the Navy and I work very hard for the respect of the men I work with. I have worked very hard for the position which I hold today. I am damn proud of my job and my country and, put in the position, I would do my best or die for this country. Just one thing I refuse to do, and that is to be the scapegoat for any one of our Navy policies . . . it [the CNO's comments] makes me feel as though all my work and pride have been in vain.[11]

In response to DOD pressure, the Navy announced in December 1986 that it was adding 1,000 enlisted positions for women aboard thirty-nine ships and two civilian Maritime Prepositioning Ship squadrons. But while it was opening shipboard assignments with one hand, it was closing them with the other. It announced that the Mobile Logistics Support Force (MLSF) was being redesignated the Combat Support Force (CSF). Six types of ships in the CSF were reclassified as "other combatant," thus ensuring that they would remain off-limits to women.

Then in February 1987, in a move reminiscent of the Army's 1981 "Womanpause," the new Chief of Naval Operations, Adm. Carlisle A. H. Trost, ordered a freeze on the numbers of enlisted women in the Navy at the current strength through fiscal year 1991.

At that point there were nearly 47,000 Navy enlisted women on duty, some 5,000 of whom were at sea aboard forty-two ships. The goal had been to have 51,300 enlisted women by 1991. Echoing the line taken by Watkins six months earlier, Trost said that the freeze was necessary to protect sea/shore rotation for men and because Congress had refused to grant the Navy the overall strength increases needed to man its dreams for a 600-ship fleet.[12]

Retired Rear Adm. Fran McKee charged that the freeze plan was "another reflection of the very fragile nature of any long-range planning concerning the utilization of women in the Navy. For years we have witnessed the cyclical use of women as a valve to adjust the Navy's manpower picture." She charged that the Navy had continually failed to meet its management challenges. "While decisions such as these are not directed at affecting morale," she said, "they do indeed have a most unsettling effect on Navy women regarding their professional future and true value to the Navy in accomplishing its mission."[13]

Naval affairs writer Donald Fraser called blaming the Navy's problems on women a "bum rap." He asked rhetorically: "How . . . could 10 percent of the Navy's enlisted members possibly screw up the ship-shore rotation pattern for the other 90 percent? Even if all of the women stayed ashore all of the time, wouldn't that still leave 467,960 [enlisted men] to rotate?" As far as he was concerned, it was a clear-cut case of a "tail wagging the dog."

In any case, Navy officials were stunned when, the day after announcing the freeze, Defense Secretary Weinberger rescinded it, saying that he was comfortable with the previously planned goals that called for an increase of 10 percent by 1991.

If Navy women were relieved at Weinberger's intercession, it was soon overshadowed by the announcement that James H. Webb, Jr., had been selected to replace Lehman as Navy Secretary. A 1968 graduate of the Naval Academy, and a Pulitzer Prize–winning author who had seen action in Vietnam as Marine platoon commander, Webb had earned a reputation of being anti-military women. In an article published in 1979 in the *Washingtonian* magazine entitled "Women Can't Fight," he argued against expanding the use of women beyond traditional, noncombat roles in the military and contended, in colorful terms, that women had no place in combat or in the service academies. Their presence in the academies was "poisoning" men's preparation for combat. His statements came back to haunt him in his nomination and congres-

sional confirmation to become Navy Secretary. Although his nomination was never in jeopardy over his views on women, Webb faced
enough tough questioning on the subject that it should have raised
his level of sensitivity to the concerns of Navy and Marine Corps
women. However, in one of his first acts after taking over his new
office, Webb, in a message to the fleet, directed that in the
promotion process, "new emphasis" be placed on the selection of
officers "who have demonstrated outstanding performance in
demanding assignments," particularly those related to combat.
This reinforced the perception that Navy and Marine Corps leaders were attempting to force women out by reducing promotion
opportunities. The effect on morale, already low, was devastating.

The gravity of the situation was not revealed until August 1987
when the DACOWITS Executive Committee made an official
fact-finding trip to Navy and Marine Corps bases in the western
Pacific. Upon their return Chairwoman Dr. Jacqueline K. Davis
reported to Weinberger and Webb, in blunt terms, that they found
the women demoralized by recent statements and policy decisions
that the women believed were designed to drive them out of the
service. The committee also reported shocking instances of sexual
harassment, job discrimination, and a lack of communication
between the Navy leadership and enlisted women. According to
Davis, the women perceive "that the chain of command does not
work in attempts to redress grievances." The women felt that they
were discouraged from taking their complaints to higher authority
and that, when they did, commanders often ignored them. In some
cases, it was a commander who perpetrated the offenses.

The gist of DACOWITS' report was picked up by the *New York
Times* and other national media, causing much embarrassment to
the Navy and Marine Corps. Secretary Webb immediately directed
the CNO to convene a study group to conduct a "comprehensive
examination of current policy on utilization of women" and its
"implementation within the Navy" and to make recommendations
for any changes. The study group visited ships, squadrons, and
shore commands, and conducted extensive interviews with more
than 2,500 naval personnel stationed at ten locations. The *Navy
Study Group's Report on Progress of Women in the Navy* was
published on 5 December 1987; within days, the Secretary announced several major policy initiatives designed to improve the
utilization, assimilation, and treatment of Navy women.

Among the actions taken was a clearer definition of "combat mission," which resulted in expanding opportunities for women to serve at sea, to include twenty-six of the thirty-seven ships in the Combat Logistics Force—oilers, ammunition ships, and stores ships. This would bring the total number of ships available to women to ninety-five. Aircrew assignments with shore-based fleet air reconnaissance squadrons were also opened. The effect of these decisions was to open 10,000 additional positions for women and greatly expand their opportunities for seagoing assignments.

Even Senator Proxmire was moved to praise the Navy Secretary: "[Webb] deserves praise for taking a step in the right direction . . . and [for] taking the lead in bringing some coherence to the present combat-exclusion law."[14]

Webb directed vigorous corrective and preventive actions in areas of sexual harassment, fraternization, treatment, and morale, and approved a number of other recommendations to improve career opportunities.

Also, at the recommendation of the study group, a full-time captain's position was established as Special Assistant to the Chief of Naval Personnel for Women's Policy. The position, to be filed by a female captain, was to focus attention on Navy women's issues and concerns, which seemed to be spinning out of control.

A follow-up study was conducted in 1990, headed by Rear Adm. Roberta L. Hazard. Among its many findings was one well known to most Navy women: that the combat statutes and related policies not only unnecessarily restricted women's assignments and impacted "negatively" on their careers, but they created the perception within the ranks of Navy personnel that "women are not equal contributors." Among the study's recommendations to ameliorate the problem were that the Secretary direct a review of all Navy units and "platform types" (that is, ships and aircraft) in the context of the combat exclusion law and OSD guidance, to ensure that women were not being unnecessarily excluded from permanent assignments; that he direct that when requirements are developed for new Navy units, ships, and aircraft, a statement and supporting data be required concerning the potential for assignment of women; and that new designs for ships of the types currently or planned to be open to women be required to provide accommodations for women.

By that time 8,000 Navy women were at sea aboard fifty-six

Navy ships and seventeen Military Sealift Command vessels. Female pilots were routinely landing and taking off from fleet aircraft carriers delivering personnel and supplies, and the training aircraft carrier USS *Lexington* was going to sea with 300 women permanently assigned to its crew. The Navy announced in 1991 that the percentage of women at sea was projected to increase from 13 percent to 25 percent by 1996. Part of the increase would be from the replacement of the *Lexington* by the USS *Forrestal* as the training carrier, with the potential for 1,025 additional billets for women.

With each U.S. military deployment, Navy women were getting closer to the real action. When the destroyer tender USS *Acadia* sailed to the Persian Gulf in June 1987 to repair the frigate USS *Stark* after the *Stark* was damaged by Iraqi missiles, there were 248 women aboard—25 percent of the *Acadia's* crew. In December 1990, Lt. Comdr. Darlene Iskra took command of the salvage ship USS *Opportune.*

As women continued to advance within the Navy, the combat exclusion law loomed larger than ever as the major impediment, not only to their individual careers, but to their acceptance as full-fledged members of the naval profession. Even so, the Navy leadership was not interested in seeking repeal of the combat exclusion law and actively opposed any suggestions along those lines.

THE MARINE CORPS HANGS TOUGH

The recruiting commercials say it all—the Marines need "A Few Good Men." Sometimes the story line changes, but the message carried on posters and in the national media comes across loud and clear.

The smallest and most combat intensive of the services, the Corps continues to project itself as the last bastion of the classic fighting man. To a Marine, this tough-edged, "leatherneck" image has been the message and the reality. All else remains secondary. In this environment, more than in any other military service, women have been something of an anomaly. If women were a necessary concomitant of the volunteer military, the Corps' leaders remained determined that it would be on their terms.

During the expansion years of the 1970s, no one seriously challenged the Marines' insistence that its mission and organization made it far less able than its sister services to absorb women into its ranks. The Corps' missions require a large portion of its forces to be dedicated to combat, combat support, and combat service support organizations, all of which are postured for immediate deployment to combat areas abroad. The Marines rely heavily on the Navy for logistical support and medical services, which normally have the highest concentrations of women.

As part of the Department of the Navy, the Marine Corps comes under the same combat exclusion law as the Navy. But its primary missions (ground combat) and organization make it more a hybrid of the Army. Although the Marine Corps never bought into the Army's complicated coding system, its policies on women's assignments are borrowed as much from the Army as from its parent service. This combination has left little room for accommodating women. Moreover, the size of the Corps compared to the others made it a less attractive target for OSD in the overall allocation of resources.

So throughout the 1980s, as controversies swirled around the other DOD services, the Marines managed to remain somewhat on the fringes. Nevertheless, the Corps was not totally immune to the pressures of the AVF or to the equal opportunity concerns that had become a fixture of American life. Both inevitably intruded, even on the Marines, effecting policy changes, strength increases, and new opportunities that would never have been envisioned in earlier times.

A major break with the past had come in the late seventies, with the decision to assign women to the Fleet Marine Force in combat service support and aviation elements. Then, during the course of the 1981 DOD Background Review, seeing the way the wind was blowing in the corridors of the Pentagon, the Marine Corps initiated its own internal studies to determine its "optimum requirement" for women. At that time, there were 6,700 women in the Corps, constituting less than 4 percent of the total strength—a proportion smaller, by a wide margin, than in the other services.

The first of two studies of women Marines was completed in 1984. It focused on enlisted women—their classification, assignment, and deployment. The second study, three years later, concentrated on officers. Both studies established centralized, detailed plans and policies for women's utilization. As a starting point, the basic policy on classifying female Marines was that they be assigned to all occupational fields except infantry, artillery, tank and assault amphibian, and pilot/naval flight officer. Men and women were to have an equal opportunity to serve in the support establishment, and women were to have fair and equitable career progression. Women Marines would continue to serve in the Fleet Marine Force (FMF), in service support groups of the Marine Amphibious Force (MAF), in aircraft wings, and in division headquarters.

However, women Marines would not be assigned to any unit in which they would likely become engaged in direct combat action with the enemy. Direct combat action was defined as "seeking out, reconnoitering, or engaging hostile forces in offensive action." Among the assignments declared off-limits were infantry regiments; artillery, tank, assault, and amphibious battalions; and forward area air defense units.

After reviewing all enlisted positions, the number open to women more than doubled—from 5,000 to 12,000. The number of officer positions open to women increased from 655 to nearly a thousand. A few new policies and additional career opportunities emerged from these studies.

Another important break with tradition came in 1984 when Corps headquarters directed that women be given defensive training to include weapons training. Of the military services, the Marine Corps was the last holdout against women receiving any kind of combat training during recruit "boot" indoctrination. But under the new assignment options, women Marines could find themselves in combat situations and should therefore be able to participate in the defense of their units.

Beginning in October 1985, female Marines were firing rifles alongside their male peers. Four months later the Corps reported that women were qualifying in the M-16 rifle on the firing range at Parris Island, South Carolina, and that they were shooting well, sometimes better than men. Pfc. Anita Lobo set a recruit range record, firing 246 out of a possible 250. "We surprised a lot of people," said Capt. Denise Van Peursem, training officer for the women's recruit training. "Everybody expected a qualification rate of about 40 percent when women started firing, and here we are at 98 percent."[15]

Before long, women Marines were routinely participating in field exercises in both the United States and overseas.

But while progress was being made, problems of another sort were surfacing. The Corps leadership was stunned by the DACOWITS' report following their 1987 fact-finding trip to Navy and Marine Corps units in the Pacific region. Revelations of sexual harassment, abuse, and discrimination were certainly not new. However, the circumstances reported in this instance were too flagrant and notorious to be glossed over as minor instances.

In response to instructions from Navy Secretary Webb, the Marine Commandant convened a task force in December 1987 to study the progress of women in the Corps. In its report, the task force confirmed the existence of the problems identified by the committee and found that, rather than being isolated instances, they pervaded the Corps. It recommended corrective action from the command level down. It also recommended some changes in classification, assignment, and deployment policies.

In general, however, the task force found the policies on women to be valid. In their view, the biggest obstacle to women's full integration into the Corps was "attitude." In testimony to Congress in February 1988, Lt. Gen. John I. Hudson, the Marine manpower chief, said: "Our policies are sound, but our actions in carrying them out were in some instances impeded by attitudes." The solution: "that the Commandant stress the significance and importance of a positive attitude by commanders toward women."[16]

The Corps' crusty Commandant, Gen. Alfred M. Gray, Jr. accepted most of the study group's recommendations, and gave his strong support to its key proposals: that sexist attitudes, sexual harassment, and exclusion from field assignments not be tolerated. His edict to the field stated that "women in the Corps are Marines and will be treated as such—with decency, dignity, and respect." But his own actions and public statements often tended to undermine his position.[17]

Gray rejected proposals from his senior officers to open assignments to Marine security forces and embassy guard units, and to allow women pilots. Gray also rejected proposals to permit women to participate in offensive combat training (arguing that it was "not in keeping with the role of women in the Marine Corps' conduct of war"), but agreed that the defense elements of basic warrior training would be made equally available to women.

Carlucci overruled the Marine Commandant's decision on embassy guard duty and ordered Gray to open it to women, producing a public confrontation with the irascible general. "I'm being hustled along here," Gray complained publicly. "I'm having the opportunity to do what's good for my people taken away from me." He added that he was responsible for the well-being of his Marines, otherwise "you can get another commandant."[18]

Shortly thereafter, the first three women graduated from the special training program for Marine embassy guards and took up their posts: Lance Cpl. Angela Hunter to Paris, France; Lance Cpl. Pamela Schrader to Bonn, West Germany; and Cpl. Marie Winslow to Geneva, Switzerland.

But, although the pressure from OSD rankled the Corps' leaders, it hardly made a dent in their determination to hold fast. The system for controlling total numbers of women was an arbitrary 50 percent ceiling on the number who could enter each of the noncombat fields open to them. Ostensibly, it was a reflection of their proportion in the general population. When there were not enough women to meet the quota, more men were assigned to the field. It was a one-way street in that the reverse did not apply. Even in fields that women preferred and dominated in civilian employment, the Marines would not allow women to exceed the 50 percent ceiling.

So although the other services were expanding the use of women, the proportion of women in the Marine Corps remained modest, going from less than 3 percent of the total in 1981 to 5 percent by the end of the decade.

AIR FORCE GOES FREE-FLOW

As the other services struggled to define roles for women within the parameters and intent of the combat exclusion statutes, the Air Force was relatively free from constraints—except those it imposed upon itself. For all practical purposes, there was no limit to the number of qualified women the Air Force could recruit and effectively employ, a fact that continued to make it the most vulnerable of the four DOD services to pressures to use more women.

The new Reagan team soon discerned that the Air Force was an important key to the overall military manpower situation. It was still in the catbird seat when it came to recruiting men and women. Even during the recent lean recruiting years, the Air Force was always able to skim off the best talent from the shrinking pool of potential male recruits, and its leaders were not inclined to share the wealth with their sister services unless forced to do so. The Air Force had no internal incentive to recruit more women. There were no quality advantages in substituting women for men. Unlike the other services in which women were required to meet higher standards than men, the Air Force applied the same standards for both, so there were no discernible differences in quality between male and female recruits.

Nor was combat exclusion a significant factor limiting the Air Force's utilization of women. The applicable 1948 law (Title 10 U.S. Code Section 8549) prohibited women only from serving on "aircraft engaged in combat missions." But Air Force policy went well beyond the law by excluding women from any job or unit assessed to have a "high probability" of direct combat or exposure to hostile fire or capture. Women were arbitrarily excluded from any job even remotely connected with a combat environment, including not only aircrews of combat aircraft without combat missions (for example, training and testing) but also crews of noncombat aircraft whose missions might take them over enemy territory or in any way expose them to hostile fire. Women also were excluded from assignments to nonflying units with missions to deploy to combat areas. These included aerial port squadrons and civil engineering units, which deploy to build and repair runways and basing facilities in combat theaters.

But it was no secret that the vast majority of Air Force jobs required skills not unlike those to be found in large civilian industrial organizations, giving the Air Force an unlimited ability to absorb women.

When, as a result of the 1981 Background Review, OSD abandoned the practice of dictating to the services annual female accessions and strength goals, the Reagan administration gave up a simple but effective tool for controlling the interservice alloca-

tion of military personnel resources. Without external management controls, the Air Force was now in a position to skim off a
disproportionate share of scarce male recruits. Many of these men
would be trained for jobs that women could perform as well or
perhaps better—men who might otherwise fill combat or seagoing
requirements in the other services.

Under the goals set by the Carter administration, one in five of
new recruits entering the Air Force in 1979 and 1980 was female.
When the new administration acquiesced to the Army's plan to
hold the line on new female accessions, the Air Force feared it
would be required to take up the slack, thus leaving more male
recruits for the Army. Air Force planners were hard-pressed to
justify such a parochial position. However, unlike the other services, the Air Force was provided little cover by the combat
exclusion law.

As rationale for limiting the numbers of enlisted women, the
Air Staff devised a complex mathematical model combining affirmative action goals and ceilings with estimates of women's "pro-
pensity" to enlist in each career field. The estimates for all career
fields were then translated into female recruiting objectives. The
model could be manipulated internally to meet predetermined
accession goals that the Air Staff thought would be acceptable to
OSD. Splendid in its presentation, it was essentially an elaborate
shell game disguised as legitimate personnel management methodology. OSD officials nonetheless bought into it, to their eventual
regret.

Congress was not so naive. In 1985, under constant pressure
from the services to allocate more funds to improve recruiting of
better quality men, Congress took on the Air Force by requiring
that 19 percent of new Air Force recruits in 1987 be women. The
goal was raised to 22 percent for the following year. In 1989,
Congress prohibited the Air Force from setting minimum or
maximum gender-specific goals on original enlistments except for
duty assignments falling under the combat exclusion law, which, as
discussed earlier, were so small as to be almost nonexistent.[19] The
effect was to establish what was essentially a free-flow enlistment
system in which men and women competed for available openings.
The Army, Navy, and Marines were allowed to continue setting
separate accession and strength ceilings for women.

Meanwhile, a new DOD policy on combat exclusion was published (DOD Risk Rule), which resulted in the Air Force having to open more than 2,700 positions to women that had been unavailable under the Air Force's combat exclusion policy. They included assignments to mobile civil engineering units and aerial port squadrons. It also opened aircrew positions in reconnaissance and electronic warfare support aircraft. Even then the Air Force dragged its feet on assigning women to these aircraft until 1990, and then only after the DACOWITS raised the issue of compliance.

The last remaining positions at ICBM sites were opened to women, and the first women launch control officers descended into the command capsules of Minuteman nuclear missiles. In addition, the Air Force's senior leadership agreed to assign women to the new MX Peacekeeper missiles as soon as they came on line.

By the end of the decade, there were 77,000 women in the Air Force, constituting 14 percent of the service. Ninety-seven percent of Air Force military jobs were opened to them, at least in theory.

THE COAST GUARD DILEMMA

The Navy's determination to seal off the primary mission elements of its fleet always stood in sharp contrast to the Coast Guard's open assignment policies. Unhindered by any combat exclusion law, and under the Department of Transportation rather than Defense, the Coast Guard continued to exercise its independence from its much larger service cousin. In 1978, the Commandant had made the decision that there would be "absolutely no arbitrary restrictions based solely upon sex" in the use of its people. Successive commandants remained true to that concept and the results were consistently impressive. "My view on the performance of women in the Coast Guard is that they are Class A!" said Adm. James S. Gracey, in a 1982 issue of *Sea Power* magazine. "They are great! They have performed up to all my expectations and beyond most other people's expectations."

By the end of the 1980s, Coast Guard vessels of nearly every class routinely were going to sea with mixed crews, from icebreakers operating in the Arctic and Antarctic to drug enforcement vessels in coastal waters off Florida. Women were commanding cutters and operating all types of craft. They were participating in and even leading armed boarding parties on drug interdiction missions at sea, and female pilots were operating law enforcement and search and rescue aircraft.

During the intervention in Grenada, Coast Guard women were assigned to the crews of vessels sent to patrol the waters around the island. The Executive Officer aboard the largest vessel, a buoy tender, was a female ensign.

Because of the Coast Guard's open assignment policy, women officers' opportunities for seagoing and command assignments far exceeded those available to Navy women. Twenty-eight percent of all female Coast Guard officers were serving at sea and five of them were commanding ships. In the case of enlisted women, however, shipboard assignments were limited—not by policy, but by the size and configuration of many Coast Guard vessels. Many vessels could not accommodate enlisted women due to lack of privacy in enlisted berthing and head (bathroom) facilities. In 1990, the Coast Guard determined that, wherever possible, existing vessels would be reconfigured to accommodate mixed enlisted crews and new vessels would be designed to provide adequate accommodations for enlisted women.

But the Coast Guard's biggest problem in sending enlisted women to sea was not having enough enlisted women to fill all the accommodations already available.

In 1990, at the direction of the Commandant, Adm. Paul Yost, an extensive in-house study was conducted of Coast Guard women. Its purpose was to examine the utilization of women in the Coast Guard in the light of national demographic trends that showed that most of the new entrants into the work force during the 1990s would be coming from the female and minority population segments. The study report observed that, although there were no restrictions on the number of women in the Coast Guard, and 100 percent of all positions were open to them, the Coast Guard lagged behind most of the DOD services in the proportion of women on active duty. Women constitute only 7.8 percent of the active duty Coast Guard, and there were no plans, programs, or policies specifically aimed at recruiting them.

As a result of this report, the Coast Guard planned to increase female accessions to 20 percent in the coming years.

*   *   *

The problem of the Coast Guard's relationship with the Navy was also addressed in the report. It was inevitable that the Coast Guard's practice of integrating crews would cause friction with the Navy because during operational exercises and in the event of war, operational control of the Coast Guard transfers from the Department of Transportation to the Department of the Navy. The question then arises as to which policies on women should take precedence aboard Coast Guard vessels. Gracey took the position early on that women should not be excluded from combat missions because removing them from crews in wartime would degrade the operational readiness of vessels while male replacements were being trained. The issue, nonetheless, remained a bone of contention with the Navy throughout the 1980s.

At one point, the Navy Judge Advocate General determined that the Navy's law did not apply to Coast Guard vessels, although the Navy Secretary could order changes to "standardize" policies of the two services. Coast Guard women lived in fear that, if the crunch came, their smaller service would be forced to capitulate to the Navy and they would be removed from crews right when they were most needed.

In 1987, on the recommendation of the Navy's women's study group, the Navy policy was changed to provide that in the event of mobilization or national emergency, women would continue to serve in the billets to which they were "permanently" assigned. This appeared to solve the Coast Guard's problem. But Admiral Yost seemed unconvinced. In the 1990 study of women, the Commandant emphasized that "women are an integral part of the ship's company, up to and including command." He echoed the concern of his predecessors, that the removal of women during mobilization would "have a deleterious effect on the operational and military readiness of their vessels."

Adm. William Kime, who succeeded Yost, determined to implement all of the recommendations of the study and reaffirmed the Coast Guard's commitment to increasing the recruitment and utilization of women. He appointed a Woman's Policy Advisor to oversee the process.

Probably the most radical new policy to be implemented was the authorization of sabbaticals for up to two years for career level enlisted and officer men and women to care for newborn children.

The expectation was that it would improve the retention of skilled personnel.

MILITARY FLYING

Flying was and is the one major operational mission common to all of the services. And, as in other fields, the key to women's participation in military flying has been the combat exclusion law. The governing statutes were simple and straightforward; the service policies implementing them were neither. The law specified only that the Secretaries of the Air Force and Navy could not assign women to duties in "aircraft engaged in combat missions." The Navy had the additional burden of complying with the statute banning women from permanent assignments aboard its combat ships, such as aircraft carriers.

As in other fields, the DOD services' policies on women flying extended beyond the wording of the law into that ambiguous area of "intent." The net effect was a confusing set of policies from one service to another and only limited access to military flying. The Air Force, Navy, and Army allocated small quotas for women (which acted as ceilings) in certain of their flying programs. The rules differed from one service to another; a type of flying open to women in one service would be closed in another. The Marine Corps continued its total ban on women flying. Only in the Coast Guard was flying unrestricted either by law or policy.

Throughout the 1980s, as women demonstrated their proficiency in different types of aircraft and mission environments, the services were increasingly hard-pressed to justify denying assignments for which women could qualify within the confines of law. Moreover, with technological advances in aircraft and weaponry coupled with innovations in the employment of aircraft in modern warfare, it became increasingly difficult to draw meaningful distinctions between combat and noncombat flying missions and/or aircraft. The fact that the services operated under different rules further complicated matters.

Under pressure from OSD, service secretaries, and members of Congress, as well as some of their own senior commanders, the services gradually relaxed their restrictions, opening additional flying opportunities for women. Although, numerically, the gains were microscopic within the totality of the armed forces, their significance to women's advancement in the military was important.

Because it has by far the largest flying requirement and the most varied missions, the Air Force was always the service most vulnerable to challenges to its policies and its methodology for determining women's access to flying programs. Although the combat exclusion law specifically applied only to aircraft "engaged in combat missions," the Air Force chose to designate whole classes of aircraft as having combat missions and therefore closed to women. All fighters and bombers fell in this banned category— even those used strictly for training missions. Also originally banned because of their roles in combat were reconnaissance aircraft, electronic warfare, forward air controllers (FACs), Airborne Warning and Control Systems (AWACS) aircraft, and C-131 transports used to airdrop troops and equipment into combat.

In other instances, although an aircraft type was open to women, certain units flying them would be closed because they flew missions in support of combat operations. For example, many Air Force women flew the C-141 transports but they were excluded from those assigned to units with combat airdrop missions.

During the 1980s, responding to a variety of internal and outside pressures, the Air Force gradually opened a wider range of flying options for women. In 1982, Air Force Secretary Vern Orr opened assignments in AWACS, considered the world's most sophisticated surveillance planes. The AWACS mission spanned that unclear area between combat and noncombat. The planes carried advanced radar to provide air traffic control over a battlefield, spot and track enemy aircraft, and direct friendly planes in for the attack.

In 1984 the SAC commander, Gen. Bennie L. Davis, approved the assignment of women to crews of the new giant KC-10 refueling tankers. They were already assigned to SAC's KC-135 fleet. Acknowledging that competition for positions on the new crews would be keen, Davis said, "I look forward to having the best crew members available, both male and female, flying SAC's newest aircraft."[20]

In 1986, the Air Force opened 1,645 positions aboard aircraft previously closed to women. The positions included pilots and technicians to crew the latest RC-135 reconnaissance aircraft and EC-130 electronic warfare or radar-jamming aircraft. A decision was subsequently made to open the high-flying U-2 and the strategic reconnaissance RS-71 Blackbird (the fastest aircraft ever built), but shortly thereafter it was announced that the RS-71 was being retired.

Even with these new openings, restrictions on women's access to Air Force rated programs continued to go well beyond the requirement of the law. In its 1988 report on job restrictions imposed on military women, the GAO cited Air Force goals on training women as pilots and navigators as an example of unnecessarily restricting women's opportunities under current statutory provisions. Instead of opening all noncombat pilot and navigator positions to women, the GAO said, the Air Force set an arbitrary percentage on the number of women it thought would be interested in or who could qualify for those openings. By that method, of 480 eligible (that is, noncombat) pilot positions, only 40 could be filled by women. The numbers and proportions of female pilots in the active inventory reflected the system. In 1989, fourteen years after women first entered pilot training, only 315, or 1.4 percent, of the more than 22,000 active duty pilots were women.

Part of the Air Force's reluctance to adopt a more open policy on women flying stemmed from deep-seated but unspoken doubts about how they would perform under the stress of combat operations. The first real-world test (albeit limited) came in 1983 during Operation Urgent Fury when the Air Force transported troops and equipment to Grenada. Women pilots, navigators, and enlisted crew members were in some of the aircraft. Lt. Celeste Hayes was a C-141 pilot assigned to the Air Force's Military Airlift Command at Charleston, South Carolina. During the operation she delivered troops of the Army's 82nd Airborne to Salinas Airfield while combat operations were in progress around the field. Asked if that wasn't considered a combat operation and therefore off-limits to women, Lieutenant Hayes replied that, since it was her time to fly by the duty roster, no thought was given to *not* letting her pull her duty. She said that she was trained and qualified for the mission and the squadron had needed all its pilots for the operation. Other Air Force women flew on C-141s during the operation as flight engineers, loadmasters, and in other crew positions.[21]

Three years after Grenada, Air Force women participated in the raid on Libya as pilots, copilots, and boom operators on the KC-135 and KC-10 tankers that refueled the FB-111s on the way to their targets. Afterward, Sen. John Warner publicly praised the women's participation, saying that it showed people "the range and type of positions women hold in the Air Force today."[22]

During Operation Just Cause in Panama, Air Force women flew and served as crew members of the cargo aircraft in support of the operation and on tankers providing in-flight refueling for the airlift operation; others serviced the aircraft on the ground. However, women were not allowed to fly in C-130s or C-141s that brought in Army airborne troops and equipment because airdrop was still listed by the Air Force as a combat mission. After Panama it was announced that the airdrop ban was being lifted and that previously closed assignments were being opened on both the C-130 and C-141. Actually, this decision had been made much earlier, but, due to institutional inertia or foot-dragging, staffers had not gotten around to implementing it before the operation started. The new openings included all aircrew positions—pilots, navigators, flight engineers, loadmasters, and flying crew chiefs.

Rated female officers and enlisted personnel welcomed each new opening but viewed them as long overdue. Despite their record of performance, the women were discouraged by the continued existence of what they considered to be arbitrary constraints on their flying options. Change came at a snail's pace and only grudgingly on the part of senior Air Force military leadership. Most of the challenging and career-rewarding flying assignments remained off-limits, and the most prestigious command and staff positions remained reserved for people who had flown combat aircraft. The women's frustration was heightened by what they perceived to be the Air Force leadership's insensitivity to their plight and lack of concern for their professional careers. As a result, highly trained, experienced women began seeking opportunities on the outside. In the case of pilots it was a loss that the Air Force could ill afford at that time.

In fact, one of the most serious problems the Air Force faced in the late 1980s was the loss of experienced pilots. Because of limitations on their opportunities to fly, women pilots were leaving faster than men. Typical of the female talent drain was Capt.

Stephanie Wells. In 1979, she had testified before Congress in support of repeal of the combat exclusion law. She believed then that she was capable of flying fighters in combat (see page 340). She continued to believe it. In 1984, after assessing her future as a female pilot in the Air Force, she decided that the grass would be greener on the outside. She found her challenges with NASA at the Johnson Space Center as a staff and research pilot and flight instructor for astronauts. She continued her military flying as a C-5 transport pilot in the Air Force reserve.[23]

Capt. Theresa Claiborne made her career decision in 1989. She had spent seven years flying mostly KC-135 tankers for the Strategic Air Command (SAC) but was not permitted to fly the B-52s she refueled. "In SAC, wing commanders have all flown bombers," she said. "As a female in SAC, there was only so far I could go." So, after sizing up her chances for advancement, Claiborne left active duty and joined a reserve unit to fly KC-135s. She planned to become a civilian airline pilot.[24]

In spite of the built-in handicaps, a number of women pilots persisted against the odds. Lt. Col. Teresa Marné Peterson, for example, who was one of the first women pilots in the Air Force, after flying C-141 cargo planes became an instructor training pilots in high-performance jets. In 1990, she became the first woman to command an Air Force flying training squadron.

Capt. Jacqueline Parker (whose photograph appears on page 379) became the Air Force's first female test pilot in 1988. "I never met an airplane I didn't like," says the five-foot-three pilot. "The fighters are all so exotic," she says. She especially likes the F-4: "It flies just like an old fighter." But the A-7 attack fighter is her all-time favorite. Her ultimate goal since the age of fourteen has been to become an astronaut pilot. Unless the policy is changed, her chances of flying in space will be better than flying combat fighters.

Capt. Troy Devine has all the right tickets for success in the Air Force. A 1985 graduate of the prestigious Air Force Academy, Devine went on to earn her silver wings. Had she been a man she would have had her pick of operational assignments. She did the next best thing by becoming a pilot of the high-flying TR-1 spy plane for the Ninth Strategic Reconnaissance Wing at Beale Air Force Base, California. For that privilege she had to sign an agreement to not become pregnant for at least a year and suffer the indignity of being tested for pregnancy every two weeks.

The supreme irony was that the U.S. Air Force trained female pilots of other NATO nations to fly its combat aircraft and, north of U.S. borders, Canadian forces were training and assigning women to fly fighters. Following a trial period, in 1987 all aircrew positions in the Canadian forces were opened to women. Capt. Jane Foster and Maj. Deanna Brassier were the first two female jet fighter pilots in the world. During training exercises, Foster did more than shoot down the myths about female fighter "jocks." Flying a CF-18 Hornet, she "shot down" with a simulated missile a U.S. Marine flying an AV-8B Harrier. Afterward, an amused witness reported that the Marine was so angry at losing to a woman that he threw his helmet across the hangar. "We like to think [flying fighters] is a man's job," said Capt. Pierre Ruel, a flight safety officer at Canadian Forces Base Cold Lake, "but it's not." A Norwegian F-18 pilot on an exchange tour with the Canadian forces explained that it was not really a matter of women flying combat. "It's more a matter of women entering the ranks," he said. "Fighter pilot has been male territory up until now."[25]

Many American female pilots believe that this attitude permeates the ranks of the U.S. fighter pilot community and that it, more than any other factor, accounts for the slowness of military leaders to relax self-imposed rules or to seek repeal of the combat flying exclusion statutes.

The Air Force's practice of banning *all* combat aircraft was undercut by the Navy's policies of allowing a few women access to some combat aircraft on noncombat missions. In contrast to the Air Force, Navy policies were aligned more closely to the law—basing restrictions on unit *missions* rather than *type* of aircraft. Navy women gained experience in types of aircraft that were closed to women in the Air Force.

As early as 1975, Lt. (jg) Rosemary Conatser (later Mariner) became the first military woman to qualify in high-performance jet aircraft. She flew the Navy's single-seat A-4L and A-4E. The following year she flew the A-7E, a frontline light attack aircraft, including practice bomb drops. For the next five years she flew in research and development test and evaluation projects for the Naval Weapons Center at China Lake, California. In 1990, Commander Mariner took command of a Navy tactical electronic warfare squadron, the first woman chosen to lead an operational aviation squadron in any of the services. By 1991 she had logged 3500 military flying hours in fifteen different aircraft and seventeen carrier landings.

By the early 1980s Navy women were already flying several types of combat aircraft (for example, F-4s, A4-Fs, and A-6Es) in flight tests and evaluations and as weapons instructors. They were also flying electronic warfare aircraft (EP-3), and H-46 helicopters, as well as transports. Jet pilots Lucy Young and Andrea Rice completed the TopGun program and became air-to-air adversary pilots for the program. Young went on to become an instructor pilot and Rice became an "aggressor" (enemy) pilot in the Navy's advanced training command.

In 1983, Colleen Nevius became the first Navy woman to qualify as a test pilot.

Lt. Barbara Bell was the first woman instructor at the Navy's elite test pilot school at Patuxent River Naval Air Station in Maryland. Earlier she had graduated number one in her mostly male class at the same school and had gone on to become the first woman permitted to qualify as an F-14 radio intercept officer. Only the law kept her from the next logical assignment—an F-14 squadron aboard a carrier. Training Navy test pilots was her next best option.

In 1987, the Navy opened pilot, NFO (navigator), mission specialist, and aircrew positions in the Fleet Air Reconnaissance Squadrons.

Although the Navy's policies were less restrictive than the Air Force's with respect to types of aircraft open to women, opportunities to fly were not much better overall, chiefly because of the added constraints imposed by the legislative ban on combat ships. The carriers were and are the center of the naval aviation universe, and the Navy's flying requirements are geared to the demands of the carrier fleet. Women aviators were routinely operating off the decks of carriers, but they could not be permanently assigned to the air units on board, the training carrier USS *Lexington* being the one exception.

Female helicopter pilots were allowed to cruise aboard the noncombat auxiliary ships that deployed for periods of up to six months at sea.

The combined effect of the two statutory exclusions and the Navy's own policies produced results not unlike those achieved by the Air Force. By 1991, nineteen years after the Navy opened flying opportunities to women, there were only 181 female pilots and 75 navigators on active duty in the Navy, constituting just 1.8 and 1.2 percent, respectively, of the two communities.

The Army marched to a different drummer from either the Air Force or Navy. Since the combat exclusion laws did not apply, the Army based its flying exclusion rules on its interpretation of the laws' intent. Using its combat probability coding system (DCPC), the Army excluded women from all fixed-wing aircraft and helicopters assigned combat missions or flying in direct combat support. But, as with the units operating on the ground, it was difficult to draw a clear line between combat and noncombat flying. Banned, for example, were the Apache attack helicopters, but women were assigned to the unarmed Black Hawk and Chinook helicopters that supported combat troops in the field.

Capt. Michelle Yarborough believes that, if given the chance, women can fly anything: "If a woman is given the training and she has the mental aptitude, the physical ability to do what's required of her in the cockpit, I feel she is perfectly qualified to fly combat." Yarborough knows whereof she speaks. An Army test pilot with the job of checking out the Cobra attack and OH-58 scout helicopters at the DOD test site at Edwards Air Force Base in California, she has flown nearly every Army helicopter with a combat mission. "You don't join the Army because it's a safe job," she says. "You join the Army for your country." This view is shared by most female pilots.

Female Army aircrew members had their first close encounter with combat action in 1983, in Grenada, when they found themselves flying operational missions into hostile territory. Lt. Kathlyn Henderson said she thought nothing of flying her OH-58 helicopter on night missions checking for snipers in the dark, dense hills of the island.[26] Then during the invasion of Panama, Army women flew Black Hawks ferrying infantry troops to landing zones and hauling supplies, sometimes under heavy enemy fire. Their days of vindication would come a year later in the Persian Gulf.

Of the four DOD services, only the Marine Corps was able to ban women from all flying, asserting that all Marine flying involved combat. Actually, some of the Corps' air missions were identical to those flown by women in the other services. For example, flying helicopters that airlift troops and supplies in support of ground troops in the field. In 1988, the internal task force of senior officers that studied the progress of women in the Marine Corps recommended that flying opportunities be opened to women. The recommendation was rejected by the Commandant. There is no indication that his decision was seriously challenged by higher authority.

Coast Guard Commandants had no such reservations. Unimpeded by law or institutional reluctance, the Coast Guard continued throughout the 1980s to utilize women in all types of aircraft in the full range of operational missions, including air/sea rescue missions and law enforcement missions on drug interdiction.

With each incremental step American women flyers inched closer to actual combat. As they met each new challenge, they demonstrated that the only limitations on American women's ability to perform flying duties in military aircraft were those imposed by an archaic law and restrictions added on by service policies. Before the end of the decade, although some diehards were still claiming that women did not have the "right stuff" to fly combat, most knowledgeable people were no longer making that claim. The official position had shifted to the political—it was now a matter for Congress to resolve. The Air Force's personnel chief, Lt. Gen. Thomas Hickey, laid it out in testimony before the Senate Armed Services Committee in March 1990. He acknowledged that there is probably not a combat job in the U.S. Air Force that women could not do. "They can fly fighters, they can pull Gs, they can do all those things," Hickey said. "They are physically [and] emotionally capable . . ." He added that "the issue is if you want us to put them there, just change the law and the Air Force will do that." But he stopped short of recommending repeal.

Repeal of the combat exclusion laws was not what the military leadership wanted and it was not what either the civilian leadership in the Pentagon or in the Congress would actively seek. Instead, the DOD attempted to give some coherence to the conflicting policies of the services.

THE DOD RISK RULE

The findings of the DACOWITS during their trip to the western Pacific led Defense Secretary Weinberger to establish a

DOD Task Force on Women in the Military in September 1987. It was to address a wide range of issues impacting on women's careers, morale, utilization, and quality of life. Among the Task Force findings were the inconsistencies in the services' applications of the combat exclusion statutes. It recommended that the DOD adopt a clear standard for evaluating whether noncombat positions or units should be closed to women.

The result was the DOD Risk Rule. Published in 1988, the rule imposed a new standard interpretation of the combat exclusion laws as the norm for the military in evaluating noncombat support units and positions from which women could be excluded. The purpose was to narrow the services' interpretations of the statutes, thus providing the widest possible latitude in assignments and career opportunities for women. Also, it was supposed to eliminate inconsistencies among the services wherein similar positions or units were opened to women in one service but closed to them in another.

The rule stated that "risks of exposure to direct combat, hostile fire, or capture are proper criteria for closing noncombat positions or units to women, provided that . . . such risks are equal to or greater than that experienced by associated combat units in the same theater of operations."

Although the immediate practical result of applying this rule was to open an additional 30,000 noncombat positions to women, service policies relative to combat remained as unclear as before and as difficult to apply in the real world. The result was a host of contradictions as theory came into conflict with reality.

The theory underlying the DOD Risk Rule was based on a faulty premise—that it is possible to protect military women from the risks of what is fundamentally a risky profession. In modern warfare, geography and circumstances, not policy, good intentions, or misplaced chivalry, dictate who will face hostilities in war. For example, had hostilities broken out in Europe during the Cold War, military women by the thousands would have been in the direct line of enemy fire because they were concentrated in support units behind the front lines, which would have become priority targets under the "deep-strike" doctrine. Modern weapons do not distinguish between combatants and noncombatants.

Other, more obvious anomalies abounded. Under Army regulations, female soldiers were prohibited from assignments to the infantry, armor, or cannon artillery. But in reality a soldier doesn't have to be an infantryman to get into a firefight, as the Army would soon learn in Panama.

Air Force women were barred from flying fighters or bombers, but those combat aircraft depended on tankers for air-to-air refueling en route to their targets, even over enemy territory. In war the tanker becomes a very lucrative target with no capability for defending itself. Women were flying them and serving in other crew positions.

Similarly, Navy women could not serve on the combat ships such as destroyers, aircraft carriers, and submarines, but they served in the crews of the destroyer tenders, submarine tenders, and other ships whose missions are to provide essential supplies, repair, and replenishment to the fleet during combat operations. The missions of these ships take them into harm's way when the Navy deploys into a combat area and make them highly vulnerable, prime targets in war because they are vital to the fleet's operations.

The ultimate absurdity was that Air Force women were assigned to launch ICBMs with nuclear warheads to obliterate enemy targets, but they continued to be barred from delivering conventional weapons in a B-52, strafing enemy tanks with an A-10, or engaging in air-to-air combat at the controls of an F-15.

Lawrence J. Korb, former Assistant Secretary of Defense under the Reagan administration, got to the heart of the matter when he observed that it is "ludicrous" to be overly concerned about the welfare and safety of military women whose jobs are to serve their country in a crisis while at the same time accepting as inevitable the obliteration of millions of civilian women and children in a nuclear exchange.

As the decade of the 1980s closed, the disparities between theory and reality in military policies, tolerated during the Cold War, were exposed by another kind of war.

PANAMA AND OPERATION JUST CAUSE

Panama was an unlikely site for a defining event in the history of women in the American military. When Capt. Linda L. Bray led thirty soldiers of her 988th Military Police Company to seize an enemy objective near Panama City in December 1989, she ignited a firestorm of controversy over the new roles of women in the armed forces. Her military objective that day was to take control of a kennel for attack dogs of the Panamanian Defense Forces, which was presumed to be lightly defended. But what was expected to be a routine military police operation turned into a three-hour, infantry-style firefight. The mission was a success and overnight Linda Bray became a new American folk hero.

One of the 770 military women who deployed with the American forces on Operation Just Cause, Captain Bray was just doing what she had been trained to do. It was no big deal to her or to the men and women under her command. But sociologist Charles Moskos got it right when he said that Bray's command of troops in the combat operation in Panama was "a shot heard around the world, or at least in the Pentagon."[27]

Certainly it was big news to the American public raised on the myth that women were excluded from military combat. And even though Pentagon policymakers knew that women might be exposed to hostile fire and might even have to shoot back, they were not prepared for the deluge of public interest in what happened in Panama. Major stories appeared in nearly every news publication in the country, accompanied—and this was unusual—by photos of Captain Bray in full field gear.

Less well publicized was action involving female pilots flying two Army Black Hawk helicopters: 1st Lt. Lisa Kutschera and WO Debra Mann. Their helicopters came under heavy fire during the operation. One had to be grounded after it was hit. A third chopper was fired on during a supply flight. When it was all over the three female Army pilots were nominated for the Air Medal, two of them to receive the "V" for valor.

The news of women's involvement in the action met mixed reactions. The Army didn't know how to respond initially. A spokesperson hastened to point out that the events had been overblown in the press. Some people lauded the women's accomplishments as an example of women's capabilities to perform as combatants. Others denigrated them, arguing that what the women had done proved nothing. One grumpy critic even commented, "The sorts of things they were doing could be done by a twelve-year-old with a rifle."

Surprisingly, the question of whether women should be in harm's way as a matter of public policy was seldom raised. The thrust of most of the discussion centered on how inconsistent and meaningless the rules on women in combat are and how blurred they become when the shooting starts.

The central figure in this controversy, Captain Bray, was surprised and unprepared for all the media attention. "The story for me was to demonstrate how well the soldiers performed. I was so thankful for army training," she said later. "That was the point of the story, but that's not what came out. It came out: 'Women in combat.'" The attention was deeply resented by many male soldiers who thought the women were getting far too much attention for their small contribution. Some of the letters she received were angry and obscene. She was especially unprepared and dismayed by the negative attitudes of other Army officers and the treatment she received from them. In the end, the treatment she received so disillusioned and demoralized her that she left the Army.[28]

The Department of the Army said:

> Capt. Linda Bray's service in Operation Just Cause focused attention on the new role of women in the Army. Like many soldiers called to serve in dangerous situations, she performed her duties admirably. The media stories about Bray's mission in Panama will be remembered as a significant event in the history of women in the armed forces.

What happened in Panama might soon have been forgotten— and the issues it raised concerning women's participation in national defense put on hold—had it not been for events several months later in the Persian Gulf.

NOTES

1. Letter published in *Army Times*, 21 September 1981.
2. Ann Wright speech for Women's History Week, at Fort Bragg, NC, on 7 March 1984.
3. "7th Trans Gp Provided Muscle to Load Cache," *Army Times*, 12 December 1983.
4. "Women GIs in Grenada," *The Houston Post*, 8 December 1983, p. 12A.
5. *Ibid.*
6. Wright, *op. cit.*
7. GAO Report, *Women in the Military: Impact of Proposed Legislation to Open More Combat Support Positions and Units to Women*, July 1988.

8. Letter to Gen. Carl E. Vuono, 7 July 1989.
9. DOD Background Review, p. 75.
10. Interview with Ted Bush, "Watkins: Navy Has All the Women It Needs," *Navy Times*, 23 June 1986, p. 1.
11. Letter to the editor, *Navy Times*, 4 August 1986.
12. "Navy Freezes Number of Women on Duty for Next Five Years," *Washington Post*, 3 February 1987, p. A19.
13. Interview with Rosemary Purcell, "Weinberger Thaws Freeze on Adding Women," *Navy Times*, 16 February 1987, p. 30.
14. Rick Maze, "Proxmire Hails Navy for Opening Jobs to Women, *Air Force Times*, 25 January 1988, p. 8.
15. Mel Jones, "Women Marines Doing Better Than Expected on Rifle Range," *Navy Times*, 27 January 1986, p. 3.
16. Testifying before the House Armed Services Subcommittee on Personnel and Compensation, 4 February 1988.
17. Molly Moore, "Top Marine Bars Widening Women's Role," *Washington Post*, 26 April 1988, p. 1.
18. Comments to the DACOWITS, 24 April 1988.
19. National Defense Authorization Act for Fiscal Year 1989. Enlisted jobs closed to women by Air Force interpretation of the combat exclusion law: combat control, tactical air command and control, aerial gunner, and pararescue and recovery (as of August 1991).
20. Air Force Policy Letter for Commanders, 15 February 1984.
21. Wright, *op. cit.*
22. "Warner Praises Women's Role in Libya Raid," *Air Force Times*, 12 May 1986, p. 15.
23. At NASA Stephanie Wells instructs and flight-checks astronauts in the high-performance T-38 trainer, trains astronauts in the G-2 Gulf Stream, which is configured to simulate the shuttle landings, and flies the KC-135 used for zero-gravity training.
24. "Air Force Flight Rules Driving Women Out of the Service," *San Francisco Chronicle*, 28 March 1989.
25. Julie Bird, "Special Report," *Air Force Times*, 4 December 1989.
26. "Women GIs in Grenada," *Houston Post*, 8 December 1983, p. 12A.
27. Editorial in the *Washington Post*, "Women in Combat: The Same Risks as Men?" 3 February 1990.
28. "Back to the Kitchen," *Washington Times*, 1 July 1991, p. 1.

CHAPTER 27

THE PERSIAN
GULF WAR

M AJ. MARIE T. ROSSI, pilot and Commander of B Company, 18th Army Aviation Brigade, was preparing to lead her Chinook helicopter unit into Iraq during the opening hours of the ground assault. On the eve before the forces moved out, an incredulous CNN reporter pushed a microphone in her face and demanded to know how she felt as a woman doing a job normally done by men in combat. Her reply clearly surprised him as well as the TV audience who viewed it:

> I think if you talk to the women . . . in the military we see ourselves as soldiers . . . We don't really see it as man versus woman . . . What I am doing is no greater or less than the man who is flying next to me or in back of me.[1]

Rossi was killed in the line of duty when her helicopter crashed on 1 March 1991, the day after the cease-fire. Her sacrifice came to symbolize for many Americans, and for military women in particular, the revolutionary changes that had taken place in women's roles in national defense.

In an astonishing lapse of military intelligence, the United States was caught by complete surprise when, at 2 A.M. on Thursday, 2 August 1990, Saddam Hussein's tanks rolled across the border of the tiny emirate of Kuwait. Within hours the million-strong, battle-tested Iraqi Army had overwhelmed the Kuwaiti forces. In one stroke, Saddam Hussein became the strongest leader in the Arab world and had destabilized the entire Middle East and the oil markets of the world.

In the days that followed, Iraqi forces moved ominously close to the Kuwaiti border with Saudi Arabia, long a friend of the United States in that troubled area. President George Bush declared an economic embargo against Iraq, froze Iraqi assets in the United States, and ordered three aircraft carrier task forces into the region to "protect vital U.S. interests." The United Nations Security Council declared a worldwide trade embargo.

Meanwhile, President Bush ordered Operation Desert Shield—the rapid deployment of U.S. military air, ground, and naval forces into the region to stop further aggression.

As war threatened in the Gulf, a big question in many American minds was whether the armed forces were ready to deploy and fight in a desert roughly 7,000 miles from U.S. shores. Neither the all-volunteer military nor what General Vessey had termed the "co-educational" military had been battle tested against a well-armed, determined enemy. Certainly, there was no disputing that the all-volunteer force of 1990 was a quantum leap from the "hollow" force of a decade earlier. Military experts agreed that, by any measure, the forces were the best quality, best trained, best equipped, best led in U.S. history. Not even the hard-line advocates of conscription were seriously suggesting a return to the draft.

However, the jury on the coed aspect of the AVF was still out. The fact that women now constituted 11 percent of the active duty military and more than 13 percent of the reserves was worrisome to many people—both inside and outside the military. Questions continued to be raised about the wisdom of placing so much reliance on the "weaker sex" for the tough, dangerous job of fighting wars. Women's ability to perform arduous, highly technical jobs in a real war was still unproven, and the reliability of mixed male/female support and combat support units in a major combat operation was still relatively unknown.

Critics of the integrated military insisted that women were the "weak link"—the Achilles' heel—of the armed forces. In a replay of the debates of a decade earlier, the conservative community and some senior military retirees were especially vocal, charging that women were a drag on military readiness and more trouble than they were worth. Detractors explained away the performance of the women during the brief operations in Grenada and Panama by insisting that their contributions had been overblown by feminists and a naive press—that neither operation had provided real proof that women were an asset to unit performance. In the absence of any empirical data to support these charges, it was contended that military leaders knew "the truth" but, for political reasons, were being muzzled.

So, evidence in Panama notwithstanding, the question remained: How will integrated male/female units perform in a real-world combat environment? In a very real sense, military women were still on trial.

DESERT SHIELD

While the President was stitching together an international coalition, and politicians debated the relative merits of economic sanctions versus military force, American troops and equipment from bases in the United States and overseas continued pouring into Saudi Arabia aboard military transports and wide-bodied jets commandeered from civilian airlines. At the beginning of September there were more than 100,000 American combat troops and support personnel in the theater, and a fourth aircraft carrier battle group was steaming toward the area. Reserve and guard units and individuals with needed skills were being activated by the thousands either to deploy to the Gulf or to replace regulars being deployed.

Amid the international hubbub, American service personnel, regular and reserve, male and female, were quietly doing what soldiers have always done when the call to duty came. They were getting their lives in order, assembling their field gear, saying goodbye to loved ones and friends, and preparing to do what they had been trained to do.

Desert Shield would be the first major U.S. military deployment since the agony of Vietnam, and the largest deployment of military women in U.S. history. According to Lawrence Korb: "This crisis will demonstrate to people that women are an integral part of the armed forces, that we couldn't do the job without them."[2]

Of all the new realities brought home to Americans by the nightly news from Saudi Arabia, none was more startling than seeing, for the first time, a U.S. soldier in full desert battle gear, loaded with equipment, and discovering that "he" was a "she." It was one of the many images that made this war so different from all the others. Replays of Vietnam, Korea, and World War II were always filled with the faces of men at war. This time many of the soldiers' faces on the TV screens, in the morning newspapers, and in the magazines were the faces of women—wives, mothers, sisters, daughters, sweethearts, the girl next door.

Although the image of Capt. Linda Bray in Panama was still vivid in the minds of the American public, it had not totally driven home the full extent of women's actual involvement in the U.S. armed forces. The Persian Gulf War did. For the first time the American public began to realize that women had become an integral and significant part of the new military, serving side-by-side with the men in the field, doing the tough, dirty, risky jobs of war.

Initially, the press, ever in search of a new human interest story, engaged in a feeding frenzy over touching scenes of young mothers saying good-bye to their husbands and children. Admittedly, it was a new twist to an old theme—soldiers leaving spouses and children to go off to war, perhaps to die. Only here the roles had been reversed: It was the wife and mother going to war leaving the husband and father at home. The media soon dubbed the Gulf operation the "Mommy War." Typifying the theme was a full-color cover photo on a popular magazine of an Air Force captain saying good-bye to her small daughter. "MOM GOES TO WAR" the title read. "With tears and brave smiles . . . thousands of American mothers are saying good-bye to their families to face the unknown dangers in the Gulf."[3]

These media images were jarring reminders of the sacrifices that many military women were now expected to make, but they were arguably no different nor more heartrending than the sacrifices of the men. Many men resented the implication that their pain was less important or that they were more expendable than the women who wore the same uniforms. Most of the women resented the implication that they were weak, weepy, and unprofessional.

Even after arriving in the desert, the women continued to receive media attention disproportionate to their numbers because of their news value in a situation where "hard" news was tightly controlled. Nevertheless, had it not been for the press, the extent of women's involvement in the Persian Gulf would probably never have been known, because the military services had more pressing concerns and little interest in publicizing women's contributions. Despite the press's tendencies for exaggeration, in general, the media images projected of women in the Gulf accurately portrayed what was going on.

For the first time since women had become a part of the military at the turn of the century, national leaders from the President on down began referring routinely to the "*men and women*" of the armed forces and to "*service personnel*" rather than servicemen. In his national address to Congress on 16 January 1991, President Bush invoked a woman's name, Army Lt. Jacquelyn Jones, among the four "comrades in arms" he quoted to rally public opinion for the war effort.

THE AGONY OF ANTICIPATION

By mid-January 1991, the International Coalition forces were well organized under American Gen. Norman Schwarzkopf. The U.N. Security Council had imposed a 15 January deadline for Iraq's withdrawal from Kuwait, and the U.S. Congress had granted President Bush authority for a de facto declaration of war. The whole world waited—holding its breath.

With 350,000 U.S. troops hunkered down in the area, Americans were steeling themselves for war with the very real prospect of heavy casualties and the likelihood of a protracted involvement in the Middle East. One of the most feared unknowns was a chemical or biological attack by Iraqi forces. Protective masks and clothing (called "chem gear") were issued to all the troops and kept close at hand. Medical personnel were trained to set up temporary facilities to decontaminate and treat victims. "Everyone knows what to do and knows how to do it, but they have never done it for real," a Navy official said.

The first medical personnel to arrive were Army, Navy, and Air

Force mobile medical units airlifted to the Gulf; they would provide care on a joint basis. Meanwhile, two U.S. Navy hospital ships, the *Mercy* and the *Comfort*, left their home ports at Oakland, California, and Baltimore, Maryland, and sailed for the Gulf area. Together they could deal with any medical emergency, including chemical warfare casualties. Combined, they had twenty-four operating rooms and eight X-ray rooms and could accommodate 160 intensive-care patients and 2,000 limited-care patients. The staffing of these theater medical facilities, ashore and afloat, was very different from that in previous wars, in that the age-old sex stereotypes—wherein women were nurses and all other medical personnel were men—had all but vanished.

Despite the tensions, the men and women in the Gulf rarely seemed to question why they were there. When asked by inquiring reporters, the usual response was that they were just doing their duty; they were there to do what they had been trained to do. They were all volunteers and proud of it. "There's not a single one of us who's here because he was forced," said a cavalryman. "We're here because we want to be here." Airman 1st Class Kimberly Childress, a twenty-seven-year-old Air Force communications specialist assigned to an Air Force A-10 "Warthog" tank-killer squadron, said she wanted to come: "It's my job." Tech. Sgt. Deborah Knight, a reservist with the 38th Aerial Port Squadron, admitted to being "scared" but said she was doing it for her son. When her unit was called up and deployed to Saudi Arabia, she had to leave her husband and four-year-old son back in Charleston, South Carolina. "[Saddam] right now is the enemy against me. He's the reason I'm here," she explained. "He's the reason I'm away from my son."

The men and women of the 2nd Forward Marine Support Group, dug into the desert close to Iraqi-occupied Kuwait, shared the tension of knowing they would be in the line of fire if and when a ground attack came but were as prepared as professional Marines could be under the circumstances. "I think a lot of us are a bit apprehensive," said intelligence officer Maj. Ginger Jacocks just before the ground offensive kicked off. "The majority of the people out here are facing combat for the first time," she said, referring to men as well as women.

There was also the looming new reality that, if the fighting started, women would die. Even though servicewomen had been killed in previous wars, many military men and women still believed that the American public was not prepared to accept it. "But they're going to have to accept it," said 1st Lt. Diana Torres, an operations officer of an ammunition supply unit, "because it's going to happen."

Once the forces were in place and ready for action, the waiting seemed interminable. The men and women shared a common boredom, loneliness, and gut-wrenching apprehension. They trained to peak levels and then trained again. They cleaned the talcumlike sand out of their weapons and vehicles, fixed their equipment, checked over their chemical gear—and then did it all again. They occupied endless hours writing home, looking for mail, playing games, sleeping, praying, and complaining about the MREs (meals ready to eat). But mostly they waited and wondered: What will it be like? Am I good enough? Will I lose my nerve? Will I leave this awful place alive?

At 11 A.M. on Tuesday, 15 January, the President signed the directive authorizing the attack, and that afternoon Defense Secretary Dick Cheney signed the "execute" order. Still nothing happened.

DESERT STORM: WHEN POLICY FACED REALITY

"They did it!" Air Force pilot Capt. Stephanie Wells wrote in her diary on 17 January. "The attack has begun at long last. As I figured, the nervousness of anticipation is gone." Even her attitude had shifted from one of almost despair and resignation at the thought of the United States going to war, to "Go get 'em and get this thing over with."

Wells' C-5 transport crew agreed that the anticipation and anxiety of waiting for the war to begin was tougher than being in it. On the sixteenth she wrote "H-hour is past. We are on the ground in Bahrain at 0800 [8:00 A.M.]. Hostilities are imminent . . . This is the most scared I've felt on this whole business." During the intelligence briefing before departing for Torrejon, Spain, she felt the adrenaline surge of anticipation. She got all her chemical warfare gear out of the bag and ready. The departure from Bahrain and the flight were uneventful, but the whole crew felt the heightened awareness. Wells thought that before the next mission to Saudi she would buy a handgun even though she hated them. "I can think of some scenarios where I might need it," she wrote.

At 12:50 A.M. (local time) Thursday, 17 January, the first fighter planes roared off the runways of the air base at Dhahran, Saudi Arabia, and U.S. warships offshore launched cruise missiles at Iraqi targets. Before 3 A.M., radar-evading F-117 Stealth fighters had demolished targets in Baghdad as Americans watched the action live on their TV screens. Operation Desert Shield had become Desert Storm. A somber President told America that the liberation of Kuwait had begun: "No president can easily commit our sons and daughters to war."

More than events in Panama, Desert Storm exposed to the American public the problems and contradictions in DOD and service policies on women vis-à-vis combat, and some of the assumptions underlying them.

During the operation, American military women did just about everything on land, at sea, and in the air except engage in the actual fighting, and even there the line was often blurred. They piloted and crewed planes and helicopters over the battle area, serviced combat jets, and loaded laser-guided bombs on F-117 Stealths for raids on targets in Baghdad. They directed and launched Patriot missiles, drove trucks and heavy equipment, and operated all kinds of high-tech equipment. They manned .55-caliber machine guns, guarded bases from terrorist attack, and ran prisoner of war facilities. They repaired and refueled M1 tanks, Bradley fighting vehicles, and earth-moving equipment. Navy women served on naval replenishment and repair ships, fleet oilers offshore, and at facilities ashore; Coast Guard women were involved in harbor security. Other women commanded brigades, battalions, companies, and platoons that provided support and services to the troops in the field. They staffed medical facilities ashore and afloat to receive, treat, and evacuate casualties.

Women also were directly involved in the war effort at installations all over the world and in the United States, supporting the gigantic airlift, sea-lift, and refueling operations, as well as combat operations launched from bases outside the immediate combat theater. While observing preparations for B-52 strikes launched from England, Sen. John Warner was struck by the extent of women's involvement. "At midnight in England, when the troops were loading B-52s [bombers] in the cold misty rain, you couldn't distinguish the men from the women," he said. "The women were loading and fusing the 500-pound bombs the same as the men."[4]

The ground crews at all these bases, as well as the many thousands of military and civilian personnel stationed at installations scattered around the world and in the United States, were as essential to the overall effort in the Gulf as those actually located in the theater.

Of the U.S. services, the Army deployed by far the largest number of military women to the Gulf. It was also burdened by the most complicated policies on assigning them. For their own protection, Army women were not supposed to serve in the front lines or in direct combat units. However, it was obvious from the beginning that front lines were not what they used to be and noncombat units regularly took casualties. In the Gulf War there were no fixed positions or clear lines in the sand—the "front" changed hourly. Units in the rear areas, where the women were concentrated, were often as exposed to attack as those at the front. Iraqi long-range artillery and especially the surface-to-surface missiles were unisex weapons that did not distinguish between combat and support troops. The men and women under Scud attacks knew they were in combat regardless of what the military called it. Their location in the rear provided little protection to the soldiers of the 14th Quartermaster Detachment when a Scud missile slammed into their barracks near Dhahran, Saudi Arabia, killing twenty-eight of them, including three women.

Army policy excluded women from serving in the direct combat units, namely infantry, armor, and cannon artillery. However, on many occasions during Desert Storm, female soldiers in support units found themselves in the thick of the action. Women assigned to units supporting the mechanized forces, for example, moved forward with the combat units into Kuwait and Iraq, often coming under enemy fire.

Moreover, women were assigned to target and launch Patriot missiles because the Army makes distinctions between *defensive* and *offensive* combat. When they were firing their missiles at incoming Scuds, the soldiers in the Patriot batteries, both male and female, must have thought it was a distinction that made a difference.

The principal source of the confusion within the Army was the Direct Combat Probability Coding (DCPC) system, which unnecessarily complicated the management of military personnel at a time when the Army could least afford it. The system was especially troublesome at the unit level, where commanders struggled to keep pace with the shifting, unpredictable demands of the war by getting the most out of the people they had. Although Army leaders in the Pentagon continued to deny it, numerous reports surfaced through unofficial channels that commanders in the field were regularly ignoring the rules and assigning their people where they were most needed—without regard to gender. "I've got a job to do and I need good people," said a combat support battalion commander. "I don't give a damn whether they're a male or female so long as they know what the hell they're doing. This is no place for screw-ups."

Other reports surfaced that Army unit commanders, to be "on the safe side," often applied their own interpretations of the rules. The commanding officer of an enemy prisoner of war camp (EPOW) in Saudi Arabia, for example, decided on his own to ban his female military police from internal prison guard duties even though they were fully qualified to perform them. Their normal primary guard duties were delegated to the male MPs while the women were relegated to answering telephones, checking IDs, issuing clothing, and delousing prisoners' clothing. One of the reassigned women had worked as a correctional officer at a civilian maximum security facility, where she had dealt with tougher customers than any Iraqi soldier. She had fourteen years of military training for the job she had been sent to the Persian Gulf to do and, like the other women, she was incensed at not being allowed to do her job. Understandably, the men resented having to take up the slack. Worst of all, the camp was short of critical, trained personnel to cope with an enormous influx of Iraqi prisoners.

Later, at the same EPOW camp, a team of five military police had to be sent in at 2 A.M. to help quell a riot. Sgt. Kitty Bussell, a member of the team, was stopped by a Saudi who told her that a woman could not go inside on such a dangerous job. Trained in riot control and armed with an M-16 rifle and pistol, Bussell refused to be turned away. "I'm as good a shot as anybody," she insisted and went in.

Women were not permitted to fly the Army's Apache or other attack helicopters; but female pilots of the 101st Airborne Division's Screaming Eagles flew Black Hawk and Chinook helicopters loaded with supplies and troops fifty miles into Iraq as part of the largest helicopter assault in military history. To the Iraqis, the noncombat helicopters flying over the battlefield were as much targets as any Apache and probably a lot easier to hit.

Maj. Marie Rossi, thirty-two, led her squadron of Chinooks during the first assault. However, she almost didn't go because of confusion over the Army's policy. Before the ground assault, Rossi's commander had informed her that all the female pilots were being replaced by men because of the combat restriction. Rossi asked him if the enlisted women on the crews were also being replaced and was told they were not. Rossi reminded him in strong terms that the same policies applied to both officers and enlisted women. He backed down.

There was confusion in the Marine Corps as well. As in the Army, Corps policy banned female leathernecks from all combat jobs and units. Its women were concentrated in the support and combat support units, which normally would have been positioned in the rear areas.

When orders first came to deploy to the Middle East, only the male Marines were shipped out; the female Marines in the same units were left behind. Five days later the female Marines were deployed, but they were annoyed that the Corps could not seem to clarify its policy. The women felt that it was demeaning to them and bred resentment among the men. "It was always my plan to bring the women from day one," the Commanding General explained defensively.

After the women arrived in Saudi Arabia, they were quartered for a time aboard air-conditioned ships while the men were sweltering in tents and warehouses ashore. The men resented the special treatment the women seemed to be getting, and the women resented being treated differently. "We are Marines," complained S. Sgt. Martha Brown, a radio repairman. "We should be treated as Marines." As the Marines settled into their positions in preparation for the ground assault, the double standard disappeared.

Then, in what was described as a "calculated risk," a huge Marine support base was set up well forward of most infantry units and nearest the border of Iraqi-occupied Kuwait. Its mission was to provide logistical support for two infantry divisions. Thus, more than 170 "noncombatant" female Marines assigned to the 2nd Forward Marine Support Group were located in one of the most forward and exposed positions in the theater. They helped set up the base in the bare desert—digging bunkers, filling and stacking sandbags, driving trucks, and setting up communications equipment. At that point Corp. Deborah Yelle, a tactical satellite communications repairman, was surprised to find herself 100 miles closer to the potential front lines than her fiancé.

When the ground offensive started, the Marine infantry units leapfrogged past the forward support group to attack the entrenched enemy. They relied on the support troops, male and female, to keep them supplied with ammunition, fuel, and essential stores. According to the Corps' Commandant, Gen. Alfred M. Gray, Jr., his women, like his men in the theater, all performed their duties like "superb Marines."[5]

The Air Force policies on assigning women were somewhat less complicated than those of the Army and Marine Corps but were often as contradictory. The law forbade women from flying on aircraft engaged in combat missions, which the Air Force interpreted as excluding women from bombers and fighters. But women were at the controls and in the crews of the jet tankers that refueled them in midair during attack missions. On one of her missions, Capt. Ann Weaver Worster flew her KC-135 tanker 250 miles into Iraq. The tankers constituted very easy and lucrative targets, since they were unarmed and loaded with precious fuel essential to the success of the air campaign. These lumbering giants were highly vulnerable to surface-to-air missiles and would have been sitting ducks for Iraqi fighters had the coalition forces not been able to gain air superiority early on. The same could have been said of the Airborne Warning and Control Systems (AWACS) aircraft directing the air traffic over the battlefield, and the transports delivering troops, supplies, and equipment. All were lucrative targets; all were defenseless; all were open to women.

In one of the more inexplicable anomalies of the war, Air Force women were routinely assigned to tactical air bases in Saudi Arabia, where they serviced, repaired, and armed combat aircraft in preparation for strike missions. The air bases were frequent targets of Iraqi Scud missile attacks and took direct hits. Navy women, on the other hand, were banned from assignments in any capacity on the aircraft carriers offshore. The missions of the bases and carriers were the same but the carriers had the protection of the entire fleet. The only exceptions for women on the carriers were those flying support aircraft bringing in personnel and supplies, but even they were not permitted to remain aboard.

Moreover, although Navy women were barred from serving on

the crews of combat ships, female sailors were assigned aboard the ships that provided essential supplies, repair, and ammunition to the American fleet during Gulf combat operations. They were also aboard the hospital ships offshore. All of these support ships would have been as vulnerable to Exocet and Silkworm missiles and floating mines as the combat ships, and they generally sailed without the protection of the fleet.

After being exposed to the media coverage of the war and seeing women's performance on live TV, the American public and members of Congress understandably began to question the logic of the rules and laws governing women's participation in the military, particularly as they related to combat situations.

SOME OF THE FACES OF WAR

The real story of American women in the Gulf War is as much about individuals as about policies. Although their experiences were different by light-years from their predecessors in World Wars I and II, the women of Desert Storm were, nevertheless, pioneers exploring the new limits of a profession often hostile to their presence. Following are a few of their stories as soldiers, sailors, airmen, and Marines doing their jobs.

Capt. Stephanie Wells' credentials as a command pilot were impeccable. Few military pilots could match her combined experience in the active and reserve Air Force and in NASA. However, as tensions escalated in the Gulf, Wells feared she might have to sit this one out. On 6 August 1990, the day President Bush made the announcement that the United States would be sending troops to Saudi Arabia, Wells had called her reserve unit at Kelly Air Force Base in Texas and was told that women were being excluded. She was outraged. "Perhaps the Saudis have said no women," she reasoned. The next day the call came—"women are NOT excluded." Within days she was flying C-5 missions all over the globe in support of the Gulf operation while still holding down her full-time job as staff instructor pilot with NASA at the Johnson Space Center in Houston, Texas.

On 29 August 1990, Wells' reserve unit, the 68th Military Airlift Squadron of the Military Airlift Command, was activated and she was given twenty-four hours to get her affairs in order and report for full active duty. Once activated, the 68th became part of the largest airlift operation in history. As a command pilot, Wells flew 600 hours in support of the operation. This included twenty-two flights into Saudi Arabia, Egypt, and the United Arab Emirates, on trips averaging fourteen days. Cargo consisted of helicopters, trucks, tanks, missiles (including Patriots), medical supplies, and food, as well as some troops. She also took trips to Thailand and into Turkey in support of the Kurd relief effort.

Sgt. Theresa Lynn Treloar, the "Ice Lady," earned her nickname by virtue of her direct, confident style and single-minded commitment to a tough and dangerous assignment—an assignment that put her closer to the battlefront than any other American woman on the ground in Iraq. So secret was her mission that her Army superiors refused to describe it or to permit photographs of her for publication. "I was given the opportunity to turn this job down," she told reporters. "I chose this and I knew what I was getting myself into when I chose it." According to Capt. Michael Mendell, the leader of the team of twenty-three men and one woman, "there were no other female soldiers in the same situation." Mendell had chosen Treloar for the assignment over the objections of higher headquarters. It was insisted that an assignment so close to the front lines would be against Army policy. The camp was only a few miles from the front, within range of Iraqi artillery. When American forces crossed the border, the unit would move forward and she with it. "She is the only woman I know who carries an M-16 rifle, a light antitank weapon, an AT-4 and grenade," Mendell said. "I would trust her to cover my back in any situation."

An outspoken, French-speaking soldier with a seven-year-old daughter at home and a "great marriage," Treloar believed that because she was a woman, some male soldiers were quick to misinterpret her professional manner for coldness and had dubbed her the "Ice Lady." The opposite male perception, she said, is that "anger in a woman reflects emotionalism."

The Persian Gulf was not the first time Treloar had challenged Army policy and attitudes. During Operation Just Cause, when her unit deployed to Panama, she had been forced to remain behind at Fort Bragg because of a battalion rule that forbade spouses from serving together on a mission. When her husband, Sgt. Charles Barbour, was sent to Panama, she said she confronted the officer who had written the rule and told him calmly that if the rule were imposed again she would divorce her husband. She meant it. "I would have just lived with my husband instead of being married to him."

Sergeant Treloar said she was proud to put her life on the line for "the American way of life" and was well aware that she was trailblazing for military women. "I always feel the pressure," she said.[6] Her activities during Desert Storm remained classified even after the cease-fire.

Capt. Cynthia Mosley, thirty, commanded Alpha Company of the 24th Support Battalion Forward, 24th Infantry Division (Mechanized). The mission of the 100 men and women of her company was to supply a mechanized brigade with fuel, water, ammunition, and anything else it needed to operate in the field. During the ground assault, the company followed close behind the advancing forces on Highway 8 into Iraq. At one point, the combat units were advancing so rapidly that they were running out of fuel. As the support unit closest to the front, Alpha Company pulled up beside M1 tanks and Bradley fighting vehicles on the side of the road to refuel them so they could continue the attack. For a while, they were supporting not only the brigade they were assigned to, but all the brigades in that area of the front. The Army awarded Captain Mosley the Bronze Star medal for meritorious combat service.[7]

Capt. Sheila G. Chewing was a weapons controller on one of the Air Force's AWACS aircraft that directed the air war over Iraq. On 17 January 1991 she helped shoot down two Iraqi fighters during one of the first dogfights of the war. During the first bombing raid on Baghdad, Chewing identified two Russian-built Iraqi MiG-29 interceptors and directed U.S. F-15 fighters in for the attack. Then she listened to the radio exchanges between the F-15 crews as they blew away the MiGs and called, "Splash two." It was the first of many such experiences for Chewing and the rest of the AWACS crews. "When that happened [bringing down an enemy plane], we really felt like we were doing our jobs."[8]

Lt. Phoebe Jeter, twenty-seven, had her moment of truth shortly after midnight on Tuesday, 21 January 1991, when she heard the words "Scud Alert" and the sirens went off. She had trained for three years in simulated war games for this moment. As commander of an all-male Patriot Delta Battery of "Scudbusters," Jeter knew that the alert was no drill—this was for real. The Scuds were coming into their area and could be carrying either chemical or conventional warheads. "Everybody was scared . . . we didn't know where they were headed." Within minutes her computer screen revealed that the Scuds were headed for her base and Riyadh. Jeter was in charge of the engagement control center from which Delta Battery's Patriots would be fired. She barked commands through her gas mask to her tactical control assistant, ordering thirteen missiles fired, which destroyed at least two Scuds.

The ultimate irony, of course, was that by the Army's Humpty Dumpty definition, Jeter and her men had not been in "combat."

Proud to be the first female Scudbuster, Lieutenant Jeter was one of the thousands of black women who served their country in the Gulf War. She was commissioned through the ROTC program and admits that she joined the Army looking for "adventure," but she learned in Saudi Arabia that, "I could do anything that I wanted to do."

Airman 1st Class Gina Maskunas-Delaney, of Killen, Texas, was a crew chief for an F-117 Stealth fighter. She scrawled a message to Saddam Hussein on the side of a laser-guided bomb being secured to the bay of her plane: "We care enough to send the very best."

Lt. Col. Ora Jane "O.J." Williams, forty-nine, from Monticello, Mississippi, was a career soldier with eighteen years in the Army when she deployed to the Gulf from Fort Bragg, North Carolina. Williams commanded the 2nd Material Management Center, a battalion-sized logistics management unit with the mission of requisitioning supplies for three combat divisions: the 24th Infantry Division (Mechanized), the 82nd Airborne, and the 101st Airborne. Her unit handled tens of thousands of daily requests for everything from ammunition and spare parts to food, tents, and clothing. "I'm here because I can do [the job]," she said confidently. Being the only female in the unit, the men sometimes would give Williams a hard time. But being black, female, and tall, Williams was used to being given a hard time. "The men are always thinking, 'Is she going to be a powder puff or is she going to pull her weight?' It doesn't make any difference," she said philosophically. "You have to earn respect and demonstrate your capabilities."

S. Sgt. Hattie Brown, thirty, of South Boston, Virginia, deployed to the Gulf as a radio operator with an air defense unit. Located at a site near the Kuwait border, she and the eight men under her supervision relayed battle reports from the field to the headquarters. "I've confronted the idea of death and I try not to be scared," said Brown, an expert marksman. "If I die, I hope I do it with pride, trying to get the enemy." Her greatest fear was making a mistake that would cost someone else's life. She planned to become a police officer after leaving the Army.

S. Sgt. Laura Long, twenty-seven, of Sandusky, Ohio, was a vehicle dispatcher with the 1st Tactical Fighter Wing in Desert Storm. She worried about her drivers during the Scud alerts, wondering if they were okay. As a supervisor, she felt that she had to stay calm so she could "be there for everybody." So, rather than run for shelter as she was supposed to, Long stayed at her post and called her drivers. She believed that if women were allowed to be in the front lines, they would do as well as anybody; if allowed to be fighter pilots, "we would be the best fighter pilots around." If she had had her way when she joined the Air Force, Long would have been flying one of the combat fighters. But she decided to settle for less. "Sometimes you have to take what you can get."

Lt. Col. Roslyn Goff, forty-one, commanded 800 soldiers of a combat support battalion. When it came time to move out through the minefields into Kuwait and Iraq, her men were as apprehensive of her ability to lead them into the battlefield as they were about the enemy. But, according to the Army citation for the Bronze Star medal after the war, Goff had "inspired her battalion to excellence under fire."

Sgt. Sherry Callahan was an assistant maintenance crew chief and boss of the team that maintained and prepared the F-15 fighter flown by the commander of the 1st Tactical Fighter Wing. She called the plane "Daphne." She was proud of the fact that it had not broken down since they got to the Gulf. "We wash it. We maintain it," she said. "We take care of it like a personal car. Except we can't take it home." Her biggest frustration as a mechanic was that, at 140 pounds, she sometimes did not have that extra bit of strength needed to fix some things right. She was grateful to the men she worked with, who she admitted helped her out a lot. "When you first get to a base in this [mechanic] specialty, the guys always have a question in their minds: Is she going to be able to carry her load?" she said. "But once they find out . . . they help you as much as they can."

Sgt. Carla Barbour-Clark, thirty, of Madison, Virginia, was a forklift operator assigned to the 438th Aerial Port Squadron out of McGuire Air Force Base in New Jersey. A divorced mother of a three-year-old daughter, Barbour-Clark worked twelve hours a day moving pallets at a sprawling air base in Saudi Arabia. When the Scuds came in, she said she thought her heart would stop. "That rush of adrenaline comes, and there's a moment of panic," she said. "I don my chem gear, and if I see someone who is having trouble with theirs, I help them."

S. Sgt. Cynthia Williams, of Glouster, Virginia, took exception to those who thought that women would not be able to hold their own in a combat situation. An air policeman with eleven years in the Air Force, Williams was assigned to the 1st Tactical Fighter Wing Security Police Squadron. Her job was to guard the gate to the air base in Saudi Arabia. Among the tools of her job was her M-16 rifle. She admitted that incoming Scuds gave her "a jolt" but that the threat of terrorism was more frightening. When asked if she would hesitate to use her weapon in a terrorist attack, Williams almost resented the question. "The gate guards are male and female alike," she said. "The women can be shot just like the men. I feel no hesitation in picking up an M-16 and going at it."

PRISONERS OF WAR

As had been predicted, women's integration into the operational elements of the armed forces would not come without a price. One of the nation's worst fears was realized on 31 January 1991 when the Iraqi government announced that it had captured an unspecified "number of male and female conscripts." Any female prisoner would receive "good treatment in accordance with the spirit of lofty Islamic laws." The only report of U.S. soldiers missing since the start of Desert Storm was of two members of a transportation battalion missing along an oil pipeline in the vicinity of the Saudi Arabia-Kuwait border. One was a woman.

Even before the POW report was officially confirmed, the experts began speculating on how an American woman might fare as a prisoner of the Iraqis. Although Army and Navy nurses imprisoned by the Japanese during World War II had not been mistreated, the U.S. military had been contending for years that any female taken prisoner by an enemy would be forced to endure unspeakable horrors. Observers of Arab culture, however, contended that a female POW might have less to fear than male prisoners because of the "revered" position of women in the Arab world. They might be exploited for propaganda purposes, but beating or sexual abuse was unlikely. "If they're [Iraqis] behaving based on the traditional laws of Arab society," observed Ashraf Ghani, an associate professor of anthropology at Johns Hopkins University in Baltimore, "they would go out of their way to be respectful to women." But he added that, considering Iraq had its back to the wall, "they might do anything."[9]

"The ones least surprised by this are the women," said retired Brig. Gen. Evelyn Foote. "It's all part of the bargain of being a soldier, sailor, airman or marine," she said. "It was certainly on my mind when I was in Vietnam in 1967."[10]

Spec. 4 Melissa Rathbun-Nealy, twenty, of Grand Rapids, Michigan, was identified by Pentagon officials three days after the Iraqi announcement that they had female prisoners. The Army said that she was one of two Army truck drivers missing in action and probably taken prisoner by the Iraqis. She thus acquired the dubious distinction of being the first American enlisted woman to become a prisoner of war, and the first U.S. female military POW since World War II.

Rathbun-Nealy had enlisted in 1989, according to her father, Leo Rathbun, because she did not have career goals at the time. She was stationed at Fort Bliss, Texas. When her unit, the 233rd Transportation Company, was deployed to Saudi Arabia in October 1991, she admitted to being scared but felt that women had the right to be in combat. After she got there she made it clear that she wanted to be close to the action if the war started. According to her father, "She told her supervisor that she didn't want to be stuck behind a desk. She wanted to do what she was trained to do." What she was trained to do was drive twenty-four-wheel trucks that transport tanks.[11]

On 30 January 1991, Rathbun-Nealy and Spec. David Lockett were driving a heavy-duty Army truck carrying supplies when they became stuck in the sand and were overrun by Iraqi troops. Both were wounded by enemy fire—she by a bullet and shrapnel in her arm, he by bullets in his chest. They were first taken to Basra and then to Baghdad. They later described their most fearful time— during the coalition air raids when they could see the bombs exploding close by.

During her first telephone conversation with her anxious parents, Rathbun-Nealy assured them that the Iraqis had taken "excellent" care of her and described her captors as "beautiful people." Her guards had called her a hero as brave as Sylvester Stallone and as beautiful as Brooke Shields. Joan Rathbun asked her daughter if she realized just how famous she had become. "Well I'm beginning to get the idea," she replied.

Americans got their first glimpse of Rathbun-Nealy when she came down the steps of the plane in the first prisoner release. The baggy yellow prisoner's suit could not disguise her quiet composure and military bearing. Even General Schwarzkopf, the usually unruffled commander of the Coalition Forces, seemed tongue-tied as he greeted her at the foot of the airplane stairs.

Maj. Rhonda Cornum's capture went unnoticed until it was over. Prior to the POW exchange, there had been no mention in the press of a second American woman being taken prisoner. And even then only the first name gave the clue—Rhonda was clearly not a man's name.

The early reports of a Black Hawk helicopter being shot down indicated that all aboard were lost. No mention was made of any crew members being taken prisoner or that there had been women aboard. Gradually, information came out that there had been survivors, but there was still no mention that a woman was involved. Actually, three of the eight soldiers aboard survived and were taken prisoner, Cornum among them.

Cornum, thirty-six, an Army flight surgeon and mother of a fourteen-year-old daughter, was assigned to the 2nd Battalion, 229th Aviation Regiment at Fort Rucker, Alabama, when both she and her husband, Air Force Capt. Kory Cornum, were deployed to the Persian Gulf.

On 27 February 1991 the call came from operations to the pilot of the ill-fated Black Hawk helicopter for a mission to rescue a downed F-16 pilot sixty miles away in Iraq. The pilot had been injured in the crash. "You have Doc Cornum on board? Do you have all of your equipment?" "Yeah," the chopper pilot replied. Cornum later recounted what happened next:

> We flew as fast as we could, over a bunch of our guys, moving east. A few minutes after we saw the last friendly convoy, we started taking small-arms and antiaircraft fire. Seconds later we got hit, then we crashed.
>
> After we tumbled and rolled, I found myself underneath at least part of the wreck. I wasn't thinking clearly enough to know why I couldn't use my arms. I used one foot to kind of push my way out from underneath this airplane. By the time I got out, the Iraqi soldiers were there.[12]

After the crash, Cornum heard a flurry of Arabic when they pulled off her helmet. That was when the Iraqis realized that their captive was a woman. "They were surprised, although not as surprised . . . as Saudi soldiers would have been," she said. "There are female nurses in the Iraqi military." Cornum was thrown over the tailgate into the back of a truck, unable to cushion the fall with her arms.

She and one of her fellow survivors, Sgt. Troy Dunlap, were first taken to Baath Party headquarters and then on to Baghdad, where they joined the third survivor, who was also injured. Except for being thrown into the truck, Cornum said that she had not been mistreated. She was given medical care to stabilize her broken arms but she would not allow the Iraqis to perform the surgery she knew was required. Her biggest problem, other than the pain, was her one-piece flight suit. With the condition of her arms she could not remove the suit to take care of normal personal necessities, and the Iraqi guards did not want to help her undress. It would have been wrong for an Iraqi man to see any part of her body. Finally, a guard took pity on her: He put a large bag over her head and helped unzip her flight suit as the bag came down. Later, Dunlap was able to assist her. "Dunlap was a real star," she later reported.

Cornum was released with other prisoners on 6 March. She was a happy but odd vision as she stepped carefully off the plane in her yellow POW garb, both arms in slings, her long hair hanging in an unmilitary fashion down her back. But Cornum never lost her characteristic cool as the crowd, led by General Schwarzkopf, greeted her and the other released POWs. How was she feeling, someone called out. "Airborne!" she shouted.

Doctor, surgeon, paratrooper, pilot, Army officer, mother, hero. "God, she's tough, she's tough," her mother said. "She could always do anything and she still will."

The two former women POWs, Rathbun-Nealy and Cornum, met briefly aboard the hospital ship *Mercy*. What was it like to meet one another? a reporter asked later. "We're both females in the Army. That's about it," Cornum replied matter-of-factly. "Gender doesn't come into play at all, to tell the truth. Nor did it the whole war, which I think is the most important thing you can come away with."

DEATH DID NOT DISCRIMINATE

In the end, Melissa Rathbun-Nealy and Rhonda Cornum could count themselves among the lucky ones. Thirteen other women would not make it home alive.

The first American women to die in a war since Vietnam and the first enlisted women ever to be killed in action perished with twenty-five of their male comrades on the night of 25 February 1991, when a Scud missile slammed into the military barracks near Dhahran.

Spec. Beverly Clark, twenty-three, of Armagh, Pennsylvania, was part of an extremely close family of three sisters and a brother. She had joined the Army right after graduating from high school. When news of her death came, her hometown was in shock. "She just was a fine all-around human being," said a former employer. "There's been a lot of tears [here]."

Spec. Christine Mayes, twenty-two, of Rochester Mills, Pennsylvania, had gotten engaged just the day before leaving for the Gulf. "She didn't really want to be over there any more than the rest of them," said her fiancé, David Fairbanks. "But that's what she got paid for; that's what she did."[13]

Spec. Adrienne L. Mitchell, twenty, of Moreno Valley, California, had just wanted to get out on her own, "to finance her own education," explained her mother. Her father, retired Air Force Chief Master Sgt. Frank Mitchell, had not wanted Adrienne to join the Army. But, like so many young people attracted to the military, she wanted to earn money for a college education under the GI Bill. After initial training she was assigned to the 475th Quartermaster Battalion at Fort Lee, Virginia, and deployed with it to Saudi Arabia. Although Frank Mitchell said he was all for women in the military, he did not approve of their serving in a combat theater. "I just do not think that the U.S. male population is ready for women in combat." Adrienne wrote home to her worried parents that she wasn't scared. "The only thing we've got to worry about is the Scud missiles." Three days later the word came that their daughter was gone. "I did 30 years . . . and didn't get a scratch," her father said. "My daughter's been in for five months, and she's dead."[14]

Maj. Marie T. Rossi, thirty-two, and the three men in her crew were killed on 1 March 1991, the day after the cease-fire, when her Chinook chopper hit an unlit tower at night in bad weather. When the news of her death was flashed by the media, millions of Americans felt that they had lost one of their own. On 24 February, the eve of the massive ground assault into Iraq, Rossi had stolen the hearts of TV viewers during an interview on CNN. "Sometimes you have to disassociate how you feel personally about the prospect of going into war and . . . possibly see the death that is going to be out there," she had said. "But . . . this is the moment that everybody trains for—that I've trained for—so I feel ready to meet the challenge."

Siblings and friends recall that even as a child, Marie was a natural leader and instigator, who was looking for new things. So no one was surprised when she entered Army ROTC and, in 1980, graduated as a second lieutenant. After serving briefly as an artillery officer, she went on to become a helicopter pilot. While flying Chinooks in South Korea she met John "Andy" Cayton, a Warrant Officer helicopter pilot. They subsequently married and had the rare good fortune to be together in Saudi Arabia, but flying in different units.

Rossi was one of the first American Army helicopter pilots to fly into enemy territory delivering troops, supplies, ammunition, and fuel to the front. She had made several flights into Iraq facing hostile fire and had come away without a scratch. "After the TV interview, we were so excited and proud," said her father, Paul Rossi. "Then came the awful news—Marie's not coming home." Her mother, Gertrude, said that it was hard to accept, but "I know Marie. My daughter would expect us not to fall apart."[15]

Warrant Officer Ken Copley, helicopter pilot and veteran of the Vietnam War, who had known Marie in her previous assignment, paid her the ultimate pilot's compliment: She was one of the most respected pilots he had ever known.

Sgt. Cheryl LaBeau-O'Brien, twenty-four, of Racine, Wisconsin, made the ultimate sacrifice when the Black Hawk helicopter she served on as a crew member was shot down near the Iraqi border.

Cheryl and her husband, Michael, probably considered themselves fortunate in that they had both deployed to the Persian Gulf and were stationed in the desert only two miles apart. Cheryl loved her job servicing helicopters in the lst Infantry Division. When she died it was doing what she wanted to do. Her mother, Lois LaBeau, had been concerned about her daughter's safety but had been told that Cheryl would be many miles behind the front lines. But knowing how committed her daughter was, Lois was not reassured. "I knew that if something needed to be done, she would never say, 'No, I'm not going. That's a combat zone.' " Michael agreed: "Cheryl wouldn't have said, 'Let it be a man.' Cheryl would have said, 'Let it be me.' "[16]

Capt. Terry VandenDolder, an Air Force reserve pilot called up to fly C-141 transports for the airlift, flew home twenty-two bodies of fallen American soldiers. Two were women. "There was great sadness and grief for the lives cut short by war but no more for the women than for the men," she says. "There were tears for each."

DEMOLISHING OLD MYTHS

Although the extent of women's participation in the war came as a stunning surprise, after the first flush of media attention most Americans seemed to take it all in stride. And, as thousands of women risked their lives in Desert Storm, many old myths that had hindered their progress in the military were demolished and replaced with new realities.

Myth: *Military women are protected from exposure to combat.* Reality: This was the principal myth exploded by the war. Whether or not military personnel were exposed to enemy attack depended more on luck and circumstance than on law or policy. Modern weapons of war did not discriminate by gender, job, or location in the combat theater.

Myth: *During mobilization for war the women could not be counted upon to deploy.* Reality: From the outset the women demonstrated that they were as committed to fulfilling their military obligations as their male counterparts. After the war the DOD reported to Congress that the deployment of women was "highly successful." Data on personnel who were nondeployable suggested that the rate for women was "somewhat higher" than for men, with pregnancy accounting for the largest difference. However, it "did not affect the overall conduct of the operation."

Myth: *Women would not be able to perform in the pressure of the combat environment.* Reality: Throughout the war the women demonstrated that, like the men, they had the right stuff. They did the jobs they had been trained to do and did them well. They asked for no special favors and received none.

Myth: *American women, accustomed to their creature comforts, would not be prepared to cope with the primitive, rough living conditions and the physical demands in a combat zone.* Reality: They did cope. Many lived like "grunts" in the field. They slept in coed tents so cramped that "if anyone turned over, you knew it," and under lean-tos set up beside the trucks they drove. They endured the blistering heat and the lack of privacy. They ate the MREs, guzzled bottled water, went days without showers, and put powder in their hair instead of washing it. In some respects they suffered greater discomforts than the men, not the least of which was the shortage of female personal hygiene supplies (rarely was there a shortage of men's shaving items). In addition, the women had to deal with the usual sexual harassment from their own male comrades and the pressures to constantly prove themselves. They also had to cope with demeaning Saudi customs that limited women's freedom of movement and often interfered with their ability to do their jobs. The knowledge that the U.S. military would not have tolerated similar discrimination based on race added to their frustration.

Myth: *The presence of women in the combat area would destroy "male bonding."* Reality: Throughout Desert Storm, the combat support units, ships, and aircrews with women performed their missions well even under direct fire. When the action started, the mixed units and crews bonded into cohesive, effective teams. According to Capt. Cynthia Mosley, commander of an Army combat support company that was in the thick of the action during the ground attack into Iraq: "When the action starts every soldier does what they're trained to do," adding that, "Nobody cares whether you're male or female. It's just: 'can you do the job?' "[17]

Capt. Carol Barkalow, a graduate of West Point who was attached to the 24th Infantry Division that spearheaded the end-around ground attack into Iraq, said she saw a new type of relationship forming between men and women not unlike the one usually described among men. She describes it as "a nurturing relationship based upon respect and sharing the same hardships."

Myth: *Men and women could not work together in a combat theater without sex getting in the way.* Reality: Although sexual tensions and harassment did occur in the Gulf War, there was no evidence that it interfered with operations. In fact, the men and women serving side-by-side in the Gulf demonstrated that they were capable of working together as teams; they could be comrades without "fraternizing"; they could share tents without sharing beds; they could share common dangers without feigning chivalry. If there were tensions within a unit, whether sexual, racial, or any other kind, it showed lack of leadership and proper training. A senior officer got it right when he commented that: "The trained soldier shows discipline—an untrained one looks for trouble and usually finds it."

Myth: *Enemy soldiers, Arabs in particular, would rather die than surrender to a woman.* Behind this myth were stories or rumors widely circulated within the ranks of the American military of earlier Israeli experiences wherein it was claimed that Egyptian POWs had killed themselves or butchered female guards rather than take orders from women.

Reality: The Iraqis were not hostile to the women nor did they resist taking orders from them. "They couldn't surrender fast enough," said S. Sgt. April Hanley, 503rd Military Police Battalion, of the Iraqi soldiers rushing forward to be taken prisoner. "They didn't care whether I was male or female as long as I was American."[18]

MP Spec. Meg Griffin, assigned to check in the Iraqi prisoners at the EPOW camp, recalled: "Some of them looked at me like, 'A female? What is a female doing here?' But none of them ever questioned my authority." On one occasion, when an Iraqi called a female MP "Bitch!" she yelled back, "Prisoner!" and that was the end of it.[19]

Myth: *The American public would never tolerate women being taken prisoner or "coming home in body bags."* Military women had been told for years that this was the reason for the restrictions on operational assignments. Even though there had been no public outcry over the American female POWs and casualties in previous wars, the myth nevertheless remained an article of faith within military circles and was a major consideration in devising the DOD Risk Rule.

Reality: Even though the press focused on the female POWs and casualties, the public generally took the news in stride. While there was speculation about whether women would be treated better or worse than male POWs, there was no public outcry. There was a national collective sigh of relief when the POWs were released, but no more for Rathbun-Nealy or Cornum than for the others—they were just better known from the media coverage.

Similarly, Americans grieved when the bodies of servicewomen were returned for burial, but no more than for the servicemen lost. The general reaction was that the men and women in the Gulf had chosen to serve their country and some had made the ultimate sacrifice. There were no claims that any one life was more precious than another.

PARENTS GOING TO WAR—AN ONGOING DEBATE

Even as old myths were demolished by Desert Storm, a new one seemed to emerge—the public's intolerance of mothers going to war.

As the troops returned home from Operation Desert Storm to public acclaim, military policymakers were already grappling with some of the difficult personnel policy issues surfaced by the war. Among them were new questions about the deployment of single parents and dual-service couples with children.

The issue of fathers going to war was not especially newsworthy, since it had always been a reality of war—it was what men did.

In that scenario, it was assumed (rightly or wrongly) that the children left behind would be cared for by nurturing mothers. Those stereotypes died with the Gulf War.

Initially, when the press hit upon the new phenomenon of the mothers deploying for the "Mom's war," a distorted picture emerged. First, it created the impression that child care was a "woman's problem" when in fact it was a personnel management issue involving many more fathers than mothers. And second, it implied that military women with children were unable to deal with their family problems when in fact most military mothers coped— without complaint.

In reality, the parenting issue was a natural by-product of the modern all-volunteer force. In earlier times the military had been predominantly young male bachelors. By contrast, the volunteer military of 1990, although still predominantly (89 percent) male, was older and family oriented, with growing populations of dual-service couples and single parents. The Pentagon reported that within the military population there were nearly 47,000 dual-service couples with children and another 67,000 single parents, two-thirds of whom were men. To ensure the deployability of this force, the services had devised policies requiring these parents to have up-to-date plans for the care of their children in the event of deployments. Temporary allowances could be made to accommodate individual unforeseen hardship cases.

Hence, the services were unprepared for the blitz of media interest in mothers and dual-service couples being separated from their children, perhaps never to return. During the initial deployments, attention focused on unhappy children left with friends or relatives because their only parent or both parents were being deployed. As hostilities commenced, attention shifted to soldier parents in the war zone who might be distracted from their duties by worries about their children. The messages conveyed by the media were touching but often mixed. Army Spec. Hollie Vallance, twenty-two, symbolized the plight of military mothers when photographs of her saying a tearful good-bye to her husband and seven-week-old daughter, Cheyenne, were published in newspapers across the country in August 1990. Vallance insisted then that she felt it was the right thing to do. Seven months later, when she returned to her family, she still felt that she had done the right thing.

Marine Lt. Col. Ruthann Poole, forty-one, said that leaving her four-year-old daughter was probably the hardest thing she had to do. "Some day she'll understand," Poole said philosophically. "She thinks Mommy's gone to the field. That's all I told her."

Michele Browne, on the other hand, was convinced she had made the wrong decision. Browne, twenty-one, an Army supply specialist, had left her three-year-old daughter in the care of the child's grandmother and regretted it. Later, at a base near Dhahran, she told a sympathetic reporter, "It's hard being a single parent and going to war. I don't want to be here."

Sometimes it was the role reversals that attracted the media's attention. Army Sgt. Cheryl Stewart, thirty-three, left her husband with their two small daughters when she deployed with the 202nd Military Intelligence Battalion. Her husband, a former infantryman, had what she described as a "case of the guilts." She said he was having a problem with his male ego. "He felt he should have been here [in Saudi Arabia] and I should have been home." Similar reports prompted one student of the women's movement to observe: "I think what's happening, in a funny way, is that men are becoming fathers and women are becoming soldiers."

In most instances, although there was loneliness and stress due to separation, the children were being well cared for by loving grandparents or other relatives and friends. In some cases, however, the service member's so-called child care plan turned out to be an empty gesture. Horror stories surfaced of small children being left unattended or in the care of unsuitable guardians. In the worst reported case, a male soldier had simply left his three children to fend for themselves with instructions on how to use his bank automated teller card. In another instance, an Army woman was arrested by military police and held for twenty-four hours at Fort Dix, New Jersey, for failing to report for her reserve duty because she had no one to care for her sixteen-month-old daughter.

There were other reports of single parents (usually young women) who had left active duty with the expectation of completing their service obligations in the Individual Ready Reserve (IRR) but were suddenly recalled to active duty. These individuals never dreamed they would be called to serve again.

Their complacency was well grounded in precedent if not in policy. During the Vietnam War, few reservists had been called up and, in fact, the reserves and National Guard had been popular and acceptable safe havens from active duty in Vietnam. There was no reason to believe that it would be any different in the future. But 1990 *was* different.

Faced with growing public concern over the matter, military leaders repeatedly explained that it was not a serious problem—that more than 17,000 dual-service couples and single parents had deployed to the Gulf and the vast majority had made appropriate arrangements for their children. Most of them deeply resented the inference that they were uncaring and irresponsible parents. They felt that a sensationalist media had blown up a storm where none was warranted. One service couple in the Gulf, when asked by an inquiring reporter how they could "bear" to leave their son in the care of others, responded to the implied criticism: "We're doing this *for* him."

The intense media attention greatly increased public awareness and sympathy for families separated by war, particularly for children left with no parent at home. Child advocacy groups argued that, during the war, many children feared that they would lose their only parent or both parents. The Children's Defense Fund supported exempting single parents and one parent of dual-service couples from combat service and giving them assignments where they could care for their children.

Members of Congress were soon inundated with inquiries from concerned constituents and reporters. Sen. John Warner, ranking Republican member of the Senate Armed Services Committee, later acknowledged that the single parent issue had caught everyone by surprise. Pressures were rapidly building for Congress to take some action.

Pentagon officials felt the political heat but opposed any change in the policy, particularly while the war was still in progress. They contended that deployment exemptions would reduce military effectiveness and be unfair to personnel who were not parents. As far as the leadership was concerned, the current policies for child care plans were adequate to the needs of both the services and the families involved. To ensure an effective military, soldiers must be available on short notice without regard for their personal circumstances. Those unable to resolve conflicts between their military and family obligations had the option of leaving the service under honorable conditions.

The House Subcommittee on Military Personnel and Compensation, chaired by Rep. Beverly B. Byron, held hearings in February 1991 to evaluate the impact of Desert Storm deployments on service families headed by single parents and those families where both parents served in the military. The main focus of the hearings was on the potentially negative effect on the children left behind. Testimony on both sides was heard, some of it highly emotional, but no recommendations emerged. Byron later acknowledged that the services' family care plans had worked a lot better than she had dreamed.

In March the Senate considered similar legislation. It was rejected after Defense Secretary Cheney and Chairman of the Joint Chiefs of Staff Colin Powell objected on the basis that changing the rules would weaken combat capability by removing key personnel from deployed units and by undermining unit cohesion and esprit de corps.

From the national security perspective, the bottom line for the armed forces must always be personnel readiness. To be an effective fighting force, service members' availability to deploy in the event of war becomes the paramount imperative. Allowing for temporary circumstances, deployability on short notice remains the fundamental difference between military service and most civilian employment. On the other hand, in a volunteer environment the services constantly have to balance military needs with the normal, legitimate needs of their people. Carolyn Becraft, an expert on military women's issues and a consultant for the Women's Research and Education Institute, laid out the policy dilemma that the volunteer environment creates: "When you have a career force that is 90 percent married, you can't tell people they can't have children. And, when they do have children, you can't tell them that, if they become single parents through death of a spouse or divorce, they will be discharged." Besides, she says, "it would be a horrible waste of talent and taxpayers' money."

Most military women, with or without children, viewed the political debate as a thinly disguised attempt to undermine women's hard-earned acceptance as military professionals. This perception was reinforced by the knowledge that the issues were being pressed by groups opposed to women's participation in the armed forces (for example, the conservative Eagle Forum). Military women insisted that, as adults capable of holding responsible military positions, they had the right to make decisions for themselves concerning the care and welfare of their own children. The ultimate responsibility for the children, they insisted, rested with the parent, not with the government.

However, the child care issue would not end with the war. There remained lingering concerns on Capitol Hill and among child advocacy groups about the wisdom of policies that separate young mothers from small children to send them off to war.

END OF THE STORM

Six weeks after it started with the launching of the air war and exactly 100 hours into the ground phase, Operation Desert Storm ended in a stunning defeat of Saddam Hussein's forces. Although he had not yet accepted all twelve of the United Nations' resolutions passed against him, his army was surrendering in the field and his country was in shambles. President Bush decided to declare victory and called for a cease-fire. Some 540,000 American GIs began to savor the thought of going home. "This victory belongs to them—to the privates and the pilots, to the sergeants and the supply officers . . . to the finest fighting force this nation has ever known," the President told a joint session of Congress.

Because of the degree to which women were integrated into their assigned units, the services and DOD had been hard-pressed throughout the operation to provide an accurate count of military women in the Gulf. In July 1991, the Pentagon reported that approximately 41,000 had served in the combat theater, a figure much higher than had been previously estimated. Military women constituted some 7.2 percent of the U.S. forces deployed, broken down by service as follows:

Military Women in the Gulf by Service

	Number	Percent of Total Deployed
Army	30,855	9.7
Air Force	4,246	7.0
Navy	4,449	4.2
Marine Corps	1,232	1.5
All DOD	40,782	7.2

Source: Department of Defense[20]

Like the men, the majority of the women (27,000) were in the active duty forces; but the highest proportion of women were in the reserves, where they constituted 13 percent of the total. Their presence among reserve officers was an astonishing 21.3 percent— or more than one in five of the reserve officers sent to the Gulf.

The Coast Guard had only a handful of women in the Gulf because most of its requirements were aboard the Navy's combat ships, which were off-limits to women.

THE ASSESSMENT

Defense Secretary Dick Cheney said on 2 March 1991: "Women have made a major contribution to this [war] effort. We could not have won without them." Commanders in the field echoed similar sentiments. According to the Coalition commander, Gen. H. Norman Schwarzkopf, American military women had performed "magnificently."

The superb performance of America's armed forces during Operation Desert Shield/Storm was the vindication of the all-volunteer force and of women's participation in it. "One of the lessons we've learned from Operation Desert Storm is the extent to which the nation accepted the significant role of women in the operation," said Pete Williams, spokesman for the Secretary of Defense. "Until then, there had always been a concern that having women involved in combat would be traumatic for the country."[21]

Martin Binkin, a manpower expert at the Brookings Institution, and author of several Brookings studies on women in the military, said he was "somewhat surprised that the American public now accepts women in dangerous and austere conditions alongside men."

Any concerns expressed earlier that women were the military's "weak link" proved totally unfounded. In fact, the Pentagon's postwar analyses of the U.S. military's strengths and weaknesses during the operation identified numerous problems and short-comings that had hampered the six-month buildup and the six-week war. *Reliance on women was not among them.*

According to the DOD Interim Report to Congress on the conduct of war, the women played a vital role in the theater of operations. The report acknowledged that "there were instances of misunderstanding concerning the application of combat restrictions" and explained that the policies were not designed to shield women from all hostilities, "but are designed to limit their exposure to a level which is less than that in direct combat." Direct combat was defined as "closing with the enemy by fire, maneuver, or shock effect in order to destroy or capture, or while repelling assault by fire, close combat, or counterattack."[22]

But whatever official face the Pentagon chooses to put on the situation, it cannot mask forever the evidence that the rules designed in peacetime for the utilization of military women were confusing and often incompatible with the practicalities of mobilizing for an efficient wartime operation. Although the conduct of the war was not hampered by these problems, they imposed unnecessary personnel management burdens on the military at a very inauspicious time.

Undoubtedly the future of women's participation in national defense for the balance of this century and beyond will be heavily influenced by the lessons taken from the Persian Gulf War. The one clear lesson that should be taken from this experience is that American men and women are capable of serving side-by-side as professionals in a combat zone, doing whatever they are trained to do, with a lot of courage and pride in a job well done.

The future will also be influenced, as in the past, by technology, manpower realities, equity considerations, societal attitudes, and by the deeply ingrained institutional conservatism of the military community. Even before the dust had settled over the Arabian desert, some skeptics were already contending that the Persian Gulf War was not a true test of integrated forces because of the war's short duration, the type of terrain, the ability to achieve early air superiority, and the low casualties. They expressed concern about women's presence in longer wars against tougher, better-equipped enemies.

Nevertheless, by war's end it had become apparent that the combat exclusion laws and policies would be challenged in the Congress and possibly in the courts, and that some would not survive objective analysis. As one editorial put it, "Early debates over the particular perils of women at war now have the quaint ring of an old John Wayne movie."

Whatever official conclusions ultimately are drawn from the Persian Gulf War, women's place in the U.S. armed forces was permanently altered and universally recognized because of it.

NOTES

1. *USA Today,* 26 February 1991.
2. *Ladies' Home Journal* magazine, December 1990, p. 93.
3. *People,* 10 September 1990.
4. Grant Willis, "Operation Desert Storm—All-volunteer Tour de Force Raises New Issues," *Money* magazine, 18 March 1991.
5. Speech to the DACOWITS at the 1991 Spring Conference.
6. Philip Shenon, "At Combat's Doorstep," *New York Times,* 24 February 1991.
7. Briefing to DACOWITS at 1991 Spring Conference.
8. Joby Warrick, "AWACS Proves to be Gulf 'Trump Card,' " *Air Force Times,* 26 March 1991, p. 11.
9. Margaret Roth, "Women Face Unknowns as POWs," *Army Times,* 11 February 1991.
10. *Ibid.*
11. Joyce Price, "Painful Support for Women POWs," *Washington Times,* 12 February 1991, p. A12.
12. Nick Adde, "Proving Their Mettle," *Air Force Times,* 15 April 1991, p. 47.
13. *USA Today,* 28 February 1991, p. 8A.
14. Nick Adde, *op. cit.*
15. LEXIS NEXIS of Media Data Services, The Time Inc., Magazine Co. Spring/Summer 1991.
16. *Life* magazine, May 1991, pp. 61, 62.
17. DACOWITS briefing, 1991 Spring Conference.
18. *Ibid.*
19. Amy Eskind, *Los Angeles Times,* 28 April 1991, p. M2.
20. These numbers were still being revised as this was written.
21. Molly Moore, "Women in the Battlefield," *Washington Post,* 16 June 1991, pp. 1, A 16.
22. Department of Defense, "Conduct of the Persian Gulf Conflict," An Interim Report to Congress, pp. 10-1, 2.

CHAPTER 28

THE END GAME

As SHE WATCHED the fighters clear the runway on their missions into Iraq, Lt. Stephanie Shaw, who controlled strike missions for a tactical air wing in Saudi Arabia, said: "I can fly that F-15 just as well as a man."

The possibilities of her doing so came closer to reality when, on 5 December 1991, President George Bush signed the National Defense Authorization Act for Fiscal Years 1992 and 1993. Included in the legislation was a provision to repeal the forty-three-year-old legal barriers on women flying combat missions in the Air Force, Navy, and Marines and, by inference, in the Army as well. Also included were provisions authorizing the suspension of gender-based restrictions on sea and land combat roles while a new presidential commission studied women's assignments in the military.

The questions about the rules on women in combat had been raised to the level of public debate since the operation in Panama. But more than any other event in history, Operation Desert Storm became the catalyst for demands to lift, or at least review, the combat exclusion laws and policies. For the first time, the debate over women in combat was no longer hypothetical—it was for real.

Critics of the existing laws, such as Carolyn Becraft, insisted that Operation Desert Storm invalidated all the combat exclusions except those prohibiting women from serving in ground combat, where greater physical strength than most women have is required.

But the war also hardened the resolve of many opposed to any relaxation of the combat exclusion rules. The strongest resistance came from many senior military officials who believed that to tamper in any way with the combat exclusion laws would open the floodgates to demands to tear down all the constraints, including the aircraft carriers, infantry, armor, and artillery, and that this could undermine the combat readiness of the U.S. armed forces.

Antagonists for and against eliminating the combat exclusions were not divided by gender; there were men and women speaking out on both sides of the issues. Some proponents of change were willing to go only so far—allowing women to enter combat flying was the logical limit. Others wanted to go all the way and tear down the entire edifice of laws and policies and replace them with a best-qualified-for-the-job rule. Few argued for pulling back to more traditional roles for women.

As the issues were widely debated in the media and within the military itself, momentum for change was building on Capitol Hill and public opinion surveys supported it. In April Sen. John McCain (R-Ariz.) told colleagues that women should be allowed to join crews of Navy combatant ships and to fly fighter planes and combat helicopters.

The following week the DACOWITS recommended at its spring meeting that the Secretary of Defense support repeal of the combat exclusion statutes, arguing as they had for more than fifteen years that the Secretary and the services should have the flexibility to fully utilize all qualified personnel based on ability rather than gender. The committee received a standing ovation from the crowd of military women present. Stating the case for the recommendation was committee member Heather Wilson, a former Air Force captain and graduate of the Air Force Academy, then working at the White House on the National Security Council. She argued that the nation would be more secure if commanders had the flexibility to use the best talents of all their men and women. "If there is one thing the gulf [war] has shown, it is this: Those who support a stronger America and those who support greater opportunity for women in the military are on the same team."

Following the meeting, and after briefing Defense Secretary Dick Cheney and JCS Chairman Gen. Colin Powell, DACOWITS

Chair Becky Costantino met with the President and received his assurances that he would consider the recommendation.

THE HOUSE ACTS

The first direct challenge to the combat exclusions came on 8 May 1991 when the House Armed Services Committee voted to allow women to fly combat missions in the Air Force, Navy, and Marines. While working on the 1992 defense authorization bill, the committee had adopted by a voice vote an amendment cosponsored by Representatives Patricia Schroeder (D-Colo.) and Beverly B. Byron (D-Md.) that would repeal the legal prohibitions against women flying military combat missions.

It had come as no surprise to anyone on Capitol Hill when Schroeder, a senior member of the House Armed Services Committee, introduced an amendment to the budget bill to repeal the forty-three-year-old statute barring Air Force women from serving in aircraft engaged in combat missions. A longtime proponent of opening all jobs for women in the military, Schroeder decided to strike at the weakest point of the combat exclusion laws. The no-flying statute was the least defensible and the Air Force seemed to have the most positive attitude. On more than one occasion its personnel chief, Lt. Gen. Thomas J. Hickey, had acknowledged that there were no flying jobs in the Air Force that women were not capable of performing. Recently, when McCain had queried the service's personnel chiefs about taking a new look at the wartime roles of women, the only one to respond favorably was Hickey: "In my own personal view, the last impediment we have [to] doing that is the law."[1]

Byron, who chaired the House Military Personnel and Compensation Subcommittee and had held several hearings on military women, saw no reason to single out the Air Force. In her view, there was no logical difference between air combat flying jobs in the other services. She proposed expanding Schroeder's amendment to include repeal of the Navy and Marine Corps ban. Much to everyone's surprise, the revised amendment slipped through with little opposition. Some members opposed to the idea let it pass out of sheer exhaustion from long hours of bill markup sessions. Others simply assumed that it would self-destruct at some point. Still others saw the issue as a political bombshell that could bring the feminists down on them if they resisted. "There were a lot of cowardly lions roaring in the cloakroom," said Schroeder, "but they wouldn't go out on the floor and vote against it . . . The Persian Gulf helped collapse the whole chivalrous notion that women could be kept out of danger in a war."[2]

The committee report noted that lifting the statutory restrictions would not mandate that women perform combat missions; those decisions would rest with the secretaries of the Air Force and Navy.

The defense authorization bill, with the Schroeder-Byron provisions, cleared the full House by a voice vote on 22 May 1991 and moved on to the Senate.

Opponents of allowing women in combat were stunned, not just because the provision to repeal the combat flying exclusion had passed, but because it had hardly been challenged. Their consternation was heightened when the defense secretary publicly endorsed the proposal. As the prevailing political winds shifted in the direction of repeal, the idea of having full control over policy in this area seemed to take on greater appeal within the upper echelons of the Pentagon. At a 23 May press conference, Cheney's official spokesperson, Pete Williams, stated the DOD position on the House bill:

> The Department welcomes the legislation, because it gives the Department of Defense the authority to decide where the line should be drawn, rather than having Congress set the limits on the role of women in combat.[3]

With Cheney's apparent endorsement of the legislation, opponents within the Pentagon were caught between a rock and a hard spot—between what appeared to be the official party line and their own deep misgivings. Those opposed to eliminating the combat flying exclusions, including many senior military officers, were convinced it would be a major chink in the wall that sealed off combat ships and ground combat units from female incursions. "They're taking the heart and soul out of the law," lamented one official. "How are we going to defend not doing a total repeal of the law?"

Even though Army laws were not directly involved, it was clear that allowing women to fly combat in the other services would, by implication, remove any rationale behind the Army's combat flying bans. The Army Secretary said that if Congress approved the legislation, the Army would follow that guidance and open that part of the aviation branch that was presently closed. But Lt. Gen. Gordon Sullivan, President Bush's nominee to become the Army's new chief of staff, was less receptive to the idea. When asked about the matter during his Senate confirmation hearings, he said, "My recommendation at this juncture would be that women should not fly in combat."[4]

The nominee to become the new Marine Commandant, Lt. Gen. Carl Mundy, Jr., took a different approach. He said he believed that women could fly planes "superbly" but had reservations about making room for them aboard Navy ships. If told to do it, however, "the Marine Corps knows how to salute."[5]

THE SENATE REACTS

When the House passed the defense authorization bill with the provision to repeal the ban on women flying combat missions, the ball then passed to the Senate, where support for opening assignments to women in the military had also been building. Senators McCain and William V. Roth (R-Del.) had taken the lead in advocating changes to the laws. Then, the ranking minority member of the Senate Committee on Armed Services, Sen. John Warner (R-Va.), in an interview on Mutual/NBC Radio, said: "If they [women] are going to take the risks in the rear, and they are willing to take the risks in the forward positions, can we as a matter of law deny that? . . . There is no safe area now in a combat zone, front or back."

On 9 May 1991, the day after the House Armed Services Committee voted to include in the defense bill the provision to authorize women to fly in combat, Warner sent a letter to the Secretary of Defense praising the women's performance in the war:

The face of war has changed significantly while our assignment policies for [military] women have been resistant to change due to what may be antiquated legal restrictions. I believe it is time that Congress again review the combat exclusion laws that limit the assignment of women to many duty positions in our armed forces.[6]

He said he was requesting hearings of the Senate Armed Services Committee to debate the combat exclusion policies.

Meanwhile, the House action had generated a national debate on the question of women in combat. All the major media publications ran features, including articles by experts and interviews with anyone willing to express a view on either side. TV and radio shows staged debates arguing the pros and cons of women in combat in general, with emphasis on the infantry. Even though Rep. Beverly Byron, cosponsor of the House proposal, protested that the line had intentionally been drawn at combat flying and that she had trouble with the idea of women going into hand-to-hand combat and living in foxholes, the public debate zeroed in on the more sensational and emotional question of women in foxholes. In the process, more heat than light was shed.

Determined to avoid being drawn into the controversy, Cheney fended off press questions by tossing the question back to Congress. "We basically follow whatever direction we're given by the Congress . . ." He was satisfied that the current policies "work well" and said he had no plans to significantly change the current arrangement.

The Senate Armed Services Committee scheduled hearings for 18 June 1991 before the Manpower and Personnel Subcommittee chaired by Sen. John Glenn (D-Ohio). It was generally assumed, even by the committee staff, that the question to be addressed was whether the Senate should go along with the House measure authorizing combat flying or go even further by repealing the combat ship exclusion as well. But it soon became apparent that the game plan was to open up the entire range of issues relating to women in combat.

This was precisely what opponents of the House measure had hoped for. For them, the fact that repeal of the combat flying exclusion had cleared the House with such ease was a wake-up call. Military traditionalists and conservatives felt they had been sandbagged in the House and were determined not to let that happen in the Senate. They knew that combat flying was the Achilles' heel of the combat exclusions because there were no convincing arguments for *not* allowing qualified women in those jobs, and public sympathies clearly supported it. The House action, in their view, threatened to destabilize the entire edifice of combat exclusion laws and policies and they were determined to dissuade the Senate from following the House down this slippery slope.

Over the years a cozy relationship has developed between the senior military ranks and members of the two armed services committees and their staffs. It is not uncommon for the military to go over the heads of their own civilian leadership to lobby views at variance with the official DOD party line, although there are inherent career risks in doing so. For retired military, however, lobbying Congress is a risk-free occupation, and they are not shy about doing the services' bidding on politically sensitive matters.

In this instance the official DOD position on the House measure to repeal the flying ban remained unclear; DOD would do whatever Congress willed but had no intention of taking the lead on what everyone agreed was a politically touchy matter. The civilian leadership in the Pentagon would welcome the authority to set policy opening assignments to women but would not actively seek it out.

There were no doubts where top military leaders stood on the issue. They were opposed to any weakening of the combat exclusion laws despite growing public and congressional support for it. And they had powerful allies in the Senate, among them Sam Nunn (D-Ga.), Chairman of the Armed Services Committee, the most influential member of the Congress on matters of national defense, and John Glenn (D-Ohio), former Marine combat fighter pilot and world-famous astronaut, who chaired the subcommittee on manpower and personnel.

Under the circumstances, military members interested in preventing the expansion of women's roles in the military felt little or no compunction about expressing their views on the Hill where they counted the most. Many who did so, both active and retired, had a lot of rank, prestige, and combat experience to give weight to their views.

By contrast, the lobbying by the proponents of opening flying opportunities for women had been mostly sporadic and ineffectual. Proponents tended to assume, naively, that public and congressional support generated by the Persian Gulf War would provide the momentum needed to push the measure through. They also thought, again naively, that they could count on support from McCain and Warner in the Senate because of their previous public expressions of support.

Immediately following the surprise action by the House, the lobbying by military traditionalists and conservative organizations against opening combat flying was intense and effective. Recognizing that there were no convincing factual reasons why qualified women should *not* be allowed to fly combat missions, the opposition employed the only tactic left to them—the "slippery-slope" argument: Repeal of the combat flying exclusions would lead inexorably to opening *all* combat roles to women, including the infantry and combat ships. The conservative coalition argued that allowing women to fly in combat would threaten the American family because it would lead to the drafting of women and sending mothers to die in foxholes. Phyllis Schlafly told the Heritage Foundation, "The oft-stated goal of the radical feminists is a totally gender-neutral society, and the military is the cutting edge of this fantasy."[7]

Much of the rhetoric was almost a replay of the emotional arguments raised in 1942 to prevent women's entry into the wartime military and again in 1948 to prevent them from being accepted in the regular peacetime services.[8]

Even though the chiefs seemed to be of one mind, the ranks of the military were split on the question of women in combat and not along gender lines. There were men and women on both sides of the issue. This split was reflected during the hearings.

In their opening remarks both Nunn and Glenn indicated that the hearing would not be limited to combat flying. The entire range of combat issues would be explored as well as the societal implications. Nunn also made the point on several occasions that if combat assignments were opened to women, they might be *forced* into combat positions against their will either through involuntary assignment changes or a draft.

With the exception of Senators Roth and Edward M. Kennedy (D-Mass.), both of whom announced at the beginning that they favored repeal, the senators present did not appear eager to buy into the House measure. Even those who earlier seemed to be leaning in the direction of removing constraints—Warner and McCain—seemed to be backing away to more neutral ground.

The Defense Department's chief witness was Christopher Jehn, assistant secretary for force management and personnel. In his opening statement Jehn said that the Defense Department had continually reviewed and expanded opportunities for women in the military but that "we have reached a point where further expansion of opportunities is very difficult within the current combat-exclusion laws and the associated policies that reflect their intent." But he stopped well short of suggesting that these impediments be removed.

Referring to the recently passed House bill to repeal the combat flying exclusions, Jehn pointed out that "it would leave intact the limitations on assigning Navy women to combat vessels." This action could inadvertently create "inequities or inconsistencies," since it would allow female aviators aboard combat ships but not women who were in other seagoing fields.

What the committee wanted from Jehn was an unequivocal statement of the defense secretary's position on repeal of the combat flying laws. They also wanted to know what the Pentagon's plans would be if the combat exclusion laws were repealed. To the senators' obvious annoyance and frustration, no matter how often the questions were repeated or how they were phrased, Jehn never gave a straight answer. Neither was it ever clear whether the assistant secretary was just following orders or was simply inept.

There were no ambiguities in the service chiefs' messages. Not always known for their unanimity on controversial issues, they were united this day behind a common objective—to convince the Senate of the folly of repealing any combat exclusion laws. From the moment they appeared in the hearing room in all their beribboned splendor, it was clear that the four chiefs were marching to the same drummer—well, almost.

All four of the chiefs spoke against making any changes in the rules that barred women from serving in combat. Their message was that there had already been enough experimenting in the use of women in the military and that the current combat exclusion laws were essential to maintaining an effective fighting force. They pointed out that all the services faced massive force reductions, restructuring of units, redefining missions, and sorting out the lessons of the Gulf War. This was not the time to put women into combat roles without first sorting out the full implications.

Army Chief Gen. Carl E. Vuono and Marine Commandant Gen. Alfred M. Gray, Jr., offered the most rigorous opposition to any changes in the combat exclusion rules. Rather than discuss the question of women flying in combat, both focused on what they perceived to be the pitfalls of opening ground combat units to women. They told the committee that removing the ban on female soldiers serving in infantry, armor, and other ground combat units would harm the combat effectiveness of the units. They did not explain exactly how, other than to suggest that women did not have physical strength or stamina and that their presence would distract male soldiers from their jobs.

Vuono commented that he had not seen a "major ground swell to change our policy" and even if Congress saw fit to change the law, "which I urge you not to do," he would favor continuing the current policies of exclusion. He was not asked the obvious question that had been highlighted by the Gulf War: *If Army women can fly unarmed Black Hawk and Chinook helicopters over a battlefield in support of combat operations, why should they not fly armed attack helicopters?*

The Army enlisted woman selected to testify supported her chief. "I don't think a female would be able to keep up with a male, where we're talking infantry," said S. Sgt. Susan Leifeste, who had served in Saudi Arabia.

Gray, who represented the only service that had no women pilots, told the committee: "We don't find that our women want change. They seem to be satisfied with what they do. They like the assignments," he said. "We believe our women understand that you need women and you need men, and they're different." Gunnery Sgt. Jean A. Amico agreed with her commandant: "I don't wish to carry a rifle, lug a pack around and live the way the grunts do."

The Marine Commandant was not asked for, nor did he volunteer, any insights on why women were not permitted to fly any of the Corps' aircraft.

Navy Adm. Frank B. Kelso II and Air Force Gen. Merrill "Tony" A. McPeak, although they personally preferred that the laws not be changed, testified that, if Congress decided to remove the exclusions, they would open up combat assignments. On the question of women flying in combat, the Navy CNO was evasive, and reminded the committee that if the combat exclusion law were lifted the Navy would have the added problems of having to reconfigure combat ships for sleeping quarters and give extra sensitivity training to previously all-male crews. He also vaguely alluded to morale problems the Navy encountered integrating women on noncombat ships (an inference not substantiated by the Navy's own studies of women aboard ships). Kelso admitted that he had some sympathy for the young woman who was obviously an excellent aviator, ". . . who can fly an airplane well and do her job very well, who sees this law as keeping her from where she wants to be and wants to go." But he pointed out that the Navy female officer and enlisted communities were divided on the issue: Some want open assignments and some prefer traditional roles.

Of all the witnesses to testify that day, the Air Force's McPeak was the most expert on combat flying. A career fighter pilot and combat veteran of Vietnam, he had probably flown most combat aircraft in the Air Force inventory. "There are some women . . . who can do this combat as well as a man," McPeak acknowledged candidly. When it came to taking G-forces, he said that women were superior to male pilots. "So it's the law that's preventing us doing this, and I find some comfort in that . . . I admit it doesn't make much sense." He also said, "Personally, I'm not eager to increase exposure of our women to additional risk . . . However, the Air Force does not believe in artificially barring anybody from doing any job." McPeak went on to say: "If a woman passes it and wants to fly the F-15, then in my judgment we should not erect a policy barrier against her doing that in the Air Force."

But the most revealing and disturbing response the Air Force chief gave that day was when he was asked if he had to choose between a highly qualified female pilot and a less qualified male pilot to fly with him into combat, which would he choose? He said he would choose the man even if it were not in the best interest of national security!

Of the witnesses who testified against removing the combat restraints, it was left to former Marine Commandant Gen. Robert H. Barrow to pull out all the emotional stops:

> Exposure to danger is not combat. Being shot at, even being killed, is not combat. Combat is finding . . . closing with . . . and killing or capturing the enemy. It's KILLING. And it's done in an environment that is often as difficult as you can possibly imagine. Extremes of climate. Brutality. Death. Dying. It's . . . uncivilized! And WOMEN CAN'T DO IT! Nor should they even be thought of as doing it. The requirements of strength and endurance render them UNFIT to do it. And I may be old-fashioned, but I think the very nature of women disqualifies them from doing it. Women give life. Sustain life. Nurture life. They don't TAKE it.[9]

Women in combat units, Barrow added, would "destroy the Marine Corps . . . something no enemy has been able to do in over 200 years."

Referring to the lobbying by military women on the Hill, General Barrow commented caustically that, "They have their own agenda and it doesn't have anything to do with national security." A senior military woman sitting in the audience observed in an aside: "I think the General's agenda has more to do with maintaining the macho image of the Marines than with national security."

After the chiefs departed and lower grade witnesses replaced them at the witness table, there was less unanimity of testimony. Two officers, Army Lt. Col. Gary Thomas, an airborne troop commander, and Marine Capt. Michael Shupp, an infantry company commander, echoed the sentiments of their chiefs. Both were Gulf War veterans and both were strongly opposed to allowing women in combat units. Not only were women incapable of performing combat jobs, they said, but their presence in combat units would disrupt the male bonding needed to be effective.

Two enlisted men, a Navy submariner and an Air Force combat air controller, did not agree with that assessment. Both said they would be willing to serve with women in combat as long as the women met the same physical and mental standards set for men. Master Chief Electronics Technician Richard Frey said that if the services made their standards and requirements equal and women could pass them, then women should be allowed to go into any field they wanted. And this included serving aboard combat ships and submarines.

Master Sgt. Glenn Palmer worked in one of the few fields closed to enlisted women in the Air Force because of the combat exclusion policy. He said he would be willing to serve with any woman who could meet the tough physical standards of enlisted combat air controller. He would "personally and professionally welcome anyone who could pass the training standards."

Apart from McPeak, the only significant testimony directly related to combat flying came from two women pilots, Air Force Maj. Christine Prewitt, and Navy Lt. Brenda Marie Holdener. Both said that being denied combat flying opportunities because of their gender, not their skills, was hurting their careers. Prewitt, a C-12 Huron transport pilot, said she had undergone the same flight training as the men and insisted that she was just as qualified to fly fighters. As for the reactions of the men to the presence of women, she had been in units where she was the only woman and the men adjusted to her presence. "Initially, there are some problems, but after you go in there and prove yourself, it doesn't matter."

Holdener, a former Navy enlisted woman, now a helicopter pilot and veteran of the Gulf War, was assigned to a helicopter combat support squadron based in Norfolk, Virginia. Her job was flying supplies to support ships at sea. Holdener said that if women were allowed to fly combat aircraft they should also be allowed to be part of the ship's company. She admitted that living on a ship had its problems, but modifications could be made to accommodate mixed crews. She insisted that the only question should be: "Can women do the job in the combat arena? I say 'yes.' " She told the committee: "I am very selfish . . . I would like to see it [the law] changed just because that would afford me more opportunities."

At one point Marine Col. Ron Ray asked rhetorically: "Why do these women want to trade the best of what it means to be a woman, for the worst of what it means to be a man?" "He just doesn't get it!" said a woman colonel.

The central question that the House measure raised was never directly addressed: *What impact would qualified women flying combat missions have on the military's ability to fight a war?* Listening to the services' star witness on the subject of combat flying, the Air Force Chief of Staff, any reasonable person would have to conclude the answer was: "*None!*" The best the Navy CNO could come up with were vague references to having to modify combat ships to accommodate women and the need to indoctrinate male crew members. He was never asked to explain how this had been accomplished aboard fleet support ships.

Instead, the combat flying issue the House had raised was buried beneath a mountain of emotional rhetoric that was overwhelmingly focused on ground combat. The testimony of the Army and Marine Corps witnesses totally obscured the fact that women are excluded from ground combat by *service policy—not by law.* Only an uninformed spectator could not have realized that this was a deliberate ploy by those who orchestrated the hearing. Why else was the witness list so heavily weighted with Army and Marine Corps ground soldiers? And why else was the testimony elicited by the senators almost devoid of any meaningful discussion of the pros and cons of women flying combat missions?

Observers suspicious of the motives of the hearing's organizers also wondered why no senior military women were asked to testify. The most noticeable absence was Rear Adm. Roberta L. Hazard, the highest ranking woman on active duty in the U.S. armed forces. She had chaired the 1990 Navy Women's Study Group and currently headed the Committee on Women in the NATO Forces. In fact, with the single exception of the DACOWITS Chair, Becky Costantino, there was a strange dearth of testimony from anyone with firsthand knowledge of the full range of military women's issues. Nor was there testimony from any of the many experts who had conducted in-depth research and studies of women's performance in the armed forces.

Military women, active and retired, left the hearing room discouraged and angry. "The last bastion of male domination of the military," a female air reserve pilot wrote on her notepad at the end of McPeak's testimony. If it hadn't been for the ban on combat flying she would have stayed in the Air Force rather than fly for the airlines. She concluded that she had made the right decision. "It's still a boy's club," she lamented.

Air Force women were especially incensed when they saw McPeak's comments on the evening news. It appalled them that their chief would openly admit that he would allow his "personal" feelings, which he accurately characterized as "old-fashioned," to get in the way of his operational judgments and women's careers. Many men openly shared that concern.

If, as many suspected, the hearings had been designed to stall the momentum generated in the House for repealing the combat flying laws, it succeeded. But that left Glenn's subcommittee in a quandary over what to recommend to the full Senate Armed Services Committee when it came time to mark up the defense authorization bill. The conflicting testimony at the hearing might be used as a basis for doing nothing but that was really no longer an option. By extending the debate to all gender-based assignment policies, including ground combat, the subcommittee had opened Pandora's box and there was no way to close it again. Nor could they count on help from DOD or the services to bail them out.

To further complicate matters, Senator Roth served notice that he was introducing a bill similar to the House-passed measure. Kennedy was with him on this.

After much deliberation, the subcommittee decided that the only way out of what had become a difficult situation was to do what Pentagon leaders are famous for when they are unable or unwilling to make a decision on military women's issues—set up a group to study it.

COMMISSION ALTERNATIVE TO REPEAL

The Senate Armed Services Committee version of the 1992–93 Defense Authorization Bill emerged on 9 July with no provision to open combat flying to women. In place of the House-passed measure, the committee proposed that Congress direct the President to appoint a fifteen-member commission to study the assignment of women in the military. The commission was to complete its work by 15 November 1992, and the President was required to submit his recommendations to the Congress a month later. If adopted, the practical effect would be to delay any action to revising the rules on combat for at least eighteen months.

Senator Roth was furious. His proposed bill, similar to the measure adopted by the House, had been tabled by the committee in favor of the commission. According to Senate sources, it was Glenn who arranged to sidetrack Roth's bill with the commission. Glenn said that the group appointed by the President would study "the social implications" and consider the attitudes of religious groups toward the changing roles of women in American society. He also mentioned that it should consider the international implications and how the United States would be looked at by other nations "who don't permit women an even place in their society." It was not clear what he had in mind.

"I am greatly disappointed that the full . . . Committee has effectively ducked the question of whether to let women in the armed services compete for fighter pilot positions," Roth said in a press release on 11 July. "Appointing a commission to perform another study is absolute hogwash." He insisted that the subject needed no further study. "As we've seen in the Persian Gulf, women have already proven themselves capable of flying in combat situations." He argued that it should not take political courage to take a stand. It was not a question of ground combat, or a draft, or of establishing quotas, he said. "I am simply talking about giving women pilots equal opportunity for equal capability—no less, and no more."

Those on both sides of the issue realized soon after the 18 June hearings that the momentum generated by the Gulf War for removing the combat flying restrictions had been stalled and that, once lost, it could probably never be revived. Passing the buck to a commission and delaying any decision on this politically volatile issue until after the 1992 election was an offer any senator would find hard to refuse. The fact that the commission idea came from the Senate's own Armed Services Committee and was backed by a formidable bipartisan coalition of Democrats Nunn and Glenn, and Republicans Warner and McCain, made it all the more irresistible.

"If they have a commission study it, it takes everybody off the hook," said a congressional staffer. "Whatever the commission recommends, Congress and the Pentagon can say, 'don't blame me, it wasn't my decision.' "

Unmoved by the power of the opposition, Roth picked up the gauntlet. He served notice that he was not going to give up easily. He was prepared to take the issue to the floor of the Senate and was joined by Kennedy. They were prepared to cosponsor an amendment to the defense authorization bill when it came up for debate on the Senate floor, which would probably be within the next week to ten days. To succeed required persuading a majority of the Senate to vote against the recommendation of the highly respected Sam Nunn and his powerful Armed Services Committee, a formidable undertaking under the best of circumstances.

Meanwhile, lobbying against repeal had been intense. A key staffer confirmed that the committee had been receiving a lot of mail and phone calls on the issue of women in combat and that it was running heavily against repeal. Conservative opponents, led by Phyllis Schlafly and her surrogate, Elaine Donnelly, had been lobbying the committee and other members of the Senate without letup. "They are covering this place like a blanket," the staff member said, adding that very little was being heard from those favoring repeal.

The fact that the flying repeal measure had sailed through the House so easily and that several senators had earlier made encouraging statements had lulled the proponents into believing that repeal of the combat flying ban was almost a done deal. Its rejection by the Senate Armed Services Committee was their wake-up call. They had totally underestimated the strength of the opposition and overestimated the depth of support within the Senate committee. Especially painful was the realization that they did have the support of Warner and McCain. Both had embraced the commission concept.

To turn the tide in the Senate, Roth's and Kennedy's staffs advised proponents of repeal that, if they wanted this legislation, they were going to have to fight for it. A last-ditch effort was organized by Carolyn Becraft, of the Women's Research and Education Institute, and Heather Wilson. Word went out to military women (active and retired), former DACOWITS members, and the vast network of national women's organizations[10] that the legislation to repeal the combat flying exclusion laws was in jeopardy and that it was necessary to urge U.S. senators by letter, fax, and/or personal contacts to vote for the Kennedy-Roth bill.

Especially crucial at this point was the active involvement of women flyers through a relatively new organization—the Women Military Aviators (WMA)—whose membership included women pilots and navigators of the Air Force, Navy, Army, and Coast Guard, active and reserve. More than a few of its members were veterans of the Persian Gulf War or had flown missions in support of the operation. Also active in the WMA were many World War II Women's Airforce Service Pilots (WASPs) who had flown nearly every type of plane the Army Air Corps had at the time (see page 64).

The WMA effort to gain support for the Kennedy-Roth bill was led by their current WMA president, Air Force Lt. Col. Kelly Hamilton, and her successor, Navy Comdr. Rosemary Mariner. Hamilton, a command pilot of KC-135 refueling tankers who had flown missions in support of Operation Desert Storm, was convinced that the current laws made no sense. She would often remind people, "I can get shot at; I just can't shoot back."

Mariner was among the first group of eight women to earn the coveted gold wings of a naval aviator, in 1974, and the first woman to fly the Navy's A-4E/L Skyhawk. She was no newcomer to the battle for women's right to fly combat. In an interview back in 1982 Mariner said emphatically that she didn't buy the old argument used for keeping women from qualifying for combat— that it was to protect them. "When you go into a profession, you want to reach the top. You take the risks with the rewards. I don't want to be protected," she said. "A child is protected. As long as women are 'protected' we will not be regarded as adult citizens."[11] After the Senate Armed Services Committee announced its decision to substitute a commission for repeal of the flying ban, Mariner organized WMA members to call upon senate offices and explain why repeal was needed, not more studies.

At that same time, the media picked up the implications of the

Senate committee's decision, and a national debate on women in combat erupted in the major print and electronic media nation-wide, often eclipsing in space and intensity the debates over funding of major weapons systems and military base closures. With very few exceptions, the press concentrated most of its coverage on the highly contentious question of women in ground combat, with emphasis on the infantry, while glossing quickly over questions of women serving on combat air missions and combat ships, which were the only congressionally imposed policies.

THE REAL QUESTION:
WHY NOT LET WOMEN FLY COMBAT?

The public debate highlighted many problems, real and imagined, associated with the introduction of women into ground combat units. But no convincing, objective evidence surfaced that could justify continuing to deny qualified women the opportunity to fly in combat, Air Force Chief McPeak's lame excuse of "personal" feelings notwithstanding. There was no evidence that women selected and trained against gender-neutral standards could *not do the job*. And, more to the point, *no objective evidence surfaced that allowing women in these jobs would impact negatively on readiness.*

To the contrary, women's own performance flying in the combat environment during Desert Storm and their record of flying high-performance aircraft, including Navy and Air Force fighters, as instructors and test pilots argued for tearing down this particular barrier. Moreover, there were weighty testimonials to justify it, beginning with Senator McCain. The decorated Navy fighter pilot veteran told the manpower and personnel subcommittee on 17 April 1991 that he saw no reason why women should not be allowed to serve as pilots of Air Force and Navy fighters and Army and Marine helicopters on combat missions.[12]

Desert Storm commander Gen. Norman Schwarzkopf told Congress, when asked about women in combat, that he drew the line at ground combat but said: "I have no doubts that women could perform in Army cockpits—any cockpits."[13] His air commander in the Gulf War, Air Force Lt. Gen. Charles A. Horner, said that restricting women in combat was "contrary to individual freedoms the military is sworn to uphold." As for flying fighter planes, this fighter pilot veteran of Vietnam said: "I think they can do it."[14]

And although many fighter jocks railed against the idea of women flying on their wing, others did not agree. Marine 1st Lt. Shaun Sadler, who flew a helicopter gunship from a Navy assault ship in the Gulf, said: "I think women are capable of doing whatever a man can do—probably better in some instances." And Air Force Capt. Timothy Leahy, a combat pilot who flew special operations missions guiding helicopters on night missions behind Iraqi lines, when asked whether women could fly combat choppers, replied that he didn't think the gender of the person would make any difference. "Physically, I don't think there is any reason why she shouldn't be able to."[15]

Even Col. David H. Hackworth, retired Army combat veteran turned war correspondent, who made a strong case for excluding women from ground combat, in the 5 August issue of *Newsweek* magazine admitted, "I myself have no problem with women in combat flying attack aircraft." He said that "many combat-experienced pilots offer strong arguments against it," but he did not reveal what those arguments might be other than to say that, "High-speed aircraft do place demands on physical strength of pilots . . . withstanding the force of 9Gs is no easy feat."

If the fog of rhetoric over women in foxholes could be cleared away, the issue of women *flying* in combat stands on its own merits. The question for the Senate to answer then, was: *Why not repeal the laws?*

Senators Roth and Kennedy determined to force the Senate to face that question in open floor debate. On 25 July the two Senators held a joint press conference and announced their intention to introduce an amendment to the 1992 Defense Authorization Bill when it came before the full Senate. Their amendment would repeal the 1948 law that excludes women from flying on aircraft engaged in combat missions.

"We are here today to talk," Roth told the press, "not about gender, but about excellence. We are here to talk, not about whether we want women pilots flying combat missions, but whether we want the *best* pilots flying combat missions . . . When our nation's future is at stake . . . we want the most highly skilled and seasoned men and women on the job."

Kennedy said that "the issue is not whether women should fly high-performance aircraft. They already do . . . as instructors of [male] combat pilots." He said, "The real issue is whether we select our combat pilots based on ability or on gender," and whether women will be barred from flying combat aircraft by 1948 laws "that are no longer relevant to today's world."

Among the people assembled in the room with the press were about fifteen uniformed Navy, Air Force, and Army women who wore hard-earned military flying wings. Their combined experiences totaled many thousands of hours in a vast variety of military airplanes and helicopters as pilots, aircraft commanders, navigators, weapons officers, test pilots, flight instructors, and enlisted loadmasters. Some had tested high-performance combat aircraft and had even taught male pilots in the Navy's prestigious TopGun school. Some were veterans of the Persian Gulf War or had flown in support of the operation.

Despite the possibility of official censure for appearing to lobby the Congress, this small band had gathered to put human faces on what had become a highly charged political debate over the future of women in military aviation. "It's time to stand up and be counted," one said. "That's why I'm here." Any one of them could explain, in personal terms, how women's military careers were directly affected by the combat exclusion laws and how their ability to contribute to the military's mission was limited.

For most of these women, time had already run out to realize any benefits for themselves even if Congress decided during the current session to expand their flying opportunities. But it was important to them to help open the doors for others. "If we don't have the courage to speak up now," said one, "then we will be letting down the younger women who look to us as examples and role models."

Four days after the press conference an article appeared on the front page of the *Washington Post* under the heading: "Women Fliers in Race with Changing Times." Staff writer Barton Gellman had ventured to the Naval Air Station at Patuxent, Maryland, to see for himself what Navy women pilots were doing in the elite Navy Test Pilot School, which trains the best of the Navy's pilots. What he found and wrote about were real people up against the limits of the laws that Roth and Kennedy wanted repealed. The article brought home the urgency for Congress to repeal them *now*, not at some vague time in the future after a commission, the administration, and Congress had finished haggling over them.

Among the women test pilots he met was Lt. Lori Melling, thirty-one, who dreamed of flying Navy F/A-18 or A-6 attack planes. If war comes again, she wants to fight. An exceptional pilot, she has taught air-to-air gunnery to male jet pilots at the TopGun school. Described as aggressive and self-confident, Melling has all the right credentials to be a fighter pilot—except the right gender. She settled for test pilot school. "I want more," she said. "I want to be able to stay on par with my male contemporaries, and I'm not . . . The Navy's all about going to sea. I'm a jet aviator and I can't go to sea." Her male contemporaries had already served their three-year tours at sea and would be planning for the next one. If she didn't go soon it would be too late.

Lt. Barbara Bell was the first Navy woman to qualify as an F-14 radio intercept officer. In 1988 Bell graduated number one in her mostly male class in jet school. She was so good she was invited back as an instructor. More than anything else, Bell wants to join an F-14 squadron at sea. Had she been a man she would already have gone as a part of the normal career progression. At the age of thirty Bell faced the same time crunch as Melling. "Unless I go [to sea] right now," she said, "it's too late."

Lt. (jg) Loree Draude has a little more time but none to spare. At twenty-three she had just completed jet school and made her first carrier landing on the USS *Ranger*. "It was pretty cool," she said. "It was almost depressing in a way. I really envy the guys who can go out and do that all of the time." Draude's father, a brigadier general in the Marine Corps, was very proud of his daughter's accomplishments.

Commenting on the women's performance, the director of the test pilot school, Capt. Thomas J. Bernsen, said: "These are exceptional ladies . . . they blew out on top of the guys to wind up coming here. . . . I'd put them up against any man, anywhere."

Gellman also interviewed two women reserve pilots—Navy Comdr. Lucy Young and Air Force Capt. Teresa VandenDolder— who had left active duty because they saw no real career opportunities for women in military flying. As the Navy's first female instructor of air combat at the Navy's TopGun school, Young used to fly the A-4 in dogfights as an "aggressor" pilot. She had flown hundreds of air combat engagements against male pilots and "splashed" a lot of them. But that was as close as the law would allow her to the real thing. She just got tired of being relegated to a support role all the time, so she decided it was time to quit. She was flying for a commercial airline.

When "Terry" VandenDolder graduated from Air Force pilot training she wanted to fly F-15s or F-16s but had to settle for transports flying cargo and VIPs. The possibility of the rules changing for women appeared so remote, she left to fly with the airlines. As reserve pilots, both Young and VandenDolder flew missions to the Persian Gulf during the war.

As copies of the *Washington Post*, one of the nation's most respected and widely read newspapers, landed on Senate office desks, the message was unmistakable: The law barring women from combat flying should not be allowed to stand.

THE SENATE DECIDES

As the members gathered in the Senate chamber at 9:30 A.M. on 31 July 1991 to begin consideration of the 1992–93 Defense Authorization Bill, everyone expected a floor fight on the women-in-combat issue. In the end it wasn't even close.

The bipartisan battle lines were drawn, with Roth and Kennedy leading the debate for repealing the combat flying ban and the big guns from the Armed Services Committee—Nunn, Warner, Glenn, and McCain—in opposition. If ever there was a David and Goliath situation on the Senate floor, this was it. Nunn decreed that future funding for the B-1 and SDI would have to wait until the matter of women in combat was settled.

It was apparent from Senator Warner's agitated demeanor when he began to speak on the Senate floor that things were not going well. Instead of one amendment to the bill dealing with women in combat there were now two: the original one laid down by Roth and Kennedy and a new one apparently still in the process of being laid down by Glenn and McCain with the backing of Nunn and Warner. When Warner came to the microphone he began talking vaguely about a change of plans and then launched into a defense of the presidential commission to make recommendations to the executive branch and the Congress on women in the military. He expressed the hope that the Senate as a whole would "see the wisdom of the position taken by the [Armed Services] committee."

Then he outlined what he felt was the deficiency of the amendment about to be introduced by Roth: It "did not address the issue," in that it would benefit only a narrow segment of women in the military—female officer pilots—without recognizing the enlisted ranks and officers who are not in aviation. He argued that if that amendment were adopted, it would create the perception that the Senate had "struck a blow to try to help women take a greater role . . . in the military" when it had not.

A "substitute" amendment, prepared by Senator McCain to be introduced by Senator Glenn, presumably would avoid these inequities. Instead of repealing any laws, the new amendment would authorize the Secretary of Defense to temporarily waive *all* the combat exclusion rules while the presidential commission gathered evidence on how women performed.

At that point informed observers watching from the Senate galleries and on C-Span TV surmised that the opponents of the Kennedy-Roth amendment had taken a head count and discovered they did not have enough votes to defeat it on the Senate floor. So, in a last desperate attempt to win votes, this new amendment was being offered in the hope that a temporary suspension of all the combat rules, as opposed to repealing just the flying exclusion laws, would swing enough votes to kill the Kennedy-Roth amendment. It was proposed by McCain and Glenn, not as a substitute but as a competing amendment, with the backing of Nunn and Warner. At first blush it must have seemed like a reasonable alternative to any senator not familiar with the issues.

Anyone familiar with the events of the preceding weeks knew that this was yet another maneuver to torpedo efforts to repeal the combat flying laws. If successful, the question of opening the full range of military flying to women would be held hostage to the presidential commission proceedings, where it could be smothered under the weight of the volatile ground combat issue, as had happened during the 18 June hearing. In the end, the strategy backfired.

Both sides agreed that the two amendments would be debated together during the two hours allocated. But Warner served notice that he, Nunn, Glenn, and McCain intended to oppose the Kennedy-Roth amendment and would urge their colleagues to do the same. Roth and Kennedy, on the other hand, took the position that the two amendments were compatible and, although they would urge acceptance of their proposal, they had no problem voting for both. So, in effect, the floor battle would be over the Kennedy-Roth amendment.

In his remarks introducing his amendment, Roth agreed that many issues of women in combat needed the study a commission could perform, but flying in combat was not one of them. A commission, he said, "will not tell us anything we do not already know about the performance of women pilots in battle." He insisted they look at the record. "We want the best and the brightest pilots in the air, not on the ground," said Roth. "We want the best person in the cockpit of a Stealth fighter or a B-1 bomber—not the second best." He pointed out that a *Newsweek* poll released that week showed that 63 percent of Americans favored allowing women to fly combat aircraft. Leaving "an antiquated barrier in place—when it impairs the maximum effectiveness of our armed services—makes no sense at all."

"Barriers based on sex are coming down in every part of our society," said Kennedy. "The armed forces should be no exception. Women should be allowed to play a full role in our national defense, free of any arbitrary and discriminatory restrictions," he said. "The only fair and proper test . . . is not gender but ability to do the job." Kennedy pointed out the irony of the most complex questions about combat exclusions related to the Army, not the Air Force or Navy. "Yet it is the Air Force and the Navy that have to contend with statutory exclusions." He said that the combat exclusions are bad for women, because they deny them an equal opportunity for service and advancement; bad for men because they place an inequitable portion of the burdens of military duty on them; and bad for national security because they deny the military the opportunity to put the best personnel by virtue of their training and skills in the most important positions.

In his opening remarks, Glenn argued that his amendment was a "much broader and much more positive step" than that of Kennedy-Roth. Rather than being limited to aviators, who were only a small fraction of military women, the amendment that he and McCain were proposing "would let all of our women in uniform participate on a test basis in all combat roles for which they wish to compete." It would look for "positive ways to improve their opportunities" while at the same time being conscious of other effects, such as the potential of subjecting women to "involuntary assignments to ground combat assault roles on the same basis as men . . . or requiring women to register for the draft and to be drafted." The clear implication was that if the Kennedy-Roth amendment were adopted, all these things would follow down this slippery slope.

The debate that followed repeated several central charges aimed by Glenn, McCain, Warner, and Nunn at the Kennedy-Roth amendment. The arguments against and the rebuttals can be summarized as follows:

The Kennedy-Roth amendment puts the cart before the horse. Ending the ban on women flying combat missions before the issue has been thoroughly studied by the commission would be unwise. It is a very "complex issue" that should be studied with all its ramifications before getting rid of any laws. There are too many unanswered questions.

"To anyone who says we need more studies, more evidence," said Roth, "I say look at the record." He cited the record of the previous fifteen years of women flying and testing high-performance aircraft, pulling G's, training male combat pilots, and performing in the Gulf War. "Their aptitude and ability have been proven here at home—but their courage and mettle were proven in the skies over Saudi Arabia, Kuwait and Iraq."

The Kennedy-Roth amendment is too narrow in that it deals only with women in aviation. If approved, Kennedy-Roth would benefit only those women who occupy roles in aviation, who constitute less than half of 1 percent of the more than 227,000 women in the active military. The commission, on the other hand, would take a much broader approach. "It would let all our women in uniform participate on a test basis in all combat roles for which they wish to compete," explained Glenn. "Our amendment would say to all military women that we are looking at positive ways to improve their opportunities" while being conscious of the negative effects of any changes in the laws. The commission should look at every job in the military and see if it can be opened up, Glenn explained. "If they determine that [jobs can be opened], then we would move in that direction."

As far as proponents of Kennedy-Roth were concerned, it was not an either-or situation. They encouraged senators to support both the Glenn-McCain amendment authorizing the temporary waiver of all combat rules while the commission completed its assigned tasks, *and* their amendment repealing the legal ban on combat flying. Allowing women to fly combat would not deter the commission from studying other areas of combat.

Curiously, it was never explained that the reason so few women are in aviation is precisely because of the 1948 combat exclusion laws that Kennedy and Roth proposed be repealed.

The Kennedy-Roth amendment would be unfair to Navy women NOT in aviation. It would leave intact the ban against women in other Navy occupations serving on combat ships. McCain complained: "I do not see how the Kennedy-Roth amendment can reconcile a situation in which women can be part of an air wing . . . aboard an aircraft carrier . . . but not allow women to be part of the ship's company." Then, in a breathtaking leap of convoluted rationalization, McCain fretted that the amendment, rather than help women pilots, would actually harm them. He explained that pilots perform many other duties aboard carriers besides flying, duties that would remain off-limits to women: "Ironically, the . . . amendment would harm women aviators in their ability to succeed and move up the promotion ladder, which all men and women both should be allowed to take advantage of."

Navy women pilots observing from the gallery listened in amazement and dismay. Did this former Navy fighter pilot, who earlier had called for opening combat flying, really not comprehend the far greater harm to their careers caused by the very law that Kennedy-Roth proposed be repealed?

Kennedy minced no words: "I am fascinated in listening to [McCain and Warner] crying crocodile tears that we have not gone far enough: that we did not eliminate both statutes . . . We are going to permit the pilots on the aircraft carriers but we do not permit other [female] Navy personnel on them, and therefore how wrong this amendment is." In his view there was complete justification for repealing the statute banning women from combat ships as well, but he and Roth were taking it one step at a time.

The Kennedy-Roth amendment is a draconian measure that would have far-reaching (i.e., negative) effects. Its adoption would lead to the elimination of all exclusion laws and force the services to open *all* combat assignments to women, including ground combat. It could also force women into combat against their wills, as men are forced.

Roth patiently explained that what his amendment would do is bring the Air Force and Navy laws more in line with those of the Army: "There is no legal obstacle . . . in the Department of the Army as to the assignment of women to combat. That could be done right now, today, if the . . . Army determined to do so." He said that his amendment did not perform major surgery, but likened it to "pinpoint laser surgery." It would simply remove the congressionally imposed restrictions that prevented women from flying combat aircraft and "give the Defense Department the authority to determine how best to use women aviators." Whether the women can meet the performance standards would be up to their superiors to determine, but the women should be given the opportunity to compete if that is their choice.

"What we are basically saying," said Kennedy, "is in the area of combat air, the determination is going to be done on ability, not gender, and if you have trouble with that, you have trouble with this amendment."

Adopting the Kennedy-Roth amendment could affect the constitutionality of the male-only draft. Opponents argued that the Supreme Court decision in Rostker vs. Goldberg, which, it was insisted, upheld the constitutionality of an all-male draft, was based on the congressional exclusion of women from combat. Hence, if combat exclusions are removed, it was speculated, there would be grounds for declaring the all-male draft unconstitutional. Thus, approval of Kennedy-Roth would probably mean that women would have to register and, if necessary, be drafted on the same basis as men.

Kennedy called the draft issue "that old chestnut," and a "red herring" and contended that opponents of his amendment had to be "pretty desperate" to drag it out. He and others pointed out that there is no draft and the likelihood of having one in the future is remote to nonexistent. What the Supreme Court really did in Rostker was to defer to the Congress in matters of military personnel policy. In effect, the Court said that Congress could make policy in this area of women in combat. Congress had chosen in 1948 to allow the services to make policy in matters of ground combat.

The example of the Israelis argues against using women in combat. McCain recalled that Israeli women fought alongside men during Israel's struggle for independence in 1948 and claimed that this "created so many problems" that women were never again sent into battle.

Although there has never been any evidence to support this claim, McCain implied that it is the reason women are currently excluded from all combat assignments in the Israeli armed forces. "It would be well for us, during our deliberations," said McCain, "to consider what the experience of another has been over 40 years of combat."

Critics reminded McCain that the British had opened seagoing positions to women on combat ships of the Royal Navy; that both Canada and Denmark were training women as fighter pilots; and that five NATO nations have no combat exclusion law—Canada, Denmark, Luxembourg, Norway, and Portugal. "Ironically," said Kennedy, "the United States Air Force has trained Danish women fighter pilots but will not train United States women pilots to fly fighter aircraft."

As the debate moved into its second hour it became more testy and personal, with angry exchanges barely disguised by a veneer of senatorial courtesy. The arguments were repeated followed by the same rebuttals. Near the end, Nunn, generally regarded among senators as the 500-pound gorilla on matters military, weighed in to convince his colleagues of the folly of adopting the Roth-Kennedy approach. He rehashed all the objections already heard and urged the amendment be rejected in favor of the commission proposed by his committee with the Glenn-McCain amendment.

Kennedy acknowledged that a commission could be extremely important and useful "in trying to find ways to enhance the opportunities for women in military service." But, he cautioned, if the commission does not view this issue *with an enlightened viewpoint, it could very well come back with recommendations that may support a more Neanderthal and archaic kind of position.* The clear implication was that the commission could not only decide *not* to open combat flying, it could also recommend turning back the clock on gains already made by women in the armed forces.

The Senate can support the commission and the Roth proposal, Kennedy argued, because:

> What we are attempting to do is eliminate gender as a classification and commit this Nation to ability as the criterion for classification . . . The

statute which is in existence at the present time, 48 years old, is archaic and Neanderthal and we should be free from it . . . I believe we should not have a Neanderthal, archaic statute, applicable to the Navy and Air Force, which is not applicable to the Army, and without which the Army was able to make progress as it has over the years.

What the military women watching found most distressing during this debate was how far McCain and Warner had swung away from statements made in the afterglow of Desert Storm. Was it a sincere change of heart based on new information or simply political expediency to satisfy their conservative and military constituencies? Whatever the reasons, the women felt betrayed.

Toward the end it was Sen. Nancy Kassebaum (R-Kan.) who brought the floor debate over the Kennedy-Roth amendment back into sharp focus. In a brief colloquy with its authors, she went over the issues raised by the opposition.

Kassebaum calmly admitted that she was "a bit confused by some of the debate I have heard." She had understood that "all we were doing was just repealing the statute that barred women from [air] combat in the Air Force and Navy."

Roth: "I would say to the senator, she is absolutely correct."

Kassebaum: ". . . this [amendment] is not saying women will be automatically in combat?"

Roth: "That is absolutely correct."

Kassebaum: "This is merely saying . . . it will be up to the armed services to make that decision?"

Roth: "Absolutely. Each of the services will have the freedom, the flexibility to do whatever they think best."

Kassebaum: "It seems to me the Army has been able to do that for some period of time. It seems to me it makes sense simply to say that this should be a decision that would be made by the armed services." Leaving this decision until a commission completes its work, she said, "only leaves further confusion and uncertainty." Congress has been accused of "micromanaging the Department of Defense: It seems to me this is one area where we clearly are, again, trying to micromanage." It makes sense "to repeal the statutory ban and let the armed services make decisions themselves."

McCain protested that the service chiefs were opposed to the proposed amendment and "I do not want to go against the chiefs of the armed forces."

"Let me ask the senator from Arizona," Kassebaum replied

calmly: "What has happened in the Army? The Army has no prohibition dictated by us. It is their own prohibition. So how do we [say] it has been a problem."

McCain shot back that the Army based its prohibition on the laws applicable to the other services. He said that no one had so far advocated the role of women in ground combat: "If the senator is suggesting somehow we should put women in ground combat roles without further study or contemplation," it would be "objectionable at best."

She replied that she was "simply saying that I do not want to be in a position of deciding . . . whether women should or should not be in combat. I have a great deal of confidence in the chiefs being able to stand on their own two feet and make that decision . . . because they understand how women can serve best."

That, as Kennedy acknowledged, was "absolutely the point" of the amendment.

There was really nothing more to be said.

The end came so quickly it was difficult to follow what had happened. With nearly a half hour still left for debate, the vote was called for. It was agreed that the Glenn-McCain amendment would be voted on first by roll call. To the surprise of no one, the vote was 95 to 3 for approval.

Then in a quick parliamentary maneuver to finally scuttle repeal of the combat flying laws, Glenn, with the backing of McCain, Nunn, and Warner, moved to table the Kennedy-Roth amendment. The motion to table was rejected by an astonishing vote of 30 for and 69 against. The Senate then approved the amendment on a voice vote.

The Senate then shifted gears so quickly to SDI that observers in the galleries looked at each other in confusion and disbelief. It was a while before the significance of what had just occurred sank in. When it did they realized that the Senate had not only adopted the House measure removing the legal ban on women flying combat missions, it had also provided DOD the authority to suspend the remaining combat exclusion law so that tests could be conducted across the full range of combat assignments while a commission studied the issues.

The Senate vote was not for putting women in combat; it was a vote to recognize women's significant contributions to national defense and for moving away from artificial, outdated barriers based on gender as the only criterion. It does not force the services or the DOD to remove all combat constraints. It does force them to reevaluate their policies without hiding behind the so-called combat exclusion laws and the "intent" of the 1948 Congress.

The intent of the Congress in 1991 was made clear during the Senate debate and by the margin of the final vote. As Senator Kennedy said: "This is about as clear a statement of what the Senate wants as you can get around here."

THE COMMISSION

On 15 November 1991, after the joint House-Senate conference committee completed its reconciliation, Congress passed the 1992 Defense Authorization Bill and sent it to the President for his signature. The new law, signed on 5 December, repealed the 1948 laws banning women from flying on combat missions of the Air Force and Navy; established a Commission on the Assignment of Women in the Armed Forces; and authorized the Secretary of Defense to waive the remaining combat exclusion law in order to conduct test assignments of female service personnel in combat positions.

The fifteen-member commission, to be appointed by the President, would have until 15 November 1992 to complete its work, with its final report due in Congress a month later. The report should contain recommendations for "such legislation and administrative actions as the Commission considers appropriate," to include:

Whether existing laws and policies governing the assignment of [military] women . . . should be retained, modified, or repealed.

Whether existing law and policies relating to other aspects of the assignment of women . . . should be retained, modified, or repealed.

What roles women should have in the Armed Forces, including what, if any, roles women should have in combat.

What transition process is appropriate if women are to be given the opportunity to be assigned to combat positions.

Whether special conditions and different standards should apply to women than apply to men performing similar roles.

The commission was specifically tasked to look at how combat readiness will be affected if women are assigned to combat roles, including physical readiness and the effects of pregnancy or other factors related to time away from work.

Also to be considered in connection with readiness are "the effects, if any, of such assignments on unit morale and cohesion." That Congress viewed male morale as a legitimate criterion for policies on assigning women provides an insight into the mind-set of those who drafted and sponsored the formation of the commission. Forty years earlier, troop morale was an acceptable criterion for excluding blacks ("coloreds") from all-white units.

Operating under the aegis of the DOD, the commission was empowered to hold hearings, take testimony, receive evidence, and secure information from DOD and other federal agencies, and to request the services to conduct tests of women in combat positions. Its work was cut out for it. In a few short months it would have to review, study, debate, and decide on a complex set of questions that have been debated for years within the Department of Defense. The questions are highly charged with visceral emotions and deeply held beliefs on both sides, with no simple answers and very little room for compromise. And no amount of testing will solve that problem.

Actually, it is not clear what useful purpose tests of women in combat roles will serve, since the results are easily predictable and the Canadians have already done it. Any objective test will show that, overall, women do as well as men, sometimes less well—sometimes better. *It is more a matter of individual than inherent gender differences.*

That is essentially what the Canadians concluded. It should have come as no surprise when they found that very few women are able to qualify for and perform jobs that require considerable physical strength, particularly in the infantry. But they excelled in other areas. Before the tests were completed, Canada made the decision to abandon gender-based policies and go with a gender-neutral system. They opened all but the infantry and a few other ground combat jobs and continued testing performance in those. Assignments on submarines remain off-limits but, according to a Canadian spokesman, that may change as new submarines come on line. There is no reason to believe that U.S. tests would produce different conclusions.

Sociologist Charles Moskos makes the point that the problem with such a test "is not that it will prove women cannot fight, but that it will prove they can." He was right, of course, but he might have added that an objective test would also prove that many men cannot. In any case, tests leave unresolved the core political policy question of whether women *should* be assigned combat roles (in addition to combat flying). That is the question the commission is expected to answer.

THE LAST LAW

The commission will have to make a specific recommendation on whether Congress should repeal the last combat exclusion law—Section 6015 Title 10 U.S. Code banning women who are not aviators from combat Navy ships. No amount of additional study or testing can provide information that is not already well known to the Navy.

As was the case with combat flying, there is no valid justification for continuing this last vestige of the 1948 laws. Here again, in all the debates over women in combat, it was never argued that having mixed crews aboard combat ships would be any different from having them aboard noncombat vessels. As the Navy itself has acknowledged repeatedly, its women on ships program has been an unqualified success. Mixed crews work very well even in the combat environment of the Persian Gulf.

If there is a valid case to be made for retaining the combat ship exclusion law, it has yet to be made and it is highly unlikely that a presidential commission will be able to find one. Even the Navy's own leadership has not come up with a defense of the existing ban except to pass the buck to Congress. In 1985, CNO Adm. James D. Watkins acknowledged to a group of female officers that it was not a question of whether women could do the jobs in combat, because they can. Only the law stands in the way, he said, repeating the Navy's party line. If Congress wants to, it can change the law. But he was not about to ask for repeal.

One of the few authoritative voices speaking forcefully for repeal is that of the former chief of Naval personnel, Adm. William P. Lawrence, who calls the 1948 law "irrelevant" and "absurd."

Navy leaders know that, even more than the combat flying ban, the exclusion of women from the full range of shipboard assignments hurts Navy women's careers, morale, and acceptance within the sea service. Their own studies have shown this repeatedly. The 1990 study of the progress of women in the Navy found that the law impacted negatively on women's careers and created the impression among the ranks of all Navy personnel (male and female) that "women were not equal partners." The study laid out the most insidious effect of the combat exclusion law:

> In the view of all Navy members . . . the law profoundly influences both the acceptance and the quality of treatment accorded to women since they are perceived to be distanced from the heart of the organization and its primary mission-achieving units.

Any woman who has served in the Navy must identify with that observation. Most Navy men today would also acknowledge its validity, while not necessarily espousing the cure.

It is hard to conceive of a situation wherein the Navy would take such a cavalier attitude toward any law having a similar negative impact on 10 percent of its sailors who are male. Instead of asking Congress to repeal the offending statute, the Navy has chosen to actively oppose any efforts to do so, while blaming its women for male sea/shore rotation problems created by the law.

Any pretense that more study or tests are required before the combat ship ban can be repealed is a cop-out. It is time for Congress to repeal this last vestige of the 1948 law and for the Navy to get on with devising more sensible personnel policies, as other nations have already done.

THE NEXT PHASE

Whatever conclusions emerge from the deliberations of the presidential commission, another milestone in women's participation in the military has been passed and there is no turning back. The next step will be to begin the process of devising new policies reflecting the new political environment and the realities of the modern military—policies that will ensure for the future the highest quality military establishment possible with the resources available. It boils down to tapping the best talents from a shrinking pool of young potential recruits to do the jobs required by a military that grows smaller but more technologically demanding each day.

That goal can best be served by a gender-neutral, best-qualified personnel system that matches individual talents and aptitudes with the legitimate, validated requirements of the jobs that have to be done, without artificial, unrelated constraints. The results of such a system will continue to be gross imbalances, ranging from high proportions of women in the traditional fields, such as medical and administrative, to few or none in fields requiring sheer physical brawn, such as the infantry and Navy Seals, with various male-female mixes in between. There will also continue to be wide disparity between the services, with the Air Force on the high end and the Marine Corps on the low. So be it!

It has been argued that if women are allowed to be combatants, it would probably hurt female recruiting. Again, so be it! Anyone, male or female, who considers joining the armed forces must be made aware before taking the oath that being in the military is not about uniforms and parades; it's not about benefits or adventure, despite some of the recruiting razzle-dazzle. The military is about going to war and war is about killing and maybe dying for your country. And, as the entire nation learned during Operation Desert Storm, being designated a combatant or noncombatant has very little to do with who lives and who dies in modern war. Anyone not willing to accept that fundamental reality of military service should find other ways to serve.

There is also a question of equity, or reverse equity, if you will: Is it right to expect military men to face the risks inherent in the military profession while attempting to protect the women who take the same oath, draw the same pay, get the same training, and wear the same uniform?

Today, an increasing number of women are saying no. As Capt. Debra Dubbe, a graduate of the Air Force Academy, who served as a navigator on a refueling tanker during the Grenada invasion, has stated, "There is no difference in women or men taking risks—or dying. I signed up to be an officer, and if it means having to die, that's what I agreed to do." A young female enlisted paratrooper who had landed in Panama with the 82nd Airborne laid it out in simple terms: "If they are going to let us wear the uniform then they ought to let us defend it. Otherwise, don't let us wear it." A growing number of men are agreeing with that view.

THE REVOLUTION CONTINUES

The final chapter of women in the military remains unwritten because the revolution is unfinished. The year 1991 marked the ninetieth anniversary of the establishment of the Army Nurse Corps, the first time women were permitted to serve as members of the U.S. military services. The changes that have taken place in the intervening years have reached far beyond anyone's most elaborate vision and have been nothing short of revolutionary when viewed in the total span of military history.

This long story has been about women's struggle to break through the attitudinal and societal barriers shaped by old but strongly maintained traditions and myths about the military institution and women's proper roles in it. That struggle was never about women seeking special privileges or double standards. It was about being allowed to compete based on ability, not gender.

It was never about proving that women can do anything a man can do, but about being judged as individuals by the same standards as men in any job for which they can qualify. It has always been about being allowed to pursue a career based on their individual qualifications rather than sex stereotypes and male norms unrelated to the job.

It was never about women's equality to the exclusion of readiness considerations. It was about the privilege of serving one's country without artificial barriers based solely on gender.

In short, women's struggle for a place in the armed forces has been about seeking the full rights and responsibilities of citizenship.

The mission of the armed forces is to provide the best possible national defense within the funds allocated for that purpose. The goal of the military personnel systems must be to provide the right people to do the job. So the bottom line is that *no individual, male or female, should be allowed or required to fill any job he or she cannot perform satisfactorily in war for whatever reason.* Gender is rarely, if ever, the best criterion.

The experiences of Grenada, Panama, and the Persian Gulf War have helped destroy many old myths and preconceived notions about women's ability to perform in the stress of a combat environment, and did much to ease concerns about the effectiveness of mixed male-female forces. The hard-liners who have held sway over policy decisions are having to face new realities and changing national attitudes. And there is growing evidence of new attitudes within the services as a new generation of leaders matures—leaders unencumbered by the baggage of the past who are willing to challenge antiquated arguments and stereotypes.

More than in the past, men are speaking out about the contributions of women to the total team effort. Increasing numbers of them, such as Admiral Lawrence, have a daughter, a wife, or a sister in the military and see no reason why she should not be able to go where and as far as her talents and hard work will take her.

The strongest support comes from men who work with women as members of the military team and judge the women by the same professional job-related standards they apply to men in the same positions.

Women have proven that they are ready, willing, and able to accept the risks and responsibilities that go with the oath they have freely taken. They have earned the right to be treated as members of the first team rather than as a protected subclass excluded from the heart of their military profession. They have earned the right to the recruiting poster's promise and challenge: "Be All You Can Be."

NOTES

1. Barton Gellman, "Combat Flights by Women Backed," *Washington Post*, 9 May 1991, p. A1.
2. John Nordheimer, "Women's Role in Combat: The War Resumes," *New York Times*, 26 May 1991, p. 1.
3. Press release, 23 May 1991.
4. Molly Moore, "Women in the Battlefield —Gulf War Role Helps Bring Shift in Attitude," *Washington Post*, 16 June 1991, p. A1.
5. *Ibid.*
6. Letter from Sen. John Warner to Richard Cheney, Secretary of Defense, 8 May 1991.
7. Alan McConagha, "Family Is at Stake, Critics Claim," *Washington Times*, 18 June 1991, p. A10.
8. The earlier opposition was having women in military fields other than nursing. For debates see pages 21–27 and 113–119.
9. Prepared statement read at the hearings.
10. Organizations included: Women Military Aviators, Inc., Women's Research and Education Institution, Women Officers Professional Association, National Women's Law Center, American Nurses Association, Business and

Professional Women's Clubs, Women's Legal Defense Fund, National Organization for Women, Federally Employed Women, American Association of University Women, and Air Force Women Officers Associated.

11. Interview with Patricia McCormack, "Female Pilot Determined to Use Her Wings to the Fullest," *New York News*, 24 March 1982, p. 28.

12. Rick Maze, "Sen. McCain: It's time to remove assignment restrictions," *Navy Times*, 6 May 1991.

13. Rowan Scarborough, "Female Fliers Earn Respect," *Washington Times*, 18 June 1991, p. A1.

14. Associated Press, as reported in *Air Force Times*, 23 September 1991, p. 9.

15. Scarborough, *op. cit.*

Appendices

THE WHITE HOUSE

April 27, 1951
EXECUTIVE ORDER 10240

Regulations Governing the Separation from the Service of
Certain Women Serving in the Regular Army, Navy,
Marine Corps, or Air Force

By virtue of the authority vested in me by the Army-Navy
Nurses Act of 1947 (61 Stat. 41) and the Women's Armed Services
Integration Act of 1948 (62 Stat. 356), and as Commander in
Chief of the armed forces of the United States, I hereby prescribe
the following regulations governing the separation from the ser-
vice of certain women serving in the Regular Army, Navy, Marine
Corps, or Air Force:

The commission of any one woman serving in the Regular
Army, the commission or warrant of any woman serving in the
Regular Navy or the Regular Marine Corps, and the commission,
warrant, or enlistment of any woman serving in the Regular Air
Force under either of the above-mentioned acts may be terminated, regardless of rank, grade, or length of service, by or at the
direction of the Secretary of the Army, the Secretary of the Navy
or the Secretary of the Air Force, respectively, (1) under the same
circumstances, procedures, and conditions and for the same
reasons under which a male member of the same armed force and
of the same grade, rating or rank, and length of service may be
totally separated from the service by administrative action,
whether by termination of commission, termination of appointment, revocation of commission, discharge, or otherwise, or (2)
whenever it is established under appropriate regulations of the
Secretary of the department concerned that the woman (a) is the

parent, by birth or adoption, of a child under such minimum age as the Secretary concerned shall determine, (b) has personal custody of a child under such minimum age, (c) is the stepparent of a child under such minimum age and the child is within the household of the woman for a period of more than thirty days a year, (d) is pregnant, or (e) has, while serving under such commission, warrant, or enlistment, given birth to a living child; and such woman may be totally separated from the service by administrative action by termination of commission, termination of appointment, revocation of commission, discharge, or otherwise.

Harry S. Truman.

APPENDIX TWO

Z-GRAM 116

7 August 1972

FM CNO (Z-116)
TO NAVOP
BT
UNCLAS//N05350//
EQUAL RIGHTS AND OPPORTUNITIES FOR WOMEN IN THE NAVY
1. THERE HAS BEEN MUCH DISCUSSION AND DEBATE WITH RESPECT TO EQUAL OPPORTUNITY FOR WOMEN IN OUR COUNTRY OVER THE PAST FEW YEARS. MY POSITION WITH RESPECT TO WOMEN IN THE NAVY IS THAT THEY HAVE HISTORICALLY PLAYED A SIGNIFICANT ROLE IN THE ACCOMPLISHMENT OF OUR NAVAL MISSION. HOWEVER, I BELIEVE WE CAN DO FAR MORE THAN WE HAVE IN THE PAST IN ACCORDING WOMEN EQUAL OPPORTUNITY TO CONTRIBUTE THEIR EXTENSIVE TALENTS AND TO ACHIEVE FULL PROFESSIONAL STATUS. MOREOVER, THE IMMINENCE OF AN ALL VOLUNTEER FORCE HAS HEIGHTENED THE IMPORTANCE OF WOMEN AS A VITAL PERSONNEL RESOURCE. I FORESEE THAT IN THE NEAR FUTURE WE MAY VERY WELL HAVE AUTHORITY TO UTILIZE OFFICER AND ENLISTED WOMEN ON BOARD SHIPS. IN VIEW OF THIS POSSIBILITY WE MUST BE IN A POSITION TO UTILIZE WOMEN'S TALENTS TO HELP US ACHIEVE THE SIZE

NAVY WE NEED UNDER AN ALL VOLUNTEER FORCE ENVIRON-
MENT AND STILL MAINTAIN THE SEA SHORE ROTATION
GOALS FOR ALL NAVAL PERSONNEL TOWARDS WHICH WE
HAVE BEEN WORKING. TO THIS END THE SECRETARY OF THE
NAVY AND I HAVE ESTABLISHED A TASK FORCE TO LOOK AT
ALL LAWS, REGULATIONS AND POLICIES THAT MUST BE
CHANGED IN ORDER TO ELIMINATE ANY DISADVANTAGES TO
WOMEN RESULTING FROM EITHER LEGAL OR ATTITUDINAL
RESTRICTIONS.
2. AS ANOTHER STEP TOWARD ENSURING THAT WOMEN IN
THE NAVY WILL HAVE EQUAL OPPORTUNITY TO CONTRIBUTE
THEIR TALENTS AND BACKGROUND TO ACCOMPLISHMENT OF
OUR MISSIONS, WE ARE TAKING THE FOLLOWING ACTIONS:
    A. IN ADDITION TO THE ENLISTED RATINGS THAT HAVE
RECENTLY BEEN OPENED, AUTHORIZE LIMITED ENTRY OF
ENLISTED WOMEN INTO ALL RATINGS.
    B. THE ULTIMATE GOAL, ASSIGNMENT OF WOMEN TO
SHIPS AT SEA, WILL BE TIMED TO COINCIDE WITH FULL
IMPLEMENTATION OF PENDING LEGISLATION. AS AN IMMEDI-
ATE STEP, A LIMITED NUMBER OF OFFICER AND ENLISTED
WOMEN ARE BEING ASSIGNED TO THE SHIP'S COMPANY OF
USS SANCTUARY AS A PILOT PROGRAM. THIS PROGRAM WILL
PROVIDE VALUABLE PLANNING INFORMATION REGARDING
THE PROSPECTIVE INCREASED UTILIZATION OF WOMEN AT
SEA.
    C. PENDING FORMAL CHANGES TO NAVY REGULATIONS,
SUSPEND RESTRICTIONS REGARDING WOMEN SUCCEEDING
TO COMMAND ASHORE AND ASSIGN THEM ACCORDINGLY.

APPENDIX THREE

UNCLASSIFIED

DEPARTMENT OF THE ARMY
PENTAGON TELECOMMUNICATIONS CENTER

COSN = SCD881   MCN = 73062/17777   TOR = 780622231
RTTUZYUW RUEADWD0419 0622227-UUUU—RUEAPPP.
ZNR UUUUU
R 032227Z MAR-78 ZOC ZEO T ALL US ARMY REPS AND ACTIVI-
TIES
FM HODA WASH DC//DAPE-MPE//
TO ALARACT
ST

UNCLAS ALARACT 004/78
ROGERS SENDS
SUBJECT: WOMEN IN THE ARMY
1. IN THE LAST FIVE YEARS THE NUMBER OF WOMEN IN THE
ACTIVE ARMY HAS MORE THAN TRIPLED WHILE AN EVEN
GREATER INCREASE HAS OCCURRED IN THE RESERVE COM-
PONENTS. THESE INCREASES AND THE ENTRANCE OF WOMEN
INTO MANY NONTRADITIONAL SKILLS PRESENT CHALLENGES.
THE PURPOSE OF THIS MESSAGE IS TO EMPHASIZE THE
ARMY'S COMMITMENT TO THE INTEGRATION OF WOMEN
AND TO PROVIDE FUNDAMENTAL GUIDANCE TO ENSURE THIS
INTEGRATION IS COMPLETED SMOOTHLY AND RAPIDLY.
2. TODAY, WOMEN ARE SUCCESSFULLY PERFORMING A WIDE
VARIETY OF DUTIES, MANY OF WHICH WERE CONSIDERED
SOLELY IN THE MALE DOMAIN JUST A FEW YEARS AGO. A
RECENTLY APPROVED COMBAT EXCLUSION POLICY OPENED
MORE SPECIALTIES TO WOMEN THAN EVER BEFORE. HOW-
EVER, EQUAL TRAINING FOR MEN AND WOMEN WAS ONLY
RECENTLY IMPLEMENTED. CONSEQUENTLY, MANY WOMEN
IN THE ARMY HAVE NOT RECEIVED ALL THE TRAINING IN
SOLDIER SKILLS NEEDED TO PERFORM THEIR DUTIES. UNIT
COMMANDERS MUST PROVIDE FOR THESE WOMEN ADDI-
TIONAL INDIVIDUAL TRAINING AS REQUIRED AND ENSURE
THEIR FULL PARTICIPATION IN UNIT TRAINING, FIELD EXER-
CISES AND UNIT DUTIES SUCH AS PERIMETER GUARD.
3. QUALIFIED WOMEN NOW HAVE THE OPPORTUNITY TO
SERVE IN ALL BUT A FEW SPECIFIC COMBAT UNITS AND COM-
BAT SPECIALTIES. IN AVAILING THEMSELVES OF THAT OPPOR-

TUNITY WOMEN, LIKE THEIR MALE COUNTERPARTS, MUST ACCEPT THE RESPONSIBILITY FOR SHARING ALL RISKS AND ENDURING ALL HARDSHIPS INHERENT IN THEIR SPECIALTY. SOME PEOPLE BELIEVE THAT WOMEN SOLDIERS WILL NOT BE DEPLOYED IN THE EVENT OF HOSTILITIES: THAT THEY ARE ONLY TO BE PART-TIME SOLDIERS—HERE IN PEACE, GONE IN WAR. SOME WOMEN ARE BEING USED IN SKILLS OTHER THAN THOSE FOR WHICH THEY WERE TRAINED AND SOME ARE BEING EXCUSED FROM PERFORMANCE OF UNIT DUTIES. THE ARMY CANNOT OPERATE EFFECTIVELY IN THIS MANNER. WOMEN ARE AN ESSENTIAL PART OF THE FORCE; THEY WILL DEPLOY WITH THEIR UNITS AND THEY WILL SERVE IN THE SKILLS IN WHICH THEY HAVE BEEN TRAINED.
4. THOSE OF US IN AUTHORITY MUST REAFFIRM OUR CONVICTION THAT WOMEN ARE AN INTEGRAL PART OF THE ARMY. WITH THIS IN MIND, WE MUST ENSURE THAT WOMEN ARE PROVIDED AN EQUITABLE OPPORTUNITY FOR ASSIGNMENT IN THEIR SPECIALTY, ARE GIVEN ADEQUATE TRAINING AND ARE HELD RESPONSIBLE FOR THE FULL RANGE OF DUTIES PRESCRIBED FOR THEIR ASSIGNED POSITIONS.
5. THE FIRST CONSIDERATIONS IN THE ASSIGNMENT OF WOMEN IN THE ARMY HAVE BEEN, AND WILL CONTINUE TO BE, THE MISSION OF THE ARMY ITSELF, AND THE UNIQUELY DEMANDING NATURE OF ARMY SERVICE IN WARTIME. WITHIN THAT CONTEXT, WOMEN CAN MAKE MANY IMPORTANT CONTRIBUTIONS; INDEED, THEY ARE DOING SO NOW. THE BURDEN WHICH RESTS ON LEADERS AT EVERY LEVEL IS TO PROVIDE KNOWLEDGEABLE, UNDERSTANDING, AFFIRMATIVE AND EVEN-HANDED LEADERSHIP TO ALL OUR SOLDIERS.
BT
    ACTION ADDRESSES
000 ALARACT (DA MEMO 105-1 APPLIES)
#0419

NNNN

                                 PAGE 02
               UNCLASSIFIED   032227Z MAR 78
                                 RUEADWD/0419

APPENDIX FOUR

DEPARTMENT OF DEFENSE
HUMAN GOALS

Our nation was founded on the principle that the individual has infinite dignity and worth. The Department of Defense, which exists to keep the nation secure and at peace, must always be guided by this principle. In all that we do, we must show respect for the serviceman and civilian employee as a person, recognizing his individual needs, aspirations, and capabilities.

The defense of the nation requires a well-trained force, military and civilian, regular and reserve. To provide such a force we must increase the attractiveness of a career in Defense so that the serviceman and the civilian employee will feel the highest pride in himself and his work, in the uniform and the military profession.

THE ATTAINMENT OF THESE GOALS REQUIRES THAT WE STRIVE ...

To attract to the defense service people with ability, dedication, and capacity for growth;

To provide opportunity for everyone, military and civilian, to rise to as high a level of responsibility as his talent and diligence will take him;

To make military and civilian service in the Department of Defense a model of equal opportunity for all regardless of race or creed or national origin, and to hold those who do business with the Department to full compliance with the policy of equal employment opportunity;

To help each serviceman at the end of his service in his adjustment to civilian life; and

To contribute to the improvement of our society, including its disadvantaged members, by greater utilization of our human and physical resources while maintaining full effectiveness in the performance of our primary mission.

(Note these are *not* identical.)

DEPARTMENT OF DEFENSE

HUMAN GOALS

*O*ur Nation was founded on the principle that the Individual has infinite dignity and worth. The Department of Defense, which exists to keep the Nation secure and at peace, must always be guided by this principle. In all that we do, we must show respect for the Serviceman, the Servicewoman, and the Civilian Employee, recognizing their individual needs, aspirations, and capabilities.

*T*he defense of the Nation requires a well-trained force, Military and Civilian, Regular and Reserve. To provide such a force we must increase the attractiveness of a career in Defense so that the Service member and the Civilian employee will feel the highest pride in themselves and their work, in the uniform and the military profession.

THE ATTAINMENT OF THESE GOALS REQUIRES THAT WE STRIVE—

*T*o attract to the Defense service people with ability, dedication, and capacity for growth;

*T*o provide opportunity for everyone, Military and Civilian, to rise to as high a level of responsibility as possible, dependent only on individual talent and diligence;

*T*o make Military and Civilian service in the Department of Defense a model of equal opportunity for all regardless of race, sex, creed, or national origin, and to hold those who do business with the Department of Defense to full compliance with the policy of equal employment opportunity;

*T*o help each Service member in leaving the Service to readjust to civilian life, and

*T*o contribute to the improvement of our Society, including its disadvantaged members, by greater utilization of our human and physical resources while maintaining full effectiveness in the performance of our primary mission.

SECRETARY OF DEFENSE

DEPUTY SECRETARY OF DEFENSE

CHAIRMAN, JOINT CHIEFS OF STAFF

SECRETARY OF THE ARMY

SECRETARY OF THE NAVY

SECRETARY OF THE AIR FORCE

CHIEF OF STAFF, U.S. ARMY

CHIEF OF NAVAL OPERATIONS

CHIEF OF STAFF, U.S. AIR FORCE

COMMANDANT, U.S. MARINE CORPS

Selected Bibliography

BOOKS

Aynes, Maj. Edith, A.N.C. (Ret.). *From Nightingale to Eagle: The Army Nurses' History.* Englewood Cliffs, NJ: Prentice Hall, Inc., 1973.

Barkalow, Carol. *In the Men's House.* New York: Poseidon, 1990.

Binkin, Martin, and Shirley Bach. *Women and the Military.* Washington, D.C.: The Brookings Institution, 1977.

Binkin, Martin and Mark J. Eitelberg. "Women and Minorities in the All-Volunteer Force," William Bowman, Roger Little, and G. Thomas Sicilia. *The All-Volunteer Force After a Decade.* Pergamon-Brassey's, 1986.

Cornum, Maj. Rhonda and Peter Copeland. *She Went to War.* Novato, CA: Presidio Press, 1992.

Goldman, Nancy Loring, ed. *Female Soldiers—Combatants or Noncombatants.* Westport, CT: Greenwood Press, 1982.

Hancock, Capt. Joy Bright, USN (Ret.). *Lady in the Navy: A Personal Reminiscence.* Annapolis, MD: U.S. Naval Institute Press, 1972.

Kiel, Sally Van Wagenen. *Those Wonderful Women and Their Flying Machines: The Unknown Heroines of World War II.* Revised and expanded edition. New York: Four Directions Press, 1990.

Morden, Bettie J. *The Women's Army Corps 1945–1978.* Center of Military History, U.S. Army, 1990.

Moskos, Charles C., and Wood, Frank R., eds. *The Military: More Than Just a Job?* Pergamon-Brassey's, 1988.

Myles, Bruce. *Night Witches: The Untold Story of Soviet Women in Combat.* Novato, CA: Presidio Press, 1981.

Rogan, Helen. *Mixed Company: Women in the Modern Army.* New York: Putnam, 1981.

Schneider, Dorothy, and Carl J. *Sound Off: American Military Women Sound Off.* New York: E.P. Dutton, 1988.

Somerville, Mollie. *Women of the American Revolution.* Washington, D.C.: National Society, Daughters of the American Revolution,1974.

Stiehm, Judith Hicks. *Bring Me Men & Women: Mandated Change at the U.S. Air Force Academy.* Berkeley, CA: University of California Press, 1981.

Stiehm, Judith Hicks. *Arms and the Enlisted Woman.* Philadelphia: Temple University Press, 1989.

Stremlow, Col. Mary V., USMCR. *A History of Women Marines 1946–1977.* Washington, D.C.: History and Museums Division, U.S. Marine Corps, 1986.

Treadwell, Mattie. *U.S. Army in World War II: Special Studies—the Women's Army Corps.* Washington, D.C.: Dept. of the Army, 1954.

Wekesser, Carol, and Matthew Polesetsky, eds. *Women in the Military.* San Diego, CA: Greenhaven Press, Inc., 1991.

Willenz, June A. *Women Veterans: America's Forgotten Heroines.* New York: Continuum Publishing Co., 1983.

Willoughby, Malcolm F. *The U.S. Coast Guard in World War II.* Annapolis, MD: U.S. Naval Institute, 1957.

ARTICLES AND PAPERS

"Academy Women: Ready to Take Command." *U.S. News and World Report,* May 26, 1980.

Adde, Nick. "Proving Their Mettle." *Air Force Times,* April 15, 1991, 47.

"All Volunteer Tour de Force Raises New Issues," *Army Times,* March 18, 1991.

"Are Women the Weak Link in the Military?" *U.S. News and World Report,* November 20, 1989: 61.

Beans, Harry G. "Sex Discrimination in the Military." *Military Law Review,* Vol. 67 (Winter 1975): 19–83.

Becraft, Carolyn H. "Personnel Puzzle." *Proceedings,* U.S. Naval Institute, April 1989.

Becraft, Carolyn H. "Military Women: Policies and Politics." *The Bureaucrat,* Fall 1991: 9–12.

Bird, Julie. "AF Women Filled Many Roles in Panama Mission." *Air Force Times,* January 1990: 6.

Bolton, Congresswoman Frances P. "Women Should Be Drafted." *American Magazine,* June 1949.

Brown, Barbara; Emerson, Thomas I.; Folk, Gail; and Freedman, Ann E. "The Equal Rights Amendment: A Constitutional Basis for Equal Rights for Women." *The Yale Law Journal,* Vol. 80, No. 5 (April 1971): 871–979.

Clarke, Maj. Gen. Mary E. "Contribution to Make." *Army Times,* September 21, 1981.

Copeland, Peter. "Army Women Went into Panama with Weapons —and Used Them," *Washington Times,* January 2, 1990: A1, A3.

Davis, Barbara. "POW Nurses: So Proudly We Hail." *The Retired Officer,* March 1974.

Davis, James A., Jennifer Lauby, and Paul B. Sheatsley. *Americans View The Military: Public Opinion in 1982.* National Opinion Research Center Report No. 131, 1983.

"Draft Women? The Arguments For and Against." *U.S. News and World Report,* April 6, 1981.

Drake, Katharine. "Our Flying Nightingales in Vietnam." *Reader's Digest* (December 1967): 75.

Dudley, Robert. "Fresh Doubts About Women in Armed Forces." *U.S. News and World Report,* July 20, 1981.

Eskind, Amy. "A Post-war Memorial Day, 1991, Arms and the Woman," *Washington Post,* May 26, 1991, D3.

"Female Air Aces of World War II." *Air Aces: The Luftwaffe Fighter Aces,* Vol. 2, No. 2 (April 1977): 64–65.

Flerovsky, Alexi. "Women Flyers of Fighter Planes." *Soviet Life* (May 1975): 28–29.

Gellman, Barton. "Combat Flights by Women Backed," *The Washington Post,* May 9, 1991: A1.

Gugliotta, Guy. "Scuds Put U.S. Women on Front Line," *The Washington Post,* January 28, 1991, A19.

Gugliotta, Guy. "A Woman's Place: In Command," *The Washington Post,* January 23, 1991, B1, 9.

Hale, Mariclaire, and Leo Kanowitz, "Women and The Draft: A Response to Critics of the Equal Rights Amendment." *The Hastings Law Journal,* Vol. 23 (1971–1972): 199.

Holm, Jeanne M. "Women in the Armed Forces." *Encyclopedia of the American Military,* New York: Charles Scribner's Sons, 1992.

Hunter, Richard W. "Military Discrimination." *Transaction Social Science and Modern Society,* Vol. 18, No. 3 (March/April 1981): 45–51.

Jolidon, Laurence. "Females on the Front Lines: No Easy Task," *USA Today,* December 13, 1990: A5.

Korb, Lawrence J. "Volunteer Army: It Deserves a Fair Chance." Op-Ed, *The Washington Post,* June 9, 1981.

Landers, Robert K. "Should Women Be Allowed in Combat?" *The Congressional Quarterly,* October 13, 1989.

Lieberman, Jeanne M. "Women in Combat." *Federal Bar News & Journal,* 37 (May 1990): 215–222.

McNeil, Donald G. "Should Women Be Sent Into Combat?" *New York Times,* July 21, 1991: E3.

Miles, Donna. "Women of Just Cause." *Soldiers,* magazine of the U.S. Army, 1990.

Moore, Molly. "Women in the Battlefield—Gulf War Role Helps Bring Shift in Attitude," *The Washington Post,* June 16, 1991: A1.

Moore, Molly. "Women Face Combat Risk." *The Washington Post,* September 12, 1991: 1.

Moskos, Charles C. "Females in the Field." *Society,* September-October 1985: 28–33.

Moskos, Charles C. "Soldier Boys: Soldier Girls." *The New Republic,* February 16, 1990: 7–9.

Murphy, Caryle. "A Slice of Americana Hits the Saudi Desert." *The Washington Post,* February 17, 1991: 42.

"One Way to Avoid a New Draft: Recruit More Females." *U.S. News and World Report,* February 14, 1977.

Quigley, Capt. Robin U.S.N. (Ret.). "Women Aboard Ship: A Few Observations." *Seapower,* magazine of the Navy League. May 1977.

Ralston, Jeannie. "Women's Work." *Life,* May 1991: 52–62.

Roe, Dorothy. "Pentagon May Seek Drafting Women if Recruiting Plan Fails." *The Associated Press,* October 17, 1951.

Salisbury, Karen. "The Women's Army Corps." *Newsweek,* May 21, 1951.

Scarborough, Rowan. "Female Fliers Earn Respect." *Washington Times,* June 18, 1991: A1.

Schmitt, Eric. "War Puts U.S. Servicewomen Closer than Ever to Combat." *New York Times,* January 22, 1991: A1, A8.

"Sex Barrier: It's Falling Fast in the Military." *U.S. News and World Report,* June 28, 1976.

"Should Women Fight to Kill?" *Newsweek,* August 5, 1991: 22–30.

"Soviet Women at War." *Anglo-Soviet Journal,* Vol. 3 (April-June 1942): 71–82.

"Soviet Women in the Great Patriotic War." *Soviet Military Review* (March 1975): 42–45.

Summers, Col. Harry G. "It's No Surprise That Women Joined Combat in Panama." *Air Force Times,* January 22, 1990.

"The Untold Story of Black Women in the Gulf War." *Ebony,* September 1991: 100–106.

Wexler, Joan G. "The Equal Rights Amendment and the Military." *The Yale Law Journal,* Vol. 82 (June 1973): 1533–57

Willis, Grant. "Operation Desert Storm—All-Volunteer Tour de Force Raises New Issues." *Money,* March 18, 1991.

"Women in Combat: Closer Than You Think." *U.S. News and World Report,* March 3, 1980.

"Women in the Armed Forces." *Newsweek,* February 18, 1980.

"Women in the Military: Should They Be Drafted?" *Newsweek,* February 18, 1980.

"Women in Uniform: Can They Save the Military?" *U.S. News and World Report,* June 5, 1978.

"Women May Yet Save the Army." *Time,* October 30, 1978.

GOVERNMENT AND MILITARY SOURCES

Beck, Col. B. G., U.S. Army. "Women as Warriors." *ARMY* (February 1981): 26–31.

Center for Strategic and International Studies. Report: "The Gulf War: Military Lessons Learned," July 22, 1991.

Commission on Organization of the Executive Branch of the Government (Hoover Commission), Vol. III. November 15, 1948.

Cooper, Richard. *Military Manpower and the All-Volunteer Force.* Report prepared for the Defense Advanced Research Projects Agency. Santa Monica, California, Rand Corporation: R-1450-ARPA. 1977.

Hancock, Joy Bright. *Recollections of Captain Joy Bright Hancock, U.S. Navy (Ret.).* Oral History. Annapolis, MD, U.S. Naval Institute, 1971.

Horton, Mildred McAfee. *Recollections of Captain Mildred McAfee, USNR (Ret.), Mrs. Douglas Horton.* Oral History. U.S. Naval Institute, 1971.

Kane, Lt. John E. "From Pariah to Professional: Women on Tugs." *Defense Management Journal,* Vol. 14, No. 1, January 1978.

Kelly, James F., Jr., Capt. USN. "Women in Warships: A Right to Serve." *U.S. Naval Institute Proceedings* (October 1978): 44–52.

Lyne, Mary C., and Arthur, Kay. *Three Years Behind the Mast: The Story of the United States Coast Guard SPARS.* Washington, D.C., The United States Coast Guard, 1946.

National Advisory Commission on Selective Service. *In Pursuit of Equity: Who Serves When Not All Serve?* Washington, D.C.: GPO, 1967.

North Atlantic Treaty Organization. IMS Secretariate. *Women in the NATO Forces.* Brussels, Belgium. 1991.

Palmer, Jean. *Recollections of Captain Jean Palmer, USNR (Ret.).* Oral History. Annapolis, MD, U.S. Naval Institute, 1971.

Presidential Recommendations for Selective Service Reform. A Report to Congress Prepared Pursuant to P.L. 96–107, February 11, 1980.

Quigley, Capt. Robin L. C., USN (Ret.). *Reminiscences of Captain Robin L. C. Quigley, U.S.N. (Ret.).* Oral History, Annapolis, MD, U.S. Naval Institute, 1978.

Quigley, Capt. Robin L., USN (Ret.). "A Requirement to Serve." *U.S. Naval Institute Proceedings* (October 1978): 52–53.

Rogers, Jim. "Soviet Women." *Soldiers,* magazine of the U.S. Army, March 1978.

Shelly, Mary Josephine. *An Interview with Lieutenant Commander Mary Josephine Shelly, USNR (Ret.) on Her Service in World War II with the WAVES.* Oral History. U.S. Naval Institute, 1970.

Stratton, Dorothy. *Recollections of Captain Dorothy Stratton, First Director of the SPARS, U.S. Coast Guard.* Oral History. U.S. Naval Institute, 1971.

U.S. Congress. Congressional Record—Senate, July 31, 1991. pp. S11412–S11437.

———. House of Representatives. Committee on Armed Services, report of hearings: *Hearings on Women in the Military,* 1988.

———. House of Representatives. Committee on Armed Services, report of hearings: *Women in the Military* (H.A.S.C. No. 101–63), 1990.

———. House of Representatives. Committee on Armed Services, report of hearings: *Women in the Military* (H.A.S.C. No. 96–72), 1981.

U.S. Department of the Air Force. Air War College. *Women in Combat Roles: Past and Future,* Marion E. Oelke and Richard J. Vogt. Research Report No. AU-AWC-88-1880, 1988.

———. Air Force Systems Command. *Women in the Military Cockpit,* Report of the Armstrong Laboratory, June 1991.

———. Air Command and Staff College. *USAF Women Pilots: The Combat Issue,* Teresa Marné Peterson. Student Report No. 88–2110, 1988.

———. USAF Academy. "The Combat Exclusion for Women Aviators: A Constitutional Analysis," Marilyn A. Gordon and Mary Jo Ludvigson. *USAF Academy Journal of Legal Studies.* 1990.

———Office of the Deputy Chief of Staff for Personnel. *USAF Mobilization, Military Personnel Requirements for Women.* Washington, D.C., June 1, 1950.

———. Office of the Director of Women in the Air Force. *History of Women in the Air Force,* semiannual reports, 1948–1976.

———. Office of the General Counsel. "Constitutionality of an All Male Draft," Memorandum, February 7, 1980.

U.S. Department of the Army. Center for Military History. *Women in Combat and as Military Leaders,* March 1978.

———. *History of the Army Nurse Corps in the Philippine Islands September 1940–February 1945* by 1st Lt. Josephine M. Nesbit. Unpublished draft in the files of the Chief, Army Nurse Corps.

———. Medical Department. *Highlights on the History of the Army Nurse Corps,* Washington, D.C., 1987.

———. *The Women's Army Corps 1945–1978* by Col. Bettie J. Morden, USA (Ret.), 1990.

———. *U.S. Army in World War II: Special Studies—The Women's Army Corps* by Mattie B. Treadwell, 1954.

U.S. Department of Defense. Conduct of the Persian Gulf Conflict—An Interim Report to Congress. Pursuant to Title V Persian Gulf Conflict Supplemental Authorization and Personnel Benefits Act of 1991 (Public Law 102–25).

————. Defense Advisory Committee on Women in the Services. Minutes and Reports of Meetings, 1951.

————. Defense Equal Opportunity Institute. *Women in Combat*, February 1991.

————. Defense Intelligence Agency. *Women in the Soviet Armed Forces*, DDI-110-109-76, March 1976.

————. Office of the Assistant Secretary of Defense (Manpower and Reserve Affairs). *Report of the Inter-Service Working Group on Utilization of Women in the Armed Services*, Washington, D.C., August 31, 1966.

————. Office of the Assistant Secretary of Defense (Manpower and Reserve Affairs), *Utilization of Military Women (A Report of Increased Utilization of Military Women FY 1973-1977)* prepared by: Central All-Volunteer Task Force, Washington, D.C., December 1972.

————. Office of the Assistant Secretary of Defense (Manpower, Reserve Affairs and Logistics). *Background Review: Women in the Military,* Washington, D.C., October 1981.

————. Office of the Assistant Secretary of Defense (Manpower, Reserve Affairs and Logistics). *Background Study: Use of Women in the Military,* Washington, D.C., May 1977, revised edition September 1978.

————. Office of Assistant Secretary of Defense (Manpower, Reserve Affairs and Logistics). *Going Strong! Women in Defense*, 1984.

————. Office of the Assistant Secretary of Defense, (Manpower, Reserve Affairs and Logistics). *Background Review: Women in the Military*, 1981.

————. Office of the Assistant Secretary of Defense (Force Management and Personnel). *Population Representation in the Military Service—Fiscal Year 1990*, July 1991.

————. Office of the Secretary of Defense. *Military Women in the Department of Defense*, 1990.

————. Office of the Secretary of Defense. *Report of Task Force on Women in the Military*, January 1988.

————. Personnel Policy Board. *Report of Conference of Civilian Women Leaders,* Washington, D.C., June 21–22, 1950.

————. Personnel Policy Board. *Subcommittee Report No. M-7-51: Maximum Utilization of Military Womanpower,* Washington, D.C., April 9, 1951.

————. Personnel Policy Board. *Utilization and Recruitment of Women for Military and Civilian Service,* Washington, D.C., February 1951.

U.S. Department of the Navy. Bureau of Naval Personnel. *Conference of District and Air Command Assistants (W),* May 16–18, 1956.

————. *U.S. Naval Administration in World War II: Bureau of Naval Personnel, Women's Reserve,* Director of Naval History, January 18, 1946.

————. Office of the Chief of Naval Operations. *Navy Study Group's Report on Progress of Women in the Navy,* 1987.

————. 1990 Navy Women's Study Group. *An Update Report on the Progress of Women in the Navy,* 1990.

————. Headquarters U.S. Marine Corps. *Women Marines in the 1980's.* 1986.

U.S. Department of Transportation. "Women at Sea" by Robert Taylor, *Transportation USA,* Fall 1977.

————. United States Coast Guard. *Women in the Coast Guard Study,* Commandant Publication 5312.17, July 1990.

U.S. Government Accounting Office. "CRS Issue Brief: Women in the Armed Forces," by Ellen C. Collier, Congressional Research Service, July 12, 1991.

————. *Military Personnel: Composition of the Active Duty Forces by Race or National Origin Identification and by Gender,* GAO/NSIAD-91-134FS, February 1991.

————. "Should Women Be Kept Out of Combat?" Beverly Ann Bendekgey. *The GAO Journal,* Summer 1990.

————. *Women in the Military: Career Progression Not a Current Problem but Concerns Remain,* GAO/NSIAD-89-210BR, September 1989.

————. *Women in the Military: Air Force Revises Job Availability but Entry Screening Needs Review.* GAO/NSI-91-199, August 1991.

————. *Women in the Military—Attrition and Retention,* GAO/NSIAD-90-87BR, July 1990.

————. *Women in the Military, Impact of Proposed Legislation to Open More Combat Support Positions to Women.* July 1988.

————. *Women in the Military: More Military Jobs Can Be Opened Under Current Statutes,* September 1988.

U.S. Marine Corps. *A History of Women Marines 1946–1977* by Col. Mary V. Stremlow, USMCR, History and Museums Division, Headquarters, U.S. Marine Corps, 1986.

————. *Marine Corps Women's Reserve in World War II* by Lt. Col. Pat Meid, USMCR, Historical Branch, Headquarters U.S. Marine Corps, 1964, revised 1968.

————. *Women Marines in World War I* by Capt. Linda L. Hewitt, USMCR, History and Museums Division, Headquarters U.S. Marine Corps, 1974.

Vitters, Maj. Alan G., and Kinger, Nora Scott. "Women at West Point: Change Within Tradition." *Military Review,* April 1978.

"Women on Sea Duty." *All Hands,* magazine of the U.S. Navy, No. 742 (November 1978): 6–10.

Index